PIMLICO

661

UN NEWSPAPERMEN

DF

Dudley Edwards is an historian, jour-
and crime writer. Her non-fiction

es *Victor Gollancz: A Biography* (winner
James Tait Black Memorial Prize), *The*

Fi *of Reason: The Economist, 1843-1993*
The Faithful Tribe: An Intimate Portrait of the
Institutions. Her nine crime novels are
es on the British Establishment.

NEWSPAPERMEN

Hugh Cudlipp, Cecil Harmsworth King
and the Glory Days of Fleet Street

———

RUTH DUDLEY EDWARDS

PIMLICO

Published by Pimlico 2004

2 4 6 8 10 9 7 5 3 1

First published in Great Britain in 2003 by
Martin Secker & Warburg

Pimlico edition 2004

Pimlico
Random House, 20 Vauxhall Bridge Road,
London SW1V 2SA

Random House Australia (Pty) Limited
20 Alfred Street, Milsons Point, Sydney,
New South Wales 2061, Australia

Random House New Zealand Limited ,
18 Poland Road, Glenfield,
Auckland 10, New Zealand

Random House (Pty) Limited
Endulini, 5A Jubilee Road, Parktown 2193, South Africa

The Random House Group Limited Reg. No. 954009
www.randomhouse.co.uk

A CIP catalogue record for this book is available from the British Library

ISBN 1-8441-3420-2

Papers used by Random House UK Limited are natural, recyclable products
made from wood grown in sustainable forests; the manufacturing processes
conform to the environmental regulations of the country of origin

Printed in Great Britain by Clays Ltd, St Ives plc

CONTENTS

Harmsworth and King family trees   vi

Preface   ix

Prologue   1

I. Heavy Baggage   3

II. A Legacy of Uncles   24

III. The Hard Ascent of Cecil King   54

IV. The Effortless Rise of Hugh Cudlipp   81

V. Cudlipp and Mr King   117

VI. Two Wars   152

VII. Bart's Revenge   187

VIII. The Eagle and the Lark   224

IX. His Uncle's Nephew   268

X. The Influence of Ruth   303

XI. The Reluctant Assassin   355

XII. Lord Cudlipp and Mr King   394

Epilogue   443

Notes and Sources   452

Index   475

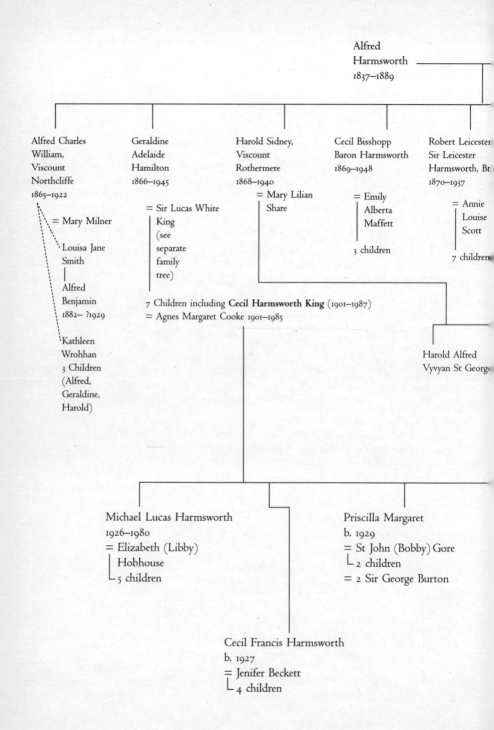

Alfred
Harmsworth
1837–1889

Alfred Charles
William,
Viscount
Northcliffe
1865–1922

= Mary Milner

Louisa Jane
Smith
|
Alfred
Benjamin
1882– ?1929

Kathleen
Wrohhan
3 Children
(Alfred,
Geraldine,
Harold)

Geraldine
Adelaide
Hamilton
1866–1945

= Sir Lucas White
King
(see
separate
family
tree)

Harold Sidney,
Viscount
Rothermere
1868–1940

= Mary Lilian
Share

7 Children including **Cecil Harmsworth King** (1901–1987)
= Agnes Margaret Cooke 1901–1985

Cecil Bisshopp
Baron Harmsworth
1869–1948

= Emily
Alberta
Maffett

3 children

Robert Leicester
Sir Leicester
Harmsworth, Bt
1870–1937

= Annie
Louise
Scott

7 children

Harold Alfred
Vyvyan St George

Michael Lucas Harmsworth
1926–1980
= Elizabeth (Libby)
  Hobhouse
  5 children

Priscilla Margaret
b. 1929
= St John (Bobby) Gore
  2 children
= 2 Sir George Burton

Cecil Francis Harmsworth
b. 1927
= Jenifer Beckett
  4 children

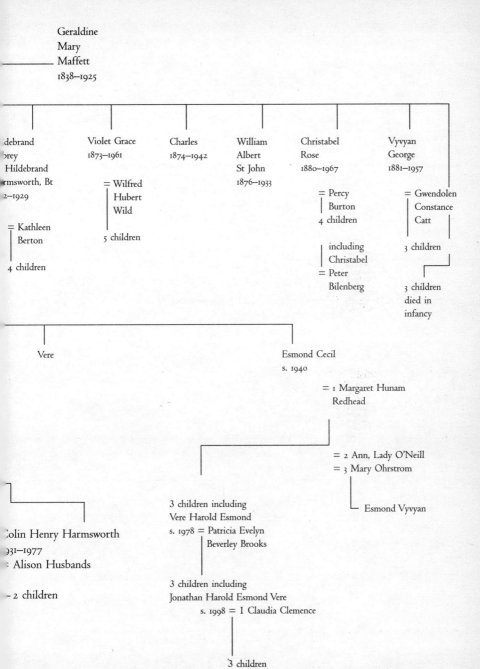

Geraldine
Mary
Maffett
1838–1925

…debrand
…orey
Hildebrand
…rmsworth, Bt
2–1929

= Kathleen
Berton

4 children

Violet Grace
1873–1961

= Wilfred
Hubert
Wild

5 children

Charles
1874–1942

William
Albert
St John
1876–1933

Christabel
Rose
1880–1967

= Percy
Burton
4 children

including
Christabel
= Peter
Bilenberg

Vyvyan
George
1881–1957

= Gwendolen
Constance
Catt

3 children

3 children
died in
infancy

Vere

Esmond Cecil
s. 1940

= 1 Margaret Hunam
Redhead

= 2 Ann, Lady O'Neill
= 3 Mary Ohrstrom

…olin Henry Harmsworth
…31–1977
= Alison Husbands

– 2 children

3 children including
Vere Harold Esmond
s. 1978 = Patricia Evelyn
Beverley Brooks

3 children including
Jonathan Harold Esmond Vere
s. 1998 = 1 Claudia Clemence

3 children

Esmond Vyvyan

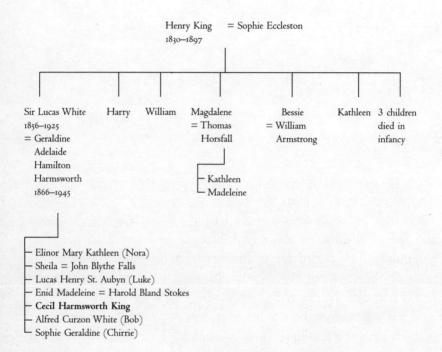

Henry King = Sophie Eccleston
1830–1897

Sir Lucas White   Harry   William   Magdalene   Bessie   Kathleen   3 children
1856–1925   = Thomas   = William   died in
= Geraldine   Horsfall   Armstrong   infancy
Adelaide
Hamilton
Harmsworth
1866–1945

                                      ⌐ Kathleen
                                        ⌐ Madeleine

- Elinor Mary Kathleen (Nora)
- Sheila = John Blythe Falls
- Lucas Henry St. Aubyn (Luke)
- Enid Madeleine = Harold Bland Stokes
- **Cecil Harmsworth King**
- Alfred Curzon White (Bob)
- Sophie Geraldine (Chirrie)

PREFACE

'YOU WILL NEVER WANT FOR A LIVING WRITING WHITE-WASHING biographies that will please people's relatives,' said Cecil Harmsworth King, then 78, to Charles Lysaght.* King has numerous descendants and few of them agree about him; however, as a family they have in common a high regard for truth and to the best of my knowledge none of them wanted a whitewash. Nor did Hugh Cudlipp's widow or his battalion of surviving friends.

What was to have been a life of King developed into a biography of both King and Cudlipp, the odd couple of Fleet Street who pooled their exceptional and complementary gifts to create the biggest publishing company in the world. At eight or nine, Cudlipp's ambitions were sparked by the success of his brother Percy on the local paper; in his teens, King was gripped with the desire to exercise power like his Uncles Alfred and Harold, the press lords Northcliffe and Rothermere.

Onlookers were often bewildered at a partnership whose principals had such contrasting backgrounds, intellects, interests and personalities. Yet they had a joint obsession: though Cudlipp was no businessman and King no journalist, both were passionate newspapermen. King would give Cudlipp his chance; Cudlipp would become King's amanuensis. And the whole quickly became immeasurably greater than the remarkable halves.

---

* Lysaght had just published an honest, sympathetic and highly-praised biography of Brendan Bracken, whom in 1945 King had described as 'trumpery'; King's opinion of Bracken went down even further over the years.

I never met Cecil King, but I would, I believe, have liked him and enjoyed his conversation. I knew and loved Hugh Cudlipp, who was of enormous help throughout all that long period when I was intending to write a book just about King; he and Jodi also gave me full access to all their papers. Hugh also extracted a great deal of fun from all the frustrations and annoyances that dogged what had originally seemed a straightforward project. I am very glad that before he died he knew I had decided – with the enthusiastic approval of the publishers and some of King's family – that the book had to be about both of them.

Cudlipp's memoirs are a delight, while King's do his own reputation terrible harm. As a writer King was as terse, gloomy and disparaging as Cudlipp was eloquent, funny and generous. King never put a cheerful slant on anything; Cudlipp never spoiled a story for the want of an amusing embellishment.* It was the hope of Cudlipp that this biography would do King the justice he seemed incapable of doing himself.

I could not have written a decent book about Cecil King without the help of his daughter Priscilla, who gave me her wholehearted trust and never flinched from telling the truth, however much it hurt. She and her husband, George Burton, cosseted and encouraged me, even though we often doubted if the biography could ever be written. Jodi Cudlipp is another cosseter who was always exceptionally good to me; since Hugh died we have become very close. Her innumerable kindnesses have included lending me her flat and correcting the proofs.

Scilla and Jodi both read the book in typescript. Scilla confined herself to correcting factual errors, but Jodi fought like a terrier for Hugh when she felt he was being pushed into second place because of the sheer weight of the King archives. Our disagreements always ended in amity and laughter, with her identifying herself as 'bossyboots' to my 'prissy historian'.

I have been in the biographical trade for a long time and I work hard to avoid allowing my personal feelings to affect my judgement: I do not

---

* Where there are several versions of any important Cudlipp anecdotes, I've chosen what seems the most accurate; where it is of no historical significance, I've chosen the most amusing.

believe that my affection for Jodi and Scilla, to whom I dedicate the book with deep gratitude, has distorted the story of Cudlipp and King.

For reasons that will become clear later, I have been involved with this book for almost fifteen years. During this period, my editors at Secker & Warburg have been uniformly supportive in strange circumstances and have always shared in any laughs that were going. My thanks to Dan Franklin, who was lucky to get out early, to Max Eilenberg, who was there during the worst of times, and to Geoff Mulligan and Stuart Williams who ultimately had the best. And my thanks also to Felicity Bryan, who was my agent on the project.

I am grateful to Howard Gottlieb, Margaret Goosetray, Sean Noel and all their staff in the extraordinarily efficient and reader-friendly Department of Special Collections in Boston University; to the London Library, as always; and to the staff of all other libraries I used.

I list my most important sources and interviewees at the back of the book and acknowledge with gratitude the help of all those listed. A special word of thanks to Bruce Arnold, Piers Brendon and Alison Hawkes for making some fascinating material available, to Laurence and Carey King for writing at length about their relationships with Cecil and Ruth, to Geoffrey Goodman and Donald Zec for reading the typescript and to Mandy Greenwood and Kate Worden for doing their jobs so well. Without Sasha Borissenko, Maureen Cromey and Johann Geronimus, who tackled my repetitive strain injury, it would have taken much much longer to finish the book.

I am blessed in my friends, but this project has been kicking around for so long and so many of them have been kind and interested and helpful at various times that it would be ridiculous to single out any except Máirín Carter and Seán O'Callaghan (who read and commented critically on all of it), Nina Clarke, Kathryn Kennison, Paul le Druillenec, John Lippitt, James McGuire, Jonathan Madden, Úna O'Donoghue, the late Gordon Lee and my niece Neasa MacErlean. As usual, my assistant, Carol Scott, was my rock.

To Jodi and Scilla

Prologue

9.35 a.m., 30 May 1968

CECIL HARMSWORTH KING, ALL SIX FEET FOUR AND EIGHTEEN STONE of him, sat behind the eight-foot octagonal desk formed by two eighteenth-century Italianate baroque tables; a journalist later described it as 'fit not merely for a King but for an emperor.'[1] Symbols of his eclectic interests as well as his status were evident all around him – in the gold and green Kermanshah carpet, the Anatolian prayer mats, the Chippendale and Hepplewhite chairs, the seventeenth-century sideboard, the Adam fireplace, the shelves of rare books on Africa and the carefully chosen objets d'art. 'A visitor hijacked to the place would assume at first glance that he was at the country retreat of a cultured aristocrat, a former Viceroy,' remarked Hugh Cudlipp later. 'What the room did not in any way resemble was the powerhouse of a world-wide publishing empire responsible not only for *Country Life* and *Halsbury's Laws of England* and other impeccable tomes but for popular newspapers and mass magazines regarded by highbrows like King himself as sensational or vulgar.'

In the basement, the rotary presses were being geared up to print over five million copies of the *Daily Mirror*, the biggest-selling newspaper in the world, each issue read by almost 15 million people. On the ninth floor, in King's suite, a portrait of the tabloid's founder, Lord Northcliffe, stared from the wall behind his nephew, Chairman of the *Daily Mirror* and *Sunday Pictorial* companies since 1951, and since 1963 of the enormous Reed Paper Group and of the International Publishing Company, the biggest publishing company in the world. Like Northcliffe in his last years, King had come to think of himself as more powerful than governments. And as Northcliffe and his brother Lord Rothermere had been instrumental in 1916 in having Asquith deposed as Prime Minister, so King was confident of toppling Harold Wilson. He had forgotten, however, that unlike Northcliffe and Rothermere, he did not own the newspapers whose policy he directed.

Four floors down, all five feet seven and eleven stone of him, was Hugh Cudlipp, King's protégé since 1935, his amanuensis, his interpreter, his trusted deputy, the person who knew him better than anyone else and the nearest King had to a friend and confidant; they were seen as a team like Gilbert and Sullivan, Marks and Spencer or (Cudlipp's suggestion) Barnum and Bailey. At 8.15 that morning, a letter signed by Cudlipp had been delivered to King's home; on behalf of the board of directors, it asked for his immediate resignation. 'Three of us who have worked with you for many years,' the concluding paragraph had begun, '– myself, Frank Rogers and Don Ryder – will be ready to see you together on Thursday morning at IPC to discuss the appropriate next stage.'

As Cudlipp later told it, King dialled 01 on his internal phone: 'I understand you want to see me,' he said to Cudlipp. 'The temperature was zero. I replied, "Yes. We will come up right away." It is curious how banal the conversation tends to be on these occasions.'[2]

As the trio apprehensively entered the directors' private lift and began the ascent, Cudlipp warned Rogers and Ryder that, although all three were expected, there would inevitably be only one chair in front of the William Kent tables. He would take that, but say nothing until they were seated too. 'I anticipated long pauses from Cecil, designed to promote in the unhappy delegation a sense of discomfort, doubt or guilt . . . There was one chair in front of the octagonal desk, and there was a long pause . . .'

CHAPTER I
Heavy Baggage

THEIR PATHS FIRST CROSSED IN JUNE 1935, WHEN PERCY CUDLIPP, Editor of the *Evening Standard*, advised his precocious young brother to answer a mysterious classified advertisement for a 'bright assistant features editor with ideas, able to take charge.'[1] 'I can still remember opening a letter from Hugh Cudlipp,' recollected King decades later. '. . . He was twenty-one but had by then seven years experience of journalism.'[2]

King was thirty-four, a middle-ranking executive and no journalist, but from childhood he had been determined to become a force in the world of newspapers that had brought his uncles riches, titles, fame and power: 'My first contact as a boy with Fleet Street was standing behind Northcliffe's chair while he was presented with a bust of himself by the fathers of the various chapels.'[3] Hubert Kinsman Cudlipp had never heard of Fleet Street when, as a boy intent on early escape from the boredom of Howard Gardens Secondary School in Cardiff, he listened agog to Percy's tales of scandals, crimes and free cinema tickets and determined to become a journalist too.[4]

Cudlipp's family baggage was light. Sturdily rooted in Cardiff, straightforwardly Welsh to the core, with his younger sister and two elder brothers he was reared in a lower-middle-class area of three-up, two-down terraces. His big rosy-cheeked father, Willie, an amiable commercial traveller in eggs and bacon, traversed the Welsh valleys 'with his order book and umbrella, a new carnation in his button-hole'.[5] Bessie Amelia Kinsman, his wife and the neighbourhood entertainer, passed on to her youngest son in abundance her talents as a raconteur, mimic and gossip – 'the life and soul of the party without the aid of gin in a street where there were no parties';[6] against stiff competition, Hugh (as Hubert renamed himself in adolescence) was to be the life and soul of another street – Fleet Street – which lacked neither gin nor parties.

Cecil King's baggage was as heavy as the trunks and tin boxes that accompanied paternal and maternal ancestors across the seas. First, there was the matter of his nationality and allegiances. He tended to describe himself as Irish, yet the preceding two generations of Irish Kings had made their careers in India as servants of the British Empire. Although Grandfather Henry King, born in Drogheda, County Louth, in 1830, was an enthusiastic proponent of Irish Home Rule,[7] he prospered in the Indian Medical Service. He and his wife, Sophie Eccleston (of Irish parentage, but a New Yorker by birth and upbringing), retired to Dublin in 1884, by which time their elder son, Lucas White, had already completed eight years in the Indian Civil Service. Their second son, also Henry, would end his career as a Lieutenant-Colonel in the 33rd Punjabis, and their elder daughter, Magdalene, lived in India too as wife to a civil servant.

Cecil's maternal grandmother, Geraldine Maffett, was of a solid Ulster-Scots background, but Alfred Harmsworth, whom she married in her home city of Dublin, was English, and they moved to London after a few years and raised their family there. Cecil himself was born in London and soon taken to India, spent most of his first two years there and then returned to London, accompanied by two ayahs, his mother (Irish-born and London-reared) and three of his six siblings; taken to live in Dublin in 1905, he was educated mainly in England, where he made his career.

Both Cudlipp and King inherited brains in abundance, but King's came with intellectual baggage and heavy expectations: the Cudlipps cared as little about their ancestry as the Kings cared much. Cecil's paternal great-great-grandfather was a bookseller and publisher; his great-grandfather, Luke White, a classics graduate of Trinity College, Dublin, became a headmaster; and Grandfather Henry had been a prize-winning classics scholar before studying medicine. With a trace of the perverseness that was to distinguish his grandson, Henry served the Empire but refused to stand up for 'God Save the Queen'.[8] His son Lucas White, Cecil's father, was the intellectual star of the family: head boy and a prize-winner at school, at Trinity he shone in logic, classics, Persian, Arabic and Hindustani, took a BA and LLB and came high in the Indian Civil Service examination; later he was to reach proficiency in Biluchi, Pushtu and Russian. That family track-record was to weigh heavily on Cecil at school and university.

When he began his career, all Hugh Cudlipp had to live up to was the steady progress of his brothers Percy and Reg along the provincial newspaper route to Fleet Street. Cecil King had the Harmsworths – the newspaper magnates Uncle Alfred (Viscount Northcliffe) and Uncle Harold (Viscount Rothermere) – and for good measure, in public life, his godfather, Uncle Cecil (MP and later Lord Harmsworth), and his Uncle Leicester (baronet and MP). More important, though, were the two men's contrasting upbringings: King emerged from privilege, coldness and tragedy an emotional cripple, who gazed like a contemptuous outsider at his fellow man and who could achieve intimacy only through sex. Cudlipp was not just clubbable; there was almost no one in the universe with whom he could not get on. Even Cecil King.

'I was born on 20 February 1901 at Poynters Hall, Totteridge, an eighteenth-century house of no distinction, now pulled down.' A very Cecil opening to his memoirs – factual, precise and dismissive. Yet his sister Enid remembers it as 'charming',[9] while a cousin described it as 'a fine old house . . . a Queen Anne mansion with thirty-five acres laid out by "Capability" Brown'.[10] Poynters belonged to his redoubtable Grandmother Harmsworth, who, as Geraldine Maffett, had married imprudently for love and fun. One of ten children of a prosperous land agent with a reputation for harshness, she was auburn-haired, plump and attractive, but with a will of steel, formidable strength of character and such uncompromising Ulster-Scots values as implacable integrity and disconcerting candour and forthrightness. 'She always said she had excellent health, but poor spirits,' wrote her granddaughter Enid, who lived with her for long periods as a child and young adult. 'She had a tremendous fund of good sense and good judgement and though [she was] nervous, I have never met anyone who could give such a formidable impression of unchanging strength, deep affection and earthy wisdom. She was a rock to which all her family clung, especially her sons. They loved and reverenced her to the end far more than their wives.'[11]

Geraldine Maffett was twenty-six when in 1862 she met the twenty-five-year old Londoner, Alfred Harmsworth, son of a green-grocer-turned-merchant and now a master at Dublin's Royal Hibernian Military School. He was handsome, charming, clever and amusing: his wife used to remark that he was the brains and she the ballast.

Ballast was certainly required, for Geraldine was fecund and Alfred Harmsworth was poor. It was her idea that he better himself by becoming a barrister: in 1864, the year of their marriage, although he remained in Dublin, he was admitted as a student of the Middle Temple in London.[12] Three years later, having reason to believe the Fenians were targeting Harmsworth, they bundled their babies (also named Alfred and Geraldine) into blankets and left their home out-side Dublin, staying successively with Ulster-Scots relatives in Dublin, Armagh and Belfast before settling in London: 'Geraldine Harmsworth left her native land with anything but a heavy heart,' said one family biography. 'Loyal in sentiment to her Ulster connections, she had no great love for Ireland, holding the over-simplified view that the North was constructive and the South destructive.'

After two years and two more children, Alfred Harmsworth was called to the bar. Although he had great ability, he was too ami-able, easygoing, convivial and fond of drink to be a success in a profession that required drive and application. He was given the odd brief and did a bit of devilling, but he preferred artistic and literary company to work; he published the occasional mediocre poem or story and in 1868 founded the Sylvan Debating Club, where he was the outstanding speaker. His family (of their fourteen chil-dren, eight sons and three daughters survived) lived in poverty, their homes increasingly down-market and their creditors ever angrier. Though they kept up appearances and managed to keep a maid, as a provider Harmsworth was a failure. Yet he was so lovable, and his sense of humour so pervasive, that his wife still adored him and his family forgave him; his tough daughter, Cecil's mother Geraldine, seems to have loved him more uncritically than she ever loved anyone else. It was a devastating blow to his family when, in

1889, at the age of fifty-two, Harmsworth followed in his father's footsteps by dying of cirrhosis of the liver;* without him, home was dreary.

Alfred senior died on Alfred junior's twenty-fourth birthday. 'It will be a bit of a struggle to keep the family in its place,' wrote Alfred to one of his brothers, 'but we will do it and we must make our folk powerful and prosperous, where the father would have loved to have seen us . . . We must all set to work to make the mother's life the happiest possible.' Young Alfred had eventually been forgiven for impregnating the maid when he was sixteen — an indiscretion that had caused his horrified parents to turn him out of the house. By then he had already become a journalist; before his father died, he had married above him and founded *Answers*, his first paper, geared towards those who, Alfred explained, had been 'taught to read but not to think'.

The most handsome of a handsome family, with blue eyes and golden hair, Alfred was a brilliant journalist, his natural instinct as an observer honed by years of looking at and listening to the world around him. He was also daring, driven and inspirational. His brother Harold, prudent and Midas-like with money, agreed to leave the Civil Service and look after the finances. Leicester, Cecil and Hildebrand joined shortly afterwards and even their clever but indolent sister Geraldine worked hard at typing, research and the odd article. Other papers followed and within a couple of years the family was prosperous; within a couple more they were rich.

But before the Harmsworths became famous, Geraldine's life was turned upside-down. In the spring of 1890, while on a visit to a Maffett relative in Dublin, she was introduced to Lucas White King — at thirty-three, ten years her senior and convalescing after an illness that had followed a stay of nine months in Moscow learning Russian. She fell instantly for this handsome, fair-haired, blue-eyed, widely travelled, serious man, and he just as quickly for this slim, striking woman with huge brown eyes, dark gold hair and perfect skin. They had met

---

* That is the accepted story, though according to an obituary of Geraldine Harmsworth in *Truth*, Alfred Harmsworth lost his common-law practice and was attending Clerkenwell Sessions 'to receive his "soup" having got cancer of the throat; his voice was almost inaudible in court'.

only five times when he had to leave for Europe, but they conducted a passionate correspondence and were engaged by June. He came briefly back to London and was a hit with the Harmsworths, who found him as nice as he was socially desirable; in February 1891, bearing a splendid trousseau for which Alfred had paid £250,* Geraldine arrived in Karachi and married Lucas King the following day. She sent a telegram to her mother: 'Married Dot [her nickname]'.

The danger signals were already evident. King, who had been separated from his India-based parents at the age of eight and reared in Ireland with relatives, was emotionally needy, sentimental and short on humour. His wife – from a family where argument and teasing were the stuff of everyday life – was confident and self-possessed, and even in the early days found it difficult to give him the reassurance he constantly craved. King used his abilities to the full, was a brave, just and industrious colonial officer and had a huge range of interests (archaeology, antiquities, anthropology, coins, flora, fauna, folklore, geography, linguistics and big-game hunting are just a sample), which he pursued with dedication. Geraldine was bone-idle: the piano she had brought from London was unplayed; although encouraged to write, she managed only a couple of articles; and nothing came of her promise to be involved in his hobbies and not just be a housekeeper ('I must be far more than that – I must be your chum as well'[13]). But she enjoyed the social life as a memsahib and took instantly to the pleasures of having everything done by servants. She had considerable managerial ability; throughout her life, in several different locations in India as in Ireland, England and Scotland, her houses were efficiently run and she had no trouble keeping servants.

King continued to rise steadily through the ranks, respected for his political acumen, his coolness in the face of danger and his conscientiousness, while Geraldine adapted easily to her improving social position. But the rise of her siblings was on a far more dizzying scale. During Geraldine's first visit home after five years in India, Alfred launched the *Daily Mail*. On the morning of 4 May 1896, the day of the first issue, as the family sat round in a circle looking at copies of

---

* About £16,000 today.

the paper, he kissed the top of his mother's head and said, 'It's either bankruptcy or Berkeley Square.'[14] The Prime Minister, Lord Salisbury, was one of those who sent a congratulatory telegram, though in private (in a reference to Thackeray's Pendennis, who started a newspaper 'by gentlemen for gentlemen') he described the *Daily Mail* as 'a newspaper produced by officeboys for officeboys'.[15] That, of course, was its strength.

A year later Alfred was in Berkeley Square, but well before that he had bought a fine town house for his mother in Marble Arch.* It was from there that – magnificent in yellow satin – Geraldine left in her mother's carriage with her mother's liveried servants to be presented at court – 'bending low to kiss Queen Victoria's tiny, puffy, purple hand with rings embedded in her fingers'.[16]

By then the Kings had three children: Elinor Mary Kathleen, known as Nora, Sheila Geraldine and Lucas Henry St Aubyn. Enid Madeleine, born in 1897, was the fourth to be born in India, but the Kings were back in England for the birth of the ten-pound[17] child who would be Cecil, two months after a Harmsworth Christmas that netted Geraldine enough money to buy herself *inter alia* a mink cape, a sable muff and a diamond brooch.

The putative godfather, Cecil Harmsworth, wrote:

My dearest Dotkin . . . Much love and thanks to you & Lucas for the honour you intend me in regard to the name of the latest arrival. I need not tell you how greatly the idea pleases me – but you won't mind my saying that it would be more in accordance with the wisdom of the serpent to name the young man after the head of the house. Of my most affectionate regard for all your scions of the race you may assure yourself – but in the rough and tumble of life sympathy & affection are not the most useful things. Nor do I know that Alfred's love for a god-child would be smaller than mine . . .[18]

Alfred had no legitimate children, and Leicester and Cecil had each given his name to their eldest sons (Cecil's Alfred had died in 1899),

---

* 2 Great Cumberland Place, where the Cumberland Hotel now stands.

but Geraldine stuck to her decision, though paying obeisance to the family in giving Cecil Harmsworth as a second name. So fair as to be almost white-haired, he was nicknamed Snowball.

The three eldest children were sent to be looked after and educated in what Enid, who was sent there subsequently, described as 'a sort of home from home' in Wiltshire;[19] Enid and Cecil were taken to Lahore. The following March they moved to Simla for the hot season, and here Geraldine reached the social heights of Anglo-Indian society in a whirl of 'dinner parties, balls, dances, lunch and tennis parties . . . races and gymkhanas . . . polo, cricket and tennis tournaments [and] amateur dramatics'.[20] She was basking in the glory of her husband, whose courage and ability had brought him promotion and honour: he was made Companion of the Star of India at a ceremony to which he drove with the Viceroy and the Maharajah of Patiala 'in a State carriage of solid silver through lines of elephants covered with red and gold embroideries and carrying howdahs of silver and gold'.[21]

Only Geraldine knew how intensely vulnerable was the private Lucas King. 'Sweetest Heart,' said a typical letter from the field. 'Two of your dear letters today came together & none yesterday. You must always write to me in the morning Sweet as I pine for my darling's letters.'[22] 'This is a long letter for your short one, darling,' he wrote a few months later. 'I think she cares for him a little now and then but no woman can love like a man, sweetheart. With worlds of tenderest love and a storm of kisses from your ever devoted Boysha.'[23]

In Simla, Geraldine became an intimate of Mary, the rich and beautiful young American wife of the new Viceroy, Lord Curzon. Enid remembered 'dancing classes at Vice Regal Lodge, and rows of tiger skins on a vast polished floor, and stools made out of elephants' feet lined with red velvet.' Geraldine's great deprivation was that the arrival of her twins caused her to miss the Coronation Durbar – designed successfully by Curzon to be the greatest event of its kind ever seen in India. Brother Alfred wrote in December 1902 from the Paris Ritz to congratulate her:

My dearest Dot
    The time for my annual screed is come & I recline comfortably before an excellent wood fire in my beloved Paris this

biting cold winter day to tell you, amidst all your oriental magnificence, bearer peons, chokedars, marlis (is that it?) & the rest of them not to forget your good & increasing brother left behind in Europe . . .

We left the dear Mother very well & happy, not a day older I think, a very wonderful old lady indeed with the modest demand for 'more freeholds' for an Xmas and birthday gift . . . Kiss the little niece for me & select nice names for the twins.[24]

The female twin was unremarkably named Sophie Geraldine after her grandmothers; she would be known as Chirrie (after the Urdu for 'little bird'). The male was christened Alfred Curzon White, and though he was given a lowly uncle as godfather (St John, the seventh son, known as 'Bonch'), his godmother was Lady Curzon; he would be known as Bob.

King received the Coronation (Durbar) medal, but he was becoming increasingly desperate to get out of the Indian Civil Service and into academia. 'His strenuous official duties in the Punjab, Mysore, Waziristan, Kohat and elsewhere,' it was later observed, 'did not prevent him from following with conspicuous success his natural inclinations for, and applying his aptitude to, archaeological, historical, linguistic and numismatic study':[25] he was the author of *The History and Coinage of the Baraksai Dynasty of Afghanistan, The History and Coinage of Malwa* and *A Monography on the Orakzai Country and Clans (N.W. Frontier)* and in 1896 had acquired a doctorate from Trinity. Tired of endless travel across vast tracts of inhospitable territory, King was anxious to have a proper home where the whole family could live together; Geraldine, on the other hand, later told Enid that she wept into her trunk when packing to leave India for the last time.[26]

Money was no obstacle: Geraldine received from Alfred (now a baronet) an allowance of £2,000[*] a year, and opposite Poynters was the Old House, which their mother owned and would make available to the Kings. In March 1903 Geraldine left India for good with Enid, Cecil and the twins.

---

[*] About £120,000 today.

'My earliest recollections are of Totteridge,' wrote Cecil King:

– my very first is of being held by Nurse Dunch, who gripped my nose while pouring medicine down my necessarily open mouth.

I can remember getting my woollen gloves dirty on the pram wheel in which I was being pushed: Aunt Christabel's wedding to Percy Burton: receiving a sovereign from Uncle Alfred [Northcliffe] when he became a peer in 1905: going home from a children's party given by Uncle Harold [later Lord Rothermere] and Aunt Lil in such dense fog that the footman had to walk in front with one of the carriage lamps to light the way. Finally, I can remember a visit to Elmwood, Northcliffe's place in Thanet, where there was a boat from an Arctic expedition Northcliffe had financed, and an alligator in the hothouse.[27]

They were in Totteridge for two years, during which time Lucas King was home for nine months. He had always been popular with the Harmsworths and Alfred was as munificent as ever, giving his brother-in-law a cheque for £500 to spend as he liked: King rented a house and shooting in Aberdeenshire, beginning an association with Aboyne and its surroundings that lasted until his death. He returned reluctantly to India as Commissioner of Rawalpindi: 'I hate the idea of India more and more every day so find me a nice home, sweetie, and *home* I will come in October,' he wrote in April 1904.[28] 'I must stick it till then, I suppose. Darling Pet life is absolutely worthless without your sweet presence.'

'In my vast experience,' wrote King's Lahore language teacher, 'I have never come across any other Officer who has taken such interest in Oriental studies and has attained such proficiency as Mr White King. He can write and speak these languages with great facility, and in my opinion is well fitted to lecture in any or all of them.'[29]

Back in Totteridge in October, King applied for the chair of Arabic, Persian and Hindustani at Trinity College, Dublin;[30] his appointment was announced the following March and he retired from the Indian Civil Service on a pension of £1,000[*] per annum. While the parents

---

[*]   About £60,000 today.

set up house in Dublin, the children went to Uncle Alfred's country house for the summer and were there introduced to their governess, Miss Amy Matthews, BA. 'Tiny, grey-haired, plain and indomitable,'[31] said Enid; and in maturity even Cecil spoke well of her: 'a strict disciplinarian and an excellent teacher. What we learned from her we really learned.'[32] She was to spend eight years with the Kings, teaching all the children except the eldest son (known when very young as Aubyn, but now called Luke), who had been at prep school in England from 1903.

Judging by the precocity of the letters Cecil wrote at three-and-a-half, Miss Matthews wasted no time. One of the earliest demonstrated the curiosity that was to distinguish him intellectually:

> Dear Mum
>   I shall be so glad to come and see my new nursery will it be pretty. was the big ship rolling about that you and Daddy went on. I am waiting to come to Ireland. I want to unpack our toy box. did a big ship carry all our things. shall I play with Enid every night downstairs. We are all quite well. Love and kisses From Snowy xxxxxxxxxxx[33]

He wrote again the day they set off for Roebuck Hall, four miles from the centre of Dublin, this time exhibiting the honesty that was to be one of his most memorable characteristics:

> We are going to Ireland to-day in a big ship, We are in the Billiard Room, Today. I hope That The sea won't Be rough, and That we won't be ill.
>   I wrote That This letter nearly all myself.
>   We are all good.
>   Snowy.
>   Sheila helped me[34]

('I remember arriving in Ireland,' recalled the adult Cecil, '. . . it was pouring with rain.[35])

Set in eleven acres, the house, said Enid, was 'solid and square, late Georgian and built of stone painted cream with a slate roof and granite portico. It was uncompromising, ungraceful'.[36] The furnishings included many valuable Indian carpets and 'oriental china, stone Buddhas, brass figures and embroideries. Our large hall was like a small museum of these things with weapons and musical instruments hanging on the walls as well as Dad's fine tiger skin'.[37] Apart from Miss Matthews, who dominated the children's lives, the staff consisted of a nanny, nurserymaid, cook, housemaid, kitchenmaid, parlourmaid, gardener and a cowman; there was also a coachman to drive the two bay horses and four magnificent carriages presented by Uncle Harold. 'The coachman's livery was of chocolate cloth with silver crested buttons and, as Dad's service allowed it, he wore a cockade on his smooth top hat. He wore white breeches and black top boots with light brown tops. Crests were painted inconspicuously on the doors of the carriages.'[38] A chauffeur replaced the coachman in 1908 when the horses and carriages gave way to a car, a Darracq, presented by Uncle Leicester Harmsworth, who owned the company.

Enid and Cecil developed diametrically opposed views of their father. Cecil found it 'impossible to reconcile the picture of the youth with an education in remote County Clare, ambitious, enterprising and brilliant, with the irascible old gentleman I knew, who had no imagination and no enterprise that I ever noticed . . . There was . . . an occasion, which I vividly recall, when he kicked me down a flight of stairs. When I asked why, I was told I knew full well, but I didn't! I supposed I was making too much noise, but I was a quiet child and this did not seem certain.'[39]

Yet for Enid, 'My father was the dearest person in life to me and much the closest, with his merry blue eyes, enormous general knowledge, his simplicity and affection . . . If something amused him, he would very nearly burst with laughter . . . he always drew out the very best in anyone he was with, making them feel twice as good and clever and happy as usual.'[40] For her, 'the happiest room in the house was Dad's study lined to the ceiling with books; there I would curl up in a huge armchair in the evenings and read while he read also, twiddling his toe out of his shoe, or rapidly wrote Persian script from right to left, while the rest of the family gossiped or played joking family Bridge (which I also enjoyed) with Mother in the drawing room'.[41] Family recollection favours Enid: 'Very nice, very mild' was their cousin Christabel Bielenberg's memory of King.[42]

Cecil's earliest recollection of his father was 'of his playing his last game of tennis. He behaved like an old man, but during the years in Ireland he only went in age from forty-eight to sixty-three . . . The contrast between my father in 1878 and my father in, say, 1908, when I can first remember him, is so great that it has always seemed to me that the explanation must be with my mother, who devitalised him and squashed him flat.'[43] Geraldine, according to Cecil, insisted on King 'being treated with great deference, but we all observed that on family matters she herself ignored him'.[44]

'The Indian climate might have been a cause,' admitted Cecil, 'but then my father spent his service in the hills of the North-West frontier and not in the plains, which must have been very trying in those days.' Cecil showed no more empathy than he did charity in his memoirs; he was either unable or unwilling to take account of the physical toll on King of the often gruelling conditions he had faced during more than a quarter of a century in India, or of the emotional vulnerability that had stemmed from a largely parentless childhood. By the time King had the permanent home he had always craved, he was prematurely old (as early as 1895, Geraldine wrote apropos a visit to their 'honeymoon places . . . Lu is getting too old, so he says, for rubbish of that kind, he was 39 the other day!'[45]); although his letters to his wife continued the habit of passionate language, their relationship suffered, she told Cecil years later, because he had lost interest in sex, which, as a true Harmsworth, she greatly enjoyed.

Geraldine and her husband now had little in common and lived almost separate lives: apart from his teaching at Trinity, and his work as a JP, King enjoyed academic and literary company; having sold his remarkable coin collection on his return from India, he now collected ancient Irish stone and bronze weapons and built up a fine collection of first editions of modern Irish authors. Geraldine had acquired a taste for grand company and had no interest in artists, though she collected some Irish glass and furniture – enjoying 'the jokes and the bargaining with her old cronies on the quays'.[46] And though both were snobbish, Geraldine was interested in having exalted connections in the present and future, while King searched for them in his past.

Having no personal experience of a normal family life, King proved ill-equipped to be a resident father and continued to leave to Geraldine the running of home and family, while she mainly delegated the care of her children to domestic staff and schools. That was a familiar story among the well-off of the period, yet Cecil appeared to regard his experience as unique. The adult Cecil felt 'as if I were an orphan brought up by step-parents, a stepfather who was completely null and a stepmother who was loveless, capricious and occasionally cruel'. In the 1960s Enid wrote that Cecil 'seems in recollection to have been a solitary, unhappy child. This puzzled me; he seemed to us so obviously our Mother's favourite and he was so physically beautiful. We knew also that he was brilliant. My father once asked me in genuine and extreme modesty if I thought it strange that he should have fathered such an outstanding son. Cecil was aloof then as he is so often described now.'[47]

Such was the forcefulness and sincerity with which Cecil was later to speak and write of a miserable childhood that his account was generally accepted as fact. And though he spread the blame pretty widely, his mother bore the brunt of it. 'A favourite ploy with my mother was to clean my ears with a handkerchief and a hairpin. This was often very painful and, I thought at the time, intended to be so. She also on occasion thrashed me with her walking-stick, coming to the bathroom afterwards when I was in the bath to inspect the weals.'[48]

'Malevolence is not the normal manifestation of the maternal instinct,' wrote Cudlipp in 1976, 'but I accept without reservation King's description of his mother and of this particular woman's effect upon this particular son. In all his writings there is but one fleeting romantic reference to her . . . He writes wistfully of her striking good looks being plainly visible in a photograph taken on her return from India: what is plainly visible in the picture to anybody who was not emotionally involved is that she was the right old bitch her son knew her to be.'[49] To an outsider, the photograph shows a fashionably dressed woman with a rather fat, masculine face, who might as well be thinking mystical as malevolent thoughts; however, Cudlipp was affected not just by Cecil's accounts of his mother, but by a tense meeting with her in the 1930s[50] in her grandest of *grande dame* modes.

Like many other readers of Cecil's memoirs, Cudlipp had been horrified by this passage:

A last episode. Ten years after my mother's death, when I was fifty-four, I woke up in a panic, having dreamt she was still alive! I had been a good son in outward behaviour, but I must have hated her. I have no wish to do anything with my hands and it has seemed to me over the years that this was because in early childhood I had wanted to strangle her with them.[51]

'I can recall, on reflection,' wrote Cudlipp, 'no phrase more stark in a description of family life. Beside it *Oedipus Rex* is a Brian Rix comedy, *King Lear* a rapturous musical, and *Macbeth* a marital romp . . . Lord Northcliffe's last wish was to be buried as close to his mother as possible. Cecil, I am sure, would wish to be buried as far away as possible from Geraldine II.'

Was she so dreadful? Once again Enid saw things differently:

Roebuck was our first and only home until we each made our own, and, until the tensions of growing up began, it was excellent, and we were always very attached to it − so clean of purpose, orderly and changeless. In the very early days Mother, though aloof and extremely reserved, was softer, creating our wonderful Christmases and leaving a bar of Cadbury's chocolate on our pillows every night. She also told us lovely cautionary stories of her own invention at lunch. She believed in monotony for children; we never went away, or even to a pantomime.[52]

Like many little girls of that class and period:

we changed after tea into white frocks and sashes and came down to spend half an hour with Mother in the drawing-room . . . I can see Bob now stretched on his tummy behind Mother's chair arranging and setting his collection of flies and beetles . . . The only times we came down to dinner at night were for Christmas and Mother's birthday on the 27th December. I can never be too grateful to Mother for our lovely Christmases. It was all so perfect. Mother, usually so detached from our childhood plans and pleasures, took a lot of trouble.'[53]

Like her mother, Geraldine was not particularly maternal: both were cut out to be matriarchs rather than mothers. As a child and adolescent, she had lived in a succession of ever rowdier houses filled with fighting younger siblings whom she was supposed to help bring up to high standards; crying was forbidden, largely because Alfred junior could not stand noise. While he led by example, she alternated between sarcasm and physical punishment to keep some sort of order. Yet there is no family evidence to suggest any resentment; her amiable father adored her and the Harmsworths were always immensely strong on family feeling. (St John Harmsworth, crippled in 1906 in a car accident on his way home from his inamorata, his sister-in-law, was kept for the rest of his life in luxury not just by Alfred but by his cuckolded brother Harold.) 'I wish I could see them all,' Geraldine wrote from Germany, where she spent almost a year with relatives when she was seventeen. 'I wonder how they are getting on without Gorks [one of her nicknames] to whip them, poor little kiddies.' Still, Geraldine was certainly a dominating personality, 'with that Harmsworth authoritative air of hers which brooked no disobedience'.[54]

Enid says nothing of brutality, but talks about parental detachment:

> Every Easter holidays my parents went away leaving Miss Matthews in charge to the despair of Luke home from Winchester. I remember Luke poignantly calling from his bed: 'It's come to a pitch, Mummy, it's come to a pitch!' in an anguish of boredom when his precious holidays stretched blankly before him once more . . .
>
> What I simply could not understand was that Mother used to tell the story of Luke's heart-breaking outburst with some amusement, which brings me to what I think is one of the biggest differences between then and now. I mean the relationship of human people with each other. I never once thought of my older relations as fallible, sensitive people like myself. They really were Olympian and had to be obeyed, however mysterious and illogical their rules might be. There was virtually no communication with them.

This failure to see his parents as people typical of their class and time, rather than as neglectful and hurtful monsters, was to intensify

with Cecil in adulthood – his own inadequacies as a parent notwith-
standing. And when in his fifties he began his relationship with the
besotted Ruth Railton, who questioned nothing, was jealous of all
his past and present relationships and so encouraged his resentments,
he was to see his past more and more through a self-pitying prism
that exaggerated and distorted. The dreadful events of his adolescent
years were to have a profound and damaging psychological effect on
him, obscuring the truth that, as Edwardian upper-middle-class child-
hoods went, his was no worse – and in many ways much better –
than most.

The family was never to be properly rooted in Ireland, where, in
Enid's words, they 'lived in an English upper class society transplanted
in Ireland, with a background of deliciously funny irrational sub-
servient characters'.[55] Cecil's favourite was Turley, the chauffeur, whose
car was far more exciting than the pony he occasionally rode; he not
only hung around as Turley serviced the Darracq, but went with him
around the seedier areas of Dublin looking for tools and spare parts.
Cecil loved too watching a blacksmith and later a fine cabinet-maker
at work, but – being 'impossibly clumsy with my hands'[56] (whether
for dark psychological reasons or genetic ineptitude) – was strictly an
observer.

The biggest lack was children of his own age. The three eldest Kings
were much older: Luke, the youngest of them, was away at school;
Enid, the fourth child, was sent most holidays to stay with Granny
Harmsworth; and Sophie Geraldine ('Chirrie') and Alfred Curzon
White (Bob), almost two years younger, had the self-sufficiency of
twins. Sheila, seven years Cecil's senior, did the best she could for her
solitary, sensitive younger brother. She was, said Enid, 'Cecil's and my
dearest possible sister from the first. She was full of imagination, and
we had wonderful games together; she cared enough to take a lot of
trouble to give us pleasure, or a surprise. She was highly nervous and
wept very easily, but she really was absolutely charming, sensitive and
loveable, unselfish and delightfully pretty.'[57]

In her efforts to entertain Cecil and take him out of himself, Sheila
'arranged for me to play the part of a Grain of Mustard Seed in the
Dundrum parish hall. I had only one word to say, but didn't say it,
but instead rolled myself up in the curtain and wept. Not long after-
ward I was billed to appear as Cupid, with flesh-pink tights and a

bow and arrow. But, mercifully, I caught 'flu and was put to bed, and thus my stage career ended.'[58]

There were few other children for Cecil to play with while he remained in the schoolroom: his diary for 1910 records little social-ising other than dance class. Enid recalls, 'It was anything but a treat for Cecil, the only boy in the class, dressed in navy blue serge and an Eton collar with long black stockings over his knees and black patent leather shoes. He looked absolutely miserable, but was awarded a box of chocolates when, after months of unspeakable boredom, he brought enough attention to bear on the problem to master the polka.'[59]

He was, in fact, happier with girls than boys. It was at dancing class that he met Enid Starkie, who used to come to the King par-ties and was one of the few Catholics in the King social circle: 'Amongst the Kings it was Cecil who was my particular friend,' she wrote in her autobiography. 'He was the nearest to me in age. In the early days of the parties our friendship was more quarrelsome than affectionate, and we used to grapple together in physical combat.'[60] The only friend to feature in his diaries before 1913 was Olif Hardy who visited, and was visited by, Cecil. He remembered it as his first flirtation: 'it was the shyest and most tentative of attachments. However, the poor girl contracted cancer of the brain, so I watched her lose successively her sense of balance, her hearing and her sight. This would have been a rather shattering experience in any case, but it was made more so by her mother, when Olif was dead, insisting that we were engaged to be married. Though this was a ridiculous idea – we were so very young – it enhanced the importance of a relationship which had come to such a grievous end.' The Mrs Hardy story seems improbable: Cecil was in fact only eleven when his diary recorded his first tragedy: 'Olif died at 15 minutes to one. Nora got a pearl necklace from Uncle Alfred.'[61]

His preference for girls made boarding school a particular trial. He had been despatched in September 1911 to an English prep school, Rose Hill, in Surrey: 'I remember very little about it except my mother in floods of tears as she left me there . . . After four terms I was so thin I was taken away from the school, as our doctor in Ireland said I would die if left there. I don't remember being badly fed, but I was miserable, home-sick and a bed-wetter, so my thinness may well have had a psychological cause.'[62] Yet his school reports were most com-

plimentary and his thinness may have had to do with his exceptionally fast growth (five feet three inches at the age of ten).

At his Dublin Protestant day school, which had two women teachers,
Cecil was much happier, though 'the boys were a rough lot and the
masters an even rougher lot':[63] his school report of July 1913 showed
him far ahead of the other five in his class. And at home there were
plenty of books, for all the family were readers. 'By the time I was
thirteen I had read more books than most people in a lifetime . . . I
was and am unable to read poetry . . . but at an early age I had read
all Dickens, Thackeray, Jane Austen, George Eliot and even Scott . . .
In addition to novels I read translations of the classics, scientific
books, books on anything I could lay my hand on.' There were also
elementary experiments in chemistry, conducted in the dirty harness
room in the stables. However boarding school loomed again.

'My darling Luke,' wrote Geraldine in July 1914 to her eldest son.[64]
'Poor old Snow has been in Winchester the last three days having his
exam for Headmaster's nomination . . . If he fails, which is most
probable, he goes to . . . Eton* after Xmas.' Cecil's diary records that
this visit to England included a round of family visits and such treats
as a play – *When Knights are Bold* – which he loved and dinner at the
House of Commons; but as an adult he explained simply that – ill-
prepared and a poor examinee – 'off I went with my eldest sister to
Winchester and, of course, failed'. Yet, though he did not win a scholarship, Cecil earned a place to be taken up the following January and,
from the outbreak of war in August, developed a new passion: 'Snow
is tremendously interested in the war, & reads newspapers all day,
knows every move & every ship – off before breakfast to see the
telegrams up at the post-office,'[65] wrote their mother to Luke, now a
graduate of Sandhurst and an officer of the 60th Rifles in India.

Six years Cecil's senior, Luke was as sociable and outgoing as his
brother was shy and introvert. 'This is the longest epistle I have ever
compiled and I hope it will please you,' he ended a four-page letter
to his 'dear Mum' at the age of twelve from prep school. 'With best
love to yourself Daddy Sheila Enid Snowie Sophie Alfred as well as

---

* With his own sons, Cecil was also to take the view that Eton was for those not sufficiently able for Winchester.

a few million kisses for each from Luke.'[66] 'My darling Mater'[67] was one form of address from Winchester in unselfconscious letters full of school happenings, codes, nicknames, negotiations over money and freedoms, jokes and amiable insults: 'Tell dad his book is beastly old fashioned. Best love to all especially tip givers from Luke.'[68]

Popular and successful at school and a prize cadet at Sandhurst, Luke had his sights set on service in India. 'I hope, dear Granny,' he wrote in March 1913 to his paternal grandmother, Sophie King, apropos the death of his uncle and godfather, Lieutenant-Colonel Harry King, 'that some day I may worthily fill his place as your soldier son . . . I only hope that when my time comes I shall be able to stand up with the bravery of my uncle.'[69] At Geraldine's request, Northcliffe had written to several military people, including Field Marshal Lord Roberts, VC, once Commander-in-Chief of the British Army, asking that they help Luke join either the King's Royal Rifles or the Rifle Brigade – both fashionable regiments[70]. The request was unsuccessful.

Luke left Sandhurst in September 1913 with the 60th Rifles,[71] and by December that year he was in Bombay. The outbreak of war the following August filled him with frustration: 'It is desperately rotten luck that we should be left out of this, the greatest war that has ever been.'[72] Geraldine, who had been very upset at his choosing to serve abroad,[73] was relieved: 'My darling Luke,' she wrote in September. 'The war is our one interest & topic – we think & talk of nothing else. I see the K.R.Rs have lost about 23 officers altogether – killed wounded & missing – if I had had my wish last year – I daresay you would have been in that list!'[74] Despite her bellicosity, she was 'so glad you are out of it – there is no fun in this fighting – it is slaughter by machinery, & I believe the noise of the artillery is simply deafening – Hell let loose in fact!'[75]

Luke was on his way to that hell soon afterwards, writing en route to the trenches that 'I hope that I will be able to uphold the honour of the family without too much loss of blood'.[76] From there in January, now a lieutenant, he thought of his brother: 'I suppose Cecil is now installed at Bathers [A. G. Bather was housemaster]. I wonder what he thinks of it. I should like to have ushered him in myself. What a nuisance this war is to be sure!'[77] 'Cecil is delighted with Winchester,' wrote his mother, '& says he is "enjoying" himself – he is in the 3rd class from the bottom – which does not appear to me to be a very good start.'[78]

From Cecil's memoirs there was no hint of any enjoyment: his house was mediocre; his headmaster 'had no relationship of any kind with anyone in my house' and was 'certainly in part a humbug'; his housemaster was a clergyman whose 'religious faith was at best tepid and his impact on his house small'; and the second master (later head-master, Dean of Christ Church, Bishop of Durham and Bishop of Winchester) was 'a pleasant nonentity with a stone-deaf wife'.[79] 'I hated almost every day of my time at Winchester and, in any case, my first term was a disaster. I am not a conformist and Winchester was a very conformist institution, so my approach to becoming a Wykehamist was not suitably reverential. I was very homesick.'

Any inference from this that home was worth missing was contra-dicted by the adult Cecil: homesickness 'is worse if you are unhappy at home. A happy home life gives you a secure base from which you can issue with confidence. But if life at home takes all you have got, life at a boarding-school is just the last straw.' Apart from the elabo-rate rules and customs, many of which he found absurd, there was the prohibition on being alone: even the lavatories were without doors. 'I didn't like little boys and I am desperately dependent on being alone part of every day, so daily life at Winchester was very heavy going for me, though the other boys took it in their stride.'[80]

During his first term Cecil contracted bronchitis, pneumonia and measles and was 'put into a small ward with another boy – a sort of death-cell. He died and I just didn't.' There were no ministering angels, just thoughtless night-nurses who kept him awake: he was sent home to convalesce and missed the summer term of 1915. 'How is my long brother?' enquired Luke in April, having himself just recovered from a wound and newly engaged to be married. 'He will be off with Chicken Pox in a day or two!'[81]

Cecil was still at home when, on 8 May, Luke was killed at Ypres. There was an early telegram: 'YOU KNOW HOW I GRIEVE FOR YOU DARLING SISTER PLEASE WRITE ME BIOGRAPHY OF DEAR LUKE FOR THE TIMES ALFRED'.[82]

CHAPTER II
A Legacy of Uncles

'MY MOTHER WAS NOT A LOVING WOMAN, AND IT IS HARD TO SAY why she took Luke's death so hard . . . However, for weeks after the news she was barely sane and entirely dependent on my hourly presence – no one else would do . . . I was not only left trying to comfort my mother, but also trying to prop up the flagging spirits of my father.'[1] Cecil's subsequent attitude to Geraldine suggests strongly that subconsciously he deeply resented the scale of her grief at the loss of Luke.

Whatever his mother's failings, she did not succumb to the temptation to extol the dead child over the living. Even Cecil could not avoid admitting this, for she told him frequently that he was her favourite child. Her extended family, however, who saw Luke often and loved him, were less aware of Cecil, and he would have been reading such letters as Rothermere's – to whose sons Luke was very close ('As for dear Luke I felt for him next to my own boys'[2]) – and his own godfather, Uncle Cecil's ('I loved your dear boy as much almost as my own sons'[3]). Uncle St John's ('The noble boy has inscribed his name on the roll of heroes and covered our family with glory'[4]) was typical of condolences of the time, when the only consolation for the death of a son was to believe that he had, as St John put it in another letter, 'nobly fulfilled his destiny. Life offers nothing greater than this.'[5]

After the summer of domestic mourning, Cecil went back to Winchester, itself increasingly gloomy and intense as the list of school dead grew remorselessly and senior boys knew they would

soon themselves be on the way to war. Cecil performed well academically, his ability was recognised and he was promoted accordingly. His obsessive preoccupation with the war continued, made
more vivid by the dramatic and very public activities of Northcliffe,
who was not only powerful through his newspapers, but strode the
public stage — worshipped, hated, feared and admired. In his own
empire he aroused strong feelings too, but he always had the gratitude of the ordinary journalists and production workers whose lives
he transformed by paying them decently. To be able to listen in private to a man more dreaded and courted by the British government
than any press baron before or since was to have a profound effect
on his serious nephew.

In Northcliffe's room at *The Times* — along with their photographs
— was a cupboard full of toys for the twenty-three Harmsworth
nephews and fourteen Harmsworth nieces.[6] 'He was, of course,' wrote
Enid, 'the most exciting person I have ever known, right in the fore-
front of his day, tingling with new ideas and ambitions, and always
on the move.'[7] His nephew Godfrey wrote:

> He personified the best that an uncle could be. He enjoyed the
> relationship. He entered genially and affectionately into its obli-
> gations and sentiments. Schoolboy Harmsworths would be
> excited by his visits to Eton, Harrow and Winchester. He always
> replied promptly to their requests for autographs of the famous,
> foreign stamps and photographs of aeroplanes, about which he
> was an evangelical. There were school holidays at Elmwood where
> he would introduce nephews to the great and give them the thrill
> of hearing him talk on the telephone to the Prime Minister.[8]

They adored him: 'Uncle Alfred has been working like Hercules
to put things right,' wrote Vyvyan Harmsworth in May 1915. 'Why
don't they put *him* in the Cabinet? — the nincompoops.'[9]

Cecil liked as well as admired this hugely glamorous figure — so
different from his quiet father: the uncle's achievements during the
First World War were to haunt the nephew during the Second.
Northcliffe was a legend: 'the rotund English nobleman who owns
half of the British publishing world, who makes and unmakes governments in John Bull's little isle according to his own sweet will,

by far the greatest single personal power in the world war' was a description in a 1917 article by a German in an American news-paper.[10]*

Now the proprietor of *The Times* as well as the *Daily Mail* (the *Daily Mirror*, which he had founded in 1903, he sold to his brother Harold in 1914), Northcliffe was powerful, patriotic, bellicose, fearless and at loggerheads with the government, defying noisily in both his papers its efforts to censor criticisms of various kinds of ineptitude. Nor was there anything about him of the armchair general. Believing his own maxim that 'The man on the spot knows best,'[11] he travelled frequently to see war conditions – often in circumstances of danger and extreme discomfort – and came back ever more vociferous in support of soldiers against politicians. It was his knowledge of what was actually happening at the front that precipitated a huge scandal over high-explosive shells, the shortage of which Northcliffe rightly believed was leading to unnecessary British casualties.

Less than a week after Luke's death, which his colleagues saw had greatly upset Northcliffe,[12] *The Times* published a report from its chief war correspondent that yet another attack had failed because of a lack of high explosives. Then the *Daily Mail* ran with the story and, though well aware that he would be accused of giving comfort to the enemy, Northcliffe began a devastating frontal attack on the most popular member of the Cabinet, the Secretary for War, Lord Kitchener. In 'The Tragedy of the Shells: Lord Kitchener's Grave Error' – the most famous leader written during the whole war – he accused Kitchener of sending to the army in France the wrong kind of shell. 'He was warned repeatedly that the kind of shell required was a violently explosive bomb which would dynamite its way through the German trenches and entanglements and enable our brave men to advance in safety. The kind of shell our poor soldiers have has caused the death of thousands of them.'[13]

The paper's circulation dropped from 1,386,000 to 238,000 overnight; a placard saying 'The Allies of the Huns' appeared across the name-

---

*   'In that single word "rotund",' added Northcliffe – who enclosed the article with one of the indiscreet and entertaining circular letters he used to send to his 'private circle', many of which are preserved in King's papers – 'he got back on me for all I had been saying about Germany for years.'

plate on the newspaper's headquarters and copies were burned on the floor of the Stock Exchange as 1,500 of its members cheered for Kitchener and jeered at Northcliffe. His brother Cecil, a Liberal MP, felt forced to resign from his minor government post.[14] But Northcliffe's nerve held: 'As regards abuse, I am a pachyderm'[15] was one of his entirely accurate boasts.

Within a few days, the Liberal government had been brought down by shells. Although Kitchener was too popular to overthrow, in the new coalition government, the vigorous, effective and ruthless David Lloyd George became Minister of Munitions; Rothermere was passed over for a ministry because of Northcliffe's attitude to Kitchener.[16]

It was the beginning of the end for Prime Minister Asquith. Northcliffe did not let up: he sacrificed his friendship with Winston Churchill by his papers' bitter criticism of the Dardanelles disaster. As he had always been able to think like the man in the street, throughout the war he thought like the soldier under fire. The recipient of innumerable communications from the front, and a frequent visitor as a war correspondent, he also saw eloquent and detailed letters from his much-loved nephew, the heroic Vere Harmsworth, son of Rothermere, who reported in detail on muddles and disasters first in Belgium, then at Gallipoli and later in France.

Northcliffe fought countless campaigns and, as a colleague put it, 'Although one never heard him boasting, his bearing suggested that he believed he had saved England from the follies of incompetent government in the conduct of the war.'[17] Yet though he was often critical, he was never defeatist, and it was perhaps his gung-ho attitude and absolute certainty that Britain would prevail that reined in his nephew's natural pessimism. 'I was quite confident we should win the War,' wrote Cecil in his memoirs, 'and somehow communicated this confidence to my parents.'[18] 'I am getting more and more optimistic every day,' he wrote at fifteen to Geraldine from school in July 1916, 'I hope you are doing so too.'[19]

Fighting had already come close to home with the Easter rebellion of 1916. Physically fearless and his Uncle Alfred's true nephew, Cecil had gone as close to the action as he could. 'While the fighting was on, I stood on the roof of the Mount Anneville [*sic*] convent . . . and watched 4.7 inch naval shells bursting in O'Connell Street. When it was all over, I drove around the town with my father to see the very extensive damage done, most of it by bullets and hand grenades, but round the GPO the damage was much greater.' Yet exciting though he found it, the experience marked Cecil, curing him 'for ever of the comfortable feeling so prevalent in England to this day that riot and civil commotion, let alone civil war, could not happen here'.[20] He would always rather enjoy destruction and seemed almost to look forward to social and political upheaval.

Northcliffe never considered himself an Irishman, and he had no strong religious feelings, but his mother – whom he idolised and visited or wrote to every day, and who was the only person whose advice he sought – was utterly determined that Ulster Protestants should not be forced into a United Ireland and required her Alfred to do his utmost on their behalf. After the rebellion, his main concern was that events in Ireland could weaken the war effort, and for a few weeks he was involved daily with Lloyd George in discussions about how to settle Ireland. 'One of the keys of the situation is Mr Murphy of the *Irish Independent*,' he told his brother Cecil, '– a man for whom I have a profound admiration. I have telegraphed asking him to come to London, and I believe if he and I got together we could settle this damnable business; but it needs to be settled *now*, otherwise the hotheads will get to work, both in Ulster and elsewhere.'[21] Murphy came to London, but to Northcliffe's intense disappointment, negotiations with Lloyd George foundered. 'He had hoped, if not believed,' wrote Northcliffe's joint biographers, 'that destiny had reserved for him a leading part in the last act of a drama of internecine history.'[22] Still, Ireland had been a mere sideshow. Back in England that June, Cecil was in his grandmother's drawing room when Northcliffe declared, 'The British Empire has had the greatest stroke of luck in its history. Kitchener is dead – drowned at sea.'[23]

The Northcliffe anti-Asquith campaign intensified after further visits to the war zones in the summer of 1916 (listening to the guns 'throating and sobbing'[24]), interspersed by visits to Switzerland and Spain to examine the nature and effectiveness of German propaganda. He did not let up, though the horrors were taking their toll on his physical and mental health, as were the misfortunes striking his family. The appalling injuries received by his nephew, Leicester's son Alfred, during the Battle of the Somme included castration: Northcliffe visited him in hospital on his way home from the front.

In October, he was greatly affected by a letter from his nephew Vere saying that he felt he might have been born 'just to live my 21 years and then fade away'. Vere feared for Rothermere, his father, should he be killed, but 'If I fall, do not mourn, but be glad and proud. It is not a life wasted but gloriously fulfilled.' He was leaving everything he had 'for the betterment of those who have suffered through the war. Most of it for the men of my Battalion. My whole being is bound up in my men, heart, body and soul. Nothing else seems to matter.'[25]

'He was much cut up,' reported a colleague of Northcliffe's, when Vere was killed leading his company in the Battle of Ancre.[26] Cecil would have read the newspaper report that Vere was 'the favourite nephew of Lord Northcliffe'.[27] Tom Clarke of the *Daily Mail* recorded a couple of weeks later that when he entered Northcliffe's presence:

> He looked across the room at me – over the top of great black-rimmed spectacles – like a somewhat benevolent mandarin.
> 'I thought you were dead,' he said.
> 'Dead?' I echoed.
> 'Killed,' he said. 'I thought there were no young men left.'[28]

Northcliffe's grief did not distract him from his assaults on 'the awful muddle', or from his discussions behind the scenes with Lloyd George on how to bring about change. His impressionable nephew Cecil was avidly reading devastating leaders that he knew to be inspired or written by his uncle. A particularly savage *Daily Mail* assault on governmental indecision in December 1916 outraged the two-thirds of the press not owned by either him or Rothermere. Denouncing 'the colossal vanity of this neurotic child Northcliffe', a *Daily News* column added: 'If the present Government falls, it will fall because Lord Northcliffe decreed that it should fall, and the Government that takes its place, no matter who compose it, will enter on its task as the tributary of Lord Northcliffe.'[29] The following day the *Mail's* headline was 'THE LIMPETS: A NATIONAL DANGER' and by the evening it was announced that the Prime Minister was asking the King to agree to a reconstruction of the government. No wonder that, the following morning, though he was well aware that there had been plenty of others plotting behind the scenes, and subsequently never claimed to have brought Asquith down, Northcliffe phoned his brother Cecil and crowed, 'Who killed cock robin?' 'You did' was the inevitable reply.*

Northcliffe was offered a seat in Cabinet and refused, but while he now tempered his criticisms of government, he continued to use his energy and influence to help prosecute the war. His effectiveness was acknowledged by the Germans, who in February sent a destroyer that fired twenty shells at his house. Although he refused the headship of the new propaganda department, he became chairman of a committee concerned with the future of aviation – one of his consuming passions. Then, two months after the entry of America into the war, after intense pressure from Lloyd George, he agreed 'with more regret and reluctance than I can express'[30] to head the British War Mission in the United States. While Lloyd George was pleased to get Northcliffe out of the country, he was also choosing a great propagandist who knew America intimately to take overall charge of the 10,000-strong British operations.

'I do not suppose many people have had such a kaleidoscopic life as I have had since the War began,' Northcliffe wrote to his 'private circle':

First, those intense four days in 1914 of flogging those political jelly-fish into action, then the row about Kitchener and the shells and the bannings and burnings of my newspapers, then Ypres, Verdun, Gorizia and the Carso, among the Germans in Switzerland, then off to Spain, a few days salmon fishing on the Tay . . . the Battle of the Somme, more visits to France, more stirrings up of the government, thirty-six hours in which to abandon the work of my life for this killing job of trying to push everything available in the United States across the Atlantic to Haig and all the meat and wheat I can get for the people at home.'[31]

_____

* As a corrective, after Lloyd George became Prime Minister, Cecil Harmsworth noted in his diary, 'The London Liberal daily papers are full of denunciations of Northcliffe, whom they regard as the arch-wrecker of the Asquith Govt. There is truth in this, of course, but not all the truth. Grave dissatisfaction with the P.M.'s leadership has been growing apace among Liberals.'

His remarkable success in a hugely demanding job in the public eye brought Northcliffe acclaim, adulation, celebrity status, exhaustion, illness and emotional strain. But back in England in November 1917, now elevated from baron to viscount, more famous and respected than ever, he let up in neither criticism of military errors nor war work. On his way from the allied war conference in Paris in December and from visits to generals, he called on Rothermere's son Vyvyan in a French hospital; he had been wounded for the third time at the disastrous Battle of Cambrai.

'They are murdering my nephews!'[32] cried Northcliffe two months later when he was told of the death of Vyvyan, who was awarded a posthumous Military Cross. 'He was a very able young man,' he wrote to a friend, 'and he told me that on all occasions when he sustained wounds, he had been in the thick of chaos and disorder, caused by ignorance of actual fighting conditions displayed by commanders.'[33]

By now, to considerable effect, Northcliffe had stepped up his assaults on the incompetence of the top brass. He had also become Director of Propaganda in Enemy Countries, in which role he was startlingly effective: so devastating in their impact were the 4,000,000 demoralising leaflets dropped over enemy territories that Northcliffe became a demon figure in Germany; he was later described as having brought about 'the moral collapse of the German people.'[34] His brother Rothermere, who had been an extremely effective Director-General of the Royal Army Clothing Factory, resigned after three months as Secretary of State for Air. According to Winston Churchill, he was 'eaten up with love' of Vyvyan,[35] whose death broke him.

For young Cecil, the high-profile involvement of his uncles, as well as the family tragedies, heightened his excitement vis-à-vis the war. Godfather Cecil Harmsworth, now on Lloyd George's secretariat, fed his obsession by showing him round 10 Downing Street.[36] Life at school had improved steadily: he passed the School Certificate in July 1917 with credits in History, Greek, French and Elementary Mathematics. In English Essay he merely passed, which came as no surprise, for, as his books show, although his opinions were always interesting and sometimes outrageous, Cecil's style was stilted, jerky and dull.

At school, as he got older, he was allowed some blessed time alone. There was also pleasant company available, for, in September 1916, his brother Bob had joined him – despite Cecil's gloomy prophecy that he had little chance of getting a place.[37]

A sunny, clever and enthusiastic boy, like Luke, Bob got on easily with his family. A poem he wrote for his mother in December 1911, when he was nine, poked affectionate fun at her voice and her weight, and letters home from Winchester were as open and familiar as Cecil's were stiff. Thus, Bob at fourteen:

Dear Mother,
    Thanks awfully for your letter . . . A 'cargo' would be extremely welcome. The only disadvantage of the last one was that the cake was rather too large, and as I could not procure a tin large enough to hold it, it became perceptibly stale towards the end. I was told (privately) that the praefects of this house decided after some discussion that it was absolutely necessary for me to fetch the papers every morning as I was so closely related to Lord Northcliffe! . . . Cecil is arranging with Uncle Cecil about next leave-out day. Hoping shortly to receive above mentioned cargo, with a smaller cake (but something else in its place!)
    I am your very loving son
    Bob[38]

And Cecil at sixteen:

My dear Mother,
    As I have not received a letter from you saying if you object to my going on a visit to my friend & as he did not seem to be very keen on having me, I wrote to him yesterday saying I could not come. My chief motive in so doing is that I find the holidays so very short, so I do not wish to spend more time away from home than I must.
    I got my tails about a month ago. They look quite smart.
    I am glad to see that half term was last Sunday & I am already beginning to look forward to the holidays.
    I enclose 20 stamps, quite nice ones. I suppose the last lot

arrived as 'silence is assent' according to the proverb.

We have a whole holiday next Tuesday when Bob & I expect to go bug hunting.

My half-term report ought to reach you about a fortnight hence.

I must stop now as I have nothing more to say, if indeed I ever did have anything to say.

With much love

from

Cecil[39]

Bob's passionate interest in insects took them on their bicycles on butterfly-hunting expeditions in the New Forest – 'the only happy days I can recall', according to the elderly Cecil.[40] They lasted for just two school years. At the beginning of the 1918 autumn term Cecil travelled from home to Winchester a day ahead of Bob. Within a couple of days he received this letter from his mother:

My darling Snow,

After all our talks, plans & jokes about submarines, the worst has happened. Our dear Bob, I am afraid has been drowned in the 'Leinster'. We have had hours & hours of anxiety mixed with hope and now must give up. Enid by a fortunate chance did not travel with Bob as she had arranged . . . Consult Mr Bather as to what you would like to do for the next few days. Would you like to go for walks with him or perhaps a chum. I am quite stunned. Our noisy jokey boy gone . . .

My love to you dear. More precious than ever if possible, now you are the only son left.

Your heartbroken Mother[41]

'My darling Boy,' wrote his father:

In the midst of my grief I cannot help feeling for you as you must be so lonely with no one to comfort you. My heart goes out to you dear son and I wish I could comfort you . . .

Of course I feel it much more than Luke's death who fell on

the field of glory but this. Oh! The pity of it . . . It was the merest chance that we have not lost two . . .

All my love my dear boy

Your heartbroken Dad[42]

The *Leinster* had been torpedoed by a German submarine on its way from Dublin to Holyhead. 'My dear Dot,' wrote Rothermere:

Enid's letter has plunged me once more into the blackness from which I was emerging. It is terrible and I feel for you more than I can say. You and I have had blows rained down on us and the unfairness of it all makes me hate this world.

I am thinking of you both very much and of the four young lives sacrificed thank God not in vain.

Always your devoted brother,

Harold[43]

'It was not till Sunday night that I heard a rumour about the Sea Boy,' wrote Northcliffe to Geraldine. 'I had read the lists with anxiety, but did not see his name. His dear sacrifice is one of those that are bringing vengeance on the Brutes for you will see that President Wilson specifically mentions this horrible crime.'[44] Bob's death, like those of Vere and Vyvyan, exacerbated the ailing Northcliffe's loathing of Germany, about which he was becoming increasingly irrational. The demands of his newspapers for punitive reparations and the hanging of the Kaiser militated against making a reasonable peace.

What made Bob's death even worse for Cecil was that, at his request, they had swapped ships. 'I still have Cecil's anguished letters from Winchester,' wrote Enid, 'where he had arrived the day before the disaster, Mother's sensible plan being to send the boys separately.'[45] (It was, in fact, thanks to Granny Harmsworth, who thought the Kings were crazy to put them in danger by sending them to school in England, that they never travelled together.) 'We were not very close, but I was naturally very shaken,'[46] was Cecil's account, but in this underestimation of the importance of Bob to him, as in so much else, his autobiography reflects his later belief that his family life and school were loveless and dreadful, and does not fit with contemporary evidence. 'I find it useless to attempt to tell you how much you are to me, dear,' wrote his 'devoted' Enid in November, thanking him for a birthday present of *The Navy Eternal*, '& I am sure the rest of us are equally tongue-tied, but at any rate I can tell you how pleased I am with your book.'[47] Rejoicing a month after Bob's death that conscription had been suspended, Cecil wrote to his mother, 'What pleases me is that I shall be able to go home and see you at last, the thing I have been praying for for all these long weeks.'[48]

Although he would become fascinated by psychoanalysis, King seems never to have recognised that the deaths of his brothers and cousins had a major effect on him. He would blame his mother for his need for strong defences ('to protect yourself, you must be seriously attached to nothing and nobody'[49]), yet this is a normal reaction to shocking bereavement. And as his character developed, he showed such classic symptoms of survivor guilt – the 'why not me?' syndrome – as self-hatred and ruthless ambition. But at the time he concentrated on building up the defensive shell that would so inhibit ordinary human intercourse.

'Cecil has had a very hard time but is bearing up bravely,' wrote his godfather, Uncle Cecil, who had gone down to spend a few days with him. 'We saw together most of the things to be seen in the wonderful old town . . . I attended a service at the College Chapel. I tell you I was proud to be seen out with such a boy & especially when . . . [someone] took him for my son! He is something altogether not of the ordinary in boys.'[50]

In that same letter, Cecil senior asked permission to be allowed secretly to pay for Cecil's university education. 'A "darling man", as they say in Ireland, gentle, cultured, weak and amusing . . . and [a] delightful talker,'[51] wrote Enid of him. Young Cecil used frequently to spend a night at one of his houses and 'he was very friendly',[52] yet said later that their relationship 'had no positive content'.[53] And the housemaster, who received no good word in Cecil's memoirs, featured differently in correspondence: 'Bather was very kind & offered to do everything in his power for me,' he wrote to his mother. 'However I came to the conclusion that the best way of occupying my mind was to bury myself in my work.'[54] His success is so doing was an early indication of his pronounced ability as an adult to compartmentalise his life; his December school report was complimentary and in January 1919 he was made a prefect.

According to his memoirs, being reserved, shy, bookish, uninterested in games and scornful of Winchester traditions, Cecil had no friends, but correspondence – which also shows him skating and playing tennis – reveals that there were a few, and even reports him enjoying himself thoroughly with Enid's friends at Cheltenham. He was innocent, though. His nickname, 'Chaste Minerva', baffled him: 'Minerva is always chaste when referred to in Homer. Why I was so called I do not know, unless there was a good deal of homosexuality, but if there was, I was certainly unaware of it.'[55] Considering that Cecil was a strikingly handsome youth, who closely resembled his Uncle Alfred at the same age, it says much about his aloofness towards his fellow pupils that no one even made a pass at him.

Cecil left school in April 1919: 'I am very sorry to say goodbye to Cecil,' wrote his housemaster; 'he has been a very satisfactory member of the house throughout his time here and has had a very honourable career. My best wishes for his future . . . I hope that we shall still continue to see something of him.'[56]

Cecil wrote in his memoirs,

Bather said goodbye and that it was doubtless a very sad day for me. I said it was the happiest day of my life. He said I would come to think of my time at Winchester very differently. I said I was sure I would not. Though, naturally, I have had unhappy days since then, it is true, as I thought at the time, that nothing afterwards could ever be so bad as Winchester.

Winchester plans to send out Wykehamists, honest, reliable, professional people. If you arrive below the standard, you are dragged up to it. If you are not one to be fitted into the Wykehamist mould, so much the worse for you. As a result there have been no great Wykehamists and a surprisingly small number of eminent ones . . . Trying to sum up the permanent effect of Winchester, I would say that the school insisted on discipline and hard work.[57]

What he did not go on to explain was why, if Winchester was so bad, he sent one of his sons there.

Anthony Sampson, author of *Anatomy of Britain*, spoke in the early 1990s of the 'Winchester factory [that] still produces the eternal Wykehamist, with his dry confidence, clipped sentences and gaucheness with girls'.[58] Hugh Cudlipp, who studied the Winchester phenomenon as he struggled to understand King, found enlightenment from Richard Crossman, the ultra-intellectual Labour minister in the 1960s, who divided Wykehamists into three categories. 'The third was "the few – their minds sharpened by six years of mental struggle with the tradition but in lifelong reaction against it . . . They are the radical throw-outs of the Public School system; and some of them even became "traitors to their class"'.'

'Those were the Wykehamists, the traitors to their class, the radical throwouts, who I met around the barricades of a changing society,' remarked Cudlipp, 'notably Crossman, Hugh Gaitskell and King.'[59] King also, added Cudlipp, had 'the brand of intellectual arrogance' associated with Wykehamists, 'but without the blend of conventional good manners that Dick Crossman mentioned was also high on the curriculum'.[60]

If King's radicalism was slow to show itself, even at seventeen he was not fully behind Northcliffe's demands for ever harsher peace terms. 'The terms are much more severe than I had expected,' Cecil wrote to his 'Hun-hating' mother after the Armistice was signed in November, 'though I did not expect them to be very mild. I fail to see how the Germans could possibly start fighting again once they are carried out.'[61]

The following autumn, in 1919, he went up to Christ Church, Oxford, Vyvyan Harmsworth's alma mater. As with Winchester, five years earlier, he had sat for a scholarship exam for which he felt ill-prepared, and failed, but did well enough to be given a place to read history. He abandoned a mild ambition to be a research scientist – an occupation he always thought would suit him temperamentally – because though he was good at mathematics, he felt he was not good enough.

According to Cecil's memoirs, his rooms were 'dark and dank'; the college was 'extraordinarily snobbish'; tennis, at which he was very good, was 'in the hands of a very snobbish set'; he was black-balled for the college debating club; and, although he was relieved to get away from the Wykehamists, who mostly went to New College, it meant that he knew almost no one. What was more, the tutors disappointed. Although he wanted to concentrate on modern history, one took him no further than the eleventh century; another was idle; a third, to whom he went for his special subject, 'Currency, Finance and banking', was a moral philosopher who knew no economics; and a fourth, John Masterman, 'took little interest in me, and was astonished when I got the inevitable second'.[62] (Sir John, wrote Professor Hugh Trevor-Roper in 1962 in a circular letter soliciting contributions from ex-pupils towards a dinner and presentation, was 'a great teacher and unfailing friend'. 'My recollection of Masterman is of a lazy snob,' responded King.[63])

'What I really got out of Oxford was an interest in history and three years in which I could be alone.'[64] King would read history intensively all his life, but already by the time he left Oxford he was developing the thesis that imbued his attitude to past, present and future. In the words of his grandson, Laurence King, who understood him better and loved him more than most, he 'tended to see [human] progress in terms of the imposition of new ideas (or a new order) by a great man on an otherwise chaotic situation. It was a very Hobbesian vision, fuelled by his experience of Northcliffe. He saw the natural condition of man as brutal anarchy, on which order and progress had to be imposed.' This pessimism would make him an often bleak and disturbing political analyst.

Immensely dismissive of his contemporaries in his memoirs, Cecil admitted to a few friends: Harold Paton, the only Wykehamist ('who was no intellectual' and became a county court judge); W. A. Pantin ('who was a medieval man, out of his element in this century. Appropriately he became a very distinguished medievalist in due course. I don't think I should have noticed this unless I had been told'); and Francis Needham ('who was of a more scholarly type and went to the Bodleian as his first job'). From their correspondence, it is clear that the amusing and very well-read Needham was immensely affectionate towards Cecil and made all the running; it was years afterwards that Cecil realised he was homosexual.[65]

'On my way through school and university,' he lamented in his memoirs, 'none of my teachers took any interest in me. As my father had played no part in my life, it is bad luck that no other member of the family and no teacher played a parental part.'[66] This seems hard, not only on Bather, but on Thomas Scott, the Dean of Christ Church, who on being promoted to the bishopric of Ripon in September 1920 wrote to Cecil regretting 'that the pressure and confusion of the time had prevented my seeing more of you. I hope you will believe, however, that I have a real friendship & affection for you, and that this will not cease now that I am going away. I shall always be glad to hear of you, or if I can be of any use to you, I shall be extremely pleased'[67]

No doubt, like his teachers, members of the family must have felt that they had tried quite hard, too. They were as kind to him as they could be, but, as Cecil admitted in his memoirs, 'I was probably fairly unapproachable'.[68]

'Unknowable' was the adjective chosen by Christabel Burton, his youngest aunt, who lived opposite Granny Harmsworth. Close to other family members, like Rothermere's surviving son Esmond (three years Cecil's senior), she would say after visits from Cecil, 'That is a nephew I do not know. He is unknowable.'[69] Uncle St John, the discoverer and marketer of Perrier water – 'subtle . . . elegant and untrustworthy, but absolutely fascinating and very good-looking,'[70] according to Enid – was, admitted Cecil, 'popular with the younger members of the family, but for some reason I was never approved'.[71]

Like other uncles and aunts, Northcliffe had been doing his best for his unknowable nephew:

One of my most vivid recollections of the Northcliffe period was, I suppose, in 1919. I was staying at Poynters, and was woken up by Northcliffe's valet. He said his lordship was leaving for Elmwood in forty-five minutes and wished me to go with him for the weekend. When I joined him in his car he hoped I would have packed, breakfasted, and shaved off my moustache. I just made it, running down the back stairs with a fried egg in each hand.[72]

Although his parents wanted him to go into the Foreign Office or take up some other gentlemanly career, Cecil had long since decided that he wanted to go into newspapers, and he looked to his Uncle Alfred for help. 'I was his favourite nephew*[73] – and though he did not believe in employing relatives after his unfortunate experiences

---

* Northcliffe took an interest in Cecil, but there is no independent evidence that he was ever his favourite nephew; cousins dismissed the idea.

with some of his younger brothers, he arranged for me to spend long vacations from Oxford in his newspapers.'[74]

In 1920 Cecil worked at the *Daily Mail* newsroom under Tom Clarke. 'I am no reporter, and was far too shy to do well then. However, I got a paragraph in the main news page about a left-handed bowman in the statuary on the London County Hall.'[75] He kept his first piece for *The Times*, a brief report on a meeting of the Veterans' Association held during the Christmas vacation,[76] and worked for that newspaper the following summer. There is nothing in his reminiscences about inspirational journalists or fascinating assignments, but he did recollect advice from Northcliffe:

> He was very insistent that anyone in newspapers, if he were to go far, must have no friends among people of position. You never knew when circumstances would change and your friendship would have to turn to hostility. If your relationship was purely professional, this could not be helped – but serious personal relationship was another matter. A part of the same advice was never to join a political party or any group with a political tinge. But for this advice, in the thirties, I should certainly have made the mistake of joining one of the popular front activities.[77]

It was good advice, but the first part would prove easy for Cecil to take, since he found personal relationships so difficult anyway. Still, despite the impression that his memoirs give of a life of almost unrelieved solitude at Oxford, his increasingly long and chatty letters to his mother suggest he was having much more fun than he had in his school days: 'A clergyman gave a lecture last night,' he wrote in the spring of 1920, 'on the relations between the sexes. There was lots of goody-goody stuff about the present abnormal times & the need for reform etc. etc. The funny part was that he called his lecture "Psychotherapy" – one of the best euphemisms I have ever heard. If he had heard some of the terse & very unprintable (nice expression that) comments on his lecture he might have thought twice before delivering.'[78]

There were balls, visits from members of his family, afternoons watching boat races and the cultivation of a moustache: 'When I come home I shall twirl my moustache (if it is twirlable then) & talk about "years of discretion" and "men of the world".[79] He saw his Dublin friend Enid Starkie, now at Somerville on the first rung of her distinguished career as a scholar of French literature: 'White King told me his son at Christ Church took Enid and some others up the river, on a picnic,' noted her father.[80] 'When I see you it all comes back,' she wrote to Cecil in 1936, 'what I used to feel about you when you were an undergraduate and I was little more than a silly schoolgirl at college; I do not think I have ever known any man more beautiful than you were at nineteen – and I have known many men – "The Daffodil" I used to call you in my own mind.'[81] And there were visits to France – the country and Paris – to stay with the family of the Comte d'Orléans, whose son Charles became a good friend ('Charles appears really to like me, strange though it may seem'[82]). There Cecil played billiards, bridge and tennis and indulged his passion for shooting, to which he had been introduced by his father in Scotland in his early teens.

'I am having a great time here,' he told his mother in March 1921. '[They] have treated me like a prince . . . They can do for me what no amount of money can do – they can introduce . . . me to the best Parisian society. It is up to us out of self-interest as well as gratitude to do our utmost for them.'[83] It was a telling appeal to his mother's snobbery, which had grown with her family's preposterous success. Lloyd George had done them proud: by now Rothermere, like Northcliffe, had been elevated from baron to viscount; Leicester, an MP, provincial newspaper proprietor and book and art collector, was a baronet; Cecil was Under-Secretary of State for Foreign Affairs (he would be given a peerage in 1939 to please Rothermere); Hildebrand was rich (he would be made a baronet in 1922); and she herself was Lady King, as – according to Cecil – Rothermere had secured a knighthood for Lucas as a present to Geraldine at a time when Lloyd George badly needed press support.[84] (However, since the elderly Cecil was a natural denigrator, it should be remembered that Lucas King's public service and academic careers were both very distinguished and worthy of acknowledgement.)

The family was yet again in mourning, this time for Sheila, who after violent rows with Geraldine (who had wanted her to marry well) had broken off her engagement to a man she loved and in 1917 had married John Falls, a naval officer whom Enid thought bumptious and self-important. In 1921 Sheila died in Dublin in childbirth – 'a terrible loss to me,'[85] said Cecil; her son John was brought up by Geraldine. Sheila had meant much more to Cecil than either Luke or Bob and it was not surprising that he needed a sympathetic woman to console him. He found her in the Christ Church deanery, the garden of which his rooms overlooked.

They had known each other for a while: in June 1920, Cecil's dance card showed him dancing with Margaret Cooke five times at a college ball,[86] and she met him sometimes at her house. 'Every Sunday in term time,' she wrote many years later, 'undergraduates flowed in for tea, some shy & spotty, awkward even to boorishness, others gay & easy, talking with light-hearted confidence of their interests, their homes & friends.' Margaret was no performer. Writing of herself in the third person, she recalled her frustration: 'she could deal with one at a time or even two, quite successfully – but she had never been able to talk about herself – take the floor in conversation, so found it hard to make much of the situation.' And since the visitors left before service at 5.00, there was no opportunity 'to prolong any conversation into a relationship . . . once or twice she went to the drawing room early about 3.30 hoping someone would arrive early.' And Cecil did:

> With a beating heart she heard what seemed like familiar steps on the stairs . . . She got up to greet him & motioned him to a chair. Could he have guessed that she had been hoping for this very thing to happen? . . . He was full of tales of his first French experience – rats running across his bedroom floor – dogs everywhere – unkempt & smelly . . . He could be quite amusing when he unbent – & she gave him all her interest & attention . . . He moved very quietly & carefully . . . His hands were rather small for his size – square & very round fingered. – they were hands that weren't used much – inarticulate hands, she thought.
>
> What could she do to make some other meeting possible? Did he ever go to lectures on excavating or something other than his history? Perhaps they might go together or meet there? Just

as it seemed as tho' something might be arranged the door opened again & in came . . . a bevy of other youths.

They met again not long afterwards after a concert in hall, where she was transported by the singing. Cecil suddenly appeared, 'towering above most of his neighbours & looking round – was it for her? He caught her eye & smiled! She smiled back asking him with her eyes to wait for her at the main door & as the crowd thinned out she made her way to him still full of song in her heart & longing to share it with him.'[87] They began to go for walks, the first time she had ever been out with a man. In June they attended two balls within two days of each other, danced together thirteen times and Cecil decided to marry her.

There is nothing of their relationship in his memoirs: Cecil's second wife, Ruth Railton, was so jealous that although he briefly mentioned Canon Cooke, Regius Professor of Hebrew, as the father of the girl to whom he became engaged at Oxford, Margaret was not mentioned by name and his first marriage was never alluded to. (Since Ruth was referred to as his wife, a confused indexer provided an entry: 'Cooke, Ruth, *see* King, Dame Ruth'.) Nor are there any letters from her in his extensive archives. But Margaret kept a great deal of correspondence, including some of her unsent letters to her husband.

'Our essential link always seems to me a spiritual one,' Cecil wrote to her in the late 1940s, 'though I am not quite sure what I mean by spiritual. At a guess I would say it was on another – and deeper level . . . It was your spirit that originally attracted me &, as I say, that is the real link between us. Sexual attraction came later, perhaps because there is some connection between these two.' 'It wasn't my appearance Cecil fell for,' Margaret recalled, 'but as me with him – the inevitable recognition of & response to each other in a spiritual way & only later came the physical attraction.'

A search for spirituality was central to Cecil's life. He envied those with faith. His parents were practising Anglicans until, after Luke's death, his mother stopped all church-going, yet he felt they had no definite beliefs. And being congenitally incapable of taking anything on trust, Cecil had to puzzle religion out for himself. At his confirmation he told his housemaster that he found it impossible to believe in a personal God and was told that this was only a little temporary difficulty. Canon Cooke – although dismissed by Cecil as 'no great scholar and an ineffective head of a family' – he acknowledged to be 'sincerely and deeply religious' and with 'a spiritual gift. I was lonely and read a great deal, as I had always done, and I suppose it was about that time that I read the *Cloud of Unknowing*, the greatest mystical book written in English, dating from the fifteenth century.'[88]

Whatever the attractions of mysticism, Cecil was tormented for decades by sexual need. To his commonplace book he added in 1963 a public letter by the poet Ewart Milne, which expressed what Cecil himself had always felt about sex:

> sex to me is suffering. This is what it means, has meant since my first pubertial longings, the fire in my head and loins, sometimes such that any woman, my mother or any other, would have helped; and what it has meant through two marriages and now into my sixties. I mean suffering identical with the pangs of Tantalus [a son of Jupiter condemned to eternal, insatiable hunger and thirst], a mental and physical hunger, a desperate longing for that which I can see, which is all around, but which I cannot touch at will – and touch, physical contact, is essential for any easement of my condition – but only, if at all, by permission; that which, even when perhaps briefly I can satiate or at least blunt its ferocity, returns next moment more urgent and demanding than ever.[89]

It was not surprising that Cecil's physical need became so urgent that he was not yet twenty-one when he wrote:

3 Oriel Street,
Oxford
21/11/21

Dear Margaret,
   I am writing to ask you a question which has been on my mind for some time. I have done my best to put it off till I am older, but without success. Will you be my wife? This is

not a sudden whim: I got my family's consent 5 months ago. I feel the question is a little less abrupt in a note than if I came & asked you personally.

Cecil H. King[90]

The same day he wrote:

My dear Mother,

Just a line to tell you that I am engaged. I am sorry I could not put it off any longer, but I tried my best & failed. By Saturday I had reached a point at which I could neither eat, sleep, work, nor even sit still, so I wrote & asked her in a little note this morning. It was so brief as to be almost curt, but now all is well. I have just spent two hours with her, but have not yet tackled Mama or Papa, who are delighted, it appears. I thought Papa would jib, but not so. Perhaps it would not be a bad idea to write to the lady & say pretty things. She is a very charming person though not very like you. I am sure you will like her nevertheless. Perhaps Girlie [Nora], too, might pen a line.

In the 8th heaven of delight,
Your very loving
Cecil

P.S. Can I ask her on a visit? Very probably she wouldn't come but what do you think about it? Write & offer any advice you can think of. P.P.S. I am writing to tell Dad & Nora

Geraldine King, who had already provided Cecil with a ring with fine diamonds[91] ('a beauty – much nicer than I expected. I am going to have it altered in a day or two as at present it is too big even for her thumb! . . . Your very, v. v. loving Cecil'[92]), wrote, 'I thought the lady *charming*, the very cursory glance I had of her . . .', responding from Scotland, where she and her husband had moved because of IRA attacks on Protestants in Ireland.[93] 'I have no doubt Cooke & Co are more than delighted, and I hope I am getting as great a treasure, as they are. You see I know little or nothing of the lady, & that little, through your eyes . . . Much love to you – dearest son. You know I will always back anything that is for your happiness & this seems to be your dearest wish. Your ever more than devoted Mother.'[94]

'My dear Boy,' wrote his father:
    Your letter last night gave me the surprise of my life, and of course I could not help regarding it with mixed feelings. I knew of course that you cared for her, but did not think you would bring matters to a head so soon. I congratulate you, dear boy, on winning a very sweet girl — she must be that if she is like her Mother — but at the same time I think you have been a bit 'previous'! It must be a long engagement, as I see no prospect of your earning enough to support a wife for a long time to come.
    However if she and Pa don't object I have nothing against it. I determined not to marry till I had £1000 p.a.* and stuck to my resolve. It may be an incentive to you to work hard and I hope it will. My dreams of a diplomatic career for you, I fear, are shattered, and you will drift into journalism, in which a living can be made more quickly.
    With my heartiest good wishes & love to you both,
    Your very loving
    Dad[95]

There were loving congratulatory letters too from Nora and Enid, and welcoming letters to Margaret.

Dear Lady King,
    Thank you so very much for your letter. I was so glad to get it & am most grateful to you for your kindness in welcoming me.
    I feel that it is a great privilege to have a man like Cecil: I have looked upon him for some time as one in whom I could place unquestioning faith and trust, & since last Monday I have realised this with increasing certainty. I hope that you will not long have any feelings of personal loss, but may only gain.

---

*   About £60,000 today.

Thank you very much for asking me to stay with you. I should love to go, & will write later, if I may, when I have consulted Cecil.

I send you most grateful thanks for your generosity from Margaret[96]

Much though they loved her, Margaret's parents were surprised that someone of the glamour of Cecil Harmsworth King had chosen her, the least striking of their four daughters. The eldest, Mary, was the beautiful, selfish and indulged child; Helen, Margaret's bigger twin, was strong-willed and amusing and, like Betty, the youngest, artistic. Though Margaret became head girl at school, was musical, artistic and intelligent and impressed those who knew her well, she was untrained, self-effacing and over-anxious to please. 'Some of my earliest recollections are of paralysing fear – fear that I was unwanted & would be lost or left behind, alternating with such utterly carefree happiness & joy that would not be denied & came so unexpectedly – at the scent of a pansy or the first primrose, a snowdrop or violet – the scent of a hot daisy.' Knowing that her mother had desperately wanted a son, Margaret had 'frantically' sought to justify her existence. Having done well in Classics at school, she had thought of going to university, but felt instead that she should stay at home with her delicate mother, who took to her bed in her forties. And she believed that both her parents were disconcerted and unhappy at the thought that she would be the first daughter to marry. Her sisters, who found her hard to understand and were irritated by her capacity for self-sacrifice, rather resented Margaret acquiring such a catch as Cecil Harmsworth King.

Her mother, Helen, wrote gratefully but worriedly to Geraldine King:

the dear things are such children one hardly feels that they realise the gravity of the steps they have taken. Still – both are rarely thoughtful & beyond their years & their great happiness is very delightful to see. Both feel sure of themselves and of each other & both agree that to know of the love between them is only an incentive to better work & to higher aims . . .

Cecil seems to be just such a man as we would wish for our

beloved little Margaret's husband & I am very thankful that he has won her. She is rather reserved – but one can hardly imagine a sweeter or a better girl. She is very anxious to show that it need not be a loss to you all that she has Cecil's love – & that perhaps she too has something to contribute to the happiness of your circle. I do hope that you will find her winsome. She has a strong nature & aims at high things – but at the same time is very gentle & unselfish.[97]

'She reverences parents too – & in no way asserts herself in difficult or wounding opposition,' Mrs Cooke wrote reassuringly to Geraldine the following month. '. . . Cecil, dear man, made my room lovely & fragrant with red roses . . . we find him a very loveable person.'[98]

Margaret recalled her visit to her future in-laws:

'I was just 20, & had never been away from home before. We travelled up to Scotland together & I was welcomed by Lady K – & two of her daughters. I was too much in love & on top of the world to think anything but how wonderful everything was, but I got rather a shock when later on Lady K looked me up & down from her majestic height & said, '*Well!* You are everything I *don't* want in a daughter-in-law – you are small, you are poor, & you have bad ankles! But,' – a radiant smile broke out on her face – 'I always wanted a daughter with red hair & I like the name Margaret, so I expect I will make the best of it!' I can say this frankly without unkind intent, as we later on became close, excellent friends.[99]

Margaret was a hit and, her mother reported to Cecil, 'found it easy to care for your Mother & Geraldine . . . & the lovely country filled her up to the brim with pleasure. She says cares disappear on the moors.' In clothes borrowed from her sisters, Margaret was taken to London to meet Granny Harmsworth:

Inwardly she was wondering what it would all be like, this astonishing family & why she would have to win the old lady's approval? Suppose she did *not* approve – what then? Nothing was going to make any difference to her & C. They would marry approval or not!

A [for Agnes, her first name] had never been about much & always loved any sort of jaunt. She sat back in her corner beaming all over her small, pink-cheeked face – her golden-auburn hair curling round it. She radiated joy & expectation – everyone in the carriage kept glancing at her because of the extraordinary sense of happiness that flamed from her. C watched her from the opposite seat, his good-looking young face relaxed & happy, his long legs stretched out right across the compartment.[100]

Everyone liked Margaret, and Cecil was determined to marry her as soon as possible. He worked hard, and his Second in the summer of 1922 was very respectable; Francis Needham, who got a First, declared that 'your school was much better & more difficult than mine. I do hope they [Cecil's parents] will be satisfied at home.'[101]

Cecil had not seen Northcliffe since the previous summer, when his uncle kissed him goodbye before setting off on a world tour, but was expecting him to set him up in a good newspaper job. Northcliffe, however, was gravely ill.

He and Lloyd George had become bitter enemies. 'During the War no one could doubt his patriotism,' wrote Lloyd George in his memoirs. 'It was sincere and fearless . . . But he could not understand comradeship in any enterprise. He only appreciated team work when he was the captain of the team.'[102] 'It's his big head on a little body that I don't like'[103] was Northcliffe's pithy dismissal of his enemy. For an enemy Lloyd George had indeed become, and he did not fight by the Queensberry rules. In April 1919 his response to Northcliffe's continual criticism of what he saw as the weakness of both the Prime Minister and President Woodrow Wilson was to imply in the House of Commons that Northcliffe was mad:

Still I am willing to make some allowance . . . when a man is labouring under a keen sense of disappointment, however unjustified and . . . ridiculous the expectations may have been . . . [w]hen a man deludes himself, and all the people whom he ever permits to go near him into the belief that he is the only man who can win the War, and is waiting for the clamour of the multitude that is going to demand his presence there to direct the destinies of the world, and there is not a whisper, not a sound, it is rather disappointing; it is unnerving; it is upsetting.

Then the War is won without him. There must be something wrong. Of course it must be the Government. Then, at any rate, he is the only man to make peace . . . So he publishes the Peace Terms, and he waits for the 'call'. It does not come . . . Under these conditions I am prepared to make allowances; but let me say this, that when that kind of diseased vanity is carried to the point of sowing dissension between great Allies, whose unity is essential to the peace and happiness of the world . . . then I say that not even that kind of disease is a justification for so black a crime against humanity.[104]

As he said 'diseased vanity', Lloyd George tapped his forehead. Just half a century later, another Prime Minister was to feel the same way about Cecil King.

Lloyd George was ruthlessly capitalising on rumours that Northcliffe was going mad, which arose from his mysterious illnesses and absences, and were gleefully spread by his enemies. He found enough energy from time to time to hound the government over issues about which he cared deeply, such as the future of Ireland, but, though only in his mid-fifties, he was essentially burned out, fat and ailing. In July 1921 he set off on what he called his 'world whirl', which took him from the United States, through Canada, to Australia, Japan, China, Korea and Indo-China and then back to Europe via India, the Suez Canal and Palestine.

In a spot-on satire, *Punch* wrote:

Lord Thanet sailed . . . on the *Megalomania* for his great world-pilgrimage, in the course of which he will visit the North and South Poles, ascend Mt Everest and descend to the centre of the earth.

Incidentally, he will investigate the opportunity for emigration to the Solomon Islands, where, on the news of his impending visit, the inhabitants have given up their anthropophagous practices, embraced vegetarianism and taken to golf.

Subsequently he will enter on a thorough examination of the

questions of Church Disestablishment in Patagonia, the introduction of safety razors amongst the Hairy Ainus, and the construction of a tunnel from the North of Australia to New Guinea . . .

Northcliffe was fêted abroad as the Colossus he had been, and his enormous appetite for information and keen eye for detail did not desert him. Yet, as the tour went on, in his occasionally irrational, rude and violent behaviour he was beginning to show the signs of the disease that was to kill him: a blood infection – malignant endocarditis – which attacked his brain and his heart. Until 1959 it was generally believed that he died of syphilis; Cecil was among those who refused to believe otherwise.

'It won't be an easy time for you, I should think – now or later,' wrote Francis Needham in July, on hearing from Cecil, who was shooting in Aboyne, that Northcliffe was severely ill. 'I wish you weren't quite such an impossible person to do anything for. But this is the sort of time when M. will be an unspeakable help – I am so glad you have got her.'[105] 'Margaret tells me the drs despair of Ld N.c's health,' he wrote next day. 'Is it what you told me? – or is he going to die? I should think he would almost rather that than be an invalid.'[106]

Northcliffe died on 14 August 1922; within a few hours messages were flooding in from kings, presidents, prime ministers, political and industrial leaders, ambassadors, representatives of many races, personages of many countries. Their tributes crowded the communications systems for two days. Newspapers at home and overseas were black-bordered.

Three days later Westminster Abbey welcomed 'the greatest mourning congregation known there for many years'[107] and the public came out in their thousands. The cavalcade of ninety cars drove at walking pace the seven miles of streets from Westminster to North Finchley, 'not a single yard without its sign of public respect:

In Parliament Square, at Victoria, at Hyde Park Corner, at Marble Arch, the crowds stretched far back until they seemed like the multitude that gathers to watch the passing of a king . . . Bus drivers stopped their engines and doffed their caps; passengers rose in respect from their seats. In many of the streets the shop

blinds were lowered. The last part of the journey was through
the scenes of his boyhood: Maida Vale, Swiss Cottage, St John's
Wood . . .'[108]

At the funeral, the coffin had been followed by Northcliffe's
brothers, 'and by young nephews, among whom there were facial resem-
blances almost unbearably poignant to some who had known him
over the years'.[109] In photographs, Cecil, strikingly like Alfred at his
age – when he was nicknamed Adonis – cut a fine but rather lonely
figure at the end of the crocodile of male mourners.

'My dear King,' wrote Needham next day:

I saw you yesterday, though you didn't see me. I was with Paton,
who had some business down that way, and we stood outside
the Abbey at 12, opposite the West Front.

What did you think of it all? Of course it was painful in a
way: all public funerals are. But I thought dignified too
(remember I was some way off & could judge better than you
who were probably hot & unhappy & loathing the whole thing),
and the crowds seemed quiet & reverent, on the whole – very.
You looked splendid, we both said. I know your justly low
opinion of praise: but I thought you must be told.[110]

Lloyd George's assessment of Northcliffe was memorable, accurate
and unkind. 'I should describe him as a great journalistic Barnum.
He had the knack of divining what the public wanted, say, a white
elephant, and of seeking one out and getting it into his menagerie.
Having got it he knew how to advertise it . . . Northcliffe did many
good things, but the truth is that he had a bad effect on the public
mind.'[111]

Northcliffe's press rival and sometime political colleague, Max
Beaverbrook, whom King was to loath and Cudlipp to love, wrote a
more just assessment in his Daily Express, remembering Northcliffe as
the 'greatest journalist England has ever seen – if we are to judge
greatness, as we must in public life, by the influence a man brings to
bear on the age in which he lives'. In establishing as well as running
newspapers, he 'created through his own efforts directly and through
those of his imitators indirectly, an entirely new public atmosphere.

The classes enfranchised in the later nineteenth century at last found a medium of instruction in public affairs and a method of making their opinions felt – not once every five or six years but continuously, from day to day. Such an achievement ranks Northcliffe finally among the makers of history.'[112]

A maker of history was what King also wanted to be. But Northcliffe's death had dealt a terrible blow to his ambitions.

CHAPTER III

The Hard Ascent of Cecil King

'THERE WAS A PERIOD,' RECALLED KING, 'WHEN I WONDERED IF HE had given effect to his promises to leave me all the family heirlooms. As he had said I was his favourite nephew, it was at least possible some niche might be arranged for me at the *Daily Mail*. However, I was not mentioned in his various wills and eventually found the same as the other nephews.' Like his siblings and cousins, he inherited £500.*

'I then had to deal with Rothermere, an uncle I hardly knew.'[1] Uncle Harold was not very accessible. Already devastated by the death of his elder sons, he now had to face life without the astonishing brother who had rescued him from a clerkship at the Board of Trade, given scope to his money-making genius and thus brought him to wealth and power. As he mourned him, Rothermere also had to deal with his brother's hugely complicated affairs. What with vast death-duties, two wills, a litigious widow and an ex-mistress determined to get a disputed legacy, there were bequests so generous (including three months' salary to all his employees) that the estate had to be broken up and Rothermere had to pay many of them out of his own pocket. *The Times* was sold to John Jacob Astor, and Rothermere took over the *Daily Mail* and most of the other papers of Northcliffe's Associated Newspapers, while the periodicals – including *Answers*, the foundation of the Harmsworth fortune – went to Sir William Berry, later

---

* About £18,000 today.

Lord Camrose. Unlike Northcliffe, Rothermere was never sentimental about his papers.

King languished in Scotland waiting for a decision about his career and yearning for Margaret. His memoirs barely touch on this period and little correspondence survives: it is mainly the letters of Francis Needham – who had become an Oxford librarian – full of gossip as well as talk of books, work and the vagaries of colleagues and land-ladies, that give clues about what King's life, prospects, state of mind and developing character were like at the time. Those King sent in reply, according to Needham, were of the 'Had dinner today'² sort.

August 28th 1922

My dear King,

I was with the Cookes yesterday from 1 till 5! – & dutifully send my report of those most delightful people.

Margaret was looking lovely, in a blue & white stripy dress, with your white fur (which I hadn't seen & like immensely), the necklace, & of course the ring. I wish you could have seen her. Helen [her twin sister] looked nice too – I think you would say beautiful when her face is in repose; but her smile is not pretty, & she has nothing of M's gentle unselfish expression. Do you mind another person's admiring your lady? – because I can't help it, please. & she is so nice to me, & protective!

And, my dear, so fond of you: why – why – *why* weren't you a fly on the wall after lunch in the drawing room yesterday! You would love to hear her talk about you behind your back . . .

Oct. 2nd 1922

My dear King . . .

About Cooke. I don't think it is any good being scornful of people like that. I know what you mean exactly; but if you are narrow (I mean if you just cut into a little bit of life & judge all the rest from that little bit, as he does) it doesn't neces-sarily follow that you are shallow . . . If you go to Cooke for what he has to give, you must admit he is kind & capable enough; but outside that he would be entirely uncomprehending – i.e. narrow. I don't pity Mrs C. one scrap . . . She is no fool, & she must have known then exactly what she was marrying.

And my advice to you, my child (I love giving advice), is not to expect more from him than there is there. Then you'll like him very much. Otherwise, you'll dislike him – and despise him too . . .

Ever yours,
Francis N.[3]

Oct. 10th 1922

My dear King,

Evidently Margaret was wrong, or you are not coming south for a while. I was summoned, Saturday evening, to go & rejoice with her – which I did; but her reason was so complicated (something about photographs & delayed letter & telegram) I didn't quite understand why we *were* rejoicing.

She said – I thought this wd. please you, though perhaps you know – 'It sounds rather horrid, but I would leave the family tomorrow to go to Cecil, if it were necessary. I think when you are engaged you don't belong to your family any more, in one way. I only realised it quite lately.' That used to be one of your troubles, didn't it? I remember your talking about it last term.

I wish you would come south: such excitement rose at the bare thought . . . Congrats. On your £500 – also to Enid . . . Ever yours, Francis N.[4]

Like many others, Geraldine King was worried about her finances; Northcliffe's affairs were not yet settled. St John advised her that autumn:

Dearest Dot,

I deeply sympathise with you. My advice to you is to cross the border on a raiding expedition. Harold is in an expansive mood. There is a proverb which says 'those nearest the fire get most heat'. Get next the fire.

In days to come my Perrier tree should be full of fruit. In those days you shall have your share. But reach up and get what you can now. There is lots about.

My love to you, dear.

St John[5]

'My dear King,' wrote Needham in November, relating how Canon Cooke had taken him to High Table, and how almost everyone there 'I hated like poison – either elderly & stupid, or young & worse (the nice ones, Feiling, Masterman [two of the tutors who had disappointed Cecil], etc. weren't there)'. Needham was full of his burgeoning acquaintance with Cecil Harmsworth's nineteen-year-old student son Desmond. 'I like him very much . . . I tried hard to find anything of you in him, but couldn't see much . . . And you? – Margaret told me just *where* you were, on Friday, but I shall like a letter when you have time.'[6]

King was in Glasgow, for Rothermere had sent him and a cousin, Hildebrand's son Ronnie, to learn at his *Glasgow Record*:

how a newspaper ran. I lived in a residential hotel, Moore's Hotel, and met Ronnie at breakfast. I had introductions to some of the wealthier citizens of Glasgow, with whom I had nothing in common, and also to some of the Ayrshire aristocracy, with whom I fared somewhat better. I was lonely, though engaged to be married.

The newspapers, the *Glasgow Record* and *Sunday Mail*, were carefully run, but neither the editor, Campbell, nor the manager, Barr, ever explained to me what it was all about . . .

Glasgow in 1922 was a raw, gloomy city to which I can have contributed nothing. In fact when out walking one day I was handed a tract *Through Crime to Christ*, so I must have looked pretty down and out![7]

'The idea of Cecil King being a reporter,' marvelled Hugh Cudlipp much later:

I mean if you're living in the Gorbals and there's a knock on the door, well you wouldn't answer it in case you're going to be stabbed in the back for a start, and if you do open it and you find this six-foot, Irish, shy, skinny, Wykehamist hesitating in front of you, you would think he was there as a decoy and the thieves were behind him. I don't know how he made anybody talk about anything because he had great difficulty putting a question to them, because he would be shyer than they were frightened. I think it only lasted a year – to the relief of the Gorbals and Cecil.[8]

Back in London, his cousin the Honourable Esmond Harmsworth, Rothermere's only surviving son – whom many within the family thought had probably been sired by St John – was now the heir apparent to what remained of the Harmsworth newspaper empire. Having served in the Royal Artillery, he had been an aide-de-camp to Lloyd George at the Peace Conference and then, with family backing, had become MP for Thanet at a by-election in 1919 at the age of twenty-one; his destiny as a newspaper proprietor was fixed. But while it was a burden for Esmond (who knew he was third-best in his father's eyes) to be required by Rothermere to 'inherit all the sacrifices of those great personages, your two elder brothers,'[9] it was torment for King (who burned to be Northcliffe's heir) to be treated as just another nephew. His prospects were modest, but there were constant reminders of the grandeur of his relations. In March 1923, for instance, he left his lowly job to travel to London so that his father could take him to the King's Levée at St James's Palace to be introduced to George V.[10] It was no wonder that it was in Glasgow that he first developed the symptoms of psoriasis, a stress-related skin complaint.[11]

There were strains too with Margaret. In March 1923 the faithful Francis Needham wrote:

My dear King,
   I don't know at all what I am to say or how I can help, but write I must, & I do ask you to remember that it is no pleasure to me to risk breaking with you (as I know I am doing now), who are so much the best friend I have.

My dear man, do you know what you are doing? – and how much pain you are able to give by what you say & write? Have you thought what a bad & great effect it is having on her health? Because if you have, & if you are acting like this deliberately to the girl you asked to marry you, you are doing what is most wrong, & you fill me with utter shame and – I never thought to be saying this to you – contempt.

King, you can't be doing that: you – who have never said one hurtful word to me, & were always, I thought, the most gentle of all the people I know when you are with the few people you are fond of.

I am talking more or less in the dark, because I don't know what the exact trouble is – but I did gather that it is about Mrs Cooke again. Surely it is a poor thing to be troubling her about, when (you said so in your very last letter, & you know it is true) you have her *on your side* over the question with Mrs Cooke; & if she hasn't learnt yet to act with you in particular instances, this (I wish you could see her as I did this evening. She could barely speak. She looked pitiably ill, & I didn't know what to do) isn't the way to change things. There is every reason – in this case at least every excuse – for a girl doing what her own mother tells her. Besides, is a habit of loyalty to the people who love you such a very bad thing after all?

Cecil, don't be angry with me. I had to write like this. I should have been despicable if I hadn't. And for God's sake write to your Margaret like a sensible man, & make her happy again.

Ever yours,
F.N.[12]

The adult King never lost his temper. He recalled in his memoirs that as a child, in a fancy-dress costume with a dagger, he had attacked another child with the knife after a quarrel; on another occasion he hurled a jelly at a small boy at a party. 'After the third episode, at Winchester, it was clear that if I allowed this to happen again I should kill someone. So I decided I must never lose my temper again – nor have I.'[13] At school, 'I developed a really lethal weapon, sarcasm. I knew what sort of remark to make or question to ask to silence anyone. It was only later that I realised what a devastating weapon this was, and one not to be used.'[14] When he renounced this second vice, King did not say, nor in his memoirs did he discuss what was to be his most damaging habit in his relationship with the loving and anxious Margot (as she was becoming known) – the levelling of destructive criticism of the kind he hated and deplored when it came from his mother.

What initially caused him resentment was what he described as Margot's 'intense attachment'[15] to her family and her tremendous sense of duty to her often ill and usually hypochondriacal mother. To the emotionally needy King, whose family could never give him enough help or love, Margot's devotion to her parents seemed both excessive and disloyal. To Margot, brought up in a house of '*great* love, beauty, culture & gentleness',[16] as well as one of profound religious feeling, there was plenty of affection and joy to spread around. 'Quite honestly, when I married,' she wrote much later to King's sister Enid, 'I did so with utter simplicity & trust in my heart – never believing all the horrors C. told me of – the list of black marks against each member of the family – I thought of you all as new people to love – to share life with . . . fun of all sorts & the simple happiness of family relationships.'[17]

But family relationships were no longer so simple. To Margot's distress, her parents could not grasp 'the situation of Cecil's & my life & means,'[18] which were that, despite all the Harmsworth millions, they would largely have to live on his salary and the proceeds of a few shares. Margot had no money: the £5 she was given as a twenty-first birthday present went on a signet ring for King and all the dowry on offer was a promise from her mother of £50 a year (which was rarely delivered). It was clear that they could afford only a modest flat without domestic help, but that was not a serious possibility for King, who had lived in privilege, or for Margot, who knew only comfort. She was later to lament that she had not started married life cooking and scrubbing for King, but so protected had her existence been that she had no idea how to run a home or even how to shop. 'I only know now . . . that I was what is known as an "institutionalized" girl – I had never rebelled against anything.' Sex was something else she knew nothing about. When King employed that foresight on which he prided himself, by telling her that he would not be capable of being faithful to her after marriage, she had no idea what he meant.[19]*

Although they did not realise it, at their core, the high-minded and devoted Margot and Cecil had very different views of what marriage was about. 'I wanted to make Cecil happy & shew him what a loving home could be – & make up to him for his unhappy childhood – by bringing up a family in the way I was – in all gentleness and love & joy,' wrote Margot years later. 'I wanted to shew that love & joy does accomplish things & that God means us to be happy, joyous people – *even tho'* we have to bear his Cross as well . . . and [I wanted] to bring joy & love to everyone I met.'[20] Tolstoy, writing to his son on his marriage, expressed King's view: 'The goal of our life should not be to find joy in marriage, but to bring more love and truth into the world. We marry to assist each other in this task. The most selfish and hateful life of all is that of two beings who unite in order to enjoy life.'[21]

Despite tensions in the Cooke family, plans went ahead for an appropriate wedding and in April, after a visit by Geraldine to Oxford, Margot wrote, 'I just want to tell you that I love Cecil utterly – my greatest wish is to make him happy, and be the best wife to him that it is in my power to be. I don't feel that anything in my life matters except this – & the sooner I can begin the happier I shall be . . . With much love, from Margot.'[22]

As she had always chosen Margot's hats and clothes, her mother chose her trousseau – some of which was snaffled by her sister Mary. Margot and Cecil were married on 23 June 1923 at Christ Church Cathedral at a ceremony conducted by Canon Cooke and a bishop, with Margot in ivory satin, diamonds and pearls, the bridesmaids wearing Rhine diamond neck-chains provided by the bridegroom, and a guest list that included many Harmsworths (though not Rothermere) and a respectable haul of social, academic and clerical high life. Rather than Francis Needham, who always declared himself too frightened socially even to accept King's invitations to Scotland, the best man

---

* When I told the worldly, octogenarian Cudlipp about this, his response was that it was akin to proposing on bended knee while hoping that your address book would not actually fall out of your back pocket.

was the Hon. John Browne (Winchester and Magdalene and heir to Lord Kilmaine), who had introduced King into Ayrshire society. 'There were,' one newspaper reported, 'many beautiful presents.'[23] An invoice from Liberty's for £93.18.10* for Shirvan rugs and Persian and Turkey carpets is a testimony to the generosity of his family.[24]

The Kings spent their honeymoon at Grand Falls, where the Harmsworth brothers had built paper-mills, in the house constructed for Northcliffe's occasional visits – sailing there and back in a cargo boat. King's favourite memory of Newfoundland was of a logging camp where the cook was using his false teeth to imprint a pattern around the tarts.[25] Vague plans for him to stay there and work fell through. 'You feel a very long way off,' wrote Needham in August, '& I am glad it isn't for 6 months after all, or I think I should have come out disguised as a grand piano in the hope that you'd give me a corner somewhere.' He had asked Mrs Cooke 'for the yellow picture of you, & she promptly gave me Margaret's – which I refused to have until she had been asked. Will you do that, please? [N.B. It shall be in my *bedroom!*]'[26]

They went to live in the house in Abercorn Place, St John's Wood, which Geraldine King had bought with part of Northcliffe's legacy. According to Enid, it was 'a large, ugly, gloomy house standing in its own grounds, with a lot of dark oak panelling and small latticed windows downstairs at least'.[27] 'The day after we returned from our honeymoon,' Margot recollected decades later:

he went to Fleet St about his future job & came back to tell me the result. I felt he looked a bit forlorn & asked the reason. This was the explanation.

He was interviewed by the man who was then Managing Director & told he would start in the Advertisement Dept. As [King] rose to go the M.D. said to him, 'Now look here, I am giving you this job but I want to make it quite clear from the start – we don't want any of the Harmsworth family in this building – & we will do all we can to break you!' . . . One thing I am sure I will never understand – & that is the psychology of

---

*   About £3,300 today.

the popular press. I have many good friends among the staff —
for whom I hold both affection & admiration, but how any one
can employ a young man with one sentence & threaten to break
him in the next is beyond my comprehension! I may say that
this M.D. had been one of Lord Northcliffe's discoveries, picked
out as a boy (almost from the gutter!) & trained & trusted until
he reached this important position.

Thus was King's disappointment and bitterness further exacerbated,
and his memoirs record virtually nothing positive from this period.
It is hard to make Fleet Street sound dull, but he managed it decades
later in his terse, dismissive accounts of the people and their jobs. At
the *Daily Mail*, 'I first had a spell with the auditors' (he sat 'on an
accountant's stool totting up figures', according to Margot[28]), 'which
gave me a view of the business from the financial end, and later I
moved to the Ideas and Business Development department under
G. H. Grimaldi.'[29] (Needham provided some much-needed colour:
'How are your twopence-halfpenny lunches?'[30])

Caird, the Managing Director, 'King thought a mean, penny-
pinching Scotsman'; Marlowe, Editor for twenty-seven years and one
of the few journalists prepared occasionally to stand up to Northcliffe,
'seemed to me a dignified nonentity'.[31] But Grimaldi 'was one of the
ablest'[32] people King ever met in his business life. 'He taught me how
to write a business letter: "Always begin with 'you', never with 'I'."'
However, his ability was limited: 'the main reason for his relative lack
of success seemed to me to be a lack of an adequate sense of direction.' Grimaldi's boss, the head of the Advertising Department, was
C. Stephen Millikin, 'a forceful and able man, who had served a term
of imprisonment' for selling shirts he didn't deliver.

Rothermere received short shrift, too. According to King, he ran
Associated Newspapers from his flat in the Savoy. 'He must have been
a superlatively able Wall Street speculator but in the more human business of running a newspaper, he seemed to me to be without aptitude of any kind. In general, he preferred to deal with the inferior.'
Other than a lieutenant who died young in 1919, 'I cannot recall any
particular talent in his entourage.' But then, from his advertising back-
water, King saw little of either the uncle or the entourage.

King kept examples of the letters, circulars and advertisements that he produced during his joyless time soliciting small ads for the *Daily Mail* and *Evening News*:

> Dear Sirs,
>   It is our opinion that we have in the Traders' Smaller Market Place, which appears in the Daily Mail every day, an advertising medium of peculiar interest to yourself.
>   This special feature with its comprehensive title is designed to introduce new advertisers, at a trifling cost, to the unique influence of The Daily Mail in building up a national demand for every kind of product . . .[33]

> Dear Sir,
>   Dance lovers all over London are looking forward to a busy Christmas dancing season.
>   To give a lead to our readers who are not all acquainted with the most attractive dancing resorts in London, we are publishing a Special Feature entitled –
>   WHERE TO DANCE
>   During the Christmas & New Year Holidays
>   – which will appear on the same page as our weekly Dancing Notes.[34]

There were panel advertisements and paragraphs in editorial columns drawing attention to how the problems of different categories of buyers and sellers could be solved with the help of a small ad:

> THE SERVANT WORRY
> There are few mistresses who have been fortunate enough to escape the servant worry. Numbers can look back upon disorder in the household through inefficient domestic help, and, worse still, nothing short of chaos through being left unexpectedly without help of any kind . . .[35]

King's innovations included offering promotional gifts of cocoa, chocolates and 'dainty' hairbrushes, which – though small – would 'master the most unruly curls'.

'I am glad you have done with advertising,' wrote Needham in January 1925. 'The other sounds much more interesting & responsible: but don't find too many instances of waste & inefficiency & corruption at first, or they won't like you.'[36] The new job was a directorship of the Empire Paper Mills in Kent, and Rothermere also gave Cecil and Margot a holiday that took them to Lisbon, Madeira, Cadiz, Athens and Constantinople.

'My dear Cecil,' Rothermere wrote in October 1926, 'I have decided that you should spend some months in the "Daily Mirror" office so as to gain more experience. Will you therefore on your return report to Mr Cowley. He will give you the same salary as you have been receiving in the "Daily Mail". Your affectionate uncle, Harold.'[37] 'Third parties', King wrote to Cudlipp many years later, had told him that 'Rothermere thought I was abler than Esmond & did not want me in the same part of the business, so he transferred me to the Mirror which he thought was on its way out.'[38]

The *Daily Mirror* had been founded in 1903 by Alfred Harmsworth as 'the first daily newspaper for gentlewomen', written entirely by women. Within a few days it was clearly a disaster: 'women,' he concluded, 'can't write and don't want to read.'[39] A male Editor, Hamilton Fyfe, was appointed and told to sack the staff: 'a horrid experience,' he recalled, ' – like drowning kittens.'[40] As a tabloid, it was relaunched in 1904 as a picture paper for men and women and was a huge success. Harmsworth helped to build its personality by leavening serious campaigning and news coverage with such stunts as having an acrobat leap from an aeroplane holding a *cri de coeur* from old-age pensioners in his teeth. He never loved it, though, viewing the *Mirror* as 'a sort of bastard child' of his journalistic family;[41] he left it to his brother Harold to manage and sold it to him in 1914, when its circulation was more than 1,200,000, for only £100,000,[*] the amount he had lost on it in its early days. The following year Rothermere launched its sister picture paper, the *Sunday Pictorial*. Both papers flourished as they fed the voracious public appetite for illustrations of war: the *Mirror* became more profitable even than Northcliffe's *Daily Mail*.

By the time King joined the *Mirror*, it had become a vehicle for the

---

[*] About £5.5 million today.

political views of his uncle, committed – as Cudlipp put it in the racy history of the paper that he wrote for its fiftieth birthday – 'to a protracted campaign for national economy, conceived and delivered with the same unctuousness and lack of verve as characterise a Sunday evening sermon on the virtues of thrift'.[42] Although under Fyfe it was pro-Labour, in the 1922 General Election Rothermere's *Mirror* (like his *Mail*) was grimly anti-socialist as well as anti-Lloyd George. It was the *Daily Mail*, in October 1924, just before the General Election, which – in its handling of the Zinoviev letter (which later proved to be a fake) – sank the Labour Party by raising the spectre of a communist revolution in Britain and swept the Conservatives into office. Ramsey MacDonald was Rothermere's scalp, just as Asquith had been Northcliffe's. And Rothermere's relationship with Baldwin was to be as bumpy as Northcliffe's had been with Lloyd George.

John Cowley, Chairman of the *Mirror* and *Pictorial* companies, did not impress King. 'I remember having a talk with Cowley when someone came into the room' was King's account of their interview. 'Cowley said, "I am just running the ruler over this young man." I remember thinking at the time that Cowley's assessment of my gifts or abilities would be of little value.'[43] Appointed Assistant Advertisement Manager, King was now in another job that he felt deliberately gave his intellect and energy little scope. Cudlipp agreed. 'He had a frightful job in advertising and I suspect that's why they gave it to him because he was selling advertising on a declining dying newspaper and he lacked the conviviality necessary in mixing with the unimaginative but rather jolly advertising crowd.'[44]

King was desperate to have influence, but not to be in the lime-light: he wanted, as he explained to Margot, to be only 'a power behind the scenes'.[45] Yet the 'unknowable nephew' was incapable of persuading Rothermere or his colleagues of his considerable abilities; he was, as Margot had early on found to her distress, disliked, distrusted or feared by most people. Yet she believed him to have 'a most special gift & future with his encyclopaedic mind & rare disinterestedness of purpose'.[46] In Cudlipp's bleak assessment, he was 'tasting the sour fruits of nepotism, biding his time, and trying on dying men's shoes.'[47]

That no one had ever believed in him or much liked him was a recurrent theme of King, exaggerated in later years. But Margot was not his only admirer. King's need for unconditional affection was more than met by Francis Needham. 'I have just got your portrait back from Rymans, framed, & now it is over my sitting-room mantelpiece: so I can't escape from you for a single hour when I am in. Not that I want to. I don't mind telling you look very handsome, in spite of the dirty ears.'[48] There were King visits to Oxford and Needham visits to London. And by early 1925 the intimacy was so great that Needham went so far as to substitute 'My dear Cecil' for 'My dear King'. It was Needham to whom King confided some of his frustrations. 'I was interested to hear about your work (I always am),' wrote Needham in mid-1925, 'but what does the "more responsible, settled job" that you want mean? A newspaper of your own?'[49] And it was Needham who helped King dispose of Sir Lucas King's library after his sudden death, *Times Literary Supplement* in hand,[50] in August 1925 — shortly after two loving letters ('My dear Boy . . . Your devoted Dad') about, *inter alia*, books, duck-shooting and the terminal illness of Granny Harmsworth, who died the same month. 'Mother is splendid,' wrote King to Margot. 'I think she vaguely expected it and her mind was ready . . . [She] has no plans. She says no one will want to have a dreary widow planted on them.'[51] (Her letters show a determined cheerfulness: 'Leicester is a dear,' she wrote to Margot early in 1926, 'and looks after me as if I was a very old lady. He spoke most affectionately of you the other day — they want your double for their son Harold. Quite a good idea for everybody concerned so I suggested their asking Helen on a visit & putting the matter in hand! But I don't suppose they will.'[52])

There were others who thought themselves close to King. 'I *am* so very sorry for you, dear Cec, in all that has happened,' wrote his best man, John Browne, on reading about the deaths of both father and grandmother:

. . . I feel for you most tremendously in your father's loss, for I know you were very fond of him.

You have had so much to bear in your life, & you have always borne it with such a wonderful, quiet courage, that I am sure the same courage will bring you though this. I am glad for you that you have Margot; before, you have always been alone, but this time it must make all the difference to you to have her wonderful help, & her sharing of your sorrow.[53]

'Darling Cecil,' wrote one of Margot's relatives, '. . . You have lost so many dear folk in your rather short life, darling – that you know sorrow more than many young folk.' She reported how thrilled Margot's sister Betty had been by the 'stories of birds sent specially by you to her. She is as proud as punch about it – and it is dear of you darling. You give them so much pleasure by your thoughts and deeds!'[54] And his old French friend, Charles d'Orléans, continued to amuse him with his problems in finding a suitable wife with plenty of money.[55]

Geraldine King had become rich, for to her legacies from Northcliffe and her mother was now added a present of £100,000* from Rothermere, who in 1926 was worth somewhere between £15 and £26 million. 'Though I had no training of any kind,' recalled King, 'I took over the management of this fund. My uncles had made so much money that I felt I must see whether I could do so too. I made about a quarter of a million for various family trusts, and then took things much more easily. Obviously I could make money if I wanted to, but it involved a life concentrated on this one objective.'[56] He had no interest in money, he explained, for 'my rich uncles were insecure and unhappy men, so wealth as a source of security and happiness, the delusion of so many people, meant for me the reverse.'[57] Yet, though King certainly never tried to become really rich, he was to live much of his adult life in fine houses among beautiful things. Occasional legacies, money that his mother and Rothermere gave him from time to time and some modest shareholdings gave him a start, and with his innately fine taste and increasing knowledge of antiques, silver, paintings and other works of art – although he bought for pleasure and sold when bored – he always made a profit.

He and Margot did not stay long in his mother's house. An attempt to move to a flat in 1924 ended with her miscarrying, but in 1926, after the birth of Michael, they moved to Park Stile in Langley – 'a darling little Queen Anne house,'[58] according to Enid. Geraldine sold the house in St John's Wood and for a couple of years divided her time between King, Enid and Scotland, but by 1929 she was inde-pendent, with a Georgian house with eighty acres near Runnymede –

---

* About £4 million today.

stuffed with Rothermere's spare antiques – and Cushnie, near Aboyne, the shooting estate she had bought two years earlier, 'which we all took to our hearts and which she handed over to Cecil after a few years. We hoped that it would have given her much more occupation and interest than it ever did, with its human family of sixty tenants, two residences, two schools, two shops, its farming, forestry and game-preserving problems.'[59]

Promising a visit to Park Stile, Needham – Michael's godfather – wrote:

I've always been on my best behaviour at Abercorn Place, because I was afraid you wouldn't like the 1926 Francis Needham as much as you did the 1920–22 one. The possibility of a 1926 Cecil never came into my head, I am afraid; but the little I've seen of him (it is up to you to make it more) was exciting and (I don't see why I shouldn't say what I think) a lot more interesting and attractive than the old Cecil. And I thought I could never like anyone more than I did him.

In the same letter, though, he was fighting still against King's habit of denigration, this time apropos their old contemporary Harold Paton: 'I can promise that if you dig just a little bit (& only a very little) you'll find him the very best & most sympathetic person you could possibly want. I don't know anyone better & wiser & more reliable over personal things. But keep off politics – like I do; & don't be nervous, but just jump into the middle of him, so to say. You won't be disappointed.'[60]

Jumping into the middle of people was not an option for King, who was dependent in personal relationships on others making the running. 'I have no idea what the man I am talking to is thinking,' he wrote in his memoirs. '. . . I have no idea whether people like me or dislike me unless they make it obvious from some overt act.'[61] In conversation, 'I am entirely dependent on the other party supplying the right response.'[62]

So most people failed him and his sense of self-doubt and futility grew. His state of mind was summed up in a passage from a letter Asquith wrote in 1892 when he became Home Secretary, which King put as the colophon to his memoirs:

Do you remember the Theban, somewhere in Herodotus, who says – that of all human troubles the most hateful is to feel that you have the capacity for power and yet you have no field to exercise it. That was for years my case, and no one who has not been through it can know the chilly paralysing deadening depression of hope deferred and energy wasted and vitality run to seed. I sometimes think it is the most tragic thing in life.

Still, 'by much importuning,'[63] after three years King persuaded Rothermere to make him Advertisement Director of the *Mirror* and its sister paper, the *Sunday Pictorial*, and give him a seat on the board. He also made an entrepreneurial leap into newspaper ownership. 'I am forgetting those Croydon papers of yours,' wrote Needham in 1930. 'Do tell me a little more – are they *Household Hint*ish sort of things, or what? – and the circulation? – and do they pay their way? The first step on the Northcliffe ladder, eh?'[64] That the venture was a failure wounded King so much that this most aggressively candid of men ignored the episode in his memoirs and suppressed a mention of them in a book that Cudlipp wrote in 1953.[65]

He was, at least, getting more opportunities to learn at first hand of countries about which he had read voraciously. 'My angel wife,' he wrote from Russia in the summer of 1932, en route from Moscow to Stalingrad:

> . . . I am very well & happy & enormously interested . . . [John] Coope [a colleague] is a nice person to travel with – no one could be nicer . . .
>
> You would love the Russians. The women are more attractive than the men, I think. They have nice strong wise faces – none of them pretty but some of them rather beautiful. Men bathe naked here anywhere . . . I have hardly seen any women or girls bathing & the few I have seen wear knickers & a brassière. I agitated to see a maternity house & eventually we were taken to see what proved to be a central hospital for pregnant syphilitics & their babies up to 2 years old! Interesting up to a point but rather grim. The social work – schools, hospitals, kindergartens & housing are all well done here . . . Yesterday we also saw a marriage & divorce bureau – very interesting. On

all such subjects their ideas are really modern.

All my trust & best love is yours my darling . . . Snow

As it seduced so many other intellectuals, the Soviet Union had already seduced King. 'I am really thrilled about the whole place . . . This five year plan is serious – very serious and for that reason alone I am very glad I came. Any talk about it breaking down or about the sullen dissatisfaction of the people is just bunk. The whole face of Moscow has been changed and in another five years it will be a model town . . . This is a new world and I am thrilled.'

It was in his travels that King most resembled his Uncle Alfred. Both of them were interested in absolutely everything, from politics to social conditions, from flora and fauna to the beauty of women. But at home, King was no Northcliffe, for there was nothing showy about his talents. The Peter Principle dictates that people rise until they reach a job they cannot do. King was an outstanding example of its opposite: the more lowly the job, the worse he did it, so as he hauled himself painfully up the ladder, he surprised people. At this period, to a man, his colleagues undervalued and underestimated him. Cowley, for instance, had refused to let him see any figures when he joined the board. King's response was to tell the Company Secretary that he would get an injunction compelling him to do so. The Secretary said he would show King any figures he wanted without Cowley knowing, so King had become well informed about the problems of the *Mirror*, which was going from bad to worse. It was, recalled King, impossible to sell advertising in a paper 'which was vaguely supposed to be doing about a million, but was in fact slipping at the rate of 70,000 a year and by 1933 was under 800,000.'[66]

Rothermere was no longer running the paper. He had been badly bruised by yet another foray into politics, which had him throwing his weight behind Max Beaverbrook's short-lived United Empire Party and conducting a vendetta against Stanley Baldwin. It was after a vicious personal attack in the *Mail* that Baldwin retaliated with the famous denunciation of the two press proprietors – that they were seeking 'power without responsibility – the prerogative of the harlot throughout the ages.'

Having been steadily divesting himself of his personal shares in the *Mirror*, Rothermere sold the last of them in 1931 and, although the *Daily Mail* Trust was still a major shareholder, Rothermere told Cowley that he had decided that he had too much to do and that henceforward 'the *Mirror* and *Sunday Pictorial* businesses are entirely under your and your colleagues' control ... all vacancies on the Boards of the two companies will be filled by you'.[67]

The triumvirate that ran the paper included John Cowley, who, as Chairman, 'was a man without ability that I could ever discern ...' said King. 'He had no initiative of his own and simply sat there to see that Rothermere's wishes were carried out.'[68] 'As caretaker,' added Cudlipp, 'he besought his colleagues to take care, and the delivery of a writ, even by a firm of crooked solicitors on behalf of a notorious scoundrel, would disturb his sleep at nights.'[69] Wally Roome, the General Manager, 'had a good deal of superficial charm and was very quick and shrewd where his personal interests were involved, ... but contributed nothing to the Company.'[70] Cudlipp concurred: 'a hail-fellow-well-met smoothie whose sincerity couldn't be trusted an inch but who was pleasant to have a drink with.'[71] Jimmy Lovell, the Finance Director 'was a nicer man, and conceived it to be his duty to mind the bawbees.'[72] 'His mission in life,' agreed Cudlipp, 'was to obstruct any expenditure on anything at all.'[73] Thus, as Advertising Director, King had no expense account and could not afford decent staff.

'The death rattle in the throat of a national newspaper is first heard in John o'Groats and Land's End,' said Cudlipp, 'when the local general store cuts its supply below a quire, and this was now happening on a grander scale throughout the country.'[74] The Editor, L. D. Brownlee, was an Oxford Blue with a passion for cricket and no sense of what his dwindling readership wanted. And the only talented people on the board were Harry Guy Bartholomew, commonly known as Bart, and Cecil Harmsworth King.

'Facially they were both strikingly handsome,' observed Cudlipp, 'but the contents were mentally dissimilar by every known test ... Bart was inventive, energetic, conspicuous, a showman, a born newspaperman but not a journalist in the sense of being able to write a sentence and knowing what it meant.'[75] 'In some ways he was like Northcliffe,' the *New Statesman* was to comment when Bart retired, 'a rough erratic genius fashioned out of an extraordinary mixture of shrewdness and naivety, toughness and sentimentality.'[76] He was much nastier than the sane Northcliffe, though.

Bart had joined the *Mirror* in 1904 as Assistant Art Director and, through a mixture of technical ability and ruthlessness, vastly accelerated the process of getting a photograph from camera to printed page. A key insight into his personality comes from his reaction to Northcliffe's instruction that the *Mirror* should give some of its best pictures to the *Mail*: 'To retain a scoop for his paper, circumvent Northcliffe's instruction, and deceive the *Daily Mail*,' Cudlipp said, he 'smashed a photographic plate across his hand, deliberately cutting his fingers'.[77]

Northcliffe had recognised his talent, making him a director of the paper in 1913 at the age of twenty-eight and during the war Bart was a war photographer, as courageous as he was brilliant. 'His personal experience under fire,' wrote one *Mirror* biographer, 'became his own standard of what a photographer should risk to get the picture. Earthquakes, wars, revolutions – the whole range of public and private catastrophe was the *Mirror* photographer's parish.'[78] However, there was little Bart could do at the *Mirror* but hope that, some day, he would have a chance to turn it into what he knew it could be.

'He had ideas, I had good judgement,' was King's comment, 'so we put our heads together.'[79] While they disliked and distrusted each other, they both knew what had to be done. Bart instinctively understood what King had concluded after a great deal of thought – that the traditional respectable middle-class readers to whom the dull, conservative *Mirror* appealed were disappearing and that salvation lay in providing an exciting, left-wing product to the young working class who had never before bought a newspaper. Instinctively radical, Bart hated upper-class snobbery and arrogance and despised government incompetence.

King's strategic and political gifts were necessary to create the conditions in which Bart could let rip. Bart had to keep quiet, for his motives for getting rid of Brownlee were all too clear; King, however, could plead disinterestedness. King was highly intelligent, a good strategic thinker, preternaturally patient and aware of many of his own deficiencies. Knowing that he lacked intuition, he learned about people from observing them closely, and though he was better at seeing weaknesses rather than strengths, he did recognise talent and always wanted to encourage it. He was also ruthless. Cudlipp described the patient, calculated, relentless approach that King would have adopted to achieve this vital change in his company. 'Brownlee is an excellent fellow, King would concede, but is he in the right job? Are we being fair to Brownlee himself? He might have a mental break- down the way things are going and we don't want that on our con- science. It would surely be kinder to give him a hint after Christmas than before, don't you agree? Who is the best among us to tell Brownlee – surely not Bartholomew? Shall I, or you, or you?'

Being so calm and measured helped, as did the authority that came from being a Harmsworth, good-looking and six feet four:

After a passage of time people began to wonder why Brownlee was still coming to the office, and Bart was content to enjoy the intrigue without any personal risk.

The Cecilian chant continued. The real problem is really no longer Brownlee – he will obviously be happier with a generous cheque and more time to dally at Lords. The problem is who will follow him as Editor. Bartholomew? Over Cowley's dead body? Then why not Cecil Thomas as Editor with Bart in another role but not directly responsible for what is being printed *that* night?[80]

'I spent last night reading and listening to the wireless,' King wrote in early August from London to Margot, who was in Scotland:

– particularly Moscow and Athlone – the latter made me almost homesick for dear dirty Dublin . . .

But my real thrill is from the office. There was a stormy meeting this morning and when the more pugnacious members had withdrawn we held a board meeting and decided to give Brownlee three months leave of absence. He will, of course, never return. It is all a bit previous, but what a relief! Now we can get a move on and in more directions than one.

It is perhaps for the best that I shall be going away so soon and then I shall return in time before things warm up in the autumn.[81]

And so the intellectual, remote, fastidious Cecil Harmsworth King, who always said that the newspaper that would suit him would have a readership of one, created the conditions for the tabloid revolution.

The good-natured, tranquil and safe pair of hands that became Editor from the outset did what Bart told him. 'Bart was the architect, Thomas was in charge of the builders – or, in the view of some, was the superintendent in charge of the madmen.'[82] And King was 'the elegant wheeler-dealer, becalming the Triumvirate, expediting the emasculation or isolation of the duds, first-aiding Bart's erratic confidence and diverting him from the sillier and merely mischievous excesses, shocking for shocking's sake.'[83]

The model was the *New York Daily News*, which had begun life copying the *Mirror*, but was now the far more successful product. Unlike the *Mirror*, which was a picture paper with news, the *Daily News* was a newspaper with pictures. The first edition that Bart directed, in November 1933, was a stunning departure from the paper's customary cosiness. 'TRIAL BY FURY – U.S. LYNCH LAW' was the lead story; 'Frenzied Mob Storm Another Gaol' the subtitle. There were shocking pictures of a well-dressed Californian mob battering their way into a prison and of the hanging body of a lynched black man. As Cudlipp put it, publishing this 'study of mass lunacy . . . was the first indication that the genteel *Mirror* intended to expose unpleasant truths as well as to report the titillating niceties'.[84]

Yet though the underdog whom King favoured was beginning to get a look-in, the radicalisation of the paper could go no faster than the Triumvirate would tolerate. Cowley was all too aware that Rothermere, through the Trust, was still the controlling shareholder, and Rothermere, seeking order and certainty in a confused world, was seen to be an enthusiastic supporter of fascism: he was friendly towards Germany and, domestically, he thought Oswald Mosley and his fascists were sensible and patriotic. 'HURRAH FOR THE BLACKSHIRTS!' shouted the *Daily Mail* in January 1934; 'GIVE THE BLACKSHIRTS A HELPING HAND,' urged Rothermere in the *Daily Mirror*:

Timid alarmists all this week have been whimpering that the rapid growth in numbers of the British Blackshirts is preparing the way for a system of rulership by means of steel whips and concentration camps.

Very few of these panic-mongers have any personal knowledge of the countries that are already under Blackshirt government. The notion that a permanent reign of terror exists there has been evolved entirely from their own morbid imaginations, fed by sensational propaganda from opponents of the party now in power.

As a purely British organisation, the Blackshirts will respect those principles of tolerance which are traditional in British politics. They have no prejudice either of class or race. Their recruits are drawn from all social grades and every political party.[85]

Cudlipp was still palpitating with rage when he wrote about Rothermere later: 'lascivious, gluttonous, Hitler-grovelling, penny-pinching, power-mad, boring old sod.'[86] Cudlipp was invariably vicious about Rothermere*; King, unusually, was rather more kind. 'I think Rothermere was a most forceful, able man, disgusted by the ineffectiveness of governments between the wars, hence his contempt for Baldwin and his admiration for Mussolini and Hitler. At least these last got something done. I really think that was about all there was to it.'[87]

There was, however, a great deal more to it than that. Rothermere, like Northcliffe, was intensely patriotic. He hated and feared Soviet communism and, like so many in the 1930s, left or right (including his nephew Cecil), his opposition to one ideology drove him – for a while – into the arms of another. Yet though his emotions had led

---

* Ms Wanda Kościa
First Circle Films Ltd
22 May 1997

Dear Ms Kościa,

Thank you for your letter of 19 May asking me to agree to doing a profile-interview about (presumably the First) Viscount Rothermere.

I enjoyed the enormous pleasure of never meeting him, and even greater privilege of never working near him as an editor. In my last few years I honestly cannot be persuaded by a fat cheque or a share-option in First Circle Films to waste time working on a TV profile for BBC2 of the lascivious, gluttonous, Hitler-grovelling, penny-pinching, power-mad, boring old sod.

Sorry, Wanda.

Sincerely,
Hugh Cudlipp

him astray, he was no fool and quickly realised he had been taken in. Repelled by Mosley's Albert Hall rally in June 1934 when communist agitators were savagely beaten up, and disturbed by his anti-semitism and anti-democratic corporatism, Rothermere withdrew all backing for him. He also, early on, got the measure of the Nazis: 'The oligarchs of Germany are the most dangerous, ruthless men who have ever been in charge of the fortunes of a people of 67,000,000 in number,' he wrote privately to the Chancellor of the Exchequer, Neville Chamberlain, in October 1934. 'Violent as they were on the 30th of June in internal politics [the Night of the Long Knives], they will be equally or more violent in external politics.'[88]

Yet Hitler was a great fan of Rothermere's, whom he believed to be 'alone among the great newspaper proprietors of the world outside Germany . . . the only one who gave himself and the Nazi movement a fair deal.'[89] Deliberately, Rothermere stayed publicly friendly towards Germany, so the *Daily Mail* line did not obviously change, just subtly altered: '[Rothermere] wants us to be very strongly armed and frightfully obsequious at the same time'[90] was Churchill's assessment.

Rothermere met Hitler later that summer and established a cordial relationship. 'Lloyd George and your brother . . . won the war for Britain,'[91] said Hitler, a man with a keen appreciation of the importance of propaganda. Rothermere deliberately, as he explained himself to Churchill, used with Hitler 'the language of butter' rather than 'the language of guns', as it was more effective in dealing with dictators who lived in 'an atmosphere of adulation and awe-struck reverence'.[92] They exchanged warm and confidential letters, and Hitler came to see Rothermere as 'one of the very greatest of all Englishmen. He is the only man who sees the magnitude of this Bolshevist danger.'[93] With his customary lavishness, Rothermere gave Hitler priceless gifts: a note with a jade bowl acknowledged Hitler's indifference to worldly goods, but explained that the present was for 'Hitler the artist.'[94] And the *Daily Mail* persisted in its perplexing and apparently contradictory line.

But Rothermere's sacrifice in painting himself as a fellow-traveller in order to obtain information useful to the British government, the military and the anti-appeasers counted for little. The government was resolutely determined to believe Hitler to be no threat: innumerable letters to key people about the German military build-up, even when accompanied by copies of Hitler's letters to him, usually resulted in patronising brush-offs from all but Churchill. 'You have been wonderfully right in your talks with me,' wrote Churchill in midsummer 1937, citing Rothermere's predictions about the 'violation of the Rhineland . . . The collapse of the Abyssinian resistance' and Mussolini's relationship with Hitler. 'My information tallies with yours that Czecho-Slovakia will soon be in the news.'[95]

'Blackshirt, collaborator, profiteer, buffoon, alarmist, international busybody, as mad as Northcliffe:'[96] it was easy to dismiss Rothermere if you did not know what he was up to. Even Esmond Rothermere, who was alarmed by the decline in circulation of the Daily Mail, had given up trying to understand his father's motives. For Cecil King, whose early career had been blighted by the death of one mad uncle who was notorious for hating Germans, it was hard to be dependent for advancement on a second who was perceived to be equally megalomaniacal but pro-Nazi. 'His enthusiasm for Hitler was deplorable',[97] he wrote primly in his memoirs. Cudlipp, in his, asked embarrassing questions: 'Did either [King or Bart] oppose in 1934 the publication of Rothermere's Fascist tirade, degrading the Mirror to the status of a recruiting sergeant for Mosley? Did either mildly propose that another view of the Blackshirts might be published in the same newspaper? Did either indicate an intention to resign with a public statement saying why?' He answered his own questions. 'The only explanation of the silence is that they knew or hoped that the end of the Rothermere influence was near at hand, and that in their resurrected Daily Mirror, matching the politics to the commercial aim, there would arise an occasion for retribution.'[98] They also, understandably, did not want to lose their jobs just when they had reached positions of some power. So, for now, they advanced cautiously.

King's stock in the wider newspaper world was rising. In London he was sitting on committees of the Newspaper Proprietors' Association, an organisation founded by Northcliffe and from 1934 chaired (poorly, thought King) by his cousin Esmond. Early in 1935 his godfather, Cecil Harmsworth, who was to have attended the Imperial Press Conference in Cape Town on behalf of Rothermere, had to drop out; Rothermere asked King to take his place. Leaving in mid-January on the Warwick Castle, King and Margot were away until May; their travels included a 5,000-mile tour of Africa, visits to

Rhodesia, South America, the West Indies and New York. For more than three months King was treated like a press proprietor rather than the Advertising Director of two undistinguished newspapers. He made contacts with senior newspapermen throughout the Empire and met the most important people in the places they visited. Margot's notes of the trip chronicle a remorseless round of lunches, dinners and banquets. 'Lunch – with speeches by minister without portfolio & Mr Moffat, P.M. of Rhodesia, a dull old man but a dear, son of missionary Dr Moffat' was a typical entry.[99]

For the first time, King found his opinions canvassed by newspapers. 'The great value of a conference of this kind,' he rather ponderously told the Jamaican *Daily Gleaner*, which referred to him throughout as 'Harmsworth-King,' 'lies in the fact that it helps the different parts of the Empire towards a better understanding. We have been to South Africa, and that very fact means that in future we shall have a closer sympathy with its aims, and a better understanding of its problems.'[100] Writing to his sister Nora from the ship taking the Kings to New York, Cecil was more frank: 'The most interesting part of the trip, I think, was the comprehension one got of the 'colour bar'. Black are black & there to be exploited & whites are born to live on the black man's labour. The bare-faced cynicism with which this view is held was quite extraordinary. The wiser spirits admitted that this could only lead to complete disaster in the end, but in the meantime it is rather fun (for the white man).' His shipmates did not impress: 'This ship is full of Americans – the very weirdest ones. They are mostly dull, vulgar & elderly with eccentric ideas of dress. Our star Englishman is Sir Montague Burton (the Tailor of Taste) – a shifty-looking little Jew from Leeds.'[101] He was more tactful a week later when in New York – in his capacity as Rothermere's nephew – he 'inspected editorial and mechanical departments' in the *Daily News* while, in his capacity as secret *Mirror* revolutionary, he was looking for inspiration.

'BRITON VIEWS N.Y. AS CITY OF FUTURE,' announced the paper. King had:

> declared New York to be the city 'most nearly typifying the metropolis of the future.'
> The swift tempo of life here, the precise and orderly arrangement

of the streets and the American construction plan were among the metropolitan characteristics which the tall, ruddy-faced British publisher believes will be adopted by other countries in time to come.

The Englishman admitted he was agreeably surprised to find that New York, despite its speed and bustle, lacked the noise of many other cities he has visited on his three months' swing around the world. He admitted, however, that he felt a slight disappointment as he viewed the skyline from the Upper Bay. 'It seems a bit too jumbled,' he said.[102]

Back home, brasher news coverage and heavier black type were gradually attracting new readers, and Young Turks were being recruited. It was King, in his capacity as Advertisement Director, whom Bill Connor and Basil D. Nicholson (J. Walter Thompson copywriters on the Harpic and Horlicks accounts respectively) had visited in 1934 with some strip cartoons; both were hired in the summer of 1935. Connor, as Cassandra, was to become the pioneering columnist of 'big-scale, incessant rudeness'.[103] Nicholson, hired as Features Editor, drove the visual transformation of the *Mirror*; he also placed the advertisement for an assistant that caused Percy Cudlipp, Editor of the *Evening Standard*, to get in touch with his little brother.

CHAPTER IV

The Effortless Rise of Hugh Cudlipp

'WHEN KING WAS AT ROSE HILL IN SURREY, PINING FOR HOME AND hating home, Cudlipp was unborn,' wrote Cudlipp in his autobiography:

> when he was duly delivered in 1913 in Wales, King was a twelve-year-old day pupil in Dublin, complaining that the boys were a rough lot and the masters even rougher. In January 1915 when King began the unhappiest days of his life at England's oldest public school, seeking solitude in a world of doorless water-closets, Cudlipp was wetting his diapers in the family pram in Cardiff. When King was studying constitutional history at Oxford, with currency, finance and banking as his special subjects, wandering around Northcliffe's newspaper empire during the vacations, Cudlipp was at Gladstone Elementary School.[1]

Hubert Kinsman Cudlipp's competitive streak was honed early. During his early childhood there was the Saturday-night ritual when Willie Cudlipp washed the four children in a zinc bath in front of the kitchen fire: first Phyllis, the youngest by two years; then Percy, the eldest; then Reg; and finally Hubert, 'by which time the water no longer resembled ass's milk . . . If Napoleon or Wellington had been cut down to that size the world might never have heard of them'.[2] A greater grievance was the way in which his brothers, seven and three years his senior, excluded him from their conversations by speaking in gobbledegook, and circumvented domestic rules against having bread, butter and jam together while tricking him into obedience. 'Boys have grown into bank robbers for less than that and it was greatly to my credit that I developed nothing worse than a suspicious nature – a useful weapon in the armoury of a journalist.'[3] And then there were their respective sizes: Percy grew to be 6 feet, Reg 6'4", and Hubert 5'7", the same height as his sister.

School meant boredom and punishment, and he 'exploded in confusion and tears at the age of ten, frightened, I guess, when my mother told me I had passed the examination (just) for the Howard Gardens Secondary School in Cardiff. The same year King, aged twenty-two, married Agnes Margaret, whom I knew and liked, much later, as Margot . . .'[4]

The only happy memory of school was the day when four professional musicians – two violins, viola and cello – visited and played Schubert to those prepared to stay on after hours. Up to then, Hubert's experience of music had been restricted to listening to Percy's gramophone, on which the brothers had graduated from popular music to a neighbour's Gilbert and Sullivan and finally to Berlioz, who sparked their lifelong love of classical music. But that afternoon, 'I stayed and then I ran and leapt and gurgled the whole mile home without touching the pavement . . . I said nothing all the evening and couldn't eat; they thought I was sickening for a fever'[5] Later, Reg and Hubert had piano lessons, but realised soon that, despite their passion for music, they had no talent.

Though school was otherwise a 'joyless purgatory', Hubert bore no malice: 'it was nobody's fault except my own that everything I learned I harvested outside the walls.'[6] His education began at home: he was brought up irreverent. There was his mother – mimicking Queen Mary, 'stately and stiff-backed but nonchalantly flapping her gloved hand in acknowledgement of the plaudits of the Cardiff crowd'[7] or telling her stories – as her youngest son would do – with more regard to theatrical effect than accuracy. A trim, histrionic, well turned-out coquette and bundle of nervous energy, 'she was volatile, impulsive, a tireless raconteur who would create an Othellian tragedy or a Ben Travers comedy from fragile over-the-wall gossip and routine family material'. There was Percy, who regarded himself – along with his family, employers and the rest of the human race – as raw material for caricature and parody. Of his childhood fame as 'Cardiff's Boy Poet', Percy's assessment was:

> I wrote in verse. Myself I saw
>   Performing wondrous feats
> As Wales's little Wordsworth, or
>   As Cardiff's pocket Keats.
>
> Yet though, at night, a hundred times,
>   I wrote till I was drowsy,
> The rhythms faltered and the rhymes
>   Were uniformly lousy.[8]

Hubert developed his own mimicking skills at the expense of the parson at the Wesleyan Methodist Chapel, the quavery-voiced Sunday school teacher, the entrepreneurial housewife who sold faggots and peas, and the muttering, spluttering, staggering drunk who horrified the tee-total Cudlipp parents. And he developed his argumentative skills at the expense of anyone who tried to teach him religion. He was unimpressed by the 'painful circus' of church, especially since he had noted that his father didn't know the words to the hymns. Although Hubert never had the patience to do more than skim books, he was a sponge for useful information. As recalled by a contemporary, at Sunday school:

> The young Cudlipp stood clearly forth as a dangerous and sub-versive heretic.
>   Mr Massey told us a story about a Birmingham chain-maker who lay dying, and in his extremity could think of nothing better than to send for Mr Massey. The man was gazing with feverish eyes at a picture of a racing pigeon he had once owned which had won many races. Mr Massey took in the scene at a glance. 'I strode up to the wall and ripped down the picture of the pigeon and put up a picture of Our Lord,' he said. Here he paused for effect, and I think we were all impressed – except Hugh. Taking advantage of the pause, he asked in a piping treble, 'Mr Massey, what do you think of the Theory of Evolution?' At that time, in orthodox Methodist circles Darwin's theories were still held to be anathema. The question caused a wave of horror through the Sunday school.[9]

He was eventually expelled on the grounds of being an atheist, a word then unknown to his mother.[10] This removed a source of income, for in addition to pinching money at home, he and Reg used to divert the pennies for the collection to purchase liquorice sticks and gob-stoppers at the only sweet shop open on the Sabbath.[11] In Hubert's case, this was supplemented by the Saturday sixpence earned for acting as the *shabbus goy* and lighting the gas and putting on the lights in the home of the orthodox Jew opposite. 'I said to Mr Belman, "if you would like me to come over during the week as well," and he said, "No, only on Saturdays", which of course I didn't understand.'[12]

The Cudlipp parents' preoccupation was with bringing up their children; otherwise, they might go occasionally to the cinema or the theatre, Bessie would read romantic novels and there was always an evening paper. Still, home was not without intellectual stimulation. From the market stalls Percy acquired poetry and novels to supple-ment Arthur Mee's *Children's Encyclopaedia* (bought by Willie on easy terms) and the Bible (which Hubert had briefly swapped for a ginger guinea-pig). Art consisted of a pen-and-ink drawing of Lloyd George that Willie Cudlipp had bought from the local artist, and mahogany-framed photographs of the Holy Sepulchre and other New Testament scenes, which he had collected as an army-canteen corporal in the Middle East.[13]

The streets, though, were full of interest. There were members of his gang to play and fight with and the drama of the occasional bloated corpse of a local suicide. There was great excitement in get-ting a lift from the milkman, who always roared with laughter when his horse farted,[14] and in sneaking a look through the pub door at 'the Bacchanalian scenes inside. Tawdry women sitting at the bar, tipsy men laughing, a spectacle of luring and noisy Hogarthian vulgarity, just like the hell . . . Mr Massey . . . had warned us about. What fun.'[15] There were annual holidays to a farmhouse or a boarding house by the sea, and the annual trip on a paddle-steamer: 'The singing of the Welsh miners who had dug the coal to drive the ship could be heard from the bars throughout the journey and I wandered as close as I dared to the scene of revelry.'[16] And there was the occasional Sunday treat to beauty spots in an uncle's car, which climaxed with a picnic 'with cucumber sandwiches and chocolate cake and cold ham and tongue and icecream and raspberries and paper cups and forks and corned beef and orangeade and salad and mayonnaise and Lea

& Perrin's and paper napkins and wasps and ants. We were warned by Bessie in advance not to overpraise the feast or gobble it up as if we were starving. 'You all make it look as if you never have anything at home'.[17]

For Hubert, 'Life began at twelve, though there were two more years to serve in the prison from which his brothers had escaped.'[18] ('Cecil Harmsworth King was twenty-five, shyly pecking around in minor jobs in the Harmsworth family newspaper empire . . . poking his nose in where he wasn't wanted and wasn't encouraged.'[19])

There was the entertainment of the Big Tent Mission, as Pastor Jeffreys called for people to give themselves to Jesus:

> A pious drunk and a black man came forward. 'There is no colour bar, my friend, in the Kingdom of Heaven,' the evangelist intoned.
>
> I had seen the black man saved several times at previous meetings and wondered if he was in the touring cast or on the establishment, helping to erect and dismantle the Big Tent. My Sunday School suspicions were confirmed. And reconfirmed some years later when the Pastor was performing at Blackpool where I happened to be a reporter.[20]

Percy would sometimes take Hubert to the Chinese laundry, where Mr Wah Kee would play the zither and his daughter would occasionally sing 'in a high-pitched nervous voice. During the war, drunks would smash Wah Kee's windows and denounce this patriotic British citizen as a "war-mongering Chink". Percy gravely assured his audience of one small fascinated boy that was the reason why Wah Kee still shuttered his windows at night.' Unbeknownst to Bessie, in 'a crummy but enchanting Chinese café in Cardiff's Tiger Bay, Percy told Hubert 'hair-curling stories, imaginary or true, of the goings-on in Cardiff's Chinatown'; identified Indians, Arabs and Africans manning the freighters that collected the coal; and pointed out a prostitute. 'Percy was a lurid Baedeker and I was an eager tourist, for the foreigners rarely left the doss-houses and dingy hotels of the docks area to saunter through the city streets except to answer charges of malicious wounding or worse at the courts near the City Hall where I was to meet them frequently as a reporter in a few years' time.'[21]

It was Willie who, though mildly supportive of the Liberals, of a conservative disposition and with no interests outside his home and his job, inadvertently politicised his twelve-year-old son who was already sympathetic to the poor. Most days, three unemployed men carrying tins and with labels around their necks saying 'PLEASE HELP TO SUPPORT FAMILY' would walk slowly down his street 'singing beautifully, mainly hymns; money would be given to them by the wives or the neighbours and when they were singing, they put their heads together and threw their heads in the air like wolves. It impressed me a great deal, this curious ritual, which went on day after day, different groups, different people, but always three.'[22] He noticed too that the most generous contributor was the Jewish Mr Belman.

Since Reg was now at work, Willie began to take Hubert with him on some of his monthly trips, with car and driver, to parts of Wales that the trains did not reach. Hubert vividly remembered May 1926, when a General Strike had been called in support of the miners, who were resisting a cut in wages. Hubert was being taken round the home towns of the miners whose songs he listened to on the steam ship, or of the unemployed who sang for pennies in his street. Willie was soft-hearted and would get into financial difficulties because he did not pursue creditors, but he was anti-union: Hubert was instinctively sympathetic. He would 'sit in the car looking at all these fascinating and decrepit dying places, because South Wales was officially desig-nated a distressed area . . . and I thought, well, there's a Tory gov-ernment and all this appalling poverty and unemployment and nothing is happening about it'.[23]

But the highlight of Hubert's childhood was the visit to London, where Percy now worked, to see the British Empire Exhibition:

I remember the journey I hoped would never end on the top of the bus from Paddington Station to Forest Hill, rubbing the steamed windows with my sleeve and looking for the elephant and castle at Elephant and Castle. I remember the advertisements in flashing, coloured electric bulbs, and the crowds in the streets at night long after Cardiff had gone to bed. The wonders of the Empire Exhibition itself merely left me wide-eyed and silent. Who could forget London?[24]

'Well, and what on earth are you going to do?' the cleverest teacher asked Hubert when he thankfully left school at fourteen. 'When I replied that I would be a journalist, sir, Mr Mathias said, "I have read now and then a humorous essay by you, usually in indecipherable handwriting, but good heavens, boy, you need far more than an errant sense of humour to review books for a newspaper. You need knowledge — where is your knowledge?"'[25]

When, at fifteen,[26] Hubert became a probationary reporter on the impecunious *Penarth News* (circulation 3,000[27]), 'King was twenty-six . . .'[28] dabbling in reporting (for which he was, by personality and temperament, utterly unsuited) and advertising.'[29] Hubert, now blissfully in his element, and in hot pursuit of his brothers, began to catch up fast.

Reg Cudlipp, who had followed Percy into journalism because of high praise for an English composition at school,[30] was the only established reporter there; he and Hubert worked in one room along with the Editor, J. K. Foster, who subsidised the paper with his milk-round, and his daughter Suzie, who kept a parsimonious eye on expenses. After six months' probation, Foster took Hubert on as a 'pupil reporter' for thirty months at five shillings a week,* which was to rise to ten in his third year. When Foster 'was not engaged in fobbing off the creditors, cadging newsprint on a promissory note, asking the printer for more time to pay, canvassing advertisements at cut-price rates or freelancing for other newspapers to try to make ends meet, he kept a strict eye upon me, always referring to me flatteringly or disapprovingly, as "Mr Cudlipp"'.[31]

Hubert graduated from reporting on Boy Scouts, bazaars and churches to town-council sub-committees and court cases concerning drunks, indecent exposure or errant motorists: 'Their tarnished names were in my dog-eared notebook before they had been Found Guilty and publicly paraded in our next issue. Their minor follies were recounted in excruciating detail for the titillation or deterrence of their neighbours.'[32] Then there were the corpses, who offered the chance of a bonus.

To win the commission that Foster paid for an obituary notice,

---

* About £10.00 today.

Hubert had to get tip-offs from undertakers and get to their par-
lours before the competing *Penarth Times*. There, as the deceased was
being laid out, Hubert would collect details of his life from relatives for the editorial write-up and collect the money for the classified advertisement, which he learned to draft expertly. 'To encourage
sympathy and trust I never declined to view the body when invited.
My stock remarks were "How peaceful he looks" or, if a woman of
reasonable age, "How beautiful". The editorial obit, a different exercise, usually ended with a puff for the undertaker on the theme of
"The funeral arrangements are in the hands of . . ." This would
ensure early information when his next client bit the dust.'[33] Mastering
the necessary professional clichés was an essential part of the job.
For such events as undistinguished weddings, for instance, '"The bride
and groom left for their honeymoon in the South" with a capital S
meant they were going to Weston-super-Mare or Minehead on the
other side of the Bristol Channel by paddle-ship but was intended
to imply a sun-baked villa among the mimosa at Cannes or Monte
Carlo.'[34]

His first setback – a libel threat – came when he was still only
fifteen. Sent to cover a soccer match between Penarth and Barry, he
compensated for his complete ignorance of sport by eavesdropping.
Inspired by a shout from a Penarth supporter, he got his 'Big Idea':

> . . . The facts were straightforward. The referee was from Barry
> . . . and Barry had won. Only a dolt could have hesitated over
> the introductory paragraph, and to get on in journalism you have
> to establish fairly soon that you are not a dolt:
> 'Few of the Penarth supporters,' I wrote, 'were surprised at
> the 5–0 result of Saturday's clash' (it sounded better than match)
> 'with the team from Barry. Nor were any of the Barry supporters
> surprised. After all, the referee himself came from Barry.'[35]

The referee was bought off with a letter in the readers' correspondence column 'severely castigating the bias of my report. It was
signed "Fair Play", and was written by me.'[36]

More serious was what happened when Hubert failed to turn up
on publication night with the results of a swimming gala. Love had
struck in the shape of Edith ('Bunny') Parnell, 'an artless sportive

virgin in a one-piece bathing suit',[37] known in the headlines as 'Penarth's Channel Swimmer', and he so far forgot himself as to take her out in a rowing boat. 'You have let the paper down,' said his editor. 'I suspend you for two weeks, Mr Cudlipp. Without pay.' Then there was the rebuke when Hubert looked mutinous when asked to deliver a few parcels of newspapers. '"Mr Cudlipp," said Mr Foster, "do you know that the early issues of *Answers* were delivered to the shops by Northcliffe himself. Are you too proud?"'[38]

The great test came when Foster asked Hubert to stand in for him at short notice and cover a performance of *The Messiah*. 'When he told me he wanted 3,000 words my first thought was that it must be the Second Coming . . . Nowadays I could cover Judgment Day in a ten-line paragraph, but the reverse order of 3,000 . . . was, in spite of my professional nonchalance, disconcerting.' As he listened to 'I know that my Redeemer liveth' ('great song which I'd not heard before, sung by a professional, beautiful, lovely tits, soprano from London doing a bit of moonlighting'[39]), 'I was very moved, but I was shit scared. Then I got the great idea.' When the oratorio was over, he stood outside the church hall and asked every member of the choir for their names and full addresses and, though it caused a big queue, everyone cooperated. The following morning he asked at the library for anything on *The Messiah* and copied the necessary information from *Grove's Dictionary of Music* and regurgitated it. 'I must congratulate you, Mr Cudlipp,' said Foster. 'I did not know you were a music critic as well as a soccer expert.' But the poster Hubert composed in black crayon (MESSIAH TRIUMPH FULL NAMES OF CHOIR) was not enough to save the ailing *Penarth News*: 'on October 12, 1929 – the same year Cecil Harmsworth King . . . was "hired" as a director of the *Daily Mirror* – I was fired when the *Penarth News* expired in bankruptcy'.[40] Foster's testimonial was generous:

I have pleasure in stating that Mr Hubert Cudlipp has been employed on these newspapers for the past year and has assisted generally in the gathering of local news, the reporting of Council meetings, social functions, etc.

He is strictly temperate, a hard worker, takes a fair shorthand note, and is well informed on musical and dramatic subjects.

I have only parted with him on relinquishing proprietorial control of these journals and strongly recommend him.

'Who,' as Cudlipp later pointed out, 'could have got pissed on five bob a week?'

To follow Percy to Fleet Street was the goal, but Hubert knew he needed more experience first. Reg went to the *Western Mail*, and within a few months Hubert joined the Cardiff *Evening Express* on a year's trial as Junior Reporter. It was around that time that he decided he was a Hugh rather than a Hubert – a name then discredited among the reading young who had learned in the immensely popular William Brown books of his fat, sneaky, cowardly enemy, Hubert Lane.

Hugh's social conscience was further stirred by the experience of waiting all night at a pithead with weeping women to hear news of menfolk trapped underground. Then there was the inquest on a woman who had died after a botched abortion using a piece of slippery elm. He came home to find his mother hiding the paper from him and broke it to her that he was the reporter. There were other inspirations: 'as "our music critic" [he] thrilled to the voices of the Welsh miners' choirs at the three Valleys Festival.'[41] Before covering concerts, Hugh would swot up on the music and would then eavesdrop for information and opinions in the bar during intervals. He became a great fan of the National Orchestra of Wales and its conductor, Warwick Braithwaite. And after a Sibelius concert, where the general view was that the brass had overwhelmed the strings, this sixteen-year-old critic wrote an attack on Cardiff City Council for being so parsimonious as to deny this great Sibelius interpreter enough strings to do the job properly:

So the next bloody day in the office the news editor said, 'Hey, Hugh, Warwick Braithwaite wants to see you in the waiting room.' So I was a bit worried about this great musician whom I've seen only in the white coattails with all the orchestra all dressed up with bloody daffodils in their button-holes. He's come to see me but he thinks he's come to meet a chap with a beard. At least I was in long pants, thank Christ.

I went a little nervously into the room and he said, 'Are you H.C.?' and I said, 'Yes, Mr Braithwaite.' 'I'm delighted to meet you,' he said. 'I've been telling the City Council until I'm mad for the past year that we must have more strings and now, thank God, the newspaper says that this is terribly important. The orchestra is delirious about it. At last, at last, somebody has seen this. I can't tell you how grateful I am.'[42]

Because no one else was interested, Hugh's duties also included standing in for the drama critic.

He had a bad moment representing the paper at the Lord Mayor's Banquet. Having expected the press to be put in the corner, he found himself at the top table surrounded by tall grown-up men. 'For the first time in my life, instead of the knife and fork we had at home, I saw a battery of knives, a battery of forks and a battery of spoons in front of me; it looked like the battle plan for Rourke's Drift. So I looked at them with mounting dismay and also at the three glasses, which was quite new to me because we didn't drink in our house until we left it and then we couldn't stop.'

When the first course came, Hugh played for time on the cutlery front by fiddling with the salt, but then a waiter arrived and said, 'Red or white?':

So I said 'What's that?' He said, 'Red or white?' So I said, 'A little of each please.' It was a phrase of my mother's about vegetables. He said, 'What?' I said, 'A little of each.' So he poured a little of each. The other chaps around – they didn't know much more than I did really, but they did know that you don't have a little of each. They did know that bit.

I had the sense there must be some order in the knives and forks and spoons or they wouldn't all be there, so I was waiting for the chap next to me to move. But he had too much sense to wait for me to move so he was waiting for the chap next to him to move. I went forward to pick up the salt to see if the Mayor had moved – he was about six up from me – and he hadn't moved.

Hugh played for time by hitting the sauce bottle and then:

the chap next to me thought, 'Well, someone's got to move', so he moved and then I moved and then the Mayor moved. I carried on with my white and red mixed; it was very nice I thought.

When I actually got the taste of it I got cracking, but then I had to get home. You couldn't have taxis, so I had to walk a good two or three miles and I was obviously pissed. It was only a two-storey house, but I was holding on to the banister crawling up the stairs. They'd go to bed about nine o'clock in our house and it must have been about eleven and then I saw the ghostly figure of my mother dressed like an archangel saying 'Where on earth have you been?' I said, 'To the civic dinner with the Mayor,' while weaving my way up, not to the loo because it was an outside loo; and when I got to the top I realised I'd made a big mistake and I had to go all the way down and out.[43]

Hugh learned a great deal on the *Evening Express*, including 'more about death, more about the death of newspapers and the acute vulnerability of Editors'. For, just six months after joining, he found the Editor dying in his office, with the blind cord round his neck. 'I closed the door and ran to the Chief Sub-editor, a man who was notorious for his stories of his own steely courage in World War One. When I informed him that the Editor was hanging in his office he fainted and slid off his swivel chair. I grabbed the News Editor and said, "Come with me – quickly." I cut the blind cord with a Boy Scout knife attached to my belt. The Editor was still breathing. He was taken to Cardiff Infirmary by ambulance – and survived.'[44] The cause of his attempted suicide was the amalgamation of the two Cardiff evening newspapers.

Out of a job again, Hugh decided to try to emulate Percy and get to London via Manchester, the best recruiting ground for the national newspapers. In July 1931 he was offered a job as a reporter, district correspondent and Sub-Editor at £3[*] a week on the *Manchester Evening Chronicle*;[45] so at seventeen he tore himself away from Bunny Parnell and set off on the train to find himself a boarding house.[46]

Percy was literary and Reg was reliable; Hugh was already a hard-boiled newspaperman, from his speedy feet to the fedora he pushed

---

[*]   About £160 today.

towards the back of his head. Despite what Mr Foster had said, he found shorthand too boring to bother with. Instead, he developed his excellent memory and improvised where necessary. His great test was to come when in Manchester he was one of those detailed to take down verbatim a portion of a speech of Lloyd George's – a job way beyond his competence. On the phone to the office, as a good Welshman he had little difficulty in making up an eloquent version of what he had listened to; the following morning the News Editor exulted that their newspaper had a hundred words not in their rival's version.'[47]

Hugh was acquiring many skills fast. From Reg he had absorbed 'the art of draining information from tight-lipped officials by pretending to know more than I knew, and rapidly acquired the science of being the Instant Expert'.[48] 'One learns the art very quickly of not asking questions,' he recalled, 'because asking questions is absolutely fatal. It puts the person on his guard and if he knows you're from a newspaper, it's inviting him to shut up.'[49] Street wisdom was Hugh's greatest asset, allied to his instinct for a new angle to an old story and his ability to make almost everyone like and trust him. What he called his 'journalist's working kit or tool-bag'[50] contained many weapons, including his 'of-course-you-can-trust-me mask'[51] and his unerring nose for what people wanted to hear. Reporting from Salford, 'a God-awful city' a tram-ride from Manchester, he had to get to know the Chairman of the Finance Committee: 'finance was never and isn't now my subject, but it was important, so whenever I referred to him in the paper I called him Salford's Chancellor of the Exchequer. This became the basis of a very good friendship.'[52]

Meeting Khrushchev 'at a caviar and vodka nosh-up in . . . the Kremlin is not a daunting experience when one has run the gauntlet of dealing with the mayors, aldermen, councillors and chief constables of provincial England. Bureaucracy is exportable. There is no basic difference between the Chairman of the Finance Committee of Salford City Council and the Chancellor of the Exchequer at No. 11 Downing Street, apart from the fact that in my experience the Chancellor is less pompous.'[53]

Salford, gripped by the Depression and devastated by unemployment, further radicalised young Hugh. 'In the police court one unemployed man who burgled to top-up his dole was followed by another,

interspersed by traffic offenders, girls nicked for soliciting, and battered wives reaching for the kitchen knife; the inquests processed sui-
cides, drunks who had not seen oncoming cars, or the victims of
illegal backstreet abortions.'[54] This 'knowledge of the grim reality of
life before death equipped me forever in understanding how "the other
half" endured and survived'.[55] His best friend in Salford was Walter
Greenwood, who was to become famous for *Love on the Dole*. Recalling
his drives round Wales with his father, Hugh said, 'The schoolboy
impressions were to be etched more deeply by my experience as a
newspaperman, and by an early fascination with the political scene
and the social conflict. I met other angry and frustrated men as life
went on.'[56] Hugh was angry himself: 'I visited slum houses that had
been denounced by Engels in 1844 in his book on the English working
class, condemned as unfit for human habitation. Men, women and
children were still living in the same houses in the same revolting conditions.'[57] But 'my See-Salford-and-Die masterpieces, indulging my
social conscience, did not wow the circulation manager. People would
not squander pennies on reading about what they had to endure; they
craved for escape.'[58]

The banishment of the Blackpool district reporter to a Swiss TB
sanatorium opened up a marvellous opportunity. At eighteen, Hugh
was now his own boss, Blackpool was a key to a healthy circulation
and his bosses were desperate for stories that could be trailed on
newspaper placards along the promenade. Blackpool was 'El Dorado
for a young newshound. Was it really the Sodom and Gomorrah of
the North as I had heard whispered in prissy Penarth?'[59] Certainly, to
Hugh, Blackpool was unbelievably cosmopolitan: the Winter Gardens
had fifteen bars allegedly representing different nations, with the
Lancashire waiters vaguely disguised as Mexicans, Chileans or whatever.

There were the usual stories from police courts and, with the help
of a friendly, honest Liberal councillor, an introduction to the intri-
cacies of municipal graft. But above all there was his education in
'the British working class on holiday before they discovered the Costa
Brava, wearing "Kiss me, Sailor" paper hats and blowing bubble gum
and cramming into the ear-splitting song-plug booths when it rained,
or into the Zoo at the Tower or the bars at the Winter Gardens:[60]

The Golden Mile was irresistible, an orgy of the bizarre, with its big wheel and exhibitions, barkers with loud-hailers beckoning the crowds to step inside and splash a tanner. Freaks. Midgets. Albinos. The Fattest Woman in the World, straight from Coney Island, America . . . Mitz, Morris and Akka, the Hollywood Apes, whose best trick, to the hilarity of those more agreeably seated, was to piss in unison on the front row . . . Ribald postcards – 'I've lost my little Willie' . . . The well-endowed nudes portraying Renowned Art Masterpieces who dare not wobble for fear of breaking the law unless you made them giggle or wiggle with a paper pellet . . .[61]

Hugh absorbed the clear message that 'the Great British Public' had an appetite 'for the vulgar, the bizarre, the prurient, for sex-in-the-raw, seeing but not touching, as well as between the sheets in holy matrimony.'[62] He sniffed out fraud – the shooting range where the big prizes were regularly won by the son and girlfriend of the proprietor, and the Big Top evangelical mission he had seen in Cardiff with the same black man being saved at every service. 'Only a cad would have unearthed these trade secrets and there was one around . . . Only a dolt could not have failed to inspire a riveting local placard a day with which to titillate the customers.'[63]

Blackpool attracted stars whom all journalists wanted to interview: Hugh's audacity came in handy. When he heard that Laurel and Hardy were coming, he went to meet them in Manchester, travelled with them back to Blackpool, gave them helpful advice on what to do when they were there and, to the chagrin of the waiting hacks, got out of the train with them with his story already written.[64]

But his News Editor in Manchester wanted more; the challenge was to get exclusives – better still, what were known as Running Exclusives. Blackpool provided the means to unleash Hugh's creativity; if there was no news, he could make news happen.

An early idea came from an encounter 'with a rather dull-looking parson. I had the good sense not to say, "Oh, who wants to talk to him." He said – talking in that parsonic language which always amuses me, "One grieves a little, does one not, about the falling congregation in one's church?" To which I replied, "Well, yes, I'm sure one does."' When it emerged that the church overlooked the Blackpool

Tower circus, Hugh suggested a special Christmas service for its per-formers – gymnasts, clowns and all, in full regalia. Naturally, he already knew the circus proprietor ('a wonderful source of stories – if you can't get a story out of a bloody lion . . .') and persuaded him that it would be good publicity.[65] And of course he had the scoop on a Friday, when the paper had its biggest circulation; on the Sunday the national press were there in force. Another Running Exclusive came from his suggestion to another worried cleric that he hold a special service to bless pets. '"Dogs, cats, goldfish, snakes – you decide how far you go."' Ahead of the pack on Friday, the following Monday he ran interviews with the religious leaders of all local denominations condemning the idea: 'one of my principles was never to suppress criticism of my own inspirations, indeed to encourage it to produce the follow-up story'.[66]

The 'vagabond impresarios who put on the sucker-shows', whom Hugh met in pubs in the Golden Mile, were invaluable. Sid was a particularly valuable source. It was he who told Hugh of his negoti-ations to bring to Blackpool Jacob Epstein's 'Genesis', a marble sculp-ture of a naked woman with Negro features in the last stages of pregnancy, representing, 'the mother of all races'. Having caused public outrage in London in 1931, 'Genesis' was bought by Louis Tussaud's Waxworks in Blackpool where, along with other Epstein works, it was exhibited in a sideshow highlighting the horrors of modern art. Sid and Hugh's collaboration had caused the prurient public to queue up in their thousands to see what had produced such headlines as 'DIS-GUSTING, SAYS BISHOP. IS EPSTEIN MAD? INSULT TO MOTHERHOOD? IS GENESIS GENIUS OR FILTH?'

Some months later the lady had lost her appeal and Sid was to substitute her with the Rector of Stiffkey, now in bad odour with the church because of his moonlighting in Soho as 'the Prostitutes' Padre'. Sid was fearful that holidaymakers would find religion a turn-off:

'I suppose', I said jokingly, 'you'll finish up with something like "SEE THE UNFROCKED RECTOR OF STIFFKEY BURNING IN HELL".

Sid's eyes narrowed as he downed the remaining three-quar-ters of his beer in one gulp. 'Bloody marvellous', he said, explaining that the Hell bit was easy; strips of red chiffon blown about by a hidden electric fan and illuminated by flashing red bulbs. 'I did it for Dante's Inferno in Barry Island five years ago . . .' On Thursday, the irreverend reverend was travelling north, *sans* dog collar, under the care of a chum of Sid's, to be interviewed by me that night for the exclusive in Friday's *Evening Chronicle*, re-written with new bits for Saturday's *Daily Dispatch*. The show opened on Saturday but the Rector was to be kept under wraps until a press conference for all on Sunday morning after a further exclusive interview with me for the *Sunday Chronicle* and *Empire News*: you worked for the whole newspaper group in those days, adjusting your style. My story for Lord Kemsley's Sunday papers judiciously contained condemnations of the show by prominent churchmen and local dignitaries: UPROAR OVER UNFROCKED RECTOR'S PUBLIC SHAME.[67]

When Hell palled, Sid grasped at Hugh's suggestion of Fasting Unto Death; Hugh would occasionally see the rector snatching a beer and a sandwich between shows. 'When he appeared in the den of an agnostic lion at Skegness in 1937 the clumsy ass trod on its tail and was mauled to death. It was not my idea or Sid's that his life should be endangered. Skegness was not in my district. The Prostitutes' Padre had decided for himself that showbiz was in his blood, and ironically his new living was the death of him.'[68]

Then there was the England soccer player who had confided in a pub that, between financial and domestic trouble, he wished he could disappear for a week. Hugh had a friend who captained a fishing trawler. 'Three days later the *Chronicle* announced: MISSING BLACKPOOL FULLBACK MYSTERY. Day after day there was no news, no clues. Had he been kidnapped? Had there been trouble at the soccer club? Suicide? For what possible reason?' The descending journalists from the nationals concocted 'theories more ingenious than my own to justify their expenses'. In due course, courtesy of a radio message from the captain, Hugh was at the dockside at the right time. 'CHRONICLE FINDS MISSING FULLBACK: Exclusive Interview'. A press conference was held, later. 'Another of my principles was never to deny access, later, to other newspapers: the wider the coverage, the more imposing the validity.'

A bonus for Hugh was the chance to socialise with the 'smart-alec by-line reporters' whom he envied on the nationals, 'often despatched to Blackpool to chase the hares I had unleashed a day or two before. I did not mislead them or point them in the wrong direction as they third-degreed me with champagne on draught in Yates's Wine Lodge; I was helpful with background but not foreground. There is no clam more clammy than a reporter being pumped by a reporter.'

The arrival of the stunningly successful writer, Edgar Wallace, to stand as Liberal candidate for Blackpool in the 1931 General Election was another gift. Hugh's offer secretly and unpaid to assemble and edit a two-issue campaigning *Liberal Banner* was accepted. 'I sensed that Lord Kemsley, whose newspapers were dedicated to supporting all Tory candidates everywhere . . . would prefer not to know of my clandestine activities.' Among the ways in which Wallace showed his gratitude was his collaboration as he left after his defeat. As he called 'Goodbye, Blackpool' through the window of his yellow Rolls-Royce to the people assembled outside the Imperial Hotel, 'a voice yelled out "Good riddance."'

> I saw Edgar lean forward to instruct his chauffeur to circle and return. Dramatically alighting from the Rolls, removing his black hat and long cigarette holder, Wallace growled: 'Who said "Good riddance"?' When nobody replied, he growled again: 'I thought so – a bloody coward'. The citizens I interviewed on the spot condemned the skunk who had insulted the famous author. All agreed that the shout had come from somewhere near where I had been standing, but none could identify the bloody coward. I phoned the exclusive of Mr Wallace's carefully timed departure to make page one of the Blackpool edition.

In old age, Cudlipp was unrepentant. 'It happened: that is the point. In creative journalism, the event does take place; it is the antithesis of the *phantom scoop*, when the prophesised event does not take place.' If creative accountancy involves juggling with figures to produce 'the most flattering picture which may be economical with the truth while falling just short of criminal concealment', then creative journalism 'is the art of causing something to occur that would not otherwise materialise' and is worth reporting: 'making news, not faking news'.

Hugh put his successes in Blackpool down to energy and a sense of fun, but he regarded it as having given him a privileged education: that was 'where I learned not only what newspapers were about, what the entertainment industry was about, what joy was about, what religion hoped to be about and so on'.[69] He gave up creating news when his predecessor came home and Hugh was recalled to Manchester to report other people's news. His ability to write colour pieces was well recognised by now; one assignment was to tour the Lancashire mill towns in a car to report on the mood and spirit of those affected by a strike in the cotton industry. Hugh was, of course, on the side of the strikers and in his dozens of interviews 'was impressed by their determination despite their poverty to hold out against these bastards.'[70] Their resilience moved him: 'the pawnbrokers' shops were filled with pledged possessions, the bookies' runners were idle, and the wives (most of them spinners or weavers themselves) told me the secret of how to make a hot-pot go further by adding water'.[71]

Hugh phoned his sympathetic story through as he travelled and it grew in each edition, reaching front-page lead by the fifth edition. But at the end of the day, in the sixth and final edition, it had disappeared completely. The Managing Editor, it emerged, though he had loved the story, had removed it from the edition that went to London as Lord Kemsley had interests in the cotton industry and sackings would probably have ensued. 'What do you then go out and do? Become a paid-up member of the Tory party?'[72] Or, as Hugh did, become committed to Labour.

Promoted again, Hugh learned about writing news headlines, graduated to headlines for funny stories and was given responsibility for editing the features pages, which he deliberately aimed at women – a lot of fashion, 'but not posh fashion.'[73] Hugh's knowledge of women was based mainly on general observation: for such an attractive, vital, confident young man, he was very inexperienced as far as girls were concerned – 'streetwise, but not bedwise.'[74] Other than the occasional fumble at boozy parties and the occasional lustful look at passing talent, he had remained faithful to Bunny Parnell, who on the strength of being the first woman to swim the Bristol Channel, had become a sports reporter first in Cardiff and then in London working for Reuters. In sharp contrast to King, who had always intended to have extramarital affairs, Hugh – though 'I covered a thousand cases and a million broken romances as a reporter'[75] – believed at the time that commitment to a woman required fidelity.

Hugh and Bunny were not lovers. His first sight of a naked woman close-up had come backstage in a Manchester theatre: after a dull interview, the actress Coral Browne stood up and – true to her mischievous form – let her dressing gown fall wide open as she asked '"Any other questions?" My notebook fell out of my hand and she said, "Well, I've got to go now," shaking my hand.'[76]

Hugh and Bunny both went to Cardiff at around this time, he from Manchester and she from London, to have a little party with their respective parents to announce their engagement. On the very morning it was to take place, there arrived a letter from someone who claimed to live in Bunny's boarding house, insinuating that she was having an affair with the Editor of *John Bull*. 'Tittle-tattle,' thought Hugh, and ignored it. The investigative antennae were switched off: it did not occur to him that, without Bunny's collusion, the writer would have been unlikely to have known his address. The engagement was formalised and he went back to Manchester, hoping even more fervently for the big break that would take him to London where Percy was now Assistant Editor of the *Evening Standard*.

It came with the arrival in the office of James Wedgwood Drawbell, Editor of the London-based *Sunday Chronicle*, who was looking for a Features Editor and was already an admirer of what Hugh had achieved. In March 1933[77] the nineteen-year-old Hugh was transferred to work in Drawbell's 'finishing school'. A master of layout, Drawbell taught Hugh a whole new range of technical and presentational skills: how to sling type, write bright headlines and crop pictures in the right place.

It was because, after two years, Cudlipp was still on the minimum union wage that in June 1935 he answered the advertisement for the job of 'bright assistant features editor with ideas, able to take charge'. When Nicholson called to say the job was on the *Daily Mirror* (well known to Cudlipp as a lame, conventional and politically Conservative duck), Cudlipp was not impressed: Bart's improvements were as yet sporadic. But when they met, the witty, brilliant and anarchic Nicholson attracted him. 'We're going to turn the *Mirror* into a real lively thrusting tabloid newspaper,' announced Nicholson. 'We haven't started yet.' He took Cudlipp to his room to view, 'surreptitiously', the template for the future, the *New York Daily News*. 'Can you start today?' he enquired. 'Otherwise I may be fired before you get here.'[78]

Lord Kemsley made it easy for Cudlipp to leave the *Sunday Chronicle*. Loyal by instinct, he would stay for an extra pound a week, he told Drawbell, but Kemsley – to whom this minor matter had eventually to be referred – stuck at ten shillings. Having enough money to enjoy himself mattered to Cudlipp, who was desperate to marry his Penarth channel swimmer.

He joined the *Mirror* at twenty-one, on £13.13.0[*] per week – 'just the man we want both for it, and for others later on,'[79] said Nicholson, in the letter of confirmation. Arriving on 1 August, for all his street wisdom, Cudlipp was disconcerted by another new boy, Bill Connor: 'When I first met Connor I felt that I was involved in an extremely unpleasant motor crash; even the exchange of orthodox civilities, the casual "Good Morning", was accompanied by the awful din of screeching mental brakes. It has never been a question of What Makes Connor Tick, but What Makes Connor Clang.'[80] Although Cudlipp's fiancée now worked in an advertising agency, he had never met anything quite like these imports from J. Walter Thompson. Nicholson, who was described by King decades later as one of the cleverest men he had ever met, educated his protégé by asking him outsiders' questions from the perspective of years spent persuading ordinary people to spend money on products they did not know they needed:

> Newspapers, said Nicholson to me at 2 a.m. in such conference rooms as the Gargoyle Club, did not know their business.
> What was the use of worrying readers about obscure revolutions in Bolivia if they could not sleep at night through indigestion? Was a pregnant woman, whose husband could not possibly afford her fourth child, interested in a Parliamentary debate on foreign affairs which would obviously result in nothing at all? What was the point of publishing pompous articles by avaricious big-wigs when figures proved that nobody would read them? Did newspapers really care what their customers read, or

---

[*] About £700 today.

didn't they know how to find out? Why had the profession of journalism attracted such little talent and originality? Had it ever occurred to Fleet Street that people didn't want to read anything at all? Or was I the sort of bloody fool who believed that the newspapers knew what they were doing?'[81]

Cudlipp threw himself joyfully into making the *Mirror* irresistible, even to pregnant women with indigestion:

REVELLER VANISHES FOR DAYS —
COMES BACK AS POP-EYED DRAGON
SHOUTING 'WHOOPEE! WHAT A NIGHT!'

was one of his favourites from that period, as was:

MATCH-MAKING MAMMIES
SHOO SPINSTER LOVELIES TO GIBRALTAR
TO GRAB A JACK TAR HUBBY[82]

Such headlines were inspired by the hysteria of the louche American publications he conscientiously studied: 'I wouldn't have passed one of these headlines myself then or since, but Nicholson received them with maniacal glee.'[83]

Cudlipp had been warned that while the news pages were changing dramatically both in style and substance, most of the features pages were to be kept as they were to mollify Chairman Cowley. He employed deviousness to deal with the letters page, a bastion of respectability and inoffensiveness, by getting permission to start a rival page for younger readers called 'Live Letters', which offered 'snappy' replies to their queries and metamorphosed into a lively problem page.

More confrontational was the manner in which he subverted the gossip page, then specialising in 'refined, soporific chit-chat on social and booksy affairs. Was it generally known that George V was an enthusiastic philatelist? Who was the tiniest débutante, the best-dressed Member of Parliament, the tallest Cabinet Minister, the most hand-some bishop? The swans on the lower reaches of the Thames were mating.'[84]

Three weeks after he arrived, Cudlipp upset more than the

Chairman when readers were told not only that the Queen of Spain had used a toothpick at a Savoy dinner, but that the corns of the actress Elsa Lanchester were so bad that she found it excruciating to dance at the Dorchester Charity Ball:

> When the item appeared her husband Charles Laughton came through on the phone, asking if I were the editor of the gossip page. I replied Yes, with suitable pride. 'Sir,' he thundered in his *Mutiny on the Bounty* voice, 'sir, I am coming immediately to your office in a fast car to horsewhip you.' I continued, a little nervously, writing a paragraph about a millionaire who had given his dance partner a double-decker bus because he liked her tango.[85]

What Cudlipp had failed to appreciate was that, in giving him his head, Nicholson was blatantly ignoring not just the wishes of the despised Triumvirate, but direct orders. 'Unruly, introspective, wildly imaginative and self-destructive,'[86] Nicholson got on well only with disciples and had no notion of how to woo his superiors. And though they both wanted the same kind of paper, his relationship with Bart – who disliked anyone who challenged him, loved secrets and hated intrusive questions – was at best uneasy. As Cudlipp recorded:

> Nicholson had often been puzzled by a whining noise that came from the process department above our room. It would rise to a screech, then droop to a plaintive, cello-like hum-m-m-m. When Bartholomew wandered in one day Nicholson put the question bluntly to him:
>
> 'Bart, who in the name of hell do you think is making that excruciating din?'
>
> The Old Man was annoyed, but admitted eventually that the noise was coming 'from an invention of mine'. Secrecy, of course, must be preserved.
>
> 'What is the invention for?' asked Nicholson.
>
> 'I cannot tell you that.'
>
> 'Well – what sort of thing is it for?'
>
> Bartholomew, angry at this impertinent, unceasing cross-examination, blurted out that his invention 'could do anything'.

Nicholson screwed up his face in wonderment and then asked: 'Can it, for instance, make love to a guinea-pig?'[87]

So it was that six months after Cudlipp's arrival, Nicholson summoned him to the roof of Geraldine House, the wedding-cake-style building constructed in Fetter Lane by Northcliffe and named after his mother. 'The wind was at gale force, it was raining, and it was impossible to light the giant Corona he had thrust into my mouth. "Bartholomew has fired me," he shouted. "He wants to see you now. I think they want to give you my job. Take it, or everything we've done will be wasted. All the other people here are fools."'[88]

King, who was always a generous employer, gave Nicholson a trip on the maiden voyage of the *Queen Mary* as a farewell gesture, and Cudlipp took over. Unlike Nicholson, he knew how to bend in the wind and, as Features Editor, he and his fellow revolutionaries learned various means of circumventing the rules and softening the impact of change on their superiors. They conducted themselves, observed Cudlipp, 'in the edgy atmosphere of an unlicensed gaming club expecting a police raid . . . [with] a code of nose-tapping, keep-it-to-yourself secrecy';[89] holding material back from early editions until Cowley had gone home was a frequent dodge.

Cudlipp's pages burrowed into the lives of readers and gave them reassurance and guidance as well as stimulation and fun. 'Are you glad you married, or sorry? What was the most embarrassing moment of your life? Is your family crazy, too? Tell us about the worst nightmare you ever experienced . . . the skeleton in your cupboard . . . your Greatest Adventure. What are your Eight Sane Rules for Happy Marriage?'[90] An American agony aunt came in to advise sensibly but racily on how far to let men go ('excessive petters should be slapped'), home-making ('cooking is just as important as Mother says') and childcare ('mix a little perfectly good and practical love into the day's routine').[91]

The relationship with readers became ever more intimate. In a series called 'Truth', prizes were offered for the best letters about what people would really like to say to their loved ones, with a number of examples provided: '"If only I could tell him about that irritating habit of his that drives me mad!" "If only I could tell him that he is killing my love by being so secretive!" "If only I could tell him of my past. It is haunting me."'[92]

Over 50,000 women filled in a questionnaire designed 'to get to the bottom of this love business': the information that emerged revealed, *inter alia*, that 'the first kiss, on average, came five months after the first "hello" and was experienced at the age of fifteen-and-a-quarter, usually between 6 p.m. and midnight'.[93] And 60,000 letters arrived in response to a course of twenty-four lessons on how to make the best of yourself.

The young, male and female, were pursued:

Knock! Knock!

Who's there?

It is the younger generation.

What is your ambition?

Youth is painfully fighting for an outlet which will offer escape from obscurity into the public eye. The *Mirror* is offering that outlet.

If you are under twenty-five and have something to tell the world about yourself and what you want, send in your entry, now. Write 100 words on 'What I Am', 100 words on 'What I Can Do' and not more than 200 words on 'What I want to Do'. Address your entry to 'Ambition'.[94]

In search of a columnist who would appeal to female readers, Cudlipp fixed on the twenty-eight-year-old ex-actor, novelist and whimsical columnist for women's magazines ('The Girl that I Marry'), Godfrey Winn. As Cudlipp put it delicately in the 1950s, when homosexuality was still against the law, Winn 'knew famous people like Louis Mountbatten, Somerset Maugham [an ex-lover], Noel Coward and Ivor Novello'.[95] 'Out of the blue,' recalled Winn, 'I was rung up and taken out to lunch in a small Fleet Street restaurant called *The Wellington* by a young man, several years my junior, with a head of dark curling hair set above a wide forehead, and the deep-set Celtic eyes of a visionary turned fanatic who gave me the impression at sight that if anyone touched him, electric sparks would shoot out in every direction.'[96]

To woo non-journalists, Cudlipp had perfected a device that he called the China Egg:

The first essential was to spot a likely man or woman of potential journalistic talent, invite him or her out to a slap-up lunch, implant an idea in his or her mind, extract that idea during subsequent conversation and draw instant attention to its excellence with suitable exclamation. My theory was that if the guest could be persuaded without undue pain, other eggs newlaid and lion-stamped by the Egg Marketing Board might reasonably be expected to follow.[97]

It was not an infallible technique, but it worked with Winn.

Winn (whose nickname was Winifred God) was soon writing 'my very own page' in the *Mirror* six days a week about his mother, his garden, his white Sealyham terrier, Mr Sponge, his pale-blue coupé (known to the vulgar as Winifred's Blue Boudoir) and his famous friends: 'the tantrums were daily and the weeping weekly, but Winn was a superlative journalist'.[98] He snuggled up to his female readers, went to tea with one of them weekly (armed with a photographer), shared with them those of his innermost thoughts that were fit to print and received many hundreds of letters every week. Paid £20[*] a week initially, he was on £40 in 1938 when he was poached by the *Sunday Express* to write a weekly column for £100: in the days of the Triumvirate, money was not yet unlimited.

The boundaries of the features pages were further pushed back with such pioneering headlines as:

POISON-PEN FIEND'S
ASTONISHING CONFESSION:
I SMASHED A GOOD WOMAN'S LIFE

HE DROVE HER FROM HOME
WHEN SHE NEEDED HELP. NOW HE ASKS
– 'WHERE IS MY DAUGHTER?'[99]

Cecil King saw the fun in all this. 'Nobody confused him with the Laughing Cavalier,' observed Cudlipp in his memoirs, 'but he did have

---

[*]   About £1,000 today.

a sense of humour . . . "Irish", he explained.'[100] Few people other than Cudlipp could locate it: 'to get Cecil to laugh,' Cudlipp said privately, 'you had to tickle his prick with a feather.' Others loved Cudlipp's outrageous stories and his swift wit, but that was not the way to woo King. During their always civil encounters, reported Cudlipp, King kept to the business in hand, 'occasionally with a twinkle in his eye . . . It was apparent he didn't like anybody very much and also apparent that he didn't particularly dislike me, though we would not be going out on the tiles together or painting the town pink. He knew a Good Idea, especially a mischievous idea, when he heard one and indeed would think up a mischievous idea or two himself: he said he enjoyed "putting the cat among the pigeons".'[101] For his part, though King saw Cudlipp as being without education or foresight, he recognised his 'galaxy of journalistic gifts. He was a brilliant reporter and sub-editor: he had acquired a wonderful technique for lay-out from Drawbell, and has a gift for timing which is quite beyond price in a daily paper.'[102] He also found in Cudlipp what he had hitherto found almost exclusively in women or the homosexual Francis Needham – someone with the desire and the ability to break through his carapace or, in Cudlipp's words, 'shout across the drawbridge'.

Godfrey Winn recalled:

> Very tall, with a deceptively quiet manner and soft flaxen hair brushed smoothly across his neat head, Cecil King, then in his early thirties, already bore a striking physical resemblance to the portrait of his uncle, Lord Northcliffe, which hung above the fireplace in his office. If I had met him at a party, an extremely unlikely supposition since he deplored such social gatherings as a waste of time and energy, I would have erroneously taken him at sight for a university don. He had the same precise, dry voice, the same pursed lips, of someone who has chosen to be a spectator rather than a participant in the hurly-burly.[103]

His increasingly forbidding exterior compounded King's social difficulties, but he continued to seek solace and wisdom from literature, history and philosophy. The publication in 1936 of a new edition of the long-neglected *Journal Intime* of the nineteenth-century Swiss critic Henri Frédéric Amiel had been of immense importance to him.

Covering decades of scrupulous self-observation, it encouraged King's introspection, but also consoled him with a sense of fellow feeling. In his memoirs he wrote that Amiel spoke of himself 'in terms which apply so well to me.' It was utterly typical of King that he gave his readers a key to understanding him that was written in difficult French and replete with nuances, yet offered no translation.[104] In English it reads: 'I am open to whoever wants to leave, I withdraw from whoever has a low opinion of me, I am silent with whoever stops listening. Thus my neighbour is always master of the relationships into which we enter. "Each man harvests according to what he has sown in me." I can do nothing other, nor do I want to. I will do without whoever can do without me.'[105] Till the day he died, Cudlipp – for all the education King made available to him – would not have read a page of Amiel in English, let alone French, but instinctively he understood what to sow in his mentor, and he harvested royally.

As Cudlipp for the moment successfully made mischief with the features, King was focusing on the politics. Moving the paper leftwards took some time. In November 1935, to Cudlipp's disgust, it stoutly supported the Conservatives. Popular strip-cartoon characters were marshalled in support:

John Ruggles: Who reduced unemployment? And the income tax?
Who reduced the price of beer? STANLEY!
Gladys Ruggles: I put my trust in Mr Baldwin.
Jane: Hip! Hip! Hooray![106]

Still, the concerns of ordinary people were colouring the paper's politics: even Godfrey Winn's column occasionally agonised about the poor and the unemployed and sought money for deserving causes. On Rothermere's instructions, the *Daily Mail* Trust had sold virtually all its *Mirror* shares, so there was no longer a proprietor for Cowley to look over his shoulder at. There was also no longer an uncle for King resentfully to beg favours from, though as a last gesture Rothermere made him a Director of the *Sunday Pictorial*, which was ailing badly. Their relationship had not improved. King was always to feel that Rothermere had treated him badly, while Rothermere hated the new *Mirror* and could not stand King: 'I really cannot bear that insolent fellow,' he told his sister Christabel.[107]

King's reputation (like Bart's and Cudlipp's) depended on the *Mirror* being a success. Although Chairman Cowley was unhappy about the vulgarity of the revamped paper, its soaring circulation made for happy shareholders. And he was easily hoodwinked. When Cudlipp began a series explaining the policies of the political parties, 'King said, "Why not include the Communists?" When I replied: "Because the Board of Directors would faint." He said, "Probably"',[108] but succeeded in persuading Cowley that on free-speech grounds there was no option.

Cudlipp generated ideas like confetti, but King occasionally came up with a major proposal. Being preoccupied with the importance of getting youth into power, it was King who suggested doing a series on the 'Under 40s' who mattered in all important spheres – science, invention, the arts, and so on. And, improbably, King came back from an American visit with a book based on a magazine series entitled 'Charm School' suggesting that it might be useful. Cudlipp turned this into the *Mirror Charm School*: 'I am having difficulty over my charm school,' King wrote to Margot. 'I want it all pseudo-psychological – "to be charming you must think beautiful thoughts" – while they are thinking in terms of nudity and deodorants. However I will get my way.'[109]

Simplifying and clarifying represented the key to the paper's political coverage. King had developed the criterion that everything should be interesting and intelligible to a bus-driver's wife in Sheffield. 'I got a little tired of hearing about [her],' recalled Cudlipp. 'It wasn't dauntingly difficult for a commercial traveller's son from Cardiff to chat up a bus-driver's wife in Sheffield or anywhere else the Wykehamist might choose to mention without notice of the question: the proletariat spoke the same language.'[110]

A key moment for the paper's future came with the scandal of King Edward VIII and Mrs Wallis Simpson.

British journalists knew that the King's lover, Mrs Wallis Warfield Simpson, had divorced her second husband in October 1936; that the King wished to marry her; that Churchill – in the wilderness, but influential – was sympathetic but Baldwin was not; and that while American newspapers were full of related stories, British proprietors and editors were operating a self-denying ordinance in the name of loyalty to crown and/or government. The uneasy silence held even after a late-November Cabinet meeting discussing options, but then the Bishop of Bradford, publicly – and, to most people, bafflingly – prayed that the King be given the grace to do his duty faithfully. Though the bishop was so oblique that it may well be true, as he later claimed, that he was referring only to the King's apparent lack of interest in religion, Bart decided enough was enough and set to work organising another conspiracy. As Cudlipp put it, the *Mirror* was always 'ready to intrude into private joy'.[111]

On the evening of 2 December 1936, from his office next door, Bart telephoned Cudlipp. 'Do not leave the building,' he instructed. 'You'll get a call in the next hour but don't ask who's phoning you. He'll tell you Cowley's son has left the office. When you get the message put your head round my door – but don't say a word if anybody is with me. Better still, say nothing at all, even if I'm alone. Understood?'[112]

Cowley junior had been told he was not required to work late and had been given a copy of the first edition of the *Mirror* to take home to his father. On receipt of the news of his departure from Geraldine House, Cudlipp duly put his head around Bart's door and grimaced. 'Sit down, Cudlipp. We're printing it tonight. Don't tell a soul. Don't ask or answer questions. Don't answer your phone from now on even if I ring.'

The third edition reported Baldwin's 'audience of the King on urgent and political matters not connected with foreign affairs'; but the final, which came out too late for other newspapers to emulate, went for broke. In its biggest black type yet, over a photograph of Wallis Simpson, the *Mirror* headline read:

THE KING WANTS TO MARRY
MRS SIMPSON
CABINET ADVISES 'NO'

During the ensuing press mêlée, which lasted until Edward abdicated a week later, the *Mirror* demanded information and thumped the royal tub. It had blown the gaff, it explained, 'with the welfare of the nation and Empire at heart. Such is the position now that the nation, too, must be placed in possession of the facts.'

Cudlipp was allowed to visit the news pages with such front-page headlines as:

God Save the King!
TELL US THE FACTS,
MR BALDWIN

And

45,000,000 DEMAND TO KNOW
— AND THEN THEY WILL JUDGE

Cassandra accused 'the Prime Minister and his Government of manoeuvring, with smooth and matchless guile, to a desperate situation where humiliation is the only answer'. The aristocracy, with their own 'sorry pageant of adultery and divorce', were hypocrites to oppose the King marrying the woman he loved.

There was no appreciation to be had from the King. Writing in *A King's Story, the Memoirs of the Duke of Windsor*, of the wickedness of the press, he recalled that his beloved had come into the drawing room holding 'a London picture newspaper . . .':

'Have you seen this?' she asked.

'Yes,' I answered. 'It's too bad.'

The world can hold few worse shocks for a sensitive woman than to come without warning upon her own grossly magnified countenance upon the front page of a sensational newspaper.

'I had no idea that it would be anything like this,' she said. Nor had I. And, trying to reassure her, I expressed the hope, but without conviction, that the sensationalism would soon spend itself.

'You do not seem to understand,' she said in a troubled voice. 'It is not only that they are attacking you personally, or me. They are attacking the King'.[113]

Considering that the photograph was a flattering posed portrait, recorded Cudlipp testily, and that the *Mirror* had been one of the few papers on his side, the Duke was either naïve, forgetful or ungrateful.[114]

Although the paper was on the losing side, its circulation went up again and there was no going back to tepid Toryism. Like illicit lovers, Cudlipp and King were stealing time together and they were developing an understanding of each other and their politics. The value of their conversations, recalled Cudlipp, was not to do with King's views on tabloid journalism, 'of which I instinctively knew more than he could ever intellectually learn, but on his wide-ranging views about the world in general, his knowledge of politics, his Time-machine forays into the future:

> where would Britain, Europe, the civilised and uncivilised world be in five years, and where would our newspapers be, saying what and to whom? And there were the mistakes the great publishing houses of Fleet Street had made in the past and were still making. We talked of Northcliffe, Beaverbrook, Camrose and the other pioneers in their particular spheres, and of war and peace and human rights and social injustice and vested interest. These were the fascinating areas of which King knew almost everything and I knew little.[115]

Both had been struck by how uninformed had been the *Mirror* about what was going on between government, press and palace: 'knowing nothing, hearing nothing, seeing nobody, suspecting everything'.[116] Once Rothermere had left, there was no one on the paper with any contacts with the great, the good or the indiscreet. Beaverbrook, the *Daily Express*'s proprietor, and Rothermere's son Esmond, now Chairman of Associated Newspapers, which owned the *Daily Mail*, were confidants of the King, as *The Times* was of Stanley Baldwin. 'The *Daily Mirror* had no contact with anybody who knew anything, not even with a footman at Buck House.'[117] 'Cudlipp and I,' recollected King, 'vowed never to be caught in the dark by some crisis like this ever again.'[118] Yet with Cudlipp restricted on the *Mirror* to features, King to advertising and the paranoid and volatile Bart in control, they had to proceed cautiously.

'King was my tutor, Bartholomew my tormentor. A sustained conversation with Bart about anything of consequence was out of the question; dialogue was conducted in expletives, abruptly begun, abruptly ended; he did not have surfeit of charm to squander on superiors or underlings. Power had come to him late in life and it was his, and his alone, to monopolise.'[119] Bart was distrustful of Cudlipp, fearful lest he was becoming close to King, whom he needed, but resented and hated. 'Bart was a loner,' said Cudlipp. 'Cecil was a different sort of loner. If you have two loners moving in different orbits, it's highly unlikely that they're going to meet and if they do there is a meteoric crash.'[120]

Cudlipp often coincided with Bart in El Vino's of an early evening; Bart usually with Cecil Thomas and a couple of toadies; Cudlipp with Bill Connor, as Cassandra, the paper's star political columnist. Bart would normally confine himself to gazing at Cudlipp with suspicion. 'It was ironical,' Cudlipp remembered later, 'that a newspaper that was successful because of its sense of human values, its compassion and its sincerity and warmth, should be produced in a climate upstairs of rumbling personal malevolence and rivalry, though there were others who worked on the landing or downstairs who formed lifelong friendships.'[121] Like Cudlipp himself.

'I was aware,' remarked Cudlipp, 'that under Cecil's shy exterior was a searing ambition and self-confidence that immunised him from the dislike of his boardroom equals. They all stupidly thought his sole qualification was nepotism. He said to me, but only in the early days in a fleeting moment of candour: "Have you noticed that our elders and betters are getting older? There isn't a surfeit of talent around, is there?"'[122] Watching him closely, Cudlipp concluded that 'unobtrusively he was packing a punch he would deliver without mercy or remorse in middle age at anyone who stood in his way. Beneath the cultivated shy exterior, but not far beneath, there was a repressed pride, an expectation of deference from others, a smooth superiority and an urge for revenge I have not witnessed in other men.'[123]

As King endured the frustrations and humiliations, and waited for signs of weakness among his elderly colleagues and further opportunities to show what he was capable of, Cudlipp extended his influence through his burgeoning relationship with Cassandra, and with Richard Jennings, who since Northcliffe's time had been writing *Mirror* leaders over the initials 'W. M.'. The donnish and fastidious Jennings was gently socialist, though more interested in poetry than politics, and the braying barbarism of Nazism horrified and gradually toughened him. When on the death of the German President in 1934, Hitler consolidated his dictatorship, W. M. wrote of this 'hysterical Austrian, with his megalomania, based on an acute inferiority complex, his neurasthenia, his oratorical brilliance, his inexperience in the government of a great people'. Yet, though the *Mirror* was more sceptical than most other

British newspapers, even after Hitler stripped Jews of their citizenship and Mussolini invaded Abyssinia, it still wanted – like its readers – to believe that reason would prevail and the dictators would stop short of war: 'What does the world and his wife want?' asked W. M. in March 1936. 'Merely to get on with their work and play.'

It was the beginning of the Spanish Civil War in July that finally convinced Jennings that, as Cudlipp, King and Cassandra already believed, peace with the dictators was probably beyond reach. Commenting on a speech of Winston Churchill, W. M. said:

> Once more it is Mr Churchill's perhaps not distasteful duty to ginger up our rearming Government in the House of Commons yesterday afternoon.
>
> He imparted an alarmist atmosphere to the proceedings.
>
> He can claim credit for having drawn Mr Baldwin's somnambulist attention to the huge, the inexplicable armaments of Germany. He speaks with authority, as one long closely concerned with the technicalities of war. Thus yesterday we seemed, indeed, back in the dark war age – with Mr Churchill again demanding his state of emergency and clamouring for a deputation to confer with the Prime Minister.
>
> It is depressing to have to admit it. But Mr Churchill is right.

The Mirror did not again falter on the anti-appeasement front.

In 1937 King secured the opportunity to prove his ability in a new field, persuading Rothermere and the Triumvirate that he should be sent to Quebec to sort out the very messy capital structure of the Anglo-Canadian Pulp & Paper Company. He was already well informed about the paper trade because of his editorship of the Empire Paper Mills, and though he had no experience of dealing with company finance, he achieved a highly satisfactory capital reconstruction. Accompanied by Margot, he went also to New York, Chicago and then to Des Moines:

> A tall, blond, English newspaper executive – Cecil King of the London Daily Mirror – saw his first cornfield Friday, reported the local paper.

Without being bowled over, Mr King was impressed.

'Iowa is such a rich country,' he said. 'The ground is so good; everything is so green.

'The small towns are much nicer than in England — more open, with wider streets and trees. And so friendly . . .

Des Moines is the only city outside of Chicago and New York Mr King is visiting, because he said he considers publishing methods on The Des Moines Register and Tribune and the picture magazine, Look, 'the smartest in the States . . .'[124]

Travel was a joy to King, not just because he was so interested and learned so much, but because he was easier with people abroad, especially, if like Americans, their simple friendliness broke down his reserve. Once again, he came home more confident than he had left. And he was determined to do something as a matter of urgency about the *Sunday Pictorial*.

Although Rothermere was the founder, he had shown as little interest in the *Pictorial* as he had in the *Mirror*: its circulation had dropped from more than 2,400,000 in 1925 to under 1,400,000. Much to Bart's resentment, the Triumvirate had resisted handing another respectable, dull newspaper to him to turn into something profitable but socially embarrassing. As a Director of the Sunday Pictorial Company, King was in a strong position to force his colleagues to see financial sense and reluctantly they agreed that the Editor should be sacked and that Bart should take charge. Bart, however, was so rude to the Chairman that he revolted and appointed King Editorial Director instead.

Having assured King that he could have any *Mirror* executive as Editor, but that he would do his best to ruin whoever took the job, Bart returned to his office and summoned Cudlipp. '"Here's a laugh", he said, "Cecil King is going to send for you shortly and ask you to become Editor of the *Pictorial*. As if you'd leave the *Mirror!* Come and see me afterwards." I was not accustomed to such comradeship and warmth . . .

'King phoned me with his polite request, "Would you like to pop down?"' So King explained the problem 'with his usual patience' and offered the twenty-four-year-old Cudlipp the job. 'It is only fair to warn you that we won't be getting any help from Bart.' Well aware that King was taking an enormous risk and that failure would be hugely damaging for both of them, Cudlipp replied instantly, 'Yes. When?':

> Among my more dramatic one-scene dramas on newspapers I retain a nostalgic memory of the meeting shortly afterwards with Harry Guy Bartholomew . . .
>
> 'Yes, yes, come in,' he said when I phoned. He couldn't wait, but the benign smile which I had rarely seen before and never saw again did not remain for long.
>
> 'Seen King?'
>
> 'Yes.'
>
> 'Did he offer you the job?'
>
> 'Yes.'
>
> He was in a boisterous mood, banging his fist on the table and laughing in a humourless fashion.
>
> 'What did you say, Cudlipp?'
>
> 'Yes.'
>
> In the closing stanzas of a menacing harangue, Bartholomew, now almost breathless with rage, eyed me distastefully and said, 'I'll tell you this, you'll not get any help from me – no help at all. That's all.'[125]

CHAPTER V

Cudlipp and Mr King

'YOU HAVE TO GET HOLD OF A SICK NEWSPAPER,' WROTE CUDLIPP decades later, 'pull it out of bed, drag it to its feet and shake it hard and often. The first thing to do is to make it interesting, and the barometer you have to watch is the one which indicates whether you are killing off the old readers by shock at a quicker rate than you are attracting new and younger readers by gay, modern methods. If this does occur you get the sack and somebody else has a go in your place. It's as simple as that.'[1]

The comatose paper that Cudlipp was required to transform into a left-wing sensational tabloid required savage and rapid change. Reading with dismay the most recent issue, Cudlipp judged it a 'conspiracy to make the English Sabbath duller'. 'Should prospective brides produce before marriage a certificate testifying to their prowess in home management?' asked an editorial, before plumping for the answer: 'Give and Take in married life is an adequate substitute for diplomas'. Early tomatoes occupied an entire page, and the clerical columnist asked 'Is Most of the World Mad?'

> The jokes page, my God, the jokes page! 'Nuts and Wine' it was called, and one and all warned me I would kill it at my peril, but I threw thirty chestnuts on the fire the first week I took over.
>
> *Another Howler*
> Deerstalking is the animal conversation between stags.
> *Canned music*

Employees in a tinned fruit factory are encouraged to sing whilst at work. They just make merry while they can.[2]

Cudlipp rapidly discovered that the staff resisted axing jokes and pointless, short editorials only because they were paid extra for them; he won their support by upping their basic pay and by communicating the sense of excitement and fun that he generated spontaneously wherever he went. He was often brash and was given to (short-lived) explosions of anger, but he bore no grudges, encouraged talent and was marvellous, mischievous company and a hilarious performer. As throughout his life, he enjoyed journalism so much that he was always surprised anyone was prepared to pay him: 'Who would mind working around the clock if every day is punctuated by the impulse of events, when the only routine is the exceptional and the unexpected, when the norm is the abnormal?'[3] For depressed, cynical hacks who thought failure was inevitable, it was intoxicating to have this young dynamo turning everything upside-down. 'The newspaper,' as he put it, 'suddenly discovered the human race.'[4] He was proud of the contrast between the first front page of 1937 and that a year later. The first:

BRASS BANDS PLAY TO CATERPILLARS

The second, which related to the most shocking murder of the time:

MONA TINSLEY'S SPIRIT
LED HER SLAYER TO THE GALLOWS

Bart, for no reason Cudlipp could ever fathom, offered him the free choice of two *Mirror* journalists, and Cudlipp chose a pair whom Bart particularly disliked and underrated, so would be glad to lose. The gifted Peter Wilson, who had joined the same day as Cudlipp but whose talents as a sports writer had been stifled because Bart hated his father (and anyway could not see the point of sport), became on the *Pictorial* 'The Man They Can't Gag' – 'my "nom de Fleet Street" which endured for some thirty-five years . . .':

If some pernickity characters inquired who 'They' were and what it was they wanted to 'Gag' me about they were in a conspicuous minority; and with the complete backing of the paper and Cudlipp, in particular, who said that even were I to be successfully sued for libel he would, the next day, write me a letter immediately extending my contract, I was able to say a lot of things I had wanted to for a long time, which few other more nervous, and less successful, papers would have permitted me to write.[5]

An Old Harrovian in a Regency waistcoat, Wilson was, said Cudlipp, 'happiest thumping on his typewriter splashed with heavy-weight's blood with the rest of the gang at the ringside.'[6] And Stuart Campbell, who had channelled his frustrations as an ordinary member of the News Desk into becoming a bolshie union representative, became under Cudlipp a fine investigative journalist.

Cudlipp merrily applied the *Mirror*'s winning formula of bite-sized news, crime, sensationalism, astrology, sentiment, social conscience and sex to the *Pictorial*, along with brilliant sports coverage. Various of Cecil King's relatives, who been shocked by the vulgarity of the new *Mirror* and *Pictorial*, were to be made even more aghast when Cudlipp decided to welcome the spring in 1938 in pioneering fashion:

I briefed the photographer meticulously. I didn't want gambolling lambs. I didn't want a tortoise — awakened early from his hiber-nation by popping him for a short time in a low oven — clawing a path through the daffodils in Regent's Park. I didn't want cro-cuses in St James's Park or any other park, and I didn't want bloody ducklings popping out of chocolate Easter eggs, cour-tesy Lyons' or Fortnum and Mason's. I told him what I did want and it arrived on my desk Saturday morning, a fragrant study at an orchard in Kent of a comely smiling model stretching her arms toward the sky through the branches of an apple tree in full blossom. The top half of the lady was also in full blossom; young, burgeoning womanhood, innocent but topless.

He took it to King. 'Cudlipp, I'm afraid you can't publish that pic-ture without showing it beforehand to the chairman, and if you do show it to the chairman you won't be publishing it.' But Cudlipp was prepared. 'I'll try,' he said, and they set off to Cowley's austere office:

The only publications on his desk were the *Financial Times* and the *ABC Railway Guide*, aphrodisiacally discouraging. He kept pigs and after we had listened patiently to a dollop of porcine patter and his vacuous views on life in general, I steered the conversation towards the weald of Kent where he farmed. I casually mentioned trees in blossom. 'Ah yes,' he said, 'they are now at their best, a sight to see, especially the apple blossom.' 'Sir,' I said, avoiding the eye of the Wykehamist, 'I am sure you will agree that it is imperative that the new *Pictorial* is accurate in everything it prints, particularly pictures portraying the countryside where so many of our readers live.

Cowley offered to help. 'I mentioned that I had with me a charming study illustrating the arrival of spring but I was concerned to be assured that the apple blossom in the background was truly at that particular stage at this very moment:

Cowley studied the picture for longer than was strictly necessary to settle the horticultural query and then pronounced: 'You need have no fear, Cudlipp, of the accuracy of this picture. My apple trees are exactly in that condition now. Full bloom. The picture might well have been taken in my own orchard yesterday.'

On our return journey along the corridors, Cecil King paused, the whole six-feet-plus of him, planted his right hand against the wall and laughed hysterically, until there were tears in his eyes. I thought he was going to be sick. I had never heard him laugh like that before or since. 'Cudlipp,' he said when he recovered his composure (we were not on Christian name terms until many horticultural scoops later), 'never do anything like that to me again.'[7]

It was around that time, according to the *Evening Standard*, that Rothermere 'aroused considerable speculation by his disclosure that he had "severed his connection with the 'Daily Mirror' and the 'Sunday Pictorial' in March 1931." Mr John Cowley, chairman of Sunday Pictorial Newspapers, spoke of it yesterday at the meeting of that company. He said that he had no idea of the reason which prompted

Lord Rothermere to issue the statement.' So who was in charge? 'There are eight directors . . . The "thruster" among them is Mr Cecil King, a nephew of Lord Rothermere and the late Lord Northcliffe.'[8] Not that King would have minded this implicit rebuke: upsetting the Harmsworths gave him pleasure.

They were both risk-takers, but King had invested far more in this venture than Cudlipp, who commented, 'Northcliffe's nephew had masterminded his own destiny strategically and tactically, encouraging talent that would one day make a team, his team, anticipating history, social and political trends, with a meticulous sort of timing so that the unexpected seemed inevitable. He called it the art of foresight. To an extrovert from the other side of Offa's Dyke his patience was chilling. It was like watching a blind man playing chess.'[9]

Had the *Pictorial* failed, there would have been other homes for a gifted young journalist, but no other newspaper proprietor would have welcomed a Harmsworth. Despite being a director, King no longer had any influence on the *Daily Mirror*, from which Bart vengefully barred him; he 'could keep contact only by subterfuge or accident'.[10] Cudlipp fared better; there was little Bart could do other than warn *Mirror* journalists to shun him. But Bart's unremitting hostility made for an uneasy life in a building where the *Mirror* and *Pictorial* shared the same offices, the same plant and some directors.

The political thrust of the paper changed drastically; the commentator who thought the Conservative Foreign Secretary, Anthony Eden, dangerously left-wing, was replaced by the ferociously anti-fascist Charles Wilberforce, whose lively, urgent, provocative and sometimes intemperate style was combined with a deep understanding of world history and politics. 'Cecil King, condescendingly and never in the presence of Mr Wilberforce himself, referred to Charles as his mouthpiece; Mr Wilberforce, a vain fellow, regarded Cecil King as his legman, but as the impartial Editor I had the sagacity to marry one man's words with another's foresight and frequently with my own convictions.'[11]

King was a dull writer and Cudlipp (aka Charles Wilberforce – a pseudonym adopted because Bart objected to him writing under his own name) still did not know much, though he had plenty of opinions. Certainly he would not have been equipped in the spring of 1938 to write the stunningly well-informed attack on the perilously muddled condition of the British Empire. 'Come with us now on a tour of this vast estate,' Wilberforce invited.[12] 'A story of foresight and brilliant planning? No! A story of a hideous muddle.' Deplorable housing and health conditions in Trinidad had been brought to light only by riots; Arabs and Jews in Palestine both had unaddressed justifiable grievances; nothing was being done to solve the Irish problem, which had the potential to end in civil war; Malta, the New Hebrides, British Honduras and British Guiana were all misgoverned and India would vote Britain out tomorrow:

> Vast as this problem is, there is a way out of the appalling muddle.
>
> We need rulers who know what they want – and who mean to get it. Who are not content to sit back in the West Indies and say: 'Sugar no longer pays,' but who will breed new strains of sugar cane with a higher yield – as the Dutch did in Java . . .
>
> We often talk about educating the native for self-government. Why not try doing it?
>
> Look at Southern Rhodesia and Kenya. What are we trying to do with these places?
>
> Is it enough to paint them pink on the map and leave it at that?

What was needed in the Empire, said King through Wilberforce – thinking longingly of what he could achieve if only given a chance – were men of mighty energy, great vision and immense administrative ability to implement a bold, far-sighted plan:

> Hitler clamours for colonies – colonies which he would exploit possibly in the interests of their inhabitants, but more probably in the interests of his Germany.
>
> We *have* colonies. We have the greatest Empire in the world. And we are doing nothing about it.
>
> The self-governing Dominions were approaching a day of reckoning, Australia because of its low birth rate, Canada because the future lay with the French-Canadians and South Africa, 'a land flowing with milk and honey', drawn from the hide of the

black man with no thought for the future when the black man outnumbers and will eventually overwhelm the English and Dutch inhabitants.

A quarter of the world in our grip . . . and we are doing nothing about it . . .[13]

A week later, drawing on an insider's book, Wilberforce savaged the League of Nations:

What a magnificent ideal it was, the League.

And what a God-forsaken mess was made of it.

'If only speeches could have made the world safe for democracy,' says the General, 'then the League would indeed have been impregnable.'

TALK!

While Europe armed to the molars.

TALK!

While the Dictators strutted before the world and thundered before their rising people.

TALK!

While Spain went up in flames and the whole world fanned the conflagration.

TALK!

To which everybody listened. And which nobody believed.[14]

The tone was even rougher in June 1938, when the article that was headlined:

THE WORLD IS SAYING
WE ARE
YELLOW

contrasted firm actions by Robert Walpole in 1739 and by Lord Palmerston in 1850, along with an uncompromising speech of Lloyd George's in 1911, to point up the spinelessness of the current British government against affronts from Brazil, Mexico and Spain:

Once upon a time the British lion sprang if you cut off an

Englishman's ear, or injured a British subject's property, or launched a gunboat.

Now you can diddle Britain out of millions of pounds and seize her oil wells. You can even kill a score of Englishmen – AND GET AWAY WITH IT!

Germany, Italy, France and Russia were no longer judging Britain by the speed with which it was producing weapons, but by its cowardice in using them.

The world is saying that the colour of the British flag is yellow.
The world must learn that the colours of that flag are Red, White and Blue.[15]

Patriotism, rearmament, strength and courage in the face of fascist evil were Wilberforce/Cudlipp's watchwords and those of the writers he hired. Using a profusion of frivolities and titillations, he hoped 'to leave the reader gasping for breath, and then, leading him gently by the hand, to whisper in his ear: "Just a moment, friend. Before you take another look at that luscious Swedish blonde in the swimming pool on page 16, there's a piece on page 27 by the Foreign Editor of the *New York Times* analysing the sources of Hitler's power."'[16]

Along with its stablemate, the *Pictorial* led Fleet Street in plain speaking about the evil that had to be confronted and the likely horrors ahead, but it was more consistent. While the *Mirror* wobbled over Munich, the *Pictorial* was savage: Munich was shameful. 'Here, I fear,' said Wilberforce, 'is what history will decide about the role of Britain. "It muddled its way into the mess by vague idealism – and it muddled its way out by betraying the cause it had so feebly espoused."'[17] And Wilberforce also showed a rare degree of knowledge, understanding and thought about what lay ahead. That autumn, in 'WAKE UP BRITAIN!' he offered 'a great Plan of National Regeneration' by which Britain could avert war by regaining her strength, morale and self-confidence. The country had to be put on a potential war footing: 'WE HAVE GOT TO WAKE UP – OR PERISH'.

Every adult should be registered for potential conscription; with the help of a great allotment scheme, food growing should be vastly extended; the Territorial Army should be expanded; there should be a physical-fitness campaign; the arrest of the falling birthrate; the rapid arming of the defence forces with the latest and most scientific weapons; and the vigorous prosecution of Air Raid Precautions. 'The Government are doing something, but we have got to have dynamite in it. We want drive and energy like never before.'[18]

If the details of King's plan were different, his thrust was the same as that of Northcliffe in the years leading up to the First World War. So too was his preoccupation with the importance of propaganda. 'How we have laughed in Britain at the clubfoot dwarf, Dr Goebbels. How we have sneered at his hell-raising speeches and his wild propaganda!' Yet like Hitler, he showed up the weaknesses of democracy. 'Once upon a time the British Democracy was a great ideal – an ideal to fight for and preserve. "Freedom of speech" meant something more than an excuse for the confusing din of 50,000,000 conflicting voices. "Liberty" meant something more than the liberty to die without a chance to protect ourselves.' British propaganda efforts were 'pathetic' . . . It was not by such puerile methods that Hitler built up his power and succeeded in scaring the world.'[19]

'*Knowing* what is going on is the lure of journalism. *Explaining* to vast audiences what is going on is the art. *Influencing*, or trying to influence, what is going on is the self-imposed mission.'[20] While only Cudlipp had the art, both he and King succumbed to the lure and shared the mission. As the duo in charge of a national newspaper, they had access to all the sources they wanted. 'King's subjects were history and politics and mine were instinct and politics', and both separately and together they built on those strengths and cultivated relationships with experts like the military specialist Basil Liddell Hart, politicians like Leslie Hore-Belisha, the War Minister (many of whose speeches Cudlipp wrote), and public servants like Robert Vansittart, Chief Diplomatic Adviser to the government.

After fewer than six months on the *Pictorial*, their sources were so reliable that Cudlipp was convinced, one Saturday night in February 1938, that Anthony Eden was so irritated with the temporising and wishful thinking of his Prime Minister, Neville Chamberlain, and most of the Cabinet that he was on the verge of resignation. So strong was his hunch that he rang Eden at home at midnight, apologising volubly for arousing him so late:

'Quite all right, Cudlipp, I'm not in bed.' *Clue Number One.*
'I understand, Mr Eden, you have resigned as Foreign Secretary.'
There was a pause. *Clue Number Two.* And then –
'Oh.' *Clue Number Three.* Any fool knows the difference between
Yes and No, but a newspaper man of any merit must be able
to divine the degree of admission indicated by that inadequate
shield 'No comment'. No fool could have misinterpreted the
exclamation 'Oh'; the pause and then the intonation indicated
his surprise that the secret could have reached the Press so quickly.
There were no parrying questions from Anthony Eden along the
lines of: 'And who has told you this curious information?' There
was no denial, *Clue Number Four.* That was the most significant
clue of all, and *Clue Number Five* was that experience had taught
me that at midnight, especially with honest men like Eden, the
instinct for stratagem or evasion and in particular downright
lying is at its lowest ebb.

Fearing a request to hold the news 'in the national interest', and
yet nervous of launching such a stunning exclusive 'merely on the evidence of the word, "Oh"', Cudlipp took a chance. 'I realise there may
be further talks and the announcement will not be made until
tomorrow, and apologise again for disturbing you tonight and so late.'

Still no denial and another pause.
Clue Number Six: clearly an announcement *was* going to be made
the next day.
'Good-night, Mr Eden.'
'Good-night, Cudlipp.'

Prudently, lest the 'Oh' had indicated a measure of indecision, to
the 'EDEN RESIGNS' headline, Cudlipp added the sub-heading:

CABINET WANT HIM TO STAY
TODAY'S TALKS WILL DECIDE

Having written the story, he rang King, who by then would have
been more than three hours into his regular eight or nine hours' sleep,
and told him the news. "'This is a major scoop," said Cecil, "how do

we know at this ungodly time?" "Oh," I replied, "I phoned Eden myself at midnight and he said 'Oh'. I will explain it all when we meet.'"[21] The resignation was announced that day. Lord Halifax took Eden's place and appeasement reigned supreme in the Cabinet.

Like Northcliffe a generation earlier, King was an admirer of Winston Churchill, with whom he was now on friendly terms, having been taken to meet him in October 1938 by Cudlipp, who was soliciting an article from him.[22] The following April they decided to wage a campaign to urge his inclusion in the Cabinet. Cudlipp kicked off on the front page with: WHY ISN'T WINSTON CHURCHILL IN THE CABINET?'

> Churchill, more than any other politician foretold the crises that Germany's rearmament would inflame. His virility and vigilance have spurred on the Cabinet remorselessly – but they still will have nothing to do with Churchill himself.
>
> No one questions his integrity, his ability, his eagerness to serve.
>
> His fame is already too gloriously illumined for friend and foe to insinuate that he could be motivated by a zest for personal splendour or material gain.
>
> But while there gathers sullenly the hurricane that threatens to wreck our generation, this one man who could stem the dark forces, this one man whom Hitler fears, is thrust into the background and forced to endure a political impotence which is as shameful as it is premature.
>
> Why isn't Winston Churchill in the Cabinet?[23]

This generated 2,400 letters, of which 97 per cent were favourable. Churchill was duly grateful and, when Bart decided he wanted Churchill as a columnist, he saw no alternative but to grudgingly allow King back into the *Mirror*'s fold as a go-between with the great man; King and Cudlipp visited Churchill at Chartwell in July. They sipped tea as he drank whisky and they listened to him as, for an hour, he predicted disaster. 'Nothing can save us,' he said. 'Nothing – except the hammerblow of circumstance.'[24]

Churchill was a powerful contributor to the *Mirror*, but not for long; when war was declared on 3 September, he was put in charge of the Admiralty. His relationship with the group would later deteriorate sharply, but they were not in any case natural allies. Bart, King and Cudlipp might agree with Churchill on how to deal with fascists, but they had no time for his class or his party and wanted a new political and social dispensation post-war. During the period when Churchill was writing for the *Mirror*, Wilberforce was mocking the incestuous nature of the Conservative Party, its innumerable aristocratic connections and the privileged background of most of its MPs. When Baldwin had first been asked to form a government, the *Pictorial* reminded its readers, 'one of his first thoughts, he said, was that it should be a government of which Harrow should not be ashamed, and the newspaper added, "What damn nonsense!"'[25]

With war looming, the Triumvirate were as sleepy and the young pretender as energetic as ever. From Quebec in July 1939, King reported to Margot: 'We shall come back with a lot of very definite proposals that serve my purpose in London and have the full backing of everyone here.'[26] 'Cowley has postponed very necessary action for too long,' he told her a week later, 'and now what with the conditions of the industry it is a matter of making the best of a bad job.'[27] Back in London in late August he was 'having a fierce tussle in the office but have still not got Roome down to any concrete war term plans for printing our papers. Cowley only came in today when he was sent for!'[28] Margot reported delightedly to her mother-in-law that:

all his schemes laid in Quebec & New York seem to have been most successfully brought to a head, & sealed & signed by all the most important people involved. I am tremendously thrilled about all this, because it really is a definite achievement on his own, & its success will give him some much-needed self-confidence.

I really feel that at last he is ready to make something definite of his life: & with some of the political contacts he has made recently I am full of hope for the future! I do hope you will believe how much I live for his achievement & success . . .

I sometimes feel that you all must think that I could prod him on faster, & spur him ahead, but I feel so strongly that my part is to watch him & support him always, but any definite step he can only take when he is ready in himself. I do believe that he is now ready to go ahead, but in some ways he seems to have been rather slow at developing, & it has taken a lot of patience to wait for this moment . . .

I have a most glorious life & can never be too thankful for the experience of being Cecil's wife. It is sometimes quite a terrific undertaking, but always infinitely worth while![29]

War was declared three weeks later, on 3 September, a Sunday morning. 'Since writing to you yesterday we have rather been through the mill,' King wrote to Margot, who was on holiday in Ireland with the children. 'I spent the night with Bart in his flat. Before leaving the office we had a very trying evening with continual postponements of Chamberlain statement and rumours of a peace deal . . . At the office we sat through until 11.15 awaiting the declaration of war while the BBC regaled us with recipes and tinkerbell tunes. The premier . . . talked far too much about his feelings.'[30] As a special edition of the *Pictorial* was rushed out, the sirens sounded. 'I noticed,' recalled Cudlipp, 'as we were ordered to move to the basement, accompanied by the anxious Mr John Cowley, that the air-raid shelter was in a state of hopeless disarray and incompletion. Had we been too busy warning others?'[31]

Cudlipp, now twenty-six, intended to fight. King doubted that, at thirty-eight, he would be wanted; later, because of his bad psoriasis, which was often uncomfortable (like wearing a hair shirt, he said) and sometimes caused his skin to bleed, he was rejected and classified as D4. Anticipating this, he had tried some months before war broke out to get a war job: he wanted, like Northcliffe, to be a great propagandist. 'Propaganda only required the skilled people we [the *Mirror* and *Pictorial*] had, some offices and typewriters and we were in business. Most of the advertising people might be unwelcome in Whitehall, but I had the same social and educational background as the senior civil servants, and I had spent fifteen years on the borderline between journalism and advertising. Surely I was just what was wanted!'[32] His enquiries revealed that in the event of war a senior politician was to be in charge of the Ministry of Information, the Public Trustee was to be a senior civil servant and the Censor to be an admiral. 'This lunatic set-up was just the first form the organisation took. It was subject to frequent changes, but one principle was immutable: no one at the MOI must know anything about propaganda, popular opinion, mass communications, or anything of the kind.'[33] When he applied for a job, he was interviewed by a junior civil servant, who told King that he would have a big drop in pay. 'I said it would be war work, so that was all right. The little man said he would let me know shortly how my application had fared. I never received an acknowledgement, let alone acceptance or rejection.'[34] Further appeals to influential people, who included Duff Cooper and Lord Reith, got nowhere and even that fixer of all fixers, Sir Walter Monckton, was to fail to find King a niche in either propaganda or censorship, not least because he was increasingly unpopular with both government and press.[35]

While Cudlipp waited to be called up, their relationship strengthened. At King's suggestion, on Saturday nights, when there was a lull between editions, they would dine together at a Spanish restaurant where they would share two bottles of claret. Periodically, King would manage to say – on paper and through increasing Cudlipp's salary generously – what he could never say in person. A letter of January 1939 was typical:

My dear Cudlipp,
    As you know, I am a warm admirer of your ability as editor of the Sunday Pictorial, but I do think your work over the week-end calls for special praise. When the whole world wanted the real authentic story, your success in getting Hore-Belisha's own account [of his sacking as War Minister] was a scoop of the first magnitude. In addition I think your tact and discretion in dealing with the whole business could not have been bettered.
    I enclose a cheque for expenses, which is intended to add weight to these remarks.
    Yours very sincerely,
    Cecil H. King[36]

9 January 1940

Dear Mr King,
    Your letter was a great pleasure for me to read.
    I can only repeat my grateful thanks to you for the help you give me, and for constant political advice which enormously helps to make these things possible.

Throughout the whole business, and any similar matters, it is a privilege to share the confidences with you.
Yours very sincerely,
Hugh Cudlipp

Yet though 'Cudlipp' and 'Mr King' were partners in adventure, as well as colleagues, King's reserve made ordinary friendship impossible. Cudlipp conversed with King; he caroused with others in pubs and wine-bars and restaurants. They knew little of each other's lives outside the office and nothing of each other's joys, sufferings or indiscretions.

Life had not all been success and fun for Cudlipp. Shortly before he married Bunny Parnell, in April 1936, his big brother had taken him for a long walk in Hyde Park and had hinted strongly that she was too friendly with the Editor of *John Bull*. Once more, Cudlipp dismissed the story as tittle-tattle. On their rainy bridal night in the Channel Islands, just after the oysters, Bunny burst into tears and asked if he thought it possible for a woman to be in love with two men. ('It's not part of the usual church service,' observed Hugh in old age. 'Here comes the bride down two aisles at once.') '"Do you mean you're in love with two men?" I asked. And she said, "I think so." The rest of the honeymoon consisted of a fortnight walking in the rain around this dreary place. I can't explain the psychology. I mean *I* wouldn't go on honeymoon and say, "Do you think it's possible for a man to love two women?" I would have saved the fare and gone off to Paris with the other one.'[37]

They lived in North London, first in a small cottage that Cudlipp had taken over from his friend Warwick Braithwaite, the conductor he had met while reviewing music in Cardiff in his mid-teens; and then, with growing prosperity, in a house in Finchley. Bunny became increasingly frank about her split affections and confirmed that the secret lover was indeed the very popular Tom Darlow, Editor of *John Bull*. 'One night she invited me to meet her from her advertising agency in a rather posh Mayfairish pub and I was saying to her, "What does this character look like?" She said, "There he is over there." Even then, for some reason, I had this blind spot.'[38] Cudlipp did, however, now feel free to have affairs of his own. There was, for instance, the 'comely and wholesome Eton-cropped graduate' who worked at Communist Party headquarters and believed in free love.[39] And there was Eileen Ascroft, blonde, talented and ambitious, who had worked for him at the *Mirror* and whom Bart fired simply because he realised Cudlipp liked her. Yet the marriage with Bunny survived even when she took off with her lover for a three-week holiday.

She died in childbirth in 1938 after a Caesarean in an expensive Harley Street clinic. That night Cudlipp went back to the office to see the last edition. 'I like the first-page lead,' he said to his assistant, who then showed him some other news that had come in, saying, "'I think this is a better human interest story than that one." I remember saying, "Don't talk to me about human interest tonight":

> As the months went by, I began to think about this and realised
> that she suddenly one day — approximately eight months before
> her death — became terribly enthusiastic about having a child,
> which, being a career lady, she had never mentioned before. So
> I duly performed. But, of course, as time went on, I realised that
> the father of the child was the editor of *John Bull*.[40]

'It was just the end of a lunatic, protracted episode'[41] was the way Cudlipp chose to deal with Bunny's death. He never forgave her, but he avoided talking about her and got on with his life, now enhanced by the intensification of his love-affair with Eileen Ascroft, now of the *Evening Standard*, who, though married, became his social consort. Eileen resented Bunny, and — at her wish — Bunny's name would always be left out of Cudlipp's *Who's Who* entry.

King, meanwhile, had his own marital difficulties, though from the outside his personal life seemed wonderful. In 1936, with the help of a present from his mother of £1,000,* he bought a lease on Culham Court, a fine Georgian house in twenty acres of grounds near Henley-on-Thames. 'I feel rather anxious about your taking Culham,' wrote Margot's father. 'It's a dreadful burden to be saddled with a house beyond one's income; but you & Cecil are the proper judges of that point and I don't think it is worth while to spend one's spirit &

---

* About £50,000 today.

strength on keeping up merely a house . . . Of course you've tried your best to find something less exacting.'[42] Perhaps Canon Cooke did not understand how much it meant to his son-in-law to be seen to be successful, and how much he enjoyed the life of a country gentleman.

King was always to claim (and believe) that money meant nothing to him, but he was measuring himself against his millionaire uncles. Although he was to tell his children from the time they were young that he would never leave them anything, he had no such reservations when it came to inheriting himself: 'The dinner with mother went off all right,' he wrote to Margot in 1932. 'The "business" did not amount to much, but I think I have got her to do some tax dodging. Even though this will not make any difference to us now, it should in time. And in any event it would prevent her leaving everything to a cats' home — for what that's worth.'[43]

Culham was a remarkably fine house for the Advertising Director of a couple of newspapers; it included five reception rooms, sixteen bedrooms, servants' hall and menservants' dressing room. 'Country houses — spacious — with white walls and mouldings, full of flowers, with an indescribable smell of their own, fragrant yet ever so slightly damp, like an autumnal wood,' wrote the novelist Antonia White in her diary, 'even in summer have a peculiar fascination for me. I am very fond of Culham with its yew-tree hedges and gardens, the rows of clean, orderly greenhouses.'[44] They also had Cushnie, which they all loved and where, as his father had taught him, King taught his boys to shoot.

Antonia White gave a glimpse of life at Culham, noting the:

> pleasure and faint repugnance of sharing, but not belonging to, the life of a family living an entirely different way from one's own. The servant turning my stockings inside out. Yet . . . in spite of all this wealth and plenty, it's impossible to have some small thing you want 'out of hours'. There only seems to be one tiny ashtray in the whole house and I am so afraid of disturbing the church-like orderliness of the place that I don't like to leave it cluttered up with ashes so every few hours climb up to my bedroom to empty it into the wastepaper basket . . . Like all rich women [Margot] likes little economies, sells the surplus

peaches from the greenhouse which cannot bring her in more than £20* a season.[45]

Antonia White was not to know that Margot was eternally worried about money, for she had nothing of her own and King was domestically parsimonious.

When war broke out, Michael Lucas Harmsworth King was thirteen and at Eton, Cecil Francis Harmsworth was eleven, Priscilla Margaret was ten and Colin Henry Harmsworth eight. The Kings had wanted many children, but there had been frequent miscarriages. It was typical of King's thoughtless and often hurtful candour that he would explain that the ideal family for him would have been the one he had read about that consisted of twenty-seven girls and one boy.[46] Though Francis was his favourite, he was closest to Priscilla, who adored him and found him full of infectious enthusiasm: 'when he would leave Cushnie it was as if the sun had gone out,'[47] she said much later.

They were attractive children whom family and friends genuinely liked. 'I loved their pretty, friendly ways,' wrote their Grandfather Cooke in 1934; 'you have brought them up to expect & give nothing but love. It is the most beautiful thing in the world.'[48] 'Your children . . . really are enchanting,' Rosamond Lehmann, another novelist friend, wrote to Margot, 'both in looks and character. When they come up close to me in a group they really give an impression of being incandescent.'[49] 'I hope you are all well,' wrote Uncle Leicester Harmsworth, 'especially that most wonderful family of yours.'[50] 'I . . . have always felt your life with Cecil was ideal,' said Geraldine King, who never lied, ' – and the dearest children in the world.'[51] Even more telling, for she wrote it in her diary, was Antonia White's comment that 'The brilliance and vitality of the King children is remarkable'.

Yet they were brought up very much as King himself had been, with servants (there were six domestic staff at Culham Court until the war began), nannies and boarding school; twice, in the 1930s, their parents were away together for months. As Francis put it, Margot 'was devoted to pa and that was the first and last always'. Michael was mature and gifted for practical constructive work, while ungifted academically,

---

* About £1,000 today.

concluded an educational psychologist, brought in to find out why the nine-year-old boy had collapsed academically at school; but he 'is obviously a particularly tender and gentle child, *affectionate* and therefore it was hard on him to have had to give up his teacher, whom he liked, and have his parents leave for a long trip'. He 'should receive signs of special and individual *affection* from one of the adults with whom he is living'.[52]

As well as emotional neglect, there were unintentional cruelties: the children wanted pets, for instance, but when Michael acquired a dog, it was got rid of without explanation when he was away at school. Although King was tremendously interested in animals, was a frequent visitor to the zoo and had had dogs as a child, his attitude to them was scientific and utilitarian. 'The welfare of animals – two legged, four legged, smooth, furry or feathered – was a dedicated mission to the *Mirror* and its principal writers,' observed Cudlipp, who loved animals:

> There wasn't a stray cat or lost dog that didn't know our phone number. We campaigned against the export of live horses from Ireland under appalling conditions, the brutal clubbing of seal pups in Canada, the crating of calves. Cecil couldn't fathom it. 'Let us fight for children's welfare, of course, but . . .' I was his lunch guest one Sunday at his Georgian mansion house by the Thames at Henley, preceded by a two-hour walk in the rain around the three or four farms on the edge of his property. 'Curious,' I said, as we hung up our dripping coats, 'I haven't seen a dog. Not one.' He looked at me with some surprise. 'Curious? You can't eat dogs,' he said.[53]

Harmsworth directness ruled, and was to take its toll on the children's confidence. It was hard for Michael to hear that he would go to Eton because, unlike Francis (known to the family as Podge), he was not thought clever enough for Winchester. 'I have written a long letter to Michael [thirteen] which I hope is all right,' King told Margot in 1939. 'I feel I must say what I think and I must try hard to consider the impression I make on him. The first part is important and easy, the second much harder, but I hope more successful than my last effort over his future.'[54]

King was an awkward father, for in conversation he still relied on others to make the running. Not that the children did not try. 'I got back last night,' he wrote to Margot in 1935, 'to find the babes finishing their tea . . . – so I got them to stand by at dinner. Francis [seven] spread the *Mirror* out on the table and read it, Colin [four] sat on the table and talked and Priscilla [six] tried to sit on the arm of my chair with her arms around my neck. They were complete darlings.'[55] The family's happiest times were in Scotland, where King relaxed completely and the children could participate in shooting parties, heather-burning, fruit-picking and other activities that involved one or both of their parents. They were expected to be industrious; during the war, they would be required to spend about three hours a day working in the garden.

Since it was thought that the tender-hearted Priscilla should not be involved in shooting, she would go to stay with Lady King, who lived twelve miles away. A loving but rather anxious child who liked to please, Priscilla would sit literally at the old lady's feet, relishing her wit and cleverness and her highly individual conversation, interspersed as it was with Hindustani and German words. Though eccentric and grand, Geraldine King had a friendly relationship with her grandchildren, who called her 'Dills' or 'Wills', and she was welcoming, generous and thoughtful to them. 'She was much the most powerful woman I've ever come across,' said Francis many years later. 'A wonderful woman for a growing child. A wonderful grandmother.' Generally kind, Geraldine, in a typically imaginative gesture, would send her grandchildren a guinea in sixpences* on their birthdays, as it made them feel positively rich. ('Dear little Priscilla,' she wrote to Margot, 'who sits on the arm of my chair & says "Wills, I love loving you."'[56]) Until she died, she would send Priscilla *Punch* every week with apple pips – for which Priscilla had a passion – slipped inside.

Geraldine King was, however, even lazier and more selfish now than when she had lived in Dublin. When her daughter Sheila died in childbirth, she had taken on the baby, John Falls, and had ignored all suggestions that it was bad for him to be brought up exclusively by doting old people and servants. Uncommonly racist and xenophobic,

---

* About £30 in fifty-pence pieces today.

even for her time, she was outraged in 1934 when she heard that her niece Christabel had become engaged to a German, and wrote to her quoting Nietzsche: 'against stupidity, even the gods fight in vain'.[57] Margot, who loved Geraldine and was a peacemaker, eventually persuaded her to go to the wedding reception, where she looked at her niece 'as if I were a reptile'. She had decided to send John Falls to Wellington, she told Margot around this time, since the school had 'no snobs, no nouveau riche, Jews, Turks or Infidels would not be bothered with the place'.[58]

Like so many of her siblings, Geraldine despised the *Daily Mirror* and the *Sunday Pictorial* (shades of her mother: 'Alfred, I don't know which of your papers is more vulgar this morning'), refused to have them in her house and, naturally, told her son how much she deplored them. Margot, to whom both Geraldine and Rothermere complained 'about the sordidness of the papers and the disgrace to the family',[59] could do nothing but pass the criticisms on and worry. Invited to meet Geraldine, Cudlipp was warned by King about her views on his paper:

> He advised me that the prudent course was to listen and say little, preferably nothing, and I wondered why he wished to stage-manage such a potentially combustible confrontation. I enquired if there was any sort of Press photograph, any at all, which could conceivably appeal to her?
>
> Yes, I was informed, *horses*. During my brief encounter with Lady King at Cecil's house in Henley-on-Thames on a Sunday morning I steadfastly pointed to a picture of a rampant stallion I had sited on the centre pages of that day's issue, and none of the family heirlooms was shattered.[60]

King was a most attentive and conscientious son and Geraldine was grateful, generous and affectionate towards his family and immensely supportive of Margot. ('She is looking very worn,' Geraldine wrote to King in October 1939, ' – what a time she has been through & then driving 700 miles – much too much for her. Put her to bed, when she arrives for a day or two. I often wonder why you don't keep a chauffeur – & less gardeners. Her father spoke to me of the strain all this motoring must be.'[61] 'Spare yourself – a *very* precious person always remember,'[62] she wrote to Margot a couple of years later.) Yet the mother–son relationship was too intense to be healthy and Margot failed to wean King away from his fixation on Geraldine, though it became increasingly hostile. Exacerbated by career disappointments and frustrations, King's resentment of his mother and his bitterness towards the Harmsworths in general continued to grow. His relationship with Margot was intense: 'I certainly take off my hat most whole-heartedly to both of you,' wrote a friend in 1930, 'for carrying on these seven years, opening your minds so gloriously to each other's families, trying to understand each other in the light of your so different settings.'[63]

Yet the process was much more painful than most people realised. King wanted absolute intimacy of body, mind and soul, and in his determination to know his wife, he subjected her to remorseless interrogation and criticism about her thoughts, her intellect, her beliefs and her emotions. Similarly, he wanted her to know and share his hopes, his fears and his sensitivities and – impossibly – to be utterly honest and yet uncritical. 'Cecil had a very special part to play in the world,' she wrote in the 1950s, ' – gifts & powers above the ordinary run of men.' But though she had struggled to give him the help he needed, 'no one can imagine what it was like to have the full force of his mind & his love & his problems focussed on one'.[64] Even the way in which he expressed his devotion could be overwhelming. On Margot's thirty-ninth birthday, in 1940, he transcribed a Tudor poem extolling the worthiest, truest, most faithful, gentlest and meekest woman on earth. And, although poetry did not really appeal to him, that Christmas he gave her a present that must have taken days to create: in a tiny notebook he painstakingly copied out, over twenty-five pages, lines of passionate verse from a range of love poets who included Shakespeare, Marlowe, Donne, Lovelace, Herrick and Villon.

'He is with Margot a complete baby,' wrote the perceptive Antonia White, 'can hardly bear her out of his sight. Margot's plan to stay back at Culham with me could not come off because Cecil refused to go to a tennis party a few miles away without her, although she had no wish to play and didn't. Out of the question, of course, that Cecil should be upset. I suppose she is absolutely the only person with whom he has any real contact. And she enjoys that: it is her power.'[65]

But Margot had to share King with his mistresses – a pain made

worse by her belief, as a deeply religious woman, that she was con-
doning something wrong. 'You are not betraying principles by forgiving,' wrote one of her few confidantes in 1938. 'Ride on the snaffle
with a very light rein . . . I think you are probably doing the best
thing in the very strange circumstances . . . Only don't take more than
you can possibly help out of yourself in the process. Try to concentrate on the children or some other problem, & deaden your feeling
temporarily in one direction.'[66]

Margot's emotional vulnerability was exacerbated by the demands
of the innumerable people who found her immensely sympathetic:
'remember what Cecil says *is* so true,' wrote another friend as early as
1933, 'that you will simply *have* to harden your heart & close your ears
to other people's troubles, as that is the only way when one is made
like you of keeping *any* vitality for oneself.'[67] Five years on, running
two big houses, entertaining many visitors, travelling with King and
worrying about her friends, her long-suppressed rebellious side was
coming to the surface. 'There is . . . a gleam in her eye when she is
thwarting someone's wishes,' wrote Antonia White, who was very fond
of her. 'Her pleasure in cutting every single one of the sweetpeas –
I almost feel *because* it distresses the old gardener so much. The ardour
with which she agreed with me that it is better to go to a hanging
than to be titillated by constantly reading accounts of one.' (That
subconscious rebellion was sometimes expressed in irrational aggression: once she persuaded King – who had never used corporal punishment on any of his children – to beat Francis on a trumped-up
charge.)

'I wish Margot weren't quite so *moral*,' continued Antonia White,
'she is so convinced that whatever she does is right and always *for the
best of reasons*. She makes a great show of liking people, wanting them
to enjoy themselves but nearly always it is *her* will which is imposed
on the others.' Hugh Cudlipp, who liked her too, noticed the same
tendency; at a function where he had explained to Margot that he
never danced and never wanted to, he found himself dragged on to
the floor because she thought he should. 'She rules Cecil,' said Antonia
White, 'by apparently obeying him in everything.'[68]

Margot's subliminal rebellion was her main survival technique. Yet
she wilted under King's insatiable need for approval, his determination to put every part of their lives under a microscope and his envy

of the intense spirituality and inner joy that so many people recognised in her. (In their early days, 'when Cecil told me I had no right
to be happy because I had not known suffering, & put me thru' all
the mental misery he could devise, my joy increased until he recognised it as something other than ordinary happiness & ceased to try
to destroy it'.[69]) 'You mention in your letter a possible reason for the
sense of disapproval I get from you,' he wrote in the late 1930s:

> In the first place I do think this is a scientific, therefore intel
> lectual, therefore a world destructive of human values. This is
> also my world, but not yours & you are quite right to be sus
> picious of it. But I am only capable of an intellectual search for
> truth & so while endeavouring to protect yourself from harm
> you should be readier to admit that this is my only possible road
> to God.
>
> As it is you are the man with the Rolls Royce perpetually
> pointing out that my motor-cycle is not nearly so good as your
> car, although you know it is all I can afford. This is perhaps
> rather over-stating the case because though you deplore my intel
> lectual activity you are also full of admiration for my intellectual
> intuition in others. You should surely only disapprove when I fall
> short of my own intellectual standards – not approve of some
> bits & disapprove of others when they inescapably go together.

Though Margot loved him deeply, she was never prepared to give
King simple adulation, and in addition to the criticism of which he
complained, both she and the children teased him. At his times of
greatest insecurity, all this rankled:

> You have at various times deplored among other things my
> work, my books, my voice, my clothes, my walk, my manners,
> my way of dealing with servants, with my office people & with
> our friends. This has all reached such a point that some of my
> less attractive mannerisms have been built up as acts of defi
> ance . . . I know I can be compelling when I put my mind to
> it, but I sometimes want to be attractive – at least not entirely
> repellent . . .
>
> When I outlined some of this to you, you said you had always

been so loyal to me. I don't mean you ran me down to other people; I know you wouldn't do such a thing; I am only talking of your attitude to me when we are alone . . .

Please don't think I am trying to be hurtful. I most sincerely am not. I think in all this it is for you to recognise that your attitude to me *has* been patronising & that this is impossible, & for me to recognise that because of my upbringing I am apt to see slights where none are intended, & to take my proper place more confidently in the future.

With all my most devoted love, dear wife

Snow[70]

But, at base, the biggest problem of all was sex. 'I have been intensely interested in sex which interest you have also deplored. But this is the basis of all my vitality, which you appreciate. My interest in sex was obviously likely to persist until I had satisfied at least my curiosity on the subject, but you objected to that, and if you take away my sexual side & my intellectual side there is mighty little left.'[71]

To King, sex was much more than an interest; it was a consuming need. Underneath that impassive expression, he was tormented by desire: the many women who found him intimidating or difficult to talk to would have been surprised to know that he looked at them through the eyes of François Villon: 'Those graceful little shoulders, slender arms and comely hands, small tits, trim, well-covered hips, perfect for holding love's jousts. Those broad buttocks, that cunt in its pretty little garden, perched on plump firm thighs.'* Despite being a good tennis player and a fine shot, he assured Margot that 'love-making is the only form of athletics that interests me in the least. It is the only handcraft too! In one form or another it is the only pleasure in life worth talking about.'[72] Assuming that women were readily available, he explained to Margot, he would wish to sleep with at least a dozen a year: 'that I don't involves a lot of restraint on my part, restraint which would be made easier if I felt that you were at all appreciative. Quite a lot of my discretion is to avoid hurting you and anyone else and it would help if the beneficiaries were nicer about it.'

---

* Quoted in King's *Commonplace Book*.

Margot had suggested that he have the occasional fling, but where 'are these women to come from, the office, our circle at home or a third sphere to be developed for the purpose?'[73]

The shortage of available women was such that King once even shocked Margot's bohemian twin sister Helen by propositioning her, and in the name of honesty, he insisted on reporting on all his affairs. Of one, he wrote to Margot in 1937, '[She] apparently thought . . . that we should go on as before.' I said maybe sometime, but not now. Hence many tears and much recrimination. I certainly shall not see her again for some time (except in the office – if she stays) probably never.'[74] Some mistresses also confided in Margot. 'I do love you for your wonderful generosity and kindness to me,' wrote Joyce Temperley, Priscilla's godmother, after being propositioned by King:

> I cannot think of anyone else who would be as 'great-hearted'. You were more right about C the other day than I realised; he does want a decision soon one way or the other and I am torn in two; on the one hand my *character* pulls me back, for such conduct is not really strictly in my line, on the other hand there is my *nature* which has for so long felt frustrated and now sees suddenly a patch of sunshine. I have written to C to tell him it is not a thing I can decide in cold blood. We must just try to get as much happiness as possible out of our friendship and probably the matter will settle itself. I am much too spontaneous a person to decide beforehand. Also, if one does a thing like that in the enthusiasm of the moment, it takes on a less serious aspect and a less important part in one's life and neither he nor I want it to be too terribly that. I feel I risk a great deal, more than either of you, for you are safe in each other for always . . . I feel strongly that, whatever I decide now, there will be a shadow across our friendship.[75]

King's sense of deprivation was made worse because he saw sex as 'my only avenue to people and the human outlook.'[76] He agonised over his inability to make human contact: 'I am secretly inflexible when it comes to admitting my real feelings,' began another key passage of Amiel's, which King believed described one of his own disabilities:

to saying what might bring pleasure, to abandoning myself to the present moment – a stupid reserve which I have never noticed without grief. I never dare to speak from my heart since I am ashamed of flattery and fearful of not finding the right nuance. I always banter with the passing moments and am emotional in retrospect . . . Fear of being carried away and distrust of myself pursue me even in moments of tenderness and as the result of a kind of invincible pride I cannot make up my mind to say to any given moment: Stay! Direct me! Be a supreme moment!*

At times King contemplated chastity, not just to please Margot but because of troubles with distressed mistresses, but he could not bear to lose 'so much colour and hope out of my life for others' benefit . . . however unselfish one is one must be left with enough to carry on with'.[77] A 'reasonably congenial circle of friends' might help disperse 'a lot of my surplus sexual feeling', he told her, but the social problem of finding friends 'from whom one gets anything back' seemed insuperable. 'If once a week one could have some sort of party at which one was not merely exchanging cutlets and talking about the weather or working to give some dull people pleasure it would be grand, but is it possible?'[78] Margot was later to torment herself because she felt she had failed to find him the right people, yet visitors to Culham included writers like Rosamond Lehmann (who later described King as one of the best conversationalists she ever met) and the biographer Michael Sadleir, while the critic Raymond Mortimer was one of the intellectuals using a gothic cottage in the garden as a weekend retreat. In truth, King's propensity to find fault with almost everyone, and his inability to initiate conversation, made a rewarding social life almost impossible. Still, the office provided him with opportunities to lunch and dine with people at the centre of things, who at least could be relied on to give him the political, economic, military and other information and political gossip for which he had an insatiable appetite. He had also the breadth of knowledge and intellectual rigour to understand what he was hearing: as early as 1939,

---

* Quoted in King's *Commonplace Book*, with a note 'So like me'.

for instance, he understood the potential of nuclear fission and, by March 1941, he had deduced that atom bombs were being developed by the British.

In January 1940, King began keeping a war diary, which ultimately ran to 400,000 words (reduced to a quarter when published in 1970). Although it is packed with military and political detail and written mostly in a pedestrian style, King was a keen observer and recorded detailed conversations like a veteran reporter. 'Had lunch with Churchill today,' he wrote in February 1940:

> The party consisted of Mr, Mrs, Miss Mary [Churchill], a Miss White (a cousin), and an American woman who talked too much. Mrs Winston is a very good-looking woman, with good eyes and good features, but rather thin, dried up, and nervy. The daughter, aged seventeen or eighteen, is a real winner: huge eyes, big mouth, wide across the eyes, and a full figure. Winston wore black boots with zip fasteners, the first I have seen.

Churchill and King disagreed *inter alia* about Hore-Belisha ('I said I thought that judged by the very low standard of the present Government Belisha was quite good'); Chamberlain ('I said he was too old, of dreary appearance, with a sorry record of appeasement, and that his speeches were dreary and lacked substance; leadership ('Churchill didn't seem to see the importance of leadership'); and Hitler ('the Germans' psychological summing up of the position is better than that of our War Cabinet'); but they parted on friendly terms 'despite my very plain speaking'.[79]

The wide range of insiders eager to talk to King is testimony to how influential he had become as a result of the success of the *Mirror* and *Pictorial*. And although Bart still kept King as much as possible out of the *Mirror*, he could not do so completely: 'Rang up Thomas [Editor of the *Mirror*],' King wrote in January 1940 after a reshuffle, 'urging on him the importance of taking the news in a very anti-Chamberlain sense.'[80] But the *Mirror* did not match the sheer impudence and verve of the *Pictorial*, the savagery of its attacks on appeasers giving it enormous influence for a popular Sunday newspaper. So too did its exposés of profiteers, petrol wasters and others too selfish to contribute to the war effort, and its sympathetic investigations into the problems of conscripts.

In October 1939, after the carve-up of Poland between Russia and Germany and a speech from Lloyd George urging the government to consider making peace with Germany, Cudlipp (who now wrote sometimes under his own name, sometimes as 'The Editor' and sometimes as Wilberforce) had written a denunciation: 'A SHAMEFUL SCHEME: WE ACCUSE LLOYD GEORGE'[81] was the headline on page 1; 'TWILIGHT OF A GOD' that on page 5; 'The time has come for The Man Who Won the Last War to pass on the torch to those who are younger' was the theme, as the need for youth to replace age was to be King's obsession throughout the war. Then, in January 1940, Cudlipp had a four-hour private meeting with Lloyd George and reported to King that he believed Britain would lose the war. So did King, but he was nonetheless determined that Germany should be given a run for her money.

King was determined to follow in the tradition of Northcliffe, to tell the truth about the inadequacies of the war effort and, by so doing, to give a lead for more faint-hearted newspapers to follow and to force politicians to take action. 'In the last war,' he told Anthony Eden (now Colonial Secretary) in the spring of 1940, 'the newspapers were absolutely uncritical until the shell scandal broke out [in Northcliffe's *Daily Mail*.]'[82] The *Pictorial* denounced unfounded optimism about German and Russian resources, poorly equipped and badly executed British operations and the sluggish leadership of industry as well as politics, wherever they found it, as well as demanding that Churchill replace Chamberlain and everywhere that age give way to youth.

King was triumphant in May 1940 when Churchill became Prime Minister. 'So at last my campaign to get rid of the old menace has come off,' he wrote, with echoes of his Uncle Alfred crowing about killing cock robin:

I consider this the best bit of news since war was declared. I do not think Churchill is young enough to win the war, but he is immeasurably better than Chamberlain. The *Sunday Pic* was the paper that hammered away at getting Churchill into the Cabinet, a campaign that the other papers took up and that got him in.

Then on October 1 last the *Sunday Pictorial* had a very good page article by Cudlipp announcing that Churchill would be the next premier. We shall reproduce part of it to show how right we are.[83]

'I would not stake out our claim so extravagantly' was Cudlipp's comment on that passage thirty-five years later:

There were other forces at work, primarily the march of events . . . and powerful forces in Parliament . . . Cecil King's campaign to get rid of the old menace had certainly 'come off', but others were there on the battlefield who had the stomach for the fight and lived to strip their sleeve and show their scars. The turbulent newspapers had erected the guillotine. It was Chamberlain who put his own head on the block and Parliament which released the cord that freed the heavy blade.[84]

Although even King was impressed with some of Churchill's fighting speeches, Churchill disappointed from the beginning by failing instantly to throw out his colleagues and replace them with the young and the virile. In June, Churchill had a long meeting with King explaining military and political realities: 'did I realise how ghastly our position was? We had won last time after four years of defeats and would do so again. Meanwhile Italy might join against us at any time, and France might be forced to back out and leave us alone to face Germany. Was this a time for political bickering?' King's reaction was predictable: 'My feeling after seeing him was that this was all quite hopeless.'[85]

The *Pictorial* and the *Mirror* continued their assaults on most of Churchill's colleagues and on 'bumbling bureaucrats, hidebound brass hats, preposterous Colonel Blimps'[86] and pacifists ('put the lot behind barbed wire' was the *Pictorial*'s suggestion), and to bolster their criticisms of old men's inertia and weakness they brought in experts like Lloyd George (seventy-seven) and Cudlipp's friend General 'Boney' Fuller (sixty-two).

In the middle of 1940, an assessment of Cudlipp came from the magazine publisher, Edward Hulton:

[A] young journalist who has kicked over the traces and is beginning to enjoy himself, slashing wildly but shrewdly, is Hugh Cudlipp . . . This month he has thrown several prettily aimed Molotoff cocktails at Mr Chamberlain. Cudlipp is an uncomfortable sort of young man to meet. He is a revolutionary. I don't mean he is filled up with a stock of ballyhoo about Karl Marx, or that he believes that every Labour Party pamphlet is an addendum to the gospels. If he were, he would be just another Bloomsbury drawing-room socialist. And that would be old-fashioned. Cudlipp is just fed up with the evil complacency which is still the order of the day in this country, and will remain so while we tolerate this domination of palsied grey-beards in every corner of our national life. Hugh Cudlipp has none of the urbane manner of his equally able brother, Percy, who edits the *Daily Herald*. He does not soothe you with well-turned phrases. His bursting impatience for genuine reform is almost irritating. When I lunched with him the other day at the Savoy he rapidly brushed away many of the cobwebs still clinging to my own mind. I left him feeling exhausted. The operation had been painful, but salutary. Write him down as another Citizen of the New Age.[87]

King's loathing of the Establishment and Cudlipp's anger combined to make the *Pictorial* a brutal critic of privilege. The temper of those pilloried by Cudlipp for having been to public school or having aristocratic relatives was not improved by knowing that the paper was run by Cecil Harmsworth King. Neither King nor Cudlipp, who lunched and dined at the best restaurants and hotels in London, blushed at Cassandra's declaration of a 'Gutskrieg' against those who dined in expensive places. Indeed, having dined with the abused Duff Cooper at the Dorchester, King suggested to Cudlipp an article about those who lived there. Called 'Grand Hotel 1940', it led Sir Malcolm McAlpine – after a lunch at the Dorchester – to draw King aside and say that he thought the *Pictorial* was worse than the communist *Daily Worker* in causing friction between class and class. 'I said I thought this bad spirit . . . was due to execrable political leadership over a long period and not to popular journalism.'[88]

Cudlipp and King had proved as courageous, defiant, arrogant, relentless, reckless, insouciant and often unfair as each other. After an

October reshuffle, Churchill was so enraged with a signed article of Cudlipp's, which said he rewarded failures and mediocrities and quoted past words of his own against himself ('There is no place for compromise in war'), that with the agreement of the Cabinet he denounced 'a certain section of the Press' as 'vicious and malignant'.[89] King's cousin Esmond, as Chairman of the Newspaper Proprietors' Association, reported to Chairman Cowley that, on behalf of the Cabinet, Clement Attlee had warned him that if the *Mirror* and *Pictorial* went on being so 'irresponsible' and 'subversive', opinion as well as news would be subject to compulsory censorship.

Bart and King went to see Attlee, who was to be Churchill's successor as Prime Minister: 'a small, shifty little man with a Charlie Chaplin moustache & no forehead,'[90] wrote King:

> – a man I should say of very limited intelligence and no personality. If one heard he was getting £6* a week in the service of the East Ham Corporation, one would be surprised he was earning so much. Furthermore he cannot face you at all: his eyes always evade a direct glance . . . My general line was to pin him down to some specific accusation. Bart's line was vague and conciliatory. Attlee was critical but so vague and evasive as to be quite meaningless. We got the impression that the fuss was really Churchill's.

On leaving, Bart and King agreed to 'pipe down for a few weeks'. In fact, compared to what King was confiding to his diary, the *Pictorial* was extremely restrained. During 1940 he moved from expecting a bloody domestic revolution to the belief that defeat was inevitable:

> I think we have no chance at all of even postponing defeat . . . when the main impact of the war hits us, we shall collapse like a house of cards.
>
> Meanwhile the ruthless efficiency of the Nazi war machine appeals to people. Personally I think the victory of Hitler would mean a much lower standard of living for all in this country,

---

* About £250 today.

Cecil at two   Hugh at three

Hugh (centre back) and his Cardiff gang

Cecil in 1910

Cecil in his teens

Cecil and Margaret, 1923

Hugh in charge in Blackpool, *c.*1931

The Cudlipp brothers in 1938; (*left to right*) Reg, Percy and Hugh

The Kings at Culham,
*c.*1943

King with Sheila Falls,
*c.*1953

With Michael
and Francis at
Cushnie

Cudlipp in 1954

With Eileen and
Jodi, *c.*1961

Dispensing champagne on *Laranda II*, early 1960s

but it will also mean the end of Chamberlainism. By this I mean that we shall be engaged on some worth-while scheme of reconstruction, & the endless obstruction by vested interests & selfish old men will come to an end. And if the alternatives are victory under Chamberlain & his old men of the sea or defeat by Hitler, I should prefer the latter. That the younger & more virile elements in the population here can get the upper hand in time to achieve anything is now out of the question.[91]

The harshness of King's position owed much to his hatred of what he saw as a moribund Establishment badly governing hundreds of millions of people in the British Empire because of snobbery, complacency and greed. He also, as ever, had his eye on the middle and long distance.

Even at his most pessimistic, Cudlipp would never have agreed with this analysis: he hated the Nazis with a passion and wanted them beaten out of existence. Both men were patriots, but King's were the instincts of the historian and strategist and Cudlipp's those of the journalist and tactician. What was more, unlike King, Cudlipp believed that ordinary British people were instinctively anti-fascist and, like him, wanted to fight. In April 1940, Cudlipp had responded to the call to twenty-six-year-olds to register,[92] asking to join the Royal Air Force's Torpedo Boats, for which he said he was 'particularly qualified'. He was relatively prosperous these days; as well as a flat in a bohemian patch of the West End,[93] he had a converted life-boat with a car engine, on which he had been exploring the Thames and the Broads.

While the Phoney War was on, Cudlipp had agreed that King could apply for a three-month postponement of his call-up. 'He is a man of quite outstanding brilliance,' wrote King to the Ministry of Information, 'being in my opinion one of the two or three ablest popular journalists of the day . . . he is quite irreplaceable and . . . to call him up . . . would seriously embarrass an important undertaking.'

The events of May 1940, when only the successful evacuation of Dunkirk prevented Germany from winning the war, caused Cudlipp to tell King that he wanted to join up as soon as possible. By late June he was chafing, using his influence in the Air Ministry to accelerate his call-up. When nothing happened, he applied to the Royal

Navy Patrol Service. And early in July he was angry to find that King had ignored him and that the application for postponement still stood. This was contrary to 'my own desires', he wrote to J. H. Brebner, Director of News Division at the Ministry of Information. 'May I be allowed,' responded Brebner, 'to express my own personal admiration of your action as it comes like a breath of fresh air after the many applications I receive from people to go on the reserved list.'

Still nothing happened, for King was as anxious for Cudlipp to stay as Cudlipp was anxious to go. Cudlipp was furious when he heard in mid-September that he had been granted a six-month deferment. 'Mr Cudlipp is extremely anxious to join one of the combatant services,' wrote a reluctant King to the ministry. 'So strongly does he feel that it is in this direction that his duty lies, that he is prepared to resign from this firm to regain his liberty of action. Under these circumstances I feel it would be wrong for us to stand in his way any longer.' Cudlipp, who could not bear to be thought a coward, was extremely upset when, in the House of Commons in early December, the Conservative MP, Quintin Hogg, in his lieutenant's uniform, asked the Minister of Labour 'why Mr Hugh Cudlipp, aged about twenty-seven years and editor of the *Sunday Pictorial*, had not been called up; and whether steps would be taken to see that any advantage granted to him was removed in order to secure the equal operation of the Military Service Acts'.[94] Ernest Bevin confirmed that his call-up had been deferred, but 'that this deferment was against the strong desire of Mr Cudlipp himself . . . Arrangements are accordingly being made to post Mr Cudlipp to the Armed Forces.'

In a subsequent correspondence with Cudlipp, with some truth Hogg accused the *Pictorial* of tilting at windmills:

Take privilege for example. You, with your immense public, are far more prominent, and far more privileged than any Duke; and while you are always ready to belabour the privilege of the so-called privileged classes, which [while it] is not actually dead, is so nearly moribund as to be unworthy of hitting, the fact that your newspaper could possibly be the subject of criticism excites you to such paroxysms of rage that you see attacks where none are intended.[95]

That letter arrived the day after Cudlipp had joined the Royal Corps of Signals, a decision made for him by a retired colonel who had interviewed him. "'Editor. Newspapers. H'mmm. Deal with messages at all? Cables? That sort of thing? Telephones?" "Yes, sir.'"

Before Cudlipp left, he wrote to King.

18 December, 1940,

Dear Mr King:

A personal note.

Thank you for giving me the three best years I could hope for. I have enjoyed every minute on the Pictorial, and we can both get some satisfaction out of the fact that the paper is now in a healthy position.

As for our personal collaboration, I can only say that I hope it will be renewed. When all is said and done, we haven't started yet.[96]

CHAPTER VI

Two Wars

WITH A POCKET FULL OF THE MAIL HIS SECRETARY HAD THRUST AT him as he ran from the office (a letter from Hore-Belisha: 'A great public will suffer through the lack of your stimulus'; a libel writ that Cudlipp forwarded with his compliments to Stuart ('Sam') Campbell, his successor; a reading list from Major-General 'Boney' Fuller; and an urgent request from Liddell Hart to let him know if his enclosed article was too frank about the government), Hugh Cudlipp set off to war.

On the train to Yorkshire, he made friends with a costing clerk in a Jewish dress factory in the East End, who in his spare time was a sparring partner ('Look at my face'), and shared his soggy seed-cake; they would remain in touch for years. When they reached Richmond station, anxious to deal with the Liddell Hart enquiry, Cudlipp told a barking sergeant that he needed to make a phone-call. Could he follow his companions to Catterick Camp by taxi? 'His eyes roved over me from feet to head and focused on my . . . black felt hat and cigar. "Get," said the sergeant, "into that fucking truck"':

> After bedtime on the second night, a portable radio was playing loudly.
>
> 'Hey-listen! It's about us. It's Godfrey Winn. Christ Almighty! And he mentioned Codlip.'
>
> To my dismay it *was* Mr Winn, and when the initial guffaws died down he was saying, 'He is now in a Nissen hut somewhere in Yorkshire. I know that his new friends will love him as much as we loved him in Fleet Street. He made me a star.'

The heroes were laughing themselves to sleep.
'Godfrey Winn's a poof, isn't he?'
'Codlip created him, he said.'
'Did he do you – or did you do him?'

Before joining the army, Cudlipp had fed his daydreams about becoming a general by sampling books about military science and strategy, starting with Clausewitz. 'Karl had concluded that strategy should concentrate on three main targets – the enemy's forces, resources, and will to do battle; I had taken the same view long before . . . I was . . . encouraged by our identity of view, and the fact that he was a Prussian indicated I was on the right lines.'[2] The dream, however, quickly faded.

Starting as a private delivering coal to officers' wives, he was put to learning high-speed morse, which bored him; and he missed Eileen, who, though she had not yet secured a divorce, was now his fiancée.[3] She came from well-off, respectable stock: 'I suppose if you work hard enough you will one day get a job on the *Daily Telegraph*'[4] was her mother's comment to Cudlipp when she heard he was connected with the *Mirror*.

Cudlipp cherished a letter from General Fuller:

You will find the Army a strange change after an editor's office; but I am convinced that you did the right thing in joining up. This war, won, lost or drawn, is the greatest experience of your generation. Never miss a great experience or for aught that any experience; because it will mean missing something real. Reality (common sense) is the only thing worth striving for in this life. The real is the true, and it is truth which makes us free; hence we end in the ideal.[5]

In May 1941 the army despatched Cudlipp to Sandhurst to be trained as an infantry officer. 'I found that running, jumping, night marching, and bayoneting straw bags while shouting "You filthy Hun"and making blood-curdling yells did not come as easily to a former Editor of twenty-eight as to the younger material who had learnt it all in the OTC [Officers' Training Corps] at public schools. I yelled my best.'[6] Cudlipp, reported King 'has been passed as expert on rifles and bren guns, but [owing to shortage of ammunition] has so far not fired one shot from either'.[7]

King, meanwhile, was coming to terms with the new Editor. 'The paper seems to me to be all right,' he wrote to Cudlipp a month after his departure. 'It lacks the fire and dash you put into it, but that is inevitable. We don't want Campbell's version of synthetic Cudlipp,' he added, before producing a splendid example of how candour can detract from a compliment, ' – so the paper will become more like Campbell himself – duller, but more serious and with more to read in it. Prompted by you when possible and when necessary that will pan out all right.'[8] Or as Margot put it to their son Francis, apropos Campbell's impending visit to speak at his school: 'he won't be such a bomb-shell as Cudlipp would have been!'[9]

In his first month without his companion-in-arms, King had to handle another serious clash with Downing Street. The previous November, the Home Secretary had reported to the War Cabinet that, following the meeting between King, Bart and Attlee, 'the tone of these two newspapers had shown a marked improvement'.[10] Trouble blew up again in January 1941, when two of Cassandra's columns enraged Churchill, who sent a message to King – whom he saw as the key figure in both the *Mirror* and *Pictorial* – to complain: 'The Prime Minister,' wrote his private secretary, 'wishes me to say that it is a pity that so able a writer should show himself so dominated by malevolence.'[11] 'Cassandra,' responded King:

is a hard-hitting journalist with a vitriolic style, but I can assure you his attitude neither to you personally nor to Mr Eden is in any way 'malevolent'. Quite the contrary. Though we continue to take an unflattering view of some of your colleagues, our criticisms are only directed to the fact that the nation's war effort is less intense than it might be – less intense than it would be if more young men were employed in positions of real authority . . .

The 'expressions of regret' for which Churchill thanked King:

give me the opportunity of saying one or two things which have struck me very forcibly in reading the DAILY MIRROR and the SUNDAY PICTORIAL.

First, there is a spirit of hatred and malice against the Government, which after all is not a Party Government but a National Government almost unanimously chosen, which spirit surpasses anything I have ever seen in English journalism. One would have thought in these hard times that some hatred might be kept for the enemy.

The second point is more general. Much the most effective way in which to conduct a Fifth Column movement at the present time would be the method followed by the DAILY MIRROR and the SUNDAY PICTORIAL. Lip service would no doubt be paid to the Prime Minister, whose position at the moment may be difficult to undermine. A perfervid zeal for intensification of the war effort would be used as a cloak behind which to insult and discredit one Minister after another. Every grievance would be exploited to the full, especially those grievances which lead to class dissension. The Army system and discipline would be attacked. The unity between the Conservative and Labour Parties would be gnawed at. The attempt would be made persistently to represent the Government as feeble, unworthy and incompetent, and to spread a general sense of distrust in the whole system. Thus, large numbers of readers would be brought into a state of despondency and resentment, of bitterness and scorn, which at the proper moment, when perhaps some disaster had occurred or prolonged tribulations had wearied the national spirit, could be suddenly switched over into naked defeatism, and a demand for a negotiated peace.

I daresay you will be surprised when I tell you that as a regular reader, I feel that this description very accurately fits the attitude of your two newspapers. I am sure this is not your intention, nor the intention of the able writers you employ. It is, none the less, in my judgment, the result. It amounts to the same thing, even though the intention may be the opposite. It has given me much pain to see that newspapers with whom I have had such friendly relations, and from whom I have received in the past valuable support, should pursue such a line. It is because of our past relations that I write thus plainly.

This letter, King noted in his diary, raised once more his wartime dilemma:

'If we criticise the Government we can be quite fairly accused of 'rocking the boat', 'causing alarm and despondency', and so forth. If, on the other hand, we give the Government our full support, we are then sharing the responsibility for all the job-bery and incompetence that are dragging this great country to defeat. Clearly the right line is some form of compromise: so far I have steered the compromise nearer to rocking the boat than to licking the Government's boots. Perhaps at this stage of the war our policy will have to be modified.[12]

King was also very mindful that the government had just suppressed the communist *Daily Worker* and *The Week*.

He asked for an interview with the Prime Minister, and to his sur-prise was granted one the same day; no one else was present. Churchill began with a tirade on the theme of his letter, concluding that 'this "rocking of the boat" (his phrase this time) might well have disas-trous results for the nation; and what were we doing it for anyway?' To King's protest that the papers supported him and several of his ministers, Churchill asked:

did this mean that we arrogated to ourselves the right of appointing ministers of the Crown? I said no, but surely loyalty to him as Prime Minister did not carry with it loyalty to Attlee as Lord Privy Seal? He conceded this point more or less. He said he didn't mind attacks on the Government: it was the malig-nancy of the attacks that annoyed him. They had contemplated a prosecution, and also denunciation in a speech on the wire-less, but had thought these measures out of proportion. I said there were no personal feelings involved, as hardly any of us knew any of the men we attacked, but that, editing a popular paper, we were bound to write of politics in terms of persons not of principles. He said other popular papers didn't; that we were different. I said we were proud to be different.

During the lengthy discussion, Churchill spoke of the 'great "artistry"' showed by the *Mirror* and the *Pictorial* 'in undermining the morale of the nation', talked *inter alia* of his political difficulties and the shortage of talent, and wished that rather than making trouble, journalists would help the national war effort.

> I said, of course they should all be working sixteen hours a day for the Government. He said: Why weren't they? I said journalists were excluded from the Ministry of Information in favour of museum officials and Foreign Office clerks, so what *could* they do? He said the journalists could not agree on who should and who should not come into the Ministry of Information. I said clearly all the ones of any consequence should be in. He said: 'There is an idea there.'

After more than an hour, Churchill rose, 'saying that I must leave now or I should be attacking him for wasting the country's time!' He saw his visitor out, and since there was an air raid, insisted on lending King his car to take him back to the office. 'Churchill *is* wartime England,' wrote King in his diary:

> England with all its age, its waning virility, its dogged courage, its natural assumption that instinct is more reliable than intellect. In Churchill the country feels it is personified, and for this reason there can be no question of his departure until after complete defeat. From his point of view he has done, is doing, and will continue to do all anyone could to win the war. He feels this, and so attacks on his Government mystify and bewilder him . . . He has no contribution to make to our future, but he personifies our present and our past.

King expressed those thoughts frankly in a letter to Churchill, which was as lucid an account of the philosophy that underlay the political message he pushed remorselessly, as Churchill's reply was a succinct statement of what so annoyed critics of the *Mirror* and the *Pictorial*:

> When you make speeches, yours is the voice of England with all its traditions, its courage, its strength and its limitations . . . This war is to you the crowning of a lifetime of public service:

to us, who are much younger, it is the first step towards a new and better England in which we shall pay our way and not live – as we did in the years 1919–39 – on the accumulated wealth and prestige of our forefathers. This does not mean that I have some future leader up my sleeve or under the bed: I haven't. I have no idea who he may eventually prove to be, but I think we shall not find him in any of the existing parties (in which I would include Mosleyites and Communists) and I think he is now much younger than I am (nearly 40).*

He offered as an example the *Mirror's* advocacy of a government statement of war aims:

Clearly to do so in anything but vague and platitudinous terms would cause dissension among your ministers and between this country and its allies. Therefore you must think that to press such a demand is essentially mischievous. But look at it from the young man's point of view. The Middle East was conquered by the Mahomedans holding a sword in one hand and the Koran in the other – and who will deny that the Koran was the more potent weapon? At this moment we want our Koran and feel its possession would be the decisive factor of the whole war. Perhaps if you have read as far as this, you will see that there is no clear answer to this dilemma. One's loyalty is just divided.

The staff here do not always see clearly what I am driving at. Mistakes occur; but behind everything printed in these two papers is the conviction I have just described expressed in terms of the tabloid newspaper – itself a raw, crude medium but very typical of its day.[13]

King was pleased with his letter – 'well expressed, I think, and entirely sincere,' he wrote in his diary. 'I must say if I were in his shoes I should be delighted with it.' Churchill was less than ecstatic:

---

* Searching for this elusive leader would be a permanent preoccupation of King's: of the three MPs about whom he enthused briefly in his war diaries, George Grey was killed in action, Garfield Weston drifted out of politics in 1945 and Raymond Blackburn in 1951.

Dear Mr King,

Thank you very much for your letter and I was glad we had a talk. All this fine thought about the rising generation ought not to lead you into using your able writers to try to discredit and hamper the Government in a period of extreme danger and difficulty. Nor ought it lead you to try to set class against class and generally 'rock the boat' at such a time. Finally I think it is no defence for such activities to say that your papers specialise in 'vitriolic' writing. Indeed throwing vitriol is thought to be one of the worst of crimes. No man who is affected with 'vitriolism' is worthy to shape the future, or likely to have much chance of doing so in our decent country.

There is no reason why you should not advocate a statement of war aims. I wonder that you do not draw one up in detail and see what it looks like. I see that Mr Mander [a Liberal MP] has tabled his war aims which seem to me to bear out what I ventured to say in the House, namely 'that most right-minded people are well aware of what we are fighting for'. Such a task would be well-suited to the present lull.[14]

King found the answer 'pretty petty . . . evidently our criticisms got very deeply under his skin'. Still, he did not feel he could make a fight of it. 'Not one of these men is any good at all,' he told his diary the same day, commenting on a minor government reshuffle, 'and most of them have had several opportunities to prove it. We shall not attack these changes, as it is clear we shall be closed down if we do, & in any case I think it is now too late to avert disaster. But the irresponsibility of such appointments at such a time is really frightening.'[15]

'It has come as a great shock to learn that you have been so distressed at the line these papers have been pursuing . . .' King wrote back to Churchill. 'However . . . we now have your point of view clearly before us. The staff have had their instructions and you may have already noticed a marked change of tone. If in future you have any fault to find with our contribution to the nation's war effort, I hope you would let us know at once.'[16]

Pleased with having achieved his aim, Churchill wrote in a friendly manner: 'I take the greatest possible interest in the DAILY MIRROR and SUNDAY PICTORIAL with which I have been associated since their association in 1915 [right date for the *Pictorial*, twelve years too late for the *Mirror*]. I shall be very glad to see you at any time.'[17] King was invited to lunch a few days later and reported the conversation at length in his diary. His conclusion was that 'after watching him very closely for two hours, I was struck by his age and his complete lack of contact with the present day. He is a great personality, very English and very human, but obviously has no idea what he is up against in Hitler.' Urging King to come and see him if he wanted anything, Churchill got the response 'that the only thing I wanted was some war work, and if he ever wanted anyone very energetic and reasonably intelligent, would he perhaps remember me?'[18]

Like everyone else to whom King appealed for work, Churchill seems to have assumed that he would be too troublesome. Even Margot had reservations. 'Cecil came home about 3 weeks ago,' she wrote to an American friend in April 1941:

> saying he'd been asked to go to Greece as a War Correspondent & left it to me to decide whether he should go or not.
>
> I never think of him as a journalist really & I'm sure anything he wrote would fail to pass the censor – so I turned it down straight away! I keep on wondering if I have made an awful mistake – but I do think he'd be very little use as a correspondent. As it is the first real job he has been offered in this war, I felt very badly about discouraging him, tho' if I had thought it just right for him I'd have packed him off at once. I think he is thankful not to have gone.[19]

For a brave man of insatiable curiosity, who loved travel and wanted to be in the thick of things, it was torture to be denied the chance to see the war close-up except as a passive victim of the Blitz. For the most part, King's diaries are a relentless round of news (mostly bad), information-gathering, gossip, rumour and denigration, but they come alive when he writes about bombs, fires and destruction, when he often conveys a sense of excitement – even exhilaration. 'It really was a memorable experience,' he wrote in August 1940 at Culham, 'to lean out of the window into the warm gloriously moonlit night & hear the throbbing of the German aeroplane engines far above me, while searchlights rather faint in the moonlight, searched round for the enemy'.[20] Bombing in London in October 'really was a most beautiful sight – leaping flames, smoke clouds lit up from below, immense showers of sparks, plumes of water, and above it all the stars'.[21] Indeed, he had quite friendly feelings for the bombers: 'M[argot] is very disturbed by all the destruction . . . I said by clearing away so many sordid buildings, it gives London the chance of a fresh start. M said – if the country has the virility to make use of it. What a crucial point this is!'[22]

In May 1941, as he often did when the air-raid sirens went off, King climbed to the roof of Geraldine House to look at what was happening to London; what ensued inspired him to what was probably his best-ever piece of descriptive reportage. It is also a vivid reminder of why Churchill was rather testy with those who wanted him to think of future society rather than present survival:

> the fun was really starting. An incendiary had fallen through the roof of our old offices in Bream's Buildings, all wood partitions and loaded up with stocks of paper and string – very inflammable indeed. I led a party over the roofs from the main building and we threw up sandbags to a man who appeared on the roof above us. He put the sand on the flames and put them out. We then went inside the building and found the bomb on the floor burning fiercely. A fireman was covering it with bags of sand. Flames were breaking out in the lift shaft just by: the bomb was setting alight the boards of the ceiling below. We went down to the lower floor, forced open the lift door and directed a stream from a stirrup pump on to the flames; meanwhile the flames were breaking out again on the floor above. Eventually they were both subdued. Elsewhere, some of the party were extinguishing a bomb which had fallen on the flat roof of Geraldine House proper.

King correctly predicted that their fire would break out again and had men so positioned that they were able to deal with it. A fire-watcher on the roof of a shop opposite had less foresight, so the fire spread to two other shops, a church and a group of factories and printing works. 'The Germans overhead were in such large numbers that you could not distinguish the sound of individual planes. About this time three incendiaries fell in the yard [and] were put out after doing a good deal of damage. The roof watchers were splendid, paid no attention to bombs, but the editorial staff mostly cowered in a corner of the basement and were useless.'

King calculated that on average every minute for five hours 'a bomb could be heard rushing or whistling through the air. Once when I was on the roof, one dropped fairly near, and one could see the flash and the column of dust from the explosion. Fires by this time were all round us.' A stiff wind drove the flames towards them. 'Bart [who was also conspicuously brave] and Greenwell [*Mirror* photographer] turned up in A.F.S. [Auxiliary Fire Service] uniform' and were prom- ised ten pumps, of which only one arrived. With no water pressure and just the office fire-fighting equipment, Geraldine House escaped being burned down only because they found a small pipe working off the mains and managed to fill a 'dam' outside their office, a previ- ously bombed building acted as a firebreak, and at the critical moment the wind changed:

> Towards morning the smoke was such you could not see that it was full moon with no clouds; the air was full of flying sparks; every now and then there was a roar of a collapsing house . . . About 4.0 a.m. I went for a walk to see what had been hap- pening in our immediate neighbourhood. I managed to get down Fetter Lane to Fleet Street (the other way was completely blocked by this time by fallen buildings, as well as by fires). Serjeant's Inn was blazing, and further on it appeared as if the *News Chronicle* were alight . . . Behind the *Express* in Shoe Lane there was a ter- rific blaze. When I got to Ludgate Circus I could see the glow from a huge fire in Queen Victoria Street, which had been blazing most of the night. Up Farringdon Street near the Viaduct the buildings were blazing on both sides of the road. Up Ludgate Hill there were big fires on both sides, and I could see a great glow the other side of St Paul's . . .
>
> St Clement Danes had been gutted, and only the spire was alight half way up to the top and sending out showers of sparks – an odd and rather beautiful spectacle.

Back at the office, printing had been delayed again because the electric current had failed, 'the metal pots in the linos had gone cold' and all the lights were out. 'However, after a ten-minute interval they came on again and efforts could be made to get the paper out. I left at 6.30 when all danger to the office from nearby fires seemed to be well over.'[23]*

King was now not just confined to newspapers, but to newspapers that had to walk that uneasy tightrope between boat-rocking and boot-licking. His influence on the *Mirror* was still restricted and he did not get on with Cudlipp's successor. 'I had a flaming row with Campbell,' he would report to Cudlipp early in 1942, 'and now hope to have less nonsense and more co-operation.'[24] That King should get involved in a row was a very bad sign. As he once put it himself to Margot, 'I tend to say nothing even if I think I am being unreasonably treated, but . . . there is a limit & when that limit comes, I speak out from my point of view, the thunder comes after the clouds have been over-head for months or years: but from other people's point of view it may come from a completely clear sky.'[25] Still, King and Campbell (like King and Bart) rubbed along together, though uneasily, and the circulation of both papers went on rising until – in late 1942 – paper rationing imposed restrictions on the numbers of copies as well as pages. Both the *Mirror* and the *Pictorial* were immensely popular with the rank-and-file in the forces, towards whom they were deliberately geared, and were virulent critics of the petty rules and pointless bureau-cracy that irritated the troops; gradually the balance had tilted once again towards boat-rocking.

In November 1941 the Home Secretary was asked if in the light of a *Pictorial* leader headed 'SECOND-RATERS', which suggested that the House of Commons might as well go permanently into recess, he would suppress the paper 'to prevent a repetition of its subver-sive articles'.[26] There was a clear distinction, replied Herbert Morrison, between speeches and articles criticising 'with a view to effecting improvements, and those which make reckless and baseless attacks throwing discredit, albeit perhaps unknowingly, on democratic

---

* Later in the war King was required to become a part-time fire-watcher and found to his disgust that he was expected to protect 'horrible old buildings in the grimmest 19th-century manner [that] would be much better burnt'.

institutions and thus perhaps breeding that mentality upon which Fascism has founded itself. I take the view – and I think that the majority of this House and of the country will agree with me – that the article in question comes within the latter category.' However, he would take no action this time.

'I have told Campbell to see Morrison and make his peace with him,' King recorded. 'If we are to get into hot water, let us get into hot water for saying something that matters – not for a feeble example of Campbell's facetiousness.'[27] Morrison explained that 'he had been under strong pressure on one or two occasions to take action of some kind', King told Cudlipp. It seemed there would be little trouble if attacks were on individuals or on specific government actions, 'but general attacks on the Government as a whole for its general conduct of affairs Morrison thinks likely to cause despondency and defeatism. Attacks on the House of Commons as a whole – as was Campbell's leader . . . are even worse . . . Anyway, everyone's nerves are frayed and one has to be much more circumspect than ever before.'[28]

The drift was also visible in the *Mirror*. Cassandra's description of the average officer as 'a hideous, moustachioed little twerp, with an impeccable record of club ties, high-class bars, and the ability to talk minced drivel' was not calculated to win friends in high places. And the paper's laceration of military errors increased with a year of disasters that placed enormous strain on the government.

In February 1942 the *Mirror* asked, 'Is it any longer true to say that we trust the Prime Minister, though we do not trust his Government?' and King commissioned a Labour MP, G. M. Garro-Jones, to write for the *Pictorial* 'WHO IS TO BLAME?', which culminated with the question 'Have we the wrong Prime Minister? Last week I would have hesitated a little and said "no." Today I say that unless the Prime Minister acts, the answer will soon be "yes."'[29] Churchill was reported to be 'in a towering passion on Monday over the criticisms of his administration, & said he "hated the newspapers worse than the Nazis"!'[30]

Breaking-point came over Philip Zec's harrowing cartoon in the *Mirror* of a torpedoed sailor on a makeshift raft in a stormy, empty sea. Cassandra's caption read: '"The price of petrol has been increased by one penny." – Official.' As Zec and Cassandra had intended, readers saw this as a rebuke to profiteers and petrol-wasters, but Churchill was one of many members of the government and the military who believed it was intended to imply that men were being sacrificed so that oil companies could prosper. Churchill wanted the *Mirror* suppressed under powers possessed by the Home Secretary, but with the backing of Lord Beaverbrook and the Minister for Information, Brendan Bracken, Morrison suggested instead a final warning. To Bart and Cecil Thomas, the *Mirror*'s Editor, Morrison delivered a harsh and stark warning that unless the paper ceased 'fomenting opposition to the successful prosecution of the war', it would be closed down. Later he told the House of Commons that 'the cartoon in question is only one example, but a particularly evil example, of the policy and methods of a newspaper which, intent on exploiting an appetite for sensation and with reckless indifference to the national interest and to the prejudicial effect on the war effort, had repeatedly published scurrilous misrepresentations, distorted and exaggerated statements and irresponsible generalisations'. In the same issue, he told the House, the leading article had stated 'the accepted tip for army leadership would, in plain truth be this: All who aspire to mislead others in war should be brass-buttoned boneheads, socially prejudiced, arrogant and fussy. A tendency to heart disease, apoplexy, diabetes and high blood pressure is desirable in the highest posts.'

In the subsequent Commons debate, the *Mirror* suffered virulent attacks but also doughty defence, most notably from Aneurin Bevan, the rising star of the Labour left. There was no vote, but it was obvious that henceforward the *Mirror* and the *Pictorial* would have to tread carefully. Cassandra, as King wrote to Cudlipp, 'feels that it would be a hollow mockery for him to continue under these conditions, so he is closing down and going into the Army – which, in any case, he would have had to do in three months' time';[31] 'the *New Statesman*,' noted King in his diary, 'rather obscurely recalls the fact that it is odd that I should get into this spot of bother, when my uncle Northcliffe got into trouble in the last war for attacking Kitchener'.[32]

Northcliffe, though, had chosen his targets more carefully than did his nephew, whose mythical 'bus-driver's wife in Sheffield' was being given little reason to trust anyone in authority. In April, King was anxious to run a story about the extravagance of George VI and Queen Elizabeth. In the interests of releasing staff at a time when labour was at a premium, King had been told, they had taken a twenty-two-roomed flat in Mayfair, which was being done up by the War Office: 'In spite of all the calls to austerity &, above all, to save labour, the flat is being done up regardless of both.' The *Pictorial* was all set to run with a detailed account of the extravagances, including silver fittings and a private lift: 'We submitted the story – written of course in a very friendly & unsensational way – to the censor, but it was turned down flat . . . evidently the censor felt that, however worded . . . this story stank so badly it was better killed.'[33] The censor, presumably, believed that since the King and Queen were seen as crucial to raising civilian morale, to undermine them would be to undermine the war effort. But that was not the way King thought: he was interested in the truth, however unpalatable, whatever the circumstances and whatever the consequences, and he did not necessarily understand the effect of the unvarnished truth on a bus-driver's wife.

What with shrinking paper supplies, the loss of many of their most able staff and the bothers with the government, the crusading heart began to go out of both Bart and King. 'We have been discussing future *Mirror* & *Pic* policy,' King recorded in September 1942, 'and feel that criticism is now futile and merely boring. The war no longer rouses interest and therefore the only possible line – until things start moving – is great preoccupation with the young, both in services and factories.'[34] More telling was the entry more than a year later deploring the cynicism of colleagues and the people they met in everyday life:

No one believes any longer in any statement by any minister, nor do they believe their newspapers, the B.B.C., or anyone else . . . professional men from doctors and parsons to judges have lost their prestige; even millionaires have lost their glamour.

Unfortunately all this has been growing for some years and now attaches to everyone in authority. It would be a long time before any new regime acquired any real confidence from public opinion. Unfortunately attacks on the powers that be do not stir people to anger and action, but rather add to the current attitude of cynicism – a lesson I have learned in the last eight years from the reaction to the politics of the *Mirror* and *Pic*.[35]

Cudlipp was later to maintain that the final vindication against the charge that the *Mirror* was helping the enemy came post-war, when it emerged that the German High Command had given orders that all its directors should be arrested when London was occupied. But being hated by the enemy does not invalidate the accusation that the *Mirror* and *Pictorial* could be damaging and demoralising to their own side. It was true that, despite his admiration for the firm leadership of Hitler, Mussolini and Stalin, his belief that the world was inexorably moving towards totalitarianism and his loathing of the British Establishment, King passionately wanted the Allies to win the war. However, as in his human relationships, he seemed unable to see the difference between constructive and destructive criticism – a distinction that Cudlipp understood instinctively and learned in the army to apply to newspapers.

Cudlipp had not been completely divorced from his old life. He frequently sent King comments on, and ideas for, the *Pictorial* and wrote the occasional necessarily circumspect column, while King regularly sent him news of the office and of the wider world. And he made the most of army life and missed no opportunity to transcend his lowly rank: 'Cudlipp came up from Sandhurst,' recorded King in August 1941,[36] '& was in the office for some time. He thinks the training on the whole good, but is appalled by the fact that equipment is still very short – we have not yet any properly equipped motorised infantry – Bren guns in short supply & ammunition is almost non-existent.'

Cudlipp dropped by again in November. 'He is now a second lieutenant in the Royal Sussex Regiment and is stationed at Ramsgate. He gets on well with his fellow officers and does a good deal of lecturing to the troops, both his own battalion and others. Morale is even lower than he had expected, but he says the men are pathetically eager to accept any leadership that is offered and can easily be enthused.'[37] King wrote to him a few days later: 'I think it would be a grand idea if you would return to us for a week when next you have some leave . . . your inspiration and ideas are badly needed and would be most welcome. The paper is dull, all the papers are dull, because we are tired and stale. Do come and give us a breath of fresh air.'[38] In January 1942, editing the *Pictorial* during his week's leave, Cudlipp reported to King that 'the subjects people were really interested in were Russia and her war effort, the break-up of family life and the problem of lice'.[39]

The army had not ignored Cudlipp the journalist. He was pushed by his Brigadier into editing two issues of the *Sandhurst Magazine*, 'a highbrow and snobbish affair for which I had neither time nor taste. Rewriting the regimental history of the 5th Battalion, Royal Sussex, while we were preventing the Nazis from landing at Margate was more to my liking.' But the big journalistic opportunity offered itself in May 1942, when he joined the *Santa Rosa*, an American cruiseship-turned-troop-carrier, to sail in convoy from Liverpool to Suez. 'It threatened two months (two months!) of weapon drill, PT, map reading and "cleanest platoon" competitions unless . . .'

Cudlipp learned from the Brigadier, who appointed him Entertainments Officer, that he was worried about how to keep the troops occupied and fit for immediate action on disembarking, and how to keep them interested in the war without any information being available. And he learned from the ship's purser-turned-custodian that there was a small printing machine on board, previously used for menus. With the Brigadier's approval, Cudlipp found six compositors and a supply of paper, persuaded the wireless operator to tune into radio news stations early every morning and on 28 May 1942 launched *Ocean News*, which began as a one-pager, shortly became a two-pager and even managed a four-page special in colour on Sundays:

> I had discovered a mass of old travel brochures. The comps and I cut out the coloured pictures of beautiful cruising girls with a razor blade and stuck them with paste (flour and water from the Army cooks) into the white spaces . . .
>
> The worthy comps and I had a small price to pay for our diligence. As the convoy had zig-zagged its way, blowing the hooters or sounding the sirens on each ship at each turning-point to outwit the German submarines, turning left around the Cape of Good Hope into the Indian Ocean, we had happily laboured in the stomach of the *Santa Rosa* in our underpants, trying to select an *i* from a *j* and an *m* from an *n* in the flickering light. There was no fan in the tiny hold where the menus had been printed in better days. Our faces were waxen and our bodies were covered with the rash of prickly heat. The smiles of the luscious athletic white South African girls in Cape Town were directed at the bronzed gods of the upper deck.

Ocean News was given complete freedom to tell the truth, even though
– as Cudlipp reminded his readers in his valedictory editorial on 22
July 1942 – most of the news had been 'of an "adverse" nature':

> Rommel drove us out of Libya. The Japs occupied the Aleutian
> Islands. The Russians were rolled back from the Don. The Nazis
> entered Egypt and split the Eighth Army in two. Tobruk fell
> while Churchill was negotiating in America with Roosevelt. From
> Britain itself came news of mounting public uneasiness, and of
> a growing demand for a Second Front in Europe.

But the little paper contained more than news; anyone who could
write was encouraged and there were reminiscences, poems, a column
from the Brigadier, reports of sporting activities on board, and reviews
of shows and events put on by the Entertainments Officer, whose
battalion had a band and a male-voice choir and who produced their
shows, *Tropical Heat* and *Keep it Clean!*

The last issue[40] extolled the Brains Trust that had run weekly; as
well as guest speakers, there was a permanent panel consisting of the
padre, an army doctor, a corporal who had worked for the League of
Nations and, of course, Lieutenant Hugh Cudlipp. The article
recalling highlights spoke of the perpetual combat between Cudlipp
and the padre: 'They clashed over the Freedom of the Press; the record
of the Church of England in the past ten years, which Cudlipp
denounced as "ignoble." When they squabbled over propaganda the
argument went on in cabins of the ship for half the night.' Then there
was Cudlipp's definition of contentment: '"I would like to be sitting
by a large fire with a brandy and a damn big cigar," he said. "Then
I would like to turn on the radio and hear the announcement that
Mussolini had died at Hitler's funeral. And then, from a room just
five yards away, I should like to hear a particularly lovely lady saying
– 'I'm ready darling.'"'

The troops disembarked in late July at Suez and went by train to
Cairo. Cudlipp was briefly a platoon commander defending the El
Alamein Line, but was then equipped with a truck, a driver, maps
and a typewriter and told to report to Major-General Harding, who
was in the Western Desert with the Desert Rats in pursuit of Field
Marshal Rommel and his Afrika Korps. He found Harding east of

Tripoli and was appointed a public-relations officer: returning to base with copy one day, Cudlipp's truck hit a mine, earning him a permanent scar on his forehead.

That Cudlipp was in a battle zone did not inhibit King from including in his gloomy letters his expectations of disaster in North Africa. Cudlipp destroyed the letters that he thought the censor would consider subversive, but he kept others. What question had he asked King that led to the enthusiastic letter of October 1942 recommending Herodotus, Thucydides, Tacitus, Froissart, Philippe de Comines, Pepys, Saint-Simon, Benvenuto Cellini and Walpole? 'The best books on the period 1810–50 are Greville's Memoirs and the Creevy papers, but they are hard to get; the others are obtainable normally anywhere in cheap editions.' (This letter, recalled Cudlipp, arrived when he was in the middle of the desert, 'near a village with two houses unlikely to have Herodotus.'[41])

King warmed to his theme:

> Obviously this list could go on and on. Have you tried any of the Russian novels? War and Peace gives one a picture of the Napoleonic wars, though of course Tolstoi was not contemporary. Did you read Lawrence's Seven Pillars of Wisdom, and its literary parent, Doughty's Arabia Deserta? This last is a great book and interesting for its style. It is no use harping on Shakespeare and the Bible, which, with Milton, are the foundations of the language, but did you ever read the Apocrypha? This is also to be had in the Authorised version of 1611; it is unfamiliar, and the Wisdom of Solomon and Ecclesiasticus are as good as anything in the Bible or elsewhere . . .[42]

'How is the reading getting on?' enquired King a month later in a letter congratulating Cudlipp on being promoted to captain:

> I remember Professor Saintsbury used to say — and he is the best critic of English literature of the last 30 years or so — that the four palladians of English literature are Shakespeare, Milton, Swift and Fielding. This is a somewhat unusual view, but I am sure you would enjoy all of them. Milton's Paradise Lost is superb stuff. The bits about God are all very well, but his Satan

is terrific – he obviously admired him much more. Swift in the
original – he mustn't be expurgated – is the sort of bitter satire
I think you might like, and Fielding's Tom Jones is a cinch. And
Disraeli's Coningsby? And Trollope?[43]

King's innocence was matched in scale only by Cudlipp's deviousness; throughout their long relationship, King was never to learn the
awkward truth that, though Cudlipp was brilliant, he was intellectually lightweight and never read a book if he could possibly avoid it.
(He did allege in his autobiography that he had five pocket-sized vol-
umes of Gibbon's *Decline and Fall of the Roman Empire* in the desert, but
there is no evidence that he did more than dip into them.)

Winston Churchill altered the course of Cudlipp's war. In January
1943, on a visit to Casablanca to meet President Roosevelt, he noticed
to his chagrin that there was no British equivalent of the American
services' newspaper *Stars and Stripes*, in which Roosevelt featured so
prominently. Harold Macmillan, Minister of State in Algiers and
future Prime Minister, sent for Captain Cudlipp, 'who,' he wrote to
his wife, 'used to write those tremendous leading articles at the time
of Munich.'[44] The newspaper should be called *Union Jack*, Cudlipp told
the British officers at Allied Forces Headquarters (AFHQ); he sat up
all night typing a report 'on faded, war-bedraggled mauve notepaper
in a small bedroom in a hotel in the company of some indigestible
salami sandwiches, a bottle of tepid *vin rosé*, and some black dried-
out cigars I had picked up in Marrakesh. They burnt with a crackle
and exuded the stench of saltpetre.'[45]

At his insistence, Cudlipp was given sole responsibility for the content, policies and staffing of the paper and was accountable directly
to AFHQ, to which he was promised access at the highest level. He
decided that *Union Jack* (or 'Onion Duke', as it became known) would
be published first in Constantine – halfway between Algiers and Tunis
and possessing a newspaper plant – after which small units under his
command would leapfrog forward as the army advanced. He also
insisted that soldiers be charged one penny, as they would never believe
a give-away sheet.

Nothing could be requisitioned in Algeria, Macmillan explained
genially, and it was up to Cudlipp to find newsprint. Having heard that
a vast consignment was arriving at Constantine station assigned to

'Psychological Warfare' – an American propaganda exercise – and *Dépêche de Constantine*, in whose office he had wangled a room, Cudlipp and his first recruit, Sergeant Thackeray (late of the *Manchester Guardian*), staged a raid by re-addressing half the shipment to *Union Jack*. 'I called this sort of exercise "improvisation".'

After the paper's launch on 21 March, Cudlipp took off for London to organise free use of press material as well as news and picture services. The BBC asked him to broadcast on the triumphant progress of General Montgomery's Eighth Army: 'of many tributes I have read or heard to that matchless legion,' wrote a reviewer, 'his was the most revealing and the most memorable. It possessed a quality of passion . . . which few can transmit . . . the language was incisive and robust . . . he is a born broadcaster . . . [with] the manner, the voice, the sensibility and the material.'[46] It was a masterly example of the fine propagandist that Cudlipp had become: 'They have the courage, those young men of Britain,' his address concluded. 'They have the determination. They have tasted blood, and they don't like the Hun. Yet – and we must recognise this – their victory would have been impossible without the skill and the energy of the factory workers in Britain, in Canada and in America. Work hard. Work quickly. The Desert Rats will soon be fixing their eyes in the direction of Europe.'[47]

Beaverbrook phoned him the next morning: 'Do you know who this is? The Prime Minister and I listened to your eighth Army broadcast last night and Winston thought it was great stuff. Good-bye to you.'[48]

In his inveterate information-gathering about aspects of the war from everyone he met – from the inner circles of government to advertising executives, colleagues, office staff, domestic staff, ex-staff, hitchhikers, wife, children and mistresses – King liked to have his pessimism reinforced. To tell him that the war was going well, morale was high, officers were efficient, a political party was united, a minister was capable, the military were content with the politicians or the new weaponry was adequate would invite derision or contempt, so people found it more rewarding to give him the bad news he craved. General Fuller was a particular favourite because his predictions were uniformly gloomy: in November 1942 he came into the office 'appalled' and assured King that 'at this rate we shall take five years and five million men before we finally fling the Germans out of North Africa'.[49]

Cudlipp was the past master at telling King plenty of what he wanted to hear so that, when necessary, he would be receptive to what Cudlipp needed him to hear. So although King's entries on Cudlipp's visit to London attribute to him a few positive remarks (admiration for General Montgomery, for instance), the majority are negative. Cudlipp was concerned, reported King, about how tired the British looked; by the number of foreigners in London; the Italian sympathies of the Egyptian government; the indifference of the French in Algiers, which suggested the utter demoralisation of the French population as a whole; the ineptitude and awfulness of American soldiers; and the failure of British raids to damage Tripoli. He was appalled by the poor quality and low morality of MPs and 'so shocked at the performance in the Commons of a drunk Arthur Greenwood, deputy leader of the Labour Party,' he told King, 'that his comment from the gallery was "Balls", for which he was very nearly thrown out.'

Cudlipp's visit was not all hard work. He 'had lunch with his brother and others at the Savage Club and met A. V. Alexander,' recorded King. 'Alexander struck him as being a sound little man wafted up far and away above the utmost limits of his capacity . . . Anyway, at 4.0 p.m. Percy Cudlipp, editor of the *Herald*, A. V. Alexander, First Lord of the Admiralty, and Hugh Cudlipp were all singing Baptist hymns (A. V. Alexander at the piano) at the Savage Club – all of them being at least slightly drunk.'[50]

Before he left, Cudlipp made a suggestion: 'He said the spirit of the 8th Army & of England were poles apart & that I really should go out to North Africa to see our war effort at its best . . . I went to see Brendan Bracken, who jumped at the idea. He says he will provide transport, letters of introduction to Alexander, Montgomery, Tedder & the French leaders.'[51] To King's bitter disappointment, the visit fell through for a series of bureaucratic reasons, culminating in the refusal of General Eisenhower's staff to issue the appropriate visa – which added personal resentment to King's growing loathing of Americans.

King's state of mind throughout the war worried his family and friends. 'Dearest Seazle [one of his family nicknames] . . .' wrote his sister Enid in June 1942:

It depressed me so much to see a sort of despairing weariness of some struggle in your face and the phrase keeps returning to my mind, 'He saved others, himself he cannot save,' you, who have helped me so much more than you can ever know!; & I wish I could do some little thing in return. We have already shared so many things, our heritage of King Puritanism & Harmsworth contempt of every rule, as also an almost overwhelming sense of frustration.

I just hope you won't forget that from whatever cause, we develop very late, so don't for one moment look upon yourself, as you say the boys do, as a 'back number'. Age has no measure in years, surely.

Also it seems to me unhealthy to live so much even on your magnificent brains without an easing of such extreme tension and & I wish you could hobnob with the simple rock bottom of our people. They won the last war inspite of all the iniquities at the top. I think they would give you a new assurance beyond this phase of dramatic history making. I often think a newspaper office is the worst place for you spiritually & wish you could find an antidote.

But of course the thing of most importance is the enormous responsibility of your great power over people, which neither you nor they can avoid, whatever the burden to you, & I should call it a sacred trust; but, darling Cecil, I only write because I love you truly, & hope you will forgive me.[52]

Enid's letter touched on King's major personal problems. All his children were clever and they all loved him, and he was assiduous in writing to them and buying them thoughtful, beautiful and interesting – though never extravagant – presents at home and abroad. Priscilla, for instance, who was precociously cultivated, tried to share her parents' interests and was a good correspondent, was sent every week postcards featuring famous pictures with accompanying commentary (Renoir's 'Girls at the Piano' – 'What do you think of this god-awful picture? Believe it or not it is by a very famous artist'; Boudin 'is a most charming French artist who has come very much into fashion recently. Rothermere had a lot of them'; Fouquet's 'Man with the Glass of Wine' – 'almost my favourite picture – I don't know why'). Yet they saw little of their father. 'Please don't go up to your office on Saturday, Daddy,' wrote the sixteen-year-old Michael, 'because I haven't seen you very much this half, and I like hearing all about the war. I will be most disappointed if you have to leave Mummy and me early.'[53] King's personality and reputation weighed heavily on them, as did his obsession with the war, and they were mocked at their boarding schools for their association with below-stairs newspapers that attacked public schools and were thought unpatriotic.

Priscilla, who was anyway prone to homesickness, tended to suffer uncomplainingly; a letter from a teacher at Downe House School in January 1942, when she was twelve, said that she was settling down, but 'she has obviously great powers of self-control and it will take some time to get to know her'.[54] In time she preferred school to home, where she did not feel particularly welcome, but she tried to help with the twenty-two evacuees, all under five. 'She is not easy in her dealings with other people,' her mother wrote later that year from Culham, 'but is learning, & her mental capacities are at last coming to the fore. Her drawing is excellent & she is now learning the violin as well as the piano . . . life comes hardly to her in most ways. She is most capable & helpful to me here.'[55] Her headmistress said of her a couple of years later that 'with so many liars and thieves about, it was a great relief to have in Priscilla someone who was unquestionably straight.'[56] Although she avoided rows, she could be determined: King was upset that she preferred to stay on during school vacations to take a music course, when he wanted her to work on one of his farms. She had to earn as a chambermaid and waitress the fees for her tuition.[*]

Her elder brothers did not suffer in silence; indeed, they were in constant intellectual conflict with their father. It was hard on Michael that both his father's papers frequently derided Eton and Etonians: he was the only *Daily Mirror* reader at the school, as it had been banned in 1939. (It was banned too at Priscilla's school, but King sent it to her daily and the headmistress allowed her to read it, as long she did

---

[*] From the time she was fifteen, Priscilla received from Geraldine Harmsworth's trust £100 a year. Worth in 1945 the equivalent today of about £2,700, it fell rapidly in value. From this she was expected to pay all personal expenses from fares and clothes to dentistry and, in 1950, the costs of her wedding, for which King lent her the money.

not show it to anyone else.) At Eton, Michael performed far better academically than the educational psychologist had predicted and was prized by his teachers for his independence of mind, critical sense and extraordinary empathy. In a letter to his formidable father he condemned Cassandra's attack on Stanley Baldwin for resisting having his iron gates removed: 'Fatuous and childish. Why attack some old man who is as good as dead for some wretched gates he won't have taken down. There are lots of your friends who have gates. Why not attack them? We have also some gates at Culham which would go to make a machine gun or two.'[57] Early in 1942, when he was just sixteen, he wrote to his father that while he thought that day's *Pictorial* 'extremely good . . . why in the leader did you say that you intended to go on criticising? Surely you will only muddle and frighten the government if you criticise every damn thing it does? I bet if we had a smashing victory you would find some way of turning it down and finding some fault with the people who did it.'[58]

'Did you actually see Morrison about the *Mirror*,' Michael wrote in March, 'or did you get a note? I can tell you there is a great deal of excitement about the whole thing here. So far I have met no one who has any good thing to say for the *Mirror*. They all want it shut down.'[59] Two outstanding teachers, George Lyttleton and Kenneth Wickham, Michael's housemaster, came greatly to like and admire him: 'a spirited and intelligent boy [with] fierce opinions about any number of things . . . [yet] no one could doubt his genuine friendliness and courtesy,'[60] wrote Lyttleton in 1941, for as Francis had pointed out, Eton encouraged the individuality that Winchester destroyed;[61] 'Michael is a grand fellow,' he wrote to King a few months later. Michael 'has come to life, intellectually and still more – emotionally, very suddenly and precociously,' wrote Wickham in the spring of 1942, 'hastened by surviving a serious illness and his awareness of the danger through which he passed, and also by the seriousness of our affairs of which he has been made chiefly aware by conversations with you. A good victory would do him as well as all of us good, though many people say that you and Michael might almost be disappointed by it.'[62]

'I disagree that Daddy has very sound judgement in politics,' the always intellectually rigorous Francis wrote to his mother from Winchester a year or so later, when King had completely written off

Churchill.* 'As far as I can see he has only knowledge. For he thinks the only way of winning the war is for Churchill to get out of power, and the only way to do that is for us to lose the battle in the Pacific which means practically that we lose the war. Because when and if we beat Germany we have still got Japan.'[63]

Friends – mostly women – expressed their concern too. The relationship with Francis Needham had dwindled away to nothing, presumably when the homophobic King finally discovered Needham was homosexual. Charles d'Orléans could not be reached during the latter stages of the war. (At the first possible opportunity after the war was over, King 'rushed over to Paris to bring Charles coffee and soap and other things I knew to be in short supply. But the door of their home was opened by his widow.' Injured as a Resistance fighter, he had been sent to a concentration camp, where he died of diphtheria.[64]) And though there were a few men whom King liked, for any kind of intimacy he relied on women. Cecilia Semphill, whose husband was an aeronautical expert and a favourite source of King's, was horrified when she ventured a criticism to see how unhappy it seemed to make him. 'What I was trying to explain was this,' she wrote to him:

> To the outside world newspaper magnates are always credited with mainly commercial motives, and in the case of your two papers this is doubly likely to be the opinion of the public. So long as you sit behind the Mirror & the Pictorial's desks you are bound to be misunderstood, except by those who know you very well. And I have such a high opinion of your ideals that I want other people to know them too . . . you have no idea what a good publicity agent I am for you, in spite of fearful odds![65]

And then there was Margot, who wanted to support King but hated the vulgarity and harshness of his papers. 'Is it true? Is it kind? Is it

---

* 'Hitler's attitude to Churchill since long before the war was that he was a dangerous madman who would pull all Europe down in blazing ruins in order to achieve his personal ambitions,' King wrote in his diary in August 1944, 'and there is something in this'.

necessary?' was the philosophy she favoured.[66] Both her parents had died, she had had a wearing couple of years looking after the little evacuees at home, prison-visiting and acting as a Berkshire JP along with all her other responsibilities at Culham and Cushnie, and she had suffered greatly from having no time to herself. Although she had many friends who admired and loved her, she was still diffident and anxious to prove herself. Antonia White wrote in 1941:

> I do *not* love you because you are courageous, public-spirited, spiritually minded, radiant, charming & full of life, though I appreciate all these things. I love you because you are the one true and only Margaret King & for no other reason whatever. And, so my dear, you can thunder at me with good works or you can complain wistfully that I never suggest you come up to London & lunch with me (although whenever I see you you reel off such a list of commitments that no one would DARE ask you to do anything so frivolous as come up to London just to chat . . .) you will not succeed in shaking this immutable rock of my affection for you.[67]

Yet though Margot had been often exhausted and sometimes ill because of too much work and worry, she had relished having a proper job to do and was bereft when, late in 1942, it became clear that the Kings would have to give up Culham. 'Taxation is making life at Culham impossible,' she wrote to an ex-employee:

> & as there is a break in our lease next March we have decided not to renew it, & now the Ministry of Health has stepped in, requisitioning the house & we move out at the end of January. My beloved Nursery has been moved elsewhere for a few weeks while we pack up & then they return & form the nucleus of a much larger nursery. It is all a great upheaval & has come on us very suddenly . . . The family are sad about leaving Culham, as you can imagine, & to me it is a very great blow. I have tried to make it a real home for the family, & the idea of a London life does not appeal.'[68]

They took a small flat in Lincoln's Inn (Priscilla slept in a former cupboard) and King invested some of the proceeds of Culham in two large farms in Cumberland ('complete with Norman keep and Roman station with early Saxon cross just over the wall'[69]) and 'a tiny village near Aberdeen . . . which has a tiny harbour and about a mile of cliffs ending in a little bay.'[70] Missing the children, Margot was also distressed because Michael had taken his father's politics to their logical conclusion, had become a near-communist and, at sixteen, insisted on leaving Eton and going to work in a Glasgow shipyard until he was old enough to join the army. It was a decision precipitated by the humiliation of having the *Mirror* run an attack on Eton so savage that one of the governors wanted Michael expelled and there was an atmosphere of bad feeling in the school, despite support from teachers. Lyttleton, who truly loved Michael ('I should be immensely proud of you if you were my own son, & so I am of my friend'), corresponded with him for years, talking books and ideas, challenging his politics wisely; he tried to encourage Michael to go back to school, but he never returned to academic education.

Now with too much time on her hands, Margot found that her spiritual and religious instincts had intensified: she talked often to friends about a mystical experience she had had in Ireland at the time war was declared. And more and more she wilted under her husband's emotional and intellectual demands. Yet they still loved each other passionately. 'The longer I am away from you,' he wrote from Quebec in 1945, 'the more I realise how much you mean to me and how very much you have given me. Looking back I see myself as a block of ice and only you would have had the warmth of love and the patience to thaw me out into a semblance of a human being. I must have seemed very cruel but I was only frozen — now, I think, less frozen and therefore better able to appreciate you . . . My heart is all yours darling.'[71]

Yet much though King loved his wife, he seemed to believe they could rationalise their way out of their marital problems. His introspection had been fanned by a deep interest in psychoanalysis,* which she hated. 'As far as our relations are concerned my sub-conscious comes into

---

* The 'morbid hobby of this unhappy man' was Cudlipp's description.

the picture in two ways,' he wrote to her during the war:

1) I am desperately seeking a mother. It is all very well to say I can't have one & what can't be cured *must* be endured etc. etc. All quite true: all habitually in my mind & all completely inef-fectual. It is one of the strangest elements in my make-up & just can't be explained away or shifted. I suppose any love for a man by a woman has some maternal element, but yours has less than most. No blame attaches to you – or me – but this want of mine does not help.

2) My sub-conscious sadism. This is very difficult to deal with. My conscious layer is very kind & my actions, which are easier to control, are usually kind. But in words I often express (unknowingly) my sub-conscious sadism & not my conscious kindliness. This is a trap constantly set for me & my success in coping is very limited. It is perhaps the main reason why I get on with people so badly.[72]

As the great introvert struggled to understand himself, the great extrovert was busy producing for hundreds of thousands of British troops what was well described as 'a miniature *Daily Mirror* in khaki.'[73] Starring the *Mirror's* favourite cartoon pin-up, Jane, whose contribu-tion to the war effort was to take off an unprecedented number of clothes, it was put together with the help of journalists and techni-cians pillaged from the services. At first thrice-weekly and later daily, the Constantine edition of *Union Jack* was joined by separate editions in Algiers and Tunis and, as the campaign progressed, papers were also produced in Sicily, Naples, Bari, Athens, Rome, Florence, Venice and Milan. As Cudlipp had envisaged, mobile self-contained news-paper units complete with Editor, editorial and technical staff, packers, administrators and radio operators leapfrogged forward. *Union Jack*, he wrote in 1947, 'has been "made-up" by compositors working with electricity, gas, candle-light, torch, blow-lamp and matches. It has been distributed to its customers by train, truck, APO, motor-cycle, tor-pedo-boat, submarine, mule-cart, Shanks's pony – and by gondola'[74] and, in southern France, by plane.

Cudlipp was determined to give the troops the kind of paper they wanted, which meant addressing sympathetically such issues as pay,

welfare facilities, demobilisation and post-war rehabilitation problems.[75] He took, for instance, as sympathetic a view of the Beveridge
Report as did King and Bart back home. His journalists included
Peter Wilson, the thriller-writer Hammond Innes and, from September
1943, Cassandra, now Captain W. Connor of the Royal Artillery, who
turned out to be an expert forger of army orders – a useful skill when
Cudlipp needed to get through US military police blockades to grab
space in yet another local newspaper office.

It was a life of occasional excitement, great periods of boredom,
much heavy drinking and marvellous camaraderie, exemplified in the
story of the cat. Connor and Wilson fell out over Catrina, a black
cat sharing their Naples apartment. Catrina was put on trial, with
Wilson prosecuting and Connor defending. The final speech for the
defence ended with an impassioned denunciation of those who – at
a time when humanity was 'locked in an ugly embrace' – would argue
about 'two penn'orth of catshit neatly deposited in the Neapolitan
bidet of a revolting Italian Fascist who has escaped to the hills until
all is safe for his return'. The decision rested with Cudlipp, who as
senior officer had presided over the trial: Catrina could stay, he ruled,
but she would henceforth be known as Latrina.[76]

There was no better companion than Cudlipp, but he was ruthless
about getting his way. Along with his charm and persuasiveness went
the guile that is a Welsh characteristic, and the toughness that was
reflected in a physical stance often likened to a boxer's:

> head forward and slightly down, tucked into his shoulders. The
> lower jaw juts forward pugnaciously, as though daring you to
> take a swipe at it. When he speaks, the words appear to be
> ground out through the partially-clenched teeth. The consonants
> slap you in the face. His hands (or are they fists?) holding the
> ever-present cigar are stabbed into the air to make the spoken
> point even more forceful, as though he were stubbing out the
> cigar on one of many aerial, invisible ashtrays hovering about
> him.[77]

The cooperation of newspaper proprietors in newly conquered towns
was won, Cudlipp recalled, 'pleasantly, as a rule, sometimes threaten-
ingly, but always successfully, decisively and quickly . . . a uniform

and a revolver on the belt worked wonders in speeding up negotiations', as did the sinister style Cudlipp had modelled on Tito Gobbi
playing Scarpia in *Tosca*. Afterwards – Cudlipp being Cudlipp – he
and the intimidated proprietors became 'of course, the best of
friends.'[78]

While Cudlipp printed the truth and took the side of the men
against authority, he trod carefully and aimed at raising morale. Yet
there were complaints about subversiveness in his and other army
newspapers, and in 1944, when the paper was championing the troops
over pay, Churchill (confusing Cudlipp with Cassandra) complained
that the Editor of *Union Jack* was the person who had written in the
Mirror with 'extreme malignancy'. The Secretary of State for War,
P. J. Grigg, sent a message to the Commander-in-Chief, Central
Mediterranean, telling him to keep Cudlipp under better control:
'Cudlipp is an extreme Leftist and though he behaved well while in
North Africa, in Italy he seems to show a tendency to use "Union
Jack" to stoke up grievances . . . keep your eye on Master Cudlipp.'[79]
Nonetheless, in April 1944 Cudlipp was put in charge of all news-
papers in the Mediterranean theatre and a major-general, despatched
to report on their editorial policy – while complaining of the 'generally unpleasant and cynical slant . . . given to the actions of
authority'[80] – acknowledged that they were widely read and well
regarded by the troops. Cudlipp was recognised as a rebel with whom
business could be done and, though he protested, he agreed to conform to official restrictions. Political restraints did not bother him.
'The war was being run by a Coalition government. Partisan politics
were suspended for the duration. Any editor who was tempted to use
official publications to politicise in favour of Right or Left would have
been instantly dismissed by me.'[81] He was to survive a Cabinet rebuke
for printing critical letters; an attack in Parliament; Churchill's private
query to Bracken as to whether it was 'really a fact that the only journalists who are any good are the malignant scum of the "Daily
Mirror"'; as well as a couple of local crises. His newspapers retained
the freedom to reflect the leftish-leaning instincts of the men who
were to bring Labour to power in the General Election of July 1945,
two months after the allied victory in Europe.

'"Union Jack" . . . seems a bright sheet . . .' wrote King to Cudlipp
in January 1944. 'It would seem to me that now is a good time for

you to come home. For two years you have been at or near the centre of gravity of our part of the war, but it would be a pity if you stayed on while this had ceased to be true.'[82] By September King was sounding desperate. 'The most important thing is for you to *get home*,' he wrote, predicting that the war would be over by Christmas. 'Come home as a lance-corporal, come home steerage, but come home. Rome just now is a back-water. Is there anything I can do this end to get you out of the Army? For God's sake don't go to the Far East unless you must. No one here takes the smallest interest in the Japs.'[83] ('Months spent in Africa, in Naples, Sicily and Rome can but have an educative influence on him,' King told Margot.[84])

By November there was still no Cudlipp, but King was positively cheerful. John Cowley had died and Bart had become Chairman of both the *Mirror* and the *Pictorial*. John Coope — an experienced newspaper executive, though a very recent addition to the *Mirror* board — was his deputy, but according to King, he 'fairly quickly ceased to be significant'.[85] There was no promotion for King, who knew that Bart would have fired him if he thought it possible to fire a Harmsworth. He remained Advertising Director of the group and Editorial Director of the *Pictorial*, but his spirits were raised by the change.[*]

Despite Bart's notorious deficiencies, he was a considerable improvement on Cowley. 'His is an unusual and forceful personality,' wrote a tactful anonymous correspondent in a trade paper. 'In it he combines the sensitivities of an artistic imagination, an inventive genius, with a shrewd far-seeing organising and business capacity and judgment . . . It does not take anyone long to discover his quick-thinking capacity and ability, and his inexhaustible drive and unflagging energy and vitality in the pursuit and achievement of success in enterprise.'[87]

---

[*] They cannot have been uplifted by a letter to Margot from Francis: 'I see Cowley has popped off. I sincerely hope that Dad will take his place as the consummation of his worthy career in Fleet Street, but at the same time I hope that he finally leaves the whole business . . . I must say I admire Dad's gumption in carrying the job through to the disapproval of many, but I do think it is time he forsook the whole blinking show. It has taken the best out of Dad, and I hope Dad won't let it take the relics, which I am sure could produce results . . . in another sphere . . . I do want to see Dad free from all the troubles of this world, it has already given him a pessimistic view on life, and God only knows what it'll do if he sticks it much longer.'[86]

'The situation, as far as the Sunday Pic is concerned, remains the same as before,' wrote King to Cudlipp. 'One thing is very certain about the new set-up, and that is that we are all going places!'[88] In February 1945 he reported that:

> the office has been slowly stirring in its sleep . . . We have been discussing various post-war developments in the way of new publications, and under the new regime you figure very much more prominently.
>
> My own position is very different – I have to protest loud and often that I can't do everything and that we must look out some new young directors as soon as demobilisation allows it . . .
>
> As time goes on it seems to me more and more necessary that you should try and get back here . . . We shall want you as soon as we can get you . . .

Much though Bart hated King, he recognised his energy and ability and, to King's delight, just before the end of the war, he was despatched to North and South America to begin the project of securing world-wide syndication for strips, pictures and features from the *Mirror* and *Pictorial*. On an overcrowded troopship largely occupied by Canadian soldiers' British wives ('a sorry lot'), he shared a small cabin with three journalists.

King always got on far better with travelling companions than with colleagues at home, because new experiences gave him something to talk about and his sheer interest in his surroundings was infectious. On board ship, despite cramped conditions and two unsuccessful submarine attacks, he reported 'not much sleep but quite an amusing time'[89] and was delighted with a *News Chronicle* journalist called Philip Jordan, 'who was the life and soul of the party, making me roar with laughter at seven a.m., a feat which I should have thought impossible. He had a wonderful story about going over the Yildiz Kiosk in Constantinople immediately after it had been occupied by Allied forces in 1918. What struck him most was a glass chute down which concubines reached the Sultan's quarters.'[90] Instead of the lugubrious letters he normally penned to her from London, King was writing to Margot about, for instance, being fascinated by the speed and scope of life in New York – 'entranced by the clothes and flower shops and amused by the superstition which prevents any semi-skyscraper having a 13th floor',[91] – from Rio full of joy at 'this beautiful place where we were together once',[92] or from Panama luxuriating in the flame trees, hibiscus, bougainvillea and bread-trees. In a gesture that was very typical of his attempts to be kind to Margot (a prison visitor so well regarded that she had become Chairman of the association of English women prison visitors)[93], he visited and reported on a women's prison in New York, the Women's House of Correction in Buenos Aires (where he thought the nuns so imbued with the love of God that he left in tears[94]) and the Chicago County Jail (where he 'refused to see the electric chair or the death cell . . . I was so appalled by the spirit of the whole place I cannot write coherently about it. It was a negation of any belief in the dignity of human nature'[95]).

To Bart he wrote regularly with detailed accounts of whom he had seen, what he had learned and which deals he recommended. There were constant problems with the sought-after Jane strip. Could it be successfully translated into Spanish? How would the *Mirror* retain editorial control? How to deal with censorship? In Buenos Aires, for instance, the proprietor of the principal English paper 'says that she would go well but must not actually show a nipple. Other authorities say that the muffling up process would have to go further than this.'[96] When he was not on long, often uncomfortable journeys, King frequently had meetings from 10 a.m. to 1.30 a.m. – a horrifying schedule for a man who so needed his sleep. He met all the newspaper people he could, visited advertising agencies and called on radio tycoons, advertising people, diplomats and anyone else who might have light to cast on marketing opportunities and the present or future of the press worldwide. No one reading his thoughtful, acute, wise and hugely informative letters could have doubted that here was someone with the ability to be a formidable businessman. Even Bart was moved to compliments. 'Cecil I think has done very well,' he wrote to Margot. . . . 'The work he had to do has been well accomplished, and the information on other matters vital to this industry from his detailed letters is enormous. The trip has been a great success.'[97]

King wrote seldom to Bart of politics, though he communicated from Texas the depressing news of 'the *immense* popularity of Churchill. All the way from Canada to Patagonia he is the tops – far more so than any other figure in the world. We all know that this popularity is largely based on illusion, but it is an important fact that the illusion is so strongly *felt* & widely spread in this continent.'[98] He did not write to the Editor of the *Pictorial*: 'I do not intend to write to Campbell,' he told Bart, 'so that you will be able to see what he does when entirely on his own.'[99] Whatever Bart's views on Campbell, on his return after almost three months away King was unimpressed. On 11 July 1945, Stuart Campbell wrote to Bart that he had no alternative but to resign:

> as the position between myself and Mr King has become intolerable. Within two days of his return he has begun a campaign of interference and studied insults that is beyond endurance.
>
> At no time during my five years in charge of the paper can I pretend that our relationship has been of the happiest. This applies not only to myself but to the staff, who during that time have also had to submit to being humiliated by him. Even so, I have tried to keep things on an even keel, accepting it as the wish of the directors that I should work under him, although on several occasions his interference has actually imperilled the production of the paper itself.
>
> His latest display of arrogance and ill manners has gone beyond that however. Having disliked the re-arrangement of our rooms carried out in his absence . . . he told me yesterday that he was having me moved into the room next to himself.
>
> I demurred, suggesting that it was at least a matter that we ought to discuss. He then said: –
>
> 'I have no intention of discussing it with you. If you were putting an office-boy into a room you would not discuss it with him so that he could argue with you as to whether he liked it or not.'
>
> At this point I told him I had no intention of being his office-boy. Neither have I.[100]

The need to retrieve Cudlipp from the army was now even more acute.

CHAPTER VII

Bart's Revenge

THERE WAS SERIOUS COMPETITION IN FLEET STREET FOR CUDLIPP'S services. King's cousin Esmond Harmsworth, now Lord Rothermere, wanted him to become Editor of the *Daily Mail*; Lord Beaverbrook wanted him for the *Express*. On hearing from Cudlipp that he felt morally obliged to return to the *Mirror* group, because – as with other staff – it had supplemented his service pay with a proportion of his civilian salary, Rothermere asked him to compute exactly what he had been paid so that he could send the *Mirror* a cheque. Cudlipp found Rothermere unnervingly like King and decided against 'swimming from one icy cold bloody goldfish bowl into another: I'd rather the cold fish I knew than the cold fish I didn't'[1].

Acting as Beaverbrook's emissary, Arthur Christiansen, Editor of the *Daily Express* (who was on 'My dear Hugh' terms), was much warmer, begging Cudlipp 'not to enter into any firm commitments and not to make up your mind positively about your future, until we have had an opportunity to talk'[2]. Yet, though he still deeply distrusted Bart, Cudlipp decided in May 1946 to return to the *Pictorial* and to King, who had faithfully informed and consulted him with such regularity throughout his five-and-a-half years in the army: 'All our plans are held up at the moment for lack of paper,' King had written in March:

the syndication idea and the possibility of acquiring a site for
a new building being the only developments just now.
  I cannot find any two opinions about the need for a shake-up

on the 'Pic', but everything is being left unaltered until your return. The worst fault in the paper is generally felt to be a lack of sincerity which is in strong contrast to the 'Daily Mirror' . . . so much that appears in the 'Pic' has 'phoney' written all over it . . . I shall be so glad to welcome you on your return.[3]

Of course it was not just that the *Pictorial* was Cudlipp's baby and that he was happy working with King; it was also that his politics and his approach to journalism fitted perfectly with the *Mirror* group. Lieutenant-Colonel Cudlipp, OBE, might be comfortable with the highest of high society, and he certainly had a taste for good and riotous living, but his irreverence and his passion for improving the lot of the common man remained as intense as ever.

The *Mirror* – 'the paper of armies without political commissars, of fighting men innocent of ideologies'[4] – had been free to push the radical message that Cudlipp's army newspapers could sell only obliquely. In the run-up to the July 1945 election, women had been urged to 'VOTE FOR HIM!' – the husband, son, brother or sweetheart in the forces whose proxy they held, or who was unable to vote because the electoral register was out of date. 'VOTE FOR THEM!' the whole electorate was urged: 'The man who would fill that chair in your home. The mate you miss at work. The pal you liked to meet in the pub.' On 5 July, the day of the election, under the headline 'DON'T LOSE IT AGAIN', Philip Zec's VE-Day cartoon was reproduced: showing a wounded soldier holding out a laurel with the label 'Victory and Peace in Europe', it had the caption, 'Here you are – don't lose it again!' This time, the *Mirror* told its readers, the 'land fit for heroes' – promised in 1918, but not delivered – must be brought into being. And while it did not specifically back Labour, the thrust of its whole coverage was that, though a hero, Churchill had a deadbeat party that would lead peacetime Britain backwards, while Labour would deliver to the people jobs, houses, health and security.

By common consent, the *Mirror* campaign had been far more influential than those of any other newspapers of the left or right. It had, however, the advantage of being in tune with public opinion: as Cudlipp always pointed out, a newspaper can help accelerate or deepen a trend, but it cannot buck it. 'We are still thrilled by the election results, to which the *Mirror* and the *Pic* are believed to have contributed a great deal,' King wrote to Priscilla. 'Just now the prestige of our two papers is sky high.'[5]

The thirty-two-year-old Cudlipp would have been an ideal editor for a paper whose motto was 'Forward with the people', and 42 per cent of whose readership was under thirty-five. But he knew there was no possibility that Bart would let him near the *Mirror*; indeed, it was only because the law obliged employees returning from the services to be reinstated that Cudlipp was even able to get back to the *Pictorial*. Within a few weeks Stuart Campbell, now reverted to Deputy Editor, had left to become Managing Editor of *The People*. 'Now the old team-mates were opposed in a neck-and-neck race to reach a 5,000,000 sale,' recalled Cudlipp. 'The position at the starting post was: *The People*, 4,767,000; *Pictorial*, 3,400,000.'[6] Despite his head-start, Campbell was to win only by a whisker.

Because of paper-rationing, Cudlipp's fiefdom consisted of just twelve tabloid pages weekly: 'After we had accommodated sport, pictures, show business and all the other furniture, plus news, there wasn't much room for manoeuvre, for much personal impact . . . But there was the precious *rapport* with the readers, the link with the "ordinary"people of the day which Stuart Campbell . . . had preserved.'[7]

While Campbell took *The People* down the path of exposures and true confessions, Cudlipp followed his crusading instincts with the *Pictorial* and specialised in controversies about issues that affected the lives of readers struggling with austerity, rationing and other postwar problems. Its newly appointed Vigilance Council, chaired by a war correspondent, looked for justice on such issues as army pensioners and marriages wrecked by the war. The *Pictorial* selected 'on a scientific basis' a proto focus group – One Hundred Families to Speak for Britain – to be consulted 'on the problems that were making their lives less joyful than they need be because the Labour Government was loath to jettison the easy social justice of rationing.'[8] Their first outing revealed that 43 per cent were waiting for a new home and they were all short of fats, tea and clothing. The One Hundred Families were consulted too before the *Pictorial* took the daring step of publishing Grantly Dick Read's *How a Baby is Born*.

Politically, Cudlipp still listened carefully to King's reflections on global history and politics, took seriously his comments and suggestions on the content of the *Pictorial* and acted as a common-sense

filter for his mentor's madder and bleaker assessments and predictions. For though there was no faulting King's intellectual grasp of
the problems facing the world, his pessimism and his contempt for
those in power distorted his analyses. Towards the end of the war, for
instance, though he had a far better understanding than most of his
countrymen of the imperial ambitions of the Soviet Union, his detes-
tation of the United States coloured his judgement: 'I cannot help
feeling that the continental history books will regard England as
Europe's quisling . . .' he wrote in August 1944. 'It was we who let
the American barbarian in & contributed to the intrusion of the
Russians.' The only salvation, he believed, was for Britain to take the
lead in setting up a western European confederacy; and his diary
records his frustration at the unpopularity of such ideas among the
people with whom he discussed politics and whom he thought absurdly
hostile to Germany because of stories of atrocities that he himself
refused to believe.* Even after the war, when there was no longer any
doubt about the horrors committed by the Nazis and the Japanese,
in his diaries, King's rage was directed at America over Hiroshima,
and at Britain over the bombing of civilians. Post-war Europe, he predicted, would collapse into anarchy and civil war, and in Britain the
clash between extreme left and extreme right would probably end in
a fascist military dictatorship.

Cudlipp had no such fears domestically, being not only an optimist, but a believer in the innate moderation and decency of the
British people and their tendency to muddle through: though he was
still a reformer, the war had tempered some of his youthful anger.
One of his key strengths as an editor was his respect for his readers.
He believed that if only the language and the thinking were clear
enough, it was possible to explain the essence of complicated subjects like economics and industry.

A classic example of the fusion of his and King's gifts was the issue

---

* 'After the last war a high proportion of the atrocity stories were found to be lies, & in
any case atrocities were by no means confined to our enemies. Whether German behaviour has really been bad this time, only time will show, but it is hard to swallow stories of 10,000 Polish Jews being murdered per day or per week, when at the same time
the same papers publish stories of the growing German embarrassment from lack of
manpower'.[9]

of August 1947, which screamed 'INTO BATTLE' and gave 'THE TRUTH ABOUT THE CRISIS'. A thoughtful, dense and detailed memorandum by King on the dollar crisis, full of suggestions for cuts, rationing and restrictions that would have had the One Hundred Families predicting riots, was transformed by Cudlipp into a crisp account of Britain's economic problems and a robust call for national unity. Where King's instincts were authoritarian, Cudlipp's were populist.

This was 'Britain's Last Chance', thundered the *Pictorial*: the American loan was almost exhausted; the Marshall Plan was still a year away and could not deal with any fundamental British economic problems; exports needed to be raised by £9 million a week; coal was being mined too slowly; and the manpower shortage was being exacerbated by union opposition to foreign workers. Further, since Attlee was not an inspirational leader, Bevin should leave the Foreign Office and take on 'the even greater task of stepping up production and stiffening industrial morale throughout the country':

> One thing is clear. The outcome of this struggle will rest – as always – with the people. They have shown time and time again that they respond more generously to straight statements of fact, however unpleasant, and to sympathetic leadership than to parrot-like exhortations on the 'work or want' theme. They know that only by their own sweat can Britain be restored to health.
>
> The cry is INTO BATTLE! Our industrial troops are ready for the great assault. Let us have a leader who can get up there IN FRONT.[10]

The controversies of Cudlipp's post-war *Pictorial* career that he recalled as most striking concerned, first, Hermann Goering and, second, the Church of England. On 15 October 1946, two hours before he was to be hanged for war crimes, Goering poisoned himself. Rumours abounded that he had been spared because the Allies feared a German backlash, yet the government, which had decided against circulating photographs of executed Nazis, made no exception for the suicide. Cudlipp broke ranks with the press and published a picture of the dead Goering in the *Pictorial*.[11] 'I have no control over the Press in these times' was Attlee's helpless explanation in the Commons. Cudlipp – who at the request of the British government had published in army newspapers photographs of piles of bodies at Belsen – was unabashed by the uproar. 'I saw every reason to publish in the *Sunday Pictorial* the irrefutable evidence that one at least of the perpetrators of genocide was no longer a member of the human race. I recall no protests from our readers.'[12]

A year or so later Cudlipp was intrigued by a book by the Bishop of Birmingham asking questions that reminded him of his heretical questionings at Sunday school in Cardiff. 'Had the tempest been stilled? Was it conceivable that Lazarus was raised from the dead? And was the miracle of the loaves and fishes a likely story?' After the third instalment was published in the *Pictorial*, the Archbishop of Canterbury sent his private chaplain to meet Cudlipp. 'His speech was measured, his demeanour grave, and the tone was Stage Ecclesiastical.'[13] Rattled because dissenting notions were being serialised in a popular paper, the Archbishop, it emerged, would like the *Pictorial* to publish a rebuttal by another bishop. 'I am also bidden to say,' said Prebendary Eley, 'that his Grace will be content if you, as Editor, freely choose that bishop yourself.' So Cudlipp chose Bishop Blunt of Bradford, whose comments on King Edward VIII twelve years earlier had led to the *Mirror* breaking the story about Mrs Simpson and had made him notorious.

'The consequence . . . was that the sensational *Sunday Pictorial* became for three or four weeks the pulpit from which, officially, the Church of England restated to the multitude its attitude to the miraculous and supernatural elements in the Christian faith.' Dr Barnes, Cudlipp noted with interest, refused a fee 'for exposing the Miracles', while Dr Blunt 'expected and received a fat fee for refurbishing the ancient legends on the order of his Archbishop. God moves in a mysterious way his wonders to perform.'[14]

The royal family were turned into circulation-boosters too: 'the *Pictorial* never hesitated to join the advisers at Buckingham Palace. It was more than light-hearted impudence, it was a reflection of the new healthy public mood of questioning authority, especially the Establishment.'[15] Yet there was never any trace of republicanism in Cudlipp's socialism, any more than there was puritanism. Announcing the likelihood of an engagement between Princess Elizabeth and Prince Philip of Greece, at a time when there was concern about the political implications of such a strong link between British and Greek royalty, the *Pictorial* polled its readership, which predictably heavily favoured love over politics. And the paper defended the world tour of the King and Queen against criticisms of extravagance.

As the circulation zoomed, Cudlipp was at a particularly happy time in his life. He had a job he adored; most of his friends were back from the war; he was sufficiently prosperous to be able to subsidise some close relatives, as well as eat, drink and enjoy himself as much as post-war London permitted; and he had what he later described as 'a joyous relationship'[16] with Eileen Ascroft, whom he had married in the autumn of 1945[17] not long after her divorce; and he was a kind stepfather to her young son, Kerry. Like Bunny Parnell, Cudlipp's first wife, Eileen was a dedicated journalist, which was rather odd in view of Cudlipp's unrepentant male chauvinism. He liked and loved women, particularly if they were pretty, sexy, bright and fun. He enjoyed looking at them, flirting with them, laughing with them, entertaining them and making love to them, but he had not the faintest sympathy with feminism of any kind. In his Charles Wilberforce persona, he wrote in 1939 apropos 'The New Woman' that:

the young woman of to-day still talks a certain amount of drivel about her career, but she'd soon forget all about it if a man worth marrying proposed to her . . . if the New Man of the New Britain is virile and courageous, the New Woman wants to be nothing more than the sort of mate he deserves.

Back to the home.

That is where the modern woman wants to go.

She will deny it until she is blue in the gills, but she wants to go back there just the same. With her cooking, and her sewing, and her man, and her baby.

As men regained their masculinity, exulted Wilberforce, women were rediscovering their femininity: 'The stylish Eton crops and closely-clipped bobs of the early nineteen-twenties are the hideous freaks of 1939. This is the age of curls and silken strands. Instead of severely-cut "tailor-mades" – petticoat dresses, frills and furbelows are "in" once more. And I should not omit the important physiological fact that women are wearing busts and waists again. (Thank the Lord!)'[18]

Of course, it was important for propaganda reasons in 1939 to promise men that virility and courage would earn them feminine,

admiring helpmeets, but Cudlipp meant it and King agreed with him.
In May 1940, King records a conversation in which Cudlipp remarked
that:

> the tendency is for women to be attracted by the ruthless effi-
> ciency of the Germans & their war-machine. This might become
> a decisive factor at a later stage. I said I thought the fact that
> since the start of the war there had been an enormous increase
> in trouser-wearing by women was due to the fact that English
> men do not seem to be doing their job, so the women take to
> wearing the pants, both literally & figuratively (though of course
> not conscious of their motives in the matter).[19]

Trouser-wearing worried King: 'a sign of the homosexuality of our
times,' he wrote in his diary in 1943; 'in Priscilla's school of 250
boarders, they all have pyjamas except for herself and one other girl
. . . The reason given is that pyjamas are warmer, but this cannot be
the real reason as houses are warmer than they used to be.'[20] And
towards the end of the war he and Margot agreed that the biggest
social change since 1939 had been the position of women. 'Everywhere
one sees women either in slacks or with bare legs. Smoking in the
street by women is general, and we are both struck by the way women
are determined to claim in every way the same freedom as men. It is
all done rather unintelligently and women are unlikely to gain by the
new attitude. But there it is, that is what they want and that is what
they mean to have.'[21]

To Bart's simmering resentment, the King/Cudlipp relationship
continued harmoniously and successfully. They even progressed to
using first names.*

Though under his chairmanship the *Mirror* group prospered, Bart
hated his two rising stars, avoided them as much as possible and bit-

---

* Cudlipp explained the process later: 'Because of public school surname protocol, which
is silly, and Harmsworth hauteur, even sillier, the transition from "Cudlipp" to "Hugh"
was a tedious process, and from "King" to "Cecil" took longer. It was like a *pas de deux*
performed on cracking ice even when we had known and not disliked each other for
more than a decade. Why did one care or try? The answer is that a friendship with
Cecil King, however tenuous, is a rewarding experience.'[22]

terly resented the *Pictorial*'s success. 'The suspicious side glance and the brusque remark,' observed Cudlipp, 'were his contributions to the working partnership; it was a coalition of dissent.'[23]

Bart cannot have been happy that King was more and more being spoken of in the newspaper industry as a rising man. 'Modern Northcliffe?' asked a gossip columnist in the *Daily Worker* in 1947, describing King in exaggerated terms as 'the principal financial and political force at the *Mirror* and *Pictorial*'.[24] Yet he was undoubtedly a key figure in the group's expansion, about which he felt more and more proprietorial. 'The Sunday Pic put on 75,000 last week!' he wrote to Priscilla in April 1948. 'It is all rather entertaining. I can remember Northcliffe's thrill when the Daily Mail first touched 1,000,000 & now the Mirror will soon reach 4,000,000.'[25] With savage newsprint rationing and high taxes on profits at home, it made sense to invest heavily in foreign newspapers written in English, so Bart needed to give King quite a lot of scope abroad – which had the pleasing consequence for both of keeping him out of the office for a few months of every year.

In the autumn of 1946, for instance, Bart had despatched King to Bombay on a mission that soon proved impossible, but he stayed on to look at syndicating and investment opportunities in the newspaper industry. With India in political turmoil as its future was being determined, there was little business to be done – but curious to see a country where so many members of his family had served, King stayed as long as possible and visited Delhi, Agra, Benares and Calcutta. But though he loved the Taj Mahal and other great Mogul monuments India mostly depressed him. His search for the spiritual essence of Hinduism in Benares caused only gloom: 'the cremations by the water-side, the hordes of crippled beggars, the crows picking at corpses . . . have a depressing effect that even the fervour of the crowds cannot dispel.'[26]

'I should love to have you with me but I don't think you would like it,' he wrote from Calcutta to Margot. 'At the moment I am in . . . a horrid hotel full of vile people in the most horrible city I have ever been in – added to which there is acute communal tension with the usual paraphernalia of armoured cars, soldiers with fixed bayonets at street corners etc., etc. India in any case is a sea of poverty that I cannot get used to. I think your heart would just bleed from the day you arrived to the day you left.'[27]

Still, for King there was more to India than business and scenery. He no longer travelled like an advertising director of a minor newspaper company. The Labour government was well aware of the importance of the *Mirror* and the *Pictorial*, and King was equipped with introductions to the key political players from Stafford Cripps – to whom he was quite close – and Frederick Pethick Lawrence, the two Labour politicians most closely involved in independence negotiations. He met Mahatma Gandhi ('a very unimpressive man to meet, small, ugly and insignificant . . . he must be one of the half-dozen greatest men of my lifetime, but I could not see it or feel it'[28]); two future Prime Ministers of India, Nehru ('rather disappointing'[29]) and his daughter Indira; Jinnah, the future Prime Minister of Pakistan ('most unattractive and a man of immense personal ambition'[30]); and Lord Wavell, the Viceroy ('a charming Colonel Blimp'[31]).

On his way home, in Australia on syndicating business, he met Ben Chifley, the Prime Minister, stayed on a sheep farm for a weekend, fell in love with the countryside and marvelled at 'the gigantic chip Australians carried on their shoulders'.[32] (Writing to Priscilla a year later from Montreal, where he was with Margot, he described Canada 'as an entirely uncultured country – better than Australia, but worse than the U.S. – if you can believe that!'[33])

King was followed to Australia in 1948 by Cudlipp, in very different circumstances. When Bart decided to try to buy from Ezra Norton that year the lurid Australian Sunday paper, *Truth*, and the Sydney *Daily Mirror*, along with James Cooke (the Financial Director), he took Cudlipp. For Bart, putting Cudlipp in charge of Australian papers would have been both a clever commercial decision and a brilliant way of getting rid of someone he hated:

> It was a Bartian mission in the classical style, conducted in an atmosphere of extravagant secrecy with false names and coded cables. Cooke and I were instructed to call him 'Guy' during the 12,000-mile journey to Sydney in a Sunderland flying boat. And all I saw of Australia on that visit was the four walls of a bedroom because Bart insisted on appearing to be alone and conducting the talks with Norton on his own. Cooke and I were not to be 'seen'.[34]

Since, according to Cudlipp, Bart was one of the world's worst negotiators and Cooke one of the best, this was a poor move.

Cudlipp was reduced to spending most of his time in Australia reading newspapers, magazines and books about the country and listening to the radio. He was as amazed as King at its chippiness, but much taken by its energy and virility. By the time the deal fell through and he left the country, having seen nothing and met no Australians, he had – fortunately as it was to turn out – 'formed the view in my dungeon that if I were to be left behind as a hostage it would not be an intolerable sacrifice'.[35]

It was in that same year that King fell in love with Africa and Africans. The *Mirror* group had acquired from their British owners the *Nigerian Daily Times* and a couple of tiny offshoots in December 1947 and, after a brief visit to Lagos early in 1948 (when he stayed with Hugh Foot, the Chief Secretary), on his return home King was made Deputy Chairman of the West African operation and left to run it as he thought fit. Although he knew Bart saw this as a further opportunity to keep him well away from Geraldine House, King was delighted. The *Daily Times* – as it was renamed – had a circulation of only 6,000 and was badly printed, but King was convinced that it had a great future and he was happy with the people he worked with. 'I think you would *love* this place & the people,' he wrote to Margot from Lagos, ' – they are so human & so sweet to the innumerable babies.'[36] 'Africans,' he wrote later, 'have immense vitality. They are warmer, more emotional, more telepathic, more personal than Englishmen.'[37] These, of course, were qualities that made Africans ideally suited to breaking down the reserve of Cecil King and, from the beginning, they appreciated him because he genuinely liked them, wanted to give them the opportunities to run the papers he controlled and was firmly in favour of African self-government. He loved entertaining Africans in London, too. His chauffeur recalled driving along Oxford Street when King suddenly shouted, 'Stop the car'. Thinking it was an emergency, he jammed his foot on the brake, King leaped out and rushed over to an enormous African in full tribal dress, embraced him warmly and arrived back and filled the car with him and his wives and assorted others.[38]

Whereas at home *Mirror* newspapers catered for the least educated, in Africa they were directed at the élite. Most local papers were intensely partisan, which King believed to be wholly inappropriate for a foreign newspaper, so he decided the *Daily Times* should concentrate on local news and sport and anything else that interested its readers. He turned it into a tabloid, provided the paper with modern machinery and cracked the distribution problem by setting up a bus service that carried papers, passengers and freight and – unlike the erratic opposition – delivered the papers to the main centres of population by 6 a.m. Painted yellow, with the *Daily Times* in red, like all West African buses these were covered with exhortations of various kinds. 'One of the *Daily Times* buses is remembered to this day by old White West-Coasters,' wrote an historian of the African press in 1979, 'as bearing the yellow and red legend "The Lord is King" – and there was many a tight-lipped British civil servant of the day who felt that the sign-writer had got the message round the wrong way.'[39]

It was King and Africa that were to give Bart his opportunity to take revenge on Cudlipp, whose success in keeping the *Pictorial* circulation ahead of the *Mirror* was a constant irritant. On 18 November 1949, Cudlipp was in London happily editing the *Pictorial*, whose circulation had now reached the coveted five million figure. King was in Enugu, in eastern Nigeria, when he happened on a story: a mining strike had led to a riot and the shooting of twenty-six miners. King pieced together the facts in dangerous circumstances ('I had a very nasty day or two,' he told Francis[40]), with great difficulty had the cable office opened and got a cable to the *Pictorial* by 10 p.m. Cudlipp, he wrote in his memoirs, 'for reasons never explained spiked the story'.[41]

Cudlipp's reasons were straightforward enough, but would have been embarrassing to explain to King. Unlike Christiansen of the *Express*, 'the patron saint of urgency',[42] Cudlipp was interested in being first with news only if the news was of interest to the Sheffield bus-driver's wife. 'On that particular Saturday night we were publishing a spectacular issue . . . and were running late. Nigeria, as Neville Chamberlain said of Czechoslovakia, was a country far away and Enugu was not close to our readers' hearts or to mine . . . It wouldn't have sold a copy and nobody knew that better than Bart.'[43] So – as he later told Dick Crossman, the journalist and Labour backbencher – he said, 'Another bloody message from Cecil. Spike it.'[44] But Cudlipp was paying insufficient attention to office politics and to Bart's longing for revenge.

The story ran in Monday's papers, Bart found out about King's cable and 'enjoyed himself for a few days sharpening the axe and awaiting the return of King from Nigeria. Christmas was coming and there were few things which appealed to him more than a pre-Christmas firing squad.' 'Although I have made up my mind how to deal with Cudlipp's ghastly blunder,' Bart wrote to King on his return, 'I have postponed action until I have had the opportunity of informing you personally. I feel, therefore, that it would be unwise for you to have any discussion on the matter until we have met.'[45] Action was then swift. 'The final Bartholomew–Cudlipp clash has come,' was how Cudlipp put it to a Canadian friend, 'and I no longer work at Geraldine House. The field-marshal has hanged his general.'[46]

Cudlipp was hugely popular with his staff, who were outraged. He had to dissuade his Assistant Editor from walking out with him and was thrilled when the next edition of the *Pictorial* carried a paragraph reporting that he had resigned his editorship and directorship of the paper, adding, 'His colleagues and associates wish him well in his new appointment.' This was so unprecedented in the newspaper world that he was amazed that Bart let it happen, concluding at last that though Bart 'revelled in acts of ruthlessness . . . when the deeds were done he was contrite, often to a maudlin degree'.[47]

Did King fight for him? wondered Cudlipp later, though 'Bart wouldn't have listened to him anyway'.[48] Crossman was told that King had 'pleaded for Cudlipp, unavailingly'.[49] Yet much though King must have regretted losing his *wunderkind*, he showed little emotion and, indeed, the reference in his memoirs to losing his 'one bid for a world scoop' suggested a lingering resentment. 'When I see you I will tell you in detail Mr King's remarks to me,' reported Cudlipp's secretary elliptically. 'No doubt they will not surprise you. Incidentally, when I told Mr Cooke I was not accepting Mr King's offer to be his secretary he said: "Do you mind if I tell Mr Bartholomew that?" And then, quickly, "I think he will appreciate your attitude."'[50]

It was perhaps because he regarded disloyalty as a cardinal sin that the normally resilient Cudlipp was so devastated: in his light-hearted memoirs, written nearly thirty years later, the hurt was still palpable. Even though a telephone call to Christiansen of the *Express*, who immediately phoned Beaverbrook in Jamaica, secured him a job within two hours, his feelings of grief and humiliation were still intense. King wrote regretting 'that we shall be working together no more. Latterly we have seen less of each other, but we had a lot of fun one way & another & I am very sorry it is all over. I hope you will be happier in your new job than latterly you were at Geraldine House, & that we may still foregather from time to time.'[51] This elicited what, for Cudlipp, was a very bitter response:

> There is nothing I can say about Bartholomew's appalling behaviour that hasn't already been said by almost everybody who matters in Fleet Street. I have never had such a fan mail, and I doubt if any other has. This at least was some comfort.
>
> Bartholomew fires me with all the subtlety accorded to a tenth-rate sub-editor who turns up late on the first morning of a month's trial. And then I get this cable from the proprietor of a firm for which I have never previously worked:
>
> 'MILLAR DAILY EXPRESS LONDON FOR HUGH CUDLIPP. IT IS WITH ENTHUSIASM THAT I WELCOME YOU TO OUR HOUSE WHERE YOU WILL BE HAPPY AND CONTENTED STOP I HAVE SOUGHT YOUR COMPANIONSHIP FOR LONG. BEAVERBROOK.'
>
> Had the Express offer not been forthcoming – and there was no reason to anticipate their welcome after I had so completely identified myself with tabloid journalism – I would have found myself in the position of having to finance my family and maintain my present obligations on £500* for the six months period until the compensation payment [of £11,000[52]] is handed to me after the annual general meeting in June, 1950. And even this £500 I would have normally received in February for my functions on the board.
>
> However, now that there is only one cockerel in the barnyard I suppose Bart's hens on the 'Mirror' will all know even more clearly when, and how often, and to whom to lift up their skirts.
>
> We have, as you say, had a great deal of fun with the 'Pictorial' together – and we *did* pass the 'People.' Perhaps we could meet

---

* About £10,000 today.

in the New Year when the dust has settled.

Yours very sincerely,

Hugh[53]

Among those commiserating with Cudlipp was Cecil Thomas, chief hen on the *Daily Mirror* for fifteen years. Writing in a letter of his shock and disgust, he added that 'Bart has done himself no good at all, as last Sunday's issue showed pretty clearly. He has so few there of real calibre, that he simply cannot afford to lose talents like yours.'[54] Certainly the appointment of a reluctant Editor, the cartoonist Philip Zec, as Cudlipp's successor did not augur well for the *Pictorial's* future.

Cudlipp made no effort to see King again, for he was not pleased when it was reported to him that King had commented, 'Well, of course, Hugh had to be taught a lesson.'[55] He knew enough from Fleet Street gossip to have no illusions about his new employer, but he was grateful, curious and anxious to learn. Believing Beaverbrook to be 'the greatest operator since Northcliffe at work and play', he had no fears about his ability to get on with him; Cudlipp was independent-minded, but there was no more accomplished courtier.

The charming, manipulative and unscrupulous Max Aitken had made a fortune in his native Canada before moving to London in 1910. By 1916, at thirty-seven, he was an MP, a knight and proprietor of the *Daily Express* and had been much involved in the machinations that brought down Asquith ('backstairs intrigues' was King's lofty assessment) and had been rewarded with a peerage. In the First World War he was briefly Minister for Information and then Chancellor of the Duchy of Lancaster until he fell out with Lloyd George in 1918. In the Second he was Minister of Aircraft Production, Minister of Supply, Minister of War Production, Special Envoy to the United States on Supplies and finally Lord Privy Seal under his great friend, Churchill.

If not quite Northcliffean in his genius, the buccaneering, populist Beaverbrook was immensely successful and, though never nominally editor of any of his papers, he directed them day-by-day – often hour-by-hour – bombarding his editors with telephone calls and mem-oranda crammed with criticisms, ideas, difficult questions, gossip and fun. By such means he took the *Daily Express* from a circulation of 300,000 to more than four million in 1950, and the London *Evening*

Standard (which he bought in 1923) along with the *Sunday Express* (which he founded in 1918) helped to make him another fortune. In Cudlipp's view, it was his ferocious energy and his inquiring mind that made Beaverbrook 'the supreme journalist'.[56] He also understood that post-war Britain was fed up with the austerity, drabness and joylessness offered by its Labour government.

There was never a moment's doubt about who was boss. Cudlipp's wife, Eileen, women's editor at the *Standard*, had been trying for months to persuade her Editor, Percy Elland, to introduce a women's page. After mentioning the idea to Beaverbrook, he instructed her to call on the Editor at 3 p.m. the following day. Unannounced, Beaverbrook arrived five minutes later, shook hands, sat down and told them to go on with their conference. 'Miss Ascroft explained that she was just about to raise with Mr Elland the notion of a daily woman's page', whereupon Beaverbrook stood up, shook hands with both of them again, 'said "Do it" and walked out. "It seems," said Elland with a smile, "that we're doing it."'[57]

Like Northcliffe, Beaverbrook used his newspapers ruthlessly in support of his own causes, which in Beaverbrook's case were often lost. He backed Edward VIII over Mrs Simpson, for instance, as well as the appeasement of Germany and subsequently of the Soviet Union – though there was no denying his patriotism. 'He has no political sense at all,' wrote his friend A. J. P. Taylor of him in 1960 in a letter to King, '. . . It is not so much a case of Power without Responsibility as Power without Sense, Power operating in the void.'[58]

Cudlipp swiftly grasped how policy was made:

The Editors of the *Daily Express*, the *Sunday Express*, the London *Evening Standard* and the Glasgow *Citizen* enjoyed absolute freedom to agree wholeheartedly with their master's voice. They were enti-tled to take the view, untrammelled, that Empire Free Trade was the solution to Britain's problems (which it wasn't), that the tra-ditions of the British Empire were inviolable and immortal (which they weren't), that British troops should leave Germany (which would have been disastrous), that the activities of the British Council abroad were a wanton waste of public money.[59]

So politically he and Cudlipp had little in common, but that did not bother Beaverbrook, who adored the company of the gifted and amusing young, and was a close and generous friend to such members of the far left as Aneurin Bevan and their mutual protégé, the journalist Michael Foot: an understood rule on the papers was that Bevan could 'be chided . . . but not savaged'. Lord Mountbatten, on the other hand, 'could be savaged but not chided',[60] for he was one of the victims of Beaverbrook's merciless vendettas; the only congratulatory cable Eileen ever received from her employer was for an article which *inter alia* criticised the hats and hemlines of Countess Mountbatten.

'Beaverbrook was ruthless, capricious, a born political intriguer, essentially a man of mischief who would use his newspaper to wound and when possible annihilate his opponents without pity or remorse; he was all of that and more . . .' wrote Cudlipp in his memoirs. 'But the redeeming factors were his bubbling sense of fun, his engaging whimsicality and his unexpected compassion for those in trouble on his staff or in politics. His personality created and dominated his newspapers. They were gay and tantalising and therefore entertaining and effervescent.'[61]

People told stories about Beaverbrook as they had told them about Northcliffe — another showman — and Cudlipp soon joyfully spread more around the pubs of Fleet Street. A favourite concerned his first visit to Beaverbrook's apartment near the Ritz:

he was bawling into the telephone: 'No. No. No. No. No. No. No. No. No.'

He replaced the handset and walked slowly around the room, his hands on his hips. He then returned to the instrument, picked up the handset and, as he jumped six inches into the air, delivered one final thunderous '*No!*' That was the end of the matter. It wasn't on. He was agin' it. And that was final.

Then there were the two occasions 'when a searching question was under discussion [and] he said, "Hugh, bring your chair over here. Not there — here!" We sat immediately opposite each other, with knees touching, and Lord Beaverbrook peering silently into my eyes. It was the loyalty test, or was it mesmerism? I peered silently back; there was no alternative.'[62]

Cudlipp revelled in Beaverbrook's decidedly individualistic style of entertaining. There was the ritual that followed meetings of the Policy Committee (where no one challenged the central Beaverbrook diktats, but the opinionated had a wonderful time), which involved his lordship's favourite toy, the Electric Rum-Cocktail Mixer (Jamaican rum and West Indian limes, 'absolutely paramount'). And there were bizarre dinners: one required a senior executive to spend half an hour with a bucket of water, four empty bottles, a kitchen funnel and a glass, testing Beaverbrook's theory that some bottles of champagne contained more than others.[63]

Beaverbrook intended Cudlipp to become Editor of the *Sunday Express* and so initially appointed him personal assistant to the egotistical incumbent, John Gordon, but Gordon had no intention of going and Beaverbrook did not have the heart to sack him. Twice Beaverbrook appointed Cudlipp Editor and failed to tell Gordon or anyone else. Despite these disappointments, Cudlipp, now given the title 'Managing Editor' ('my detail man', as Gordon called him), turned down an offer from Bart – relayed by Philip Zec – to go to Australia to run the *Mirror* group's new newspaper and radio stations. He stayed not just because of his distrust of Bart, but because Eileen did not want to leave London.[64] In any case, he was enjoying Beaverbrook and learning a lot from both him and Gordon, who – though impossible – was a sub-editor so great 'only fools could not learn from him'.[65]

Back at Geraldine House, the *Pictorial* had deteriorated, though it was still required reading for those interested in politics – not least because of the effervescent and controversial column by Dick Crossman, whom – at King's suggestion[66] – Cudlipp had hired in 1949. The *Mirror* was still hugely influential and had passed the *Express* in circulation, though under Silvester Bolam, who was in tune with Labour puritanism, it tended to be on the worthy but dull side. Solidly supportive of the Labour government, it was passionately anti-Conservative.

The narrow Labour victory in the February 1950 General Election was attributed to the *Mirror*'s explicit support; it was no less partisan in October 1951, when Attlee went to the country to try to win a workable majority. In 1950 the paper had backed Labour for its 'fairness and humanity'; this time it played on the fears of the electorate about Soviet imperialism, the Korean War and the escalation of the arms race. The reiterated question was 'Whose finger do you want on the trigger?': the implication was that Churchill was a warmonger. On election day the *Mirror's* front page carried photographs of Churchill and Attlee with a drawing of a large gun under the headline 'WHOSE FINGER?' – the accompanying text made it clear that Labour was the choice for 'peace with security'. Cudlipp was in Beaverbrook's flat when Churchill phoned. 'The question was simply, "Shall I sue?" and the answer was simply, "Yes. Issue a writ, Winston."'[67]

Churchill won the election but pursued his case. On being convinced by his lawyers that the campaign had been too general to be libellous, he sued and settled out of court over a previous unsubstantiated allegation that he had advocated a preventive war against Russia. Since he was seventy-seven and the *Mirror* was forever extolling the virtues of youth, Churchill must have enjoyed instructing that his damages be paid to the Church Army Charitable Homes for Elderly People.

King had been biding his time and concentrating much of his energy on making a success of the group's African interests. Finding the right Europeans was always a problem. 'Why over forty per cent of the men we sent to West Africa went to pieces, sometimes within days, was never clear to me,' wrote King in his memoirs. 'I suppose they suddenly found they were more important than they ever could be at home and just couldn't take it.'[68] It was the other way round with King, who revelled in being seen as a great, benign father-figure. Frank Rogers, a provincial *Daily Mirror* journalist who in 1949 was appointed Editorial Director in Lagos, was fascinated by how King seemed to change personality when he came to Africa: becoming affable, articulate and relaxed with everyone, he treated people with great respect and kindness.[69] Also, he loved the climate, which always greatly improved his psoriasis, which was at best a minor nuisance and at worst a torment.

It was King's habit when in Africa to take members of staff individually to lunch. One of the journalists, Babatunde José, refused the invitation because it was Ramadan and he was fasting. King's response was to send him on a pilgrimage to Mecca, Medina and Jerusalem, from which he returned with great prestige: 'he was an instrument in the hands of God to be my mentor from a reporter until I succeeded him as Chairman of the Daily Times in 1968'.[70] 'In all my working life my warmest relationship was with Babatunde José,' wrote King as an old man. 'He regards himself as my son and I am proud to accept the compliment.'[71]

Inefficiency and procrastination that drove Europeans mad in Africa and would have infuriated King at home seemed not to bother him at all: his fascination with other cultures made local problems a source of interest and often amusement. There was, for instance, the matter of witchcraft. Lunching one day with one of the African managers:

> I noticed he had two black dogs. I made some comment and he said that when they had difficulty with the rotary press they would sacrifice to Ogun, God of Iron, and away the press would go. I asked what the ceremony consisted of and he said you made a pile of old iron in the machine room, poured on it a libation of gin, and then sacrificed a black dog, pouring its blood over the pile. This ceremony was quite harmless, and I never knew whether Alfred believed in it as fervently as his staff.[72]

Then there were the difficulties he faced when in 1950 he founded the *Daily Graphic* in Ghana. First, it was announced that important Gold Coast chiefs — who believed it to be a Colonial Office front — intended to declare a boycott. King went to meet them and made a speech that won them over. Then the Nationalist Party, which was led by Kwame Nkrumah, who just happened to be Editor of the propaganda sheet known as the *Evening News*, declared a boycott, and on its launch the *Daily Graphic* sold only one-fifth of the expected 10,000 copies. This was resolved by a fluke: the *Graphic* tipped five out of seven winners and two seconds in the Accra races and its circulation soared. The same approach as that of the *Daily Times* — news, sport and no political opinions, combined with an efficient delivery service — worked so well that ultimately the paper's thirteen competitors were put out of business.

King had also had the opportunity in London to show his managerial strengths in a public role, when in 1948 he accepted Herbert Morrison's invitation to become Chairman of the almost moribund British Film Institute. Although not much of a cinema-goer and not in tune with public taste (he had been bewildered in May 1940 by

the popularity of *Gone With the Wind**), King took the job very seriously; he managed to develop some sense of common purpose among
the sixteen governors, fired the Secretary and replaced him with the
gifted young Denis Forman, who would end up as Chairman of
Granada. Forman would regularly visit King in what he described as
his 'drawing-room study' in Geraldine House; he was much impressed
by the butler in a dark coat who had black-velvet gloves for the coal
and white-cotton gloves for the drinks. King would sit in his high-
backed eighteenth-century leather armchair and Forman would sit in
the smaller one opposite. King recognised Forman's ability, gave him
all the support he needed and let him rip; Forman thought King a
'brilliant' Chairman.

An example of King's style was his handling of the row that erupted
over the BFI's newspaper, when its Editor, Gavin Lambert, savaged
Sir Michael Balcon's *The Blue Lamp*. Balcon, the head of Ealing Studios,
was a natural target for Lambert, who – along with his Oxford contemporaries and friends Lindsay Anderson and Karel Reisz – was a
Young Turk bent on radicalising what they derided as cosy British
cinema. They were 'Angry Young Men' a few years before the term
was coined.

The story of the rookie copper and his mentor, Police Constable
Dixon, whose brutal shooting causes his protégé to follow doggedly
in his decent footsteps, was widely lauded and hugely popular, but
Lambert thought it sentimental rubbish. The highly volatile Balcon
was livid, and rang Forman asking if he intended to fire Lambert.

King called a special meeting of the governors and said: "'Either
you have an editor who does what he thinks is right or you have
somebody who keeps a house journal. Which do you want?" Put in
those terms they didn't want to come across as creeps. So he said,

---

* He and Margaret had to leave early, partly because she was so distressed. 'The first third
anyway is all about the young men going to war & subsequently casualty lists, widows
& scenes of the wounded. After all we are already having some of this & soon are certain to have more, so why pay to see it acted on the screen? One would imagine that
at a time like this one would have to pay people to come and see it. There was one
good remark by Clark Gable acting the part of Rhett Butler – in which he refers to
the "cause" of the Southern States. He says their cause is the desire to live in the past,
which is precisely what we in England are fighting for to-day. I hope to God we can
change it in time'.

"It's important that the editor doesn't cross the boundaries (which he might have done in this case), so we'll have an editorial committee."' This body, which consisted of Forman, Lambert and the critic and BFI Governor Dilys Powell, never actually met. Almost half a century later Forman recalled gratefully how adroitly King had handled what could have been a disastrous breach between the old and the new.[73]

After four years of the King–Forman partnership, the BFI was revolutionised; its membership had risen from 3,000 to 38,000 and the National Film Theatre had been founded. On a visit to the United States in 1955, Marlon Brando and Cecil B. De Mille were two of the guests at a lunch in honour of King given by the Association of Motion Picture Producers to mark 'his outstanding effort to bring about a better relationship between the American film industry and the English movie fans'.[74] Yet King was never again asked to chair a similar body. 'Was this forgetfulness on the part of the civil servants? Or had I trodden on some important ministerial or official toe? I don't know.'[75]

What was remarkable about King's performance during that period of Cudlipp's absence was that, at the same time as he had lost his closest and only completely trusted colleague, he was going through dreadful turmoil in his private life, which had followed a number of family upheavals. First, there had been the abandonment of Culham ('I must admit that I will never be reconciled to living in London,' Margot told Michael. 'I just feel cramped and stifled all the time & when I am in the country I feel a new creature'[76]); then his mother's death in October 1945: at seventy-nine she had a heart attack when she sat so heavily into a chair when out playing bridge that the chair went over backwards. King visited her and left when she seemed stable, but she later took a sudden turn for the worse and realised that she had only a few hours left. Undaunted, 'she sat up in bed, reading *The Times* and dictating arrangements for the funeral to my sister, Chirrie, over the top of the paper'.[77]

'Just think of her as the grand old lady – and great character – who was all your life attached with so much affection to her handmaid,' wrote King to Priscilla.[78] And for posterity he wrote a history and thoughtful analysis of his mother. 'Over the years I have often wondered how it was that this woman with all the beauty, the brains and the force of character in the world absolutely failed to achieve anything,' he mused. The nearest he came to explaining some of her characteristics 'was to suppose that she had a very lively and original intelligence and a very sensual emotional nature', but could give rein to neither without threatening the social position she so prized.

> She got bored with the people she met but was quite incapable of kicking over the traces and taking up with people who could have given her more . . . Her attitude to her children in general was immense pride in them in theory coupled with fairly con-sistent disapproval of everything they did. In my case there always seemed an element of resentment against me – perhaps because I took the social security they had won for me rather as a matter of course and so felt I could associate with the sort of people my parents had avoided.[79]

While King's portrait of her was critical, it showed none of the hatred that he later alleged he had felt for her. Rather than dancing on her grave, he went out of his way when in India to visit the church in which she had been married.[80]

Margot had been more upset than King by the death of his mother and of his uncles Cecil and Leicester – all of whom had been very fond of her – and she was becoming increasingly fragile. Although well enough to continue her work with prisoners and on the bench, and to accompany King to the United States in the autumn of 1947, she began to suffer from a depression that took the form mostly of self-loathing but sometimes of intense aggression. By early 1948, when they left their small Lincoln's Inn flat and moved to Chelsea, she was deteriorating steadily. Neither of them was to enjoy their Georgian house facing the Thames: on five floors with a large studio at the top, it was hard to run and Margot was never to be well enough to apply herself to turning it into a comfortable home. According to a young relative who lived there on and off for years:

> [109] Cheyne Walk was a tall house (112 steps, I think, from top to bottom) and the rooms were organised in such a way that a change of activity inevitably involved a journey up or down at least 35 of them. There was no central heating [King found it

uncomfortable and had it removed], the banisters on the stairs were rickety and the whole décor was dark and rather forbidding. Other people have described the atmosphere as hostile or gloomy, although I don't think I regarded it as that, since as far as I knew, it was perfectly normal.[81]

Margot was away a good deal, saw doctors, psychologists and psychiatrists and stayed with friends, relatives and in rest homes when – increasingly – she needed to get away from her husband. King had explained to her during the war that he thought 'the sub-conscious elements in your character seem to me to be 1) a terror of being left behind and 2) an intense attachment to your family (perhaps really your Mother)'.[82] Margot castigated herself on these and other grounds, including, particularly, mental sloth: 'what Cecil has had to cope with all these years – poor man. It is a terrifying thought – my obstinacy – & my negative power – & when I see my beloved family & their frustrations I am appalled – but am still unable to cope with the tension I feel every time I see them or go back to Cheyne Walk. I suppose only patience & will power will do the trick but nothing can give me back the precious years of waste!'[83]

The children were having difficulty in reaching their expected potential. Michael had been disappointed by his co-workers in the Glasgow shipyard, whom he failed to rouse behind the communist standard, and though – once more against his parents' wishes – he joined the Fleet Air Arm at the first opportunity, he was in Texas still in training when the war ended and would not be demobbed until the late 1940s. King had been optimistic about him in a letter to Cudlipp early in 1944, talking of how Michael loved and was obviously loved by the people with whom he worked. 'After his success at Eton and at Clydebank I feel he will fall on his feet anywhere.'[84] But now Michael was bored and frustrated, and worried his parents by spending all he earned and having no plans for his future. King had visited 'our precious Mike' in Texas in June 1945 ('he is really trying hard &, good flyer or no, he is a son to be proud of'[85]), but had little comprehension of those gifts that had so impressed some of Michael's teachers.

'You are very much the sort of person who reacts principally to the people or circumstances around you,' wrote Margot to Michael at the end of 1946, in a letter she probably did not send. 'This can be an invaluable asset – if not carried too far. But in the long run, one mustn't allow circumstances to dominate one . . . one must develop one's own individuality & independence . . . I have had to learn this very lesson myself . . . No one can live your life for you, nor can they be at your side so constantly that they can stimulate your interest and activity.'[86] Based back in Britain a few months later, Michael wrote to his father, thanking him for a wonderful evening celebrating his twenty-first birthday:

Up till now I have never proved myself worthy of all the kindness, patience and good faith with which you have brought me up. Your words have not always fallen on deaf ears by any means and I shall try not to fail you, and will endeavour to fulfil all the possibilities with which you have endowed me. There have been many times when I have hurt you and caused you anxiety. I believe that those times are over for well and good. Time alone can show whether I shall prove myself. I also thank you for the way in which you have settled my financial debt to you – & shall pay it off as you suggested.[87]

Michael tried, but the great sense of purpose that characterised his mid-teens seemed to have evaporated. He was as strikingly good-looking as had been his father and his great-uncle Northcliffe in their youth and was in trouble over women on several occasions. Having dropped out of formal education at sixteen, with only a School Certificate, he was poorly qualified in a competitive job market. He drifted into a job with Reuters and, in the journalistic world, his conviviality and humanity made him sought-after socially. His parents were disconcerted when, after many changes of mind on her part,[88] he married the highly attractive, tough-minded, divorced Libby Hobhouse, five years his senior; she was already the mother of a daughter by her first husband, the Hon Michael Eden, and – although this was not generally then known – of a son by the landowner, scientist and public servant, Harry Walston.

Francis, by his own assessment, had gone through a bad patch after Winchester, where he had starred academically and athletically, and worried greatly about his lack of drive. Like Mike, against his parents' wishes he had joined up at the first opportunity, which in his case was towards the end of the war, after two terms at New College, Oxford. 'I would hate to think,' he wrote to his parents, 'that I would not give such a scrappy bit of work as my life to my country'. Having originally hoped to be a fighter pilot (there was a row when King wrote, 'I do not approve'), and then a marine, he found himself an educational officer in the navy. Nearest of all the children to his father in his intellect as in his striving for the spiritual through the use of reason, he wrote his parents letters of merciless candour and precocious intellectual depth.

Like his father too, Francis was plagued by sensitivity, introspection and a sense of being apart: 'It struck me while taking a lesson the other day, a 2 hour lecture on history,' he wrote to King in 1946, 'how much I know *about* people and things; but how few people and things I know. It makes conversation so much harder to know the reactions of people, and yet not to be able to create the desired reactions. I don't think reason is strong enough to achieve both at the same time, instinct must come into it.'[89]

The problems at home weighed most heavily on Priscilla, especially after she left school, partly because her brothers were away and partly because she so desperately wanted all those around her to be happy and harmonious. She went to University College London in 1947, and that winter King wrote that he was 'so pleased that your excellent brain is at last beginning to function. Learning more & more is one of the great pleasures of growing older & I am glad you are now finding that out.'[90] But she lived at home, which restricted her independence, and like most girls of her generation, her longing for a husband and family took precedence over thoughts of a career. She was popular: 'I hated to let her go,' wrote one family friend. 'It was such a joy to have her. She is charming, clever & intelligent, besides being beautiful and good company!'[91] Yet there was a shortage of suitors: in the upper-middle classes to which the Kings belonged, there was deep distaste for marrying into 'a rag' like the *Mirror* unless there was plenty of money to compensate for the social embarrassment. Margot's plan to hold a dance for Priscilla's twenty-first birthday outraged King; instead there was a supper for twenty at home and a present on her plate on the morning of her birthday of £1.

At nine, according to his classics master, Colin the baby was 'a true mixture of Michael's slap-dash and Francis's indolence with the marked ability of both'.[92] Like Priscilla, he had real musical ability;[93] perceived as the most brilliant of the children, he was nonetheless sent to Eton, where he did effortlessly well. Though polite and affectionate in his letters, Colin had even less intimacy with his parents than had his siblings, first because of Margot's busy life and then because of her illness. In 1949, in a rather curious response to a long letter from King, he thanked him for having sent him to Eton and then explained that it had turned him from a conceited and over-confident boy into a cynic who did nothing except for effect. 'Perhaps, because of my over-critical attitude I look on the bad side of everyone first but at least I am not now deceived by a persuasive exterior as I used to be.' Being forced to stay at school longer than he had wanted had taught him tolerance − how 'to bear if not to overlook the imperfections in others which are so prominent in myself. Boredom, unintelligence, and narrow-mindedness I have discovered will make up the minds of most of those with whom I will live in future years.' However, he had learned to love people for their own sakes and was 'only perfectly happy and content when I am talking to others preferably about them-selves'.[94] In 1950, after a course at Grenoble University, Colin would do his National Service in the Coldstream Guards[*].

By the end of 1949, when King was in Africa, there was a crisis over Margot, who had lately been under the care of his sister Enid. Her condition had now been exacerbated by a difficult menopause and a sequence of medical advisers with different diagnoses and pre-scriptions: restless and anxious, she would stay with none of them for long. 'She is quite impossible,' wrote Priscilla, who adored her, but was emotionally exhausted. King wrote to Francis from West Africa, a few days after his exciting experience of the Enugu riots: 'I have had a couple of letters from Scilla & also two from Mama from which I gather what a serious turn for the worse occurred after I left. I am desperately sorry you should all have been drawn into this, but I gather Enid was at the end of her tether . . . I gather you have been coping manfully & I am most grateful. I have cabled to Munro authorising

---

[*] King found Colin's Eton and Guards manner insufferable, cancelled the plan to send him to Christchurch and despatched him instead to work in Canada in the paper busi-ness.

the [electric shock] treatment he prescribes.'[95] Margot resisted this. The doctor 'said I was a true "Mediterranean" type – who couldn't face loss – & must have electrical treatment to help me move on to the evening of life! He is practical & sound – but I am of course indignant! I *don't* want to develop by outside electrical mechanics – but by my own internal electrical equipment.'[96] But such treatment at the time was thought to be a cure-all, her family was desperate and so she unhappily agreed. Ever afterwards Margot felt that she had been badly damaged by this experience; certainly, it did not help her. She and King struggled on through the early 1950s, but she spent ever more time away.

Three of the four children – and particularly Priscilla – usually tried to humour their father, but Francis was uncompromising. Demobbed and at Oxford, and still unhappy, he wrote a devastating letter to his father in the spring of 1950. The event that had distressed him followed a cocktail party given by his parents:

> what upset me terribly was the last few words you said before going to bed. 'The party went alright, don't you think? The nicest and the best of all the people there, I thought, were the four of you.'
>
> I had hopes that Mamma's illness and indeed the unhappiness of us 3 older ones would make you try to change your attitude to us. But here you were on the same old theme.

The problem, believed Francis, was that King's peace of mind was all-important to him, so he liked to have a preconception of what his children were – 'quietly contenting yourself that you hadn't done too badly with a family of the likes of us four' – rather than being 'disturbed by the constantly changing and developing relationship that is needed between a father and his children'. Relationships might become fixed when children were grown up, 'but this only happens after a great deal of striving and struggling', whereas King had:

> transported yourself ahead of time into the security that this fixed relationship has to offer, and looked on us all as definite persons long before we had learnt anything about ourselves and become anything like definite. In my own case I was an intellectual

before I had learnt to use my brain, Scilla a great character of a woman before she had won for herself this title, and Mike a loveable nature, before he knew how to love and be loved . . .

If you remain the same person that I think you've been, on the "I am, that I am" basis (and nothing can change me), then if I go home at all, we shall be having an eternal scrap, and I shall do my best to make life unbearable and to change you, because I think that that way of life is impossible, certainly 'unnatural,' and that Mamma will be quite unable to return to, or perhaps find, a happy way of life that way. If on the other hand you do earnestly want to be sympathetic and helpful and I'm sure at times that you do, then I'll do everything I can to help and to be helped.

You are such a stimulating person, but your stimulation lies in this that you set people on their mettle – they try to answer for themselves and defend themselves against your barrage of criticism. This has really been no help to the four of us . . . do be prepared to accept me and everybody for what we are, and for us to accept you at least for what you are not, an impene-trable and impregnable tower of strength.

Francis was struggling to do the right things in his life, he said, 'but in truth I am in need of a great deal of help, for otherwise life will always perhaps be too hard for me, and this I beg you to give.'[97] Life would be hard for Francis – though not as hard as it already was for his mother: the Breton fisherman's prayer – 'Dear God be good to me – the sea is so wide and my boat is so small' – was to be very important to both of them.

King tried to respond helpfully: 'evidently my letter had at least said one thing right,' he reported to Margot after a long conversation with Francis, '– that he carried too much armour.'[98] But he felt help-less, and without Margot he was even less capable of dealing with emotions.

'I think at times you think I am too bottled up,' he had written to her in the late 1940s, '& so in general terms I am writing to say what at the moment is going on in the bottle.' He had given up seeing Joyce a couple of years earlier, he reminded her, 'because I thought if I did she would get married . . . And in any case it was hard to keep any relationship going with Joyce because — as far as my experience went — she was interested in sex & domesticity but nothing else, so conversation always flagged.' Further, he wanted to see if he could not 'get on without Joyce, or her equivalent. So on all grounds I walked, not very gracefully, out.' Joyce had indeed married, and King had tried:

> keeping the 7th Commandment for a spell, but, for whatever reason, it didn't work & I began to feel my life was falling in on me. Something had to be done & why not the old, though not very successful, recipe? So with deep misgivings I embarked on Deborah. Misgiving because with my appalling sense of futility, I see too clearly where it will all end up if it is a success — or a failure. However, you can't stand still wringing your hands & I dived in — only to have it proved to me once more that I am incapable of having a stable relationship of any kind with anyone.

He and Deborah got on very well, he told Margot; 'she laughs at me in a way I like & is very sweet to me'. However, she obviously would not agree to a sexual relationship, so he had the choice of 'walking out some time soon or really making a concentrated effort over a period to get her to change her mind.' That would be a bad idea 'as the impression I would be liable to create if successful would be far too great. So I feel sorry — partly because of Deborah, whom I am fond of — but more because I so often feel lonely & my attempts to escape from my loneliness have every other possible consequence except the one I am trying to create.' He hoped this did not sound like criticism of Margot: 'it is not meant as such. There is nothing you can do about all this.'[99]

Though this was unlikely to be helpful to a woman in a state of intense mental turmoil, in his clumsy way King tried hard to be reassuring. 'My darling Wife, don't worry so. I am quite prepared to wait for anything you want to give me,' he wrote subsequently, '& my "experiences" as you call them, won't make any difference. You are always my precious little wife whom I have wanted to love cherish & protect, but have not known how . . . It means everything to me that at last you are on the mend.'[100] But though Margot sometimes improved, she still could not cope and, late in 1950, a burden was put on her that she could not carry.

John Falls, whose birth had killed King's sister Sheila and who had been brought up by his grandmother, was killed in a plane crash along with his wife in November 1950, leaving three children. One set of relatives had offered to take the two boys, seven-year-old Patrick and five-year-old Nigel, and another set Sheila, who was six months old. 'But it seemed to me essential,' wrote King to Priscilla – now in Montreal at McGill University and desperate to be back home with St John (Bobby) Gore, who had jumped the hurdles to become her fiancé – 'that the little family should be left together and if that were to be so, then I was probably the only person who could take the job on . . . I have not yet got quite round to the idea that for the next twenty years we shall be bringing up another family!*'

'The view of doctors and others', he continued, 'is that this may be the perfect solution to Mama's troubles. I devoutly hope so, because if she proves unable to cope then indeed, I am in the soup.'[102] On Boxing Day he wrote that he had been unwell over Christmas. 'I have a lot of worries in the office & what with that and things here I more or less collapsed, but am now brisker again. Mama copes well with the children but is by no means herself again. She seems miserable, resentful, rebellious & is quite satisfied that John & Kit's death are all her fault.' The bright spot was Sheila, 'a very intelligent, friendly baby'. Then, the following day, he had to report the death of his first grandchild, Hugo. 'Poor dear Mike, the baby was the most wonderful thing that had ever happened to him.'[103]

King tried hard with his new family. Patrick, he told Priscilla, a couple of months after they were orphaned:

is very observant & intelligent. He seems aloof and self-centred, but I may be wrong. Nigel may not be as straightforward as he

---

* This generosity was to surprise many, but it was utterly in keeping with King's kindness to people in the sort of trouble he could understand. Cudlipp later reported that King: 'would stop to listen patiently to mental defectives or reeling drunks who importuned him on the rare occasions when he was walking in the streets. The death of Bernard Gray, our war correspondent, in a submarine in the Mediterranean was not a matter for a note of condolence to his widow. Cecil visited the family and advised on the education of the children for more than twenty years and I was unaware of it until Mrs Gray told me.'[101]

seems, but to all appearances is a dear little boy, full of life &
go & clearly very happy. He is also pretty intelligent.

I always wanted a second daughter called Sheila – and here
she is. She has *bright* blue eyes, is very friendly, rather precocious
about walking, very fond of her food, observant and *very* determined. She strikes me as more like my Mama than any other
members of the younger generation.[104]

The boys were sent to boarding school, there was a nanny and Margot
did her best, but she was too disturbed and restless to spend much
time at Cheyne Walk, so the burden of parenthood fell mainly on
King and on Priscilla, Sheila's godmother, who spent with them as
much time as she could spare after her marriage to Bobby in the
summer of 1951. 'To start with,' remembered Nigel:

> our existence centred around the resident nanny, governess or
> *au pair* of the day and more so after Uncle Cecil's separation
> from Aunt Margot in about 1952, when these people filled the
> role of principal female in our lives. They seemed to come and
> go very quickly and without really trying, I can count eight by
> 1956. I don't think they went because we were any more abom-
> inable than other children but more because of the house itself
> and its atmosphere . . . These nannies varied, from the kind
> through the incompetent to the conventionally cruel and,
> whether intentionally or not, acted as a buffer between us and
> Uncle Cecil. We all had breakfast together and weekend lunches,
> but otherwise our lives ran on different tracks and I cannot
> remember many occasions when he involved himself in our
> day-to-day routines.[105]

With the boys mostly away, King's private life now centred around
Sheila and his books, as family friends had largely faded from view.
He concentrated ever more on his work, and on his plans to displace
Bart. By late 1951 he had concluded, as he put it later to a *Mirror* his-
torian, that Bart 'now nearly seventy, was in his dotage and had to be
disposed of'.[106]

Certainly Bart was drinking too much; Philip Zec, the *Pictorial*'s
Editor – worried that Bart was becoming incoherent and unreliable

– had failed in the summer to persuade him to resign. Out of sheer frustration Bart had made a disastrous investment in Australia. Even more disastrously, he went to Australia to try to sort out the problems and thus gave King his opportunity.

'Cecil set about his task with his usual patience and calculated ruthlessness,' wrote Cudlipp. 'As a furniture remover, once his mind was made up, he was without equal even in an industry accustomed to furniture removal. The Cecilian chant was heard again. Were they to wait, at their peril, until Bartholomew did something monumentally stupid? Wasn't it in Bart's own interest that he should go now, before his reputation lay in tatters?'[107] King was ready for Bart when he came back from Australia, where he had left James Cooke, one of his allies on the seven-man board.

An emotionally exhausted Philip Zec told Dick Crossman the inside story over lunch. 'About a week ago,' Crossman wrote in his diary, 'Cecil King (a nephew of Northcliffe and a great big, beefy, rather silly fellow, who lives in Chelsea, is a Wykehamist [like Crossman] but is otherwise insignificant) rang a flabbergasted Zec to say that he and three other members of the board had decided to ask for Bartholomew's resignation.' Over lunch:

> King explained that, along with Bolam, the present Editor, a stooge who is solely the creation of Bartholomew, he had come to the conclusion some weeks ago that Bartholomew was in his dotage and must be got rid of . . .
> When Zec saw Bart that afternoon, he advised him that there was nothing to do but clear out. Bart asked how that could be possible and slowly realised that Bolam had given the casting vote against him. At this he broke down, after which they both drank a bottle of whisky together. For the next four days Zec was chiefly engaged in trying to get Bartholomew to write the four necessary letters of resignation. He kept on crying and saying, 'How could Bolam do it to me?'

One difficulty, Zec told Crossman, 'was that, although Bart joined the *Daily Mirror* at the age of fourteen and had built it from absolutely nothing to where it is today, he has never taken a penny out of the firm and has no shares, so that resignation meant complete penury.

Zec spent a great deal of time arranging for a pension of £6,000* a year and trying to get a cash payment out of all the subsidiary companies, totalling £20,000.'[108]

The moral Crossman drew from this story was 'the extraordinary irresponsibility of a board of directors who are not in any way responsible to anyone, even the investors . . . As a result, a palace revolution could take place at any time when four votes could be collected against the chairman.' As Zec had remarked as they parted, '"I'd always told you politics was a dirty game but I take it all back now that I've seen what happens in Fleet Street."'

Just before Christmas the press announced the unexpected resignation of H. Guy Bartholomew from the chairmanship of the *Mirror* and *Pictorial* companies:

> In an official statement issued by the respective companies it was said that the resignation had been accepted with regret. Mr Bartholomew, aged 67, wrote that his advancing years and an earnest desire to promote the advancement of younger men had moved him to this decision. He would, however, remain as a director until the end of the financial year.
>
> Cecil Harmsworth King has been elected chairman of both companies in his stead.[109]

'A bloody adding machine that thinks it's Northcliffe' was Bart's comment to the left-wing journalist Francis Williams about his successor. And Williams wrote much later, in his history of the world press:

> He was bitter, too, about the frequent comparison made between King as an intellectual and himself as a semi-illiterate . . . He was altogether lost without the *Mirror*. And indeed he was its true creator. He had made it the genuine voice of those 'lower orders' of whom the British ruling classes had been so long afraid, the champion of the women who flooded into the factories

---

* About £100,000 today.

during the war, and of the men in the ranks of the fighting services; earthy in its patriotism, ribald in its attacks on bureaucratic authority, tenacious in its criticisms of what it regarded as national inefficiency or complacency, delighted in for its frankness, its rough language and its strip cartoons.'[110]

The company that King had taken over by now included – in addition to the *Mirror* (now the most popular daily paper in the world), the *Pictorial, Reveille* (which had a circulation of 100,000 when Bart acquired it after the war and now sold three million), the West African newspapers and the huge Canadian paper mill – a Melbourne daily and six Australian radio stations. The press was intensely curious to know about this fifty-year-old executive of whom hardly anyone knew anything. One who did was J. Thurston Thrower, who had been Managing Director of the *Croydon Times* Group when it was briefly owned by King.

'Cecil King does not often "make news",' he wrote, 'but he has certainly done it this time. In the press and advertising clubs – and pubs – big names are forever being bandied about, but it is rare for King's name to come up: yet he has been doing a full-time newspaper job within 100 yards of Fleet Street for over a quarter of a century.' Though much of his time had been spent on advertising:

it would be wrong to think of King as 'an advertising man.' Actually, he has had an exceptional all-round experience with the *Daily Mirror* and the *Sunday Pictorial*; in addition, as proprietor of the *Croydon Times* Group he acquired early on in life a complete, overall picture of a medium-sized press unit. First and foremost he is an administrator of the highest calibre. Quiet and reasonable, he possesses rare judgment and business acumen.

Tall, blond and handsome, King is a good shot and in his time has been a fine tennis player. Although to some he may appear a trifle aloof, he is one of the most charming men imaginable 'off parade.' He is a man of exceptional culture and a great reader ... So far as politics are concerned, I would hazard a guess that, whatever party he in fact votes for, deep-down he is completely detached and independent.'[111]

It was King's politics as well as the Northcliffe connection that fascinated the press. Because the group was owned by some 80,000 investors, none with a controlling interest, pointed out the *New Statesman*, the *Mirror* board 'is completely free from financial pressure. This puts a tremendous responsibility on the new chairman of the combine, Cecil King. Like "Bart" before him, he is free to make of this group of newspapers exactly what he will. An exciting and terrifying prospect even for the nephew of the great Northcliffe.'[112] Bartholomew's 'sudden departure . . . is likely to have tremendous political consequences,' said the *Sunday Express*, 'and may indeed shake the strength of the Socialist party more than the departure of any of its political leaders'. Would King swing the papers away from Labour? was the question being chewed over by press and politicians alike. A French newspaper assured its readers that Winston Churchill had sent an ultimatum to King threatening to use his libel action to ruin the *Mirror* unless Bart was fired immediately. Under King, a convinced conservative, it was explained, the paper was expected to change direction.[113]

King took all the fuss calmly. 'I have just finished my first week as chairman,' he wrote shortly before Christmas to Francis, who (like Michael) was now working for the *Mirror* group:

> – and very hectic it has been, too. The wildest rumours have been flying about about my intentions. Most of them are complete nonsense, of course, & the rest forecast my plans on subjects I have so far had no time to consider.
>
> At the moment I do not see a way out of our Australian difficulties but all the rest is obviously soluble in time. I am afraid I shall have much less time for West Africa, though I will try and keep an eye on it. My difficulty is that I have not only to do my own work, but also to deal with the accumulation of untackled problems that has been piling up for years.[114]

Within a few weeks King left to visit Canada, the US and Australia. By the time he returned, in early March 1952, he had reached some decisions. 'Mr King prides himself on his ability to take the long view and to choose the right men,' the *Guardian* had written at the time of his elevation. 'He has great financial shrewdness. He is a strange man to find at the head of a tabloid newspaper. But he is a nephew of Northcliffe and has inherited the famous forelock and perhaps something of his uncanny flair for knowing what interests the common man and – more important – the common woman.'[115]

King knew that flair was missing, but he knew just who had it. 'Let's get together and make a dent in the history of our times,'[116] he wrote to Cudlipp.

CHAPTER VIII

The Eagle and the Lark

'I HAVE BEEN HONOURED TO WORK FOR THE BEAVERBROOK PRESS,' wrote Cudlipp to Beaverbrook's son in late March 1952, 'and leave it with complete admiration and much personal regret. It was simply a choice between driving my own Jowett Javelin* or continuing to ride for a third year as a handcuffed, blindfolded passenger in John's Rolls Royce.'[1]

'I have lured Hugh Cudlipp away from the Sunday Express,' King announced to the Australian Chairman, Jack Patience, '& he will be reappointed Editor of the Sunday Pictorial in about 3 weeks. He is in my opinion the best editor in this country & would be used temporarily in Australia if need arose.'[2]

·After a brief holiday, Cudlipp was back in Geraldine House in mid-April along with Mary Ellison, the secretary he had taken with him to the *Express*. 'Ever since Phil Zec was suddenly kicked upstairs and Cudlipp came back,' Crossman wrote, 'the *Pic* has been in a complete commotion, with Cudlipp changing everything round and trying out every sort of sensationalism.'[3] Crossman had expected to be sacked, as he was too left-wing for King, 'but the two of them went for a week's tour, studying circulation, and they are probably smart enough to realise that the circulation they are stealing from *Reynold's News* [a socialist Sunday newspaper subsidised by the Co-operative Wholesale Society] might slip back without a regular Socialist column'.[4]

There was consolation for Crossman in losing the Editor who

---

* A comfortable middle-range car first produced in 1947.

thought like him: 'Actually, he interfered far less with my column than Zec has done but that was because Cudlipp took it less seriously and also because he doesn't happen to be a serious-minded Socialist.'[5] And then there was the excellent advice that Cudlipp gave Crossman: 'With the column so very well established and everybody who matters reading it, I think you can afford to be a little more personal. Moreover, the one thing that I have learnt by being on the *Sunday Express* is that personalisation is the secret of readability. So let's have more about Churchill and Attlee and less about Conservative and Labour.'[6]

Perhaps because of his long experience of King, Cudlipp was unfazed by Crossman's formidable intellect. Denis Forman witnessed Crossman being subjected to a classic, blunt Cudlippean put-down just after the 1952 Labour Party Conference. 'Dick had been going to make a speech from the floor attacking the government's handling of foreign affairs and he was going to be the firebrand who would set the conference alight and get the government to change their policy.' However, having been elected to the National Executive, he changed his speech and was loudly booed. '"All these bloody communists in the front row, they all started booing me and stamping their feet", he told us. And Hugh Cudlipp said, "Dick, it wasn't like that at all. They looked at you and they said, 'Here's a guy who was claiming to be our leader and our rabble-rouser and now he's got a job he's changed his tune. Boo!' That's what it was, Dick."'

At thirty-seven, Cudlipp was doing for the third time the job he had first taken on at twenty-four, but after the initial burst of activity, this time his editorship was part-time and sporadic. The first big distraction came when King decided that the need had indeed arisen to get Cudlipp involved with the 'Australian Misadventure'. There were two major problems. First, having on a second attempt failed to buy *Truth* from Ezra Norton, Bart had bought the ailing Melbourne *Argus* to console himself. ('Wrong paper, wrong city,' as Cudlipp put it pithily in his memoirs.[7]) And second, he had also acquired a chain of radio stations, precipitating an attack of righteous nationalism by the Australian government, which censured the transaction and put severe limitations on the extent of foreign ownership in broadcasting companies.

With the *Pictorial* gaining ground and strengthened by staff whom Cudlipp had wooed from the *Express* and the *Mail*, he was despatched in the autumn, accompanied by Eileen, to spend four to five months in Australia as King's personal representative. King held a farewell dinner for them, which Crossman had expected to be 'a jolly affair':

> Actually it was the stuffiest formality. Hugh, his wife and I were the only journalists there and the rest were managing directors, executives, etc. Cecil King is so shy that he only conducts conversation in a whisper, which his guests all follow. Moreover, he was too shy to propose the toast to Hugh, far less to make a speech, and ended the dinner at ten o'clock by passing a message across to one of the directors, saying that he would like them to break it up because his wife was waiting at home.[8]

In addition to Cudlipp's editorial gifts, King told an Australian colleague, 'He has an excellent all-round knowledge of this business. He will soon join the board of one of our English companies & may well then become the director primarily concerned with our Australian interests.'[9] Within two months this prediction had become a reality.

The *Argus* had already lost about £1 million,[*] a vast sum for the *Mirror* group, whose two newspapers had the previous year made a profit of just £1.5 million between them – 'and the drain was waiting for the second million and possibly the third'.[10] In Melbourne it was in competition with the *Age*, a dull paper with the priceless advantage of a near-monopoly of the lucrative classified advertisement market, and with the *Sun Pictorial*, which was vibrant and well run by Sir Keith Murdoch's *Melbourne Herald* group. Cudlipp's job was to make the *Argus* profitable, but though in his four months there he made great improvements in the paper, raised staff morale greatly and did much, as King put it, 'to create outside a better feeling towards the paper',[11] the project was ultimately doomed.

For five years Cudlipp and King visited Australia alternately. ('He usually went during the English winter and I during the English summer,' Cudlipp wrote. 'It took me some time to figure out why those long journeys always left him looking bronzed and healthy, whereas I became increasingly pallid. Then I rumbled it. He was having

---

[*] About £16 million today.

two summers every year and I two winters. Wykehamists!'[12]) But in 1957 they at last accepted that, as King put it, 'if there is no room for a paper, there is no room, and editorial excellence will not alter this'[13] and decided to cut their losses. Threatening noisily to launch an evening paper to compete with the *Melbourne Herald*, they sold out to their putative rival for a decent price, subsequently sold their radio interests to a television company and got out of Australia with a tiny profit.

King had enjoyed Australia for the light, the terrain, the politics, its sheer scale and its energy. 'The whole vast island or continent is being transformed,' he wrote in his late sixties, 'while here we wrangle for years before building a few miles of new motorway.'[14]

Cudlipp's Australia was, of course, much more convivial than King's. No longer imprisoned in a hotel room, during his long stay he drove and flew vast distances, quickly came to enjoy Australians ('I liked the Aussie bastards and I was not a Pom they despised'[15]) and formed friendships that went way beyond the *Argus* staff. Among them were three memorable newspaper proprietors with whom he contemplated various deals that ultimately came to nothing.

There was Ezra Norton, who had treated Bart so badly – 'a lone wolf who deserved and relished his unpopularity . . . in almost every aspect of his personality he was a four-letter man'[16] – a natural curmudgeon made worse by his ulcers:

'I'm a bastard,' he said to me over the champagne and oysters in the *Malmaison* dinerie. It was his favourite diet, not normally prescribed for ulcers.

'Ezra, I know you're a bastard,' I replied. 'Everybody says so. They can't all be wrong.'

'No, you don't understand. I really am a bastard.' I believe he was only boasting.

After a dinner-table chat about his piles, he told me a touching story about his father, John Norton, generally accepted as the greatest rogue unhanged in the present century's history of Australia.

Norton had used *Truth* to destroy his enemies, but his son assured Cudlipp he should not believe everything he heard about him. '"Mind

you, he knocked me about a bit, but at heart he was sentimental.'''
After the second bottle of champagne, pressed for an illustration, 'he
obliged with this romantic vignette':

> When I was a boy, I remember sitting with my father on the
> balcony of our house in Pitt Street. It was a Sunday and the
> people strolling along the road were returning from the morning
> service. 'Come over here, son,' he said, and he put his arm around
> my shoulder.' There was a tear in Ezra's eye as he continued.
> 'Look at them,' said father, 'look at them in all their Sunday
> finery, the bloody hypocrites. Never forget this, my son. When
> you carry on my great work in *Truth*, keeping up its traditions,
> without fear or favour, you will be in the same position of trust
> as me, always able to pour a bucket of shit over the lot of them.'[17]

King's reminiscence about Norton was confined to a lunch where
'sour and ill [he] discoursed on his piles', but he added the arresting
story that relations between Norton and Sir Frank Packer (owner of
the Sydney *Daily Telegraph*) had become strained 'as there had been an
episode at the races when one of Norton's men held Packer while
Norton is said to have leapt on his back and bitten him in the face'.[18]
'"You will like Frank Packer,"' King told Cudlipp. 'When I first
met him and we exchanged a handshake, Frank said, "I'm interested
in women and horses. What are you interested in?"'[19] 'My Wykehamist
upbringing had not allowed for such an introduction,' commented
King sadly in retrospect, 'and my response must have been disappointing.'[20] Had King been prepared to admit their common interest,
they could have had much to discuss: 'The sexual element in Australian
society,' he observed, 'is very different from that in America or Canada
. . . In British Columbia you sell even machine tools by showing a
buxom young woman drooping her breasts over the machine. In
Australia . . . this element was largely absent. Perhaps as part of the
same attitude, while Australian men are the handsomest in the world,
their womenfolk would not rate high in any international beauty
rating.' This King blamed on the huge Irish-Catholic population: 'In
Ireland the men tend to drink too much and are prone to fight.'[21]
Packer was also a yachtsman and heavyweight boxer ('a useful background for a newspaper proprietor in that country,'[22] observed

Cudlipp) and Cudlipp and he were delighted with each other. Years later they were lunching in the Savoy in London when a television tycoon told Packer that a friend of his, who was an especially talented writer, would shortly be leaving for Sydney. Would Packer see him, if armed with a letter of introduction?

'Oh,' said Frank, not too pleased. 'What's so special about him?'

'Well, he's a hunchback,' said the tycoon.

'We've got plenty of writers. I eat them for breakfast,' said Frank. 'In your letter stress the hunchback bit – I haven't got any hunchbacks.'[23]

Most successful and impressive of all was Sir Keith Murdoch, whose journalistic career had taken off because of Northcliffe's encouragement, and whose business career had taken off with the help of Northcliffe's money. In some circles nicknamed Southcliffe, he showed his gratitude to the Harmsworth family in the way he treated King, and he quickly took to Cudlipp:

The day after our first meeting in Melbourne, Australia's financial centre and most mannered metropolis, Sir Keith took me to the war memorial, an imposing edifice affording a view of the city itself. He was wearing a cloak, like Northcliffe's cloak and like Northcliffe's nephew's cloak. He affected the style and speech of the cultured English gentleman of standing; the corset of Australia's twentieth-century respectability fitted him perfectly.

'I am worried about my son Rupert,' he said. 'He's at Oxford and he's developing the most alarming Left-wing views.'[24]

Unlike Norton and Packer, each of whom made the proposition in a urinal, Murdoch did not offer Cudlipp a job, for he died that year; the alarmingly left-wing Rupert would not seriously impinge on Cudlipp for almost twenty years.

The 1952–3 correspondence between King in London, North America or West Africa and Cudlipp in Australia sizzled with plans and plots and set the tone for the way in which their partnership would work now that they were in charge. King was thoughtful, calm and authoritative and knew exactly what he wanted. Cudlipp – quick, volatile and intuitive – could not wait to make it happen. As Cudlipp put it in retrospect, King was an eagle who had finally and majestically taken off.*

'My policy,' King told Cudlipp:

is to acquire a staff that can produce at least as good a paper as the present Mirror and a better one than the present Pictorial in your absence. As I see it your role must be to give the papers direction and drive without becoming encumbered with day-to-day routine. In time we may want to launch out in all sorts of directions and you must be free to leave Geraldine House with confidence knowing that all is well. At present the papers have little editorial policy and no discernible political direction. Our papers can have a lot of political fun – particularly just now when the Labour party is leaderless and policy-less. Let's plunge in! We have been too long in newspapers to take our eyes off the main ball – our customers and the quality of the product – but we can do that and still have some impact on events.[26]

There were complicated negotiations and numerous staffing problems. King was trying to buy Lord Kemsley's Scottish papers and he wanted a new editor for the *Mirror* and a replacement for Cudlipp, whom he intended to make Editorial Director of both newspapers. Jointly choosing the right people was greatly complicated by intercontinental communication difficulties and the ups-and-downs of negotiations in different continents. A typical Cudlipp cable, trying to head King off from making any rash choices, went from Melbourne to Quebec and began:

YOUR LETTER ON FUTURE PLANS MY OPINION IS NENER AS ACTING EDITOR MIRROR . . . EILBECK IMMATURE FOR PICTORIAL EDITORSHIP FOR SEVERAL YEARS STOP ADVOCATE EILBECK ASSISTANT EDITOR MIRROR IN CHARGE OF FEATURES STOP EYE CAN

---

* 'You were a different kind of bird,' I suggested to Cudlipp. 'A sort of chirpy small bird that flew very young.' 'That's right,' he said. 'A pissed lark.'[25]

THEN TRAIN HIM AS FUTURE TOP EXECUTIVE PUTTING HIM IN
CHARGE OF MIRROR DURING NENERS HOLIDAYS STOP VALDAR AS
EDITOR PICTORIAL STOP BOLAM OR SUFFERN FOR GLASGOW STOP
IF GLASGOW DEAL COLLAPSES BOLAM FOR AUSTRALIA . . . CON-
SIDER LONDON EDITORIAL . . . DIRECTOR NECESSARY HERE IN
VIEW POSSIBLE EDITORIAL CHANGES SEE LETTER STOP IF
GLASGOW DEAL IS ON SUGGEST GIVE BOLAM CHOICE GLASGOW
OR AUSTRALIA STOP IF CHOOSES GLASGOW SEND SUFFERN TO
AUSTRALIA STOP . . . SUFFERN NOW WASTED ON REVEILLE . . .
SUGGEST BEST TITLE FOR ME UNDER YOUR PLAN IS EDITORIAL
DIRECTOR AND EDITOR IN CHIEF MIRROR PICTORIAL GLASGOW
MELBOURNE STOP THIS ENSURES IMMEDIATE EDITORIAL CON-
TROL YET DOES NOT UNDERMINE INDIVIDUAL EDITORS
AUTHORITY AND STANDING WITH THEIR OWN STAFFS . . .[27]

'Your new editorial plan is exciting,' Cudlipp wrote subsequently,
in a letter elaborating on the strengths and weaknesses of various
members of staff ('A little soon to make Eilbeck Editor of the
Pictorial; don't you think? If we had to knock a few rough corners
off – which you had to do with me – that would be easier than putting a few rough corners *on*, which is the problem with Eilbeck.')

I believe that we could get both the 'Mirror' and the 'Pictorial'
really singing in a very short time. It is in many ways a pity that
Bolam has not made the grade. He is a very decent fellow, loyal
to the firm, but I know you have felt for some time that the real
drive was coming from [Jack] Nener . . . We should have tremendous fun with the new editorial set-up and worry the other
morning papers no end . . .'[28]

King's big idea for the *Mirror* and the *Pictorial* was that:

while publishing all the froth better than anyone else, we should
publish all the essential important news, and get it as authoritative and as well informed as this can be done. The Asahi
Shimbun has $4\frac{1}{2}$ million sale in Japan and is the most authoritative paper as well, so why not the Mirror?
   As I see it, we should cut to the barest bones the space given

in our news columns to serious news. But we should cover such subjects as dollar balances, North African unrest or Korea as often as occasion demands by means of very well-informed, very-simply written and very short feature pieces. A day's 'take' of news of Nato or Uno is usually quite unintelligible even to the expert, but taken in one, two or three monthly doses, should be much more intelligible to our readers and might well actually save space. Anything of this kind would require several experts on such things as economics and foreign affairs – people who don't exist on the staff at present. Our whole range of contacts is entirely inadequate. We have no single contact in the Tory Party; our Paris office is not really functioning; our New York office is nothing resembling what it should be . . .[29]

On Cudlipp's recommendation it was decided to dispense with Bolam completely. ('With Editors – and I say this with the greatest respect for those sorely-tried gentlemen – I feel a clear-cut break is the only way. You can't really demote an Editor – he has to go when the top man has lost faith in him. It is the fairer way in the end, and Bolam is a straightforward character who would not appreciate being humbugged.'[30]). Amid innumerable other changes and challenges, King concluded that Cudlipp was urgently needed back at Geraldine House. Cudlipp was itching to be back, not least because the *Daily Sketch* seemed to be spoiling for a fight: 'They have entirely purloined the Daily Mirror technique, and this means that we must rapidly develop the Daily Mirror on new and fresher lines.'[31]

'I am most anxious to get cracking immediately I return', he wrote to King at the New Year:

Coronation plans [Elizabeth II was to be crowned in June 1953] are urgent on both papers, and we must take every advantage of the splendid opportunity. Since you get back on Jan 25, and I will be at your service on Feb 5, is it possible, do you think, to

---

* 'May I comment,' wrote Cudlipp to me four decades later in a note attached to this long letter of King's, 'that this letter (among many others) indicates Cecil's terrific grip on the whole business?'

complete the Bolam–Nener change so that I can operate on the day I return? My suggestion is that you announce the whole new set-up simultaneously, saying that a further announcement will shortly be made about the *Pictorial* editorship . . . Best wishes for the exciting New Year before us.[32]

And exciting it was. Before Cudlipp got back, King had done as he requested and appointed Colin Valdar of the *Express* as Editor of the *Pictorial* and replaced Bolam with Nener. Jack Nener, who remained as editor until 1961, was someone hard to forget. He was described by one of his successors, Tony Miles, as straight from Central Casting's idea of a tabloid editor: 'crinkly silver hair, dapper bow tie, gravelly voice, gruff warmth, volcanic temperament.'[33] The journalist Audrey Whiting described him as 'an absolutely awful man to work for, dreadful beyond belief. He swore like a trooper. The language was awful, but it was deliberate. It wasn't until I actually married him and got to know him terribly well that he would laugh.'[34] 'In a hard-swearing Street,' recalled Keith Waterhouse:

Nener was acknowledged as the grand master of invective and abuse.

When, as Editor, he was taking part in some journalistic levee at the Midland Hotel, Manchester, he was colourfully holding forth in the lounge when an inoffensive 'civilian', as non-newspaper types were termed, approached him and asked, 'Excuse me, sir, would you mind moderating your language, as there are ladies present?' Nener, mistaking him for one of the seething mob of hacks who had more or less total control of the lounge, roared, 'Do you know who I am? I am the fucking editor of the fucking *Daily Mirror!*' 'Yes,' said the civilian mildly, 'I rather thought you might be.'[35]

Mirror staff, and Fleet Street in general, revelled in accounts of conversations between Nener and his deputy, Dick Dinsdale, usually overheard in the lavatory. The sub-editors, records Alan Watkins, 'like most people who work long shifts in unchanging company, had a number of catchphrases or joke sentences. One of them – it comes from the film of *Tom Brown's Schooldays* rather than from the book itself – was':

'Flashman, you are a bully and a liar, and there is no place for you in this school.'

Nener was overheard asking:

'Who's this Flashman, then, Dick?'

'Flashman? Flashman? I don't think we've got anyone of that name on the paper, Jack. Is he a reporter or a sub?'

'I don't give a fuck what he is, but get rid of him fucking quick. He's a bully and a liar.'

Yet though Nener's strong personality was felt throughout the *Mirror*, he was only technically the Editor, 'looking after the engine room and giving the crew their orders while Cudlipp, with a wave of his cigar, took the wheel as mood or inspiration decided'.[36] For feature writers like the young Keith Waterhouse, Cudlipp was a fertile source of ideas. 'From time to time I would be called up from my little cubbyhole to join him for the "elevenses" – a glass of wine or something stronger – that would embark me on some journalistic spree . . . I was sent aboard a banana boat in Liverpool Docks to investigate "the screwiest strike of all time"' – a demarcation dispute over whether the screw-holes in a piece of aluminium-covered wood should be bored by metal workers or carpenters – 'and meanwhile the bananas are still on the trees.'[37] From such polemics evolved such front-page signed Waterhouse leaders as 'How Long Must the Day of Rest Remain the Day of Rust?'

It was the genius of Cudlipp, observed Crossman's wife Anne in the mid-1950s, that 'each time he does a newspaper stunt, it's as though it's the very first he's ever done and he's as excited as a child and as skilled as a craftsman of fifty'.[38] It was a genius that communicated itself to his colleagues. 'Usually wearing an electric-blue suit,' wrote Waterhouse:

[Cudlipp] would appear in the newsroom some time after lunch, head thrust challengingly forward like that of an enquiring tortoise, teeth clamped on an outsize cigar, as he dissected and improved upon news and features page alike, in a normally amused voice that seemed to be forced down his nostrils without becoming nasal in the process. It was a striking performance and soon the more impressionable souls among the executives were copying the Cudlipp suit and the Cudlipp stance and the Cudlipp manner of speech.[39]

He would listen to ideas, but he got his own way: if necessary, as Alan Watkins points out, 'he could be an appalling bully'.

Everyone quickly got to know Cudlipp; few of them knew King. Waterhouse wrote that King was:

a patrician and remote personage, both figuratively and physi-cally, since he towered above everyone else in the building. In some effort, apparently, to unbend a little and get to know some of his staff, he had given a series of Christmas parties in his office at which, however, he spoke to nobody except his most senior executives. In the case of the features department this was not altogether surprising, since to a writer we turned up more or less drunk, having been celebrating at a lesser altitude earlier. King's expression as someone tapped out his pipe in a valuable Chinese vase distinctly said, 'Never again!'

The distinguished feature writer and biographer, Donald Zec, was intimidated by King because he seemed so aristocratic and Zec thought he had no sense of humour. Climbing the spiral staircase in the office one day, Zec met the descending King on the second landing, did not know what to say, lost his nerve and began to tell him a joke. So small that he felt he was addressing King's navel, Zec realised he was telling the wrong joke in the wrong way to the wrong person, and in a panic began to raise his voice and slap King on the arm for emphasis. 'Eventually I was shouting, "It wasn't the wife, it was the mother-in-law" and when I came to the end of the joke there was deathly silence.' King retraced his steps upstairs and Zec his downstairs; suddenly, from two flights up, he heard this enormous laugh.[40]

In an interview, King was asked how policy decisions were taken – 'by you individually, or by you and Hugh Cudlipp, the editorial director, or does it emerge as a general body of feeling from a round-table discussion?':

'It emerges,' said King. 'No one can dictate to Bill Connor – Cassandra – what he shall print in his column. No one can dictate to Vicky what he shall put in his cartoons. But the general policy trend of all the little features in the *Mirror* is roughly parallel. This is not done by instruction. This is done by a general group feeling that that is the course to pursue. If there is any difference obviously I have the final say and that's it.'[41]

In practice, this meant that King determined policy and Cudlipp transmitted it. Six days a week, when both were in London, Cudlipp would visit King's office, talk over news and ideas and then talk forcefully to his editors and other journalists ('I thought we'd do this, this, this and this. Get the picture? Got the idea?'). King and Cudlipp almost always agreed, though there were occasional differences of emphasis. In 1953, for instance, from Australia, King wrote a rare criticism:

I have looked at the Mirrors over the period of Stalin's death and do not feel they rose to the occasion. Stalin was the greatest political figure since Napoleon and, it may be, greater than he. Yet the Mirror does not make this point – in spite of my cable . . . I think the death of Stalin should have been treated in two stages – (1) the greatest political figure of our day is dead, (2) this is probably on balance a danger to the peace of the world. As to whether the official grief of Churchill and Attlee is sincere or appropriate is a side issue and surely should not have been put on the front page on the day.[42]

That they did not see eye to eye over this was more than anything a reflection of how raw power fascinated King, and how fascism – of the left or right – revolted Cudlipp. Such disagreements were always civilly debated. King did not throw his weight around; he disagreed with but tolerated, for instance, the *Mirror's* traditional opposition to capital punishment.

Reflecting contemporary Fleet Street, the papers were produced on an ocean of alcohol. Visit Cudlipp before 11 a.m. and you would be offered a beer (unless it was a day of celebration, when there would be a champagne conference at 10.30); after eleven he would open a bottle of white wine. While King, Cudlipp and senior journalists like the Political Editor, Sydney Jacobson, would tend to go to separate lunches with influential people (aperitif, wine, brandy), most feature writers would drift at lunchtime to the Falcon, the nearby pub better known as No. 10 or Winnie's, after the 'chain-smoking, gin-sipping archetypal landlady, a kindly, corseted figure inside which a chucker-out for ever lurking in readiness to bar anyone who overstepped the mark'.[43] *Mirror* and *Pictorial* reporters went to Barney Finnegan's further up the street, for there was a strict demarcation in Fleet Street's pubs. Senior people from various newspapers could, however, meet in the Old Cock, where Cudlipp might lunch on Saturdays, or El Vino, where early evening he could usually be found having a glass of champagne before looking in at the paper, perhaps disappearing to dine (aperitif, wine, brandy) and then returning to see it go to bed.*

Alcohol used to exacerbate Cudlipp's pugnacity. Crossman, who for all his socialism was an intellectual snob, was perennially in a state of wonderment at the ways of Fleet Street and was shocked by what was just another evening in the life of Hugh Cudlipp. In September 1953, with Cudlipp firmly installed as Editorial Director, Crossman was desperate to discuss with him what he should write about the forthcoming

---

*   A combination of his quick temper and his deep loyalty to friends made Cudlipp fall out with El Vino one lunchtime in 1957. Tom Baistow, a *News Chronicle* journalist, was drinking with a group that included Cudlipp, Cassandra, Sydney Jacobson and Vicky, the great cartoonist whom Cudlipp had brought to the *Mirror*. Baistow took from behind the counter the curly-brimmed bowler of the manager, Frank Bower, who dressed like an Edwardian, and stuck it on Vicky's head. 'As it fell down to his ears, he spread his hands wide in a caricature of a Jewish dealer and said: "Anyvun got any old clothes they vant to sell?"'

'At that moment Frank appeared from the other end of the bar, saw his beloved bowler on an alien head and roared: "How dare you take such a disgraceful liberty! Hand that hat back at once. If anything like this ever happens again I shall not permit you to frequent this establishment." Immediately I explained that it was my rather childish idea of a joke. "Never try such a trick again or I will ban you too," he declared imperiously.

"If that's how you treat a harmless bit of fun I don't know whether I'd want to use your *pub*," I replied, knowing the word would wound.

"I for one won't be using it again, you pompous old publican," said Hugh Cudlipp. Turning to us, he added: "Let's find a more congenial place where the landlord's hat isn't as tight as this fellow's." And we walked out. Not just because Bower had been so pompous but because we suspected that he wouldn't have created such a fuss if I had put his bowler on an Aryan head.

With typical Cudlippian panache, Hugh celebrated our act of self-abnegation by throwing a splendid lunch at the Café Royal at which we were each provided with a curly bowler that was ceremoniously punched through the crown when the brandy was served. Typically, also, Cudlipp was the only member of the group who never again set foot in El Vino.'[44]

Labour Party Conference, where supporters of his friend and ally Aneurin Bevan were to wage war on the Labour Establishment. Cudlipp eventually suggested supper at 10.30 at the Bagatelle:

> I found him there with Eileen and Rex North [a *Mirror* and *Pictorial* columnist] in a crowded, small room, with an appallingly noisy West African band. Rex North's wife was the one cabaret turn. Shouting through the band, we talked until two in the morning.
>
> Cudlipp started by telling me that he had been reading all of Aneurin Bevan's speeches and was going to launch an attack on him on the front page on Sunday. We sparred for an hour or two and at about one o'clock (I think Hugh had been drinking since about seven) he said that he probably wouldn't do a story on Aneurin Bevan and would leave me to do Morecambe in the column. He continued to repeat his line that I twiddled Phil Zec around my little finger but he was Editor, and he, Cudlipp, wasn't going to tolerate a Herbert Morrison or a Bevan and that the *Mirror* Group should be really independent. However, at another point he observed that it was the job of the *Mirror* Group, if they believed in Socialism, to launch their own constructive Socialist programme. Hugh is totally and absolutely incoherent but, curiously enough, he enjoys my company a great deal and is, I think, deeply mystified why I have got myself mixed up with that terrible man Bevan. I am sure Eileen keeps his hatred well fanned.
>
> I managed to get away at about half-past two in the morning. Fleet Street is a very extraordinary place. What is it that makes men like Hugh Cudlipp become the responsible (!) Editors of enormous circulation newspapers? What is it that makes people like myself write in them? Finally, what are the ethics of my going on writing the column when the paper has denounced Nye, as it will have done on Sunday?[45]

As indeed it did. Posters all over Morecambe publicised 'END THE BEVAN MYTH', the *Pictorial*'s savage attack on Bevan's 'vanity, arrogance [and] spleen'. 'Hugh feels he must assert himself as Editor in the political field,' concluded Crossman, and '. . . wants to show that he has some political ideas as well and I hope he feels better after his orgasm'. In Crossman's view, the article 'enormously assisted the Bevanites and the only person it really damaged was me, since a great number of left-wing delegates were, I think, shocked at the idea that I was writing for such a paper'.[46]

The mystery of 1950s' journalism is how papers ever came out. In the case of the *Mirror* group under King and Cudlipp, a key to success was that they bought talent lavishly and indulged it. King might be frugal in his private life, but he thought it short-sighted to be a penny-pincher with journalists. Like Northcliffe, he paid probably the highest salaries in Fleet Street, and he always encouraged staff to travel. 'I think it is an excellent idea for you to go to Australia via the Far East,' he told Cudlipp in 1953. 'As you say it enlarges your knowledge of the world. The Australian assignment is a dreary chore and if you can get fun out of it by showing Eileen more of the world, why not?'[47] Cudlipp likewise encouraged staff to broaden their horizons, open their minds and travel at every opportunity. 'First-rate idea,' he responded, when Crossman asked if he could go to Egypt at the *Pictorial*'s expense.[48]

In June 1953, a few months after Cudlipp's return from Australia, the *Mirror* could brag that it had broken another world record by selling more than seven million copies of its coronation issue. In August, in a letter from West Africa, King wrote, 'I should like to say that no one could have been a better collaborator than you have been these last 15 months or so. It has been a great pleasure to me to work with you and the results have been spectacular! Thank you.'[49]

There was an opportunity for celebration that October with the fiftieth birthday of the *Daily Mirror*. In his spare time in Australia, Cudlipp had written its history. 'Nobody will read a book telling *chronologically* the story of a paper (other than The Times),'[50] he had told King, when an early draft by another journalist was found wanting. This must be a frank, amusing and personality-driven account, insisted Cudlipp, with dramatic episodes such as the on-off relationship with Churchill and a contempt of court case that had resulted in Bolam going to jail for three months in 1949. So Cudlipp took on the job himself, and *Publish and Be Damned!* was written with tabloid readers in mind and crammed with incident, anecdote and bite-sized information.

Criticisms of the modern *Mirror* were examined and defiantly rejected. Bolam's classic late-1940s' defence of sensationalism was given pride of place:

> Sensationalism does not mean distorting the truth. It means the vivid and dramatic presentation of events so as to give them a forceful impact on the mind of the reader. It means big head-lines, vigorous writing, simplification into familiar everyday lan-guage, and the wide use of illustration by cartoon and photograph.
>
> To give two examples. We used it during the war to launch a VD campaign which was vitally necessary for the welfare of the Forces when a too-timid Government Department had the facts and dare not use them. We used it again when the national eco-nomic crisis demanded an explanation to the public which the Government, not expert in these matters, was leaving bewildered and ill-informed.
>
> In both cases we were widely praised for our enterprise, and our methods were at once followed by the Government. To-day the need for sensational journalism is even more apparent. Every great problem facing us – the world economic crisis, diminishing food supplies, the population puzzle, the Iron Curtain and a host of others – will only be understood by the ordinary man busy with his daily tasks if he is hit hard and hit often with the facts.
>
> Sensational treatment is the answer, whatever the sober and 'superior' readers of some other journals may prefer.
>
> As in larger, so in smaller and more personal affairs, the *Mirror* and its millions of readers prefer the vivid to the dull and the vigorous to the timid.
>
> No doubt we make mistakes, but we are at least alive.[51]

Such serious passages were well encased in classic *Mirror* froth. 'CAN A WOMAN HATCH EGGS?' was the title of the first of forty-three short chapters, with underneath:

> '*Cock-a-doodle do*' – The Mirror *tackles the problem of Higher Production – Elephant Sees Editor, Drops Dead – The Colorado beetle racket – How to assassinate your reader's pets and blow up their houses*

The first story told of bed-bound Peggy, persuaded by the letters editors to try hatching eggs, whose mission ended in deep disappointment.* Next was a vignette of Bart thrashing out with staff and economists how to help raise productivity. As they agreed that the solution was fewer restrictive practices and 'Work. Work. Work', they were interrupted by hammering from construction engineers overhead; Bart's immediate response was to scream for somebody to get upstairs 'at once and stop that bloody noise!' The elephant, Babs, one of three owned by the paper and paraded for charity, was led into the Editor's room and promptly dropped dead. The *Mirror's* patriotic offer to pay £10 for the corpse of any Colorado beetle found ravaging potatoes was withdrawn when it emerged that barrow-boys had been inspired to import them from France. The pets in peril were puppies with headcolds, accidentally recommended a lethal potion, and the endangered readers were those who followed an ill-considered fuel-saving tip. Entwined around these escapades was some hard information about circulation and the paper's anti-fascist record.

The trickiest areas for Cudlipp, which drew on all his considerable resources of cunning and charm, were the portraits of Bart and King, culminating in the last chapter:

'YOUNGER MEN':
The end of The 'Bart' Legend – A nephew of Northcliffe takes command – The Bartholomew–Cecil King collaboration – When a genius erupts – The paper's policy – Character of the new Chairman

Cudlipp was as generous about Bart's virtues as he thought King would permit, and as discreet about his vices as he could be without distorting history and boring the reader. He tiptoed around the Bart–King relationship in a style that certainly could not have been accused of sensationalism: 'Over the years Cecil King had a certain influence upon his predecessor which the older man resented. It was this resentment which clouded their association and occasionally led the volatile "Bart" to plan petty discomfitures he would later regret

---

* Several girls at Priscilla's school experimented equally unsuccessfully with eggs in their bras.

and reverse.'[52] King, he explained, 'wholly admired "Bart's" gifts and knew that the eruptive nature was a corollary of his genius'. Mendaciously, he added that 'King's respect and affection were profound for the active volcano on whose slopes he had resided, sometimes uneasily, during the two rousing decades in which the *Mirror* was being transformed.'

Handling the portrait of King that concluded the book was even trickier; King wanted the truth, but he wanted the truth as he saw it. Cudlipp needed to be tactful, but he wanted to avoid seeming sycophantic. In *Publish and Be Damned!*, as in everyday life, he often struggled to stay on that tightrope, leavening the respectful – occasionally even portentous – appraisal ('Cecil King is essentially a Harmsworth, scion of a family which has enjoyed genius, wealth and power, and more than its share of tragedy') with disarming candour and a hint of *lèse-majesté*:

> The forbidding factor in King's relationship with the rest of the human race is his aloofness, and few have vaulted the stile. Once over, old hikers report, the going is harder. His demands on his colleagues are exacting, but his trust, once placed, is complete.
>
> A sycophantic biographer would be hard put to it to explain away the more ascetic aspects of his emotional make-up. The aloofness could be accounted for by the shyness which afflicts other men of unusual tallness, but there can be no such pleasing vindication of the imperious gusts which on occasion cause trepidation in those around him . . .
>
> I have seen hardened debaters emerge from their first conference bearing the demeanour of men who have failed to penetrate the sound barrier; small comfort to them to hear of other pilots killed in the attempt.

That would have pleased King. As would this:

> It is now known in Geraldine House that when the new Chairman sets out on a business mission overseas and asks an executive or a writer to accompany him, the travelling companions are under surveillance, their characters are being weighted, their knowledge probed.

They return with stories of how the tall man fought his way through a mob of four hundred excited gibbering Indians to buy a ticket for a native cinema in Bombay; of how he stopped his car in the Australian bush to pick a wild flower; of his request to a pagan tribesman in Nigeria to demonstrate his prowess with a bow and arrow in return for a handsome tip; of the loud guffaw that astonished a group of nude African villagers when King discovered that the total equipment of their mud hut consisted of a sleeping mat, an eating bowl – and a selection of Hollywood pin-ups stuck to the wall.[53]

King was sent the text in draft:

30th January 1953

From: Mr Cecil King   To: Mr Hugh Cudlipp

In your chapter about myself there are some very amusing bits, but the general effect seems to me rather unintelligible.

From my point of view I should say that my good points are: –

1. I am a good organiser;
2. I have a vast fund of knowledge on almost every subject except music; and
3. My aloofness is an aid to good judgement of men and situations. It makes me a good critic.

From the point of view of the business my weakest point is that I am very shy and aloof and so find it difficult to establish any very satisfactory relationship with anyone.

A minor point is that I should rather no mention were made of the Croydon Times, a failure of long ago. On the other hand the British Film Institute, of which I was a very successful chairman for four years, might well be mentioned in passing.

Cudlipp followed instructions faithfully, but retained as much of the diverting material as he could. 'I think you have greatly improved the end,' commented King on the next reading, 'and have now no important criticisms to make. However . . . There are some allegedly typical judgments of people in Chapter 43 that I should not make, and anyway there are too many.'[54] In the published version, those surviving apophthegms that followed the sentence 'In his laconic, candid opinions of other people lie the clues to his own character and aspirations' were:

> 'That goose will never be a swan.'
> 'Dishonest.'
> 'A catalogue of his shortcomings would be tedious.'
> 'No fire in his belly.'
> 'Not ruthless enough.'
> 'You can see he is the boss of the department as soon as you walk into the room.'
> 'He is not the sort of man you would hand your hat and coat to' [this was apropos Attlee].
> 'Yes' – and this is the highest accolade of all – 'he *could* set the Thames on fire.'[55]

At King's request, Cudlipp also removed the lines '"I like him"(never important to me) and "He has a sense of duty."'[56]

Looking towards the future, Cudlipp exulted that while competitors had expected a period of consolidation and a move to the right under the new Chairman, 'more developments have in fact been considered during the past eighteen months than ever before in the company's story'. In his first year alone, King had been to 'Australia, Nigeria, the Gold Coast, Germany, America twice and Canada once'. It had become clear that the *Mirror* 'would not only remain an independent paper of the Left, but would be free of influence by individual politicians. King privately exchanges ideas with all factions of all parties, and thus ensures that his top executives are inoculated against pressure from any one source.'

The peroration read like a call to arms, though it was a call that had already been sounded by King himself, albeit in private. 'There is evidence that the paper is becoming more, and not less, political,' wrote Cudlipp:

> that it is striving for new methods of presenting serious news as well as light and human items. With a circulation of more

than 4,500,000 the *Mirror* claims to be read every day by 11,000,000 people. An immense power for good lies within its grasp.

Can it achieve its popularity and at the same time raise its prestige? If this goal is achieved Cecil King's name will be fourth on the list of the men who have decisively influenced the *Mirror*'s history.

The first was Lord Northcliffe, who founded it and built up its circulation to over a million. The second was the first Lord Rothermere, who killed its reputation as a newspaper but created the company's financial structure with a genius unequalled since his death. The third was Bartholomew – brilliant, truculent, mercurial – whose own pulse beat in unison with the pulse of the masses and who drove the paper so far and so fast that for the second time in its fifty exciting years it carries under its title the magic words –

THE BIGGEST DAILY SALE ON EARTH

FORWARD WITH THE PEOPLE[57]

Colin Valdar, the *Pictorial*'s Editor, persuaded a reluctant Crossman to review the book, which he found 'racy and in parts really brilliant, the work, as you might expect, of a talented thug'. An anxious Cudlipp asked Crossman to see him and, when shown his draft, said:

'I can't have myself mentioned. It's the book to be reviewed, not the author.' To which I replied that it was against every principle of *Daily Mirror* journalism to leave out personalities

Hugh then said we'd better let the Chairman adjudicate and up I was wafted to the Chairman's inner sanctum. Cecil King solemnly sat down and read the review and said he had no objections to the passages about Hugh. Then came a passage where I had written that the *Mirror* started as a circulation stunt and got its social conscience in the war. King really got very angry. 'That's just not true,' he said. 'Do you imagine that our advertisers were pleased when we attacked appeasement and supported left-wing causes? Do you imagine we weren't all risking our jobs? We did it because we believed in it. And then the circulation came.'

I said that the book had given me the other impression but

I certainly didn't want to write what was untrue. 'Ugh, the book!' King said. 'After all, it's only a publicity stunt.' Wisely or unwisely, I said, 'Now I've got you. I'm asked to review a book on its merits and you suddenly say it's a publicity stunt. You're all schizophrenes here. You really don't know when you're crusading and when you're making money.' I must say King laughed a good deal.[58]

The print run was 40,000 and the reviews generally good. At the Foyle's Literary Lunch for *Publish and Be Damned!*:

The speakers included important and serious people with important and serious things to say, but though the luncheon went on until 3.45, neither Lord Beveridge nor Sir Norman Angell ever got a chance of making their speeches. Instead of the few wise and witty words expected by way of Chairman's introduction, Mr Randolph Churchill spent twenty-five minutes virulently abusing the popular press as a whole. Lord Rothermere was his most battered target, but Hugh Cudlipp and the Daily Mirror had their share of trouncing. When he had finished, Cudlipp, white with passion, threw the notes of his prepared speech aside and began by telling us of undignified incidents in Mr Churchill's past. He retorted so effectively that he soon had the Chairman on his feet competing with him for command of the microphone. It was one of those scenes which, as the saying goes, are 'unforgettable'; those who missed them 'would have paid £100 to be there'.[59]

Winston Churchill's angry, disappointed, drunken son Randolph – who would himself become a columnist for that most vulgar of tabloids, the *News of the World* – was complaining not just about the *Mirror*, but about press standards in general. He particularly enraged Cudlipp with the suggestion that newspapers conspired to deny the existence of their 'Dog-Don't-Eat-Dog' agreement. 'I have never noticed any reluctance for dog to eat the *Mirror*,' wrote Cudlipp later about this dispute, 'nor has there ever been any reluctance for the *Mirror* to wolf any offending member of the canine species, from a mongrel like the *Daily Sketch* to a sporty dog like the *Daily Express*, and the highest-bred hounds like *The Times* and *Telegraph*.' As for the *Mirror*, it 'has ladled out eulogy and censure without stint, selecting dog and lamppost as the facts merited'.[60]

(Cudlipp's favourite dog and lamppost story concerned the *Mirror*'s response to the *Telegraph*'s 'tut-tut' when the *Straits Times Annual* showed the British Commissioner-General walking across a beach hand-in-hand with the daughter and niece of a chief, both of whom were naked from the waist up. 'It is surely unnecessary,' said the *Telegraph*, 'for even a pro-consul to follow so closely the adage "When in Rome do as the Romans do".' The *Mirror* 'was not standing for a piece of prudishness like this, and it promptly published the offending print across six columns, with the headline "THE PICTURE THAT SHOCKED THE DAILY TELEGRAPH".[61])

Still, though Cudlipp and King thought themselves socially radical, when it came to sex, their radicalism was restricted to heterosexuality: both were revolted and alarmed by homosexuality. 'Vicars, teachers and choirmasters passed in sordid parade through the court columns of the *News of the World*,' wrote Cudlipp in 1962, 'but Parliament, press and public alike evaded any serious discussion of the homosexual problem.'[62] Cudlipp decided to apply to this issue a favourite device he called 'The Green Light': 'say it first, get away with it, and others will follow. At all events say it first.'[63]

Shortly after Cudlipp's return to the *Pictorial*, he organised a three-part series called 'Evil Men' which, as he later put it, 'stripped the subject of the careful euphemistic language in which it had always been concealed. Doctors, social workers and the wretched homosexuals themselves recognised this as a sincere attempt to get to the root of a spreading fungus.'[64] To Crossman the series was 'lurid';[65] to James Cooke, the Financial Director, it was an outrage: 'he burst into my room in a state of unprecedented anger,' recollected Cudlipp. '"I have cancelled our own newspaper from my newsagent," he said; "I am now going up to the chairman to demand that he takes action." I replied: "I wouldn't if I were you, James. It was his idea."'[66]

'Evil Men' lifted the 'veil of secrecy' that was helping 'an unnatural sex vice' to get 'a dangerous grip' on Britain. The problem, the article warned, was underestimated because the public thought all homosexuals were '"pansies" – mincing, effeminate young men who call themselves "queers"'. The truth was that the 'obviously effeminate' were a small minority; unknown to the public, 'perverts' could be found even among 'generals, admirals, fighter pilots, engine drivers and boxers'. There were warnings about the rampant spread of this vice and its potential for corrupting society, as well as proposals by a psychiatrist that institutions be established wherein homosexuals could be kept until they were cured.

'This was Cudlipp's great scoop,' wrote Patrick Higgins in his *Heterosexual Dictatorship: male homosexuality in postwar Britain*, 'the breaking of the "last taboo", a sequence of articles that presented a completely negative and hostile picture of male homosexuality and was intended to titillate and terrify the readers of the newspapers, to promote ignorance, intolerance and hatred.'[67]

King was dead when Higgins's book was published; Cudlipp bought it, but did not talk about it – a sure sign that he was upset. Quite apart from his natural indignation at the suggestion that 'Evil Men' was somehow a more important scoop than the many hundreds he had pulled off in his time, he would have understood the attack no more than King. They were creatures of their time; from their perspective, the public was being rightly informed and warned about a form of sexuality they both believed to be bad for its practitioners and dangerous for the young. King particularly would have seen it as entirely consistent with the highly effective *Mirror* campaign he inspired during the war that told the truth about venereal disease. Nor was there any doubt about the genuineness of their concern for the vulnerability of children at boarding school to paedophile masters. During the mid-1950s they were rightly proud of the *Pictorial*'s role in disgracing the principal of the London Choir School, a bogus priest, whose degeneracy extended to inviting outsiders to participate in sex with pupils. And there was enough evidence of child molestation to justify the *Pictorial* campaign for the protection of children in private schools.

Yet, like many heterosexuals at that time, they muddled homosexuality with paedophilia and therefore entitled Higgins to describe the *Pictorial* as intermittently campaigning for a witch-hunt against ordinary homosexuals. Because of King's solitary life at Winchester and Cudlipp's progress from a Wesleyan Methodist background to an aggressively macho world, they were less understanding and far less tolerant than much of the Establishment; many of those they commonly lambasted as reactionaries were relaxed about what they or their contemporaries had got up to in school dormitories.

There were differences of emphasis between them: in practice, Cudlipp was much less bothered about homosexuality than King. Although even in old age his viewpoint was as aggressively heterosexual as ever and he still made fun of 'queers', he enjoyed the company of many homosexuals and revelled light-heartedly in gossip about gays in the cathedral town to which he retired. King's attitude to homosexuality was close to being one of pathological loathing; he was, said Cudlipp, obsessed with homosexuals in high places, particularly the Foreign Office,[68] and saw them in every bed: 'The number of people he mentioned to me over the years as homosexuals led me to ponder whether *homo sapiens* could be relied upon any longer to propagate the species.'[69] In old age, asked by a putative biographer about Oxford friends, King mentioned Francis Needham and Harold Paton, but dismissed them by saying that he had 'discovered' they were 'homosexuals';[70] it seems more than likely that he felt Needham's sexual orientation had somehow retrospectively sullied their intimacy, and that produced a sense of personal betrayal that drove the *Pictorial* crusade.

It was King who, through Cudlipp, spearheaded the assaults on upper-crust homosexuality. 'There has for years existed inside the Foreign Office service,' thundered the *Pictorial* in 1955 – revisiting the defection to the Soviet Union in 1951 of the spies and 'sex perverts' Guy Burgess and Donald Maclean – 'a chain or clique of perverted men.'[71] One of King's protégés, the Labour MP George Brown, wrote in the same issue of the feudal, aristocratic and effeminate nature of British diplomats. Another, Alf Robens, Shadow Foreign Secretary, revealed how enemy agents blackmailed 'perverts'. Increasingly the Conservative government was attacked as decadent for failing to root out homosexuals from education and the public service.[72]

In 1957 the Wolfenden Report recommended that homosexual activity between consenting adults in private be decriminalised, but that male prostitution be made illegal. The *Mirror* and the *Pictorial* were in support, but only because they argued that 'vice' was best kept out of public view. They majored on prostitution and their tone was as harsh as any right-wing newspaper.

Homosexuality's avenger came in the shape of the flamboyant American pianist and showman, Liberace, whose hysterical welcome in London in 1956 had provoked Cassandra into describing him as:

> a deadly, winking, sniggering, chromium-plated, scent-impreg-
> nated, luminous, quivering, giggling, fruit-flavoured, mincing, ice-
> covered, heap of mother love . . . This appalling man – and I
> use the word appalling in no other sense than its true sense of
> 'terrifying' – has hit this country in a way that is as violent as
> Churchill receiving the cheers on VE Day. He reeks with emetic
> language that can only make grown men long for a quiet-corner,
> an aspidistra, a handkerchief and the old heave-ho.
>
> Without doubt he is the biggest sentimental vomit of all time.
> Slobbering over his mother, winking at his brother and counting
> the cash at every second, this superb piece of calculating candy-
> floss has an answer for every situation . . . There must be some-
> thing wrong with us that our teenagers longing for sex and our
> middle-aged matrons fed up with sex, alike should fall for such
> a sugary mountain of jingling claptrap wrapped up in such a
> preposterous clown.[73]

Most upsetting of all to Liberace was the passage 'He is the summit
of sex – the pinnacle of masculine, feminine, and neuter. Everything
that he, she and it can ever want.' Liberace had suffered in the United
States from tabloid innuendoes about his sexuality and other sneers
from the British press had bothered him, but Cassandra outraged him.
'It hurt me,' Liberace said later. 'People stayed away from my shows
in droves.' Convinced that it was the implication of homosexuality
that was damaging his career, Liberace decided he would make the
Cassandra article a test-case; if he won, no one would ever again dare
to question his sexuality.

To strengthen his defence, in the words of his biographer, he
'defagified' himself, eschewed the sequinned jackets and adopted pro
tem a conventional style of life. 'On my word of God, on my
mother's health, which is so dear to me,' he explained in court, 'this
article only means one thing, that I am a homosexual, and that is
why I am in this court.' Cassandra's was 'the most improper article
that has ever been written about me. It has been widely quoted in
all parts of the world and has been reproduced exactly as it appeared
in the *Daily Mirror*.'[74] Asked if he had ever indulged in homosexual

practices,' Liberace lied with élan: 'No, sir, never in my life. I am against the practice because it offends convention and it offends society.'

It took three years to get the case to court, where it provided the British and American press and public with immense enjoyment, but it was devastating for Cassandra, who went through many days of torture in the witness box being ruthlessly cross-examined by Liberace's counsel, Sir Gilbert Beyfus. Although Cassandra fought back initially, he was never as good in speech as on paper and Beyfus often put him in the wrong. With echoes of Churchill's wartime condemnation, Beyfus dismissed Cassandra as 'a literary assassin who dips his pen in vitriol instead of ink and is hired by this sensational newspaper to murder reputations and hand out to the public day by day these sensational articles on which its circulation is built'.

Even the much more ebullient and confident Cudlipp felt outclassed by Beyfus, whose selective quotes from *Publish and Be Damned!* were devastating. Cudlipp did not enjoy 'being revived by playful pats so that I could be caught again'.[75] Still, like Cassandra, Cudlipp occasionally scored:

> Beyfus: Up to quite recently it would be a quite frequent sight to see both of you drinking in a Fleet Street bar?

> Cudlipp: Most certainly. In El Vino, where barristers meet after their cases and where we meet after our newspapers.[76]

'Might I suggest,' said Beyfus in his closing speech, declaring his intention of trying 'to match the language of Cassandra', that 'this newspaper is vicious and violent, venomous and vindictive, salacious and sensational and ruthless and remorseless? I do not think that is quite up to Cassandra's standards, but it is the best I can do.'

The case cost the *Mirror* what was then the enormous sum of £8,000[*] in damages, plus £27,000 in legal costs. It was then that Liberace coined the phrase 'I cried all the way to the bank!' That they knew he had perjured himself shamelessly did not make Cudlipp and King like

---

[*] About £110,000 today.

homosexuals more. (When Liberace died of AIDS in 1987, the *Mirror* suggested that his estate might like to return the money.)

Higgins sees the 1950s as a time when, in pursuit of circulation and hence advertising revenue, the popular press hysterically demonised those who could be presented as different: sexually (prostitutes and homosexuals), socially (criminals, single mothers and welfare dependants) or racially:

> In this way an incredible amount of poison was released into British society, with some terrible cultural consequences.
>
> This process of demonisation was constructed around the notion of normality which newspapers suggested were the characteristics shared by the broad mass of their readers: ordinary, decent, honest, hard-working, and above all else respectable. Every reader, it was assumed, was completely heterosexual; if single, they aspired to marriage, and when married they aspired to become parents, remained faithful to their partner and dedicated themselves to providing a good home for their family. Of course many of the journalists shared these prejudices. Fleet Street in the 1950s was overwhelmingly male and dominantly heterosexual, as reflected in what they wrote.[77]

Cudlipp, said Higgins, was 'the man who more than any other orchestrated many of these developments'.[78]

Higgins's demonisation of Cudlipp not only omits the role of King, but also completely ignores their compassionate and radical record on social and economic policy, as well as on race. The *Mirror* was famous, for instance, for 'Shock Issues' on child cruelty and neglect, squalid housing and the loneliness of many old people. Francis Williams rightly attributed to it and the *Pictorial* 'a large part in creating a more liberal social climate in British middle and lower middle class society'.[79] But then, Higgins's is a single-issue book. Yet his perspective is refreshing. It is as rare to find people who loathed Cudlipp as it is to find those who loved King, but Higgins certainly packed an interesting punch:

> Cudlipp's own political philosophy was extremely naïve, completely without any historical understanding and with absolutely no comparative dimension. It revolved around the special role

of the press in the political and social life of the nation and on a sentimental regard for the people. He cast himself as their tribune. There was clearly a sexual dimension to this struggle against the establishment, which was often depicted as effete, smooth and unmanly in contrast to Cudlipp and his allies, who were presented as masculine, virile and *totally* heterosexual.

Had Cudlipp met Higgins, he would have pointed out that understanding the historical dimension was King's job; would have made no apologies for being a body-and-soul newspaperman; and would robustly have suggested that his success in his work, and a huge range of friends who crossed the spectrum from royals to bus conductors, demonstrated that he indeed had an understanding of the British people as a whole that was far too deep and realistic to admit of sentiment. On the sexual dimension, he would have grinned and pleaded guilty to being typical of his world and the 1950s.

Despite the expensive punishment meted out by Liberace, bringing 'The Green Light' to bear on homosexuality had been good for sales. Doing the same for royalty was even better.

As an editor, Cudlipp's first serious engagement with royalty had come shortly after he took over the *Pictorial* in the autumn of 1937. When Compton Mackenzie delivered proofs of *The Windsor Tapestry* – for the serialisation rights of which the *Pictorial* had paid the enormous price of £5,000[*] – Cudlipp discovered it was dull. What had been expected to be the authorised story of the Duke of Windsor dealt mainly with ancestors about whom *Pictorial* readers would care little. The forty-eight-year-old Cudlipp looked back fondly on his youthful impudence:

Compton Mackenzie was on his way to London . . . when the *Pictorial* announced, bold as brass, that it no longer wished to serialise the book. Being the *Pictorial*, the announcement was not made in a modest and becoming manner; the book, I told our readers, was marred by a single chapter entitled 'Heritage', a section in which the distinguished author had devoted his talents

---

[*] About £240,000 today.

to a skilful dredging operation into the not so salubrious past of the Royal Family. That exercise, I decided in a moment of excessive royal fervour, would embarrass the reigning King and Queen – come to think of it, a facile but saleable proposition.

I dispatched the £5,000 cheque, and to prove it printed a facsimile of the missile on the front page: THE CHEQUE THAT ENDS A DISHONOURABLE DEAL . . . Compared with [Malcolm] Muggeridge's essays on royalty, Mackenzie's effort was a royalist homily: he was, after all, merely chipping a little off the old blocks, their ancestors. But 20 years ago the fact that Queen Charlotte, more than a century earlier, 'always had to exercise a good deal of care in discouraging too much affection between the Royal children' was dynamite to the *Pictorial* and it said so.[80]

The ensuing publicity was good for the *Pictorial*. It was even better for the *Sunday Dispatch*, whose Editor trumped Cudlipp and won a massive increase in circulation by giving Mackenzie £1,000 to write twelve lively articles based on his now notorious book.[81]

Royalty always sold papers, so just after the circulation triumph of the coronation in June 1953, Cudlipp was delighted by the growing rumours of a Princess Margaret romance. *The People* – the first paper to mention it – spoke of 'scandalous' but 'utterly untrue' rumours that she was in love with a divorced man. As hints began to appear in other papers, Cudlipp decided on another poll: *Mirror* readers were asked to vote on the loaded question:

Group Captain Peter Townsend, 38-year-old Battle of Britain pilot, was the innocent party in a divorce. He was given the custody of his two children and his former wife has recently married.

If Princess Margaret, now 22, so desires, should she be allowed to marry him?[82]

Yes, said 97 per cent of the 70,000 voters; 'unwarrantable and disgusting intrusion into the affairs of that Royal personage,' said the president of the Methodist Conference, and the Press Council condemned the article as contrary to the best traditions of British journalism. There was a long hiatus during which Townsend was banished to Brussels from his position at court, but in the spring of 1955 the *Pictorial* reported that Margaret would soon have to make up her mind whether, on reaching twenty-five – the age at which she no longer had to ask her sister's permission to marry – she would renounce her rights of succession; the *Mirror* quoted Townsend as saying 'the word cannot come from me'. In August the *Mirror* produced a front page that would be reproduced all over the world. Cudlipp's headlines were:

The Princess is 25
on Sunday.
Will she wed? When
will she announce
her decision?
COME ON
MARGARET!
PLEASE MAKE UP YOUR MIND!

Press reactions were forthright: 'hitherto unreached depths of self-importance, impertinence and plain bad manners' (*News Chronicle*); 'inexcusable vulgarity (not to say cruelty)' (*Yorkshire Post*). But this was a classic case of 'The Green Light', for after a couple of months in which Margaret, her family, the Cabinet and the public agonised about whether she could marry outside the Church and yet retain her royal title, public role and Civil List income, the rest of the press followed the *Mirror* in demanding a resolution of her dilemma. 'One by one,' observed *The Economist*, 'British newspapers have slipped off the leash to comment upon her problem, each in turn criticising the bad taste of the others that have spoken before it.'[83]

It was Cudlipp who gave a job to Malcolm Muggeridge in 1957 when he lost his column on the *Sunday Dispatch* for the crime of writing in an American magazine of the need for royal reforms. And the *Mirror*, like 80 per cent of its postbag, supported John Grigg (Lord Altrincham) when he was viciously attacked for criticising the exclusivity of court life – a theme that the *Mirror* had been pushing since late 1956, when Keith Waterhouse wrote a series called 'The Royal Circle' and concluded that 'The circle surrounding the throne is as aristocratic, as insular and – there is no more suitable word – as toffee-nosed as it has ever been'.

A particular target was the coming-out and husband-hunting season of well-born or well-heeled debutantes, the two high spots of which were being presented at court and attending Queen Charlotte's Ball; the stunt that emerged from this campaign in 1957 was a perfect example of how the *Mirror* worked in practice. The idea started with Marjorie Proops, the fashion-artist-turned-agony-aunt who had trained on the *Mirror*, been lost in 1945 to Percy Cudlipp's *Daily Herald* and then been tempted back to the *Mirror* in 1954. (One of her articles around this time inspired 27,000 letters.) She proposed to Cudlipp that she select four Proops' Debs and entertain them to 'a swanky dinner' in the West End.

> 'Fine,' I said, 'but let's make it a Debs' Ball – a sumptuous affair to which we can invite 100 *Mirror* Debs from all over the country. Girls who are working for their living at typewriters, or in factories, or standing behind counters.'
>
> 'And let's hold it at the May Fair,' said 'Tommy' Atkins, the Mirror promotions director, 'and give them all £15* to buy a new white dress. And send the *Mirror* Deb of the year to the Isle of Capri for a fortnight's holiday in the sun.'
>
> 'And put them up for the night in London. And have a huge cake – a bigger cake than Queen Charlotte's,' said Jack Nener, then editor of the paper. 'And have them all flutter down the stairway.'[84]

As soon as this was announced, Norman Hartnell, the Queen's dressmaker, offered to design a dress for the girl chosen as *Mirror* Deb of the Year. At the ball, the music was provided by the society debs' favourite bandleader; guests included a cousin of the Queen Mother and a clutch of peers, ambassadors and statesmen; Eileen Cudlipp taught a clerical friend of Princess Margaret's to 'rock'n'roll'; and real deb Henrietta Tiarks, who later married the Marquis of Tavistock, was there to congratulate the winner. Cudlipp was adept at charming

---

* About £200 today.

the toffs, who were equally good at showing they could take a joke. When, later that year, Buckingham Palace announced that debutantes would no longer be presented at court after the 1958 season, the *Mirror* solemnly announced that it would hold its last Debs' Ball the same year.

Cudlipp believed the *Mirror* deserved credit for what in 1962 he described as 'the revolution at the Palace', which became obvious from 1957 (reductions in protocol, the use of television, Prince Charles going to school), but he made it clear, as he always made it clear, that 'it was not the popular press that *caused* it, but public opinion *reflected* by the popular press. Campaigns in newspapers succeed only if they are in tune with public opinion which already exists, or if they stimulate with new ideas and information – The Green Light – a process of thought already formed in the mind of the masses.'[85]

Despite all the fun, a campaign such as this demonstrated the underlying seriousness of the King–Cudlipp *Mirror*, which Francis Williams assessed in 1969 as having wedded:

> the tabloid form to the examination of public affairs to an extent that had previously scarcely seemed possible. The decision to do this was taken as a deliberate act of policy based on the conviction that mass readers were becoming steadily more interested in public affairs and anxious to be informed about them. This decision aroused a good deal of derision when first made and was dismissed by many in Fleet Street as a high falutin' notion bound to fail. But it proved brilliantly successful.
>
> Nor is the seriousness any the less significant for being intermittent, based on the sensible principle that for the *Mirror* to ram run-of-the-mill serious news down its readers' throats day after day would merely bore them, but that to splash a really serious issue all across the front page and perhaps across the whole of the middle pages as well in brash, simple language under large black headlines not only makes them read it but makes them say to themselves, 'Well by God, if the *Mirror* thinks it's that important it must be.'[86]

Though on an issue like the modernisation of the monarchy, Cudlipp's egalitarian instincts would have driven such a campaign with or without Cecil King, King's interests and influence were obvious in many of the paper's preoccupations – for all that they were filtered through the personality and talents of Hugh Cudlipp. Looking back on his family history, King's favourite grandson, Francis's son Laurence, reflected rightly that 'Northcliffe's great achievement was to create newspapers which reflected the interest and language of the public at large. The *Mirror* took this further. It was the first news-paper not only to present the world from the perspective of its mass readership, but also to campaign systematically on their behalf. It defended the interests of its readership, not its shareholders. This had at least as much to do with Cecil King, the patrician at war with the Establishment, as it did with Hugh Cudlipp, the inspired journalist who provided the words . . . King and Cudlipp together,' he added, 'created a *Mirror* with an almost Reithian mission to inform its read-ership'.

King's contribution would be overshadowed by later dramatic events, but there was no doubting the importance of his contribution. There were, for instance, the *Mirror*'s 'Spotlight' pamphlets, written by experts and often dealing with such issues of deep interest to King as Africa (on which he remained fervently anti-colonial), the Common Market (he was an early believer), the future of television (he embraced and invested in commercial television) and the Anglo-American partner-ship (which in the post-war world he always wanted strengthened).

So impressed by the pamphlet on justice was the Attorney-General, Sir Reginald Manningham-Buller, that he wrote a private letter of congratulation to the Editor, while the Lord Chief Justice, Lord Goddard, wrote a long commentary on its recommendations and agreed to have the gist of his views published; the headline was 'HOW LORD GODDARD IS TRYING TO SPEED UP JUSTICE.'[87] And Cudlipp was delighted when Winston Churchill's Parliamentary Private Secretary and son-in-law, Christopher Soames, phoned the *Mirror* on a Saturday to request urgently several copies of the pamphlet on defence for the benefit of ministers discussing the issue with the Prime Minister at Chequers.[88]

Churchill, like most politicians, paid a great deal of attention to the *Mirror*. A Cudlipp editorial in late 1952 urging him to bridge 'the great Atlantic Gap . . . as the crowning act of his great career' elicited a letter: 'My dear Harmsworth King, It is a long time since we have corresponded directly and much has happened for good or evil in the meantime. But I thought your article in the DAILY MIRROR was so very fair and friendly that I should thank you for it . . .'[89] King was away, but 'it was written from the heart', responded Cudlipp,[90] who, unlike King, shared the admiration and affection for Churchill felt by the general public, although thinking he should have retired years before.

Within a few months it was back to normal bad relations. When in June 1953 it was announced that the seventy-eight-year-old Churchill had been ordered by his doctors to rest, the *Mirror* – rightly suspecting that he was sicker than was being admitted – broke ranks with the largely pro-Churchill press and asked, 'Should Churchill Retire?'

Lord Moran, his doctor, recorded two months later that Churchill asked if he had read the *Daily Mirror*? 'As it was handed to me, I read the big headlines on the front page: "What is the truth about Churchill's illness?"' Pointing out that the *New York Herald Tribune* said that he had had a stroke in June, had made a near-miraculous recovery, but was thought unlikely ever again to be able to take on the day-to-day leadership of the United Kingdom, the *Mirror* asked if there was any reason 'why the British people should not be told the facts about the health of their Prime Minister?':

Is there any reason why they should always be the last to learn what is going on in their country?

Must they always be driven to pick up their information at second hand from tittle-tattle abroad?

Churchill, who had indeed had a bad stroke from which he had made an astonishing recovery, observed grimly: 'Five million people read that. It's rubbish, of course, but it won't help at Margate [the October Tory Party Conference].'[91] Margate went well and Churchill carried on, but so did the attacks. '"The *Mirror* is suggesting I am past it and that I ought to resign,"' he complained to Moran in January 1954. '"Read it," he growled, passing me the paper. "Why do I waste my time over this rag? I am being bloody tame."'[92] In April, Churchill made a ferocious and misconceived onslaught on an aspect of Labour's record on nuclear weapons, which misfired so catastrophically that he completely lost the ear of the House. 'In the lobbies we all discussed why Churchill had done it,' recorded Crossman, who had been singled out in the disastrous speech:

> It's the *Mirror* and the columnists and the cartoonists who have got under his skin. He has never forgiven us for 'Whose Finger on the Trigger?' in the 1951 election . . .
>
> I rang up Hugh Cudlipp, who was in bed but immediately leapt up. When I got to his house he took me round to the office in the car and I watched him dealing with the *Mirror* Editor, Jack Nener – Nener may edit but Cudlipp disposes. Then we celebrated at the Press Club until three o'clock in the morning, drinking a great deal more whisky than I care to remember. But Hugh was as elated as I was. If we are the gutter press, we had provoked Churchill to enter the gutter with us and thereby probably ruin himself.[93]

'Twilight of a Giant' was the front-page headline.

Still, Cudlipp was always generous. When Churchill turned eighty in November 1954, the *Mirror* declared a truce, produced a souvenir issue and sent £1,000[*] to his birthday fund. And when he resigned on 5 April 1955, during a newspaper strike, Cudlipp wrote to his old hero regretting that he could not publish 'the special issue . . . to mark the end of your historic occupation of No. 10 Downing Street' and enclosing the photograph of him with the Queen he would have used on the front page. This was typical of Cudlipp, who strove to remain on good terms with those he savaged in the course of duty. The following year, during an East–West summit, he made Churchill an offer that few newspapers could have contemplated: 3,500 guineas[†] for an article on the talks: 'The Daily Mirror, with whom you have had so many battles and friendly moments, would be proud to publish this article in our own country.'[94] Churchill civilly refused for statesmanlike reasons; Cudlipp kept this and all

---

* About £16,000 today.
† About £55,000 today.

other correspondence with him among a small cache of his treasures and described Churchill in his autobiography as 'the greatest Englishman of all time'. In his, King wrote Churchill off as 'a gifted adventurer'.[95]

The *Mirror's* anti-Conservative and anti-Establishment crusade was handed a present in 1955 by R. A. Butler, Chancellor of the Exchequer. In his attempt to persuade the British people to exercise economy, he urged that 'We must not drop back into easy evenings with port wine and over-ripe pheasant'. Cudlipp rang Donald Zec:

'Why don't you give a Port and Pheasant party to a dozen ordinary people, maybe a char or two, to test out the chancellor's notion?'

'Like when?' I asked.

'Tonight,' he said.

The Savoy and the port posed no problem, but 'my insistence on over-ripe pheasant mildly irritated the banqueting manager'. The problem lay in plucking from the streets of London appropriate guests:

It is only when you actually hear yourself mouth the words that the exquisite idiocy of it all begins to dawn.

On the corner of Baker Street I accosted an 'average worker' (well, he wore overalls) with: 'I wonder whether you'd care to have dinner with me at the Savoy Ho . . .'

'Gittahtovit!'

I gottahtovit.

Having failed with a German tourist and a few secretaries who thought him a dirty old man, Zec spotted four men digging a huge crater in the pavement.

'Good afternoon, gentlemen,' I said, peering down into the hole. (As I recall it, the rain on the brim of my hat poured down into my trousers.) 'The *Mirror* is putting on a private dinner party at the Savoy Hotel tonight. Just a few friends, nothing formal. [AM I MAD!?] I wonder whether you'd all care to come along?'[96]

Advised 'to piss off', he resorted to a friend with an eclectic spread of acquaintances, who provided him with a suitable group that included a bus-driver, a canteen assistant, a dental nurse, a fishmonger, a porter and a charwoman – a category always dear to the *Mirror*, which once held a highly successful Charladies' Ball at the Savoy. This event was less popular. '"Blimey, don' 'arf pong' is a fair summary of the reaction to Mr Butler's main course . . . But the definitive verdict . . . came from a chap who declared uneasily. "I don't know whether to eat it or step over it."' 'Port and pheasant?' Zec told the *Mirror* readers. 'They can take it. They can leave it. They're hardly likely to get it. I don't think they want your port and pheasant, Mr B.'

While the *Mirror* always made it clear it was on the left, it made a point of demonstrating that it was no poodle of the Labour Party. '"The *Mirror* might not be able to win you the next election"', Cudlipp told Crossman in December 1954 as they discussed the party's deficiencies, '"but, if we turn against you, we can certainly lose it for you." If it isn't lost already, this is certainly true.'[97] During the election campaign of 1955, one front page enquired:

THE ELECTION:

ARE THE OLD MEN

AGAIN GOING TO TELL US

WHAT TO DO?

Churchill's successor, Anthony Eden, it was noted approvingly, had reduced the average age of the Cabinet. 'There are *nearly* as many stupid young men as there are stupid old men, but YOUTH is adaptable and can learn, AGE is peevish, obstinate and past learning.' Attlee, the Labour leader, was seventy-two and the Shadow Cabinet's average age was sixty. If elected, would 'the New Boys' get a chance? Eleven Labour politicians under forty-five were featured, of whom ten would be in the next Labour government eight years later. This was an indication of how good were the contacts of King, Cudlipp and Sydney Jacobson, the experienced journalist whom Cudlipp had appointed Political Editor late in 1952 and who had become Cudlipp's closest colleague: 'we called it the collaboration between the minorities, the Welsh and the Jews . . . Sydney shared with me the ability and desire to communicate what we knew to those who didn't, and in straight-forward language all could comprehend. He also believed, as I did, in the philosophy of Josh Billings, the American humorist: "It is better to know nothing than to know what ain't so."'[98]

King had wanted the *Mirror* group to take the line that '"We are pro-Labour but not this time,"' recorded Crossman, 'meaning, of course that the Labour Party was so divided and poorly led that the *Mirror*, its strong supporter, could not conscientiously recommend it as a government. This would have been the most harmful thing pos-sible.'[99] However, Cudlipp and Jacobson were sufficiently persuasive and ultimately the *Mirror* advised its readers that, though Labour was unlikely to win, they should vote for it, to 'KEEP THE TORIES TAME' – a ploy described by *The Economist* as 'superbly clever'. They rounded on the party after the Conservative victory, accusing it of having lost because its leaders were 'TOO OLD, TOO TIRED, TOO WEAK'; the party was 'BAFFLED, BEWILDERED and BETRAYED' by internal feuds; and its organisation was 'RUSTY, INEFFICIENT and 'pathetically INFERIOR to the slick Tory machine'.

Attlee had a cerebral thrombosis that August: 'Cecil King is mer-ciless to his opponents,' wrote Crossman. 'Every other paper reported that Attlee is now getting better from a slight indisposition.'[100] When he resigned a few months later, the *Mirror* backed youth in the leader-ship election in which Hugh Gaitskell (forty-nine) beat Aneurin Bevan (fifty-five) and Herbert Morrison (sixty-six) was humiliated. King wrote to him.

My dear Morrison,
    This is just to say how shocked I was by the figures of yes-terday's ballot. You have given incomparable service to the Labour Party, to the L.C.C. and to the country and this does indeed seem a churlish return for all your devoted work. I was one of those – as you know – who felt the Labour Party needed younger leadership, but I had hoped that this result could be achieved without such grievous hurt to yourself. With much sympathy.[101]

'My dear King,' wrote Morrison, thanking him for his letter. 'It was kind of you to write, especially as the Mirror played its part in producing the result. I appreciate your kindness.'[102] This civil response would bizarrely be described in King's memoirs as: 'I wrote him a friendly letter but got a reply saying that his defeat was due to me! This was, of course, nonsense.'[103]

King found Gaitskell, another Wykehamist, 'a most difficult "buttoned-up" character',[104] but Cudlipp and Jacobson were very friendly with him and acted as informal advisers and sometimes speechwriters:

For one of his performances [at the Labour Party Conference], Sydney and I had been consulted separately. We stood together at the back of the hall, neither knowing that the other had contributed to the speech but each recognising the style when the passages were intoned from the platform with suitable gestures.

Gaitskell dealt at some length with education in the middle of his speech.

'Very good,' I said to Sydney.

Then Gaitskell came to his conclusion, an all-out parody of the Tory Government for 'absentee landlordism', delivered with unusual gusto and humour. It happened that in that particular week nearly every Tory Minister was abroad and I handed the words to Gaitskell instead of using them in an editorial.

'Nice peroration, Hugh,' said Jacobson.[105]

The relationship between Gaitskell and the *Mirror* group was consolidated in 1956 over Suez. After President Nasser of Egypt announced the nationalisation of the Suez Canal, King's first instinct was to back Eden if he resorted to force. Cudlipp and Jacobson[106] persuaded him that since all the British left would oppose an invasion, the *Mirror* must follow suit. So it was that – in tune with Gaitskell – the *Mirror* urged collective international action: one front page had a photograph of Eden with the headline: 'SI SIT PRUDENTIA' ('If there be but prudence'), the words on the Eden coat of arms. And once what Cudlipp called 'the Suez military brigandry'[107] began, the *Mirror* conducted a savage campaign against what it saw as 'the culminating blunder in Eden's disastrous Middle East record'. 'HAVE SEEN FRIDAY'S PAPER CONGRATULATIONS ON YOUR QUITE MAGNIFICENT HANDLING OF SUEZ DISPUTE,'[108] cabled King to Cudlipp from Accra. Cudlipp performed well in the public arena, too. 'On television the other evening you impressed me again with one new and significant fact,' wrote the editor of *The Economist*. 'Whether you like it or not, you have become a distinguished public figure, to look at at any rate . . . For weal or for woe you are steadily living down the enfant terrible, the prodigy – which is the right result of the rolling on of the years, to say nothing of the deeds done.'[109]

As international pressure forced the British and the French to agree to a ceasefire, King wrote a warm letter to Gaitskell, congratulating him 'on the way you are handling the Suez crisis'.[110] 'May I say in turn,' responded Gaitskell, 'what a wonderful job the Daily Mirror has done in rousing public opinion on this issue. Whatever Eden may say, I do not think there is any doubt that public opinion here and abroad has once again forced him to withdraw.'[111] As Suez had divided the nation, so it divided the *Mirror* readership: 'How to lose 70,000 readers' was the rueful title of the relevant chapter in *At Your Peril*, a book about the press that Cudlipp published in 1962. '*Si sit prudentia*, or whatever, the readers were all for bashing the Wogs'[112] the *Mirror* swiftly softened its tone.

Expansion rather than contraction was the normal state for the *Mirror* group. King had come close, in 1954, to merging with the ailing *News Chronicle* group – a deal scuppered by the sudden death of the go-between – but a year later he and Cudlipp made their first important acquisition. From Lord Kemsley (with whom King had been negotiating on and off for three years) they acquired his *Glasgow Evening News*, *Daily Record* and *Sunday Mail*. The loss-making *Evening News* was promptly sold to its Glasgow rivals, and the *Record* and the *Mail* in effect became respectively the Scottish edition of the *Mirror* and the *Pictorial*. Simultaneously Kemsley sold two newspapers that were printed in Manchester and the machines were switched to producing northern editions of the *Mirror* and the *Pictorial*, which could now go to press hours earlier than hitherto. It was exclusively for the northern edition that Cudlipp asked for 'a realistic, down-to-earth, essentially northern in flavour'[113] cartoon character and thus inspired Andy Capp, 'the boozy, cunning, ribald, idle wastrel'[114] that achieved worldwide fame.

'My colleagues thought my motives were nostalgic,' recalled King, 'as it was there [Glasgow] that I started my career. I am not influenced by nostalgia but, in this case, by the prospect of a very advantageous extension of our business.'[115] And advantageous it was, not just because King had shown characteristic patience and shrewdness in waiting until market conditions brought the price down: commercial television (into which the *Mirror* group had bought at the right time and the right price) was threatening a frightened newspaper industry, and rising costs for wages, transport and paper favoured those newspapers whose circulation (and hence advertising sales) were rising. Kemsley – the man who twenty years previously had let Cudlipp go to the *Mirror* rather than give him an extra ten shillings a week – had been a master of over-centralisation and mismanagement, unlike King, a clear-thinking strategist who believed in letting good managers get on with it. On the day of the changeover, Cudlipp flew to Manchester and King to Glasgow to explain the new dispensation to the staff and later hold a celebratory dinner in Glasgow with their new senior executives.

A story of Cudlipp's illustrates how odd were this couple, but how success and excitement cemented their relationship:

It was snowing on Christmas Day in 1955. My wife Eileen Ascroft and I were peering over the Thames from our first-storey window, sampling an early champagne cocktail, waiting for neighbours and friends to join us for drinks and turkey. Among them were two handfuls of Editors and writers of one sort or another, politicians stranded in London that day, an actor or two, a sprinkling of trade union leaders and their wives, and a detective from Scotland Yard – a Santa Holmes on overtime – who was keeping an eye on an unsavoury case in Cheyne Walk, Chelsea, where we lived. Cecil King's house was Number 109, appropriately near World's End, a mile further away from the sea than No. 9, where we lived.

(Spiritually, as King might have put it, it was light years away from No. 109; its most important room was the basement with a life-sized wax model of a Chelsea pensioner seated in a rocking chair at the doorway; 'The Chelsea Pensioner' was the first of the pubs that Cudlipp would create for his friends in a succession of his houses.)

'Cecil's in the front garden,' said Eileen, 'in the snow. Did you ask him to the party?'

'No. You don't invite Cecil to parties, especially a Christmas party.' There was no knock on the door. He had delivered a letter and was retreating into the blizzard, a gaunt and solitary figure with an undersized trilby perched uneasily on his head and his hands stuffed into the pockets of a shabby raincoat . . .

Dec. 24 1955
My dear Hugh,
    At this season of goodwill I feel impelled to write and say how happy I have been working with you this past year. Not only have we had great success and much added prestige, but certainly I have thoroughly enjoyed myself in the process. As you know, I am a rather inarticulate character about my feelings, but I should like you to know that I regard you with warm affection and great respect.
    Yours ever,
    Cecil King[116]

It was less than three years later when King swooped on another prey. Cudlipp was touring Russia:

observing Khrushchev and his henchmen at diplomatic parties in the Kremlin, looking at Soviet life in general, and making notes for what would be a vivid and balanced pamphlet called 'Stop Press on Russia' . . .
    When the significant cable arrived in Sochi, on the Black Sea, I was engaged in the domestic duty of a little amateur coiffure for my wife, Eileen Ascroft, owing to the absence in that part of Sochi of professional assistance. I had washed the wool, applied the rinse, and set half of the head in pin-curls. When I read the cable the other half was left dripping wet. It said:
    THINKING OF BUYING UNCLE'S OLD BUSINESS IN FAR-RINGDON STREET STOP CABLE YOUR VIEWS BUT DEAL MAY HAVE TO BE COMPLETED SWIFTLY WARM REGARDS CECIL KING.[117]

CHAPTER IX

His Uncle's Nephew

BY THE TIME CUDLIPP GOT BACK TO LONDON A DEAL HAD BEEN done with Michael Berry, proprietor of the *Daily Telegraph* and the controlling shareholder of the magazine publishers, Amalgamated Press. Sold in 1923 by Northcliffe's executors to James Berry (later Lord Kemsley) and his younger brother Sir William (later Lord Camrose), the company was known in the publishing world as 'The Sleeping Giant'. The world's largest periodical and specialist publishing house, it owned forty-two weeklies, twenty-three monthlies and twenty annuals, including *Woman's Journal*, *Woman's Illustrated*, *Woman's Weekly*, *Marilyn*, *Roxy*, *Valentine*, *Jack and Jill*, *Girls' Crystal*, *Tiny Tots*, *Popular Gardening* and – the two survivors from Uncle Alfred's day – *Home Chat* (on its last legs) and *Sunday Companion*.

Leaving Cudlipp and his colleagues to see the deal through, King went on his annual visit to West Africa. 'Where's Cecil?' asked Michael Berry of Cudlipp, after a meeting at which he reported AP board objections to the price on offer for the rest of the shares. 'I told him – in Africa. "He's certainly playing it cool," he said.'[1] There were plenty of complications, but £18 million* later, in early January 1959, King could say to Cudlipp, 'Well, let us go to Farringdon Street and see what we have bought':

Cecil King and I walked from the quadrangle of Geraldine

---

* About £250 million today.

House, named after Northcliffe's mother, and down the hill of
Stonecutter Street to meet Harold Snoad at Fleetway House.
Snoad had toured the world with Northcliffe as assistant secretary and was now managing director of the great publishing
house. We were introduced to the principal executives and the
editors, for the directors had all met previously at a get-together,
or fall-apart, cocktail party in King's room at the *Mirror* . . .

The business . . . was conducted with an olde worlde charm
which, for visitors from the violently competitive arena of newspapers, was hard to assess. The top floor, which housed the
boardroom and directors' dining-room, was fenced in by the
warning sign 'Private'. In the entrance hall there hung a portrait
of Prince Charles and Princess Anne at the ages of approxi-
mately six and four, a picture which had been reproduced on
the front page of *Everybody's*. Young ladies in uniform worked
the lifts, most of them, it seemed to me, accompanied by an
even younger trainee. And the lifts were full of artists with
'roughs', poets with rhymes, frustrated men with 'dummies' for
new magazines, women with trolleys of tea and buns, and disappointed authors – going 'down' . . .

'There will have to be changes,' said King, as we walked back
to Geraldine House.[2]

'Financially the purchase proved a bonanza for us,' wrote King later.
'The value of two subsidiaries, the Imperial Paper Mills and Kelly-
Iliffe [trade and technical periodicals], was greater than the price we
paid for the whole.'[3] And there was another bonus in the shape of
the company's holdings in Southern Television, which had to be sold
because of the ban on dual holdings in commercial television and
fetched well over £1 million.

The main subsidiaries were well run, but the consumer publications were in serious need of modernisation. 'Cecil King,' commented the *Observer* later, 'impatient of incompetence and tradition,
moved into the peaceful offices of the Amalgamated Press, and was
appalled by what he saw: the methods, and even some of the staff,
had often hardly changed since his uncle's day.'[4] 'The truth is,'
explained King bleakly to the board, 'that all the immense effort
by the board and staff in this building, scurrying busily around,

does not succeed in exchanging two halfpennies for a penny. This is no time for protocol.'⁵ As the *Observer* saw it, King 'quickly changed the staff around, merged superfluous magazines, renamed the venerable old firm the Fleetway Publications, and painted all their vans bright pink'.

The policy was swiftly to give a thorough facelift to the magazines by investing in new technology, putting good people in the right jobs, promoting young talent, easing out the old and bringing in outsiders where necessary. ('I have never attended so many farewell parties in so short a time,'⁶ observed Cudlipp.) To Cudlipp's dismay, for he hated any hint of nepotism, among the new recruits was Eileen Ascroft, who had worked only briefly on a magazine. Charged with modernising the women's magazines, she soon became a Fleetway director.

Yet though there were some improvements, an influx of newspaper people was a strange way of sorting out a magazine company, and good people were fired. 'What about the people there already?' an interviewer asked King some years later. '"There are no good magazine people," he said firmly.'⁷ Jodi Hyland, brought in to revive *Woman's Illustrated*, became a close friend of Eileen's, but felt that, though she was a true newspaperwoman, Eileen never really fully understood magazines or their readers.

The underlying problems were stark. Commercial television was eating away at advertising revenue; general magazines were going out of fashion; the highly profitable women's magazine market was overcrowded; competition was cut-throat; and, as in the newspaper world, the costs of paper, labour and promotion were soaring. Because of its huge holdings in paper mills and its substantial investment in television,* the *Mirror* group was luckier than most, but King realised that rationalisation was an urgent priority if Fleetway was not to be a serious liability: he gazed fixedly at Odhams, his only serious competitor.

Odhams had reacted to the *Mirror* takeover by buying Hulton's and Newnes, the other important magazine publishers, for £1.8 and £12.3

---

* The initial investment of £400,000 in ATV bought a 13.2 per cent holding; by 1968 it was a 21.8 per cent holding worth £16 million (about £170 million today).

million* respectively. Among its prize assets were *Woman* and *Woman's Own*, which had circulations of 3.2 and 2.4 million, well ahead of the 1.5 million sales of Fleetway's biggest title, *Woman's Weekly*. Apart from the overlap of women's magazines, the advantages of common ownership were obvious in the field of specialist and technical journals. Such Fleetway titles as *The Architect and Building News*, *Motor Cycle*, *Poultry World* and *Wireless World* competed with Odhams's *Architecture and Building*, *Motor Cycling*, *Poultry Farmer and Packer* and *Practical Wireless*.

King had long known the new Odhams Chairman, Sir Christopher Chancellor, until recently General Manager of Reuters, of which King had been a director between 1953 and 1959; Michael King had worked abroad for Reuters and Chancellor's son-in-law worked for the *Mirror* group in West Africa. In conversations and on paper, King proposed to Chancellor a merger by an exchange of shares, which 'would bring about important savings, would look after the threatened over-capacity in the photogravure side of the printing industry and the wasteful proliferation of women's magazines which can only continue to operate at a loss'.[8] Despite their earlier relationship, Chancellor distrusted King, misinterpreted his proposal as a covert takeover bid and fled into the arms of Roy Thomson, who in 1959 had bought the Kemsley chain of newspapers, which included the *Sunday Times*.

'A merger was worked out and announced on television,' wrote King. 'There on the screen were Roy and Christopher announcing their indissoluble marriage. The TV interrogator asked if there was any likelihood of a counter-bid. Roy said no one had the money to make one. This was a bit much, so I reached for the telephone, alerted my colleagues, and in fact we made a successful counter-bid. We should probably have done this anyway, but the stimulus that evening was Roy's remark.'

Thus, baldly, King summed up a sensational takeover battle that created an uproar in the Labour Party and, because of the monopoly implications, became the subject of questions to the Prime Minister and caused the setting up of a Royal Commission on the Press. As an alternative to the proposed £70 million Odhams/Thomson merger, Daily Mirror Newspapers Ltd offered £32 million in shares for

---

* About £25 and £170 million today.

Odhams. Between the *Mirror* group, which was worth about £50 million, the £9-million Sunday Pictorial Newspapers (which partly owned and was partly owned by the *Mirror*) and the £33-million Fleetway Publications, *pace* Thomson – even without the huge A. E. Reed paper and packaging group – King had plenty of money at his disposal. Coldly the *Mirror* board announced that should the Odhams/Thomson merger go ahead, 'It would be the intention of the Daily Mirror upon becoming controlling shareholder of Odhams to use its powers to cause the whole of the Thomson interests, including the participation in Scottish Television, to be sold.'

Thomson's enthusiasm lessened visibly, but Odhams put up a valiant fight for several weeks. King – described by the *Observer* as 'Northcliffe's not unworthy nephew[9] – was all over the newspapers at home and abroad. 'KING EMPEROR?' was the query on the cover of *The Economist* – which showed King's face surrounded by a selection of his improbably titled magazines. 'The King and Thomson bids are symptoms of the present state of press economics,' it pointed out perceptively, 'of the relation that has developed between soaring costs and prices, between cut-price circulations and massive advertisement revenues, between restrictive (even Luddite) practices throughout the business and the built-in bias towards bigness as the only surety of survival.' 'Tough Press Czar' was how the *New York Times* described King when the deal was done: 'Britain has known many powerful publishers but none has ever ruled such an empire as the one he heads.'[10]

Interviewed by Jocelyn Stevens, editor of *Queen*, King appeared 'incredibly relaxed . . .':

'Why, I've got nothing else to do.' This on an afternoon when the biggest battle of his life was at its height. 'Battle? I suppose you mean Odhams. It's a holiday. We've never enjoyed ourselves so much. Don't forget I'm Irish – I enjoy a fight . . . I didn't start this takeover business, but anyone who knows me knew that I couldn't let Thomson get away with it. Thomson – I hope you won't mention that man in the same breath as myself.'[11]

Stevens was talking to King in his suite on the ninth floor of the new eighteen-storey *Mirror* and *Pictorial* building. 'THE HOUSE THAT

14,000,000 READERS BUILT' was the *Mirror* headline on 8 March 1961. 'This dominant, dynamic building, rising 169 feet above Holborn-circus, London, E.C.1, is the finest, most efficient newspaper head-quarters ever known . . . It took five years to build and equip. It cost more than £9,000,000.* The new Daily Mirror building is a GIANT that sets the world an up-to-the-minute exciting standard in news-paper enterprise.'12

It was not mentioned that, in addition to printing presses capable of producing five million papers nightly, King had in his room the only coal fire in the smokeless zone of Holborn for which, after immense difficulty over planning permission, and at great expense, a special flue and chimney were incorporated.

The holiday-camp supremo, Billy Butlin, pictured cheerily glass in hand at the opening ceremony, was a suitably proletarian icon to bal-ance the image of a solemn Cecil King unveiling the commemorative plaque. In the happy position of 'Living and working here in this Taj Mahal,' said King (giving hostages to those who would point out that he was comparing his building to a tomb), 'is what I truly believe to be the finest staff of journalists and technicians . . .:

> I am proud that this commemorative plaque bears my name. And I am especially gratified that my middle name is Harmsworth – after my uncle, Lord Northcliffe – who has been my inspiration and the inspiration of so many of us in Fleet-street.
>
> When Northcliffe founded the Daily Mirror to chase some more cobwebs from the Fleet-street of those days, even he can hardly have foreseen that it would continue to startle and out-strip its rivals half a century later.

There was some muted reassurance for those unhappy with the takeover: 'It is my view that fears which have been expressed – fears of monopoly – will not be justified by the manner in which my Board conduct the affairs of this group in the future. We will behave pre-cisely as we have behaved in the past – improving, expanding and

---

* About £120 million today.

encouraging, with the true cognisance of our duty to the public as well as to our shareholders.'

In his interview with Jocelyn Stevens, King produced no such platitudes. Describing his company as 'better administered and better run than any comparable organisation in the world', King explained that he had achieved this through delegation. 'There are four people in this set-up who matter. Myself, Hugh Cudlipp, James Cooke, the financial director, a man of enormous integrity, and [Ellis] Birk, our legal advisor. We are all entirely different and that is why we are so successful . . . They respect me and I respect them. Besides us there are twelve others. The remainder take their orders.'

King had never been known for his tact, but his arrogance was becoming ever more pronounced. Once his family had dispersed, there had been no one to curb it. Much though Margot adored him – and despite the best efforts of doctors, clergy, friends, children, relatives and King himself – she could not live with him and, from the early 1950s, they saw little of each other. 'I am writing to say that I am glad I have such a nice daughter-in-law,' wrote King to Libby in the autumn of 1951, 'and that I am coming to look upon you as a much-loved element of stability in a family which otherwise might fall to pieces.'[13] Margot would stay occasionally at Cheyne Walk, but no longer socialised with him publicly and, for most purposes, left him to look after Patrick, Nigel and Sheila Falls. '"At 2.30, be at the front door, booted and spurred"[14] would mean a weekend outing to the cinema, the Zoo or a museum,' wrote Nigel many years later. 'It was not unknown for him to play hide-and-seek on the walk back from garaging the car . . . in the days when he still drove. Of all the visits, the ones to Kew Gardens were probably those which he enjoyed most and we found most dull.' King taught them some games, but beat Nigel so easily at chess that they never played again. They breakfasted together, and while the children were not actively encouraged to join him in the studio in the evenings, he did not object to them watching television there while he read. But he had no idea how to hold conversations with children and was never able to achieve with the boys anything like the happy relationship he had with Sheila, who had become the emotional centre of his life. As Priscilla had been, she was physically affectionate and would jump into his arms when he arrived home from the office, which he left promptly at 5.30. They ate together, she adored him and would sit on his lap and talk to him uninhibitedly. 'A pretty little bundle of wool', she was much loved by Tom and Doris Langley, who lived with King in Chelsea as chauffeur and cook. One of her favourite activities was dancing with Doris to band music.

Langley, whom King had first met when he serviced King's Rolls-Royce, was asked by King post-war to look after the *Mirror's* seven cars. Then, when King became Chairman, Langley became his chauffeur. It was Langley who found him the number plate CHK 44 (King was not prepared to pay a large sum for a more significant number) and with difficulty persuaded Rolls-Royce that – though King was neither an ambassador nor royalty – he should have a flag-holder behind the Silver Lady emblem, thus enabling him to fly a red flag with the slogan 'Vote Labour' during the 1964 election campaign.

Just as King's relationship with Turley, the family chauffeur in Dublin, had been one of the easiest of his childhood, so was his adult relationship with Tom Langley. They liked, respected and trusted each other and were good companions. Though he never forgot King was his employer, Langley felt he could say anything to him; in the mid-1950s, after King's inattentiveness caused a second accident with the Rolls that badly squashed the bonnet, Langley persuaded him to give up driving and henceforward drove him also at weekends or found him a substitute driver.

Sometimes Langley would drive King to Cushnie via his two Cumberland farms, where they would stay overnight with the tenants. King would sit in the front for company and to leave space for hitch-hikers: male, female, young or old, whatever they looked like, King loved talking to them. Hopeless though he continued to be at social small talk, he found voluntary conversation with strangers liberating. Once, having picked up two hitch-hikers who were heading for Edinburgh, King put them up at one of the farms and delivered them exactly where they wanted to be in Edinburgh.

Langley drove King to Ireland several times, taking the ferry from Stranraer to Larne, for there were business interests in Northern Ireland and negotiations in Dublin over the banning of publications (references to contraception were enough to get the censors going; the *Pictorial* was allegedly banned because it ran a picture of a nun playing a trombone[15]). In Langley's observation, King got on well in

Ireland not just because the Irish were as informal and gregarious as West Africans, but also because they were flattered that a British-educated and British-based captain of industry described himself as Irish and was obviously very proud of his heritage.

The Langleys were very fond of Cecil, Margot and their children, with all of whom they kept in touch after the break-up of the family. Indeed, when King offered the Langleys a free holiday anywhere they liked, they chose to visit Colin, then working in Quebec for the Anglo-Canadian Pulp and Paper Mills. For his part, King took an interest in the education of the Langleys' son and arranged for him the apprenticeship that he wanted in print design; he did so well that he ended up a millionaire businessman in America.

The three Langleys had moved into Cheyne Walk after King and Langley found the drunken housekeeper upside-down in a dustbin with her bare legs sticking out. The Langleys found their employer hopelessly impractical and in need of having an eye kept on him to make sure his jacket matched his trousers and that he wasn't covered with dandruff or flakes of psoriasis. They also helped him with his skin treatments, including coal-tar baths that left a terrible mess. Denis Forman recalled that in the early 1950s King's psoriasis was appalling – 'much much worse than most people knew'. King would have to leave the room and put on ointment every hour and a half or so, yet he sometimes had raw bleeding patches and his coat would become covered with scales. Forman never saw skin trouble so bad with anyone else in public life. King, he said, was terribly sensitive about it and incapable of laughing it off; it was never mentioned in the family.

Despite the permanent presence of Sheila, and Priscilla's attempts to cherish her father and the Falls children as well as her husband, King was under enormous emotional stress and desperately lonely. The family friends had gradually drifted away, for without Margot's softening influence King had become less and less approachable. Socially, his rewarding times were almost always abroad: 'I travelled the world with him,' recalled Ellis Birk. 'A more charming, delightful person you couldn't imagine. A lovely, lovely man . . . His knowledge of the flora and fauna of any country in the world was amazing . . . He'd go to bed at 9.30 and then I could have fun.'[16] 'The last few weeks have been an adventure,' wrote King's sister Enid:

far outreaching the great distances we travelled & the wonders of the whole world we saw in the Queen Elizabeth herself, New York & so many kinds of gigantic enterprise in Canada.

Really I cannot tell you what an inspiration you have given me to live afresh, what a measure of satisfying thought to enrich the rest of my life. I have met more people in the last three weeks than almost in my life before.[17]

King asked his daughter-in-law Libby to accompany him on another expedition, and when she said that she and Michael would love to, he explained that the invitation was confined to her.[18] Thinking his intentions not confined to the platonic, she did not go, but Priscilla did in 1952, very happily, for they shared many interests — both intellectual and aesthetic — and on their own she found King a wonderful companion and teacher. She also acted as his hostess at Cheyne Walk on the rare occasions he wanted to give a dinner party. Sometimes he might ask some men around to talk politics. Denis Forman, for instance, was occasionally asked to Cheyne Walk at around eight o'clock, when the regulars were Cudlipp, Sydney Jacobson, a few younger reporters and usually a politician, for exclusively political talk.

Most of King's interests were solitary. As well as reading, there was collecting, which for him was a hobby rather than a passion and all part of the acquisition of knowledge. 'It was mental exercise,' said Martin Norton of S. J. Phillips, from whom King bought silver and jewellery for decades after the war. 'When he had mastered a particular area, he would lose interest and move on to something else. He had a good eye and was a quick learner. At one time he collected Irish silver because an ancestor King in Ireland had been a silversmith. Then one day it was Spanish, South American silver, then church silver.'

King never bought anything very expensive and was uninterested in whether it was cheap or dear for what it was. He would buy what he wanted, if it were within certain limits, and never bargained, since he trusted the dealers he used. Some items he kept; others he sold; he was not what Norton would have considered a serious collector. Coins, porcelain, pictures and pots interested him at times, and among his valuable books was a superb collection relating to West Africa.

The financial rewards of collecting were of little interest to him. Although he could be very tight-fisted, he was not miserly. He applied himself to increasing considerably the value of the Falls children's trust fund, which he spent exclusively on their education. He enjoyed stopping by the post office in the Rolls and picking up the children's allowance: 'This is real money,' he would say. Tom Langley treasured the memory of the affair of the Vandyke portrait. Presented to Geraldine by one of her brothers, it was regarded as the most valuable item in the King family. When King decided to sell it, Langley was charged with bringing it down from Cushnie and taking it to Sotheby's. A few days later, King called in to find out the valuation and came out laughing. 'How much do you think I'm going to get for it?' he asked Langley, who refused to guess. 'Fifty bob [£2.50] for the frame,' replied King, still laughing. 'It's a terrific fake.'

By the mid-1950s there was no longer any prospect of the Kings' marriage being repaired. Margot was still the lovable, affectionate woman she had always been, but her waywardness, unpredictability and occasional descent into paranoia, delusion, self-loathing and rage exhausted and horrified her family and friends. She had been persuaded to live in the country in her father's old rectory near her sister Betty Pinney, looked after by the retired Cushnie factor and his wife, who were deeply attached to her and the King children. Betty, who had always had a soft spot for King, wrote to Libby that he had had a raw deal: 'we're all bloody as a family and stinking neurotics. But it sticks out a mile or did at Christchurch so he should have known. Come to that I'm not sure my old Ma wasn't a great deal more fly than Cecil ever gave her credit for. She told him straight he was marrying the wrong daughter.'[19] A couple of years later King wrote in desperation to Betty:

Margot has now been ill for 4½ years. In that time I have not myself seen any real wish on her part for a genuine recovery . . . But if she won't recover, what are we to do?

The usual course of melancholia cases is a steady mental deterioration, but this is not happening. In fact in some ways Margot is clearly getting better, not worse. But her firm determination not to face recovery (oh! quite sub-conscious) makes her ups and downs of minor importance. A necessary consequence is a reluctance on her part to stay anywhere for any length of time.

He thought Margot lonely through her own choosing:

with her gift with people; with oceans of time, enough money & a car she could make her house a social centre – if she wished it that way – but she doesn't . . . Don't forget that her last house was this, which she denounced because it was so noisy!

My doctor friends, the family & our family friends all think of Margot's present form as a permanency – more or less. So she must be jollied along. There *is* no long-term solution to these cases.[20]

'Many thanks . . . for your very kind and frank explanations,' wrote the Falls children's other grandfather in May 1953. 'I am deeply grieved over your and Margot's troubles, and touched by your devotion to the children . . . you have my entire confidence and admiration & I wish I could do more to help you and them.'[21]

'Colin, in the black & white outlook of the very young,' wrote Enid to King, 'thinks you ought to marry again, but feels that he can't suggest it himself. Somebody who would give you continuity of a sort & intellectual support from a feminine angle. On the other hand if Margot really showed a determination to help herself the children would rally round. At present he & Mike just feel bitter about the misrepresentation of you.'[22]

King still had sporadic affairs, but he was desperate for companionship and for someone to look after the children. 'I would have gone mad or committed suicide if I'd stayed with Mama,' he told Francis. In 1955 he began a relationship with the extraordinary Ruth Railton.

Ruth was a good pianist and a competent conductor – particularly of choirs – whose touch of genius was the ability to spot musical potential even in tiny children. King's cousin, Christabel Bielenberg, attended some auditions with her and was amazed by Ruth's ability to discover a musician through the operation of sheer instinct. In Wales Christabel heard her tell a very minor harp player that she was on the wrong instrument. Ruth arranged violin lessons for her and she achieved some distinction.

Though she seemed frail, Ruth had the single-mindedness, energy and will-power of a great crusader. In 1946 she decided to found a children's orchestra:

> I was consumed with the desire to find and help our outstanding musical children. I was convinced that even a hundred, properly taught and inspired, would over the years change the attitude of my country to musical performance, and raise its standards.
>
> It was the eternal amateur outlook in England that puzzled me. Everything was allowed as long as it was for fun and a good time was had by all, and the results didn't matter.[23]

That was not Ruth's way: in 1946 she scraped together the money to found the National Youth Orchestra (NYO), in 1947 she put the organisation together, cut through red tape, as Musical Director persuaded fine musicians to agree to teach her pupils, tried and failed to get education authorities interested, attracted 2,000 letters by sending posters to music shops, and for three months toured the country auditioning 1,000 children and choosing 110 to be trained during their summer holidays. The first annual public concerts were in 1948 in Bath and Cambridge; the first concert abroad took place in Paris two years later. What most people had thought impossible became a great success.

The *Mirror* group liked children's causes: for years the *Pictorial* organised the National Exhibition of Children's Art (King's idea; Cudlipp's execution). In 1952 Philip Zec heard that the NYO needed another sponsor and took Ruth (then thirty-six) to lunch with King. 'I shook hands with a very tall man,' wrote Ruth in her musical memoirs, 'with plenty of greying hair, and very blue eyes – partly sad, yet quick to sparkle – but as he sank somewhat heavily on to a chair my first impression was of a man burdened with sorrow. He ate just one course, very quickly, and pushing utensils aside leant on the table to talk to me. I only remember the last question, "What do you do for money?"'[24]

The *Mirror* became the NYO's sponsor, with appropriate guarantees about leaving full authority over musical and educational policy to the NYO Council: Ruth rejected out of hand the suggestion that the NYO might be renamed the *Daily Mirror* Youth Orchestra. And, as Ruth (who had a propensity to write and speak in the style of P. G. Wodehouse's Madeline Bassett) tells it, Paul Cave, the *Mirror* journalist who acted as liaison officer:

> was the first to experience my unfortunate loathing of personal publicity. I had to explain I was trying to create the utmost beauty in music for its own sake, showing the young how to strive for it, and sometimes their fresh faith and love of doing it touched emotional peaks that adults cannot. Promoting *me*, as the *Mirror* expected, was horribly irrelevant and I would have none of it. 'But most people would give anything to have their picture on the front page of the Daily Mirror,' sighed Paul.
>
> How difficult I was as I directed promotion of me to promotion of the orchestra and its purpose! How impossible I was to insist on no stories about individual children – no photos that would cheapen our intentions or standards in the eye of the schools!²⁵

The *Daily Mirror* were superb sponsors, helping with premises, printing, publicity and administration in return for a small mention on the NYO programmes. But a difference of opinion in 1954 with the Executive, who wanted her to stick to the musical side, convinced Ruth that there was a plot to undermine her. She resigned and went to see King, whom she barely knew:

> I was nervous, but he was easy to talk to. I said I just wanted him to know that I'd resigned, and not hear it second-hand or from a newspaper. The reason wasn't so easy to explain without letting any of my colleagues down. He asked where the meeting was, and wrote a letter while I waited. Then he looked up and said, 'No Musical Director, no *Mirror* money,' and arranged for the letter to be delivered immediately to the meeting by hand.²⁶

According to Ruth, she and King met infrequently until, in 1955, they went to America in June on the same ship. She was on NYO business, and since there was a train strike, King offered her a lift to Southampton. He stopped the car at Winchester to look at the cathedral and, not realising that the form was to let him show one around places, Ruth stayed gazing down the nave. When he emerged and said, 'You didn't come with me', she replied, 'Oh, but I was so happy looking at that beautiful nave.' She did not realise until later that he had fallen in love with her then. On the ship, she was in third class, but ate with him in first. He wanted her to go to Canada with him for a week, but she refused because of urgent duties at home.[27]

Whatever about love blooming in the cathedral, the truth was that the joint voyage had been planned. 'I am taking Miss Ruth Railton,' he wrote to the American Embassy in May 1955, 'a member of our organisation, to entertain for me while I am away. My Canadian companies have an extensive business in the United States and I shall be meeting all Miss Railton's expenses while she is away.'[28] It was presumably on that trip that there emerged what the *Winnipeg Tribune* called a few months later, in a profile of 'the new Napoleon of Fleet Street', 'the new, mellow King'. On a visit to a lumber camp in Quebec, 'he bent over a juke box, studied the titles and put in a coin. His nervous hosts, awed by the big man's presence, relaxed and smiled at the tune – it was a song about king-size hugs and kisses.'

Shortly after they returned, and not long before he set off abroad again, King told Enid that he wanted a divorce from Margot. 'I am afraid that the next few months will be a horrible strain, so far away, with enormous business decisions to make, and your very home at stake,' she wrote. 'Even if Margot is co-operative, there will be much that is distasteful & if she will not agree it will be difficult indeed having got this far with someone very dear to you.'[29] Margot was not amenable, partly because she did not realise that Ruth was different from other mistresses, and partly because she could not bear to let him go. 'Last night poor Margot King was here – *very* bad indeed,' wrote Antonia White in February 1956:

Cecil now wants a divorce so that he can marry some new love. Her loyalty to him is a kind of idolatry. 'I love every breath that comes out of his body' she said weeping. Accuses herself as usual. Impossible to reason with her. Says he is one of the great men of the century. And a SAINT! Yet he has always been unfaithful to her, at times cruel, and now won't even allow her in her own house. He is a very rich man and allows her a mere pittance and now talks of buying back some of the jewellery he gave her so as to give it to his mistress. Her delusions still range from thinking herself an appalling sinner to pathetic belief in her enormous capacities and brain. Why must such innocent creatures as Margot suffer so?[30]

By now Ruth and King had decided to live together as Mr and Mrs King; she set about changing her name by deed poll. With no possibility of divorce in the foreseeable future, Ruth was sufficiently besotted with King to defy convention. She had plenty of courage, which she needed, for she was a clergyman's daughter (her father had recently died) and her mother and sisters were horrified. On the grounds that the NYO now had the Queen Mother as a Royal Patron, she also thought it necessary to inform the Executive Committee, whose Vice-Chairman, John Newsom, later told Cudlipp the story:

> she said she had a personal statement to make herself at that day's meeting . . . and as Newsom approached the place where the meeting was held he noticed sitting humbly on a chair outside, the huge and immediately recognisable figure of Northcliffe's nephew, Cecil Harmsworth King.
>
> And Ruth went before the committee and said that she was about to share a residence with the prominent press tycoon who was humbly sitting on the chair outside the meeting and that if they didn't like this arrangement that she would be happy to resign and it was for them to decide. They decided that she should not resign and then Cecil King was invited to join the meeting and no further references were made to what is now a recognisable consecrated form of habitation but at that time was just slightly unorthodox even in musical circles. The interesting point is that Cecil – who was not a man who enjoyed humiliation – was prepared to put himself in this position because of his passion for the lady.[31]

King also had people to tell. It had been a long time since they dined together socially, but one day he said to Cudlipp:

> 'What about a spot of dinner tonight?' – as if we were frequently on the tiles together in Soho. He announced the rendezvous as

Jardin des Gourmets, 5 Greek Street, a favourite haunt of mine. I arrived early to tell the waiters that I was not the host, had never seen them before in my life and warn them not to top up my glass with their usual well-tipped impetuousity.

Cecil and I sat adjacently, never an aid to conviviality unless the other diner is a lady, and an additional barrier if one of the diners is six-foot-four tall.

After a marathon meal, with silences relieved between courses by a few reminiscences and exchanges of political gossip, he ordered brandy, supervised the filling of the glasses, then turned solemnly toward me, saying: 'This is confidential until I indicate otherwise.' He announced the separation from his wife, Margot, the mother of his four children, with the words: 'I am making new domestic arrangements.'

I was too familiar with the protocol to say 'Oh,' or to ask why, where, when or with whom.[32]

Then there was family. Priscilla remembers that when her father explained that he was going to share his life with another woman and she asked who this was, he replied gravely, 'I can't tell you at the moment. Let us call her Marilyn Monroe.' Since Ruth was curve-free, and no man but King was known to have found her sexually attractive, King's choice of pseudonym would cause amazement.

Enid, who was shocked, wrote to Libby that paradoxically she felt for Ruth, 'as I can't imagine that she knows the half of what she has taken on & from what I could judge is very sensitive, & has made her difficult decision on the highest motives possible under the circumstances, that is, to make an affectionate home and ambience for Cecil & the children. I tremble to think how much she may be hurt, even destroyed, & can only meet her with compassion if I have to.'[33] A letter in February 1956 from R. A. Skelton, the Falls children's maternal grandfather, congratulated 'you and the good lady on an honest & courageous arrangement, which I trust will give both of you contentment and happiness. I am deeply sorry for Margot and you; her condition is evidently worse than I realised. It has been a profound disappointment that your guardianship has not given the children a mother. I am wondering & hoping as to the effect on the children of the new régime.'[34]

Since 'Mrs Ruth King' had a busy career, Skelton wondered if she was 'intending to sacrifice it in part so as to be an efficient mistress of your household and a gentle mother to the children'. Would she be going abroad with King or staying at home? 'Has she met the children, and will they take to each other?'

King responded:

I welcome this opportunity of saying that Ruth is a very gentle and loving person who has devoted the last ten years of her life to the musical education of the young. No one could be more anxious than she to be a loving mother to the children – particularly to Patrick who needs love even more than the other two.

She will still keep on with some of her interest in the musical world but only to the extent that is compatible with maintaining a happy home. She will come with me on some of my travels, which are likely to be curtailed now I shall have more to keep me at home. She has not yet met the boys, but has been to the house on several occasions when Sheila was about. I don't think you need worry – the children will gain a mother and will not be any longer unsettled by the rapid turn-over of my domestic staff.[35]

There was no doubt about Ruth's commitment to King. 'I knew her as a ferocious conductor before she embarked on Cecil King,' said Denis Forman. 'She moved in there with great purpose and took Cecil over and in many ways sort of saved him. He was going to pieces.' King needed a woman as strong as a Harmsworth matriarch yet wholly submissive. Ruth appeared ideal: she idolised King and had a capacity for blind loyalty and self-abnegation. Unfortunately for his family, she wanted him all to herself. Unfortunately for his colleagues, she believed him to be infallible and a man of destiny. And unfortunately for everyone in their orbit, the malevolence that bubbled beneath a superficially sweet surface was matched by energy, cunning and zeal.

Like King, Ruth lived on her own planet. His was a grey and flinty place, where he lived – as Cudlipp put it – as 'a squatter on a commanding peak from which he observed and deprecated the follies of the rest of humanity'. Hers was more complex, for, unlike King, and partly because she was as stupid as she was gifted, Ruth had a startling absence of self-knowledge. She pictured herself occupying a bower of metaphorical fluffy clouds and pink roses from which she exuded love, kindness, sensitivity, spirituality and truth; in reality, although in the public sphere she could do real good, in her private life she was jealous, merciless, fiercely manipulative and an inveterate liar and fantasist.

Before Ruth moved in with him, King had taken the precaution of having her handwriting analysed. He had been greatly impressed a few years earlier by an American graphologist, who, allegedly knowing nothing about him, had written a lengthy analysis of his character and abilities so startlingly accurate in the main (analytical, sceptical and introspective mind, behind-the-scenes string-puller, outstanding organiser, good delegator, excellent intellect, passion for absorbing new information, sense of beauty, unresolved emotional problems in his unconscious, mania for travel, dissatisfied and disillusioned, can be 'very outspoken and bitterly frank or resort to abruptness' and has the basic conflict of 'craving for affection, understanding and sensitivity while simultaneously protesting against the possible domination by the individual from whom he wishes to obtain emotional gratification') as to dwarf the misses (understanding and appreciation for the arts and music, in personal relations 'utterly charming, humorous, sensitive and alert . . . a generous host who knows how to entertain his guests royally'). One line that King left out when he printed this in his memoirs and which was blacked out in the typescript, clearly referred to the sadism about which he used to write so eloquently to Margot, for otherwise the next sentence ('Despite strong instinctual upsurges he has repressed the latter which adds to his contact difficulties in intimate situations') makes no sense.

However, given Ruth's full name and one of her personal letters to King – which, if it ran true to form, would have contained much about her feelings – the London graphologist was not working according to the dispassionate scientific criteria that King would normally have required. King got what he sought: an analysis that conformed absolutely to Ruth's view of herself and to his view of the kind of woman he wanted. Right in many important respects, it was glaringly wrong in others.

The handwriting showed 'vitality and rhythm, coupled with energy, will-power and independence . . . great ability – even brilliance – in the mental field, far transcending the normal. This could cause envy and dislike from lesser folk, especially as it is masked by such a gentle disposition.'

Ruth had developed:

a habit of under-estimating herself deliberately in order to avoid conflict, as she is diplomatic: being deliberate it does not damage her natural confidence. She could be at times impatient, and too outspoken and frank: a person of absolute honesty and integrity. She could hold great confidences and secrets; would never betray: courageous: uncompromising: very cautious and with an infinite capacity for detail.

The writer is very finely tuned, constantly moving on a very high vibration. She is intensely sensitive to atmosphere, environment, people and colour. She possesses great intuition and foresight and is highly spiritual – in fact continually drawn towards the spiritual plane of thought. She should excel, and at a very high level indeed, in music, art, or literature. She shows also strong leadership coupled with brilliant mental development in the imaginative field; well above normal intellectually with great visionary powers; psychic. She is likely to be a fine influence with others – unconsciously – especially with the young. There is a very strong emotional current running through this handwriting, and an outlet must be found for this very powerful force to achieve greatness in the field of her choice. Complete freedom of action is necessary when working or leading. There is shewn also a normal and very strong sexual trend.

Ruth's opposing qualities ('strong, yet delicate', for instance) combined 'to form an integrated balanced personality'. And in a blunder that matched his conclusion about Ruth's honesty, the graphologist added: 'Generous and compassionate, she cannot know the meaning of jealousy.'[36]

The Langleys found Ruth unprepossessing and were surprised that such a successful and attractive man could not do better. They conceived a deep dislike of her within a day of her moving in, when Doris Langley entered the room where King and the six-year-old Sheila would sit before dinner and found a change in the domestic arrangements: it was Ruth, not Sheila, who was sitting on King's lap. As Doris put it, it was necessary for Ruth 'to show Sheila who was Number One'.

King would have had to work hard to find anyone more unsuitable than Ruth for the roles of homemaker, mother, hostess and companion. For a start, she was a driven musician with no outside interests or domestic gifts and without any eye for beauty. She had never cared about her surroundings, happily living in garrets while she created the orchestra. King was a peculiar mate for her: as a small child he could not carry a tune, and in adolescence the top third of his hearing was destroyed by measles. 'Cecil couldn't recognise "God Save the Queen",' said Cudlipp. 'People thought he was a republican. Had to be nudged in the ribs. Tone deaf! and he had to marry a bloody orchestra.'

Ruth might look, sound and claim to be gentle, but she was a martinet. 'Those who endured her auditions were apt to describe them as the most harrowing experiences of their lives,' wrote an obituarist. 'The school, too, was apt to be wearing on the nerves of the more timid. When some of the pupils became noisy in the corridors, Dame Ruth stopped one of the offenders and demanded: "You! Don't speak! Tell me what you think you are doing!'37 It was by the exercise of severe, uncompromising discipline that she created an orchestral tradition out of a floating population of children. Christabel Bielenberg, who travelled with King and Ruth and the NYO a few times, was deeply impressed by how brilliantly everything was organised, but said Ruth was such a dragon that even the conductor was afraid of her:38 in that world, she was a sacred monster.

Reviewing in 1994 Ruth's book about the NYO, an ex-member — who joined three years after Ruth retired as Musical Director and Ivey Dickson, her colleague for ten years, took over — wrote that:

> [it] was always said that Dickson's régime had liberalised things, that she was Khrushchev to Railton's Stalin. In retrospect, she seems more like Brezhnev, a bureaucratic consolidator, protecting the institution from change. All the basic routines set up by Railton remained in place, not least the routines of order, discipline and surveillance. If beauty could have been secured through regimentation, the NYO would surely have done it. There were clothes inspections, shoe inspections, musical inspections, inspections of deportment, inspections of attitude, inspections of

behaviour . . . Everything the orchestra did was rigorously controlled: tuning up, turning pages, coming onto the platform,
leaving the platform, sitting down, standing up . . .

After each rehearsal, imperfections such as a dropped pencil, a
turned head, a slouch, a sneeze or cough ('in the NYO we do not
cough') were:

> brought up in a roll-call of error at the end of the rehearsal.
> Before concerts the obsession with uniformity became feverish,
> expressing itself deliriously in the sewing up of boys' trouser
> pockets: not, as might be thought, to impede self-abuse at the
> climax of some dithyrambic tutti, but to prevent white pocket
> linings from flashing distractingly under the bright lights on
> stage.
> The will to order was rationalised by both Railton and
> Dickson as a practical and artistic necessity . . . It sounds so
> reasonable, but the reality was tinged with a worrying irrationality.
> Taken as it was to such extremes, it began to appear that the
> order was not there for the music but the music for the order.

Ruth 'kidded herself that she was working to "serve the marvellous talent in British children"', but 'was only ever interested in a tiny
proportion of them'. And she was clear from the start that what she
was after was not just their musical ability, but their souls: 'I chose
not necessarily the most advanced players . . . but always those with
that . . . special inner quality . . . My role in auditions was to discover the spiritual potential as well as the musical talent.' The manner
of rejection could be brutal: 'They simply reeled from the experience,
as who wouldn't who'd set his heart on becoming a musician and had
just been given to understand that, sorry, he was simply second-rate
– not just as a musician but as a person (no "special inner quality",
no "spiritual potential").'
It was Ruth's idea to invite more children to NYO courses 'than
would comfortably sit on an average concert platform . . .':

> Concerts were the apogee to which we were all being driven; and
> on the very morning of the concert, at the dress rehearsal, when

group excitement was approaching its wire-strung peak, a small margin of players, perhaps five or six, would be asked to leave the stage because there wasn't enough room for them . . . Nothing better captures the spirit of the NYO as it was under Ruth Railton and Ivey Dickson than this gratuitous little cruelty masquerading as an artistic imperative.[39]

Sheila and the boys desperately needed affection; instead Ruth was dutiful. She resented them all, but especially Sheila, whom she saw as an ever-present responsibility and a competitor for King's attention. She betrayed her jealousy in endless – possibly unconscious – little cruelties, like decreeing that in this gloomy, unheated house Sheila, because it was good for her moral fibre, should have lino in her cold bedroom rather than carpet. There was no more dancing with Doris Langley, who was afraid to intercede or intervene in case Ruth got her husband fired. (Langley stayed working for King for several years, but he and Doris moved out not long after Ruth arrived; she found an Italian couple who spoke little English to act as butler and cook.*)

There were also serious cruelties; among the worst was that as soon as she moved in to Cheyne Walk, Ruth told Priscilla, who loved the children and was very close to Sheila, that in order to avoid them having divided loyalties, she was not to get in touch with them for two years. Subsequently she consistently refused to allow any of them to spend holidays with Priscilla. If the boys did not have school friends to stay with, along with Sheila they would be despatched to Raiton relatives or as paying guests to people they did not know. In 1960, when Ruth had, as usual, turned down Priscilla's offer to have the children for the holidays, Sheila said apropos her forthcoming visit to Ruth's sister: 'It will be my tenth birthday when I'm there. What shall I do about it?' 'I hope,' said Ruth, 'you will be grown up enough not to mention it.'

Ruth had neither a sense of humour nor of fun, so she would noisily do her duty by the three children without having any urge to

---

* Ruth warmly welcomed the news that they were to have a baby. They left when they could no longer bear her insistence that it be brought up in accordance with her diktats.

make them happy. It was torture for her to have to take the Falls children around London to dentists and doctors, and school outfitters and railway stations, when she could have been talent-spotting in Swansea, but that was a necessary part of being Mrs Ruth King, so she did it – all the while convincing herself that she was doing a wonderful job and that any failing in the relationships was entirely the fault of Patrick, Nigel or Sheila. Nigel, who trod the acceptable route from Scaithcliffe, the family prep school, through Winchester to Cambridge caused the fewest problems; difficulties with Sheila, who had a miserable time trying to live up to Ruth's requirements, were attributed to what Ruth saw as her innate nervousness; and when Patrick, who had suffered most from his parents' deaths and was the most vulnerable of the three, got into trouble at school, at work and with the law, Ruth wrote him off as suffering from evil Harmsworth and Falls genes.

Ruth was very keen on genetic explanations, which (except in the case of Northcliffe – whom she believed had marked out King as his heir apparent) mostly came down to Harmsworth bad, King good. Cecil King, she believed, was exclusively made up of King (scholarly) and Maffett (creative) genes: since he spoke well of Granny Harmsworth, Maffett was good. Any King children or grandchildren who were in favour were Kings; if they offended her, it was their Harmsworth or Cooke side coming out. Enid became a Harmsworth when she was clearly embarrassed that King and Ruth shared a bedroom in her house.

All King's children were sorry for their father and their Falls cousins, and hoped that Ruth could make them happy; all sent her warm, welcoming letters when she moved in. According to Ruth, Colin (whom she called 'My Colin'), who had known her slightly before she met King, told her and others that she was the mother he never had. According to Cudlipp, Colin was himself a manipulator; he certainly knew how to play Ruth and, since he had the priceless advantage of rarely seeing her, they never fell out. Michael had the handicap of being married to Libby, who had been at school with Ruth; they loathed each other. Ruth – who habitually applied to others her own worst characteristics – wrote off Michael as stupid and always spoke of 'Libby the liar'. Francis was popular for a time, for he said all the right welcoming words when in West Africa he met Ruth for the first time, but she would later decide that there were two Francises. One, who said kind things to her and brought thoughtful presents, was the Cecil Francis; unfortunately, there was also the Margot Francis, who said things critical of her or King. Essentially, Ruth's view of the boys was that they were unworthy of their father and wholly failed to give him his due as a great, great man, but that they recognised what a wonderful loving person she was, though their relationships with her were undermined by jealous wives.

Priscilla tried hardest but could do nothing right; Ruth simply could not bear King's obvious affection for her. The first time Priscilla came to stay with them, Ruth accused her of coming only because she wanted her father's money. 'I said "My father always made it very clear to us that he wasn't going to leave us any money", but Ruth persisted.'[40] Ultimately Priscilla told her father, who ticked Ruth off, but the floods of tears merely cloaked an increased enmity. For the rest of her life Ruth would denounce Priscilla to anyone who would listen for a range of sins from deceit and avarice through theft and snobbery to self-delusion and even lesbianism.[41] As for Margot, although Ruth had to admit that she and Cecil had loved each other, Ruth told everyone that she was insanely possessive and evil. Margot had loved Cushnie and been loved by the people there ('Cushnie, Finden, Cumberland, all need attention and I sit idle and bitter in Dorset . . .,' wrote Margot to her-self. 'I don't want him to take her to Cushnie – our shady bed.'[42]). Ruth could not fit in at all with the people at Cushnie and no one was prepared to work for her. Ultimately, King gave up the struggle and put the estate up for sale on the grounds that he was too busy to get up there often. (The farms would go later.) It was a blow to Margot and the children, and, indeed, to King himself,[*] but it was what Ruth wanted. And, by and large, Ruth got what she wanted.

She needed all her ingenuity to hold on to her career. King's vision was that Ruth would put him first, nurture him and share his inter-ests, put the children second and dabble in music when he and they were otherwise engaged. Having been used to a wife who read serious books and could talk about serious issues, King confused Ruth's hero-

---

[*] 'I often have in my mind's eye', he wrote at eighty, in the introduction to his *Commonplace Book*, 'my heather-covered mountain (about 2,000 feet high), the Cairngorms in one direc-tion and, on a clear day, the sea, thirty miles away, to the east.'

worship for intelligent interest. He had not spotted that she had no understanding of, and no genuine interest in, any world outside music – and even there, she was instinctive and non-intellectual. (Since with Ruth the word was the deed, she put 'interested in everything' under recreations when she made it into *Who's Who.*) She would listen raptly but uncomprehendingly as King talked of art and politics and history and literature, was adept at pretending to enjoy what he showed her when they travelled, but left to herself she would never look at a picture or read a newspaper or book.

Ruth was an impresario. Music, no more than anything else, did not exist for her unless she was centre-stage. She would, for instance, never listen to music at home and amazed Priscilla's second husband, who was passionately interested in music, when he realised that he seemed to know far more about the subject than Ruth. Tony Delano of the *Mirror*, who met her several times when she travelled abroad with King, came to exactly the same conclusion.

King might as well have asked Laurence Olivier to stay at home listening to records of other actors as ask Ruth to give up the NYO. She was genuinely torn between her devotion to King and her visceral need to use her exceptional gifts to find, marshal and present young talent. And whatever she had promised King during their courtship, she was determined not to choose between him and the NYO. She scaled down her involvement, but held on to the Musical Directorship. Soon King was attending rehearsals and going on the occasional concert tour and she was claiming that he indeed had an ear for music.

Dennis Barker's obituary of Ruth summed up brilliantly why she got her way so effectively:

> Her methods were invigoratingly unconventional, drawing on a vivid imagination combined with a ruthless talent for realpolitik. She once settled a difference of opinion on the interpretation of Stravinsky by announcing crushingly, 'Why, I danced at the first performance of The Rite of Spring!' By the time the opposition had worked out that she could not have been born at the time, their case had been lost and she had moved on.[43]

A journey with King, Ruth and the NYO began, said Christabel

Bielenberg, with Ruth telling a long story about how on an earlier occasion she had told the pilot there was a bomb on board, and he landed and she had been right. And then Christabel met 'a terribly nice person who'd been on the former trip when it was supposed to have happened, and it was complete invention'.

There was the occasion when the NYO visited Holland; as Ruth was making a speech, a waiter presented her with an envelope. She opened it, clutched at her heart, appeared close to fainting and explained that it was a death-threat aimed at her because of her role in the Dutch resistance during the war. A sceptic found the waiter afterwards and asked where the envelope had come from; he said the lady had given it to him beforehand and told him when to deliver it to her. Perhaps most startling of all was Ruth's assertion to a young relative that she was a gifted sexual performer who had learned her art in a Parisian brothel.

Ruth applied fantasy and realpolitik to all her relationships: it took quite some time for King's children, brought up to venerate truth above all other qualities, to realise what kind of person they were dealing with. Yet no one dared to challenge her, for she could turn on tears, a heart flutter or hysteria at will. King himself, who disapproved of divorce and never got over having one failed marriage, shut his eyes to reality and basked in Ruth's devotion.

Did Ruth lose a fiancé in the war? In January 1956, did she have an operation for a cracked pelvis that went so badly wrong that she was in dreadful pain and a steel jacket for ten years? Did she really have Margot's evil spirit exorcised from Cheyne Walk because she alleged she was being strangled in the night? Did she become pregnant with twins and have a miscarriage? The best guesses are: a) doubtful, b) exaggerated, c) probably, and d) no, for when Priscilla asked King about it, he said, 'sometimes I have to take a large pinch of salt.'

There were limits to how fully Ruth could keep King's children and grandchildren away from him, but she did her best by lies, denigration and emotional blackmail. One ploy was to tell King that one or other of them had been invited to dinner and had failed to turn up, but though he had suspended all critical faculties where Ruth was concerned, this was a device that could work only infrequently. Mostly she ignored his family as much as was possible, and King acquiesced.

'Please try to help Scilla,' wrote Margot:

She wants to love you so much and needs your love so much: but she is bewildered by your form of expression . . . She tries as hard as she knows to be loyal and loving to you and to face the difficulties of her life bravely and realistically. She knows Bobby is not the right husband for her . . . So much of her is wasted, but she does try to do her best and doesn't spare herself in her home.

She wants to love you so much – to find some sort of relationship with you, but the uncertainty of your appearance and movements – at times when she can only see you for a matter of seconds in the early morning and such like – can't really get either of you anywhere.[44]

But Margot had no influence any more: she was merely an obstacle. 'She is vacillating between wanting help,' wrote the head of the alarmingly named 'Re-education Centre' to King, 'and on the other hand, not wanting to get well unless she were to resume her old relationship with you, which I fully realise is quite impossible. I pointed out to her that this is nothing more or less than emotional blackmail.'[45]

Michael in particular put enormous effort into persuading Margot to agree to a divorce, which she did miserably in 1961; King and Ruth were married in October 1962 from her brother's house within three days of the decree absolute. 'My news will surprise almost all of Mr King's colleagues and staff,' reported the *Evening Standard*'s diarist. 'For no announcement has been made. Dr Railton [she had been given an honorary LLD by Aberdeen University in 1960] is a shy and retiring woman, utterly dedicated to the orchestra which she created and disliking the publicity it inevitably brings her.'[46] Those surprised included King's children, none of whom had been told that the wedding was taking place. Having read it in the press, Priscilla sent a congratulatory bouquet to Cheyne Walk; it was returned with a note from Ruth saying that she had found this offensive, since she and King had been spiritually married for seven years.

Ruth's possessiveness required her to undermine even those of King's children with whom she got on from time to time, which cannot have helped professionally the three sons, all of whom worked in King's empire. None benefited from their relationship with the Chairman; King used his influence only to get them their first jobs.

'The great point is that you like & are interested in human beings, because if you keep that, you are bound to have a full & worth-while life whether you go into politics or the church or the scholastic profession,'[47] George Lyttleton had written to Michael in 1943, but when Michael was finally released into civilian life his energy and optimism had dissipated. His first job after the Fleet Air Arm had been in industry. When, in 1949, he decided to leave for the Reuters job because of 'the gravitational pull'[48] of Fleet Street, the Chairman of his firm told King that Michael had greatly impressed management with 'the objectivity and shrewdness of his reporting'.[49]

In 1952 King arranged with Cudlipp that Michael should join the *Mirror*. He shared a room with Keith Waterhouse:

> on such an egalitarian paper [he] overcame the double disadvantage of an Eton education and being the Chairman's son with pleasant imperturbability . . . [He] was out most of the time – the diplomatic correspondent's day started with the Foreign Office press conference in the morning, followed by bar billiards at Winnie's until closing time* ('Should anyone want me, say I've been called to No. 10,' he would tell the news desk secretary ambiguously), followed by tea in St James's clubs with mysterious contacts.[50]

El Vino's was full of groups, each with 'a kind of prince to whom all others defer when he is holding court,' said *Queen* in 1963. '. . . with politics [it is] Derek Marks (*Daily Express*) and Michael King (*Daily Mirror*).'[51] 'It can have been no easy task to plough a furrow distinct from the paternal path, but any emotional problem was resolved in his early days with the *Mirror*,' recalled a diarist a few years later:

> One evening as a group of us walked over from the old Geraldine House wedding-cake building in Fetter-lane to Number Ten (The Falcon Pub . . .) chairman King slowed his Rolls and called over: 'Can I give you a lift home, Michael?'
> 'No, thank you,' said Michael. 'I'm having a quick one with

---

* Pubs closed for the afternoon at 2.30.

the boys first.' Old colleagues who remember the incident recall it as the day Michael King publicly chose his side of the fence.[52]

King would give Michael a lift to the office so as to listen to his political and newspaper gossip and interrogate him about what was going on inside the *Mirror*. 'Papa is very glad of your support, I'm sure, dear Mike,' wrote Margot a year or so after he joined the paper, '& you must be delighted to know that you are a help to him . . . The more you can support Papa in your work the better for him – & he needs all the help he can get.'[53] Sharing King's passionate support for British membership of the European Community – on which he was tremendously well informed – Michael enlisted the support of many European journalists. Yet King showed no sign of valuing him: as Peregrine Worsthorne put it, King was 'cruelly unappreciative'.[54] Edward Pickering, Editor of the *Daily Express* from 1957 to 1962, was one of those who believed that Michael had real ability and could be a very good political correspondent, were he given the opportunity and the scope. 'But there was a weakness. I offered him a job outside the organisation. I said, "Michael, why don't you leave? Clearly, you know, you're not going to get anywhere." He said no, because he felt he couldn't go and work for a rival organisation while his father was still running this one. Cecil wouldn't have forgiven him.'

Pickering thought he should defy his father, but Michael could not bring himself to do so. His fierce loyalty and the 'beautiful and forgiving nature'[55] that Lyttleton had admired so much, were inimical to his own interests. He had the high-sounding title of Foreign Editor, with little scope to write more than a few lines; in search of something worthwhile to do, he also worked for MI5. Although he and Libby got along quite well, and she was loyal to him in her fashion, he was hurt by her affairs and spent much of his life lunching, dining and drinking with colleagues and friends.

'Dearest Papa,' he wrote in 1962, when the *Mirror's* new Editor, Lee Howard, was proving a disappointment:

I hope you know that I am as much concerned about the future of the paper as anybody else. It is my life and therefore I have given a great deal of thought to the problem. The names that we have discussed as possible editors will not, I think, fit the bill. Obviously they are all vital ingredients. Rightly, & not too soon, the Mirror has been trying to change course a bit & revise the formulae of the past. It is, I believe, essential that this should continue. But it cannot be done by people who defer instinctively to what former editors might have done when presented with a problem.

This is a reaction I have witnessed too often. A forward look, cautious maybe, with some imagination is essential. An interim solution could make matters worse. I have 4 suggestions to make: Jacobson, Derek Dale (whose talents are not being used), Charles Wintour, Editor of the Evening Standard, and lastly your very devoted eldest son.

Mike[56]

Howard stayed on: Michael never stood a chance. 'If anything happens here,' King said to Pickering, who joined the Mirror in 1964, 'the one thing you must ensure is that Michael doesn't take charge.' It would be 1967 before Michael nerved himself to leave.

While King had never recognised Michael's abilities, which were beyond his understanding, he respected Francis's intellect, but gave him no preferential treatment either. Francis had wanted at various times to be a farmer or to go into social work, but instead chose to go down the family route. After Oxford, where he married Jenny, a scholar of Somerville, he spent a year alone in West Africa working on Mirror newspapers. After a year back home on the editorial side of the Manchester Guardian and Evening News, he returned to Africa with Jenny and worked in both editorial and management on the Daily Graphic. He did well and was respected and liked by Frank Rogers, who ran the Lagos operation for three years from 1949. By 1957, when Francis moved to London, he had spent a total of six years in Africa – the last two as General Manager – and was proud of his role in training up an African team to take over the Daily Graphic.

From a job as Assistant Editorial Manager on the Mirror, he moved to be Editorial Business Manager at Fleetway Publications, but though he was appointed to the board in 1962 and did his job competently, like many other Mirror imports he had no experience in periodicals and was therefore not in a world where he could shine.

Colin had more scope on the business side in the Anglo-Canadian Pulp and Paper Mills and was steadily promoted, even after he came back to England. Cudlipp, who never liked him, believed that King had put him into the job as a spy. But then King used all sorts of people – including Cudlipp – as spies. In any case, Colin was the furthest from King's real sphere of interest, was emotionally more liberated from him than his siblings and the most professionally successful of the three boys; in his early forties he was prosperous and in *Who's Who*.

King's treatment of his sons was becoming the stuff of Fleet Street legend. 'Unlike the Berry boys – all of whom sat on their father's board in the days of the Kemsley empire,' wrote a waspish commentator in 1962 '. . . the King sons have all had to work their way up from near the bottom. Of the three Michael, as the Mirror's foreign editor, is the best known. Ranks as one of the best diplomatic correspondents in Fleet Street, and enjoys a wide range of popularity . . . Runs an Austin Countryman estate car: a key indication that family connections allow him exactly the salary (and the power) that his position demands – but no more.'

True, King was not a proprietor, and he showed no interest in building up his small shareholding, but he seemed to take a perverse pleasure in encouraging his sons to go into his businesses, giving them much less help than the first Lord Rothermere had given him, and then making it difficult for them to leave. Although he loved them in his peculiar and inarticulate way, he regarded as proper objectivity what was in fact often a gross underestimation of their abilities.

'The children,' as Ruth put it, 'had been brought up "Papa will provide", very much Harmsworth. "Papa will provide" for every move, every job, every everything. They somehow expected that the level of school and house, the level of money which they had been brought up to would be there for ever.'[57] That was unfair to Margot and to the King children, all of whom were naturally high-minded about money. Michael, at sixteen, fiercely assured his mother that he 'would renounce any money I might get from Dad . . . it's against my principles to live on money I haven't earned.'[58] Francis, at seventeen, had written to Margot from Winchester, after Bart's accession to the chairmanship, 'I can't believe that Dad would stay just to increase our inheritance:

it would be a most worthless cause' – a sentiment his siblings would wholeheartedly have agreed with.

Still, as they got older, it rankled that while their father had benefited considerably from family generosity, he was not only determined that they would inherit nothing from him, but disapproved of giving them anything while he was alive. Francis Needham, the great friend of his youth, had once discussed King's attitude to money: 'As you know, we are completely different over money-matters: you (if there is a mean in such things) are perhaps a little too much on the prudent side; I am certainly much too much the other way – stupidly methodless & spendthrift.' Resisting King's clearly somewhat reluctant offer to waive a £20 debt, Needham added, 'Remember the Harmsworth parasites: I don't want to turn into *that!*'[59]

King ensured there was no possibility of any of his children becoming parasitical. In order to feel morally on high ground, when he sold Cushnie he passed to them exactly the amount he had inherited himself, split three ways; Priscilla was ruled out because she was female, although she was later given a valuable painting. And that – apart from the occasional cheque and the odd covenant to help with school fees – was that.

King's justifications were lofty: he loved his children, thought it important they make their own way, feared making them dependent and fully intended to leave his money to his grandchildren. Though with inherited money, a handsome salary and an unlimited expense account he was able to live and travel like a rich man, he had no interest in money for its own sake, had built up little capital and never thought himself well-off. With modest incomes and growing families (Michael and Francis each had four children, Priscilla and Colin two), all of them could have done with some help and it seemed perverse that so little was forthcoming. Even more perverse was that King broke the terms of the family trust fund to buy Cheyne Walk and put it solely in his name. Libby, who was a self-confessed snob who had expected to benefit from the Harmsworth connection, was most annoyed; Priscilla, feeling rejected by her father and persecuted by Ruth, felt most upset. In their belief that father should help their families, both Libby and Priscilla were products of their class, gender and time.

The longer King lived with Ruth and the more she dilated on the avariciousness of his children,* the more implacably mean with them he became. The nadir occurred when, in desperation, Priscilla decided to beg him for help in paying for speech therapy for her son William, who could not then talk intelligibly. Unable, because of Ruth, to see her father privately at home, she asked his secretary for an appointment and was given a date three weeks ahead. When they met he turned her down curtly and, when she asked if Langley could take her home because she was crying so much with humiliation, King refused. Yet he was fond of William and never failed to send him postcards whenever he was abroad. His grandson Laurence, whom King would help with a business venture, saw his point of view:

> People tended to look to him when they got into scrapes. These were not the circumstances in which he would help them (unless they were fundamentally in need) because it encouraged the tendency that led to the scrape in the first place. Instead, he would tell them what their mistake had been and, sometimes, what they should do to get out of it. Advice of this sort is never welcome. However, when they were pursuing a positive line, he would encourage and reward them. This is why some say that he helped them when they least expected it. But the policy was entirely considered and consistent. He never acted on impulse to buy affection.

That was true. As King was altruistic towards the Falls children, so he would later provide a seven-year covenant worth £500[†] a year to help educate a gifted grand-nephew. In neither case had he been asked to help; he had met what to him was an obvious need. Unfortunately for his children, their adult needs did not fit his criteria, his reluctance to help just seemed harsh and there was no denying that his instincts were parsimonious. He believed himself generous in

---

* As the sale of Cushnie and all its contents was going through, Michael and Priscilla went there to say goodbye to the locals; as they left, Ruth demanded they open their suitcases for her inspection.

† About £7,000 today.

the modest allowance he gave Margot (which swiftly shrank with inflation), but it bore no relation to his own affluence.

Even Ruth suffered. Since he had told her that Margot had no idea of the value of money, she was determined to show herself in a much better light, so she scrimped and supplemented the small housekeeping allowance with her own money and never complained. The house remained uncomfortable and cold because she would not ask King to spend money on it. Domestically, she had to make huge adjustments – not least because she liked late nights and late mornings and he liked to be in bed at 9.30 p.m. She did everything she could to please him and her capacity for self-sacrifice became legendary. When his psoriasis was bad, it made sharing a bed uncomfortable, so Ruth would sleep in a camp bed alongside.

As Denis Forman said, Ruth saved King. Despite all the trouble she caused with his family and with friends and colleagues as they got to know her, she had rescued him from despair and offered unfailing worship. Ruth might not understand what he was talking about, but she could be relied upon to tell him that everything he did was right, that he was a genius and possessed of rare spirituality. Within five years of her moving in with him, partly because of the confidence she gave him, King had become the biggest and most famous publisher in the world. Unfortunately, Ruth was now intent on his becoming the saviour of his country.

CHAPTER X

The Influence of Ruth

'HE IS A DICTATOR WHO SEES NOT A SINGLE CLOUD ON THE HORIZON,' concluded Jocelyn Stevens of King in February 1961 after the Odhams takeover. As he had with Fleetway, King blithely fired some very good people, whose gifts in the magazine market he simply did not understand. Yet he was full of confidence. *The Economist* warned him against being too sanguine: 'accession to such an empire puts, even in the economic sense, greater responsibilities on the emperor and on the satraps he appoints. Mr King would have no excuse to give to his newly enfranchised shareholders if the strategic direction of the combine to end magazine combines turned out in the end to be as sloppy as that of Odhams – and Fleetway – looks on occasion to have been.'[1]

Much would depend on the head satrap. Still Editorial Director of the *Mirror* and *Pictorial* and a director of ATV, since 1959 Cudlipp had also shared with King the managing directorship of the *Mirror* group, which involved him in the dreadful daily headaches caused by rampant unions; moreover he now presided over Fleetway. 'The experienced newspaperman can always detect,' wrote Arthur Christiansen, the ex-Editor of the *Daily Express*, during the fight for Odhams, 'in which direction the energies of Hugh Cudlipp are being concentrated':

When the *Mirror* launches a political crusade, or a don't-shoot-the-tiger campaign, or a plea that Britain must Export or Die, or a Page One accusation that Dr Fisher [Archbishop of Canterbury] is a poor fisher of men, Cudlipp's concentrating on the *Mirror*. When the *Pictorial* cleans itself up, and hires Sir

Malcolm Sargent, Dame Margot Fonteyn, and an art critic and induces Malcolm Muggeridge to do a six-subject column, Cudlipp's concentrating on the *Pictorial*. When the *Woman's Mirror* takes full-page advertisements in all the papers, both the Cudlipps are concentrating! The combined power of Mr and Mrs Cudlipp over the livelihoods of hundreds, maybe thousands, of newspaper men and woman, even benevolently exercised as they have always been, are going to be immense and terrifying.[2]

King had offered the chairmanship of Odhams to Jocelyn Stevens, who rejected it on the grounds that no one could oversee that number of magazines, so the job was given to Cudlipp along with all his other responsibilities. '[Cudlipp] now has to show,' said an *Observer* profile:

> whether he is as good at being a tycoon as he is at the blatant art of compelling millions to read his headlines and like his gimmicks. Since the *Mirror* group includes, besides the *Mirror*, *Pictorial*, *Herald* and *People*, a large slice of the magazines published in Britain, and more than half the women's magazines, together with such oddments as a one-quarter stake in Associated Television and extensive newsprint interests, Cudlipp's talents will have plenty of chance to reverberate.

The profiler mused on his achievements:

> People who come up the hard way make their friends (and enemies) uneasily anxious to know just how they did it. Hugh Cudlipp, the fierce and still-practising journalist from Cardiff who is second only to Cecil King in the huge *Daily Mirror* group, did it by ambition, sweat and insight into human nature . . . [He] is one of those earnest, clever, bold, rhetorical men who seem to have been given a hard push at an early age, after which they have never been able to remain still. At the age of forty-seven Cudlipp cultivates tycoonery: telephones interrupt, the gin is offered freely, the cigars look like truncheons, the jokes to subordinates are sometimes tinged with meaning, and Cudlipp's charm alternates rapidly with Cudlipp's brusqueness. He has always been direct, with an edge in his voice . . . His strength,

says one of his editors, lies in the 'uncomplicated forcefulness of his personality'.[3]

Cudlipp's persuasive genius had been employed in the campaign to win the support of the Labour Party and the unions for the *Mirror* takeover of Odhams, for there was widespread fear about what King would do with the failing *Daily Herald*, founded in 1911 as a strike bulletin: editorial policy in industrial affairs was dictated by the divided Trades Union Congress, which owned 49 per cent, and in political affairs by the fractious Labour Party. Francis Williams and Percy Cudlipp had been two of the distinguished editors who had failed to make this muddled and cash-starved official party newspaper a paying concern: circulation was running at 1.4 million and falling steadily, and the paper was losing £500,000[*] a year. Though Odhams had made a deal with the TUC that gave the paper more autonomy, it kept its cloth-cap image.

Most opponents feared King would close the paper down or amalgamate it with the *Mirror*; Gaitskell was one of those who would prefer to see the *Herald*'s fate in the hands of the pragmatic conservative Roy Thomson, rather than have any more of the press under the control of a maverick such as Cecil King. After tremendous press coverage and frenzied plotting in all camps, Cudlipp found a way of making peace with the labour movement: King promised that every effort would be made to make the *Herald* profitable and guaranteed that it would be kept going for a minimum of seven years.

Once the *Mirror* had secured Odhams, in the spring of 1961, at Cudlipp's suggestion, King held a series of cocktail parties in his office to enable senior editorial staff of the new publications to meet *Mirror*-group directors. Cudlipp recalled:

At the end of the marathon get-together was the *Daily Herald*'s night, with its Editor John Beavan and his principal editorial staff as the guests. Cecil wasn't there that evening, nor was I accompanied by any other IPC director of any particular importance in the eyes of the guests except Ellis Birk. I knew in that

---

[*] About £6.6 million today.

lonely moment that the *Daily Herald* was being baptised as 'Cudlipp's baby' . . . It was dumped firmly in my lap. The prospects of success were zero. I no doubt had everybody's best wishes, especially Cecil's, but no condolences.[4]

Naturally Cudlipp hurled himself at his new challenge, but King did not make it easy for him. Within a few months the *Observer* saw a 'patent difference of opinion between Cudlipp, who is sinking large amounts of his formidable energy and large quantities of *Mirror*-group money into the *Herald*: and his chairman, Cecil Harmsworth King, the shrewd nephew of Northcliffe, who would like to be rid of the *Herald*, and says so in public – "the cross I have to bear," he called it in Washington last month.'[5]

'I was absolutely staggered to read of your speech in Washington,' wrote George Brown, the deputy leader of the Labour Party – who had been an important intermediary with Gaitskell during the negotiations over the *Herald* – '. . . I am hanged if I can understand what such a speech can do except depress everybody, your friends and the Herald staff alike, and, of course, encourage those who were not convinced at the time. I do beg you to take an early opportunity of sounding as though, whatever your original feelings were, you are now determined to make the Herald something of which you will be proud.'[6] King – who had once graciously forgiven a drunken outburst from Brown over one of their lunches[7] – responded with a low blow: 'I am surprised that you, of all people, should be so ready to reprove when a friend drops a clanger. We are doing our best with the Herald – I think with success – and what I said was in answer to a question, at the end of a large number of questions. It, of course, never occurred to me that I should be quoted in Washington, let alone elsewhere.'[8] But the damage was done: henceforward the *Herald* would be known as 'King's Cross'.

Had he become master of the universe, King would still have stuck to his 9.30–5.30 day, with the occasional evening engagement, and would have continued his regular travels around his empire (including a completely disproportionate amount of time in Africa), leaving Cudlipp to deal with the day-to-day demands. Christiansen was right to wonder if the new burdens that Cudlipp was taking on would tax 'even his seemingly inexhaustible energies'.

They seemed not to, at least initially. Still only forty-seven, Cudlipp believed he could do anything and adored being a Fleet Street legend in his own lifetime. He had long ago outstripped the elder brothers in whose footsteps he had faithfully trodden. In 1953 the three (celebrated in print as 'the astonishing Cudlipps . . . polished Percy, studious Reg, ebullient Hugh'⁹ who 'had burst out of Cardiff to Manchester and London like a radio-active cloud'¹⁰) had had a riotous celebration of what turned out to be a very brief period when all of them were editors of national newspapers: the same year Percy – who was thought insufficiently malleable – was fired from the *Daily Herald* after thirteen years; Reg would stay with the *News of the World* until 1959.

Even with all his new responsibilities, Cudlipp milked every moment of his life for maximum enjoyment. He was up at dawn, absorbing newspapers and news programmes, sparking off and carousing with the best journalists in the business, eating in fine restaurants with the powerful and the interesting, acknowledged as the inspiration behind the most successful newspaper on earth – and now he was a tycoon to boot. He had an insatiable capacity for friendship and talk, laughter and non-stop stimulation, and the mental and physical stamina to cope with little sleep, innumerable challenges and a great deal of alcohol.

Weekends were not for rest, but for sailing with friends on the Thames or across the Channel, with the office on the other end of a radio telephone and on his head Bertie, an obliging parrot acquired by the *Mirror*'s publicity department to cry 'Read the *Daily Mirror*! Read the *Daily Mirror*!' at apposite moments.*

Cudlipp and Eileen were professionally the most successful couple in Fleet Street, but although they were cushioned by housekeepers and chauffeurs and secretaries, the pressure on both was intense. There were varied responses to her: Priscilla thought her enchanting; Crossman

---

* After the death of the mongrel that loved swimming and could be yanked back on board with a boat hook, Cudlipp had acquired an elegant and haughty-looking successor, which was stretched out on his office carpet yawning one Saturday morning when King called in. 'That's an Afghan hound, isn't it?' 'It is.' 'What's its name?' 'The Caliph of Baghdad.' King considered for a moment. 'What on earth do you call it for short?' And, without missing a beat, Cudlipp replied, 'Cecil Harmsworth King.' It was one of those jokes King could not get.

could not stand her; and to Ellis Birk she was 'a she-devil', who believed her achievements were undervalued and was very jealous of Cudlipp. Professionally she was popular and a good boss, and Jodi Hyland, editor of *Woman's Mirror*, who spent a great deal of time with them, thought the Cudlipps got on well, liked each other and had a great deal of fun – though she thought Eileen was coldly over-ambitious for both of them. Still, the Cudlipps' was a high-octane relationship with many rows and neither of them was sexually faithful.

Cudlipp had always been a tremendous flirt: Peter Wilson remembered how nervous he felt in the late 1940s when, at his request, Cudlipp threw a dinner party for the boxer Joe Louis at which he flirted relentlessly with Louis's wife. According to a journalist who knew him well, 'like many people in his position in those days, Hugh had a fancy for the wives of his junior colleagues. He was not above exercising a bit of *droit de seigneur* – not that he needed to.'[11]

The Cudlipps were mutually tolerant. When Eileen found her drunken husband in bed with the housekeeper, she did not make a major issue out of it ('every dog is allowed one bite,' she told Jodi); after all, she was rumoured to have had an affair with one of the chauffeurs. And when she began an intense and rather obvious affair with one of his closest colleagues, Cudlipp – if he guessed it – did not make a fuss. Anyway, it made it easier for him to pursue his affair with Jodi Hyland, with whom he had fallen deeply in love.

Blonde, lively and extremely pretty, Jodi had come on the scene in 1959. Until she was fourteen she was brought up in Florida by her Yorkshire mother, the widow of a civil engineer. Irene Hyland, known as 'Fling', was beautiful and adventurous: 'My first paid job,' said Jodi, 'was washing bottles for Ida, the lady bootlegger who operated next door. I worked in a large cage in the company of a tame racoon hidden from the eyes of any prying prohibition officer.' Fling supplemented their income by hiring out at a dollar a day the unexpurgated copy of *Lady Chatterley's Lover* she had acquired in Paris. She also cleaned up once in a card game partnering Al Capone – one of the stories with which she would regale her audience in Lancashire, where she settled in 1934 with her second husband, David Jones, a solicitor. A childhood in which she took second place to a wildly attractive and amusing raconteur and wit with a huge personality was perfect training for the future Mrs Hugh Cudlipp.

Jodi never wanted to be anything but a journalist. The prejudices of the time prevented her from achieving her ambition to be a news reporter; after working on a local paper in Southport, she took a job in London on *Woman's Own*, where she earned the title 'chief features writer and ace reporter'. She had barely started when war intervened. She joined the army and was sent to Bletchley Park, where her agile mind and investigative instincts were employed in support of the code-breakers. Post-war she advanced swiftly in the world of women's magazines, spent two years as a reporter in Australia, returned to edit *Debutante*, then *Girl*, and became assistant to the Editor of *Woman*, which had the largest circulation of any magazine in the United Kingdom.

After taking over Amalgamated Press, King asked Jodi to come and see him. 'Do you read the *Mirror*?' he asked. 'I did this morning,' she replied. 'Well,' he answered, 'I daresay we can struggle along without your tuppence halfpenny' and there the interview ended. Apart from the businessman Charles Clore, King was the only man with whom Jodi simply could find nothing to talk about.

Like everyone who worked in Fleet Street, Jodi had long known of the famous Cudlipp brothers and had heard Hugh described by journalists as 'Dillinger', 'Public Enemy No. 1' and 'Little Daddy' to King's 'Big Daddy'. She met him first, with Eileen, at a party and shortly afterwards Cudlipp took her to lunch and offered her the editorship of *Woman's Illustrated**. 'What I now remember most was that as I accepted his offer, he put his hand over mine across the table and said: "I hope this will be the beginning of a long association."' Asked afterwards what she thought of him, she replied with a laugh that she would like to take a second option.

At work and socially, Jodi soon became a friend and confidante of Eileen; although she never became fond of her, she liked and admired her and, of course, found Eileen professionally useful. Jodi knew more about magazines than her boss and was a useful adviser. They played chess together sometimes (which annoyed Cudlipp, because they

---

* Under her editorship, although the magazine was much improved, it was axed in the rationalisation that followed the take-over of Odhams; she then became editor of *Woman's Mirror*, a *Daily Mirror* offshoot.

weren't concentrating on him) and even borrowed each other's clothes. Gradually Jodi began to spend a great deal of time with them as a couple, especially on the boat, where she became a frequent member of the crew and shared with Eileen the cooking and the chores. Eileen was uninhibited about talking to Jodi about Cudlipp, since Jodi spent so much time with them both that she had often experienced him being impatient, demanding, self-indulgent, mischievous or irascible. 'If you ever go out to dinner with Hugh,' advised Eileen, 'always eat up your first course, because you may not be there for the second.' A colleague would later recall:

> It was not all sweetness and light. Brilliance has its price. Cudlipp had his black moods. Sometimes he would merely snap and snarl, but when the demon was really in him he would blow his top and assault with verbal violence somebody who had said the wrong thing. His contrition, after one of these attacks, never failed and was often expressed by a pay rise for the victim, or even promotion.[12]

Cudlipp was indeed, at this stage of his life, increasingly given to rows and to storming out when he had been drinking even more than usual. Dick Crossman, who was unusually temperate for his time and profession, dreaded those evenings when conviviality turned sour. 'Suddenly we had flared into one of those blazing rows,' he wrote of an encounter in the autumn of 1959, when he had enraged Cudlipp by appearing to impugn his integrity by getting his lawyer involved in a negotiation with the *Mirror*. '"I'm not going to have any of your damn lawyers again," [Cudlipp] said. "Once again you can't trust me . . ." And he flared out in a flaming row. Next morning a quiet little voice rang up and said he would send me a draft letter . . . which I could show to my lawyer. He hoped that was all right.'

Jodi was also aware that at work Cudlipp had his deficiencies. He was, for instance, incredulous when she bought the serial rights of Joy Adamson's *Born Free* ('In love with lions? Jesus!'), which for little money gave the circulation an enormous boost and began the vogue for true-life animal stories. And he used to engage in sneaky manoeu-vres like making *Woman's Mirror* bear a proportion of the cost of a completely unsuitable serial that he wanted for the *Sunday Mirror* (as the *Sunday Pictorial* had been renamed). A master of resolving conflict and finding compromises to keep the show on the road, he was no less adept at getting out of the frame before problems became obvious, or getting out from under them nimbly and fast.

It was Jodi whom Eileen told about her long-standing affair with a married colleague and of her intention to leave Cudlipp for him: 'Every dog has one life,' she said. Jokingly called 'the Heiress' because she was due a considerable sum from a trust fund, Eileen had never got over the feeling that she had married – in one of her phrases – 'beyond the green baize door'. 'You're a fucking snob, Ascroft' was a refrain of Cudlipp's, conscious that his wife felt she had been responsible for educating him socially – as King felt he had done intellectually: 'I feel I've done all I can for Hugh,' Eileen told Jodi. By then Jodi, still involved with a married man she had met at Bletchley, had fallen in love with Cudlipp; their affair had begun when Eileen had stormed off the boat at Honfleur after a marital row, leaving them alone.

For a denizen of Fleet Street, Jodi was exceptionally monogamous: Bletchleyman and Cudlipp were the only two lovers she ever had. Then Cudlipp set about seeing off the opposition. He had once told Jodi a joke about a woman who, having left her husband George, was setting off to exotic places with her lover. A friend in whom she had confided enthused, 'How romantic. It will be wonderful.' 'Yes,' said the errant wife, 'but it won't be the same without George' – a phrase that became part of Cudlipp's and Jodi's private language. Knowing she was going to Italy on holiday, Cudlipp got hold of the passenger list and confirmed his suspicion that she was accompanied by Bletchleyman. As they were leaving her flat for the airport, a telegram arrived that said simply, 'IT WON'T BE THE SAME WITHOUT GEORGE'. That would be the message Jodi would put on the flowers at Cudlipp's funeral. Just for now, it was enough to administer in Italy the *coup de grâce* to a relationship that had lasted almost twenty years.

Although officially Eileen did not know about Jodi's affair with Cudlipp, any more than he officially knew about hers with their joint colleague, Jodi had a sneaking suspicion that Eileen had deliberately pushed them together so that she would feel less bad at leaving home. The futures of all of them were uncertain, when, on the morning of Sunday, 30 April 1962, Eileen died.

With Jodi's help, the previous weekend the Cudlipps had moved into the house that Eileen had built and paid for on the Thames at Sonning and had given a supper party for a few dozen friends and neighbours. Eileen had written a note of appreciation to Jodi, telling her to call on them to help her move to her new cottage in Barnes. In the intervening week Cudlipp's *At Your Peril* had been launched with various celebrations, and on the Saturday night the Cudlipps went to a boozy party at the house of one of their new neighbours. Exhausted, Eileen left the party before Cudlipp and, being a bad sleeper, as there were no curtains yet in the bedroom, she drove back to their London house. 'Hugh,' said her note, 'Sorry to desert you but I had to try & get some sleep. As you know I haven't slept for nights – probably the excitement of the book. After Dr Thomas' excellent pills & a good night's rest I'll be down feeling fine.'

Dr Thomas's pills made the 47-year-old Cudlipp a widower for the second time. 'I do not forget the devastating ordeal in the bleak office of the West Middlesex coroner,' wrote Cudlipp in his eighties, 'where the name of the vibrant Eileen was referred to in the past tense; giving evidence myself, and hearing the evidence of the pathologist Dr Donald Teare ("The difference between a normal dose and a lethal dose of the sleeping drug, Carbrital, which she had apparently taken after a party, was very small, and that in her fatigue she might have forgotten how much she had taken.")'[13]

Saying that he was 'quite satisfied there is no question here of suicide and that she was caught by her desire for sleep,' the Coroner returned a verdict of accidental death by Carbitral. Although not an obviously happy person, Eileen was healthy, prosperous, popular and full of plans for the future, but Fleet Street being Fleet Street, and despite the absence of any evidence, many friends and most enemies preferred to believe she had committed suicide.*

Cudlipp was devastated and overwrought after Eileen's death and, a few months later, by Percy's; if anything, his alcohol consumption increased – at a time when King had been forced for health reasons to become a teetotaller. Although he was never seen to be under the influence of alcohol, King for years drank copiously. Arriving home

---

* In 1998, Cudlipp's *Times* obituary said that Eileen had killed herself.

in the evenings, he would have a treble gin-and-tonic and a bottle of wine, but he also drank heartily when in company, which made him more talkative. 'Cecil King stayed for two and a half hours,' wrote Crossman, his host, of a party in January 1958, 'drank a great deal and talked to everybody, mainly because it was the evening on which the bank rate report had been published and he was furious with it as an outrageous whitewash.'[14]

'When Cecil drank, Cecil drank,' observed Tony Delano, who met him on many of his overseas tours. 'The press attaché in Rome agreed to have a party for him and he asked for Martinis. He had a curious knack of leaving his glass away from his body and pretending not to notice when it was filled and he'd empty it in one gulp. He drank a lot, showing no visible signs – must have got through a good quart. And he insisted that wine be ordered in magnums – didn't like bottles – and always very good vintages.' (King was similarly a voracious eater who would finish his plate when most people were on their second forkful and whose breakfast usually consisted of two fried eggs swallowed in two gulps.)

From time to time King had gone off alcohol to try to alleviate his psoriasis, but in 1961 his doctor surmised that peripheral neuritis due to alcohol might be why the soles of his feet were becoming painful: 'It was a rather poor family history; one or two relatives had died from cirrhosis of the liver and one or two with heart attacks. So I felt he might keep up the family tradition unless something pretty desperate was done so that was why I took him to a specialist.' The specialist told sixty-year-old King to give up alcohol completely; that he would survive by several years the two sons who drank heavily suggests the doctor had a point. He went home that evening and, according to Ruth, threw himself on his bed in despair and said, 'I can never have a drink again.' He never did.

Teetotalism made it more difficult for King to relax; he became if anything more intolerant socially and much more censorious about excessive alcohol consumption than in his drinking days. According to his doctor, who had become a friend, he arrived downcast one morning:

I said, 'Something troubling you, Cecil?' And he said, 'Yes, I'm very troubled. I'm just about to sack the first editor in Fleet

Street.' He was discussing Cudlipp, who had not been behaving very well, perhaps drinking too much. But Cecil was disturbed by the quality of the work he was putting into the newspaper. He was not writing as well as he used to, not editing as well as he used to. I said, thinking it might have been to do with drink, 'Do you think that's sufficient to dismiss him? Why not give him one more trial. And be quite frank and say the work is not good enough and it is because you're drinking too much: stop drinking or cut it down to reasonable proportions: one more chance.'[15]

After a difficult meeting with King, Cudlipp gave up spirits (except for brandy, on the grounds that it was distilled from wine), and although he was prone to the delusion common to serious drinkers that wine does not count, he cut back considerably on his alcohol intake. Yet his position was still not secure. It was around this time that someone reported to King that his right-hand man had told a derogatory story about him. 'Derogatory' was not the right adjective, but Cudlipp certainly told innumerable hilarious stories at King's expense, as he did at his own and everyone else's. 'He was a great actor *manqué*,' wrote his colleague John Beavan of Cudlipp. 'He would act out an anecdote with brilliantly invented satiric dialogue and could hold and delight any company. Sometimes the acting was in the mind of a political leader at a time of crisis. Cudlipp would play the main part and we supplied the supporting cast. In my time I played Home to his Heath, Brown to his Gaitskell, Callaghan to his Wilson.' And, no doubt, King to his Cudlipp.[16]

'Without preamble', according to Jack Nener, giving his recollections to Cudlipp some years later, King announced at a board meeting 'that he had evidence that Hugh Cudlipp had been denigrating him behind his back to other people; that the situation was impossible and that he had no alternative but to consider your dismissal. This was followed by a dead silence.' Nener then:

stumblingly tried to convey . . . that some directors were often working under great strain, and things might be said under tension or even in thoughtless jest which, out of context, gained an exaggerated importance . . . Nobody else said anything and after a long pause the Chairman indicated that the matter was closed. I understood from that that he contemplated no further action . . . You may remember that soon afterwards you joined me . . . and that, strangely enough, neither of us mentioned the board meeting . . . I did not want to talk about it unless you did and you did not, apparently, wish to do so.[17]

What had stunned the board was the notion that King thought he could operate without Cudlipp to implement his ideas, solve his problems and generally act as his conduit to reality. Yet these two episodes made Cudlipp – ever the pragmatist – aware how expendable he now was in King's increasingly clouded eyes. He was aware that 'in the rarefied world inhabited alone by Cecil there would be a vacancy for another puppet on a string. Svengali would mould or create another person, or Frankenstein another monster.'[18] Still, the marriage of convenience held together.

The following year Cudlipp married Jodi,* who had 'gently picked up the pieces and put me together again to my eternal gratitude'.[19] ('Hugh Cudlipp or no Hugh Cudlipp,' her mother said to him, 'you couldn't do better than my daughter': 'about time too,' said Eileen's son Kerry.) Despite her love of journalism and her excellent career prospects, Jodi had decided that – third time around – Cudlipp needed a full-time wife to cherish, stabilise and mellow him. They contemplated having children (Eileen had once had a miscarriage), but decided against – wisely, Jodi soon realised, when she saw how bored Cudlipp was by children. The only drawback for Cudlipp was that musically they were as ill-matched as the Kings; Cudlipp was as passionate as ever about music and Jodi was as tone-deaf as King.

Practical, pragmatic, equable and affectionate, Jodi was philosophical about Cudlipp's thoughtlessness: the summons as she was up a ladder in Sonning painting a ceiling to get to the office within an hour, dressed for the white-tie dinner he had forgotten to tell her about; the instruction to get a big car (he didn't drive – too accident prone)

---

* 'On our way into the registry office on 1 March 1963,' remembered Jodi, 'for the first time we exchanged our full real names. He was Hubert Kinsman Cudlipp and I was Joan Latimer Hyland. We had both settled for something that looked better, more modern, in type.'

despite the problems of manoeuvring it around London traffic; his inability to stay at a play for more than one act ('I've got the idea. Now let's have dinner'); the way he stole her best witticisms; the blithe manner in which he left all practical matters to her; and – despite his generosity – his general hopelessness about anniversaries, birthdays and presents. But these aspects of Cudlipp were, to her, no more than minor irritations in an exceptionally happy and companionable marriage. 'Living with Hugh was like living with Battersea Power Station,' she once said. 'I never saw him depressed.' She loved the warmth, the energy, the joy, the laughter and even the ever-present danger of an explosion,* and revelled too in their social life and in being Cudlipp's hostess on land or sea for, however elevated his job was, stuffiness was never allowed to creep in.

Unshockable, Jodi's sharp wit complemented Cudlipp's story-telling. A typical comment of hers followed the account of the colleague who had run into serious trouble with his mistress: 'he bit off more than he could screw'. Having got used to Harold Wilson's celebrity-studded parties in Downing Street, she was surprised at a dinner given by Ted Heath to hear what she thought to be madrigals. Asked if she had ever been to Downing Street before, she replied, 'Oh, yes, but not since the Cultural Revolution.' 'Drop that bone, Cudlipp' was what she would whisper at parties if he seemed to be getting too chummy with an attractive girl (women of all ages were always girls to the Cudlipps). Ridicule was the tool she used with Cudlipp's female admirers: the most threatening did not long survive being referred to as 'Miss Mouse'.

Cudlipp's circle loved her, for although she behaved in many ways like a traditional wife in handling all domestic responsibilities and allowing her husband to occupy centre stage, she was also a great companion who hugely enjoyed the company of his friends, in the Cudlipp homes, on the Cudlipp boat, in other people's houses, in pubs, clubs and hotels and at parties and on travels abroad. With no experience of politics but vaguely left-wing instincts, Jodi was 'chucked into the

---

* Jodi remembered 'battling away in an argument with Hugh about no-one-remembers-what; and crying out in angry anguish as the torrents of tongue-lashing fell about my head: "What do you want me to do? Jump out of the window?" To which his growled reply was: "If you take on the lions, you must expect to hear them roar!"'

deep end of the political pool where the big sharks of Left and Right circled, and Hugh was no swimming instructor';[20] quickly she learned that being a politician did not preclude you from wanting fun. Like Cudlipp, she took great pleasure in introducing people like Frank Cousins, the General Secretary of the TGWU, to Tory neighbours in Sonning. Forty-two when she married the forty-nine-year old Cudlipp, she was streetwise and confident, and while happy to be a helpmeet, kept her critical faculties honed. 'I'm the pigeon bearing the message,' explained Cudlipp after a spat with Jodi over her correction to a favourite story; 'Jodi flaps along behind with the erratum slip.'

There was no place for an erratum slip in Cecil King's home life. 'She thinks he's God' was a constant comment from family and colleagues, and so Ruth did. But King, equally uncritically, embraced her vision of herself as a woman of rare spirituality and much more. 'My wife, I believe, is what is called a sensitive,' King wrote to a reviewer of a book about auras:

> she was giving musical auditions to children, one of whom was brought by his Indian teacher. When she advanced to shake his hand, he fell on his knees and bowed low before her and said it was improper for him to touch her because she had a blue aura. So when she came home she asked what an aura was, as she had never heard of such things. I found a little book on the subject, knowing almost nothing about them myself. Since then, on two occasions at least, Indians in Sikh turbans have bowed to her in the street and made respectful greetings to the 'lady with the blue aura'.[21]

'At the family house in Margate,' King wrote in 1970, 'where her father was vicar, a railway ran at the bottom of the garden and she used on occasion to see if by sheer will power she could stop a train – and she could. As a child she never thought these gifts strange; she assumed that everyone had them. As she grew older and learned that they were not universal, she became more self-conscious about them and then they began to fade. This is a normal experience.'[22] Mentioning this in his memoirs, Cudlipp also told how Ruth had claimed to have delayed a flight when she and King were late: 'It is a good thing, from the nation's point of view, that her gifts are not widely known to the unions,' he commented. 'Dame Ruth, in a mood of petulance, could bring the nation's transport to a standstill.'[23]

Like most of the stories King told of Ruth's psychic powers, these were unaccompanied by independent evidence, but his faith was unshakeable. He claimed to have long been interested in extra-sensory perception (ESP), but as with so much that concerned Ruth, he was deluding himself: he had shown no more than mild and occasional curiosity. Indeed, in his 1942 diary, he had referred to Stafford Cripps's wife, with whom he was on very friendly terms, as 'a crank because at one point she referred to her husband's Indian trip, and said that when she was returning from Moscow she *knew* he would have to make this attempt . . . She spoke as if she believed herself to possess something like clairvoyant properties.'[24]

It was not until after he met Ruth that King went public on ESP and began actively to search for promising research projects. The International Publishing Corporation (IPC) – as King's empire was named in 1963 – gave seven-year covenants of £1,500 annually to the Society for Psychical Research (SPR) and £5,000* to the Psychophysical Research Unit, founded by three young female Oxford graduates. 'Mrs King is very right,' wrote Sir George Joy of the SPR, after the three of them had visited the unit, 'when she says that if one is determined to pursue an objective, regardless of the means to carry it out, and willing to make any sacrifice that it involves – help comes from unexpected quarters – as in this case.'[25]

'CECIL KING GIVES £35,000 TO DREAM GIRLS' was a *Daily Express* headline that caused both unease and mirth among King's colleagues. The relationship with the young women quickly soured. To a blithe letter from the unit's Director, Celia Green, asking if he would like to finance a fund-raising tour of America ('This might cost £2,000 to do properly'[26]) King commented, 'I have made many visits to the U.S., travelling "en prince", but I never needed "£2,000."'[27] 'Is she going round the bend?'[28] King enquired of Joy when he received what he reasonably described as a 'preposterous' letter with mingled demands and complaints. John Beloff, the Edinburgh University psychologist to whom IPC provided £1,000

---

* About £65,000 today.

annually to pay for an assistant, was professionally impeccable, but was unable to report anything very encouraging from their research into parapsychology.[29]

With so little genuinely in common, for the Kings the world of the paranormal became an important joint interest. Ruth could feed his introspection with satisfying insights like that about his 'invisibility', which she accepted unquestioningly. King had long been convinced that he could become invisible when he chose – passing those he did not wish to speak to on narrow pavements or at parties without being seen. Paul Johnson recalled seeing:

> the great Cecil King walking down Fleet Street, a foot above the normal line of sight and equally unaware of ordinary people trudging by. King's great height and aloof personality which, as it were, edited out other people from his sight were at the root of his belief that he could make himself invisible. No doubt when I glimpsed his march down Fleet Street he believed his magic was working, reasoning that if he could not see people, then they could not see him, though, in fact, his figure was so striking, not to say alarming, that other pedestrians peered up anxiously as the grim monolith strode past.[30]

Sceptics might have attributed this to the other party's wish to avoid an uncomfortable person, but as King (with Ruth's help) decided, it was all a matter of the pulses one sends out. Nor was it surprising that Ruth built on the evidence of her exceptional intuition in the sphere of music to keep her fascinated and gullible husband fed with dreams, prophecies, intuitions, insights, curious encounters and psychic flashes. 'There was an E.S.P. programme last night on B.B.C.2,' wrote King to Joy, on a rare occasion when one of Ruth's pronouncements could be tested. 'At the end we were shown the backs of six playing cards (ducks taking off from water). Ruth immediately said, "Well, the third card is a 3 of Diamonds." This is so unlike her usual style that I pass it on.'[31] 'I am afraid,' responded the BBC producer to whom Joy passed the letter, 'that the 3 of diamonds can only count as a "near miss" for the third card, which was in fact the ace of diamonds.'[32]

'Near misses' were hits, failures were forgotten, uncorroborated stories were accepted as fact. In his lecture on ESP to the Royal Institution in 1969[33] ('one of the must embarrassing experiences of my life,' said Priscilla), one of several such anecdotes King told was of how (in his absence) Ruth had been visited by a total stranger who had sensed her pain, had telepathically guessed where she lived and made her feel much better just by touching her. 'My wife was sitting in her dress-maker's showroom,' began another, 'when a woman came in – a complete stranger. My wife suddenly knew that the woman would be dead in four days. She came up to my wife, thanked her profusely and said it was necessary for her to know, but her doctor wouldn't tell her. My wife hadn't said a word.' King was, how-ever, able to corroborate that Ruth claimed to have a vivid dream of a fire at a Donegal hotel at which they had stayed. 'I said did this take place last night? She said she did not know, as for these people in that sort of mood the recent past, the present and the near future seem simultaneous. The hotel was burnt to the ground three weeks later.' But then Ruth was given to much foretelling, which was as doom-laden as her pessimistic husband could desire.[*]

King's use of corporation money to support what his colleagues thought was lunacy was blamed on Ruth, whom they found at best irritating, garrulous, ignorant, stupid and patronising: the night before the 1964 General Election she even succeeded in alienating the direc-tors' wives. Jodi Cudlipp remembered:

On the eve of the election she ordered (and that's the right word) all the directors' wives to a drilling of the parts they were going to be told (by her) to take at the Mirror's Election Night Party – in the Board room and other apartments nearby. She had us, like her poor little music students, standing in a circle around her while she held court telling each of us where we were to be, what we were to do, and when we had to arrive to do it. There were several rather grumpy faces and quite a bit of surly mut-tering when – all of a sudden (obviously prearranged by Ruth)

---

[*] In the spring of 1968, having been told by Ruth that she had seen in a dream enormous cracks in the façade of the headquarters of the Mirror group, King instructed the Managing Director, Percy Roberts, to have the building resurveyed by the original architects. The fee was £10,000, no faults were found, but King was deposed shortly afterwards.

– King arrived, all admiring smiles at his wife. None of us wives wanted to let our husbands down by obvious insurrection, so we kept our unwilling peace, while Ruth explained her plans for us to Cecil, and as she talked, sort of cuddled up to him and, believe it or not, actually reached up (and it was quite a long way even for her long fingers) to actually twist and caress the lapel of his suit as she gazed up adoringly at his face. He almost wriggled with pleasure. And the object was to show us all who was really the boss. However, she didn't actually subdue us girls; one or two of us later got together to agree that we weren't going to stay put in those rooms she had appointed us to. I certainly didn't.

Those closest to King found her sinister: 'I thought when I first met her she was a very sensible and nice woman,' recalled Sir Edward Pickering, who had come in 1964 from the *Daily Express* to succeed Cudlipp as Editorial Director of the *Mirror*. 'I changed my view about her at some point. She was scheming and led him into all sorts of paths too like Extra Sensory Perception and so on which really caused everyone to be slightly horrified.'[34] 'The dramatic change in his personality, his attitudes and his behaviour came after he took up with Ruth,'[35] said Sir Frank Rogers, who had known King from 1949 and was Managing Director of IPC from 1965. 'Married to his first wife he was a man of substantial humility. The whole thing began to go wrong when he married Ruth. Margot was a wholly beautiful person – the exact opposite of Ruth', who was, Rogers said, 'an extremely evil influence; I use that word with some care and thought. He became a completely changed man.' 'Evil' was the word used also by Ellis Birk. 'To have that gift along with wickedness – evil – of that level, most odd.'[36] he said. 'The tragedy with Cecil was his second marriage. The woman was a maniac.'

In the early 1960s Cudlipp was presented with a particularly farcical situation when King called him in to complain about the quality of the music on ATV, in which IPC was the principal shareholder: Cudlipp and Birk, both directors of the company, should do something about it. Cudlipp pointed out that the music was confined largely to jingles and *Sunday Night at the London Palladium* and that to dictate to ATV would be like an outsider telling the *Mirror* to use another typeface. 'Cecil said rather testily, "But the music is bad.'" He and Birk could not just say this at a board meeting, said Cudlipp; they would need a practical suggestion:

> He [King] said, 'I have a practical solution. I could arrange for Ruth to be the musical director, or adviser, or whatever you think fit.' So I said, 'Well, Cecil, you get on very well with Lew Grade.* Why not write him a letter and just put the idea to him?' 'I think that's the way to approach it,' agreed Cecil. 'It should come from me.' Now curiously enough the Wykehamist, though highly and expensively educated, couldn't write a letter the way the Welsh uneducated could, so I could see the struggle going on: he couldn't say 'I've read all those books but I can't write'. As I so often did, I said, 'Look, Cecil, shall I draft something?' and he said that would be very helpful.

So Cudlipp dictated a friendly letter talking of King's affection for ATV, saying that the music wasn't as good as it should be and advising Grade to appoint Dr Ruth Railton. King signed it unaltered, it was delivered by hand at about 5 p.m. and within an hour Cudlipp's secretary reported, 'Lew Grade's on the phone; he seems to be bursting a blood vessel' and put him through. 'He said, "Hugh, a terrible thing's happened. I've had a letter from Cecil King." "What's it about?" "I don't think we ought to mention this on the phone. Val's† with me in a state of bloody apoplexy. Can you for Christ's sake come round?"'

The champagne was open when Cudlipp arrived 'and they were shaking'. Grade thrust the letter at Cudlipp. 'I read it and said, "Yes, what's the trouble?" "That madwoman? We've met her, you know. Nearly stopped the bloody studios the night she was here. King can't be serious."' Cudlipp suggested a few ideas for a letter, 'and they looked at each other. "You know what to say," I said, and then Val said, "Well, you don't know how to bloody say it, Lew. Tell him the

---

* ATV Chairman.
† Val Parnell was one of the most powerful men in variety, Grade's closest associate on the board of ATV, originator of *Sunday Night at the London Palladium* and uncle of Jack Parnell, creator of one of the greatest television orchestras in the world and ATV's Musical Director.

truth." They were very vulgar, charming, violent showbiz chaps; there was no bloody Wykehamist crap around."' They grabbed at Cudlipp's offer to draft something and that evening a holding reply ('very interesting idea, looking into it, just a touch of the forelock-tugging') was delivered to IPC.

'Have you got a minute?' asked King the following morning, and when Cudlipp arrived in his office, he flicked the letter across the eight feet of baroque tables ('he was rather good at that – whoosh, and it would land in front of you') and complained that it had said nothing. 'They can't say yes straight off, Cecil. There are unions involved. You have to be a bit patient.' Three days later King announced – in one of his favourite phrases – that he was 'spitting mad' there was no further word from Grade; Ruth was asking when she would be starting work. So another Cudlipp letter signed by King was delivered to Grade, expressing surprise at having heard nothing further.

Summoned by Grade, Cudlipp found 'a scene of disarray. Val said, "Look, we can't go on farting about." I said, "Shall we take Railton?" And then they were moaning – one was Jewish, one was Irish; there was bloody wailing from one and the other was dancing Irish jigs.' Provided once again with a secretary and champagne, Cudlipp drafted a letter speaking of their serious consideration of this eminently practical idea, described problems with advertisers and then produced the killer fact that the unions were so up in arms about the idea of taking on someone who was not a member of Equity that they were prepared to have an all-out strike. A delighted Parnell sent for the union representative, who readily agreed to be quoted as saying that he would call an all-out strike if a non-member was put in charge of the music. It was an argument that King accepted without reservation; the letter Cudlipp wrote and King sent accepted that the matter was at an end and thanked Grade warmly for his cooperation.[37]

What bemused all those who knew him well was that King, with his passion for facts, dispassionate judgement and truth, should have surrendered all scepticism where Ruth was concerned. True, according to his chauffeur, King would occasionally tick her off after she had made a gaffe so egregious that even he noticed it, but for most purposes he revelled in her adoration and suspended disbelief. IPC colleagues exchanged incredulous gossip and giggles about their Chairman's wife; of how, for instance, she had met Birk's mother at a concert and told inherently ludicrous stories about her past as a ballet dancer and a spy, or of her tales to others of her exploits as an Olympic rider, a Dior model, a ballerina, a resistance fighter and a psychic help to the police during a murder hunt. ('I doubt,' remarked Cudlipp, 'if even Ruth could have done all these things at the same time.')

They watched with dread as King became more and more arrogant and autocratic and infinitely more interested in meddling in politics than in running the enormous conglomerate that required his undivided attention. Some of those who knew him best had feared he had the potential to be a megalomaniac; now, with Ruth's encouragement, he was well on his way.

Cudlipp fought a continual rearguard action to save King from himself. There was, for instance, the matter of the bronze medallion that King wanted struck to celebrate the *Mirror*'s diamond jubilee: King on the front, Northcliffe on the back. Through guile Cudlipp prevented King from becoming a complete laughing-stock in Fleet Street by persuading him that an image of symbolic figures reading against the background of the *Mirror* building would be more appropriate than Uncle Alfred. Then there was the political history of the *Mirror* that King decided was necessary because he wanted a book that would immortalise his own contribution. Cudlipp suggested for the job the novelist, journalist and Labour MP, Maurice Edelman, with whom King kept closely in touch from the beginning. Paul Johnson put his finger on the key defect of an otherwise useful and competent book when he wrote of 'the subtle process of de-Stalinisation . . . carried out on Bart's image'. Two of the trio who had created the modern *Mirror* were alive: Bart, who was dead, 'is portrayed warts and all. Messrs King and Cudlipp are – portrayed.'[38] Cudlipp was more amused than anything else about how his contribution was downplayed to King's benefit ('It has always seemed to me that I was the organiser behind both Bart and Cudlipp,' King told Edelman in a letter. 'Cudlipp in the early stages and Bart at no time would have done much without my judgement to use the bright ideas and avoid serious blunders.'[39]). But, having a passion for getting facts right, Cudlipp was shocked when after the book's publication a correspondent pointed out a shabby omission. A paragraph quoted from A. J. P. Taylor's *English History, 1914–1945* included the sentences: 'The *Mirror* had no proprietor. It

Lagos, Christmas Eve, 1958

The Chairman, c.1962

Jodi and Cudlipp, back from honeymoon, 1963

King at a factory opening in Killingworth, 1965

IPC AGM, 1968
(*Above*) Ruth and King
(*Right*) Cudlipp and King

(*Facing page*) Launching *Strictly Personal*, 1969
(*Above*) Cudlipp, Ruth and King
(*Below*) King and Cudlipp

Unveiling King, 1970; Jodi, Cudlipp and Ruth

Ruth and King;
Dublin, mid 1980s

Jodi and Cudlipp;
Spain, mid 1990s

was created by the ordinary people on its staff . . . The *Mirror* was, in its favourite word, brash, but it was also a serious organ of democratic opinion.' As Cudlipp pointed out in his memoirs, the three dots replaced: 'and especially by Harry Guy Bartholomew, the man who worked his way up from office boy to Editorial Director'; it is not clear whether it was King who took out the phrase, because he did not agree with it, or Edelman, who was faithfully giving the received King version of the *Mirror*'s history.*

Still, despite worrying portents, what the *Sunday Times* called 'the potent double-act'[40] of King and Cudlipp looked to be prospering:† the 1964 headline – 'THE MIRROR TOPS 5,000,000' – signalled what was probably the happiest day of their partnership, for to both of them (in King's words on the *Mirror*'s sixtieth birthday) the paper was 'still, as it has always been, the heart and fulcrum of our activities.'[41]

'Over the years I have watched the growth of our paper from a circulation of under a million when I joined it in 1926 to its present dominating position as the biggest and best newspaper in the world,' wrote King in the house journal.[42] 'This is no sudden success. It has been worked for with huge energy, much ability – and a little bit of genius.' 'What surprises me is that we aren't smug about it,' said Cudlipp in a two-page spread inside; 'we have restrained ourselves with becoming modesty to a front page splash on June 9, a bonus all round for all the staff, gifts to the pensioners, a "do" at the Dorchester for the advertisers, plus a Special Shock Issue of STET. Only the good Lord knows what they would have done at the *Daily Sketch* if they had passed the one million mark.' Among the reasons he gave for the paper's success was the 'silent but tremendously important revolution' it had undergone in the previous few years: 'the tabloid that began in 1935 as the popular daily for the working class has now become the daily for the middle class as well, and may well end up as the paper for all the classes – eventually, perhaps, as the national morning newspaper for a truly classless society'. The working classes had reached

---

* The frontispiece was a portrait of King.

† In 1963, Cudlipp received an accolade that would always mean a great deal to him. Lord Beaverbrook, with whom he had maintained a warm relationship, sent him a copy of his book on Lloyd George and wrote on it: 'To Hugh Cudlipp. He has seized my mantle. This book is from his friend & admirer, Max Beaverbrook.'

the Promised Land: 'the real division in public opinion was no longer based solidly upon injustice (or envy) but upon the gap between the generations'.

It was that thinking that also informed the *Sun*, the newspaper that IPC launched that autumn in place of the *Herald*, which Cudlipp had come to hate: 'it was a bloated, listless boa constrictor suffering from fatty degeneration of the heart'[43] and its readers were old, male and poor. At Sydney Jacobson's request, Cudlipp had made him Editor – moving John Beavan to the political editorship of the *Mirror* group – but the circulation continued to decline. 'It is one of the curious anomalies of Fleet Street that this feeble, old-fashioned, unprofitable journal should be published by Cecil Harmsworth King', observed *Newsweek* in the autumn of 1963. 'International Publishing Corporation, Ltd., a $300 million group of newspapers, magazines, and books dedicated to entertaining, enlightening, and influencing the masses without losing a penny'[44] was stuck with the *Herald*.

Early the previous year the IPC board had discussed the *Herald*. 'They talked and from the talks emerged three alternatives: to continue pouring money into a fast failing paper; adopt a *laissez faire* approach and let it run down until 1968 when the crippling legal ties with the TUC ran out; or, sever the ties and produce a new paper – either by re-launching the *Herald* or starting afresh with a new name and a new image.'[45]

Cudlipp was keenly in favour of the third and riskiest option, which the sceptical King left him free to explore. Jocelyn Stevens had shown interest in being in charge of a new paper, but Cudlipp fought off his challenge. The Cudlipp energies were now focused on this new adventure – one of the most difficult aspects of which was successfully persuading the TUC to sell IPC its 49 per cent and agree to replacing the *Herald* by a new paper of the left. The paper was to be geared, said Cudlipp, to 'a middle-class couple, aged 28 with two children, and living in Reading'[46] or, as the *Sunday Times* put it, 'the aspirant affluent never-had-it-so-good, all-mod-con, technocratic and meritocratic young husband and wife'.[47]

Cudlipp 'has been in charge of the whole operation,' said Sydney Jacobson at the *Sun*'s launch in September 1964, '. . . the creative drive, the administrative drive and the inspiration that has gone into the planning of this paper derives very largely from Hugh Cudlipp.' No, said Cudlipp. 'What we are all doing, for good or ill, is, in fact, the collective thoughts of at least ten of us.'[48] Jean Rook, then on an IPC magazine, wrote eloquently later – in terms that delighted the elderly Cudlipp – of how he recruited her:

> One Friday afternoon, IPC's great Welsh chief, Hugh Cudlipp
> . . . called my office . . . . Could I see him? Now? Cudlipp was
> the sexiest man who ever made woman draw heavy breath. He'd
> a voice like a Welsh harp and looked like a cross between Richard
> Burton and Owen Glendower. Wicked rumour among IPC's
> female staff had it that he was a sexual fiery dragon, and every
> woman who worked for him secretly burned to see his forked
> and swishing tail.
>
> His summons was almost disappointingly strictly business. 'How
> would you like to be fashion editor of my new *Sun*?' he beamed.
> 'More than my life,' I replied, dazzled.[49]

King was now enthusiastic, IPC was spending an enormous amount of money on advertising, and the press at home and abroad gave enormous coverage ('Le Napoléon de la presse' was the headline over the photograph of King on the cover of *France Observateur*;[50] 'Will we now call Mr Cecil King Le Roi Soleil?' enquired the *World Press News*[51]). 'The still-under-wraps, not-yet published *Sun* had been the talk of Fleet Street, radio and TV for weeks,' recalled Jean Rook. 'Its rising was to be a new, shining era in journalism . . . [It] was to be a brilliant morning broadsheet which would singe the eyes out of worshipping readers. And any journalist who joined it would be an overnight star. It didn't happen that way, of course. The *Sun* rose, as in a fog, like a damp cinder.'

There were many reasons why the *Sun* turned out respectable and dull, of which the most important were that, because of the fear of union trouble, the original brilliant design was shelved; the paper had been largely designed by committee; Cudlipp was fifty, not twenty-eight (the age of his target readers) and, though he did not realise it, was – like his senior colleagues – now a member of the Establishment; none of them had any of the instincts of their mythological Reading couple; and, catastrophically, the planning group had been deluded

by the market research of Mark Abrams, which proved to their satisfaction that the British people now wanted more intelligent and
thoughtful papers. Unfortunately for IPC, that was just what people
said: apropos the *Sun*, remarked Matthew Engels, 'they didn't tell
strangers with clipboards that they wanted breasts on page 3'.[52]

Within a few days it was clear that the *Sun* was a failure; selling
3.5 million on its first day, it was down to 1.75 million within four
days; unloved and under-financed, it staggered on through the 1960s
with its circulation slowly sinking down towards a million. Within
days of the launch, Cudlipp's attention was back on the *Mirror*, for
there was a General Election due the following month and he was in
his element as he sought to drive his readers to the polling booths
to vote Labour.

The Labour Party had learned the hard way that wholehearted support from the *Mirror* could not be taken for granted; journalists and
politicians viewed the ambivalent relationship with fascination. On
the one hand, *Mirror* support for the party and individuals was well
known. In 1956, at a time of internal warfare within the party, when
the *Mirror* had consistently backed moderation, in response to a congratulatory letter from King for a Party Conference triumph, Hugh
Gaitskell asked King if he could 'again say how much I feel we owe
to the Daily Mirror which throughout has handled all these difficult
political issues with clarity, vigour and commonsense and has given
us great encouragement just when we needed it?'[53] It was well known
too that the *Mirror* helped and subsidised Labour MPs like Alf Robens
and George Brown, whom King took on as consultants in the early
1950s at a time when they were thinking of abandoning politics for
financial reasons. Yet it was equally well known that *Mirror* support
could never be counted on and that King disliked Gaitskell, was contemptuous about many party members and had very individual views
on foreign and domestic policy. He was also an admirer of
Conservative ministers like Ted Heath and Reggie Maudling and the
up-and-coming Geoffrey Rippon, to whom IPC paid a retainer of
£1,000* a year when the Tories went into opposition.[54]

There was never any danger of Cudlipp toying with backing the

---

* About £12,000 today.

Tories and his instinct was to back Gaitskell against his internal critics: in the spring of 1958 – when the Labour Party was rowing over nuclear weapons – he told Crossman that he had been 'under great stress from what he called "the Olympian Wykehamist", i.e. Cecil King, to switch the paper's line and go for what he called, "neutralism and anti-H-bombery".'[55]

Yet the mercurial Cudlipp's support for any particular Labour party line could not be guaranteed. Probably mischievously, he worried Crossman in the autumn of 1958 by 'flirting with the idea of swinging the *Mirror* to the Left. "As you're bound to lose next time," he told me, "let's lose on a fine anti-privilege campaign."'[56] Yet at Crossman's instigation, in 1958 Gaitskell persuaded Cudlipp – who was about to go to Russia – to produce the party's policy pamphlet. 'Cudlipp has produced the glossiest layout, with the most brilliant, simple idea . . .'[57] noted Crossman a few days later. '[He] has been a schoolboy about his work. He had the idea one afternoon, worked most of the night, got the rough layout done in the morning and since then has been ringing me up on and off and making arrangements. Will it be too glossy? Will it be dismissed as a publicity stunt? All I know is that, if this is no good, no one can do any better in selling the Labour Party policy.'[58]

'It has been shown what a few people can do if they are given the chance,' he wrote after the pamphlet's publication. 'Quite literally, this policy statement is the product of three men – Hugh Cudlipp, Sydney and myself – working with Hugh Gaitskell, plus all the *Mirror*'s skilled machinery and layout staff.'[59] In May 1959, a few months before the General Election, he made another revealing entry:

> Today I went to a most characteristic lunch in a private room at the Café Royal. Present: the two Hughs, Sydney and myself. I got there a few minutes late to find Hugh Gaitskell quaffing a Bloody Mary, while the other Hugh and Sydney were drinking their first huge champagne cocktail. At half-past one we sat down to caviar and vodka, followed by Scotch salmon and claret . . . For the first time, I heard Hugh admit the possibility that it was quite probable we should lose the Election and that there would be a tremendous rumpus inside the Labour Party.
>
> At this point Hugh Cudlipp said, 'You appreciate, of course,

that the *Mirror* will be absolutely loyal to you right up to the final day of the Election campaign. But, if you lose, we shall turn right round. From that moment on we shall be all out for a genuine radical movement and we shall be tearing to pieces the old men and the old institutions which are holding us back.[60]

Three months later Sydney Jacobson warned Crossman that Cudlipp would be telling him 'that the column will come to an end some time after the Election, because the paper isn't going to be as Labour as all that':

> Sydney added that in his view the real reason was the purchase of various magazines which had been overpriced and lost £1 million* already, apparently owing to the printers' strike. In order to break even, the *Mirror* would have to make even more money, and anyway Hugh was getting impatient with its present form and with the Labour Party. So he wasn't going to have a political columnist . . . What a classic Marxist story about the capitalist press! This is the only thing which made me sad. We had tried, with considerable success, to make the *Mirror* into a semi-serious popular paper, to build up confidence in it. Now all this is to be destroyed because of a loss on some magazine.

But then, because Crossman strove to be intellectually honest, he added, 'But even that isn't true. One of the factors, as I pointed out to Sydney, was Hugh's increasing disillusion with the Labour Opposition, a disillusion partly fed by Sydney and myself. If Labour had been a real going concern, on the up grade, the coming idea, Hugh Cudlipp and Cecil King would not have pulled out on it or at least they would not have pulled out without much more compunction.'[61] But it was one of the disadvantages of the close relationship between senior people at the head of the *Mirror* and Labour that King and Cudlipp were privy to malicious gossip and tales of

---

* About £14 million today.

backstabbing, as well as the finer points of party policy.

There was no such intimacy with the Conservative party. King's letters to ministers about the politics of West Africa, information that he gleaned from politicians and journalists he met on his travels or whatever comments and suggestions he wished to make on foreign policy were received with the utmost courtesy. Though there were Tories who loved Cudlipp's company, they were wary of him. Senior members of the government would lunch or dine with *Mirror* people, invite them to functions or ask them to pop in for a chat at Number 10 or Number 11 Downing Street, but being on their guard, they kept their confidences and their dignity. When in the late 1960s King disparaged the members of the Tory Cabinet at a lunch with Cudlipp, Jacobson and Iain Macleod, Leader of the Commons, Macleod stood up and said, 'I'm sorry, Hugh, but I'm damned if I'm going to listen to King any more. What kind of a Minister does he think I am?' and walked out. When Jacobson and Cudlipp returned from making their apologies, King, 'who was eating heartily, said, "Well, well! What an odd fellow. I was telling the truth. I had heard he could be moody."'[62]

Cudlipp's backroom work for Labour in the run-up to the General Election included helping with a brilliant anti-Tory pamphlet and, of course, mobilising the *Mirror* ('THE TIME HAS COME FOR THE TORIES TO GO! WHY? See Monday's *Mirror*. WHY? See Tuesday's *Mirror*. WHY? See Wednesday's *Mirror*. WHY? See Thursday's *Mirror*'), but the soothing message of continuing economic prosperity skilfully purveyed by Eden's successor, Harold Macmillan, brought the Conservatives back with a majority of 100. That the *Mirror* was less than heartbroken was made clear by a leader headed 'Good Luck!':

No sour grapes. The *Mirror* batted for the losing side. Mr Harold Macmillan, leader of the Conservative Party, will lead Britain and speak for Britain at the Summit.

That is the nation's verdict.

Democracy is good enough for this newspaper.

'All seems to have changed,' said an *Observer* profile of 'KING OF THE MIRROR' the following month:

The legend 'Forward with the People' has been dropped. The

political commentator, Richard Crossman, has been fired, along with Jane, the strip-cartoon heroine. After a crescendo of political argy-bargy before the election, politics have virtually disappeared. Instead, a campaign to capture youth has been announced, heralded by the new teenage Americanised strip heroine, called not Jane but Patti. To the urgent questions confronting the Labour Party, the *Mirror* – which has often called itself the 'National Newspaper of the Left' – has had nothing to answer yet . . . King's own explanation of the *Mirror's* change of heart is simple enough: 'Women readers particularly have had a bellyful of politics.'[63]

'The Accent is on youth,' announced the *Mirror*. 'The accent is on gaiety.'

Still, if in the interests of increasing circulation, *Mirror* readers could have a respite from politics, there was certainly no moratorium. A row over a US spy-plane shot down over Russia in May 1960, and Khrushchev's consequent wrecking of a France–Soviet Union–United Kingdom–United States summit, inspired one of the most famous *Mirror* front pages:

Mr K!

(If you will pardon an olde English phrase)

DON'T BE
SO BLOODY
RUDE! PS

Who do you
think you are?
Stalin?[64]

'On the U2 plane issue, and Krushchev's performance at Paris,' wrote Cudlipp to King, who was abroad, 'I quite appreciate that the anti-Russian line the Mirror took might well seem excessive to you at that distance. But praise for the Mirror has been tremendous. We were vulgar but honest, and after all, that is what the Daily Mirror is all about . . . as a newspaper we have been very fair to Russia for many years, and it would have been unutterably feeble of us to weaken the Western front when it was being so savagely challenged.' Some union leaders were still demanding unilateral nuclear disarmament, 'but no party could ever get back to power on a cowardly policy of this nature'.[65] Cudlipp might still be on the left, but unlike King, who always rated firmness as the key quality of a government, he was impervious to any of the attractions of totalitarianism and, additionally, the horrors of appeasing militant and insatiable printing unions were giving him a more jaundiced view of the working class.

Like the rest of Fleet Street, *Mirror* newspapers suffered from over-manning, restrictive practices, threats, stoppages, strikes and printers' gagging of press comment. Mindful of his group's profits, King was coy about criticising the unions publicly, but he missed no opportunity to savage newspaper management; even before the *Mirror* group acquired Fleetway and Odhams, his bluntness incurred admiration from those fed up with blandness, as well as deep resentment from his targets. The Newspaper Publishers' Association* (NPA) was denounced in 1958 as 'the most spineless jellyfish of all the employers' organisations'.[66] King was no kinder about the Press Council: 'I think it's a futile body to which we lend no support; we will not allow our people to be elected to the Council; I will not take part in any votes electing members to the Council; we ignore the body altogether.'[67]

Three years later, as the guest speaker at a private meeting on the state of the press, King was frank about the situation in Fleet Street.[68] The unions made it almost impossible to secure agreement to introduce any new methods of production and, 'with one union or another, in one printing office or another, at least every other night we are threatened with a complete close-down. It is an absolute nightmare . . .' As things were going, he expected only a couple of provincial papers and three London dailies to survive. 'If the NPA faced the unions with a cohesive, sensible, just policy they would not find the unions unreasonable. But if proprietors run away when they see a trade union, what can the general secretary do but follow up?' The only hope was for employers to stop the trade unions picking off individual titles by adopting their principle that 'if one stops all stop'.

'Are we not due for a little more leadership?' asked Peter Dallas

---

* As the Newspaper Proprietors' Association had been renamed.

Smith, Managing Director of *The Economist*. 'We are in the presence of the ablest person of the lot – are we really right to listen to him approach this matter defensively?

'We look at the Canadian unions and see they keep their word. Can't the "Mirror" influence people to believe in fair play, and to believe that unions should be taught to keep their word? This is a crusade, and the biggest and ablest man in the Press can and should lead.'

Jealous, lazy and selfish proprietors were the problem, said King. It would take a long time to get things sorted out. 'I think things are moving in the right direction. I am doing everything I can, but a chain is only as strong as its weakest link, and you have no idea how weak it can be.'

Later that year, to the credit of the publishers about whom and whose newspapers he was often publicly rude, King became Chairman of the NPA and, in an effective but dictatorial way, began the slow and painful process of putting some backbone into more timid colleagues; he would succeed on a few occasions in galvanising them to face down the unions.[69] When he realised regretfully that monopoly considerations would prevent him from taking over *The Times*, one of Northcliffe's old papers, he acted with some degree of selflessness by encouraging its takeover by Lord Thomson of the *Sunday Times*, whom he despised. King – and less frequently, but no less forcefully, Cudlipp – were articulate and combative in defence of the press, arguing in evidence to the Royal Commission on the Press, in print and on radio and television, against censorship, for libel-law reform, against restrictive practices and in favour of press proprietors acting as 'deeply engaged onlookers': 'the job of newspapers in all countries [is] to provide exact and unbiased news,' King declared at an NPA dinner. 'Equally important, to engage in perpetual and probing criticism.'[70]

King was also so candid about the shortcomings of the foreign press as to cause great offence – particularly in the United States: 'Cecil Harmsworth King created a sensation in a speech before the National Press Club in May, 1961,' wrote an American journalist in November 1963, 'when he charged that American papers were "acres of soggy verbiage". How does he feel about it now? "I can't see the slightest improvement or change in the press since my last visit . . . [except that] some of the soggy papers have dropped dead", he said here last week. "American newspapers are just as dull, dreary and dreadful as ever."'[71] 'My criticisms . . . are made with friendly sorrow, not with malice,' King told the American Society of Newspaper Editors in 1967, 'and they are mild and moderate criticisms. I merely deplore that you are producing unreadable, unmanageable newspapers, without a message.'[72]

Africa, however, was handled with great tact: 'the idea that Europe should simply teach and Africa should simply learn . . . was always odious,' he told a group of African Ministers of Information:

> The civilisation of independent Africa . . . is going to be one of the vital and original developments in this century . . . Long provoked by hostile newspapers in the past – whether abroad or, in East Africa, at home – African governments may tend to feel that all criticism, even when it's meant to be constructive, is to be condemned. That's perfectly understandable. But the fact remains that the real victim of the suppression of constructive criticism is the credibility of government information.[73]

Such appeals cut little ice with the dictatorial African governments that were stamping out press freedom. 'It is sad to us who did our best to help Ghana to see her going back so fast in so many ways,' King wrote privately the following year. 'In fact, at the moment, all our African pupils are disappointing.'[74] And between 1963 and 1975 the *Mirror* would scramble out of Africa.[75]

Yet much though King relished being a revered guru of the newspaper industry, being boss of the biggest publishing firm in the world no longer offered him enough scope for the exercise of power and influence on the scale to which he aspired: it was to politics that more and more he began to devote his mind, his passion and his ambition.

As the heads of IPC, both Cudlipp and King had access to the most powerful people almost everywhere they visited. On his first visit to Africa in 1965, for instance, Cudlipp had confidential and illuminating talks with a clutch of presidents and prime ministers who included Ian Smith of Rhodesia, Hastings Banda of Malawi, Kenneth Kaunda of Zambia and Julius Nyerere of Tanganyika – on which he reported to King (and in some cases to the Prime Minister) with his customary insight and punch.[76] 'My darling Daughter,' King wrote to

Priscilla in October 1963 from Washington, 'I am in the middle of a political whirl seeing everyone who is anyone. For some reason I am being treated like visiting royalty – I had 45 minutes with Kennedy, which is unusual. He asked me what I thought was wrong with the United States – difficult question to answer off the cuff.'[77]

To Ruth he wrote of the shabby route into the White House, from which 'unimpressive* secretaries and such were leaving', and of the deficiencies of the waiting room, but also of how – hugely by King standards – he had taken to Kennedy: 'He is more impressive than I expected, still inexperienced but still learning. A big perhaps a great man in the making. We got on very well. He kept on looking at me in an appraising sort of way . . . He talked of British Guiana, British politics, his difficulties in South America and so on.' To Kennedy's question on the United States, King 'offered the opinion that the United States is the leader of the Western world and that she is too diffident about it. I think she should assert her leadership more definitely. Finally, I urged him to come to England and promised him a wonderful reception.'[78] Kennedy's murder three weeks later led King to write an unprecedentedly positive article:

> After spending a very intense five days in Washington interviewing his closest associates, and nearly one hour with the President himself, I was enormously impressed. He was clearly a big man with a big team round him, and I formed the opinion as I listened to him that here was a man still learning. He wanted to listen, not only to talk. Here was a notable, shining example among most of the men I had met in high places in our own and many other countries.[79]

Back home the men in high places continued to disappoint. Sir Alec Douglas-Home, whom King thought 'would make a good vice-chairman of a sub-committee of the Berwickshire County Council,'[80] failed to impress when he had King to lunch alone shortly after becoming Prime Minister in October 1963,[81] yet he also incurred King's

---

* Altered to 'unremarkable' in the published version in 'President Kennedy', in *Without Fear or Favour*.

wrath on other grounds. 'In December 1963,' recalled the journalist
and politician Bill Deedes, who was then Minister Without Portfolio:

> Cecil King of the Daily Mirror group summoned me to an audi-
> ence. In the presence of Hugh Cudlipp, he began to let fly at
> me on the arrogance of Ministers, their failure to consult him
> – or indeed to appear in the least interested in anything his
> newspapers had to say. He thought Ministers would benefit from
> the sort of advice his stable could offer. In effect he wanted to
> be closer to the inner ring of Government decision-making. Like
> Rothermere and Beaverbrook before him, Cecil King was seeking
> a dangerous bargain. As I noted at the time, his newspapers
> would support policies on which he had been personally con-
> sulted – and such consulation would then become a condition
> of this support.

King was the only person who would attract a condemnatory judgement in the autobiography of the notoriously charitable Deedes, who
later tried to understand his attitude:

> To some extent, setting aside his extraordinary vanity, King was
> a victim of social change. The days had passed when senior
> politicians and newspaper proprietors could count on meeting
> together round London's dinner tables. In any case, such dinner
> parties formed no part of Alec Home's routine. When invited
> by King to luncheon in order to discuss television, of which the
> *Daily Mirror* claimed to have much knowledge and experience,
> Alec Home had refused . . . King wanted occasional signs that
> what his newspapers said weighed with the Government. In that
> case, I retorted, they must stop demanding that this Minister or
> that be sacked – as the *Daily Mirror* often did. No Prime Minister
> in his senses could take such instructions from a newspaper. I
> had difficulty in persuading Cecil King even of this. We parted
> with a low opinion of each other, though I was heartened to
> hear from Cudlipp in the lift that the Labour Party were expe-
> riencing the same difficulties with King.[82]

In the case of the Labour Party, King's inability to get on with

Gaitskell no longer mattered, as Gaitskell had died in January 1963 and had been replaced as leader by Harold Wilson, the candidate of the left, who defeated the *Mirror's* candidate, George Brown. Wilson was very unwilling, Crossman explained to Jacobson, 'to follow Gaitskell's example and accept invitations to eat and drink heavily with Hugh Cudlipp and Cecil King. Couldn't I do this job for him? Sydney explained that they are both reformed characters who don't drink so much and would not resent Harold drinking nothing. But he would have to have relations with them himself.'[83]

Wilson had no option but to become a courtier. Quite apart from the power of the *Mirror*, the newspaper had, as Alan Watkins later observed, 'a special place in the mythology of the People's Party. That place had become steadily less exalted during the 1950s. But even in the 1960s Hugh Cudlipp and his acolytes would descend on the party conference like a gang of desperadoes, to find themselves flattered and indulged by the mightiest in the land.'[84]

A couple of months after his election as leader Wilson was worrying publicly about 'the "growing disregard" of the rights of a free press'[85] and echoing King's frequent demand for an effective Press Council with 'independent initiative*.' Wilson's emphasis on the need for modernisation in all aspects of British life was also extremely palatable to the *Mirror*; it was Cudlipp who suggested to him that technological Britain should be the theme of what became known as the famous 'white heat of technology' conference speech in the autumn of 1963.[86]

Like other senior Labour politicians, Wilson gave regular briefings to John Beavan – whose life was spent garnering information from politicians and reporting back to the Chairman in detailed memoranda – and he was always available to King and Cudlipp personally and quick to write grateful letters about *Mirror* coverage. 'My dear Cecil,' he wrote by hand in October 1963 after his first – and triumphant – Party Conference as leader: '. . . I must write . . . to express my warm appreciation for the way the Mirror treated Tuesday's debate. They have in fact been first-class this week, but Wednesday's paper

---

* King would drop his opposition to the body when an independent chairman was appointed the following year.

was, from our point of view, out of the world . . . I doubt if a single issue of any paper has ever done quite such a political job.'[87]

While they believed he was a very effective leader of the opposition, neither King nor Cudlipp could warm to Wilson (though Cudlipp enjoyed his wit); in February 1964, Cudlipp told King how impressed he had been at a lunch by the charm, integrity and humour of Alec Douglas-Home: 'There is a distinct possibility that his likeability will, from a personal leadership point of view, outweigh Harold Wilson's militant dislikeability.'[88] Yet Wilson made himself so compliant that eighteen months after he became leader, King could write to Alf Robens, who was seeking financial help for a Gaitskell Memorial Foundation, that 'We here had no particular reason to be grateful to Hugh Gaitskell, and personally I think the leadership of the Labour Party is now in safer hands.'[89] 'Wilson is lunching with Mr King on Thursday,' wrote Beavan to Cudlipp in July 1964. 'But he is also most anxious to have a talk with you . . . The election manifesto is prepared . . . he wants a touch of gold dust in it. And so he will ask you whether you can go through it and add some sparkle.'[90]

The *Mirror* group enthusiastically backed Labour in the General Election that took place in October 1964, just a month after the ascent and descent of the *Sun*. The theme was the thirteen wasted years of Conservative government and the need to replace 'diehards' and 'weary willies' with new young men with new ideas. Cudlipp had not lost his touch: 'The BEST qualification for a job in the Tory Government,' stormed the *Mirror*, 'is to be related to Mr Harold Macmillan, the former Tory Prime Minister':

> As surely as the knee bone is connected to the thigh bone, the Soames are connected to the Churchills, the Churchills are connected to the Cavendishes, the Cavendishes are connected to the Macmillans, the Macmillans are connected to the Devonshires, and the Amerys and the Dilhornes and the Homes – and old Supermac is everybody's flippin' uncle.

'King always took a passionate interest in these campaigns,' wrote Cudlipp, 'goading my team on with daily enthusiasm, delighted with my slogans and angles and stunts . . . Our front pages had more power on one morning than a million pamphlets or a hundred speeches in the drill halls, parks or schools in the provinces.'[91] King also contributed a series of articles to the *Sun* on some of his favourite gloomy themes: the need to reform failing institutions ('Parliament promotes men who carry no weight; the Churches propound a view of religion which is not acceptable; the Law Courts administer the Law, but not what is felt to be Justice; the medical profession seems to be more concerned with its fees than its patients'[92]); the deficiencies of business management ('Too many old men cling on long past their ability to contribute anything. Too many jobs are given to school friends or to relations'[93]); and the lack of administrative ability in the public service ('the "old boy" network . . . is a serious menace to our whole future'[94]). His leaden prose was as unlikely to win converts to Labour as was the 'Vote Labour' pennant he flew from his Rolls-Royce.

The election was a close call: 'In the Labour stronghold, over on the top floor at the Daily Mirror offices,' reported the Financial Times, 'early depression . . . changed to later elation, and Mr Cecil King's custom-made scarlet bow tie became positively awry.'[95] Labour won a nerve-rackingly small majority of five; one of Wilson's first acts as Prime Minister was to offer to make King a life Baron. King refused: Wilson later told Edward Pickering the story:

He said that the real break between the two of them came over W's refusal to confer on Cecil an hereditary peerage. According to Wilson, Cecil was offered a life peerage and refused it. Wilson explained that he had decided against giving hereditary peerages and that in future he would give only life peerages. Cecil went further and said that what he really wanted was an earldom – presumably, said Wilson, because this would enable him to out-rank Viscount Rothermere. Wilson again indicated that he would not confer any hereditary peerages. Cecil again came back to him and said that he had been looking at precedents and discovered that during the 19th century – Wilson seemed to think that it was in Scotland – an earldom had been conferred as a life peerage. This was again refused.[96]

Wilson did not – indeed, could not – budge and King did not

forgive him. Margot recorded that as early as the 1930s he had wanted to be Lord Harmsworth (a title awarded in 1939 to his Uncle Cecil).[97] A senior newspaper executive well placed for political gossip had heard talk in 1951 of King being given a peerage by Churchill if he agreed to tone down 'the present vitriolic policy of the *Mirror* . . . A peerage would be almost irresistible to any Harmsworth. But dramatically to change the *D. Mirror*'s policy would inevitably mean a loss of sale – probably a crippling loss, and that is more than King's colleagues & shareholders would stand for.'[98] Impossible though it is to imagine King selling his soul for a title, there is no doubt that he hankered after one. Unfortunately, he no longer had realistic expectations.

So why, having failed to get his earldom, did King ever afterwards claim he had not wanted a peerage? 'You do get remarkably honest people who at some stage of their lives start telling lies because somehow they conceive that that's the truth,' observed his colleague Frank Rogers, when reflecting on King; he concluded that Ruth's lying was contagious.[99] It was Ruth, too, who bore much of the responsibility for King's growing megalomania. A note in her 1964 appointments diary gives a flavour of the honour that the frustrated prophet received in his own home: 'For the benefit of this beloved island of ours & for the world. For years no political leader. We must have LEADERS. The world has never gone through such a difficult time. Europe could be again 72 years old – standing man to man to White House Moscow & China but the one man is C.H.K.' A final phrase – 'Little pipe-smoker' – dismissed Harold Wilson.[100]

In public, King often described himself in modest terms. In a profile that Cudlipp wrote with trepidation around this time, he quoted King telling a Canadian reporter, 'I'm just a humble seeker after knowledge.' But, added Cudlipp, 'Elsewhere the same man said: 'I see nothing wrong with power as long as I am the fellow who has it.''[101]

Cudlipp recorded in his memoirs an unnerving occasion when:

Cecil told me the curious story of a telephone call the evening before at his home . . . He was reading a book in French and Ruth, who was tidying up things around the house, answered the intruder. 'When I finished the book I asked who had phoned. Ruth told me it was an anonymous caller, a man who spoke in a cultured accent. He would not give his name, but he said to

Ruth, "You are married to a man of destiny, do look after him," and then rang off.

Cecil told me this story unsmilingly.[102]

King was now as unreachable as he was unknowable: Cudlipp – frantically trying to limit the damage King might do to IPC and the Labour Party – found him less and less receptive to criticism; his children could do nothing but ignore or humour him; and his sister Enid, the only member of his family with whom he had had any intimacy in many years, had died a painful and brave death in 1961. Ruth's possessiveness grew ever more intense; their move in 1965 from Chelsea to The Pavilion at Hampton Court cut them off even more from family and social contacts. In that same year Ruth reluctantly yielded to pressure from King to give up the musical directorship of the National Youth Orchestra and henceforward confined herself to freelance work.

In the autumn of 1964, Antonia White was a jaundiced commentator:

Cecil King on the wireless last night . . . produced a more disagreeable impression on me than he ever did in his life by his voice and manner – incredible pride and self-satisfaction. And *coldness*. That contemptuous self-satisfied laugh. Well, he's got the power he wanted. But I don't think he'll ever be a great man – only a *large* one with a passion for power and a very able manipulator and business man. Cudlipp is what Basil Nicholson used to be to him but Cudlipp is a *real* thug. That is what he really admires . . . 'the finest journalist in the world.' C.K. . . . might have been all right if he hadn't been a Harmsworth. He isn't human any more. Only a glimpse of humanity when he said he loved the country. Margot still loves him with all her heart in spite of the abominable way he's treated her. He still won't arrange to pay her alimony after two years.[103]

King, of course, had not intentionally treated Margot badly; it was just that neither he nor Ruth saw any reason why she should have any more money than she needed to maintain a modest style of life: they would have had even less sympathy with her had they known that she was paying for alternative medical treatment for Antonia

White. Nor would everyone have agreed with White's assessment of King's character: some of those who knew him in private life, and others who knew him only from public appearances, were clear that he was in pursuit of the good. Just before she died in a Bristol hospital, where Priscilla brought King several times to visit her, Enid sent a loving farewell to 'my darling brother', which spoke movingly of her delight at feeling the affection that had brought him to her and thanked him – 'the only source from which I learned the supreme importance of the spiritual life.'[104]

Austin Williams, vicar from 1956 to 1984 of St Martin-in-the-Fields, the church in Trafalgar Square that he turned into a refuge for the lonely, homeless and desperate, had been introduced to King by Ruth, and became and remained an admirer. Like King's doctor, Edward McClellan, Williams once accompanied King abroad and delighted in his knowledge, the breadth of his interests and the fascination with religion that he explored not in church services but in his books and thoughts. In 1966, at a stage when King was widely loathed in government and press circles, Williams invited him to give a lunchtime address in his church: 'It is an important occasion for me,'[105] King told Priscilla, who was present along with – according to a press report – about 200 people, including Hugh Cudlipp, King's butler and other colleagues. The 'heavy price' mankind had paid for 'the miracles of the modern age', said King, was a loss 'in dignity, in wisdom, in happiness'. Religion and science were not antagonistic: 'all truth is of God . . . and people who complain that they do not understand what God's purpose is, are, I think, being unreasonably arrogant. What they can hope to learn by prayer, which requires great patience and humility, is what God's purpose is for them *now*.' Sin was 'an inhibiting factor' in establishing a relationship with God; 'persistent sin with heartfelt penitence is a prohibiting factor. In these days sin has come to mean, for reasons that escape me, sexual sin. Without minimising the gravity of sexual sins I would like to point out that . . . there are others that are even more destructive. Envy, hatred and malice, for instance.' Then there was despair, to which the Catholic church was right to attach so much importance, because 'despair is to doubt the power and omnipotence of Almighty God'.[106]

It was an address that owed much to the decades King had spent examining and interrogating Margot, whose genuine spirituality and mysticism had so fascinated him: only the previous month, Antonia White had recorded that Margot – who was coming to terms with life without King and had left despair behind – 'has this incessant sense of the presence of God. She talks incessantly of the over-whelming *joy* she feels, the absolute confidence . . .'[107] It owed much too, to Amiel, whose *Journal Intime* King so treasured and from whom he quoted: 'We always need the infinite, the eternal, the absolute.' Cardinal Heenan wrote to King saying that he had read 'your mag-nificent address' in *The Times*, and remarked that 'If all the ordained ministers of the gospel could speak so clearly we would be in a happier condition in the Church!'[108]

Harold Wilson would not have recognised the spirituality of King, for it was on him that King's growing megalomania was focused. With his tiny majority and looking for the right moment to call another election, *Mirror* support was vital for Wilson, who sought to bribe and please its controllers, particularly King. There was, for instance, the matter of a damehood for Ruth – who already had an OBE. Responding to Wilson's request a few weeks after he became Prime Minister that he suggest some suitable names for honours, King had put forward first: 'Dr Ruth Railton (my wife) – a D.B.E. for services to the musical education of the young. She founded, and has run for 17 years, the National Youth Orchestra, which is the best thing of its kind in the world'.[109]

Owing to a hiccup in the system ('after a lapse of twelve months she has now been offered a C.B.E., which, of course, she is declining,' complained King to Wilson[110]), it was not until mid-1966 that Ruth received her damehood. In the interim, King had been appointed in March 1965 to a directorship of the Bank of England.* 'There were two interpretations in the City of Mr King's appointment' was one newspaper comment: 'one, simply, that he brings a breath of fresh air to the bank, and another that it may be the result of a policy decision to include a newspaper representative'.[111] The reality was that Wilson hoped it would shut King up: 'You say that a lot of [Wilson's] appoint-ments have been made for political expediency,' noted a television

---

* A diarist mentioned that Priscilla had commented, 'Respectability at last!'; Ruth failed to see the joke and put it down to Priscilla being a snob.

interviewer after a controversial speech of King's four months later. 'Why do you say this?' 'Because I think it's true,'[112] replied King. Equally politically expedient was Wilson's query at lunch in Downing Street in August: 'Would I accept a peerage and a post as Minister of State in the Board of Trade in charge of our export drive?'[113] It was an offer that King turned down ('I do not feel that this is a sphere in which I could deploy my talents to best advantage'[114]) and indeed regarded as an insult.

By now King was not only disillusioned with Wilson, but hoping to see him succeeded as Prime Minister by Ted Heath, who, with the backing of the *Mirror*, became the leader of the Conservative Party in July 1965: 'I am delighted at your success — not only for your own sake,' King told Heath, 'but also because we shall have, in due course, the right Prime Minister for this country in its present troubles.'[115] Like Heath, King had long been a passionate European. 'A fortnight ago,' Cudlipp told the Royal Commission on the Press in 1962 by way of illustrating how he and King worked:

> the chairman thought it was time we began to explain the common market to the British public which I set about doing with enormous zeal, as I am greatly in favour of the common market. Hence it is being explained beginning last Thursday in the 'Daily Herald', and tomorrow in the 'Daily Mirror', but from then on we do not have long conferences about it . . . I enthuse the editors on this issue, and they also by happy coincidence are in favour of the common market.[116]

With de Gaulle's veto in January 1963 the issue had dropped out of the public eye, until — as he confided to Jean Monnet, with whom he was on warm terms — King had caused the Labour MP Woodrow Wyatt to write a pro-Europe article in the *Sunday Mirror* 'as a warning to Wilson that I remained as strong a "European" as ever'; to his surprise, several newspapers had followed suit.[117] King presided over a series of editorial conferences for French, German, Eastern European and Russian representatives of the press, organised by his son Michael and, of course, by Hugh Cudlipp.

Heath and King were agreed on much more than Europe — not least the need to curb union power — and Heath had the bonus of being approved of by Ruth because of his passion for music: 'Ruth says jokes about deep-frozen smile quite unjustified; that he is warm, nervous, and shy,'[118] King told his diary in November 1965. Not that King was starry-eyed: Heath would be a better Prime Minister than Maudling would have been, he wrote in his diary, 'but I am getting sadly disillusioned. Over the years one new P.M. after another has proved inadequate or useless, even when great things were not expected of them.'[119]

Yet as he sought the right moment to call an election in the hope of winning a decent majority, Wilson continued to appease King. When in December 1965 the *Mirror* produced a highly critical front page ('WATCH IT, HAROLD!') warning Wilson against intervening militarily in Rhodesia, where Ian Smith had declared UDI,[120] and instructing him to concentrate more on the domestic economy, Wilson was so desperate to get the *Mirror* back on side that he summoned Cudlipp to Downing Street that afternoon, gave John Beavan an interview at Chequers that weekend and had King to lunch on the Monday. 'Really, world statesmen ought to be able to take a few knocks from Mr Hugh Cudlipp and Mr Cecil King without becoming rattled,'[121] protested Alan Watkins. 'We are in a situation so fluid,' said another commentator, 'that one editorial by Cecil King in the *Daily Mirror* panics the Prime Minister into a complete right-about-turn. And right's the word.'[122] Cudlipp having firmly refused any honours, in a further sop Cassandra was knighted the following month.

Wilson's obsequiousness made no difference: 'Since an election became imminent,' observed a media commentator in March 1966 in a *New Statesman* article headed 'King v. Wilson', 'King has been showing sporadic and oblique signs of his displeasure with Mr Wilson. The message became loud and clear in that familiar "bloody shovel" editorial style when the two main parties published their manifestos: the *Mirror* applauded Heath's promises on the Market and union fronts and slammed Wilson for failing to toe the King line.'[123]

'The *Mirror* policy has been as critical of the Government as any paper, though we have not supported the Tories,' wrote King in his diary at the beginning of the election campaign of March 1966. 'How could we when we were hysterically pro-Labour at the last election only seventeen months ago? But my aim has been to break loose from any close connection with the Labour Party, as I think both on the balance of payments and on Rhodesia Wilson is going to run into horrible trouble before the end of the year.'[124] 'We have had no word from Wilson since the election was announced,' he wrote ten days later:

> — a contrast to the almost tearful requests for help last time. I take it that he knows he is going to win the election and is showing us where we get off.
>
> We have come out for Wilson in the end, after being very critical in the early stages. This is attributed to my friendship with Heath, but, of course, has quite other reasons. Wilson in seventeen months has shown his lack of the qualities needed in a prime minister — particularly foresight and administrative ability. I think he will lead the country into a frightful mess, and our constitution does not provide for a situation in which a prime minister with a large majority leads the country astray.[125]

Wilson's estimate was that the *Mirror* campaign cost the Labour Party 750,000 votes, King wrote a few days after. 'John Beavan saw him this morning to arrange an interview for tomorrow. Wilson very friendly; sent nice messages to Hugh; said he was writing to me and has agreed — at my invitation — to speak at the Jubilee Dinner of the N.P.A. So evidently our Harold knows on which side his bread is buttered.'[126] On holiday the following month, Wilson sent King a handwritten letter offering 'the very warmest thanks' and 'my appreciation of the tremendous help all your group gave us in the election'.[127] 'The more restrained support we gave you on this occasion was partly due to misgivings over the implementation of the Prices & Incomes Policy, partly due to misgivings over your European attitude, and partly due to the wish to avoid a landslide,'[128] was the response. And a private meeting at Downing Street yielded the conclusion that Wilson is 'an optimist basking in a sun of his own imagining'.[129]

What George Brown once described as the endless discussions with Wilson about how to involve King and keep him quiet[130] bore further fruit. In the summer of 1966 he was appointed a member of the National Parks Commission and a Director of the National Coal

Board.* 'I suppose I might be considered a queer bird for the job,' he told *The Times*, 'but I have been fairly successful in the business world. I know how many halfpennies make a penny, and I suppose that they felt that someone of my experience would be a help.'[131] Questions elsewhere about a possible conflict of interest, should his newspapers wish to criticise the Coal Board or the Bank of England, were ignored, yet for that very reason King refused to allow IPC's Managing Director, Frank Rogers, to join the Prices and Income Board.[132]

Under intense pressure from King to turn the *Mirror* guns on Wilson, Cudlipp bought time by persuading King to communicate his criticisms by letter: 'people are talking of a British de Gaulle or a National Government,' he told Wilson in June. 'These are counsels of despair and surely show the urgent need for you to become the man of the hour.' Instructions as to how to reach this happy state included controlling wages and hence inflation; launching a pro-Common Market campaign designed to win the hearts and minds of the British and the 'Continentals'; pulling militarily out of South-East Asia; dampening down expectations for a good outcome in Rhodesia; ceasing to try to be Foreign Secretary as well as Prime Minister; and sacking five of his ministers. 'But above all, what the country needs is leadership – a clear account of what sacrifices you demand of the country, and firm decisive action in implementing the policy you have decided on . . . We, at I.P.C., can be a great help and are very willing to be just that, but you are the conductor of the orchestra: we are only one of the players.'[133] 'It was despatched with Cecil's good wishes,' commented Cudlipp, 'but was predictably received with the same enthusiasm with which a guest at an early sixteenth-century feast would accept a chocolate meringue from Lucrezia Borgia.'[134] The Downing Street lunch that followed was 'a deep disappointment' to King, who 'didn't feel I got through to him at all; that I'd been invited as a flattering gesture to keep me quiet'.[135] It was not the possibility that Wilson might fall that was alarming King. 'Actually what bothers me

---

* In December 1966 the government scrabbled at the bottom of the barrel and offered him the chairmanship of the National Council of Health Education, which he declined: 'the work would be mildly interesting,' he wrote in his diary, 'but I cannot take on any more'.

most is that Parliamentary prestige is at a very low ebb and we cannot carry on like this without a demand for a dictatorship, which might be a great success in the short term, but which we should ultimately come to regret.'[136]

Nothing Wilson did could dent King's conviction that he was a failure on his way out. Ruth agreed. 'She had not had any conversation with him since . . . a year ago,' King recorded in July 1966. 'R. saw a marked deterioration – fatter, worried, more bewildered, and so *small*.'[137] 'Lunch with Cecil King,' wrote Dick Crossman a few months later:

> Suddenly he said to me, 'Well, this Government is not going to last, you know, more than a year.' 'No,' I said, 'I think this Government will hold out for four years before the election.' 'No, I didn't mean the Government,' he said, 'I meant the Prime Minister. He's not going to last. He's failed. We need younger men.'
>
> I looked up and saw the glint in his eye and remembered he was the nephew of Northcliffe. There opposite me was Cecil King seeing himself as the kingmaker, the man who put Harold in and would pull him out. We then had a long argument about failure and Cecil said to me, 'What can you think of a man who when I attack him for cowardice thanks me warmly for my help? And on two later occasions thanks me again and again for helping him when I really attacked him? What do you make of a character of that kind? Look at his indecision about Europe, about Rhodesia, about everything. It's hopeless. He's a man who cannot act and cannot administer. He must go.'[138]

It was the same message that he produced relentlessly to the parade of politicians who accepted his invitations. For two years after the 1966 election, as Cudlipp put it, King 'was the deathwatch beetle in Wilson's power-house, ceaselessly expressing his misgivings to Wilson's own Cabinet Ministers, overtly encouraging disloyalty and disillusion among the Prime Minister's entourage, stopping short only of advocating open revolt'.[139] In lectures, speeches, interviews, broadcasts and even at IPC's annual general meeting King criticised, recommended and dictated: 'Suddenly, chairman King seems busting to emerge from the profitable shadows which he has been content to fill for most of his working life,' wrote a press commentator in late 1966.[140]

Cudlipp laboured to 'avert or at worst delay a public cleavage between [King] and the Labour Prime Minister and above all to prevent an overt and acrimonious dissociation between the *Mirror* and the Labour movement, stranding the newspaper high and dry with no committed policy or political direction other than an impotent anti-Tory stance'.[141] In a lengthy letter from Madras, in March 1967, he tried to steer King away from a full-frontal attack on Wilson, which he warned might pull the whole party together behind him and badly damage the *Mirror* by leaving it open to accusations of seeking to usurp or sidestep Parliament.[142] 'But King's crusade against Wilson had reached the obsessional point of no return.'[143]

What about a National Government under another name, with new faces, some of them not politicians? King asked Roy Jenkins in February 1967, suggesting Lord Robens,[*] Lord Beeching,[†] Lord Shawcross[**] and Lord Sainsbury.[†] 'He did not fancy the idea.'[144] In May, lamenting to Ted Heath that television programmes were treating Parliament and ministers 'with total derision' and that the public shared their contempt for politicians, King said that 'if we are to save our democratic institutions something drastic will have to be done'. Should 'serious efforts [not] be made to bring in people from outside who do command public respect?'[145] Heath was no more enthusiastic than Jenkins.

Would King be interested in joining the government? asked Jim Callaghan, the Chancellor of the Exchequer, in September:

I said when the Government was formed I thought Robens, Sainsbury and (possibly) myself were inevitable, as we had

---

[*] King thought well of Alf Robens, his erstwhile protégé, whom it was widely believed would have become leader of the Labour Party instead of Wilson, had he not in 1960 accepted Macmillan's offer of the chairmanship of the National Coal Board, which required him to give up his parliamentary seat. A tough and pragmatic moderniser, he and King were in broad agreement about economic and social policy as well as being like-minded directors of the Bank of England.

[†] As Chairman of British Railways in the mid-1960s, Beeching became a byword for retrenchment.

[**] Labour MP turned businessman, Shawcross disliked Wilson, thought King an able businessman and, though he never knew him well, he and his wife occasionally socialised with the Kings.

[†] Sainsbury undertook a wide range of work in the public sphere, as well as chairing the very successful family business.

experience of administration and so few others had. I had been asked before they took office by Jim and George Brown if I was prepared to help and I had said yes. I had therefore accepted a directorship of the Bank, a membership of the Coal Board and of the National Parks Commission. Was this really the best use to which they could put my experience and ability? He said that the F.O. was occupied by George and the Treasury by himself, so I couldn't have those. I said, 'But why should I join a sinking ship?' Jim said it wasn't sinking . . . I said if they offered me a place in the Government, I would consider it . . . I recalled that I had been offered the job of understrapper to Douglas Jay* which I should have regarded as a bitter insult if I had been of a vindictive nature.'[146]

Rumours about King's lunches with politicians, civil servants and businessmen flew around Whitehall and Fleet Street. '. . . other Ministers find Mr King somewhat tedious,' wrote Peter Jenkins in the *Guardian*. 'Those who attend his *tête-à-tête* lunches have grown tired of the three-band gramophone record which, they say, consists of running down the Government and the Prime Minister in particular; complaining about the trade unions; and griping about the poorness of British management by comparison with the International Publishing Company.'[147] 'Something extraordinary seems to have taken hold of Cecil King,' reported the *Observer* in October, '. . . it is going round that King has got the idea that some time soon there will have to be some sort of National Government. It would be led by Denis Healey, and would include Lord Robens and Lord Beeching. Some people are even saying that King would not decline a post himself.'[148] Eyebrows were raised too at King's public criticisms and at the constant *Mirror* criticism of the government from an increasingly right-wing perspective. The communist *Morning Star* spoke for many when it asked, 'Isn't it time the Labour movement told Mr Cecil King and his Daily Mirror to go and get stuffed?'[149]

---

* According to *Private Eye*, their enmity had arisen in the mid-1950s 'when King was attacking Attlee at a fashionable left-wing party. "If you think that" shouted Jay, "you're more of a fool than most people take you for" – a statement which was not of great assistance to Mr Jay's future public relations, and one which has earned him constant abuse and ridicule from the *Daily Mirror*'.

Mirror assaults on Labour, and its revelations during the Party Conference about George Brown's drunkenness ruptured his and King's old friendship* and caused general outrage. As King wrote in his diary, Jim Callaghan told him amicably that 'it was supposed in some quarters that the critical attitude of the *Mirror* was due to my disappointment at not being given high office. I said no government post was as good as the one I have.'[150] There seemed no limit to Wilson's ability to swallow his anger: 'An hour with Wilson yesterday evening,' recorded King later that month:

> . . . The summons seemed to be to offer me: (1) a peerage (is this the fourth or fifth time?); (2) a Privy Councillorship; (3) he had been going to offer me the Paris Embassy, but after de Gaulle's statement in the afternoon veto-ing British entry into the Common Market there was now no point in going to Paris. I refused the honours and the interview amounted to a desultory chat. Any approach to reality was brushed aside.[151]

'Should business take over No. 10?' asked the *Observer* in December. Lord Robens was lying doggo since having said that the country should be 'run as Great Britain Limited with a damned good chairman and managing director and a damned good board'. Businessmen, the paper commented, were gripped with frustration at the government's inability to solve Britain's economic problems and were developing a contempt for politicians. 'Few of them, therefore, see a coalition as the answer to Britain's malaise. Says International Publishing's Cecil King: "A coalition will just make people yawn. We are coming near to the failure of parliamentary government." As King sees it, the politicians have made such a hash of our affairs that people must be brought into government from outside the rank of professional politicians.'[152]

King was coming close to making a hash of the affairs of IPC. Convinced that the choice was between growth or stagnation, he had continued to acquire and expand rather than consolidate, and there were serious management concerns about many parts of the empire.

---

* At a Foreign Office party shortly afterwards, Brown shouted drunken insults at Michael King about his father.

In 1963 he had edged out and himself replaced the Chairman of the Reed Paper Group, which was partly owned by IPC, and had also driven out the Managing Director, who found his interference intolerable. King's strategy of acquisition for acquisition's sake adversely affected Reed's profits, but he seemed incapable of focusing on the group's problems. He conscientiously carried out his public duties as Chairman of various companies – the awards ceremonies, the visits to factories at home and abroad, the speeches to the likes of the Printers' Pension Corporation or the newspaper retailers or the anniversary speeches – but he listened less and less and showed decreasing interest in running his empire, while extolling his own virtues as a manager and criticising others. His speech at the IPC annual general meeting in 1965 had an all-out attack on 'fuddy-duddy bosses' and called for all executive directors to retire at sixty-five or earlier. Did that include him? asked the *Financial Times*, noting that he was sixty-four. 'I said that *executive* directors should retire at 65,' he explained. '*Chairmen* should go at 70, and I shall. Mind you, I think they should be banished sooner if they get decrepit. I hope I shan't be decrepit until long after I'm 70, but I'd go if I were.'[153] The 1967 AGM speech consisted mainly of a violent attack on the 'feeble, fumbling way' in which the government was being run.[154]

'In the last years of Cecil's reign,' recalled Edward Pickering in a letter to Cudlipp a decade later, 'his increasing impatience with the day-to-day running of the business had become apparent. Board meetings lasted less than half-an-hour, never got round to matters of policy.'[155] Michael King, who might have told his father about the rising tide of resentment, instead shocked him by finally abandoning the *Mirror* for a well-paid job as Chief Information Officer of the Confederation of British Industry. One associate who did try to warn King was Ellis Birk.

When King had toppled Bart in 1951, he had invited to dinner young Birk, the senior partner in the *Mirror's* solicitors, who had become a non-executive director. 'King ordered two bottles of claret. "I've asked you to come," he said, "because you're about the only person I can speak to. How should I comport myself?" I said, "The one thing you can't do is comport yourself like Bart did."'

During dinner Birk told him how he thought he should comport himself and at the end King said, 'Will you make me a promise? Will you promise me that if I am not behaving in the way in which you said I should behave, you will come back to me and tell me so.' Birk agreed. 'I went back twice, but though King listened, nothing changed. So I decided not to bother doing it again.'[156]

The moment of truth for King's colleagues came in February 1968 at IPC '73, a crucial three-day conference of directors and senior management organised by Frank Rogers to look at the organisation and future development of IPC. 'Cecil attended for one evening only,' recalled Cudlipp:

> tonelessly reading a ghosted after-dinner speech, and amusingly answering earnest questions. He dealt at some length with the State of the Nation, a subject close to his heart, and then more perfunctorily with the current state of IPC . . . The regal manner in which he spoke, rather than what he said or didn't say, seemed to be remote or unreal. His established colleagues were patient, but he made no impression at all upon the young: it was also clear that the young . . . made no impression on him.[157]

When an observer referred to King as 'the old man' who had come to dinner one evening, 'there were some signs of uneasy, semi-suppressed mirth . . . it was embarrassingly apparent that at any rate among some sections of the assembly Cecil King was no longer regarded with awe or even reverence'. There was general agreement among senior executives that King 'stood between the company and progress,' wrote Pickering, 'that his attitudes were too patriarchal and feudal and that a change was absolutely necessary.' King believed he was coming close to toppling Harold Wilson. His colleagues were becoming intent on toppling King.

CHAPTER XI
The Reluctant Assassin

CECIL KING COULD NOT BE SACKED FROM THE BOARD WITHOUT A unanimous decision by all thirteen directors. Only Hugh Cudlipp, Deputy Chairman and anointed successor – to whom loyalty was an article of faith – had the authority, the cunning and the persuasive powers to bring this about.

'Hugh Cudlipp is kingpin around here,'[1] had been King's assessment in March 1961, shortly after the Odhams takeover. As King's enthusiasm had subsequently waned, he flirted heavily with Jocelyn Stevens – talking to him over many a lunch about publishing and his need for a successor and comparing him favourably with his own sons. To Stevens's embarrassment, he became known in some quarters as 'the prince', which went down badly with Cudlipp and others in IPC. Finally, sometime in 1963, King invited the thirty-one-year-old Stevens for a drink at his office, where he was introduced to 'grim-faced IPC executives' as having just joined the organisation. Since no such deal had been made with King, Stevens stormed out: on his way down the corridor Cudlipp appeared through a door asking agitatedly, 'What happened? What happened?' Ruth – whom King often used as a go-between – failed to persuade Stevens to change his mind, and henceforward King behaved 'like a spurned lover and a petulant child' and afterwards disparaged him publicly at every opportunity.[2]

In 1964, in an IPC shake-up, Cudlipp became Deputy Chairman and in January 1967 on television King remarked, 'One has to provide for one's succession, which I have done. If I fell under a bus this afternoon Mr Hugh Cudlipp will take my place.' It was an issue that had never been discussed with Cudlipp, let alone with the board of directors, but its impact was lessened by King's announcement that he had decided to stay on until he was seventy.* Cudlipp's responses to both pieces of news were confused: 'Hugh wanted to be chairman,' said Ellis Birk, 'and he didn't want to be chairman. At one moment he'd be getting mad because he wasn't chairman and thought he had merited it and the next he'd be mad because he was going to be.'³ Yet from early in 1968 Cudlipp had little option but to set about replacing King, for he, more than anyone, realised how the megalomania was taking over.

In addition to his loss of interest in running IPC, many other aspects of King's behaviour were worrying Cudlipp. Although he did not realise that King was keeping a diary, he was alarmed by the insouciant way in which King betrayed confidences: 'he regarded indiscretion as a cardinal virtue and public service. Guests left his dining-table like racing pigeons with messages of foreboding . . . The assumption of confidentiality by others was regarded by him as a licence to blab.'⁴

Always a mighty gossip, King repeated tittle-tattle 'that on the barest scrutiny was unlikely to be true . . . relaying without reservation what anybody said about anybody else, however prejudiced, however callous, however tainted by their own self-interest'.⁵ And while political indiscretions could be injurious to the Labour government, financial indiscretions gleaned from his Thursday morning meetings at the Bank of England were potentially dangerous for a country that was going through a serious economic crisis. King found, said Roy Jenkins, who replaced Jim Callaghan as Chancellor in November 1967 after the devaluation of the pound, 'a natural affinity with Maurice Parsons, the sour and unbalanced deputy Governor', who gave King the ammunition to act like 'Savonarola denouncing the improvident sins of the Florentines'.⁶

Then there were Saturday mornings. King had always liked to come

---

* King was still theoretically keen on youth, but his views on age had changed. When in January 1967 Wilson defended the sacking of Douglas Houghton on the grounds that 'he couldn't keep a man of sixty-eight in the Cabinet when men of sixty-four were being removed in the middle ranks', King commented in his diary that 'this is, of course, pure nonsense. Why exchange a useful little man of sixty-eight for a total dud, like [Patrick] Gordon Walker, of fifty-nine?'

to the office on Saturdays and talk to colleagues. Edward Pickering, who joined the company in 1964, recalled:

> He would ring me at about 11.00 and I'd go up there and we'd sit and chat, sometimes about newspapers, sometimes it was pure Fleet Street gossip, sometimes it was French literature. I greatly enjoyed his company and liked him very much. An extraordinarily interesting man to talk to . . .
>
> Through his contacts in the City and so on, he really could talk in ways that did focus your mind on various avenues. I remember discussing an article with him and suddenly he talked at length about the entry of the Continental Jews into this country and the way in which after the war the whole of banking was transformed by a comparatively small group of Jewish bankers. Now at that time I'd never even thought about such a thing . . . but when you did think about it it was absolutely true and it was a marvellous view of what was going on in the City of London. Now that sort of thing he was extraordinarily good at . . . And that went on until he suddenly began to have great ideas about running the country.[7]

It was early 1967 when King invited Cudlipp to devote Saturday mornings:

> to a mutual review of world and home affairs on the recurring theme of national bankruptcy and the crumbling of British society as we knew it. I enjoyed these sessions not only because of my respect for King's integrity and knowledge. It is, however, fair to say that anybody less inured to his encircling gloom would have jumped from the ninth floor in desperation after any average session. Schopenhauer . . . would have cut his throat on the Ghordies Anatolian prayer mat to relieve the tension.[8]

'The whole world seems to be sliding downhill,' King wrote in mid-1967:

> In China, in Vietnam, in the Middle East, in Central Africa, in Nigeria, things are going very badly. Even the United States is

in dire trouble with a war it cannot win and riots by Negroes in cities all over the United States . . . Our relations with [President] Johnson are deteriorating; our relations with the Chinese could hardly be worse. We have antagonised both sides in Nigeria and both sides in the Middle East. Where *do* we go for honey?[9]

King confidently expected his long catalogue of impending social and political disasters to culminate in violence and bloodshed, after which a new administration would take over, sort out the economy, cut back on defence commitments and bring the country into the European Community. Most of his policies appealed to Cudlipp; it was the proposed means of putting them into practice that worried him. Jodi recalled:

Hugh thought and hoped that by the Saturday morning chats he could control Cecil's mad ambitions. Hugh really suffered on those Saturdays, hated them (because they kept him from his boat and fun) but knew they were a necessary part of his life to guard the *Mirror*. He wanted Cecil – but a tamer Cecil – as chairman, but Ruth wanted more power for her man, and made him believe (with fawning flattery) he was that Man of Destiny who could rule the country, if not the world. Hugh's fight was indirectly with Ruth, whom he was powerless to influence. He could only hope that this man who had always seemed so reasonable, would see reason if it was pointed out to him. Sometimes, momentarily, he seemed to, but then went home to the witch and got another load of pie from her cracked sky.

The King–Cudlipp debate about what the anticipated new government should be called was finally resolved when King jettisoned 'National' and 'Coalition' in favour of 'Emergency'.[10] Much time was expended on deciding which 'new men, or old men refurbished would come to the fore, available and eager and acceptable and effective at the crucial moment. We were short of potential saviours.' Robens was always a candidate, Arnold Weinstock of GEC often, and other businessmen were added to, and subtracted from, the list that lived in the top left-hand drawer of one of the baroque mahogany tables. Lord

Mountbatten,* who was as handsome, popular, energetic and distinguished as he was ambitious and vain, was pencilled in as the titular head of government.

> There was no need to search for the *éminence grise*, and [King] had no doubt at all that the *Daily Mirror* would have a massive part to play during the constitutional upheaval. What was uncertain was whether the new regime would send for Cecil Harmsworth King or King send for the new regime; what was certain was that the moment was near at hand. Cecil's World in the last half of 1967 and the first half of 1968 was sincere, patriotic, exciting, but also whimsical and hallucinatory: it was the closest exercise to walking on the water in the history of aquatic sport.
>
> Early in 1968 he surprised . . . Frank Rogers by casually remarking that he expected to be playing some part in the running of the country, adding: 'Of course I shall be taking Hugh with me.'[11]

By February 1968, King's obsession with Wilson was causing increasing alarm at high levels of the Labour government. On the 6th he had lunch with Anthony Wedgwood Benn, Minister for Technology. King thought Benn had his head in the sand about another imminent devaluation.[12] Benn thought:

> that he [King] was slightly unbalanced. Second, if it was true that this was being said in the City and to him, it was almost certain this was getting abroad and therefore the confidence problem was serious. Third, when this situation developed, he was in a position to trigger it off. The entire weight of IPC would be thrown against Wilson in favour of a coalition . . . This is something that simply cannot be ignored.

Benn reported this to Wilson, who 'was rather agitated and excited

---

* Admiral of the Fleet, Earl Mountbatten of Burma, KG, PC, GCB, OM, GCSI, GCIE, GCVO, DSO, FRS, etc., Supreme Allied Commander, South East Asia (1943–6), Viceroy and then Governor-General of India (1947–8), First Sea Lord (1955–9), Chief of UK Defence Staff (1959–65).

. . . and said that Cecil King was mad – a view with which I would not really disagree.'[13]

Cudlipp became seriously worried a couple of weeks later when he heard reports of King's behaviour in France, where he was spending a few days sitting for Graham Sutherland. King had mooted to Cudlipp the idea of a portrait*: 'What would our colleagues think of the idea, and wouldn't it be better, anyway, if the idea came spontaneously from them?'[14] Cudlipp arranged for the expression of the spontaneous idea and suggested Sutherland, whom he had met at a dinner party: 'I was entranced to learn in my correspondence with him that his fee was at that time £5,000† from the waist up but £10,000 for a full-length portrait: who wants to paint pants, anyway, and who wanted to preserve Cecil's for posterity? We settled for "waist up".'[15]

Peter Stephens, the *Mirror*'s Paris bureau-chief, was at King's right hand from his arrival on 14 February. 'During dinner that first night he chatted freely about his ideas of a replacement cabinet consisting partially of non-politicians – with himself playing a leading part – but he was infinitely more interested in talking about – or rather, attacking – Harold Wilson and the economic plight into which he had driven Britain. "Timing is vital. He has to go, but I have to time everything with great care."' Stephens asked King one evening what exact role he thought he should have in a new government. 'There was no reply for a while so I said: "Do you see yourself as a minister without portfolio going around sorting out each ministry and putting it on its feet?" Right away he answered: "There's an awful lot that needs sorting out and that might be a very good idea. I'm not quite sure yet."'

Stephens accompanied King to a series of meetings and meals with a galaxy of senior people, who included French politicians and newspapermen, an American businessman and the Chairman of Sotheby's: to everyone he talked obsessively and with staggering indiscretion about how Wilson was a liar, the economy was in an appalling

---

* This fine portrait hangs in the National Portrait Gallery. 'The dominant impression is of ruthless honesty coupled with complete informality,' wrote the *Daily Telegraph*'s Terence Mulally on its unveiling. 'Cecil King's jacket hangs baggy and creased, and above it the face is deeply lined and worn'.

† About £50,000 today.

state, a second devaluation of the pound was nigh and would lead
to the collapse of the government and, since the Conservatives were
no alternative, new men would have to save the situation.[16] To
Stephens's further alarm, King continually stressed that 'as a director
of the Bank of England I have a fair idea of what is going on and
I know they do not issue true figures. They fake them.'* On 19
February Cudlipp telephoned with the news of a *Guardian* front-page
story:

Making a new start with a
Coalition Government
MR CECIL KING
LEADING THE
SOUNDINGS

These soundings, it was suggested, assumed that Wilson and Heath
would be bypassed, Robens would have a dominant role and King
would play a major part:

The leading figure in all this seems to be Mr King himself and
the proposal is that if an embryonic coalition were found to exist,
a number of people and newspapers would, at a given signal, all
announce simultaneously their separate convictions that the Wilson
Government should be superseded by a radical coalition . . .

Readers were reminded of various Harmsworth uncles, with special reference to Northcliffe and how he helped Beaverbrook replace
Asquith with Lloyd George – and were told that King had sought
office from Wilson.

While Cudlipp was tickled by the idea that any other newspaper
proprietor or publisher would ally himself with the highly unpopular
King, he was concerned by the story's implication that King 'regarded
himself as a power outside Parliament which was greater than that which

---

* This dramatic assertion referred to an internationally agreed practice not to disclose
  short-term drawings made under central bank swap agreements; it had been observed
  also by the previous three Chancellors.

existed within' and wanted him to issue a rebuttal. King's reaction was 'Why should I . . .? They can say what they like',[17] but Cudlipp prevailed and a rather weasel-worded denial was issued: 'It is quite untrue to say that I have been "leading the soundings," it said *inter alia*. 'I have certainly been sounding the leaders – it is a publisher's duty to know what is happening* . . . a coalition at this moment is just not on, and will not become so unless the political situation deteriorates still further, which it may.'

Press coverage was at its height as a backdrop to the IPC conference where King alienated virtually his entire senior management.[18] He was pleased with the press attention. 'The whole episode is interesting,' he observed in a complacent diary entry, 'as it would not have been given the prominence it was unless people are thinking in terms of a National Government. *The Times* gave me a cartoon† yesterday.'[19] 'The issue,' wrote Cudlipp, 'was of some significance in a democracy. What was in question now was the divine right of King.'[19a]

A couple of days later, commenting on a savage attack by Peter Jenkins in the *Guardian*,[20] King noted: 'The general theme is a bit confused, but is mainly on the lines that King is too powerful; we want no Northcliffes here. The *Guardian* is not an influential paper any longer and if it comes to open warfare I have all the guns in both verbal dexterity and coverage.'[21] He made no comment on *The Spectator*'s view that speculation about a coalition government headed by Robens and King was proof that satire had gone too far.[22] 'Cecil was unduly sensitive to criticism in his youth,' wrote Cudlipp:

---

* 'The joke was supplied to Nice from London for the denial statement as part of our usual service,' wrote Cudlipp.

† 'The Prime Minister,' wrote Cudlipp, 'was depicted as a confused little man walking hesitantly up the steps of an imposing State building; the formidable Cecil, labelled 'Coalition Government', was standing in his way and there was a 'Thinks' balloon above Harold's head saying:

> As I was going up the stair
> I met a man who wasn't there.
> He wasn't there again today.
> I wish, I wish he'd stay away.

impervious to it in middle age, and relished it in his vain maturity. The disapproval of little and ignorant men was merely a spur, irrelevant or amusing . . . As the principal gunner in the King's Royal Artillery and the captain of the Praetorian Guard I was in fact apprehensive: the political thinkers on the editorial staff, two or three of whom were of high calibre, were as concerned as the *Guardian* about the robust manifestation of Northcliffe's ghost. So was I.[23]

He was made even more apprehensive when, on 26 February, an alarmed Stephens came over from Paris to report in person on King's visit; on top of everything else, he believed King's memory was going. 'He frequently repeated things several times during the day having obviously forgotten that he had already mentioned them.' While Stephens was in London, 'the pound slumped on foreign exchange markets and in the *Daily Mail* city column of February 27th or 28th this was attributed to alarmist rumours coming from the Continent'.[24] All this fed the anxious discussions among such close Cudlipp allies as Birk, Pickering and Rogers.

Cudlipp organised a dinner[25] in early March for the group's editors and political writers. After King's familiar soliloquy, Sydney Jacobson, by now Editorial Director of the *Sun* and the *People*,[*] opposed a 'Wilson Must Go' campaign for several reasons – not least that it would strengthen him and probably invite a counter-attack along 'power-without-responsibility' lines. John Beavan, Political Editor of the *Daily* and *Sunday Mirror*s and the writer of most of King's speeches and articles, responded to King's statement that money would lose its value and the country would have to live by barter with the remark that King 'would be able to live for years on his fabulous collection of old silver. I got a brush-off for this sally.' Beavan said also that he believed the papers should be on the outside looking in, rather than

---

[*] 'My impression was that if Cecil King ever did read the *People* he held it with a pair of tongs . . .' wrote Bob Edwards, its Editor from 1966 to 1972, in his memoirs. 'Nothing about his manner or surroundings indicated that his principal role in life was to head three yellow papers strictly aimed at the servants' quarters, with the exception of the *Sunday Mirror* which might catch the mistress's eye if she happened to see it lying on the kitchen table.

involved inside politics. No one was forceful except George Gale, who had occupied the Cassandra slot since the death of Bill Connor the previous year, and who took as much a dislike to King as King took to him. Gale went on the attack, pointing out:

> that a government required the ability to sustain a Parliamentary majority and so on – elementary stuff, but apparently neces- sary – and I ended up by asking King how he proposed to engineer his *coup d'état*, and did he propose collecting Alf Robens, Lord Beeching, Old Uncle Tom Cobbley and all into a charabanc and driving to the Palace and saying to the Queen, 'Ma'am, here we are, your new Government of National Recon- struction'? My contribution to the discussion was received rather coolly.[26]

King thought the dinner a failure; he did not realise that from his point of view it was a disaster. Up to now, those agitating for his departure were mainly management; now, as Edward Pickering put it, the dinner 'had alerted the Editors to the dangers of his contin- uing dominance, had set in train the events which finally led to his departure'.[27]

The following day, at the request of the Governor, King attended the Bank of England and promised that, should he become 'person- ally embroiled in political controversy', he would resign from the Court.[*] This did not prevent him from giving a half-hour BBC inter- view a few weeks later that produced such headlines as the *Observer*'s 'WILSON MUST GO, SAYS CECIL KING'.[28] He was pleased that his remarks were 'taken up in a big way by all the newspapers this morning. Cudlipp says this is a new departure, snapping our last links with the Labour Party. He sees a new situation arising in which there is open warfare between Parliament and the press. He thinks this was coming anyway, but we had meant to delay it.'[29]

'And still nobody from the crowd . . . asked the simple question, *Who in bloody hell does Cecil King think he is?*' remembered Cudlipp in wonder:

---

[*]   The following day, 7 March 1968, King was elected a member of the Committee of Treasury, the inner group of seven Bank directors (there were eighteen in the full Court).

It was now accepted or assumed, especially by Cecil, that he occupied some undefined, unelected but absolute position of authority and responsibility in the country, indeed in the Western world, which few people challenged. His knowledge, knowing far more than anyone he had met, his commanding height, his soft voice, his benign patience with the frailties of others, combined to give him the mystique of a twentieth-century Delphic oracle, dispensing like Apollo or like Zeus at Olympus the answers to inquiries about current public events.

(All this, of course, Cudlipp could have added, was infused with a now overweening self-belief engendered by an obsessive wife who truly did believe that – together, and with sufficient faith – they could walk on water.) 'Rebuking Prime Ministers and encouraging their potential successors,' Cudlipp continued. 'Adjudicating on the merits or failings of industrial tycoons and indicating to such Secretaries of State as cared to listen the course of economic salvation. Adjusting foreign policy. Gently jostling Britain into its next niche in history . . . It was either a performance of unparalleled statesmanship or the greatest con trick of our political era.'[30]

That the media gave King so much attention was, Cudlipp concluded, because his views 'were sincere, uninhibited, different, provocative', and he made for 'compelling television; he said what he believed to be true, however outrageous the view might be, and the audience liked the avuncular, effortless, world-weary style in which he specialised'.[31] King was also adept at tossing in snippets of tantalising information; in January 1968, for instance, on *The Frost Programme*, he created much press speculation by mentioning that he had turned down a government job. That shrewd analyst, Francis Williams, spotted something very worrying. 'Frost . . . did not question [King's] assumption that his influence is vastly greater than that of almost anyone else including Cabinet Ministers.' In truth, said Williams, *Mirror* readers took no notice of 'front page barrages':

. . . Blasts in black type may make a stir, they rarely make up mind. Mr King, who is far and away the most able manager of popular newspapers now operating and not only a man of intelligence but also in many ways a very nice one, used to be well aware of this.

I remember him saying to me a good while ago that a popular newspaper could . . . not start a wagon rolling and certainly could not stop it or reverse its direction, but once it had started it could give it a push. This seems to me to be true. But it is a long way from the sort of influence Mr King seemed to be claiming for himself in his cosy chat with Mr Frost. In that chat he also claimed that he was constantly aware of the presence of the Almighty beside him. It is a pity it does not induce a little less of the arrogance that is the occupational disease of newspaper proprietors.

What was more, Williams pointed out, the *Mirror* was losing its old talent for wagon-spotting. 'It was notably late in latching on to the snow-balling impact of the Back Britain movement . . . too busy giving Mr Roy Jenkins orders in three powerful pieces to notice what was happening under its nose.' With Cudlipp's help, recommended Williams, King should get the *Mirror* back on track. 'It will be a pity if excessive delusions of grandeur get in the way of the job it can really do.'[32]

Yet to most people, as Cudlipp put it, King came across as a disinterested pundit with no axe to grind, at a time when it was not necessary to be a pessimist to be afraid of an economic crash. Even Cudlipp was by no means certain that King's terrible prophecies might not prove to be right.

'King was surrounded by yes-men; and this was his trouble' was the view of George Gale, and there is a measure of truth in that. For one thing, though his politically minded colleagues were uneasy about his solutions, they did not much disagree about his analyses of the problem and, through long habit, on the whole they brought him the news he wanted to hear. 'There are still some people who believe that the party will cling together out of fear,' wrote Beavan in a bleak memorandum about the state of the Labour Party, 'that the economy could look healthier, that the government could slowly climb back, that even Wilson could be rehabilitated. But the "some" who believe this are very few.'[33] Even when it came to the areas where they differed from King, there was no longer any point in disagreeing with someone who did not listen. Containment was the major objective: it was a good day for Cudlipp when, for instance, he could persuade King to refuse to organise a meeting of top people from five countries to sort out the Middle East ('The story will be that "Cecil King is now trying to run the international crises"'[34]). 'The outside view of how the *Mirror* was run was no doubt that the headstrong Cudlipp and his Editors and experts, all talented in their different ways, were kept in check by the discerning Cecil King, tightening the reins, prescribing caution, tempering the undisciplined enthusiasms of younger men with sage advice,' remembered Cudlipp:

> The reverse was now the truth. There was not a single soul on the editorial staff who had not doubted the wisdom of a 'Wilson Must Go' declaration, first me in writing from Madras and then independently others. But they were now regarded as uncomprehending men of goodwill but small stature and uncertain spirit who could not expect to measure up to the ultimate and fiery test of leadership. Omega was for him alone and he was deaf to any warning.[35]

One Saturday morning, once more discussing Mountbatten as the titular head of an Emergency Government, King added, 'The trouble is that he is not the sort of person I know.'[36] Cudlipp had been friendly with Mountbatten for a long time and indeed could wave a 'My dear Hugh . . . Yours ever, Dickie' letter he had received that very morning. (By now those who revelled in Cudlipp's company included a phalanx of such Establishment figures as Harold Macmillan and the Archbishop of Canterbury.) Coincidentally, that Saturday evening Edward Pickering, who was representing the *Mirror* as Mountbatten's guest at a Burma reunion, had a conversation with him about the state of the nation that culminated in Mountbatten saying he wanted to see Cudlipp urgently. They met on Monday morning, Cudlipp reported to King, and Mountbatten discoursed eloquently on how he 'had brought the house down' by telling his audience 'that if the Burma Spirit galvanised the country now there would be no problem':

> Important people, leaders of industry and others, approach me increasingly saying something must be done. Of course, I agree that we can't go on like this. But I am 67, and I'm a relative of the Queen: my usefulness is limited: this is a job for younger men, and obviously talent and administrative ability which does not exist in Parliament must be harnessed. Perhaps there should

be something like the Emergency Committee I ran in India. I
didn't want the job for obvious reasons and agreed to do it only
if there was no publicity . . . Don't you think the situation is
similar here? . . . it could only be done by somebody with intelligence, leadership, and administrative ability.

Mountbatten's big idea was that Barbara Castle, Secretary of State
for Employment, should be called in and persuaded to rouse the
national spirit. Cudlipp – who thought the idea 'nebulous, naïve, political cloud-cuckooland' – persuaded him out of it with the argument
that, if approached, Castle would instantly tell Wilson. King 'had also
been thinking along the lines of an Emergency Administration or
Emergency Government,' Cudlipp explained to Mountbatten. 'The
crux of the problem was that the nation had lost faith in Mr Wilson
and the Socialists and still had no faith in Mr Heath and the Tories
. . . Labour still had a vast majority in the House; the head of a
Coalition Government . . . would have to be a Labour Minister –
Jenkins?[*] Healey?[†] No longer Callaghan[**] . . . When the ultimate crisis
came the Tories, who would certainly not serve under Wilson, would
serve under Jenkins or possibly Healey.

Mountbatten suggested 'a private meeting of some sort: what
did I think?'
    H.C. 'I think it is important you take no personal initiative
of any sort. You should wait until you are approached.'

---

[*] Roy Jenkins, at the time the *Mirror*'s favourite minister, wrote in his memoirs that he
'cultivated my *Mirror* relations carefully', lunched or dined regularly with Cudlipp and
other senior editorial people and got on well with King, saw eye-to-eye with him on
Europe and mostly left him to do the talking; Jenkins was 'able, highly intelligent, very
charming, very persuasive', King told Robin Day in his BBC interview of 31 March 1968,
before paying a backhanded compliment: 'His Budget was a wonderful piece of stage
management and public relations.'

[†] Denis Healey, a recipient of King lunches, was one of few other ministers for whom
King had a good word. 'The best Minister of Defence we have had for many years,'
King told Robin Day. 'I don't agree with his policy about buying expensive planes we
can't afford nor clinging to our position east of Suez, but he has run the Ministry of
Defence better than it's been run for many years.'

[**] 'A charming Irishman from South Wales' was all King would say to Day about Callaghan,
whom he thought intellectually negligible.

M. 'I certainly don't want to appear to be advocating or supporting any notion of a Right Wing dictatorship – or any nonsense of that sort. Nor do I want to be involved at my age.* But
like some other people I am deeply concerned about the future
of the country.'

They agreed on a meeting with King: Mountbatten pressed for the
inclusion of Sir Solly Zuckerman, the government's Chief Scientific
Adviser and well known to both Cudlipp and King, 'whom he
described as now utterly disenchanted with Harold. Z., he said, was
"a great planner – immediately welcomed by successive U.S. Presidents,
also on the Continent, also in USSR".'[37]
In a follow-up memo, Cudlipp told King that 'Mountbatten's principal point was that nothing much could be done about the developing situation, anyway, unless the *Mirror* was behind a move in a
particular direction. He seemed to believe that T.V. could "crusade":
I pointed out that it can only report.' In addition to Zuckerman,
Mountbatten suggested as '"useful people"' Lord Beeching, an Air
Marshal 'just about to be kicked out because of his co-operation and
dedication', three senior civil servants (William Armstrong 'will waste
his time and talents as head of the Civil Service'), Jim Callaghan, Roy
Jenkins, Reggie Maudling and Alec Douglas-Home ('The people trust
him, perhaps alone of the politicians'), a couple of obscure businessmen and 'Jimmy Carreras – "great go-getter". Carreras, whom I
know well, is a film tycoon (flashy, sexy, cheap films) whom Dickie
has met through the Variety Club. The name surprised me.'[38†]
Cudlipp fixed a meeting for 8 May 1968; Mountbatten's son-in-law,
Lord Brabourne, 'who had little respect for King's wisdom or discretion', felt that the meeting 'would be a fruitful field for mischief' and

---

* He was eight months older than Cecil King.
† In his memoirs, Cudlipp dealt very charitably with Mountbatten's muddle-headed ideas:
'whereas Cecil King's approach to the "forthcoming crisis" was essentially political (chop-
ping down the Rt Hon. Harold Wilson) and economic (sweeping measures under a new
regime in which he would himself be playing a leading part), Lord Mountbatten's
approach was more circumspect and philosophical. Political manoeuvre, in favour of
whatever person or persons or faction, however lofty and disinterested the motives, was
none of [his] business . . . What he was hoping for was a massive resurgence of the
British spirit.'

begged his father-in-law to cancel it,[39] but, fortified by knowing Zuckerman would be there, Mountbatten went ahead.

In his memoirs Cudlipp described how King:

> expounded his views on the gravity of the national situation, the urgency for action, and then embarked upon a shopping-list of the Prime Minister's shortcomings. He spoke with his accustomed candour. He did the talking and I sat back in my chair to observe the reactions, detecting an increasing concern on the part of the two listeners. He explained that in the crisis he foresaw as being just around the corner the Government would disintegrate, there would be bloodshed in the streets, the armed forces would be involved. People would be looking to somebody like Lord Mountbatten as the titular head of a new administration, somebody renowned as a leader of men who would be capable, backed by the best brains and administrators in the land, to restore public confidence. He ended with a question to Mountbatten – would he agree to be the titular head of a new administration in such circumstances.
>
> Mountbatten turned to his friend: 'Solly, you haven't said a word so far. What do you think of all this?'
>
> Sir Solly rose, walked to the door, opened it, and then made this statement: 'This is rank treachery. All this talk of machine guns at street corners is appalling. I am a public servant and will have nothing to do with it. Nor should you, Dickie.' Mountbatten expressed his agreement and Sir Solly departed.
>
> Only a minute or two elapsed between Zuckerman's departure and King's. Lord Mountbatten was, as always in my experience, courteous but firm: he explained explicitly but briefly that he entirely agreed with Solly and that that sort of role, so far as he was concerned, was 'simply not on'.
>
> His Private Secretary, John Barratt, accompanied Cecil and me to our car.[40]

King's diary entry was very different:

> Hugh and I called on Dickie Mountbatten at his request at his flat at 4.30. He insisted that Solly Zuckerman should be there. Dickie spoke of him as a man of invincible integrity and as one

of the greatest brains in the world . . . Solly seemed embarrassed by this and hurried away as soon as he decently could. Dickie does not really have his ear to the ground or understand politics. After Solly had gone, Mountbatten said he had been lunching at the Horse Guards and that morale in the armed forces had never been so low. He said that the Queen was receiving an unprecedented number of petitions, all of which have to be passed on to the Home Office. According to Dickie, she is desperately worried over the whole situation. He is obviously close to her and she is spending this weekend at Broadlands. He asked if I thought there was anything he should do. My theme was that there might be a stage in the future when the Crown would have to intervene: there might be a stage when the armed forces were important. Dickie should keep himself out of public view so as to have clean hands if either emergency should arise in the future. He has no wish to intervene anyway.[*][41]

When the events of that meeting became a matter of public dispute between King and Cudlipp, King would rightly point out that his was a contemporaneous note, but Cudlipp could point to correspondence with Mountbatten and Zuckerman in the mid-1970s that supported his version. Both versions were flawed: King's, because of his inability to hear what he did not want to hear; Cudlipp's, because in retirement he had a deep disinclination to hurt the feelings of people he liked and because he was, indeed, relying on the memory of other people with reputations to defend: after Mountbatten's murder he would be more frank.

The truth of what is periodically sensationalised by conspiracy theorists as a failed coup[†] was almost certainly that Cudlipp, on King's

---

[*] King would tell *The Times* in April 1981 that he had omitted this entry from the published version of his diary (1972) because he regarded the entry as 'confidential, especially the part about the Queen'. His comment on the discrepancies was: 'Old men forget. It happened thirteen years ago. I had a note of it, and they did not.'

[†] Authors of innumerable pieces of tedious nonsense written on the so-called coup include the fanciful Nigel West, and Peter Wright of *Spycatcher* fame, who thickened the fog by saying that King was a long-term contact of MI5. It was Michael, not Cecil, who had connections with MI5; as Cudlipp often pointed out, Cecil would have been a strange recruit since he could not keep a secret for ten seconds.

behalf, instigated the meeting; that Mountbatten at some stage – probably before Zuckerman's late arrival – said what King recorded; that King spoke as apocalyptically as Cudlipp described; and that Mountbatten, who loved to think of himself as a man of destiny, was briefly beguiled by King's flattery. 'Dickie was really intrigued by Cecil King's suggestion that he should become the boss man of a "government",'[42] Zuckerman noted in his diary during a revival of the story in 1975. Knowing Mountbatten well – indeed, having heard him in the 1940s fantasise about how he might be the man to pull the country round[43] – Zuckerman wanted to take no chances and hence intervened decisively: 'Dickie at first wanted to hold me back,' he told Cudlipp privately, 'but I insisted on leaving[44] . . . I wonder what [he] would have said if I hadn't been there.'[45] Zuckerman would later admit that 'treachery' might have been the wrong word to use.[46]*

It was Zuckerman's words and action that brought Mountbatten rapidly to his senses, led him abruptly to terminate the meeting,[47] to write in his diary of 'Dangerous nonsense', to tell Zuckerman the following day 'that he greatly regretted that he had ever consented to the meeting[48] and (according to what he told Cudlipp a month after the meeting) to report the entire conversation to the Queen.[49] In 1978 Mountbatten would go one better by telling *Time* magazine that King 'came to see me . . . and said would I take over the country, to which my retort was to kick him out . . . King was a man filled with *folie de grandeur*, saying "I can fix it." I said, "This is rank treason. Out."'[50]

Unperturbed by the loss of his putative titular head of government, King decided that the overthrow of Wilson could no longer be delayed. As King had pointed out in a BBC interview a couple of years previously, when he and Cudlipp disagreed, he said, 'I'm the Chairman', so Cudlipp 'had neither the power to suppress nor the ammunition to negotiate yet another postponement . . . I could not dissuade a bull from entering a china shop by standing between the bull and the china; a more fruitful tactic was to save some of the

---

* It was no surprise that King omitted Zuckerman's words from his diary or that subsequently he should have denied they had been said. Cudlipp, in 1981, rather than saying what he believed – that King and Ruth had little grasp on reality when it came to King's past – offered the kindly but implausible explanation that 'Solly said it and Cecil didn't [physically] hear it'. He convinced nobody.

valuable crockery and as far as possible subdue the bull.'[51]

Two days after the meeting with Mountbatten, on Friday 10 May, when the newspapers were full of Labour's (long-predicted) humiliation in the local elections, three-quarters of the front page of the *Mirror* was occupied by Cecil King. Beside his photograph[*] was an article of which, unusually, he had written even the headline himself: 'the summary dismissal of a Prime Minister,' wrote Cudlipp in 1994, 'was a moment in his life he wished to share with no one except the historians'.[52]

ENOUGH
IS ENOUGH[†]
By Cecil H. King,
Chairman of the International
Publishing Corporation.

The results of the local elections are fully confirming the verdicts of the opinion polls and of the Dudley by-election.

Mr Wilson and his Government have lost all credibility: all authority.

The Government which was voted into office with so much goodwill only three and a half years ago has revealed itself as lacking in foresight, in administrative ability, in political sensitivity, and in integrity. Mr Wilson seems to be a brilliant Parliamentary tactician and nothing more.

If these disastrous years only marked the decline of Mr Wilson and the Labour Party, the damage to our political self-confidence would be serious enough, but the Labour Party came into power with such high hopes from its supporters because it took office after thirteen years of dismal Tory administrations.

We can now look back nearly twenty-five years to the end of the war and see that this country under both Tory and Labour administrations has not made the recovery or the progress made

---

[*] The caption was: 'CECIL H. KING, Chairman of the International Publishing Corporation. The Corporation publishes the Daily Mirror, the Sunday Mirror, the Sun, The People and the Daily Record and Sunday Mail in Scotland.'

[†] The article appeared also in the *Sun* and the *Daily Record*.

by others, notably the defeated Japanese, Germans and Italians.

We have suffered from a lack of leadership and from an unwillingness by successive Prime Ministers to make any serious attempt to mobilise the talent that is available in this once great country of ours.

Frequent Government shuffles mean that in any case very few Ministers are long enough in any office to master their subject.

Since 1964 we have had three Ministers responsible for the vast area of our economy covered by the Ministry of Fuel and Power. In the same period, we have had four Ministers of Education, which means that, effectively, Mr Wilson has had no Minister of Education. And the same applies to other Ministries.

We are now threatened with the greatest financial crisis in our history. It is not to be removed by lies about our reserves, but only by a fresh start under a fresh leader.[*]

It is up to the Parliamentary Labour party to give us that leader — and soon.

The article caused a sensation. At around midnight, when King had been in bed for a couple of hours,[53] the early edition hit the streets and the Editor of *The Economist*, Alastair Burnet, remarked on a television election special that 'perhaps the biggest loss which Mr Wilson, at any rate, has sustained tonight, is the loss of the *Daily Mirror* and Mr Cecil King'. 'There is nothing new about this,' said Tony Benn on the same programme. 'We have all been expecting this for months. Cecil King has been saying this to everybody who would listen to him privately for a long time.' King was entitled to his opinion of Wilson, but this article was a 'grave dereliction of duty' by a member of the Court of the Bank of England.[54] Ellis Birk wrote to Frank Rogers privately that he thought the short paragraph about the financial crisis 'outrageous. He bluntly accuses the Governor and executive Directors of the Bank of England, the Treasury and the Chancellor of the Exchequer of lying. In addition he preaches impending catastrophe for sterling.'[55]

---

[*] Cudlipp had failed to persuade King to take out this paragraph, but by prevailing on him to remove the word 'monthly' before lies, he saved a few pieces of china.

Calls from Labour MPs for King to be removed from the Court of the Bank of England were pre-empted by the announcement that he had resigned the previous evening. Roy Jenkins had seen this 'unopened, urgently delivered letter from King at the top of my box' just after 9 p.m. following a whole 'grinding' night at the Finance Bill Committee and then a morning at Cabinet and an afternoon visiting party workers in Birmingham:

> I decided to have dinner first, and when I read [the letter] afterwards was so sleepy that I could hardly take it in. He appeared to wish to resign from the Court of the Bank of England on the ground that he might be engaging in a greater degree of political controversy. It all sounded fairly hypothetical and leisurely, although I ought to have been alerted by the last sentence which desired the resignation to take effect 'forthwith'* . . . I did not react until eight hours later when the newspapers were placed upon my bed.[56]†

The King statement – particularly his sinister reference to 'lies about our reserves' – sharply exacerbated the fall in both sterling and equities precipitated by the government's election losses, dominated newspapers at home and featured strongly abroad; as many commentators pointed out subsequently, foreign (even more than domestic) investors assumed he knew more than he did: 'what Mr King let out of the bag,' said the *Telegraph* later, 'was a cat which was never in it.'[57] All that day Jenkins was under heavy pressure from Wilson to assert his loyalty and repudiate King; the *Mirror*'s championing of him over previous months had already done him damage in the mistrustful eyes of Wilson and his entourage, and they were not minded to believe his story about why he had failed to react to King's letter the night before. 'I can't afford to get into an argument

---

* 'Dear Chancellor, As I am becoming more and more involved in political controversy, I think it will be more convenient for the Bank of England if I resign from the Court. This is therefore to tender my resignation, effective forthwith. Yours sincerely, Cecil H. King.'
† 'Dear Mr King, I have received your letter of May 9, and note that you have resigned as a director of the Bank of England. Yours sincerely, Roy Jenkins.'

about the financial situation because there's a run on the pound today,' Jenkins told that ex-protégé of Cudlipp and King, Dick Crossman, now Leader of the House and Lord President of the Council, 'and, as for reasserting my faith in Harold, I shall be accused of doing it precisely because I am conspiring against him.' So Crossman, who was privately a bitter critic of Wilson, wrote a press release for a constituency speech he was due to give that night, describing King's article as 'character assassination' and 'reminding the country that Cecil King was the nephew of Lord Rothermere and Lord Northcliffe, the two megalomaniac press lords who tried to dictate to Prime Ministers'[58]: 'I cannot recollect an episode which has brought Fleet Street into such disrepute since the attempt of the *Daily Mail* and the *Daily Express* to drive Stanley Baldwin out of the premiership and the leadership of the Conservative Party.'[59]

Cudlipp remembered King throughout this period as publicly calm and privately intensely excitable about his 'crusade': 'I had a front-row seat and shared many a talk and impulsive phone call. He was acting out of character. Cecil King was on the rampage, exhibiting the same boyish ebullience he publicly displayed in the General Election of 1964.'[60] He had to be persuaded by Cudlipp and Pickering not to take out full-page advertisements in all the national newspapers to reproduce his article; in truth there was no need, since the media loved the story. The duo also prevailed on him to drop from a press release the report of the private conversation with Callaghan the previous year, in which King had by implication been offered and had refused a Cabinet position.[61]

King appeared on that Friday night on two television programmes, 'cheerful, chuckling and unrepentant'[62] according to *The Times*, making it clear that he knew no secret figures – since Bank of England directors were just 'a bit of trimming on the cake' who did what they were told – but reiterating his insistence that Wilson was finished. Wilson brushed the controversy aside, but Crossman had thrown plenty of meat into the media feeding-frenzy. 'CROSSMAN LEAPS TO WILSON'S AID' was a *Times* headline on 11 May: 'Mr King's diatribe,' wrote its political correspondent, 'is more than likely to close the ranks of Labour MPs behind the Prime Minister.'[63] 'The newspapers are pretty hostile,' wrote King in his diary on Saturday, '. . . and so are the politicians. Crossman launched an attack on me yesterday, but it was very poor stuff . . . There is to be a further piece by me in the *Sunday Mirror* tomorrow, but from then on we shall have to play it by ear . . . the range of selection [for Prime Minister] is narrow and uninviting.'[64]

The impact of King's second article, which was more of the same, was swamped by the rest of the Sunday newspapers, which were generally united in condemnation of what they considered to be King's irresponsible remarks about the country's finances: 'he has caused a financial panic by giving the impression of saying something new when not doing anything of the kind,' said the *Observer*, which, with the *Guardian*, King had once described as 'fellow-travellers of the *Mirror*.'[65] 'And he has done this because he wants to overthrow the present Administration . . . Mr King appears to be enjoying his perverse moment of political power (even if it is only negative power) as if it were some kind of fulfilment. The spectacle makes Mr Wilson look a straightforward character by the side of the devious Mr King.' King's call for a new Labour Prime Minister would in present circumstances mean replacing Wilson by Jenkins, said the *Sunday Telegraph* – no friend of Wilson's. 'The idea that such a change would produce a stronger and more effective Government, more firmly based in popular support, shows a strange and almost frivolous ignorance of the current mood both in the Labour party itself and the country at large.' 'Mr Cecil King's inept "Wilson Must Go" call has had the inevitable effect of rallying Labour M.P.s to Mr Wilson's side,' said the *Sunday Express*. And Cudlipp's old boss, John Gordon, wrote of King's TV appearances, 'I was told he looked a fool. He babbled, and said nothing coherent because clearly he didn't know anything. Why does a man make so public an ass of himself? Well, King Cecil has for some time been showing signs that he aspires to be a maker and breaker of Governments. Perhaps even to be Prime Minister. It's a sort of hereditary family condition.'[66] King phoned Cudlipp at home to talk over the Sunday coverage; they had an argument about what the *Mirror* would run the next day, during which Cudlipp reminded him of their guiding principle that – unlike Beaverbrook – they would not conduct vendettas. *Mirror* coverage, therefore, though it did not please Downing Street, did not please King, either.

'Stacks of mail this morning,' recorded King on Monday, '– mostly hostile, but an encouraging letter from Robens.' In the House of Commons, noted Crossman, dealing with the King affair, Roy Jenkins put on 'a superb performance. He withered him up, dealing with King with an olympian detachment[*] . . . more than 150 Labour M.P.s have now signed an Early Day Motion saying that King must be sacked from the N.C.B.' 'There was to be a meeting of the Coal Board to meet . . . nine M.P.s who are members of the N.U.M.[†] and two peers,' wrote King the following day. 'I was met at the door of Hobart House by the publicity man of the Coal Board who told me the M.P.s would walk out if I attended. In spite of this, Robens would prefer me to come, which I did. The M.P.s, a sorry-looking lot, then walked out. As a result I had a long talk with Alf, who is in good form and delighted with my piece.'

'What a stroke of luck Cecil King has been to Harold,' reflected Crossman the same day:

As one Tory put it, he was the only flaw in a perfect day of Tory victory news last Friday. At once he provided the positive factor required for rebuilding Harold's reputation. This was confirmed to me when Alma Birk[**] rang me up in the greatest distress to tell me how terrible life had been, that the directors were now all working together to try to get rid of Cecil King, that her husband, Ellis, who had been in Paris was now considering whether he should resign from the *Mirror* board and that she had persuaded him to stay on and fight the King influence. She also told me that 98 per cent of the letters which the Daily Mirror and the Sun had received were pro-Harold.[‡]

The growing public perception, as a Wilson biographer put it, was of Wilson 'triumphing over a self-inflated and illegitimate opponent'.[67]

---

[*]   'JENKINS SWATS THE CECIL KING GADFLY' would be the view of *The Times* the next day; 'KING-SIZED REBUFF,' said the *Daily Mail*; 'Judging from the unusual cheerfulness of Labour backbenchers yesterday . . . you might almost have thought Mr King had sacrificed himself in the interests of party morale,' commented the *Guardian*.

[†]   National Union of Mineworkers.

[**] Journalist and Labour politician and from 1967 a life peer.

[‡]   According to a *Mirror* internal report on 18 May, there were eventually only 200 letters about King's article, of which two-thirds were pro-Wilson.

Despite the vicious press coverage, the failure of the great and good to back him and the almost total absence of public support of any significance, King did not doubt his own judgement. To one of his few supporters, the MP Desmond Donnelly, recently expelled from the Labour Party, he wrote:

> At present I am assuming a fresh financial crisis that will bring the Government down. There would probably be no time for a General Election, so there would be an Emergency Government – at first perhaps Labour, but soon widened to include Tories and others. Roy might well, under these circumstances, go down with Wilson. In any case he is too weak to last. Denis Healey would do the job better, but he is not liked on either side of the House . . . A General Election would result in the destruction of the Labour Party, a huge Tory majority and the official Opposition might be Scottish Nationalists. I doubt whether a Government of such a character under conditions of crisis would work. I think Heath would soon find himself in the same situation as Wilson does now.[68]

The negative press coverage rumbled on; on 22 May Francis Williams commented sadly that 'Uncles Alfred and Harold . . . Harmsworth have finally taken over in Holborn Circus and not all of King's horses and all of King's men are going to find it easy to put Cecil together again, although many of them are now trying desperately hard to do so.' It was too early to say what damage King had done to Wilson or to the country, but 'what he had most certainly managed to do is to revive among politicians of all parties dying suspicions of personal newspaper power arbitrarily exercised'. Someone should 'take Mr King by the arm and persuade him that "enough is enough" for publishers as well as Prime Ministers'.[69] *Private Eye*'s front cover consisted of a statement from 'Cecil Harmsworth Gnome' that 'A new Prime Minister is needed to lead the nation on the road to recovery. It is not for me, a mere lunatic, to suggest who that man should be. Suffice it to say that he should be none other than myself.' Inside, in its spoof 'Mrs Wilson's Diary', Mary Wilson answered the phone to a giggling caller who said he was Lord Northcliffe:

'I draw your attention to today's *Mirror*,' said the voice. 'I have spoken. Let the people tremble. My car is at the door, and I will take up residence later in the day at Number Ten. The eagles are flying high.' 'Is that you Mr King?' I queried, recognising the speaker's Wykehamist tones and fleshy chuckle. 'Cut out the Mister,' replied the Press Lord, 'my destiny is accomplished. I am the seven-eyed Beast of the Apocalypse.' At this the line went dead, and a few minutes later Mr King rang back to apologise, saying he had had another of his turns, and that they were getting more frequent recently.[70]

Also damaging to both King and the *Mirror* was a letter to the *New Statesman* by Lord Wigg, a senior Labour figure, congratulating an *Evening Standard* diarist on 'his challenge to what he calls "the implicit acceptance of the myth" that it was Cecil King and not the late Harry George Bartholomew who produced and perfected the journalistic formula which made the Mirror our largest-selling daily newspaper'. The Edelman history of the *Mirror*, Wigg continued, 'it seemed to me, was a build-up for the living Cecil Harmsworth King at the expense of the long-dead Harry George Bartholomew – a friend of mine whose honesty of purpose leaves a memory which I still cherish'.[71] Wigg devastatingly drew attention to the doctored quote from A. J. P. Taylor that showed both Edelman and King in such a demeaning light.

This had been a terrible period for IPC editorial and management alike. Senior *Mirror*-group journalists and editors feared their relationship with the Labour Party was near to collapse. Aneurin Bevan's widow, Labour icon and Chairman of the party, Jennie Lee, had pinpointed well the damage King was doing the paper in the eyes of the party membership: 'The *Daily Mirror* sometimes seems to be a friend and ally, but this is a kind of mirage. What is now plain is that its relationship with the Labour Government is that of a Trojan horse – it likes to be within the gates, but within the gates to ensure that Socialist principles are not put into practice.'[72] 'There are no enemies of the party at the *Daily Mirror*,' a distraught Alma Birk had told Crossman three days after King's article. 'Alma's terrified female social agony about the clanger King had dropped was a tremendous revelation,' he commented. 'The one thing the *Mirror* doesn't like is failure or being made to look silly and this is what King had done for them over the weekend.'[73]

There had been some protests at a board meeting on 14 May after King told the story of the MPs' walk-out at the Coal Board, 'and,' according to Ellis Birk, 'treated it as a joke':

> Hugh then said that he considered it to be a very serious incident in relation to the *Daily Mirror*. I then said that as he had written his article as Chairman of IPC I must dissociate myself from it, since I considered it irresponsible and damaging to IPC and the *Mirror*. I debated with him shortly on the subject of 'lies' and 'the financial crisis'. The purpose of this was to make some sort of protest, without causing an immediate bust-up: too many Directors were absent.[74]

Afterwards Don Ryder, whom King had recently installed in his place as Chairman of Reed (which bored him), complained to three colleagues:

> that as a commercial operator he was being placed in an impossible position by C.K.'s outbursts: how could he have serious and continuing discussions with Government departments with this immediate background?[75] . . . There is a deeply disturbed feeling around and this incident has helped powerfully to crystallise views about the future – and the near future at that! Hugh now accepts from me the proposition that he must be in the van if and when any action is taken.[76]

So 'Enough is Enough' – though not the cause – provided the opportunity for King's removal. Birk, Pickering and Rogers, all of whom greatly liked King but believed he was on his way to ruining the company, were prime movers in nerving Cudlipp to wield the dagger. At the weekend he walked with Jodi round and round the garden of their Barnes cottage, talking about King and answering questions that he posed himself. 'You don't have to say anything,' he said. 'You don't have to answer anything.'

Once he made up his mind, Cudlipp was ruthless in winning over the directors and efficient in organising the method of despatching

King. 'I made these conditions: first, that any director I saw would be seen in the presence of another director and never the same one; second, that during the inquiry the question of succession was not brought up by anyone at any time: third, that any views expressed by any director, before any two other directors – one of whom was me – would have to be repeated before all other directors', and 'that I would be in sole charge of the tactics. Once the decision was made there could be no second thoughts.'[77]

It required only a majority vote to remove the Chairman of IPC, but Cudlipp knew that to leave King as a director was not an option: 'a King who is no longer king could scarcely be expected to behave as a constructive courtier under a new regime and monarch.'[78] He knew also that the break had to be clean and final. King had liked to deal with his directors in chats by his fireside, one to one: this time they had to present a united front and yield no ground:

> A request to depart in three months' time, or in six months, or even in a year would have been received with amused contempt, and any notion that the matter could be amicably resolved at a board meeting in the presence of the Chairman could only be suggested by Cecil himself or by somebody who had never met him. Nor could I or others accept that a man who unilaterally announced staying on until seventy in spite of his own rule about retirement at sixty-five would be likely to consider a second opinion on the same matter two years later.[79]

As he organised King's overthrow, Cudlipp had to maintain normal relations with him and deal with the political rumour-factory that was feeding on Cabinet dissension and paranoia. 'I have been informed by top-level ministerial sources,' Birk had told Rogers, 'that they consider this episode to emanate from C.K.'s megalomania and that no one else at IPC is tainted by it, although it is recognised that Hugh must have been involved.' A week later, at a drinks party given by the Chancellor, Wilson was friendly, telling Cudlipp that 'My problems are only Queen-size. I preferred the literary style of the Monday editorial ("No Vendetta") to the Friday piece ("Enough is Enough")', while Crossman told Cudlipp in the hearing of a dozen or so people that 'Cecil is a fool; a Wykehamist should know better. Doesn't he understand? We'll never get rid of the little man now. Cecil's attack is Harold's insurance policy. He's given him security for life.' Cudlipp was unnerved by a glare from Mary Wilson and by the very audible advice given on the doorstep by the *New Statesman* Editor, Paul Johnson, that 'It is time you got rid of King. He is turning the *Mirror* into a proprietor's newspaper.' 'Cudlipp looked startled,' Johnson recalled later, 'as well he might; by then the putsch must have been in its final stages of preparation, and any leakage could – indeed must – have been fatal. But the secret was kept.'[80]

A meeting of the entire board – with the exception of the Chairman – was discreetly called for 29 May: a few days beforehand Jocelyn Stevens was at a dinner party where Birk and Cudlipp were talking 'cold-bloodedly' about getting rid of King. It sounded to him like loose chatter, until he was drawn aside and told, 'We really mean this – and we're going to do it on Thursday.'[81] Frank Rogers's wife, who was very fond of King, was so appalled when she learned of the plans to oust him that she even threatened to tell him what was going on. And Paul Hamlyn – whose publishing firm had been bought by IPC in 1964 for £2.25 million*, who headed the Corporation's book division, owned ten times as many IPC shares as all the other directors put together and greatly liked and admired King – was most reluctant to see him overthrown.

As the Kings dined *à deux* in his private dining room before going to a concert, the directors were in another part of the *Mirror* complex. Having failed to persuade anyone to join him in saving the man he 'adored', Hamlyn 'succumbed to the united pressure of the other directors. "I felt pretty ashamed," he admitted later.'[82] Cudlipp would afterwards authenticate the account given to *The Times* by an anonymous participant: 'every director expressed the view that Mr King should go. They made their point, it is said, with dignity, reluctance and a genuine feeling of sorrow for the man who had given so much of his life in the service of the group.' Then each one of them signed this letter:

---

* About £27.5 million today.

May 29 1968

Dear Cecil,

I have been instructed to inform you by letter of some decisions which have been reached by all your IPC colleagues.

They were reached with great reluctance, and solely in what all believe to be the long-term interests of the Corporation. It is also fair to you to say that the views increasingly expressed by directors over the past year or so had reached a stage where a discussion among ourselves could no longer be postponed.

The feeling is that your increasing preoccupation and intervention in national affairs in a personal sense rather than in the more objective publishing sense has created a situation between you and your colleagues which is detrimental to the present and future conduct of the business of IPC.

It has been decided that the retirement age for Chairmen of the IPC should be sixty-five, in keeping with the rule laid down by you for all other directors; that you should therefore retire immediately as Chairman.

It has also been decided that I should succeed you as IPC Chairman.

The decisions were unanimous on each point, and I enclose the formal request for your resignation signed by all of your co-directors in accordance with the provisions of the Articles of Association of IPC.

It is also the wish of the directors of IPC that you should simultaneously resign as a director of the Reed Paper Group.

It is the desire of every one of us that in any announcement we pay full and very genuine tribute to your tremendous contribution to the expansion of the company during your seventeen years as Chairman.

Our view, again unanimous, is that the best course would be for you to announce your resignation tomorrow, Thursday.

Three of us who have worked with you for many years – myself, Frank Rogers and Don Ryder – will be ready to see you together on Thursday morning at IPC to discuss the appropriate next stage. The decision of your co-directors was that an announcement should be made as early as possible on Thursday.

Sincerely,

Hugh Cudlipp[83]

It was Cudlipp's idea that the Company Secretary should deliver the letter by hand to King's house early the following morning. Birk was not happy about this, believing, rightly, that this method would be widely seen as both brutal and cowardly. But Cudlipp insisted, for he had never forgotten that at the 1956 dinner where King told him he was 'making alternative domestic arrangements', he had also said that 'during periods of frustration and unhappiness', he often thought of suicide: '[that confidence] weighed deeply with me on the night we were deciding just how Cecil's dismissal should be imparted to him. A letter affording him the opportunity for discussion with Dame Ruth would be less "spectacularly brutal" than a sudden announcement on the ninth floor of a building towering over Holborn Circus.'[84] 'The intention was to give him the opportunity to ponder, discuss the situation with his wife, in whose judgement he had abounding faith, and resolve his attitude before he came to the office at, I guessed, the normal scheduled time. It would be impossible to forecast Cecil's reaction to the dismissal, but it would be unlikely to upset his programme; nothing ever had.'[85]

When later that morning Cudlipp, Rogers and Ryder apprehensively sat in front of King's desk, Cudlipp opened by asking for his reactions. Was he prepared to resign? There was a long pause, 'with Cecil's eyes focused firmly and accusingly on me:

Frank Rogers, sitting on my right, broke the silence: 'I would like to say, Cecil, that –' (King's head turned slowly to Frank to give him the benefit of the formidable glare I had received for the previous minute) 'all your colleagues hold you in high esteem and affection. You should not doubt this. We have done what we think is right for the Corporation, and that is our duty as directors. But the affection . . .'

Cecil King: An odd way of showing it.

There was another long pause, and the beam from the lighthouse turned again on me. 'Resign? Resign today? Certainly not.

It would look as if I had been found with my hand in the till. Certainly not.'

Pause.

Cudlipp: I'm sorry you take that view, Cecil. You leave me with no alternative but to go back and consult the board.

King: You can go and consult anybody you like.

Pause.

It seemed to me, nevertheless, that he had not yet said his ultimate piece and had carefully considered in advance just what he would say and when he would say it. That was his style.

Don Ryder spoke next, as the glare revolved accusingly to him: 'I would like to say something that Hugh will probably not say himself, but I think should be said. You should know that this is in no way, and has not at any time been, a revolt led by Hugh against you.' Don said more on these lines, but the expression on Cecil's face was not encouraging to a dissertation on the subject of loyalty.

'I think,' said King, 'we have had enough insincerity for one morning.'

Cecil then turned to me with the same matchless slow motion: 'If you wish to say to me that the time has come for me to go, I don't want to outstay my welcome. Far from it. In two or three months' time, or something like that . . .'

Pause.

Cudlipp: I will discuss this suggestion with our colleagues and, of course, will let you know within an hour or so what their reply is. Will you be in the office all day?

Cecil, opening his arms in a gesture of lofty patience and a hint of resigned boredom, said, 'I am at your disposal'.

Later he was asked by a newspaper whether the meeting was cordial. 'Well,' he said, 'you could hardly say it was riotous.'[86]

The trio were agreed that they would resign rather than see a stay of execution, convinced as they were that, rather than organising his retirement, King would 'conduct a subtle campaign to dominate his colleagues one by one, selecting first the weakest or most emotional or most gullible, and to hold rigidly and triumphantly to his original intention to retire at seventy and not a day, or an hour, or a minute sooner'. The directors met again and unanimously agreed to fire King and organise meetings for 5 p.m. at which they would tell the staff. A second letter went to King in the early afternoon:

> May 30 1968
>
> Dear Cecil,
>   Frank Rogers, Don Ryder and I reported back to all members of the board after our discussion with you this morning. All your remarks were conveyed in full.
>   The unanimous view of the board is that the decisions which were made last night cannot be revoked or altered in any way.
>   The letter of request which was delivered to you this morning stands. Accordingly, therefore, you have ceased to be the Chairman and a director of IPC.
>   An announcement will be made later today.
>   All the directors regret that the announcement cannot, as things stand, be made in the form of a resignation.
>   Sincerely,
>   Hugh Cudlipp

King rang his son Francis, still a director of Fleetway, and told him he wanted Francis to be the first to know that he had been sacked:

> Francis said he was very sorry but asked, courageously, was his father really surprised? 'Why do you say that?' King asked. Francis explained that as his father had chosen to resign from the board of the Bank of England owing to his involvement in political activity it was not altogether surprising if the directors of a public company also felt it was inappropriate for their chairman to be so heavily involved in a political campaign. 'They never told me that,' said King.[87]

Not even Cudlipp had predicted what King would do next: 'I rang up B.B.C. News and ITN[*] and told them I had been dismissed and

---

[*] Independent Television News.

wished to appear on the six o'clock news . . . ITN then interrupted a showing of one of the Epsom races to put out the fact that I had gone – and this was how the *Mirror* staff, including the editor, learnt that I was out';[88] 'down-the-line communication,' wrote Cudlipp, 'so noble a concept among middle management at seminars, took another nose-dive'.[89] IPC issued a brief statement confirming that King was no longer Chairman or a director and that Cudlipp had been unanimously elected in his place.

'Sensational news' was Tony Benn's assessment in his diary. It was particularly sensational to all those people who assumed that King – who for years had spoken publicly of 'my editors', 'my newspapers' and 'my publications' – actually owned IPC.

His 'huge face saddened into a bloodhound look,'[90] King told Reginald Bosanquet of ITV that his dismissal was 'a counter-attack by the Labour Party members of the board' to an article that had in fact been written with the agreement of Cudlipp and the editors. Had he put up a fight? 'There is nothing to be done about it. If your colleagues ask you to go, you go.' Were he and Cudlipp still friends? 'I should have thought there was a certain chill about our relationship today, wouldn't you think?' 'Can you think in your own career of anything parallel, that you might have done to someone else?' 'Well, I removed my predecessor, Mr Bartholomew.' Who were the Labour members of the board? 'I should think Mr Cudlipp and Mr Ellis Birk would play a leading part in that. Mr Ellis Birk has been a devoted Socialist all his life, his wife was made a life peeress . . . I would have thought those two would be the most politically minded, and would be anxious to turn the paper back to a warmer attitude to the Labour Party than had been apparent lately.' Would there be anything in the company's preliminary accounts – due to be published the next day – 'which might indicate why the company is dissatisfied with you, apart from – as you say – the political aspects of your behaviour?' 'Well, the accounts as everybody knows are going to be unsatisfactory. But I have no particular responsibility. There are certain areas of the company doing less well than we hoped earlier in the year . . . I just think it is interesting that the *Daily Mirror* and Mr Cudlipp will now presumably switch over to the support of the Labour Party just in time to nail his flag to the mast of the ship as it goes down.' 'Do you see the Prime Minister's hand in this particularly?' 'Oh, I should have thought not.'[91]

The second TV transmission ended with a comment from Cudlipp on King's suggestion that he had been dismissed as a Labour counter-attack: '"The most endearing aspect of Cecil's complex character was always his Irish sense of humour." Those fifteen words were the single statement I made during the fracas: it seemed fairer and wiser to leave the public entertaining to Cecil.'

'What,' asked the BBC interviewer of King, 'does it feel like now to be on the receiving end?' 'Well, I hope I have treated the people I have dispensed with with more courtesy than I received in my turn.' 'You have had no feeling of courtesy today? The actual announcement, really, is quite pleasant – it pays tribute to you. Are you suggesting this was done in a rather dirty fashion?' 'Oh no, not dirty fashion, but the first warning I had was when I was shaving this morning . . .'

Did Cudlipp's promotion mean that he was a Wilson supporter? 'Oh, I don't think so, no; for some considerable time he has been a Roy Jenkins supporter.' 'Really? So are we likely now to see a line in the *Mirror* supporting Jenkins, and continuing to criticise Mr Wilson personally?' 'I should have thought not too openly promoting Mr Jenkins – might be damaging to Mr Jenkins – but the underlying idea is certainly that, yes.'[92]

'Cecil described the letter as "curt",' reported Cudlipp:

> which it wasn't, and made much of the point in his marathon television appearances that he received it while shaving, as if that denoted some macabre or sinister intent; one has to be doing something or other between eight and nine a.m. . . . In private [his] mood was icy anger, in public buoyant truculence . . . In most of his off-the-cuff reactions he behaved with restraint and disdain, even with wry humour, but not initially with abuse or recrimination: that came later. The philosophical attitude hardened as he built up an impressive indictment.[93]

The press coverage the day after the sacking was lavish, gleeful, yet sympathetic and full of inaccurate details about who was responsible and why. As the *Guardian* pointed out, while an ex-director of the Bank of England flailing against Harold Wilson was in danger of 'finding himself like Desmond Donnelly, a small bored paragraph on page 19', the way 'back to the banner headlines was to get the boot'. The *Express* had a scoop:

> As she waited anxiously at home last night, Mr King's wife, Dame Ruth Railton, said: 'I am proud to stand beside such a man. I think anyone who puts his country and its needs before himself and his office is a man of great courage.'
>
> Dame Ruth . . . was waiting outside the big iron gates of her Thames riverside home . . . She went on: 'What my husband did was not a petty personal attack on one man, but was for the good of the country. He doesn't count the sacrifices he has had to make.'
>
> But she added: 'This certainly isn't the end of the road at all. It might be the end of the newspaper road but there are many other things than that.'
>
> It was the cook's day off and Dame Ruth had prepared dinner herself. 'My husband is half an hour late, and I've burnt the toast,' she confessed.
>
> Mr King held several directorships. 'But I don't know if he has got any jobs left. There wasn't time to ask him this morning,' said his wife cheerfully.

The story ran strongly abroad too: 'LION OF FLEET ST JUNGLE FELLED,' said the *New York Post*; 'KING OF FLEET ST IS DEPOSED', the *Melbourne Herald*; 'BRITISH PRESS MAGNATE OUSTED', the *East African Standard*. During that day, as King sat in his suite dictating responses to telegrams and letters, holding meetings 'to tie up loose ends' and planning what possessions were to go where, Cudlipp was holding his first board meeting as Chairman, after which IPC reported a 33 per cent fall in profits and a cut in its dividend from 21 per cent to 18 per cent. Next day the *Financial Times* commented that IPC had been an unrewarding investment over the previous five years. 'For a Harmsworth,' observed one journalist, 'it was a mortifying conclusion to a brilliant newspaper career.'[94]

Helped by off-the-record briefings, the general press consensus came swiftly to be that King had been fired for managerial rather than political reasons, though there were those who thought Wilson had been involved.[95] And there was much happiness at Westminster, where the *Guardian* reported that 'it was in sunshine all the way. Ministers were asked time and time again "Will you recognise the new Republican regime?" The word for it all was glee, unmitigated schoolboyish glee – a giant toppled from his beanstalk.' Michael Foot was one of the Labour MPs who celebrated with a motion headed 'For King and Cudlipp', which called on the House to wish King a long retirement uninterrupted by the demands of public service and urged Wilson not to appoint Cudlipp as a director of the Bank of England.

King clung to the explanation for his dismissal with which he could live: 'I was stabbed in the back for my views,' he told a *Sunday Express* interviewer,[96] 'but I will not retract a single one. Harold Wilson is leading this country into a financial crisis and he must go. I was fired because I wrote that, but what I said will come true, mark my words.' King was interviewed 'on the sun-drenched banks of the Thames outside his seventeenth-century home near Hampton Court', in a tweed jacket, shirt and tie on his knees, weeding.

Cudlipp, that same day, was photographed in the *Observer* in a jumper and shirt in the living room of the Sonning bungalow: 'a home for Mr Polly rather than Tiberius'. The new Chairman was so determined to be circumspect that, as the interviewer arrived at 8 a.m., Cudlipp was dictating quotes to Jodi: 'When my name was proposed as Cecil's successor at a formal meeting,' was one, 'I offered to retire from the room so that a free discussion could take place. I was told that was quite unnecessary: then I was unanimously appointed.'* 'Away from Jodi's typewriter,' commented the interviewer, 'Mr Cudlipp's manner is friendly, but no longer – in the *Mirror*'s favourite epithet – "outspoken". Will the *Mirror* once more support Mr Wilson? Mr Cudlipp ponders. "I think policy should be based on events, full point. Let us wait for events to happen, colon: I would never be guided by preconceived notions or personal considerations, full point. If I were to make a statement about politics, I'd be removed from the chairmanship, end quote."'[97]

---

* 'The one thing that amazes me', said Frank Rogers later, 'is that we did all allow him to take it on. But there was the feeling certainly with me that he'd done hugely good work in the company brilliantly over the years and if he wanted it, well, let's give him a go.'

The *Sunday Times* interviewer, who met Cudlipp in his office, was similarly struck by his habit 'of practically subbing *your* copy before it's out of *his* mouth . . . "Right then, get this down. Open quotes. I've the greatest personal admiration for Cecil King. He taught me the larger view of publishing . . . He taught me to plan five or 10 years ahead instead of thinking only about what is happening tonight – and that's something they don't teach you in Cardiff."'[98]

The directors had anticipated that King 'would go flat out to win all sympathy against his ruthless, heartless colleagues', and there was certainly a feeling in many quarters that they had been unnecessarily brutal. In the City, commented a *Sunday Telegraph* journalist a week later, '*schadenfreude* at the great man's discomfort' had given way to 'disgust and disquiet about the whole affair . . . the manner of Mr King's dismissal, the backstairs intrigue, the Board which apparently lacked the guts to confront their man or to vote him out except at a secret meeting to which he was not invited'.[99] It was an accusation the injustice of which caused Cudlipp much anguish; he was comforted by a column in the *UK Press Gazette* written by Colin Valdar, once the Editor of the *Pictorial*:

> In his forty years in newspapers he [King] has pruned good colleagues – John Coope (vice-chairman, after 37 years with the *Mirror*, at the time King overthrew chairman Harry Guy Bartholomew), James Cooke (the financial architect of growth from *Mirror* into IPC), Philip Zec and many more – when he thought their season was over. And he did it with no less brutality than he has just endured. He didn't invent the technique: but he was an experienced exponent.[100]

What made Cudlipp incandescent, though, was the result of a hare started by a television journalist when he suggested that Sir John Ellerman, IPC's largest single shareholder, probably had 'an important part to play in this whole thing'. Next day the *Daily Mail* was trailing Ellerman as 'one of the prime movers behind the scenes', and *The Times* said that Birk was his representative on the board. Ellerman had been the subject of paranoid speculation during the war at the height of trouble between the government and the *Mirror*, until it emerged that he owned only 150,000 shares out of a total of 5.6 million; in 1968 he had a similarly small but significant shareholding in IPC – as he had in thousands of enterprises – and impinged not at all. Birk was legal adviser to the Ellerman business, but scarcely knew him and was not, and never had been, his representative on the board. But he and Ellerman were Jews.

Once Birk denied the story, it died. Yet in Cudlipp's memoirs he reported there had been 'a monstrous fabrication' alleging that King 'had been kicked off the Board because leading British financiers were worried at his criticisms of the British economy and that "Jewish bankers" had paid out £2,500,000 in bribes, presumably to some or all of the directors of IPC to get rid of him . . . No newspaper, creditably, reported or commented upon this psychopathetic gossip.'[101] What made this so particularly preposterous, as Cudlipp pointed out, was that King had become evangelical about the contribution of Jews to the British economy: the only article he ever signed in the *Mirror* before 'Enough is Enough' was about twelve Jews whom he considered to be shining examples of industrial leadership: 'nobody I ever met was more pro-Semitic than Cecil'.

What Cudlipp was too discreet to disclose in his memoirs was that the purveyor of this monstrous fabrication was Ruth.[102]*

---

* That Ruth had Jewish friends and colleagues in the musical world makes this even more baffling.

CHAPTER XII

Lord Cudlipp and Mr King

To free himself to do his new job properly, Cudlipp handed over all his editorial responsibilities to Edward Pickering: overnight, his forty-year career as a journalist came to an end. 'He takes over at a particularly difficult time in the company's history'[1] was a quote he provided to an interviewer.

IPC, observed one financial journalist on 2 June 1968, 'has always been a jam-tomorrow company ever since Cecil Harmsworth King stitched it together five years ago . . . Mr Cudlipp will have to demonstrate pretty quickly and pretty conclusively that he knows how to open that jam-pot'.[2] 'The new chairman is a brash extrovert and a journalist of high ability,' wrote John Gordon, 'though he failed with Mr King's magazines and The Sun. He now faces harsh, difficult and different problems. Far wider than merely journalistic ones. He will need a stout heart, cool judgment, and a touch of genius to carry him through the testing times ahead.'[3]

Cudlipp's immediate task as Chairman was to deal with the loose cannon that was his predecessor; his most urgent was to calm City nerves about IPC; and his most important thoroughly to reorganise the dishevelled empire he had inherited.

The King broadsides were met with tact and generosity. IPC spokesmen stressed the debt owed to him and the affection in which he was held. He was given as much time as he liked to clear his office[*]

---

[*] 'When Dame Ruth dramatically told the Guardian "He has to have all his things cleared up by today,"' said Cudlipp, 'she was misinformed or misquoted.'

and was lent his company Rolls; he was allowed to keep his Reed directorship until the end of the year when, he said, he had always intended to resign, and during that period had a room in the Reed building on Piccadilly.

The only IPC director to visit him in his new office was Paul Hamlyn,* some weeks later: 'Cecil King swivelled his chair around so that his back faced his visitor and said nothing. Hamlyn stood there for nearly an hour and finally said, "Look, Cecil, this is as difficult for me as it is for you."'4 'He was in a very emotional state', recorded King, 'but evidently regards me with affection . . . [he] said that if he hadn't signed the document he would himself have had to go.'5 Their friendship was resumed. Ryder was the only other director whom King forgave and continued to lunch with, since he and Ruth had convinced themselves that this leading assassin was a reluctant conscript.

Early in June, King and Cudlipp civilly discussed the forthcoming IPC Annual General Meeting: if attacked, said King, 'you can count on me to defend myself'. But, he added, 'a slanging match between us wouldn't help anybody and certainly wouldn't help IPC. We would both be too good at it.'6 'As I was chairman of I.P.C. for the whole period covered by the accounts,' he told Cudlipp in July, 'I think it appropriate that I should make a brief speech . . . So I am writing to ask you to provide an opportunity in the course of the proceedings. My remarks might take ten minutes: they will be polite & they will be factual.'7 Cudlipp sent King in advance the text of what he would be saying about him and promised that he would have no difficulty in 'catching the Chairman's eye'.8

Other than the occasional interview and two articles in the *Financial Times* warning that the danger ahead was as great as that faced by the country in 1939, King had been largely out of public view; now he enjoyed teasing the press about what he intended to do at the AGM. 'I shall be there and I will make a speech. I shall certainly not be there to talk about the weather.'9

---

* One of the Jewish entrepreneurs whom King so admired, Hamlyn went from barrow-boy to publishing multi-millionaire. Known to be 'chillingly ruthless' in business, he became a great benefactor of the arts and ended his career as Lord Hamlyn.

He arrived early and 'strolled cheerfully through the shareholders shaking hands and exchanging greetings'.[10] When Cudlipp arrived, 'Cecil, flanked by the stalwart Dame Ruth[*], was already prominently seated in the front row, peering at the ceiling or glancing impassively at the excited people around him, a figure of calculated calm awaiting his moment'. He left his seat briefly to lean across the table and have a word with Cudlipp about timing and thus gave photographers the picture of their dreams.

Cudlipp welcomed King; read out in full the letter asking him to resign; spoke of the 'high respect' in which he was held; denied it was 'a political upheaval' caused by his *Mirror* article (cries of 'Rubbish' and 'Nonsense'); pointed out that only one member of the board was a member of the Labour Party; confirmed that he had agreed with King's criticisms of Wilson's administration, while regarding his dire prophecy about the economy as 'personal'; reiterated that the problem lay in 'the quantity, the pre-occupation, the personal intervention in national affairs'; took responsibility with all other directors for the decline in IPC profits; reported that King had received a compensatory payment of £35,000[†] – a year's salary – in addition to full retirement benefits; and invited him to address the meeting ('Acclamation').[11]

Despite King's early conviction that he had been sacked for political reasons, as early as 8 June he had decided that 'obviously Cudlipp wanted my job'[12] and was already predicting that he would fail. Malcolm Muggeridge, he noted in his diary, liked Cudlipp, 'but thinks him a weak man, quite incapable of holding his job as chairman of I.P.C., from which Muggeridge expects him to be ousted within a year'.[13] King had 'pondered a long time over what to say' at the AGM 'and decided to say it without notes. It is easier in this way to be forceful and to put one's views over'. His account of events was simple:

> Very briefly I told the shareholders, of whom there were about seven hundred, that the fall in profits was mostly for reasons out of our control, but part was within; that I had made certain provisions for the management of the corporation after my retirement

---

[*]   And with Priscilla in the audience.
[†]   About £360,000 today.

and these were not altogether successful; and finally told them exactly what happened on May 29th. The meeting was clearly on my side and I had a wonderful press. My speech read well, as well as sounding good at the time.'[14]

It was much more riveting and less one-sided than that. As Cudlipp remarked, 'It would be ungenerous not to give Cecil King credit for his histrionic performance.' 'Hemlock and Molasses came intermingled,' commented the *Guardian*. 'A genial, pink-faced figure: Churchillian slurred *s*'s coming over the amplifier',[15] King explained to the shareholders that for three years he had been testing out managers with a view to having IPC ready for his retirement. Cudlipp, Deputy Chairman ('clearly cast as the snake in the grass in Mr King's script'[16]) was 'the best popular newspaper editor in the world', but 'not really the conductor of an orchestra, which is what one expects of a chairman – he is more of a first violin, but a very good first violin'. Frank Rogers had done 'a magnificent job' in charge of printing problems in the *Daily Mirror*, but as Managing Director of IPC, 'a very much larger and more complex job', had spent too much on central services, had failed to produce enough profit from some new enterprises and had neglected to appoint a Marketing Director; he 'has not established himself as Managing Director of the Corporation; I think he may still do so; I think he should be given time'. Gordon Cartwright, the Finance Director, 'the third leg on which the future top management was to rest', had made various blunders – including unreliable financial forecasting – and had 'not stood up and had I still been chairman, I would by now have taken steps to strengthen the financial team'.

To the relief of the other directors, King then turned 'to the dreary personal affairs of myself': no director had ever expressed dissatisfaction with him; had he been told at a board meeting that they wanted a new Chairman, he would have had to accept that with good grace, but they lacked the courage to do so: 'The thing was just a conspiracy of a particularly squalid kind . . . I had been a member of the staff for 42 years, a member of the board for 39 years, chairman for 17 years, and I was given three hours to clear out. I was even asked, with a piece of absolute unequalled effrontery to help them in the manoeuvre by going quietly and not telling people what had happened.'

This was, however, his 'swan song'. 'Still looking and sounding like Father Christmas at Harrods', in *The Spectator*'s view, he concluded, 'I do not propose to go on hawking my grievances round. I think it is a sorry thing that my career in Fleet Street should have ended in this rather melodramatic way, but it was not of my choosing and therefore I will sit down having first wished you all, and even the board, who have treated me, I think, particularly badly, all well. Thank you. (Acclamation).'

He 'bowed out of the jungle with the worst possible grace,' commented the *Guardian*, ' – as he himself would gleefully admit.'

To the delight of journalists, it was a rowdy meeting. Cudlipp selected the most memorable headlines:

SQUALID PLOT – CECIL KING (*Evening Standard*); MR CECIL KING'S BITTER ATTACK ON IPC BOARD (*Financial Times*); MR KING FIRES HIS PARTING SHOTS (*The Times*); CECIL KING SPEAKS OF 'CONSPIRACY' (*Daily Telegraph*); MR KING GROWLS HIS WAY OUT OF THE JUNGLE (*Guardian*), and on another page the *Guardian* headlined its fuller report: CECIL KING'S 'SWAN SONG' OUT OF TUNE WITH IPC'S NEW CONDUCTOR.

While King's performance was greatly enjoyed, Cudlipp also received an excellent press. The *Investor's Chronicle* thought him 'well equipped to take on the role of conductor' at the AGM: 'His patience in dealing with a series of inept questions (why is it that the lunatic fringe generally have the most to say on such occasions?), his refusal to be drawn into an acrimonious discussion about the manner of his predecessor's going, his persuasive tongue, all combined to soothe the 1,000[*] or so shareholders who crowded into the Café Royal to hear the real low down on Cecil King's sacking.'[17] Although King's criticisms of the accuracy of forecasting methods were thought rather unsettling ('CECIL KING CASTS SHADOW OVER IPC FORECASTS'[18]), the criticised directors were re-elected by an overwhelming majority ('THE GREAT REVOLT THAT NEVER WAS'[19]).

King's association with IPC was henceforward tenuous: announcing

---

[*] Estimates varied between 500 and 1,000.

that he did not intend to retire to his bathchair with his bread and milk, he went on having lunches most weekdays with diplomats, businessmen, bankers and politicians, from whom he avidly sought, and to whom he enthusiastically passed on, bad news. There were some dinners and other social events too, with Ruth gamely helping to gather and analyse information. 'Mrs [Denis] Healey was saying to Ruth the other day how wonderful it is that the members of the Cabinet have found a new unity. R. thinks the confidence being breathed around by ministers is a planned confidence trick.'[20]

'I thought when I retired that some charity would ask me to be chairman,' King said some years later. 'I was ready to be useful and no one asked me to be.'[21] He occupied himself giving talks on topics from management to Europe to ESP, giving radio and television interviews and, while there was a demand, writing dismal and rather leaden articles for broadsheets.* 'Though no longer a newspaper proprietor,' Wilson remarked laconically in his memoirs, 'he had no difficulty in finding press space for his views and throughout 1968 and the following year, even when our payments were in strong and growing surplus, he steadfastly maintained his watch for the financial doom which never came.'[22]† There were also travels abroad facilitated by the *Mirror* and meetings with influential people: General Gowon in Nigeria, Dean Acheson in Washington, King Faisal in Saudi Arabia and Georges Pompidou in Paris, whom King told the world was heading for another 1929 and that after riots in Britain the military might seize power.[23] No more than ever could King's imagination encompass the notion that Britain might, yet again, muddle through.

In France the Kings also visited Sir Oswald Mosley, four years King's senior and once leader of the British Union of Fascists. 'He

---

* Typical were 'The declining reputation of parliamentary democracy', 'Finding talent for the House of Lords' and 'Why the Labour Conference was inadequate'; he also earned £500 (about £5,000 today) a year and a car for a short time as a consultant to *The Times* in 1968/9 when it was resuscitating the idea of a coalition government.

† 'On 2 September [1969] Cecil King resurfaced with a long jeremiad in *The Times*,' Roy Jenkins wrote in his autobiography, 'saying that the universal feeling in the City was that on present policies and under the present Government there was now no prospect of ever getting the balance of payments right. But by then King's sense of timing had become almost infallibly wrong; 2 September was the exact day when hesitant balance turned into headlong surplus.'

was by far the cleverest English politician of the 1930s,' King told the *Mirror*'s horrified Peter Stephens: 'He is an extremely brilliant man and he could still make a useful contribution.' Asked if he was thinking of including him 'in your replacement government', King replied, 'Why not? People have forgotten about his past.' 'The impression left on R. by Mosley is how sensitive he is,' King noted. 'But like Enoch Powell and others in the past, he has a curious look in his eyes which comes and goes. R. thinks he has moments or periods when he is a compelling influence on others, of which he is afterwards unaware. So that when he protests that his movement was not a bullying, Jew-baiting one, he sincerely believes this and does not realise the character or misdeeds of some of his followers under his influence.'[24]

Over the next few years the Kings and Mosleys would meet to talk about imminent disasters. 'This morass in which we wallow,' King told a gathering of business economists in 1971, 'is called by its apologists the Permissive Society but morally it can more accurately be described as the Supremacy of Evil . . . Even some catastrophe is to be preferred to the slow steady decline which has been the fate of this country for so long. A catastrophe, as has been shown by the Germans and the Japanese, at least provides an occasion for reaction and recovery.'[25] 'Cecil's story was basically the same everywhere . . .' wrote Peter Stephens from Paris in 1972 to Cudlipp; 'he was cheerfully pessimistic about any subject he raised', assuring Jean Monnet, who disagreed, that Heath had little chance of getting the House to support joining the Common Market. 'Cecil explained that eventually there would be a dictator in Britain. "Perhaps not next year, but it is certainly coming because parliament is totally discredited."'[26] On that visit he and Ruth again lunched with the Mosleys. 'There is, perhaps,' proffered Cudlipp, 'a magnetic force that draws together in the barren twilight of their lives, in their loneliness and their final rejection, the Men of Destiny upon whom inadvertently or wisely destiny did not call.'[27] Certainly King's sense of helplessness preyed on him: '"Power," he told a German journalist in 1970, "is what I miss most. The feeling that millions listen to me. That I can give orders to thousands."'[28]

Enoch Powell was another Man of Destiny whom King courted and greatly liked, but as he came to doubt if there really was a role in public life for Mosley, he was agnostic about Powell's potential for national leadership, finding his personality as fanatical as his conversation was reasonable and rational.[29] However, from the spring of 1971 there was yet another Man of Destiny towards whom the Kings were drawn and whom they were convinced had the real stuff of greatness.

With the eruption in 1969 of violence, King developed a deep interest in Northern Ireland, which gradually became a crusade. Ruth was President of the Ulster College of Music; early in 1971, as she was now perforce Cudlipp's replacement as King's go-between and political confidante, she was despatched to call on the Reverend Ian Paisley, then the 'Protestant Unionist' MP, 'to urge him to see his future in an all-Ireland setting'. 'Surprisingly, she found him a warm and humble man of prayer, borne down by the burden of responsibility that he felt was laid on him by events.'[30] King took a great liking to Paisley, whom he thought a strong personality, a fine orator and a man of peace. To Paisley, a new MP who felt lost and despised at Westminster, it was both comforting and heady to be taken seriously and treated kindly by people of such status and apparent influence; the Kings would even pick him up at the airport and take him home to dinner, where he learned a great deal about how Westminster worked.

King had an impressive grasp of Irish history and politics, was often right in his criticism of vacillating British policy in Northern Ireland, and delighted his new friend with his radicalism. Utterly convinced that the future of Ireland could be settled only by Paisley and the IRA, he felt merely contempt for the middle ground of nationalism and unionism. It helped that the Kings had got to know Paisley during a brief period when he was confused and open to advice – at times wanting to keep the status quo, at others seeming to see the possibility of a federal Ireland, and then again seeing himself as a future Prime Minister of an independent Northern Ireland. 'Paisley enjoyed this surprising new friendship,' observed his biographers, 'and the chance to talk politics with someone who was on intimate terms with the most powerful men in the country.'[31] Yet Paisley was too parochial and naïve to know that while King still had access to people in power, he had very little influence.

The Provisional IRA were similarly naïve and misled. Joe Cahill, a lifelong member of the IRA and then on its Army Council, told his biographer thirty years later that 'one of the most surprising mediators was Dame Ruth Railton', whom he thought charming and intelligent. 'She was married to Cecil King, who would have been what is now called a "press baron". She had several meetings with Dave [Daithí] Ó Conaill* and myself. She had a big innings [a great deal of influence] with the British prime minister, Edward Heath. This was through classical music. He was into that in a big way and so was she.'[32]

The Kings were on visiting but not intimate terms with Edward Heath. King had been surprised to be asked to his carol service in December 1968, where Heath 'could not have been more friendly . . . There was no political talk. Ted always puzzles me. He is a nice man and an honest one. He is capable and works extremely hard, but fails to get across to the public at all. He has no understanding of politics or public opinion but then that is true of most politicians these days.'[33]

A couple of months later Heath 'rather gave me the impression of being displeased at having to lunch with me. However, he warmed up and by the end was almost communicative . . . At one point he asked what names I proposed to submit to the Queen for my Businessman's Government. I protested that the B.M.G. had never been my idea but Robens's, and the episode passed over, but it was not entirely a joke nor entirely friendly.'[34]

A civil relationship continued, but King's disillusion was growing: 'Heath is the hero of the hour,' he wrote after the surprise defeat of Labour in June 1970, 'but how long will he so remain?;'[35] the following day, the Cabinet appointments 'filled me with alarm and despondency'.[36] Heath would disappoint him in government and King would early conclude that he was a disaster (in Peter Stephens's view, 'mainly because he will not listen to Cecil's advice'), but while King wrote him off as a politician, he was always quite fond of Heath.

About Ireland, the Kings were as naïve as were their Irish protégés about their mentors. They were much influenced by 'newspaper contacts' who told them that the Provisionals 'were brave men with the interests of Ireland at heart . . . They said they could shoot Paisley any day, but saw in him a man doing his best for his constituents and his flock'.[37] In truth, the IRA appreciated Paisley's role in polarising Northern Ireland and regarded him as a heaven-sent benefactor who won them recruits every time he produced a public tirade against Catholicism or a bellow of 'No Surrender'.

---

* David O'Connell, then on the IRA Army Council.

As Paisley was hopeful that the Kings would induce Heath to ditch Brian Faulkner, leader of moderate unionism, so the IRA nurtured delusions that they could persuade Heath to promise to get out of Ireland; all were labouring under the misapprehension – still entertained today by Cahill's biographer – that King wielded tremendous political power and that Ruth was an intimate friend of Heath's who sometimes acted 'as his unofficial representative'. 'On one occasion,' remembered Cahill, 'we asked her some question which she could not answer. She said, "Hold it until I make a phone call," and she called Heath on his direct line from her house.'[38] Or pretended to. While King still expended much thought and time on other looming catastrophes, Ruth had got her teeth seriously into solving the Irish problem. 'Ruth told me when [Cecil] wasn't listening,' reported Peter Stephens, 'that she had spent two whole nights with the I.R.A. – "My Provisionals!" – drawing up a plan to solve the whole mess. She didn't go into details.'[39]

Heath did occasionally discuss Ireland with the Kings. He asked them to dinner *à trois* in August 1971, but though on this occasion King's diary suggests that he talked much more sense than nonsense, none of it made Heath change course.[40] 'Ruth had thirty-five minutes with Heath yesterday,' King recorded in February 1972. 'Ted plays with his cards very close to his chest, and anyway one wouldn't expect him to be expansive. He struck Ruth as essentially a religious man – more of a monk than a politician. He clearly has no understanding of, or acquaintance with, Ireland and the Irish.'[41] Alas for the Kings, their own understanding of Ireland was also gravely limited.

Not that King had failed to do his homework. As he showed in his brief book, *On Ireland*, published in 1973, he had an often acute grasp of the worst aspects of British policy in Ireland: apropos the Penal Laws, which discriminated against non-Anglicans: 'The laws were ferocious, the implementation of them capricious. No policy in Ireland was ever carried through to its logical conclusion'.[42] 'British governments . . . do not yield to persuasion – only to violence or the threat thereof,' was the lesson learned by the Irish over Catholic Emancipation. And in a telling few sentences with which few historians would disagree, he concluded that 'Throughout Anglo-Irish history the story is one of half-hearted coercion followed by half-hearted conciliation . . . :

If you want to see British governmental incompetence at its worst, study Whitehall from a stance in Ireland. The English were powerful enough, though not ruthless enough, to turn Ireland into a colony of helots. They were rich enough, though not wise enough, to turn Ireland into the friendliest of neighbours. So the Irish problem has bedevilled England off and on for eight hundred years and the end is not yet.[43]

There was much that ministers could have learned in conversation with King about Irish history; however his grasp on contemporary Ireland was so distorted through the irreconcilable Paisley/IRA prisms that his prescriptions lacked any sense of reality and made his judgement rightly suspect. Nor was he realistic about the options open to a British government: his penchant for authoritarianism made him incapable of understanding the inhibitions of the body politic that he had spent his life studying. So by and large, people of power and influence did not think his advice worth having.

Yet in his last years in England, King could still make a mark. *Strictly Personal*, written before his dismissal, came out exactly a year later after a great deal of what King described as 'hoo-ha'[44] following its serialisation in the *Sunday Times*. The publishers took fright after his statement that Mohammed Jinnah, the President of Pakistan, was 'obviously homosexual, and I don't like homosexuals', led to a sit-in at the *Sunday Times* office and 'all but led to the burning down of the British High Commission office in Pakistan'.[45] The baseless allegation was excised, along with the grotesquely unfair description of Beaverbrook as an evil man who turned young men into drunkards out of sheer sadism, which had distressed and infuriated Max Aitken.[46]*

Invited to speak at the Foyles Literary Luncheon in King's honour, Cudlipp declared himself to have only one special qualification: 'I am

---

* 'One of the enigmas I failed to unravel,' wrote Cudlipp in his memoirs, 'was Cecil King's loathing of Lord Beaverbrook.' The allegations about ruining young men were based on a remark of Stafford Cripps's, which King included in *With Malice Towards None*, published in 1970. In 1984, his essay in *The Beaverbrook I Knew* was a spiteful piece called 'The Evil Adventurer' and contrasted sadly with Cudlipp's honest and affectionate portrait of the best and the worst in a man he had loved.

one of the few people mentioned in *Strictly Personal* who escapes the Cecilian lash – I, who more than anybody else, might have expected nine or ten strokes of the best! I am not denounced as are the other victims of his frank pen, as a humbug, a nonentity, mean, penny-pinching, dishonest, illiterate, or buttoned-up. Nor even as a compulsive or crude womaniser. Nor even as a high-grade mental defective.'[47]

Reactions to the book were mostly bewildered ('what has Mr King got to be so disappointed about'[48]), sad (Francis Needham, who hadn't seen King for 'more than half a lifetime', was upset that Margot was ignored[49]), hostile or – in the case of the Harmsworth family – furious at what his cousin Desmond, Cecil Harmsworth's son – whose late mother King bizarrely accused of torturing animals – described in a letter to the *Sunday Times* as 'extraordinary malice' towards his dead relatives. Brutal and arresting indiscretions, appraisals and often ill-founded gossip were scattered about with casual cruelty. To the particular distress of Enid's family, although King drew heavily on her private memoirs in ways that he did not acknowledge, frank criticisms of relatives that she had never intended to be made public* were gaily attributed to her, while her compliments were largely ignored. There was no acknowledgement of any affection or kindness in his background, just an almost adolescent collection of grievances. Where Margot had tried her best to make King see the positive in people's behaviour, Ruth was pathologically bent on vilifying those she targeted as the enemy: her retrospective vendetta against the mother-in-law she never knew was waged so successfully that King expunged from his recollections all the love and clung exclusively to the hate.

Being so hard on his own mother appears to have made King think he had a licence to be nasty about everyone else's. He seemed to look on the whole thing as a joke: family protests had no effect† except when he was challenged by his favourite and formidable cousin Christabel Bielenberg. Christabel – who would always be grateful for

---

* Her reminiscences began: 'This is a private and confidential story of my childhood intended for my own immediate family only.'
† Leaving the Shelbourne 'we were greeted by Margaret Mansergh, my first cousin & one of the Wild twins,' he told Priscilla a few months after moving to Dublin. 'They were particularly indignant over what I said about their loathsome mother (& my godmother). However, last night all was apparently forgiven.'

King's crucial encouragement when she showed him the first part of her astonishing account of her life in Nazi Germany[50]* – read with anger the description of her mother: 'She was kind and friendly, but lacked brains or any sort of drive, judgement or purpose. Enid likened her to a large red jelly!'[51]

When in Ireland, where the Bielenbergs lived, King would sometimes ask them to lunch. After reading *Strictly Personal*, Christabel turned down his first invitation, but on the next occasion accepted: 'I stood in the hall of the Shelbourne and said, "Cecil, I've come to see you. I'm not coming to lunch and nor is Peter, unless you apologise for what you said about my mother." I really think he nearly exploded. Ruth grabbed my arm – it was a terribly dramatic scene and he went puce. But then he said "Chris Mary,† if it hurt you what I wrote about Aunt Christabel, I apologise deeply."'[52]

The enmity aroused by *Strictly Personal* did not in any way inhibit King. *With Malice Towards None*, an abridged version of his wartime diaries, was 'the most misleading book title since Mr Emmanuel Shinwell displayed his political scalps in "Conflict without Malice".'[53] He garnered publicity from attacking some political icons in his launch speech: Attlee was 'a miserable little drip' and Violet Bonham-Carter 'an altogether dreadful woman . . . she used to ring up Cassandra and harangue him like a fishwife'. Referring to the diary's extraordinary candour – as unsparing of King himself as it was of others – Malcolm Muggeridge mused on King's 'strange withdrawn personality':

> so alive to the action of the contemporary drama, so eager in a way to take over one of the leading parts, yet precluded by something ironic and detached in his own personality from ever finding lines to say or a role to play. A journalist by instinct, a mystic by temperament: trying to sub the Cloud of Unknowing into a

---

* In the mid-1960s she asked him to read the typescript of the first half of her book because she knew 'he would give it to me straight'. King rang her from home less than an hour later, said 'I've read it in the car coming home and if you stop writing it I'll never speak to you again' and hung up. 'It gave me great courage at a time when I needed it.'

† Her family nickname.

Cloud of Knowing. A tycoon without a balance-sheet, a seer without a message, a gossip without a club.[54]

Without Fear or Favour, a slim volume of rather dull articles, excited little interest in 1971, but the following year *The Cecil King Diaries, 1965–1970* – originally intended to be 'With Charity Towards All' – caused so much outrage that, in Cudlipp's words, 'the goodwill and sympathy Cecil enjoyed during and after "the palace revolution" were wantonly dissipated . . . I have yet to meet the articulate apologist, except King, who will attempt to explain away, or excuse, or rationalise the outrageous disclosure, without the permission or knowledge of his guests, of the private talks that took place in good faith over the dining-table with an educated and trusted host.'[*]

In Cudlipp's view, the fabric of any democratic press was based on the exchange of confidences, to such an extent that journalists chose to risk imprisonment rather than reveal their sources, but King had 'pitifully dishonoured the traditional code. Not for money which he did not need, or for notoriety which he had already achieved, or for any ideological purpose, which is customarily the defence of the spy. The decision was simply *To hell, I'll tell* . . . King told *all* in his diaries.'[55] Nor did he hesitate to show himself in a bad light, along with almost everyone else: Harold Wilson was hardly surprised to learn how disloyal were many of his colleagues, but he was horrified to discover that when King had been told in confidence the date of the 1966 General Election, he had passed the information on to Ted Heath.

King's responses to cries of betrayal were 'blandly indifferent or

---

[*] Christopher Mayhew, MP, proposed in a letter to *The Times* in November 1972, that rather than issuing disclaimers, the traduced should record for posterity their own impressions of King and conversations with him. Their first meeting had been at a banquet in the late 1950s when King asked Mayhew how his campaign against commercial television was going. 'I told him. He then said that if, which he doubted, my views ever carried weight with my party leaders, it would be necessary to start a "Mayhew must go" campaign in the *Mirror*. I replied that he could say what he liked about me in his bloody papers. From then on we sat in silence, while the fish, meat, sweet and savoury courses were served; and I have never spoken to Mr King again – wisely, as I now think. He made a most unfavourable impression on me, an arrogant and stupid man, I thought, quite unfit for power in a civilised society'.

breathtakingly bombastic', wrote Cudlipp, 'unbelievable if they had come from any other public figure':

> 'If I don't want something quoted I wouldn't say it.'
>
> 'Political commentators are so mealy-mouthed. They proceed on the well-established principle that if you scratch my back I will scratch yours.'
>
> 'In some quarters it seems to be thought immoral to take down and publish remarks made in the course of a friendly lunch. These conversations were at no time supposed to be secret.'
>
> 'How can one make a breach of confidence three or four years after the event? If I'd published the conversations the next day it would have been a different matter.'[56]

'A great hoo-ha',[57] was King's assessment in his diary, as he reflected complacently on the buoyant sales resulting from 'the torrent of abuse in the papers'.[58] Other than mentioning that various people were now being reticent over lunch, he gave little sign of being aware of the consequences of his breaches of confidence, well summed up in a Christmas poem in *Punch*:

> Hark the herald angels sing,
> 'Who will eat with Cecil King?'
> Lonely at his Yuletide board
> Glooms the uncreated lord.
> All his guests have left the hall,
> They were 'useless,' one and all.
> All that winging, all that wooing,
> No one told him what was brewing.
> Even Harmsworths need renewing
> Constantly, if harm's worth doing.[59]

The second volume of diaries, covering 1970–4, with a cast of characters gradually diminishing in numbers, importance, interest and frankness, 'was, among other things', wrote Hugo Young, 'proof that man's indomitable ego can survive even the most crushing evidence of his insignificance'.[60] Although there was some diverting gossip and interesting information on Ireland, it was dominated by King's unattractively contemptuous opinions of others and his increasingly ludicrous and dangerous predictions:

> I said we were heading for a dictatorship, either of the Right or the Left, and much would turn on the attitude of the Army. Greenhill [recently retired head of the Foreign Office] said the Army could play no part . . . I said a sufficiently ruthless man, with all the machine-guns and the power of the Government behind him, could surely be decisive. Greenhill would not agree, but when I said, 'Then you think a Communist takeover inevitable?' he wouldn't answer. He seemed to me quite futile.[61]

Not in King's diary, because it happened in the autumn of 1975, was an event that further harmed his reputation when it was made public after his death in 1987. He had been invited, as a retired press baron, by an informal dinner club of students at the Army Staff College. 'To their growing astonishment,' wrote the military historian, John Keegan, who was present:

> he devoted his talk to an apocalyptic survey of the state of Britain, in which one institution after another – Parliament, civil service, police and media – was dismissed as bankrupt of leadership. It closed with the statement that only the armed forces could save the country from chaos.
>
> I had no doubt I was listening to a treasonable attempt to suborn the loyalty of the Queen's officers. And neither did they. The Staff College course is composed of the brightest young captains in the army, noted for their ability to give lecturers a difficult time in the question period.
>
> For half an hour after King's extraordinary conclusion he was subjected to questions which began as hostile and grew increasingly derisive. King, who had clearly hoped to flatter his audience, became defensive, then irritable and finally silent. When it became clear that the chairman was not disposed to protect him from his tormentors, he rose, announced plaintively, 'I want to go home,' and left the room unescorted to find his chauffeur.
>
> His second – was it his last? – attempt to play the *caudillo* had spluttered out like a damp squib.[62]

The second volume of diaries was peopled largely by Yesterday's Men – 'has-beens, second-raters and fringe politicos', said Hugo Young, sounding as dismissive as King himself. The venomous left-winger, Emmanuel Shinwell, was one of the few who won approval: 'he is a grand little man. His theme was that he has known all the political leaders since 1903 (he is now eighty-nine) and what a miserable lot of puppets they were!'[63] It was a diary by a man whose own day had gone: as one reviewer pointed out, it was 'unlikely to cause a hoo-ha. Mr King is nothing like so near to the centre of affairs; even his obiter dicta on the press are largely hear-say. And the new heroes are few now . . . As Mr King moves off to Ireland, he tends to cast his mantle over Ian Paisley.'[64]

By the time this book came out, in October 1975, the Kings had been in Dublin for almost a year. In his review, with great empathy, Bernard Levin wrote elegiacally:

Those who figure uncomfortably and unexpectedly in his limelight will bid him good riddance: those able to take a more detached view of this book will, I think, realise that it is the work of a deeply patriotic man, who causes mischief not for mischief's sake but to warn his countrymen to take action to save themselves before it is too late, and who, concluding finally that they will do no such thing, despairs.[65]

There were other reasons why the Kings left England. First, their beautiful Wren house – The Pavilion in Hampton Court – was no longer a practical proposition. With four reception rooms, staff accommodation and 2½ acres, it was financially demanding and, since King begrudged spending money on full-time staff, he struggled with the garden and Ruth with the house.* With the publication of *Strictly Personal*, he had alienated the Harmsworths; and with the diaries, most of his friends and acquaintances. Others he had discarded himself.

---

* An undated note gives a flavour: 'My darling Love, I have left everything on the kitchen table for breakfast – even the eggs beside the pan . . . and the right amount of tea in the pot . . . I'm already in my mind on my way back, and at the moment – I'm a very unwilling departee. So here is my message of devoted LOVE and to start the day on a good note, from your "flu'ey" jaded, "nervy" wife'.

At the Foyle's lunch for *Strictly Personal* he saw John Beavan – who had written articles, speeches and lectures for him for seven years and had been one of his travelling companions – and as Beavan wrote in an obituary of King 'hissed at me that he thought my review most ungenerous. We met again a year later when his portrait . . . was being unveiled. I hoped he had got over his irritation and I approached him with a smile. King caught my eye, froze and turned away. We did not speak then, or ever again.'[66] London had become an unwelcoming and lonely place.

Convinced that Ireland would greet him with open arms, and intent on continuing their work with Paisley and the IRA, Ruth decided on emigration. Another prime motive was to keep King further apart from his children and grandchildren: none of them was well off, air fares were extremely expensive, travel by land and sea took a long time, King's awkwardness and poor hearing made telephone conversations difficult, and Ruth had chosen a house with just one spare bedroom. As King grew more isolated, it did not take long to convince him that he had been rejected by the English because of his Irishness and that his place was among his own kind – in Ruth's view, sensitive, spiritual and mystical people who would share his sense of humour. 'This book . . . is an attempt by an Irishman to explain to Englishmen why the Irish are as they are' was the opening to *On Ireland*, written by a man who had spent in total no more than a few weeks there in the previous fifty-five years.

The Kings left in November 1974, when King was seventy-three. 'I like being back in Ireland,' he told Priscilla a month later, 'but of course I am cut off from the family. Entertaining is easy. All you have to do is keep the glasses filled and they will talk all night – or until you suggest that you want to go to bed. And the talk is good. The trouble with the Irish is that they have little sense of time and no idea of organisation. So it is murder to get anything done.'[67]

Hugh Cudlipp had retired the previous year at the age of sixty. In his memoirs he looked back on the inheritance from King with which he struggled as Chairman for just five years:

In the publishing expansion, breathtaking in its speed, there was conquest without consolidation, and we became unenviably the world's biggest printers in an industry strangled by restrictive

practices. The massive mantle was King-size. It fitted Cecil perfectly, but the shareholders would have been much, much better
off with the more modest set-up in Bartholomew's will. In financial terms the *Daily Mirror*, the perennial Derby-winning racehorse, became a cruelly overburdened moke, deprived of oats
because of other hungry animals in the stable.[68]

The mantle certainly did not fit Cudlipp. Musing many years later
on what had gone wrong, Ellis Birk remembered: 'Probably when we
were both drunk in a taxi, he'd say "Ellis, you must make me a promise.
Never, never allow me to become chairman of IPC." One of the
shrewdest comments that he ever made. Finance was not his thing.
Corporate affairs not his thing.'[69] As Cudlipp himself said:

What was needed was a new mind uncommitted about past
events and utterly unsentimental, a ruthless pruner, a cold diagnostician, a steely administrator. Cecil King had built up a publishing empire mighty in size but had failed to reorganise and
rationalise it with sufficient speed . . . By moving me to a different sphere we transformed a competent Editor into an uninspired example of the sort of Chairman who was really needed
at that juncture to embrace the activities of the whole group.
What was required was not a good first violinist or even a conductor but a ruthless surgeon who would cut and cut deep.[70]

Still, 'in his first six months as chairman, Hugh was absolutely
superb', recalled Pickering. 'He went into the City and charmed every
bank. It really was a marvellous performance. I was with him on several occasions and it really was extremely good and very inspiring.'[71]
Cudlipp tried hard: 'A great deal of my time now,' he told the *New
Statesman* towards the end of 1968, not altogether convincingly, 'is now
spent on questions like diversification into the electronic processing
of information.'[72] With shareholders and institutional investors calmed,
alongside Rogers and Pickering he addressed himself to the loss-
making *Sun*, whose guarantee of existence would come to an end in
January 1970. The choices were: turn it into a tabloid (as well as technically difficult, it seemed commercially crazy to set up an in-house
competitor to the *Mirror*), amalgamate it with the *Mirror* (would have

breached the promises given in 1961 and maddened the unions), close it down (would have cost 2,000 jobs and probably closed down all IPC publications indefinitely) or sell.

In mid-1969 the IPC board flatly refused to publish the *Sun* beyond January. Robert Maxwell made an offer, but retreated in the face of commercial realities, and the paper's demise seemed certain. A *Spectator* competition provided the verse:

> O what a wond'rous thing
> Has mighty Cudlipp done!
> He who deposed a King
> Has now put out the Sun.[73]

That was written before Rupert Murdoch expressed interest.

Murdoch had begun to look seriously at English newspapers early in 1968, having for a time, as he later told a journalist,[74] been thinking: 'is Cudlipp all that damned good? You know, they all think he's God. Or is Cecil King God, or something? Maybe one could mix it over here . . . it was almost bravado.'[75] '[He has] improved since I saw him last,' observed King in December 1968. 'I have no idea why he wants the *News of the World*, though apparently it will give him greater standing in Australia.'[76] Murdoch, who bought the *News of the World* at the beginning of 1969, was concerned with much more than Australia, where he had already made a reputation as a ruthless predator.

'When Rupert Murdoch entered Fleet Street,' said Matthew Engel, 'it was as if a gunslinger had smashed open the swing doors of a Dodge City saloon and found himself staring into the snug bar of an English country pub. Everyone looked up briefly, then tried to go back to their pints.'[77] 'You cannot publish a paper for a public less educated than the readers of the *Daily Mirror*,'[78] King had said in 1964; in November 1969, Murdoch bought the *Sun* for something in the region of a nominal £60,000* and set out to prove him wrong; his crucial decision was to appoint Larry Lamb, who had served ten years on the *Mirror* and who instantly understood what Murdoch wanted.

---

* About £600,000 today.

Cudlipp had understood well the old breed of Australian news-paper proprietors, but, as one of his protégés, the Australian John Pilger, realised, 'he did not understand the younger, colourless Murdoch'. The new *Sun* came as a terrible shock; 'he knew,' said Pilger, 'he had made a ghastly mistake.' Cudlipp invited *Mirror* stalwarts to a dinner at which Lee Howard:

> spoke briefly and dutifully about the *Sun* sinking without trace in a few months' time, then sat down looking decidedly unwell. Cudlipp's performance was vintage, but equally unconvincing in one respect and deeply convincing in another.
>
> He mocked 'the dirty digger', by listing the regular features the *Sun* had stolen from the *Mirror*, 'liveliest letters' from the *Mirror*'s 'live letters', a strip called Scarth similar to the *Mirror*'s Garth* and, most contemptuous and wounding of all, the *Mirror*'s old masthead slogan, 'FORWARD WITH THE PEOPLE.' He went on to outline the *Sun*'s character and its potential, radical appeal in a climate of reaction and intolerance; the supreme journalist that Cudlipp was, he had unwittingly defined the threat which his scorn could not conceal. He had done it so well that when he had finished speaking there was no murmur of approval, just silence and foreboding.[79]

For months, according to Pilger, there was 'an almost breathless wait on the editorial floor for the arrival of the first edition of the *Sun*.' Cudlipp, who had smuggled the first nipple into a mass-market newspaper in 1937, watched in horror as the *Sun* – now a tabloid – fulfilled its new owner's desire for 'a tearaway paper with a lot of tit' and sales soared. As unerringly as the young Cudlipp had found the heart of the British public, so Murdoch found its erogenous zone.[80] 'The Murdoch competition has obliged us to lower our standards (why not admit it?),' wrote Cudlipp to King in 1971, 'but the present state of the battle is not unnerving . . . I wonder if you were right, when you said to me many years ago, that we might be wise to start a "pop" tabloid to undermine the *Mirror*? As I grow older but

---

* Garth was a handsome spaceman; Scarth a bare-breasted spacewoman.

possibly not wiser, I am inclined to think that you were right.'[81]

The *Sun* was only one of Cudlipp's troubles. 'He found the chairmanship a great weight,' said Pickering. 'He wanted to get back to putting the front page together.'[82] Though he could perform magnificently as a front-man for IPC, at home and abroad, Cudlipp was simply unequipped for the core functions of the Chairman's job. 'The troubles of IPC are well known,' commented *The Economist* in January 1970: 'the Mirror Magazine is losing more than budgeted, the price of the *Daily Mirror* cannot be put up for fear that readers will desert to Mr Rupert Murdoch's *Sun*, the women's magazines are ex-growth, and printing continues to lose money. In addition, Mr Cudlipp almost certainly prefers to write rather than to manage . . .'[83]

'He had all the wrong skills,' said Frank Rogers. 'A chairman needs to be objective and without emotion if he is to get the best out of the people round the board table and lead them to sensible decisions. Hugh was a hugely emotional person; that's no sort of background to be the chairman of a big corporation.'[84] Or, as King put it gleefully in the *Sunday Times*, 'Hugh Cudlipp is a good, popular newspaper editor but the more judicial role of company chairman is not his meat.'[85]

To the relief of his close colleagues, Cudlipp realised early on that he was the wrong man in the wrong job. Corporate vultures were gathering when, in January 1970, in a move suggested by Rogers, Cudlipp approached Don Ryder. In Bob Edwards's words, it was the second 'shock wave . . . Its impact was almost physical.' Editorial executives and management were summoned to Pickering's office:

> Pick could take the drama out of the parting of the Red Sea.
> In flat tones he announced the extraordinary news that Reed's,
> a partly owned IPC subsidiary producing newsprint and corrugated paper in its own mills, was to become the controlling company of IPC with Don Ryder, someone most of us had scarcely heard of, as chairman . . . Hugh remained chairman of IPC and became deputy chairman (editorial) of Reed. The humiliation for us was almost as great as we imagined his to be . . . Reed's balance sheet was now what mattered.[86]

Still, Cudlipp was back in his own milieu: '[He] looks a different man,' Ryder reported to King over lunch a few months later, 'and concerns himself with editing the *Mirror*'.[87] There were plenty of good working and social times with his colleagues and old friends, many of them in the pub — complete with authentic bar with beer handles and engraved mirrors, pianola and Victorian flocked wallpaper — that he and Jodi had transported from London to an old cottage in the Sonning garden. There were sociable jaunts to lunches in a Sonning pub in the red-sailed Chinese junk that Cudlipp had custom-built in Hong Kong, and expeditions in his motor yacht, which still served as a floating newsroom and from which he would still dictate many a paragraph over his radio: 'He was a pleasing sight,' wrote Bob Edwards:

> with wind against tide rounding Cap Barfleur in a Force Five, skipper's cap firmly wedged on his head, a badly-chewed enormous cigar from Lew Grade clamped between his teeth, glass of red at his side, peering through the spray for the next buoy. These voyages invariably ended at some delightful small restaurant in northern French towns like St Malo, Deauville or Le Havre, which were often the rendezvous for new members of the crew carrying bundles of the latest newspapers and gifts for the boat.[88]

Enjoyment permeated his travels, too. A classic story emerged from the visit he, Jodi and Geoffrey Goodman made to the Far East in 1973. China was still almost virgin territory to Westerners at this time and the nervous Chinese Embassy required putative visitors to undergo an induction course. Cudlipp chose Goodman, who had romantic communist leanings, to endure this on behalf of the three of them. Goodman, who at Jacobson's instigation, had fled the *Sun* after the Murdoch takeover to become the *Mirror*'s industrial Editor, had quickly become one of Cudlipp's intimates: when he was offered a safe Labour seat in 1970, Cudlipp persuaded him to turn it down on the grounds that he would have much more influence as a *Mirror* columnist than he could ever have as a back-bench MP. 'Sure, it was wonderful flattery and I succumbed, completely,' he wrote after Cudlipp's death. 'Nor have I ever regretted it. No one I have worked for in journalism ever matched the brilliance, the inspirational qualities, the real professional friendship as well as leadership of Hugh Cudlipp. Nor the capacity to bollock his friends, most of all those he admired.'[89]

The trio were staying at the Mandarin Hotel in Hong Kong just prior to going to China and, since Goodman shared Cudlipp's pleasure in the good life,[*] he was relieved that arrangements had been made to avoid too much deprivation in the land of Mao. Cudlipp was armed with a box of fifty large Havana cigars presented by Lew Grade; the *Mirror*'s local representative provided twelve bottles of Château Latour, Cudlipp's favourite wine; and the Mandarin Hotel insisted on providing a chauffeur-driven Rolls-Royce to take them to the train. As the car set off, Goodman burst out laughing: 'Well, I've often dreamed of going into the People's Republic of Red China, but never thought it would be in a Rolls Royce driven by a uniformed Chinese chauffeur, and with a crate of Château Latour in the boot!' Required to walk into China over the Lwow Bridge, they were relieved to find coolies available to carry the luggage and wine. In Peking, they were accompanied by an enthusiastic guide who was very anxious to improve his English and to whom Goodman lent a sexually explicit novel. Jodi asked him to take her to a department store and on the way he chatted about how 'Geoffley' was teaching him all the modern words in English, and had lent him a book. 'It is velly good,' he told her, 'there is fluck on every page.' On further questioning it emerged that Goodman – with help from Cudlipp – had given the guide an intensive course in polite English for foreigners, which included such colloquialisms as 'Would you like to take a piss?'

The good times could not block out the truth that Cudlipp was failing to find a formula to fight off the challenge of the *Sun*, while yet saving the *Mirror*'s soul. *Sun* circulation, which had been 800,000 when Murdoch bought it, rose to two million in 1971 and three million in 1973, while the *Mirror*'s fell steadily.[†] While Cudlipp could console himself that – *Sun* or no *Sun* – Murdoch would have started a new tabloid, it was nonetheless anguish for him to see his own failure turned into a smashing success that he despised. His beloved *Mirror* – which in 1968 had been 'Newspaper of the Year' in recognition of its superb foreign coverage – was remorselessly

---

[*] 'My kind of socialism will allow everyone to smoke good cigars, drink good wine and have a Bentley' was Cudlipp's response to those who accused him of champagne socialism.

[†] The *Sun* overtook the *Mirror* in 1978.

dragged downmarket in the wake of the *Sun*. In 1988 Cudlipp would speak with fury of how Murdoch transformed the tabloid world:

> It was the dawn of the Dark Ages of tabloid journalism, the decades, still with us, when the proprietors and editors — not all, but most — decided that playing a continuing role in public enlightenment was no longer any business of the popular Press. Information about foreign affairs was relegated to a three-inch yapping editorial insulting foreigners.
>
> It was the age when investigative journalism in the public interest shed its integrity and became intrusive journalism for the prurient, when nothing, however personal, was any longer secret or sacred and the basic human right to privacy was banished in the interest of publishing profit — when bingo became a new journalistic art form — when the daily nipple-count and the sleazy stories about bonking bimbos achieved a dominant influence in the circulation charts.[90]

'We all knew exactly what he meant,' said Geoffrey Goodman in 1998, in his obituary of Cudlipp. 'And we all understood the underlying anxiety in his own heart that he, inadvertently, might somehow have helped it into existence.'[91]

It did not take long for Cudlipp to realise he was the wrong generation to fight Murdoch; in September 1972 he wrote to Ryder that his two predecessors had stayed on too long and that he would retire the following year when he was sixty. 'So long as I am here as head editorial man the Editors will lean on me (or me on them) . . . the time is coming when they should have the opportunity of displaying their own virtues and making their own mistakes without the benefit of my leadership and judgement.'[92] His press release explained that 'our newspapers especially appeal to the younger generations, and I feel that it would be an unpardonable vanity for a man of over sixty to have the final word on editorial plans and policies'.[93]*

---

* Or, as he put it in October 1976 in the Mirror Group staff newspaper: 'I'm still a great admirer of the female breast, but I think the daily tit-for-tat battle should be conducted by the under-40's'.

In a private letter written in 1971 not long after his own retirement, Lee Howard spoke for many when he told Cudlipp:

> I doubt if you ever knew what you, personally, contributed to my enjoyment of life. I doubt if you knew that every time you went away on a trip or for a holiday, part of the fun was gone; you wouldn't be ringing up, or coming down, or calling me up to your office – and life was therefore duller and quieter . . .
>
> I now think you're the best newspaperman in our field there ever was, and I'm delighted to have worked with you and for you. When you became chairman of the group I was very much split in two; one bit of me was really proud that a journalist from normal beginnings, like me, could rise to be the head of the biggest publishing group in the world; and the other bit thought it a bloody imposition that anyone should take you away from *us* and waste at least some of your time on goddam figures . . .
>
> I could never understand why anyone was ever frightened of you, although I knew that one or two silly people were. I suppose they hadn't seen the almost absurdly kind side of you . . . I can think of no more genuine tribute to you than that, once you had told me, when we arranged my going, that you would do the best you could for me, I didn't have to worry.[94]

'The farewell parties for Hugh are now part of the Fleet Street legend,' wrote Bob Edwards, by then Editor of the *Sunday Mirror*:

> A river steamer was hired to take almost the entire *Daily Mirror* staff to a banquet at Greenwich.* By the time it arrived most were drunk on champagne. Buns and insults were hurled, but the marvel today is about the money that was spent. I decided, for Hugh's sake, to make the *Sunday Mirror* affair at the Café Royal a little less boisterous . . . I told the executives, 'Everyone

---

* An eight-page *Daily Mirror* mock-up distributed at Greenwich had a variation on the famous Khrushchev front page: 'HUGH', it said at the top. '(*If you will pardon an old familiar headline*) DON'T BE SO BLOODY RUDE! PS How dare you leave without our permission'.

can get as pissed as they like afterwards but they are not allowed to throw buns.' A large replica of his boat faced Hugh at the far end of the room, and he sat next to me giving his character reading of various colleagues. There were Board parties, IPC magazine parties, and parties in Manchester and Glasgow. If the total cost was less than £50,000* I should be surprised. It was not just a lot duller and less dangerous when he had left. The *Daily Mirror* was a lot less important.[95]

Cudlipp had always made it clear that he abhorred working journalists accepting honours that might compromise their independence, but shortly after he had announced his retirement, on the recommendation of Edward Heath (whom he had helped behind the scenes to make the Common Market case), he became Sir Hugh. In 1975, on Harold Wilson's recommendation, he became Lord Cudlipp† of Aldingbourne in Sussex, whither he and Jodi had moved with their pub, their animals and their gipsy caravan shortly after his retirement.

Cudlipp would remain too much of an irreverent *enfant terrible* ever to be able to see himself as the member of the Establishment he had become, yet his knighthood was welcomed by an enthusiastic telegram from Prince Philip[96] and his maiden speech in the Lords concerned the importance of maintaining unchanged all the traditional ceremonial of Parliament: bows, robes and all.[97] Still, he would not enjoy the Lords much, for he did not like making formal speeches and could not bear to listen to anyone else's. He would never, though, lose his appetite for speaking in public informally. 'He danced deliciously through every prime minister from Lloyd George to Thatcher,' noted the reporter of a talk that he gave to the Chichester Society when he was eighty-one. 'Mixing reminiscence with anecdote, evaluation with occasional impersonation, he delivered a lecture which

---

* About £360,000 today.

† Wilson was generous to the *Mirror*. Beavan had become Baron Ardwick in 1970 and Jacobson was ennobled in 1975. Cudlipp was ambivalent about the honour and consulted Jodi on whether he should become Lord Cudlipp. 'Your decision,' she said. 'I'm already Lady Cudlipp. All I'll get out of it is a "The".' She would later feel that the more raffish 'Sir Hugh' suited him better.

was as amusing as it was thought-provoking. Chamberlain, he recalled, was staid and starchy; Attlee, formidable but dull; Eden rich in promise, tragic in fulfilment; Douglas-Home, like an amiable tortoise.'[98]

With the help of Jodi – now chauffeur, secretary, gardener, organiser and eventually housekeeper – in a retirement that lasted a quarter of a century, Cudlipp would continue until his last few months hugely to enjoy gossip and friendship and life. He had always refused to join anything that might in any way reflect on his independence, but now joined the Labour Party,[*] the Garrick[†] and – proposed by Heath – the Royal Southern Yacht Club. In Chichester[**] he was in the thick of everything, keenly involved in the Festival Theatre and the annual festivities; new friends of the left-wing atheistical Cudlipps included cathedral canons and members of the Conservative Club. When the moral decline of the *Mirror* became embarrassing, Cudlipp would tell strangers who enquired about his occupation that he was a retired deck-chair attendant from Bognor.

The Cudlipps' relationships were without angst. They got on well with his sister Phyllis and brother Reg, and with his stepson Kerry and his family,[‡] old friends stayed close; reunions were numerous; and in Spain (where the Cudlipps bought a villa in the early 1980s), Sussex and London the gaiety was constant and shared by Jodi's mother, whose zest for life appealed to her son-in-law. Domestic enjoyment

---

[*] In 1981 he joined the Social Democratic Party, having 'waited in vain for a return to sanity in the Labour Party' and believing its espousal of unilateral nuclear disarmament and withdrawal from the Common Market to be 'disastrous for our country'.

[†] He was always utterly unapologetic about opposing women members; in Chichester he set up two all-male clubs in order to get men away from their wives – or, as he would put it, 'the girls'.

[**] In 1988 they moved into a flat beside the cathedral; they had no pub of their own, but there were two close by.

[‡] With her boyfriend, Kerry's daughter Merry was shot dead in Angola in 1992. Cudlipp was distressed, but stoical. 'With almost half the African Continent, which I know reasonably well, in turmoil of one sort or another,' he wrote in response to a letter of sympathy from Tony Benn, 'I was not over-enthusiastic about their idea of a safari for two in a second-hand Land Rover, well-equipped as it was. Apart from obvious warnings, it would be ludicrously inappropriate for an oldie to try to persuade an intelligent young woman doctor and a fit-as-a-fiddle young Army lieutenant to think up a cosier idea, like a trip to the London Zoo. They spent their last week in Europe with Jodi and me at our villa not far from Algeciras, their departure point.'

was enhanced when Jodi bought Cudlipp the parrot Bobbie, who replaced the defunct Bertie; a loquacious bird, his repertoire included 'Publish and be damned', 'No comment. Tell the press to go to hell' and 'Vino blanco seco, por favor', which was all the Spanish Cudlipp ever learned.* Even when he was terminally ill, Cudlipp would be up at 6 a.m. critically reading several newspapers and telling Jodi what was wrong with them.

There was occasional work. From 1974 to 1976 he was a member of the Royal Commission on Standards of Conduct in Public Life and in 1976 became part-time head of the Counter-Inflation Publicity Unit, set up at Harold Wilson's request by Geoffrey Goodman, who had his old boss, Sydney Jacobson, as his deputy. When Goodman was recalled to the *Mirror*, he was asked by Jim Callaghan, the new Prime Minister, to persuade Cudlipp to take on the job: Whitehall was no place for Cudlipp; its denizens failed signally to 'Get the Idea' and jump to it. After about eighteen months he found the pretext to have the unit honourably stood down and thus saved the Exchequer £1.5 million.

Seven years on, in 1984, Robert Maxwell bought the *Mirror* group and offered the seventy-year-old Cudlipp a personal consultancy which he accepted in the hope of limiting the damage Maxwell might do. For a couple of years he fully earned his annual £10,000[†] by giving at a weekly meeting and in numerous memoranda excellent advice that Maxwell rarely followed[99] – much of it to do with the importance of supporting the editorial staff, whom he refused in principle to comment on, other than positively. Conspicuously ignored was his tactfully expressed but forceful recommendation that the *Mirror* should not be festooned with photographs of its proprietor.

Being partial to engaging scoundrels, Cudlipp quite liked Maxwell and was rather embarrassed later when he discovered that he was a serious crook; it bothered him particularly that while as

---

* As Cudlipp was smuggling the parrot into a hotel en route to Spain on one occasion, a functionary asked what was under the cover. 'Books,' said Cudlipp. 'Talking books.'

† About £19,500 today; asked to name his fee, he told Maxwell he wanted to be 'your lowest-paid employee so that I can tell you most of the truth'; he deliberately asked for a sum that would not inhibit him from walking out.

a Reed pensioner his income was safe, many of his ex-staff had been
robbed by Maxwell. A press report of a lunch in honour of the
Cudlipps held by some old colleagues* in December 1991, a month
after Maxwell had died and the truth had come out, described 'a
small elderly man with bow tie and fierce white hair', who toasted
happier times and growled that the Reed group 'should never have
sold out to a man like that in the first place'.[100]

Cudlipp's main work in retirement, inevitably, was writing.
'Symphonies, concertos, operas – Beethoven, Bach, Shostakovich,
Sibelius, Schubert, Mozart, Mahler, Tchaikovsky – would blast through
the house,' recalled Jodi, 'the music silencing the parrot, trembling the
chandeliers, as Hugh sat there scribbling, scribbling, scribbling.' There
was an attempt at a play, which Jodi thought no good and persuaded
him to forget about. There were articles and plenty of correspondence[†] and, above all, there was *Walking on the Water*,** which was as
sparklingly written and affectionate about his family as King's memoirs had been flat and bitter. It was much enjoyed by reviewers for
its pace and fun, even if there were doubts about the complete reli-
ability of the ancedotes or the genuine humility of the self-criticism.
There was, of course, general fascination with the portrait of King,
which took up almost half the book and was, in truth, brilliant.
'Cudlipp is not very persuasive about Cecil King,' said Peter Preston,
who felt too much of the book was based on cuttings. 'The scantiness
of recollection is compensated for mostly by adjectives expressing fear,

---

* Bob Edwards, Geoffrey Goodman, Mike Molloy (Editor 1975–85), Marjorie Proops,
  Keith Waterhouse and Donald Zec.

† Cudlipp specialised in writing cheering letters to people on any reasonable pretext. Typical
  was that to Harold Macmillan – of whom he was very fond – in September 1973. 'I
  must write to tell you of the immense pleasure and political fun I and a good dozen
  of my colleagues on the newspapers in our group enjoyed listening to your superb performance on television on Wednesday night. We were all at the Liberal Party conference . . . Maybe we needed some political sustenance of a different brand. Anyway, I
  said: "Let's lay on a splendid buffet supper and some bottles of Latour and listen to
  Harold." I formally report on behalf of us all – Sydney Jacobson, Terry Lancaster, John
  Beavan, Matthew Coady, Victor Knight, etc., etc – that we unanimously voted it the
  best political evening of 1973'. 'My dear Cudlipp,' began the response, 'I cannot adequately tell you how much pleasure your letter has given me'.

** It was dedicated 'TO JODI AND EILEEN and all the labourers in the vineyard of Fleet
  Street, including the Proprietors and Lord Goodman' (Chairman of the NPA from
  1970–75).

pity and other suitably heroic or tragic notions. King had the hex on Cudlipp, but we never find him doing things remotely as impressively as Cudlipp did them . . . King walks off the water, therefore, curiously diminished.' But then, concluded Preston, that was probably because of the simplifying and popularising approach that 'the greatest tabloid journalist of the lot has brought to events all his life and now brings to his own life story'.[101] Paul Johnson thought the story of King was told 'magnificently . . . King's downfall illustrated the elementary truth that, if you want to play Northcliffe, you must own the equity'.[102]* Most perceptive was Sheila Black, a journalist who had greatly admired King and been 'much estranged' from Cudlipp after the putsch: 'there is much tenderness, much that shows how close these unlikely colleagues were. Their slow, painful struggle to some kind of understanding friendship, rarely if ever expressed except in laborious handwriting or occasional anecdotes told while the complimented friend was well out of earshot, comes out beautifully. The final pain and separation after the head-on collision left an obvious scar in each.'[103]

Walking on the Water scarred King further. Up to then, while the old relationship had by no means been restored, he had been softened by Cudlipp's thoughtfulness in making the *Mirror* support network available to him wherever he travelled, by the IPC party to celebrate the Sutherland portrait and by his warm, generous and gossipy letters. King had even written to Cudlipp in 1971 that he had been 'much impressed' by a television programme that he had made about deprivation.[104] Then came 1976 and the Cudlipp memoirs.

With the help of friends and colleagues, Cudlipp had gone to enormous lengths to establish the facts, set the record straight and produce a likeness of King that would do both of them justice. He was also driven by a compulsion to justify himself to the world – and, indeed, to himself – for what Ellis Birk was right to label parricide. His deep admiration and affection for, and fascination with, King permeated *Walking on Water*: if there was any animosity, it stemmed from an unconscious anger that King's megalomania had resulted in the destruction of their partnership and had thus

---

* Of 120 million IPC shares, King owned 46,000 and Cudlipp just over 13,000.

severely damaged the newspaper to which they had given much of their lives.

Cudlipp knew King would be displeased by much of the book, but he had not realised that even the truth offended now, for King's seclusion in Ireland with Ruth as his main company had taken him further into a fantasy land. To Cudlipp he put on a brave face:

> It is better written than its predecessors and very well researched. The main blemish is that there is *far* too much about me. Though you say I am one of the three most impressive men you have met,* in fact one wonders why the poor soul labelled Cecil King in your book merited more than a paragraph.
>
> There are various inaccuracies with which I will not bore you, but the interview with Mountbatten, at which I was present, had no resemblance to the one described in your book.
>
> The plans and ambitions attributed to me at the end of my time at the Mirror are purely fanciful.[105]

'I have really been more upset by Cudlipp's book than by the burglars,' King told Priscilla, after he and Ruth had survived having been tied up for hours in their Dublin house:†

> Though an informative biography, in substance it is a demolition job on me. I have no objection to him saying I resigned from the human race in early youth nor when he makes me out as a kind of animated ice-berg bereft of all human feelings. But it's a bit much when he states that I was bent on organising a government under Mountbatten, or when he says any notice of dismissal was handed to me at 8.15 a.m. because if it had reached

---

* The others were Lloyd George and Churchill; however, said Cudlipp, while King had 'the essence of greatness', he 'did not and could not achieve it' mainly because of his pathological pessimism.

† King – always a brave man – made light of the robbery. 'It came as a shock when 3 masked men burst into our sitting room waving their guns,' he wrote to his niece, Audrey Verity. 'They knew we had a safe & demanded the key at gun-point. In the safe were some of my gold coins and all Ruth's jewellery!'; he then moved to another subject. Ruth later claimed that he had been terrified and that, when tied up, she had kept him going by reminding him over and over again that they had each other.

me later in the day my colleagues were afraid I would have committed suicide. Cudlipp's ingratitude one had assumed but this malice in his book – 8½ years after my departure – was not to be foreseen.[106]

By then the Kings were in denial about a great deal, not just about the Mountbatten episode and the reasons why King had been fired by his board,[*] but even about what he had said about himself in *Strictly Personal*. Ruth denounced Cudlipp publicly and privately for alleging that King had ever spoken of suicide, yet King had specifically discussed his self-hatred and how he had 'always wanted to commit suicide.'[107] Fed by his wife, bitterness towards most people in his past was further poisoning Cecil King: a prize example was the 1978 interview with the Press Association, the transcript of which caused much hilarity in journalistic circles. Esmond, the second Lord Rothermere, had just died:

PA: Good morning, Mr King. I'm very sorry to trouble you at a difficult time like this, but I wonder if you would like to give us a tribute to your cousin who has just died in London?

Mr King: You've got a bloody hard job. He was a shit. Cold, money-grubbing and completely unsuited to the job he held. When he took over the *Daily Mail* it was the best newspaper in Fleet Street. Look at it now. When he took over the *Evening News* it was the best evening newspaper in the world. Now look at it. Dreadful rags, both of them . . . I know you want a tribute, but I can't honestly say anything good about the man.

I suppose Vere will be the third Viscount. Well, there was always a suggestion, a very strong suggestion, that he wasn't his father's son. He doesn't look like Esmond at all . . . I honestly

---

* In February 1971, King recorded in his diary that Heath had told Ruth 'he had not yet got to the bottom of the part played by Wilson in my expulsion from the *Mirror*'; in 1981 he told Bruce Arnold that Heath had told him that Wilson was involved . In 1983, in an interview with Eamonn Andrews, King gave a totally distorted account of the Mountbatten affair, which contradicted his own diary, and even floated the notion that the Labour government had told IPC directors that he was planning a coup in order to have him fired and get the *Mirror*'s support in the 1970 General Election.

have no idea who his father is. I don't think any of this would go out on PA, do you?

PA: No.

King: Neither do I.

PA: Well, what we can salvage, feeling as you do about him.[108]

Cudlipp was one of those who treasured and laughed at that, but he continued to seize any opportunity to keep in touch with King; in 1980 he sent him a copy of his *The Prerogative of the Harlot*,* an enjoyable romp through the lives of Northcliffe, Rothermere, Beaverbrook, William Randolph Hearst and Henry Luce, to which King responded with defences of Northcliffe and Rothermere: being nasty about his relatives was the prerogative of a Harmsworth. 'Your picture of Beaverbrook is so wildly flattering it is impossible to comment on,'[109] he concluded. There was further contact the following year, when the so-called Mountbatten coup reached the headlines once again, after loose talk by Harold Wilson and his once right-hand woman, Marcia Falkender, about an MI5 plot, and after an enterprising journalist misquoted *Walking on the Water* as speaking of a 'military coup'. A telegram arrived from Cudlipp to King as he was giving an angry interview to *The Times*: 'ALL THIS TALK ABOUT AN ALLEGED MILITARY COUP IN 1968 HAS NOT COME FROM ME AT ANY TIME AND IS GROSSLY UNFAIR ON YOU STOP I HAVE EMPHATICALLY DENIED ON RADIO AND TELEVISION AND IN PRESS INTERVIEWS TODAY THAT EITHER YOU OR I EVER HEARD OF SUCH RUBBISH HUGH CUDLIPP.'

King was so pleased that his letter of thanks ended 'From your old colleague'[110] and Cudlipp's response was near-ecstatic: 'I am relieved and happy that this noisy incident has done something to get us a little nearer a restoration of that relationship with you which meant so much to me during most of my life.'[111] In his subsequent article for *Encounter* in September, Cudlipp's anxiety to exonerate King from any wrongdoing was palpable, yet only a month later King's bitterness resurfaced. 'From 1951 to 1968 I was the editor-in-chief of the Mirror group of newspapers (in fact if not in name),' he wrote in 1981

---

* Jodi, who thought the title had a pretentious ring, failed to persuade him to call it *The Paper Tigers*.

to Piers Brendon, who was writing a book about press barons. 'Cudlipp played more or less the same role as Christiansen played with Beaverbrook at the Express.* Cudlipp was always a disloyal colleague anxious to tell everyone that he ran the group and that I only licked stamps in the post department!'[112] But then King's entire view of his past had become distorted and mean-spirited: 'it was not Guy Bartholomew who transformed the Daily Mirror,' he wrote in 1982. 'His importance was that he was a director of the Mirror Company since 1914 and I needed his help with the Mirror board.'[113]

Though they could not admit it, after the initial honeymoon period, the Kings' life in Dublin was a great disappointment. King's main pleasure lay in his daily visits with his battered old suitcase to the Donnybrook shops, where he chatted about food and weather and the news to shopkeepers and customers, who, in echoes of Africa, offered him warmth and informality that made him blossom in return; probably his best friend in Ireland was a friendly nun in a local convent to whom he could chat about religion. 'He was genuinely awed by this elderly gentlewoman who had, as he said, set her hand to the plough and never faltered,' wrote an observer. 'In the world's terms, her education and her gifts seemed not to have been exploited. But Cecil – so often accused of megalomania – understood the scale of her aspiration. He saw that she had clung to her vocation, even when it had been difficult.'[114]

King desperately sought a simple faith. 'Tomorrow we are having tea with an old widow of 80,' he wrote when he was seventy-six. 'I picked her up on a bus. She is a real saint – her face shines with her childlike faith. All her life has been devoted to others and she is entirely happy.'[115] It was in the spirit of practical service that he marched one day, Ruth by his side, into a derelict local Huguenot graveyard and set about tidying it up.

Public life offered little. There were occasional discussions about Northern Ireland with politicians and diplomats, but the Kings had little contribution to make to politics, except to offer cups of tea separately to Paisley and David O'Connell. 'We have been making yet

---

* Unusually, King asked Brendon not to quote him: 'It is the truth that hurts . . . and I don't want to be caught up in a slanging match.'

one more attempt to help towards a settlement in Northern Ireland,' King wrote as late as 1980. 'But how does one overcome the mistakes of many decades of weak British governments?'[116] Ruth would always believe that they could have sorted out Northern Ireland, if Downing Street had done what it was told.

While through O'Connell, whose star was fast falling, the Kings kept up some peripheral contact with the IRA, it was Paisley whose politics King adopted. He kept his interest in British and American domestic politics and foreign policy, denounced Jimmy Carter ('absurd and incompetent') and Ronald Reagan ('stupid, ignorant and lazy'), but his rage and contempt were particularly reserved for the British government's handling of Northern Ireland. After Margaret Thatcher, in 1985, signed the Anglo-Irish Agreement and infuriated the entire unionist population, she became the chief target of his scorn. Up to the time he died, King was still predicting civil war.

In Ireland King was asked to give the occasional talk, speech or interview, wrote a few articles and book reviews, sat for a while on the board of a small current-affairs magazine, had some slight involvement with a few charities and was President of the Irish Association of Non-Smokers, but for the most part he was forgotten. Socially he could not fit into a world dominated by pubs. Even on the dinner-party circuit the Irish thought about having dinner just as King was ready for bed, and increasingly he refused to adapt. Ruth – who, unlike King, was a thundering snob – would attribute their lack of Irish friends to a shortage of 'our kind of people', but in truth people for the most part found him intimidating and rude and Ruth garrulous, boring and peculiar. King spent most of his time reading and took up playing the stock-market as a hobby; in 1981 he wrote that he had made himself 'a fortune'.[117]

Ruth did freelance work here and there as an adjudicator, was a governor of the Royal Ballet School until 1974, became involved in children's theatre, put on concerts, sat on the board of the National Concert Hall and took an interest in some musical children, including the milkman's daughter, whom she helped along the path to professional musicianship. She extolled the Irish regularly for their spirituality and 'kindness, human sympathy, participation, love of conversation', but, like everyone else, they let her down with great regularity. 'My wife . . . tells me that Irish children have a quality in their music quite different from that of children from other parts of these islands,' King wrote not long after they arrived. 'It is a spiritual quality and so of unique value in this materialistic age. Yet it does not seem to be sufficiently appreciated by the musical establishment, who are more concerned with technical excellence, not understanding that it is this spiritual quality which distinguishes the artist from the gifted technician.'[118] 'To work [in Ireland],' she wrote in a letter in the late 1980s, 'IMPOSSIBLE – SO IMPOSSIBLE. They can't even see that one can read their little minds . . . no confidence, picking brains, stealing ideas, knifing each other, jealous of experience – social climbers – "touchy"– oh, dear. But I don't *have* to work with them! If I'm of interest, and they need me, I let them USE me and get out in time.'[119]

'I don't know how Cecil puts up with that nut,' Peter Stephens once remarked to his wife. 'She replied, "I guess she massages his ego pretty regularly."'[120] Ruth did more than that. By cutting him as far as possible adrift from his family, encouraging him in his arrogant disregard for the opinions of others and overlaying this truthful man's view of the past with a miasma of lies and fantasy, she also made him completely dependent on her. Priscilla's first husband Bobby Gore was one of those who concluded that, by the time King realised what Ruth was like – 'evil' in Gore's view – he was too old and tired to face the truth, so he blocked it out and made the best of things. 'Neurotic, malicious and hysterical,' said the notoriously charitable Michael King of her in 1968; 'she prevents anyone getting to him'.[121] And that was before she held a seventieth birthday party in London for King to which none of his children was invited.

What had now become King's sometimes breathtaking meanness cast a shadow over family relationships. First there was Margot. Though she remained deeply in love with King, she had recovered fully from her breakdown in the early 1960s and was a source of strength, support and great affection to all the family.* She met King annually at a rather tense dinner with a few grandchildren or at an occasional lunch with Priscilla. She was, however, chronically hard-up. In 1974, when King, who was on a large pension, sold the lease of

---

* 'She was unpunctual, inefficient and had all sorts of faults but was intensely endearing' was the assessment of George Burton, Priscilla's second husband.

The Pavilion for £110,000[122]* Margot was still on the allowance of £133 a month awarded at the time of their divorce in 1964; it had halved in value. She steadfastly refused to say one word of criticism of King, or even of Ruth, and her finances caused dissension with her children, for she became greatly distressed when they offered to ask King to give her more. Not until 1980, when the value of her allowance was down to just over one-fifth, did King increase it, and then he merely doubled it.[†]

'A lot of my furniture is being sold at Sotheby's on November 8 in the morning,' he wrote to Priscilla in November 1974. 'My bits are at the end of the sale.' When Priscilla, whose marriage had broken up and who was living in badly furnished rooms, asked if she could have any unwanted furniture, he told her to go to the auction. As with the possessions, so with his papers; without consultation with any of his children, King sold his own and his family papers to Boston University, which gave him £10,000 and an honorary doctorate.**

Yet despite all King's parsimony and insensitivity and Ruth's baleful presence, King's children and some of the grandchildren still tried to keep some relationship going – not helped by Ruth's habit of intercepting and destroying letters to King from those she had taken against, if she thought she would not be found out. Of all his children, King had always had least to do with Colin, the family's Golden Boy, whose siblings had protected him as far as possible from family troubles. Able and pleasant, he could also be abrupt and aggressive and had a chip on his shoulder about not going to university. Yet he was professionally the most successful of the four children, was already on the Reed board and was tipped as a future Chairman. He visited Dublin in 1975: 'Colin was here for two days,' King told Priscilla. 'He is concerned with a merger of their parent company and their wallpaper ditto. He seemed in good heart, though putting on weight again.'[123] Within a few months, at forty-four, Colin had a coronary from which he died some months later. The funeral 'was a dismal

---

*   About £700,000 today.
†   £133 in 1964 was the equivalent of £258 in 1974; in 1980 it was £627.
** During the period before the papers were actually delivered to Boston, Ruth got rid of many letters from Margot, children and grandchildren as well as correspondence she thought did not reflect well on King.

occasion', King wrote to Priscilla, who had just arrived in India. 'I flew over for the day as the only way I could express my love for Colin & my sympathy with his family.'[124] He said nothing of his feelings. At the funeral, King and Michael were observed shaking hands and exchanging letters.

Until King went to Dublin, Michael continued to meet him quite often, usually in company, to talk politics or introduce him to interesting people. Apart from one appearance by Colin, Michael (because he moved in political circles) was the only King child to appear in the diaries, and he appeared often ('Mike to lunch; he had a crumb of information'[125]). In 1974 Michael would have read in the second volume of diaries: 'We had been surprised some time ago to be rung up by 10 Downing St and asked for [Mike's] telephone number. It appears that Ted wanted him to prepare the precis of the White Paper on Europe . . . Mike's value as a journalist lies in his contacts – he is no hand with his pen. However, he says they were very happy with the result.'[126] Then there was the occasion when 'Mike . . . produced two interesting ideas. He is not an original thinker, so I suppose he picked up the ideas from the people – political and industrial – with whom he mixes.'[127] It says much of what King had become that he neither understood nor cared that it would hurt to have your father publicise to the world what he thought were your inadequacies.

There were others with a higher opinion of Mike. 'Dearest Mike,' Colin wrote in 1972 after another promotion in Reed's. 'I value your good wishes more than anyone's. I am confident that if you had had the luck I have had you would have done much better . . . You may not realise it but in recent years I have learned a lot from you and have realised how much I depend upon you.'[128] Then there was the President of the CBI, who in 1973 poached Michael to be head of public affairs at Imperial Tobacco, where for the first time in his life he was well paid.

But as Francis had pointed out to King decades previously, he formed his views of his children early on and did not modify them. When Michael died of a heart-attack at fifty-four, 'I provoked a storm,' King told Priscilla, 'by saying in my letter of condolence to Libby that dear Mike was not a man of great talent but he achieved his success as everyone liked him – and some loved him. I showed the draft to Ruth and we thought the letter to be an affectionate tribute to my dead son. But Libby said it showed how I had always underestimated Dear Mike.'[129]

King had had a mild stroke some time beforehand and did not attend Michael's funeral ('*too* much travel tiredness & emotion . . .' said Ruth to Priscilla. '*There was no other reason*, except plain lack of strength & old age. In spirit we are both there . . . Mike was a true friend to me. I shall miss him desperately.'[130]) He did, however, offer to go if his absence suggested 'any lack of affection or respect.'[131] and he did travel to the memorial service. 'Thank you for the offer of dinner,' he wrote to Priscilla, 'but I think not. What with the service and subsequent lunch . . . I think that is all I want to see of the family. It would indeed help if you picked us up at Durrants Hotel. I think it might be best if we arrived at the church just in time. I'm very anxious not to be near Margot. I don't mind where we sit but above all I don't want to end up with Ruth on one side of me and Mama on the other.'[132] At the service, according to Peregrine Worsthorne, 'while the eulogist was rightly extolling Michael's many virtues, 'What a load of tosh,' the father was heard to say, "far too complimentary." Cecil King had always been cruelly unappreciative of this son, but nobody thought he would commit the ultimate outrage of carrying his prejudice to the grave's edge.'[133]*

'My darling – and only – Son . . .' King wrote to Francis after Mike's death.[134] Francis rarely saw his father ('It was indeed a loving gesture of yours to travel here and give me a glance of you in your middle age,'[135] King wrote in the early 1980s). As always in their relationship, there was often brutal frankness, anger, intensity and deep hurt: Francis, who had retired early from IPC to work in the charity world, was the child least likely to humour his father and the one most interested in unsparing analysis. Fighting for a better financial deal for his mother, he told King that she had always avoided asking

---

* 'Ruth has a psychic friend, Maeve,' King wrote to Priscilla a few months later, 'who always tells her that she is surrounded by a crowd of "beautiful people" who have "passed over!" However, the other day she announced that the beautiful people had been joined by "Mike". He was not happy while he was here, but is quite happy now. We have never mentioned Mike nor that I had lost a son, but she picked it up somehow. I don't really believe that this sort of information comes from the next world, but whence does it come? She says my aura is a scintillating one, constantly throwing off sparks!'

them to make her case as she 'wanted most steadfastly to protect Mike and me from your fury and hostility'. Ruth, trying to protect King, had 'cocooned' him 'and we have not been able to develop a more adult and mature relationship with you and particularly so since your retirement . . . your womenfolk have [always] served as your protectors, even Scil is now engaged on the task – and your menfolk have had to keep their distance. Does it have to continue to be like this?'[136]

It did continue like that, but Francis succeeded at least in getting King to be slightly less mean with Margot* and, without causing a breach, attacked ferociously King's attempts to control how she spent her money and where she lived. 'As I have told you in the past,' King said during their correspondence, 'you have always been my favourite child – perhaps because so much in your character resembles mine.'[137]

That might have been so in theory, but in practice it was Priscilla to whom King was closest, not least because she had always made more of an effort with their relationship than her brothers combined; even after he went to Dublin they corresponded very regularly, she rang him frequently and visited when she could afford it and Ruth would allow it. He seemed genuinely pleased when in 1975 she became engaged to George Burton, Chairman of Fisons, yet when she begged him to come to the wedding and Burton wrote to tell King what it would mean to her, he refused.† He was glad to see Priscilla happy, however, and took to Burton when they met. Yet barbs came through: 'He is such a *nice* man. He seems to me a shade too optimistic but if this weren't so, he would not be such a welcome member of the establishment.'[138] 'My darling daughter, It must be very entertaining watching your social life leap from peak to peak. But after a Thatcher grand dinner, what future social Everest remains to be scaled?'[139]

Sheila Falls was very attached to King too, but (like Michael's

---

* Complaining that she had an old-age pension of £1,300 (which still left her a long way short of the 1964 settlement), after pressure from Francis, King grudgingly bought her an annuity of £2,000. Margot died in her sleep in 1985.

† That Priscilla became Lady Burton when George was knighted two years later annoyed Ruth greatly. As adept as ever at displacement, she was forever accusing her of snobbery; 'Scilla's gone grandly off to France', she announced on one occasion, when the Burtons had left for their annual fortnight in a *gîte*. She was also irritated that Priscilla became a governor of several schools and a highly effective charity worker;' she always ignored her MBE.

daughter Lucinda – of whom King became very fond when she spent three days with him when Ruth was at a music festival) Ruth's ability drastically to undermine her self-confidence by striking at her weakest points made visiting Dublin a torment.

Ruth was a mistress of finding ways to keep King in his cocoon. 'Dear Pscilla*, (& George) . . .', she wrote after Michael's death. 'My own view is that the stimulus of your visit, & all the past family memories it would evoke more vividly, is not what he needs *NOW*. I think rest, & relax this coming week . . . Please don't think it sounds ungrateful, when you'd offered to come, but due to recent events in my own family, I'm not really up to "visitors" just now.'[140]

Much to King's pleasure, for he really liked seeing them, several grandchildren did battle through, particularly those who instinctively grasped that they had to make the running. Priscilla's son William had known King well as a small child and they stayed fond of each other. Francis's daughter Sarah had a close relationship with him when she was at boarding school and needed someone to write to. Always a conscientious correspondent, he responded, and they developed a relaxed, jokey relationship; at a difficult time in her life, he 'believed in me . . . when I was miserable . . . I used to think of him and stick my chin up and carry on'. He would later cast her – as he had cast Priscilla – in the role of matriarch and was uneasy that Sarah was not putting having babies before her career. Sarah's brother Roger and his wife Zena became favourites too, not least because they were endlessly patient with Ruth; and Colin's Lorna and children were accepted, though King was irritated with her brother Robin because he took a long time to choose the church over banking.

It was Francis's son Laurence who became closest of all the grandchildren and endured all the wounds that Cecil inflicted unwittingly and Ruth wittingly when he was a vulnerable adolescent. On Laurence's first visit to Dublin, he arrived nervously at the front door at the time agreed. The door was answered by Ruth: 'This is *so* inconvenient but you would insist on coming at this time.' His self-confidence shattered by this blatant lie, he spent the whole weekend tongue-tied. 'What a

---

* Priscilla signed herself Scilla in family correspondence; for forty years, Ruth resolutely wrote to her as Pscilla.

monster she was,' he reflected later. 'And how clever in a low way. She always knew exactly which buttons to press to undermine you.' Yet he surmounted all the obstacles she put in his way, until he had become so important to King that she could do their relationship no damage. 'I'm on your side,' King would say to Laurence, and his support mattered desperately to an emotionally insecure young man. Through sheer persistence he kept close to King in letters and visits. When Laurence wanted to set up his own publishing firm, King was wise, interested and financially generous: 'the influence my grandfather had on my life was considerable and wholly benign. I loved him very much.'[141]

In turn King was deeply fond of Laurence, who kept him closely in touch with his ups and downs in business, was the only person who sought his advice regularly on matters where King felt he had something to give, published the kind of intellectual and artistic books King admired and was also serious-minded and religious. And then there was Carey, a writer and journalist with a special interest in Russia, who married Laurence and became very close to Cecil. 'Laurence loved Cecil dearly,' she wrote:

and the two seemed to derive great strength and comfort from their relationship. Cecil decided, early on, that he approved of me, and I was frequently asked to stay in Dublin, often without Laurence. The two old Kings refused to call me Carey, as most people did. They insisted on Caroline. I did not mind, since it was clear from the beginning that Cecil was a law unto himself. It was also clear, to me, that his friendship was worth having. Time spent with Cecil soothed the spirit. He focussed all his great attention upon anyone he talked to. As he looked at you, he weighed you up. His heart was good, and his judgements never malign . . .

He was totally uninhibited. He would question every orthodoxy, and saw no need to edit himself to avoid giving offence. He despised the complacent and the undriven, and he wanted them to know it. Talking to him could be exhausting, as he unremittingly catalogued this world's ills. But he had the most beautiful voice, soft and expressive. It was not deep, and would rise as he talked of folly or told old tales. He was playful. He loved a joke, and would collapse with laughter, tears running down his cheeks.

Like Laurence, Carey thought Ruth a monster — but a monster whom she also was prepared to endure for Cecil's sake. 'It is difficult to describe the ferocity of Ruth's hatred of Ireland', she recalled.

My memories of outings with Ruth in Dublin are of mortifying embarrassment. There was the time at the Concert Hall when she wheedled her way up to some Irish grandee and asked him to evict a scruffy old woman from the premises. It was predictable that the 'tramp' that Ruth pointed out so viciously was the man's mother.

Another, horribly similar occasion involved the Dame clutching another nobleman by the arm, graciously sympathising with him for having to live in Ireland.

'But I am Irish'.

'No you're not, not real Irish.'

'Yes I am.'

'Oh no, you're like Cecil, not real Irish at all'.

Ireland brought out Ruth's ghastly gentility.

Knowing he had done badly with his sons, and fearful of alienating Laurence too, King used to route criticism through Carey. It was in the same spirit, they concluded, that, recognising his own autism, he had handed most human interaction over to Ruth and was largely unaware of what she was doing. Carey recollected:

She was poisonous and had no interest in other peoples' feelings or needs although she had a unique ability to wound. Cecil yearned for God, and for Truth. Ruth offered him bogus mysticism and a quicksand of lies. He felt himself unable to communicate so he entrusted his most crucial relationships, with his children and their families, to a mad, malevolent woman who was clearly possessed with loathing for all his descendants.

Ruth needed other peoples' pain. She fed off suffering and humiliation. At his best, in old age, Cecil was gentle (all right, he was also awkward and capable of astonishing rudeness) and articulate and had a unique ability to transform the moment, creating happiness as he pottered around the village, and leaving people he talked to nobler and stronger.

In hideous parallel, Ruth could conjure misery and humiliation from nothing. There was the awful incident when, with great fanfare, she offered to send a Dublin woman with a terminally ill husband and a severely handicapped child away on a magnificent holiday. Ruthlike, she graciously produced a cheque that would hardly have covered a day trip to the seaside. It was a number of such incidents that left the rest of us shivering with shame.

She herself, I think was just astonished at the ingratitude of the poor.

Did King have no idea what she was like? In the view of Carey King:

> only rarely did he seem to see what was going on. Then he could lose his temper. I remember one occasion when Laurence and I were staying in Dublin. At breakfast Ruth was being her dreadful worst, harassing Laurence about putting the butter-knife in the marmalade, or some such. She was not doing this in grand-motherly fashion: concentrated spite was pouring out of her, torrents of apparently unstoppable hatred. 'Wherever did you grow up?' she spat, snatching the offended knife.
> 'In MY FAMILY', Cecil roared.

'It doesn't matter what you do as long as you stick to it,' King had told Laurence from an early stage, and listening to King and studying him through the years with compassion and curiosity, Laurence came to conclude that King had emerged from childhood terrified of disorder and muddle and that it was this fear that informed his distrust of democracy, his pull towards authoritarianism and his determination to stick to a course of action once embarked on including staying married to Ruth.

When he was seventy-five and eighty, King's family held dinners for him in London (organised by Priscilla) at which he insisted on sitting beside Ruth. The text survives of the largely self-pitying speech he made at his eightieth about his youth.* When it was not self-justificatory,

---

* 'The great tragedy,' his granddaughter Geraldine, Michael's daughter, wrote to Priscilla afterwards, 'is that having realised how his childhood had been, he inflicted the same kinds of pressures and coldnesses on his own children'.

much of the introduction to his *Commonplace Book*,[*] published in 1981, was in the same vein. Yet the meat of the book, reflecting as it did King's interior life, was a remarkable testimony to the tortured but cultured, enquiring, open-minded and often humorous[†] man who lurked sadly behind the thick and scaly carapace and seemed able to identify almost exclusively with anguished dead sages. 'The present condition of the world is diseased' was a telling quote from Kierkegaard. 'If I were a doctor and was asked for my advice I should answer create silence, bring men to silence – the word of God cannot be heard in the world today. And if it is blazoned forth with noise so that it can be heard even in the midst of all other noise, then it is no longer the word of God. Therefore create silence.'[142]

'For over 65 years I have sought to establish a link between myself and the purposes of the Almighty,' King told Francis in 1984, 'as they appear to my limited vision . . . Though it may appear that for 15 years or so I have retired from life, this is not so, as I see it. I have been of an age when active participation in events is no longer appropriate, but instead I should be gaining – and displaying – wisdom – wisdom acquired by sitting humbly at the feet of the Almighty.'[143]

In old age, Laurence thought, King achieved serenity, but then it was to Laurence that King wrote most about the spirit. In addition to his isolation, he had a great deal to endure from arthritis, acute psoriasis and the effects of his first major stroke in the autumn of 1984. Still, there was no mistaking his distress when in 1985 he heard that Priscilla had cancer. 'I remember so well at Park Stile when I was told that I had a daughter – and I thought this was the greatest day

---

[*] The only book of King's to have been dedicated to anyone, this was 'To my dear grand-children Jonathan, Geraldine, Lucy, Richard [Michael's children], Roger, Laurence, Sarah, Andrew [Francis's], Catherine, William [Priscilla's], Lorna, and Robin [Colin's]; and my sister's grandchildren whom I adopted when their parents were killed, Patrick, Nigel, and Sheila; and my only great-grandchild Emily'.

[†] It is hard to imagine another octogenarian including in a book assembled for his grand-children a quote from Flaubert apropos Arab women shaving their private parts: 'How much time you will squander later on, dreaming by the hearth of hairless cunts beneath cloudless skies!' When I first met Hugh Cudlipp, who was by then also an octogenarian, I showed him this extract in a (successful) effort to surprise him. A couple of hours later, walking through Chichester, Cudlipp grabbed my arm, pointed at a shop-window containing naked mannequins and cried triumphantly: 'There they are. Cecil's hairless cunts.'

of my life! So your news was a shock. I am much moved by the thought of your pain and anxiety.'[144] He rang her one day and said, 'I managed to get through to you', but Ruth interrupted and he had to stop. 'My darling daughter,' he wrote later. 'It seems you are showing great courage in the dreadful tests to which you have been submitted. It is apparent that the result has been a great enhancement of your character. To me such an enhancement is the result of your moving into a nearer relationship with the Almighty.'[145] After Priscilla's treatment had finished and King had had another stroke, Ruth told Priscilla not to visit; but George had an excuse to go to Dublin on business and took Priscilla with him. When she called on King and he saw that she looked well, he cried. 'There you are,' said Ruth. 'I told you not to come.'

King's ambition was to have a good death. 'Surely a dignified death is one of the greatest accomplishments – to round your life off so that you go without reluctance when the play is over,' he had written in 1968 in a *Times* article that was one of the best he ever wrote. He would go long after he had expected the play to be over, on 17 April 1987, when he was eighty-six, and he had a long period of partial paralysis, but he conducted himself throughout with courage and dignity and found consolation in spiritual reading and reflection. Ruth caused havoc and resentment in the hospital with her demands and complaints, but nursed him with conspicuous and selfless devotion. She prevented Francis and Priscilla from seeing him for fourteen months before his death, but allowed Laurence to visit towards the end and Carey to nurse King for the last week.

'When I arrived to stay at Greenfield Park in Holy Week, 1987,' remembered Carey:

> Ruth greeted me in traditional style. 'Cecil told the nurse that you were coming to stay and that you were very beautiful. So when she sees you she won't know who on earth you are'.
>
> It was hell in the bungalow that week. Ruth would not leave the nursing to the private nurses who came in for parts of the day, nor would she do it herself. Although she was still feverish in her devotion, she was appalled by the physical aspects of looking after a bedridden patient. Her histrionic incompetence at basic nursing tasks made the dying unnecessarily messy.

Ruth nagged and harangued the nurses mercilessly. Whatever they did was wrong. Despite the pain and emotional chaos all around, the Dame constantly found time to tell the nurses what she thought of the bog Irish.

Cecil had moments of lucidity right up until his death, but at other times he rambled. It would seem, for hours on end, that the spirit we loved had gone for ever, and then he would be back.

He was struggling, but the old man was determined to be in control of his going. But whenever he seemed to be about to die, Ruth would shriek at him not to leave her, screaming and howling. And yet she begged the doctors to sedate him, even though she knew that this might hasten the end. She could not stand his illness, and would not allow him to die. It was not what you would call a calm environment.

Finally, on the morning of Good Friday, Cecil was dozing softly, and I was sitting with him. Ruth was in the kitchen, whipping round disinfecting things, maniacally arranging kitchen implements.

I remember praying that this dear old man would be allowed to depart in peace before Ruth had a chance to start screeching again. In the end, Cecil chose the moment, and he died with enormous grace. Despite the madness all around him, it was a dignified quietus.

Cudlipp was not invited to the funeral. He died at eighty-four over a decade later, on 17 May 1998, having dealt with his own last illness with similar courage and dignity and with never-failing humour.* Telling a journalist in 1997 that he was tired of being interviewed about the past 'for TV programmes and newspaper look-back-but-not-in-anger articles', he added that 'nostalgia seems to be about the only medical problem which hasn't affected me'.[146] The day he died, Jodi wrote to Bob Edwards, Geoffrey Goodman, Keith Waterhouse, Donald Zec and Terry Lancaster that 'As you will already know Hugh left this morning for the place where all good editors go, but for the

---

* 'It's a celestial cull of the Cudlipps,' he announced, when he heard that his surviving siblings were also ill.

past several days he has been scribbling away at a MSS [addressed to them] and I found it a while ago and decided to type it up. He was unfortunately called away before it was finished, so I know you will excuse any errors and omissions.'

'Millions of people are putting up with the double-cancer problem in circumstances far less congenial than mine,' he had written:

how many others can doze off with a full view of the illuminated steeple of Chichester Cathedral? My top problem is acute breathlessness caused by faulty Old Labour heart valve failing adequately to supply New Labour lung with sufficient oxygen. This makes the sort of social chat, lies, innuendoes and downright calumnies we all enjoy over two or three bottles – regrettably impossible for me. Who wants to sit next to a Trappist monk who can't drink and who can only breathe deeply when looking at a steak he can't eat?

The old editor sent each of them an appreciative message about their Fleet Street achievements and managed an optimistic comment about Kelvin Mackenzie, the new broom at the *Mirror*. He did not admit he was dying, but he nonetheless wrote a valediction: 'this note is to say "Thanks for the memories", with no reply of any sort needed.'[147]

EPILOGUE

RUTH WAS DEVASTATED BY KING'S DEATH. HER SUGGESTION THAT 'that great and good man of peace, Dr Paisley' should give a reading at the service almost gave the Church of Ireland authorities at St Patrick's Cathedral a corporate seizure. She then compounded this by asking if they would be broadminded enough to allow her to invite Catholics to the service.

As Paisley was seen in Dublin as a raving, religious bigot who thought all but Free Presbyterians doomed and called the Roman Catholic church the Whore of Babylon and the pope anti-Christ, the St Patrick's clergy were horrified at the idea of giving him access to their pulpit. And being on close and friendly terms with innumerable members of the Catholic clergy and laity, they were equally appalled at Ruth's implication that they would be reluctant to hobnob with those whom she clearly thought to be their social inferiors. Paisley did not read at the service; but he can be courteous and gracious, and after many phone calls Ruth succeeded in badgering him into attending what he regarded as a heretical service in a heretical church.

Paisley attended the funeral service as an ordinary mourner, as did David O'Connell. A man with as low a tolerance of heretics as Paisley, O'Connell had split from the Provisionals the previous year when they decided to recognise the Irish parliament; he was now a senior member of Republican Sinn Féin.[*] The British Ambassador and Babatunde

---

[*] The political wing of the Continuity IRA.

José and a colleague from Nigeria added to an unusually exotic but sparse congregation. Ruth had organised a moving and musical service; afterwards King was buried in the graveyard at Calary Church which had family connections. When it was all over, Francis, the old Africa hand, armed with a bottle of gin, summoned the Nigerians to a corner of the car park and poured a ceremonial libation.

Mike's obituaries, King had said to Priscilla in 1980, 'say the right things though a bit fulsome as obits always are'.[1] He would not have had that complaint about his own, which with their talk of his 'burgeoning', 'boundless' and 'formidable' ego, his 'dynastic yearnings', his 'self-importance' and of 'hubris and nemesis', brought scant comfort to those who had loved him. There were, of course, many tributes to his strengths as a publisher, but King had alienated so many people that there was little evidence of affection. The exception was the Nigerian *Daily Times*, which led with 'CECIL KING (Father of modern TIMES) NO MORE'. José provided a long tribute that described him as 'a great man, liberal, kind-hearted and affectionate to all those who came in contact with him'. They had last spoken by telephone on King's birthday the previous year. 'Five days after, he sent me the following cable: "THIS IS TO LET YOU KNOW THAT I AM AT THE VERY END OF MY LIFE AND SO ASK ALMIGHTY GOD FOR HIS BLESSING ON YOUR WISE AND FRUITFUL LIFE."'[2]

King had died during an exciting moment in the government's long-running campaign to ban Peter Wright's *Spycatcher*. The Mountbatten 'coup' was raked over again, John Keegan's account of what he thought to be King's seditious talk to army officers was published in the *Daily Telegraph* and within a few days of King's funeral, a Labour MP, Dale Campbell-Savours, named him in the Commons as a conspirator with MI5 to topple the Wilson government. Ruth told the press that on his deathbed King had told her to say he had never been a spy and had loved his country: 'My husband was a great patriot. He loved Britain but a prophet is never accepted in his own country, I suppose.'[3] While she did not know why Campbell-Savours had made the allegation, 'nothing in this ephemeral world surprises me'.[4] The following day, Tony Benn's diary extract about the lunch with King that caused him to conclude he was mad featured prominently in the *Guardian*. Cudlipp's renewed efforts to challenge the King/MI5 coup-story once more failed to kill it: it popped up alive and well as late as 2002 in a tawdry book of Windsor-related conspiracy theories; for a change, this time it alleged the plotters intended to persuade the Queen to dismiss the government, and linked not just King but also Cudlipp to MI5.[5]

King had always said he would leave nothing to his children, but the general impression had always been that his money would largely go to his grandchildren. Three months before he died he gave each of them shares worth £10,000[*]. The following month he changed his will and left everything to Ruth (who took the precaution of summoning a doctor to certify that he was of sound mind). King's estate was estimated at £1,303,627[†], which was a gross underestimate of the value of his possessions.

A benign view was that King had decided that this would give Ruth something to do and help keep her part of the family. Ruth described the will as a symbol of his total trust in her; what seems likely is that the vulnerable old man yielded to her request to demonstrate that trust. It seemed odd that no member of King's family was asked to be an executor and that he should have chosen a Dublin solicitor and a nephew of Ruth's.

Ruth moved to a small flat crammed with their possessions, kept the Sutherland portrait in the hall and talked to it: 'My darling husband told me this morning to do X, Y or Z . . .' was a frequent motif. A frugal woman, she had no interest in money for its own sake – only for the power and attention it brought her. For fourteen years it brought her plenty.

There were the prizes and the charities and there were the grandchildren. The former were straightforward enough. To commemorate King, Ruth would offer annually a few thousand a year for, for instance, a music scholarship, for the best nurse at the hospital where King had been a patient, for a travel scholarship for a young journalist, for an award for a young businessman or for research into psoriasis. This was the minimum sum that would guarantee many busy days meeting and corresponding with people to discuss the prize/award, its purpose, its scope, its funding, the judges, and so on. At its most simple, there would be inspections and ceremonies and lunches and dinners,

---

[*]   About £17,000 today.
[†]   About £2.2 million today.

but such projects offered scope for drama and misunderstandings, betrayals and recriminations, and heart flutters and complaints to anyone and everyone about those who had let her down: the judges who had made bad judgements; the trustees who had maladministered; the prize-winners who had shown ingratitude; and all those who had in some way slighted her.

With the grandchildren it was much more serious.

To have access to King, it had always been necessary to pretend to be an admirer of Ruth: 'We've had two visits from Laurence and Roger,' King had written once. 'It is rewarding that these two very different young men obviously look to Ruth and me to guide them in this very difficult commercial and spiritual world.'[7] People talked about being free of her and her machinations once King had died. 'I cannot tell you how divisive Ruth was,' Laurence King said once. 'I used to think that when he dies, I'm going to take her into a room and just shake her and shake her and shake her until she realises quite what she's done to us.' But of course he did no such thing, for, like many of the other grandchildren – dislike or loathe her – it was difficult to be tough with an apparently frail and broken-hearted seventy-one-year old. So Ruth exploited her bereavement and her money.

Most of the grandchildren needed money in a middle-class kind of way. For the many parents among them, King's frequent stressing of the importance of a first-class education had fuelled the belief that he would help with school fees and, though mainly disappointed on that score in life, it was a considerable blow that he had failed to help out in death.

Had Ruth wanted to keep people happy and avoid family resentments, all she had to do was divide up a million or so between the grandchildren and the three Fallses, but that was the last thing she wanted. Knowingly or not, she set about persecuting the entire King family with a combination of emotional and financial blackmail and downright lies and character assassination. She tucked into Lucinda King early on, reproaching her for having failed to come to Dublin when King asked for her; that Lucinda was afraid that the company of Ruth would give her a nervous breakdown – as it had already given one of Enid's grandchildren – was not an excuse she felt able to give. 'You will always have to live with the remorse, that a very special loving kind grandfather thought your inner qualities special . . . and

asked only that you would visit him . . . it was a great sadness to him
and to me as I know how deeply it hurt him. Now it is too late to
have what those wonderful arms would have given you: what those
far-seeing eyes would have revealed to you: what that great wisdom
would have showered on you.'[8]

She offered Lucinda, as she offered all the King family, help from
'just an ordinary feeble creature over-flowing with the fullness of all
the love he gave me' and taking with great seriousness her responsibilities properly to discharge the 'sacred trust' of the obligations that
King had passed to her. All her relationships, Ruth kept explaining,
must be based on '*trust*' – a euphemism for doing and saying whatever it was Ruth wanted done and said. Her incessant prattle about
trust and love, and the spirit and auras, would call to mind Emerson's
'The louder he talked of his honour, the faster we counted our spoons'.

Ruth corresponded with the King clan, met them in London, where
she bought a small Chelsea flat, or paid visits to their homes. In
talking of the family, she would speak mostly of how this one or that
one relied on her for spiritual guidance, how difficult it was for such
a weak woman to cope with the demands they made on her wisdom
and love, how another had shown such gross ingratitude as to make
her ill, and so on and so on. When any of them plucked up the
courage to ask for financial help, there would be much discussion
with her dead husband, after which in most instances the decision
would be postponed or a small amount given, with a promise to think
about the rest at another time when she was stronger. In the case of
parents trying to decide if they could afford to send their child to a
private school, giving them a term's fees with no future guarantees
was a most effective form of torture. Often, they would castigate
themselves for looking for money, but then inevitably the thought
that what would have helped their family might go by default to
someone else spurred them to make another effort or be insincere
just one more time. The manner in which Ruth relayed news of one
to the others caused maximum mistrust among family members. Why
was she so keen on Cousin X? Was Cousin Y staying with her in
Dublin because he was sucking up to her? Did she give Cousin Z
help with fees? And if so, why, when my son needed it more, was he
refused?

Being kind and attentive to Ruth was not enough: it was also necessary to be hypocritical or risk being put on the list of enemies. Some members of the family – like Priscilla – could never win her approval, but others would be cast out for no reason they could under-stand. Nigel Falls wrote to Priscilla that 'I have, effectively, been kicked into touch in that quarter: she has decided to limit her goodwill (not quite her words, but certainly her meaning) and she has said goodbye to us. It would have been quite funny if it wasn't so odd – she spent a weekend with us in August, after which she wrote a cool, polite thank-you letter – end of story. As you may know, I was at one time an executor of her will, but for some reason this was quietly forgotten and the honour now rests with her nephew and, I think, a Dublin solicitor.'[9]*

Sometimes they fought back. Ruth was so unpleasant to Priscilla that George Burton banned her from ever coming to their house; and after a barrage of feline criticism of their home, William Gore's wife moved Ruth to a local hotel and brought in an exorcist. Yet, like most of the Kings, Priscilla and her children still stayed in touch. The family even kept their tempers when they discovered she had com-missioned a magnificent silver-gilt cross† for St Patrick's Cathedral in commemoration of King and had told hardly any of the family about the dedication ceremony.

Charities and the King and Railton families were Ruth's hobbies, but she also kept involved in the musical world and the church, and some who had little to do with her thought her as gentle as she looked and took her rhetoric as reality. She would sometimes stay with Ian Paisley, who remained grateful for the kindness he had received from the Kings, and Ted Heath was one of those who included her at the occasional lunch or dinner. Dealing with her musical autobiography – *Daring to Excel* – caused much misery at Secker & Warburg, which was lumbered with an unreadable and unreliable book and its hyster-ical author because of Ruth's hold over its owner, Paul Hamlyn. Ruth told everyone who would listen of the inequities of the copy-editor, who was so traumatised by her sufferings that long after the book

---

* Laurence King, who was to be her literary executor, fell out of favour at a crucial time and was also replaced by Ruth's nephew.
† By the artist Gerald Benney, it cost £250,000.

came out she would leave the building if Ruth were in it. That the book went largely unreviewed was attributed by Ruth to a conspiracy by the musical establishment. The one lengthy review described it as 'cloyed with talk of service and the nobility of the life of service (virtues Railton assumed she exemplified and expected others to emulate) while at the same time making it plain that to serve the NYO was to serve Ruth Railton. Anyone who declined to do so unconditionally was written off as weak, as not made of the right stuff, a traitor.'[10] In art, as in life.

Secker were to go through further misery over the biography of Cecil King.

Not long after the 1981 resurgence of the Mountbatten story, Ruth had decided that King must have a biography, 'to correct the current image of myself and my career',[11] wrote King to Bruce Arnold, an English journalist, art critic and biographer who had lived in Ireland for decades. 'In you,' explained Ruth to Arnold later, 'I genuinely felt was a poetic & sensitive gift, an understanding of newspapers & politics, & most important, one able to see the spiritual within the outer man & everyday events.'[12] By this time, only a few months after Arnold began the project, it was being scrapped, as his synopsis had caused King great distress – and Ruth, she alleged, 'a minor heart attack'. Arnold had liked and been greatly interested by King, but he was already coming to the conclusion that he could not do the book; Ruth was muscling in at every juncture, demanding that they develop the story together, holding meetings behind King's back and telling Arnold terrible things about King's family while insisting he should not meet them. King and Arnold parted amicably, and King compensated him generously for his wasted time.

After King's death, Ruth approached Paul Hamlyn about a biography and the project went to Secker; as King had liked one of my books, Ruth asked to meet me, and having decided that I had a white aura and a sensitive Irish soul, she proposed me as biographer. Despite her protracted campaign to have everything done on trust, she eventually had to agree in writing that I would have full access to papers, the right to quote anything I liked and that she would have no veto. By the time Secker had been through those negotiations and then *Daring to Excel*, its editors – like me – had some idea of what we were up against. Ruth's efforts to stop me from seeing Cudlipp, Priscilla, or, indeed, any but the very few people she thought (usually wrongly) could be relied on to say the right things, were ingenious and often disconcerting.

In time, Ruth would create a bond not just between me and Secker, but between me and members of the King family; we certainly never lacked a topic of conversation. To distinguish one Ruth from another, Cudlipp helpfully christened her Strewth, and thus she became known to many of us, including the publishers. There was the charming editor – known to be the kindest of men – who when I asked him for the latest news about Ruth just sobbed 'hate, hate, hate, hate, hate' down the telephone. His equally kindly successor learned to deal with Ruth's hour-long tirades by putting the receiver down gently on his desk, and making a cup of coffee and chatting to colleagues for twenty minutes before picking it up again.

When Ruth detected signs of insubordination and finally con-cluded that I was not going to write the book she wanted ('Cecil was a man so great he could have saved the world'; 'ours was the greatest love story of the twentieth century'), my white aura turned black, the torrents of denigration flowed behind my back and in the mid-1990s, en route to spend one last week in the King archives in Boston, I was told by the embarrassed archivist that Ruth had forbidden me access. Her executor was instructed to continue the ban; fortunately, the horse had already bolted.

I decided to let the whole project lapse temporarily: I did not have the stomach for a legal fight with an octogenarian and did not have the heart to tell her I had decided to write a joint biography of King and Cudlipp. Nor, like family, friends and ex-colleagues, could I have brought myself to tell the truth about her publicly in her lifetime.

Ruth died on 23 February 2001 at the age of eighty-five. She had thought better of her early promises to distribute King's possessions around the family and had sold almost all of them. She left the Sutherland portrait of King to the National Portrait Gallery and the bulk of her fortune of £4.6 million was left to the Cecil King foun-dation (on which sit no Kings) and to members of the Railton family. To the Kings she left the £1.18 million that she always alleged was the sum King meant them to have. It was a will that took no account of need and could most kindly be described as capricious. Colin's two children, Robin and Lorna, were left her apartment and its contents and £250,000 each, the rest was divided unevenly between the other nine surviving grandchildren,* the fourteen legitimate great-grandchildren (Geraldine's daughter was ignored) and Nigel and Sheila Falls.† King's children were not forgotten: Francis was left £5,000 in gratitude for his 'loving kindness and generosity'; Priscilla was left the same 'with loving forgiveness'.**

Dennis Barker ended his frank obituary with a suitable epitaph. In her widowhood, he wrote, Ruth would attend National Youth Orchestra concerts and open meetings, 'laughing at any suggestion that she had ever intimidated anybody: a creative fantasist to the last'.[13]

---

*   Roger was killed in a car-crash in 1995.
†   Patrick predeceased her; his £10,000 went not to his children, but to Robin's.
**   Since they were enjoined to spend the money in 'personal enjoyment' and memory, Priscilla took much pleasure in spending some of it on a lunch to help the great-grandchildren get to know each other better.

NOTES AND SOURCES

The most important collections of papers used in this book are:

1. The Cudlipp Collection, Cardiff University Library
2. The Cecil King Collection – which includes King family papers – in Special Collections, Boston University
3. Family papers in the possession of Lady Burton, King's daughter Priscilla

I have talked to and interviewed innumerable people about Hugh Cudlipp and Cecil King, of whom only a few are cited in the text or the endnotes. Most important were:

The late Hugh Cudlipp, his widow Jodi, brother Reg, sister Phyllis Stratton and step-son Kerry Mackendrick;

Cecil King's daughter Priscilla Burton, son Francis, son-in-law Sir George Burton, daughter-in-law the late Libby King, grandsons Laurence, Richard and Robin King and William Gore, granddaughters Catharine Gayner, Sarah Ingram, Geraldine King and Lucinda Woodcock, granddaughter-in-law Carey, niece Audrey Verity and her late husband Hugh and great-niece Sheila Spence;

Ruth King, to whom I listened for many many hours and who was illuminating in her own way;

Bruce Arnold, the late David Astor, the late Peter and Christabel Bielenberg, the late Lady Birk, Ellis Birk, Natalie Brook, Tony Delano, Sir Maurice Dorman, Sir Denis Forman, Geoffrey Goodman, St John (Bobby) Gore, Alison Hawkes, the late Brian Inglis, Tom and the late Doris Langley, the late Lord Longford, Charles Lysaght, Dr Edward McClellan, Martin Norton, Sir Edward Pickering, Doug and Chantek Porcas, the late Marjorie Proops, the late Percy and Paula Roberts, Sir Frank Rogers, Rudolf Schwarz, Lord Shawcross, The Reverend

John and Hazel Treadgold, Keith Waterhouse, the late Reverend Austen Williams, Donald Zec.

I am indebted to the following for permission to reproduce illustrations: Jodi Cudlipp, Priscilla Burton, The Cecil King Collection in Special Collections at Boston University and Chantek Porcas; the picture of Hugh Cudlipp on *Laranda II* is © Henri Cartier-Bresson/Magnum Photos.

Abbreviations

AMK	Agnes Margaret King
AYP	Hugh Cudlipp, *At Your Peril*, London, 1962
CHK	Cecil Harmsworth King
CKD	*The Cecil King Diary, 1965-1970*, London, 1972
	The Cecil King Diary,1970-1974, London, 1975
ES	Enid Stokes's unpublished memoirs, Box 29, Boston
GH	Geraldine Harmsworth
GHK	Geraldine Harmsworth King
HC	Hugh Cudlipp
HC pp.	Hugh Cudlipp papers, Cardiff University Library
LK	Libby King (or papers shown to me by Libby King)
LWK	Lucas White King
MK	Michael King
MS	From the unpublished version in the Cecil King Collection in Boston
PB	Priscilla Burton (or papers in the possession of Priscilla Burton)
PABD!	Hugh Cudlipp, *Publish and be Damned! The Astonishing Story of the Daily Mirror*, London, 1953
RDE	Ruth Dudley Edwards
RK	Ruth King
SP	Cecil King, *Strictly Personal: Some Memoirs of Cecil H. King*, London, 1969
WMTN	Cecil King, *With Malice Towards None: a war diary*, London, 1970
WOTW	Hugh Cudlipp, *Walking on the Water*, London, 1976

Box numbers relate to the King archive in Boston University

NOTES

Prologue

1 John Gordon, quoted in *WOTW*, 273
2 *WOTW*, 352

Chapter I Heavy Baggage

1 *WOTW*, 49
2 *SP*, 108
3 *SP*, 58
4 *WOTW*, 29
5 *WOTW*, 14
6 *WOTW*, 15
7 He was a supporter of Charles Stewart Parnell, cf. Parnell to Henry King, box 31, 3 May 1883, 17 August 1891
8 *ES*, 8
9 *ES*, 30
10 Reginald Pound and Geoffrey Harmsworth, *Northcliffe* (London, 1959)
11 *ES*, 21 (reproduced by CHK in *SP* without attribution)
12 I am indebted to Audrey Verity for her unpublished typescript, *The Kings in Imperial India*
13 Box 11, 4 October 1890
14 Interview with Christabel Bielenberg
15 S. J. Taylor, *The Great Outsiders: Northcliffe, Rothermere and the Daily Mail* (London, 1996), 35
16 *ES*, 33

17 Box 12, LWK's records of children's births
18 Cecil Harmsworth to GHK, box 15, 18 March 1901
19 *ES*, 40
20 Verity, 223
21 Verity, 210
22 Box 9, 24 January 1902
23 Verity, 219, 4 March 1902
24 Alfred Harmsworth, box 14, 8 December 1902
25 Obituary from learned society, box 8
26 *SP*, 67
27 *SP*, 17
28 Verity, 245, 15 April 1904
29 Box 7, 26 June 1904
30 Box 7, 10 October 1904
31 *ES*, 42
32 *SP*, 18
33 Box 17, n.d.
34 Box 18, n.d.
35 *SP*, 18
36 *ES*, 47
37 *ES*, 50
38 *ES*, 52
39 *SP*, 16
40 *ES*, 127
41 *ES*, 49
42 Interview with Christabel Bielenberg
43 *SP*, 16–17
44 *SP*, 16

45 GHK to GH, box 12, 6 September 1895
46 *ES*, 50
47 *ES*, 92
48 *SP*, 72
49 *WOTW*, 264
50 This took place at Henley-on-Thames in the late 1930s; *WOTW*, 263
51 *SP*, 72
52 *ES*, 53
53 *ES*, 59
54 Enid Starkie, *A Lady's Child* (London, 1941), 138
55 *ES*, 53
56 *SP*, 24–5
57 *ES*, 87
58 *SP*, 20
59 *ES*, 55
60 Starkie, 138
61 Box 17, 13 January 1913
62 *SP*, 23
63 *SP*, 23
64 Box 16, 9 July 1914
65 GHK to Luke, box 16, 23 September 1914
66 Box 16, 26 January 1907
67 Box 16, 1908? 10 October
68 Box 16, 1908? 19 September
69 Box 16, 24 March 1913
70 J. Lee Thompson, *Northcliffe: Press Barons in Politics 1865–1922* (London, 2000), 213
71 *SP*, 28
72 Luke to GHK, box 16, 12 August 1914
73 LWK to GHK, box 8, 12 November 1913
74 Box 16, 23 September 1914
75 GHK to Luke, box 16, 29 September 1914
76 Luke to LWK, box 16, 19 December 1914
77 Luke to LWK, box 16, 22 January 1915
78 LWK to Luke, box 16, 12 February 1915
79 *SP*, 29–30
80 *SP*, 30
81 Luke to LWK, box 16, 23 April 1915
82 Box 14

Chapter II A Legacy of Uncles

1 *SP*, 32
2 Box 15, 13 May 1915 to GHK
3 Box 15, 13 May 1915
4 Box 15, Thursday, to GHK
5 Box 15, Friday, to LWK
6 Tom Clarke, *My Northcliffe Years* (London, 1931), 112–13
7 *ES*, 97–8
8 Pound and Harmsworth, *Northcliffe*, 650
9 Box 15, 20 May 1915
10 Box 14, 15 October 1917
11 Pound and Harmsworth, 508
12 Pound and Harmsworth, 510
13 *Daily Mail*, 21 May 1915
14 Pound and Harmsworth, 479; Cecil Harmsworth to GHK, box 15, 17 June 1915
15 Taylor, *The Great Outsiders*, 181
16 Pound and Harmsworth, 480
17 Clarke, 90–1
18 *SP*, 34
19 Box 18, 17 July 1916
20 *SP*, 35
21 Pound and Harmsworth, 501
22 Pound and Harmsworth, 501
23 *SP*, 58
24 Pound and Harmsworth, 505
25 To St John Harmsworth, quoted in Pound and Harmsworth, 511
26 Pound and Harmsworth, 512
27 21 November 1916, box 18, paper unknown
28 Clarke, 104
29 Clarke, 105

30 Pound and Harmsworth, 529
31 Box 14, p.14, quoted in Pound and Harmsworth, 580
32 Pound and Harmsworth, 621
33 Quoted in Pound and Harmsworth, 620
34 Taylor, 188
35 Taylor, 229
36 *WMTN*, 49
37 Box 18, CHK to GHK, 17 July 1916
38 Box 16, 22 October 1916
39 Box 18, 20 June 1917
40 *SP*, 32
41 Box 18, 11 October 1918
42 Box 18, 15 October 1918
43 Box 15, 18 October 1918
44 Box 14, n.d.
45 *ES*, 77
46 *SP*, 33
47 Box 18, 22 November 1918
48 Box 18, 12 November 1918
49 *SP*, 36
50 Box 15, 21 October 1918
51 *ES*, 109
52 *SP*, 81
53 *SP*, 39
54 Box 18, 16 October 1915
55 *SP*, 32
56 Box 8
57 *SP*, 33
58 *The Oldie*, November 1994
59 *WOTW*, 265
60 *WOTW*, 271
61 Box 18, 12 November 1918
62 *SP*, 47
63 Box 42, 21 May 1962
64 *SP*, 46
65 CHK interview with Bruce Arnold
66 *SP*, 39
67 Box 18, 13 September 1920
68 *SP*, 39
69 Interview with Christabel Bielenberg
70 *ES*, 120
71 *SP*, 89

72 *SP*, 66
73 Esmond Rothermere and Geoffrey Harmsworth to Hugh Cudlipp, *WOTW*, 263
74 *SP*, 59. However the absence of letters home during those vacations suggests that Cecil may have spent less time at the papers than he remembered.
75 *SP*, 93
76 Box 33
77 *SP*, 59–60
78 Box 18, 19 February 1920
79 To GHK, box 18, 19 February 1920
80 Joanna Richardson, *Enid Starkie* (London, 1973), 44
81 Richardson, 44
82 To GHK, box 34, 22 September 1921
83 Box 34, 29 March 1921
84 *SP*, 15
85 *SP*, 71
86 Box 34
87 PB
88 *SP*, 214
89 30 August 1963 in the *New Statesman*, quoted in King's *Commonplace Book* (Sussex, 1981), published when he was eighty, which contains the quotations that he believed summed up his character and personality
90 PB
91 Box 34, Nora to CHK, 29 November 1921
92 Box 34, CHK to GHK, 1 November 1921
93 Box 8
94 Box 34, 23 November 1921
95 Box 34, 23 November 1921
96 Box 12, 26 November 1921
97 Box 32, Helen Cooke to GHK, 28 November 1921
98 Box 32, Helen Cooke to GHK, 14 December 1921
99 PB, n.d.

100 PB, n.d.
101 Box 34, 2 August 1922
102 Quoted in Taylor, 197
103 Quoted in Taylor, 197
104 Quoted in J. Lee Thompson, *Northcliffe: Press Baron in Politics 1865–1922*, 325
105 Box 34, 15 July 1922
106 Box 34, 16 July 1922
107 Pound and Harmsworth, 883
108 Pound and Harmsworth, 884
109 Pound and Harmsworth, 884
110 Box 34, 18 August 1922
111 Quoted in Thompson, 396
112 Quoted in Thompson, 398

Chapter III The Hard Ascent of Cecil King

1 *SP*, 94
2 Box 34, 25 February 1929
3 Box 34, 2 October 1922
4 Box 34, 10 October 1922
5 Box 15, 16 October 1922
6 Box 34, 15 November 1922
7 *SP*, 94–5
8 Interview, 23 November 1996
9 Taylor, *The Great Outsiders*, 194
10 *The Times*, 14 March 1923
11 *SP*, 95
12 Box 34, 27 March 1923
13 *SP*, 22
14 *SP*, 37
15 CHK to AMK, circa 1949, PB
16 PB
17 PB, probably unsent
18 PB
19 PB
20 PB, unsent letter
21 Quoted in King's *Commonplace Book*
22 Box 34, 26 April 1923
23 Box 34, 29 June 1923
24 Box 34, Liberty's invoice, 1923
25 *SP*, 184
26 Box 34, 6 August 1923

27 29 Abercorn Place, NW8. ES, 133.
28 PB
29 *SP*, 95
30 Box 34, 11 November 1923
31 *SP*, 95
32 *SP*, 96
33 Box 35, 21 February 1924
34 Box 35, November 1924
35 Box 35, 25 February 1924
36 Box 34, 29 January 1925
37 Box 34, 26 October 1926
38 HC pp., 1 January 1953, CHK to HC
39 Quoted in *PABD!*, 10
40 Quoted in Pound and Harmsworth, *Northcliffe*, 278
41 Pound and Harmsworth, 391
42 *PABD!* 34–5
43 *SP*, 97
44 Interview, 23 November 1996
45 PB
46 PB
47 *WOTW*, 54
48 Box 34, 12 May 1924
49 Box 34, 20 July 1925
50 *ES*, 132
51 *PB*, 24 August 1925
52 PB, 20 February 1926
53 Box 34, 3 September 1925
54 Box 34, Donna, 4 November 1925
55 Box 34, 1 December 1925
56 *SP*, 40
57 *SP*, 40
58 *ES*, 134
59 *ES*, 135
60 Box 34, 18 June 1926
61 *SP*, 40
62 *SP*, 38
63 *SP*, 99
64 Box 34, 1 June 1930
65 HC pp, CHK to HC, 30 January 1953
66 *SP*, 100
67 *PABD!* 273
68 *SP*, 98
69 *WOTW*, 51

70 *SP*, 99
71 *WOTW*, 51
72 *SP*, 99
73 *SP*, 99
74 *WOTW*, 51
75 *WOTW*, 53–4
76 Quoted in *PABD!*, 48
77 *PABD!*, 50
78 Maurice Edelman, *The Mirror: a political history* (London, 1966), 39
79 *SP*, 100
80 *WOTW*, 52–3
81 PB, 2 August 1934
82 *PABD!*, 67
83 *WOTW*, 61
84 *WOTW*, 55
85 Quoted in *WOTW*, 62
86 HC pp. 22 May 1997, to Wanda Kościa
87 *SP*, 76
88 Quoted in Taylor, 298
89 Quoted in Taylor, 300
90 Quoted in Taylor, 290
91 Rothermere to Lady Vansittart, quoted in Taylor, 294
92 Quoted in Taylor, 301
93 Taylor, 301
94 Taylor, 294
95 Taylor, 307
96 Taylor, 312
97 *SP*, 76
98 *WOTW*, 63
99 PB
100 Box 36, 18 April 1935
101 Box 36, 27 March 1935
102 *Daily News*, 25 April 1935
103 *PABD!*, 132

Chapter IV The Effortless Rise of Hugh Cudlipp

1 *WOTW*, 270
2 *WOTW*, 13
3 *WOTW*, 16
4 *WOTW*, 270
5 *WOTW*, 23
6 *WOTW*, 23
7 *WOTW*, 15
8 *WOTW*, 28
9 *WOTW*, 19
10 Interview, 23 November 1996
11 *WOTW*, 18
12 Interview, 23 November 1996
13 Interview, 23 November 1996
14 Interview, 23 November 1996
15 *WOTW*, 24
16 *WOTW*, 22
17 *WOTW*, 22
18 *WOTW*, 23
19 *WOTW*, 32
20 *WOTW*, 24
21 *WOTW*, 25
22 Interview, 23 November 1996
23 Interview, 23 November 1996
24 *WOTW*, 27
25 *WOTW*, 31
26 Cudlipp's memory that he started as a reporter at fourteen was inaccurate: he was fifteen in August 1928 and began work in December. However, he may well have begun at fourteen as an office boy.
27 *The Newspaper Yearbook 1997* (ed. Dennis Griffiths), (London, 1997)
28 Actually twenty-seven
29 *WOTW*, 270
30 HC pp, 12 January 1955, Claude Cockburn in *Punch*
31 *WOTW*, 36
32 *WOTW*, 36
33 *WOTW*, 38
34 *WOTW*, 38
35 *WOTW*, 36
36 *WOTW*, 37
37 HC memo to RDE
38 *WOTW*, 37
39 Interview, 23 November 1996
40 *The Newspaper Yearbook 1997*
41 *The Newspaper Yearbook 1997*

42 Interview, 23 November 1996
43 Interview, 23 November 1996
44 *WOTW*, 43
45 HC pp.
46 HC pp., career details
47 Interview, 23 November 1996
48 *WOTW*, 39
49 Interview, 23 November 1996
50 *WOTW*, 71
51 *WOTW*, 71
52 Interview, 23 November 1996
53 *WOTW*, 33
54 'For Balliol read Blackpool' *British Journalism Review*, vol. 6, no. 2,
55 *The Newspaper Yearbook 1997*
56 *WOTW*, 26
57 *WOTW*, 44
58 'For Balliol read Blackpool'
59 'For Balliol read Blackpool'
60 *WOTW*, 45
61 'For Balliol read Blackpool'
62 *The Newspaper Yearbook 1997*
63 'For Balliol read Blackpool'
64 Interview, 23 November 1996
65 Interview, 23 November 1996
66 'For Balliol read Blackpool'
67 'For Balliol read Blackpool'
68 'For Balliol read Blackpool'
69 Interview, 23 November 1996
70 Interview, 23 November 1996
71 *WOTW*, 43
72 Interview, 23 November 1996
73 Interview, 23 November 1996
74 Interview, 23 November 1996
75 Interview, 23 November 1996
76 Interview, 23 November 1996
77 HC papers
78 *WOTW*, 49
79 HC pp., 12 June 1935
80 *PABD!*, 132–3
81 *PABD!*, 81
82 *PABD!*, 80; *WOTW*, 59
83 *WOTW*, 59
84 *WOTW*, 56

85 *WOTW*, 56
86 *PABD!*, 78
87 *PABD!*, 79
88 *WOTW*, 59
89 *WOTW*, 60
90 *PABD!*, 83
91 *PABD!*, 84–5
92 *PABD!*, 83
93 *PABD!*, 85
94 *PABD!*, 87
95 *PABD!*, 110
96 From Godfrey Winn, *The Infirm Glory* (London, 1967), quoted in *WOTW*, 57
97 *AYP*, 31
98 *WOTW*, 57
99 *PABD!*, 83
100 *WOTW*, 82
101 *WOTW*, 81
102 *SP*, 108
103 Winn, 347–8
104 23 July 1873. 'J'ouvre à qui veut sortir, je me retire de qui veut m'estimer moins, je me tais avec qui cesse d'entendre. Ainsi le prochain est toujours maître des relations qui nous rapprochent. "Selon qu'il a semé chacun récolte en moi." Je ne puis rien changer à cela et je ne le désire point. Il faut qui se passent de moi, je me passe d'eux.'
105 A translated version appeared in King's *Commonplace Book*, published when he was eighty, with a note saying 'How like me!'
106 *WOTW*, 64
107 Interview with Christabel Bielenberg, 26 September 1995
108 Interview with HC
109 10 August 1937
110 *WOTW*, 81
111 Edelman, *The Mirror: a political history*, 49
112 *WOTW*, 71
113 Quoted in *PABD!*, 92–3

114 *PABD!*, 93
115 *WOTW*, 82–3
116 *WOTW*, 99
117 *WOTW*, 70
118 *SP*, 107
119 *WOTW*, 83
120 Interview, 23 November 1996
121 *WOTW*, 67
122 Interview, 23 November 1996
123 *WOTW*, 271
124 Box 36, 10 July 1937
125 *WOTW*, 84

Chapter V Cudlipp and Mr King

  1 AYP, 47
  2 *WOTW*, 88
  3 *WOTW*, 401
  4 *WOTW*, 91
  5 Peter Wilson, *The Man They Couldn't
     Gag*, (London, 1977), 111
  6 *AYP*, 49
  7 *British Journalism Review*, 1994
  8 Box 36, 5 April 1938
  9 Interview, 23 November 1996
 10 *WOTW*, 89
 11 *WOTW*, 96
 12 *Sunday Pictorial*, 3 April 1938
 13 3 April 1938
 14 10 April 1938
 15 12 June 1938
 16 *AYP*, 51–2
 17 9 October 1938
 18 18 September 1938
 19 9 October 1938
 20 *WOTW*, 401
 21 *WOTW*, 92–3
 22 HC pp, HC to Winston Churchill,
     12 October 1938
 23 23 April 1939, Edelman, *The Mirror: a
     political history*, 77
 24 *WOTW*, 100
 25 *WOTW*, 102
 26 PB, to AMK, 9 July 1939

 27 PB, to AMK, 14 July 1939
 28 PB, to AMK, 28 August 1939
 29 Box 32, 11 August 1939
 30 PB, to AMK, 3 September 1939
 31 *WOTW*, 102
 32 *SP*, 114
 33 *SP*, 115
 34 *SP*, 115
 35 *WMTN*, 33, 36, 41, 66, 67, 69
 36 HC pp, 8 January 1939
 37 Interview, 24 November 1996
 38 Interview, 24 November 1996
 39 *WOTW*, 81
 40 Interview, 24 November 1996
 41 Interview, 24 November 1996
 42 PB, 16 November 1935
 43 PB, 6 January 1932
 44 Antonia White, *Diaries 1926–1957*,
     vol. 1 (ed. Susan Chitty), (London,
     1991), 137
 45 *White*, 38, 20 June 1938
 46 Interview
 47 Interview
 48 PB, 8 March 1934
 49 PB, 19 November, n.y.
 50 PB, 31 August 1932
 51 PB, 23 January 1940 (?)
 52 LK, report, 20 June 1935
 53 Interview,
 54 PB, 6 July 1939
 55 PB, 11 July 1935
 56 PB, 27 September n.y.
 57 Interview with Peter and Christabel
     Bielenberg, 26 September 1995
 58 PB, 27 September n.y.
 59 PB, April 1950, MS
 60 *WOTW*, 263
 61 Box 36, 2 October 1939
 62 PB, 10 September, circa 1941
 63 PB, Elizabeth to AMK, 25 July 1930
 64 PB, n.d., to Enid (XLVIII), prob-
     ably not sent
 65 White, 138, 20 June 1938
 66 PB, Dorothy L.P.

67 PB, Alicia Brown (Lady Edmon-
stone), 11 September 1933

68 White, 138, 20 June 1938

69 PB, n.d., to Enid

70 PB, n.d., but late 1930s

71 PB, 10 August 1937

72 PB, missing first page, but in envelope with letter of 10 August 1937

73 PB, missing first page, but in envelope with letter of 10 August 1937

74 PB, 9 August 1937

75 PB, n.d.

76 PB, to AMK, 10 August 1937

77 PB, to AMK, 10 August 1937

78 PB, missing first page but in envelope
with other letter of 10 August 1937

79 *WMTN,* 8 February 1940

80 Box 37, MS, 5 January 1940

81 15 October 1939

82 *WMTN,* 20 March 1940

83 *WMTN,* 10 May 1940

84 *WOTW,* 117–18

85 *WMTN,* 7 June 1940, 51–2

86 *WMTN,* 47

87 'Thinking Aloud', August 1940,
World Review (HC pp)

88 *WMTN,* 11 December 1940

89 *Pictorial,* 6 October 1940; *WMTN*

90 Box 37, *MS,* 12 October 1940

91 Box 37, *MS,* 17 June 1940

92 Correspondence in HC pp.

93 31 Shepherd Market, W1

94 4 December 1940; Edelman, 142

95 14 December 1940; *AYP,* 75–6

96 HC pp.

Chapter VI Two Wars

1 *WOTW,* 144

2 *WOTW,* 147

3 HC pp, Fuller to HC, 25 December
1940

4 'She did it Her Way', *The Oldie,*
January 1940

5 HC pp, 25 December 1940

6 *WOTW,* 148

7 Box 37, *MS,* 27 May 1941

8 HC pp, CHK to HC, 14 January
1940

9 PB, 13 October 1941

10 Quoted in *WOTW,* 131

11 Correspondence in box 36, quoted
in full in *WMTN*

12 *WMTN,* 28 January 1941

13 *WMTN,* 3 February 1941

14 *WMTN,* 5 February 1941

15 Box 37, *MS,* 8 February 1941

16 *WMTN,* 11 February 1941

17 Box 36, 13 February 1941

18 *WMTN,* 19 February 1941

19 PB, to Walton Butterworth of the
US Embassy, 21 April 1941, probably
not sent

20 Box 37, *MS,* 18 August 1940

21 Box 37, *MS,* 28 October 1940

22 Box 37, *MS,* 19 October 1940

23 *WMTN,* 11 May 1941

24 HC pp, 27 January 1942

25 PB, n.d., but during the war

26 The question came from William
Craven-Ellis, 20 November 1941

27 Box 37, *MS,* 20 November 1941

28 HC pp, 22 November 1941

29 15 February 1942

30 Box 37, *MS,* 21 February 1942

31 HC pp, 25 March 1942

32 *WMTN,* 28 March 1942

33 Box 37, *MS,* 5 April 1942

34 *WMTN,* 24 September 1942

35 *WMTN,* 233–4, 2 November 1943

36 Box 37, *MS,* 10 August 1941

37 *WMTN,* 18 November 1941

38 HC pp, 22 November 1941

39 *MS,* 13 January 1942

40 HC pp, *Ocean News Final,* 22 July
1942

41 Interview

42 HC pp, 18 October 1942

43 HC pp, 25 November 1942

44 Harold Macmillan, *War Diaries* (London, 1984), 6 September 1943

45 *WOTW*, 153

46 W. E. Williams in *The Listener*, 22 April 1943

47 HC pp, 15 April 1943

48 *WOTW*, 157. King, however, on 18 April (*WMTN*), records that Beaverbrook rang to congratulate Cudlipp on an article in the *Pictorial*, which was far less likely: probably a communications muddle.

49 Box 38, *MS*, 3 November 1942

50 *WMTN*, 18 April 1943

51 Box 38, *MS*, 29 April 1943

52 Box 39, 4 June 1942

53 PB, MK to CHK, 24 June

54 PB, 23 January 1942

55 PB, AMK to Hoopie, 28 December 1942

56 PB, 30 October, CHK to MK

57 PB, 2 March, n.y.

58 22 February 1942

59 PB, 22 March 1942

60 PB, Michaelmas 1941

61 PB, 25 November, n.y., but from Plymouth

62 PB, 8 April 1942

63 PB, n.d.

64 *SP*, 204

65 Box 39, 2 and 7 April 1943

66 PB, notebook, post-1955

67 PB, 15 October 1941

68 PB, AMK to Hoopie, 28 December 1942

69 PB, CHK to Priscilla, n.d.

70 PB, CHK to Priscilla, 12 July 1944

71 PB, 30 June 1945

72 PB, n.d., but no earlier than 1943

73 Robert Connor, *Cassandra, Reflections in a Mirror* (London, 1969), 69

74 *Union Jack*, 25 October 1947

75 S. P. MacKenzie, 'Vox Populi: British Army Newspapers in the Second World War', *Journal of Contemporary History*, vol. 24 (1989), 665–81

76 Connor, 71–2

77 Connor, 68

78 *WOTW*, 159

79 Quoted in MacKenzie, 'British Army Newspapers'

80 MacKenzie

81 HC pp, HC to S. P. MacKenzie, 17 July 1988

82 HC pp, CHK to HC, 12 January 1944 (though dated 1943)

83 HC pp, 4 September 1944

84 PB, n.d.

85 *SP*, 118

86 PB, n.d.

87 Box 39, *The Newspaper World*, 18 November 1944

88 HC pp, 15 November 1944

89 PB, n.d., Friday

90 *SP*, 187

91 PB, 1 May 1945

92 PB, 15 May 1945

93 PB, CHK to MK 22 November

94 PB, n.d.

95 PB, to AMK, 10 June 1945

96 Box 39, 24 May 1945

97 Box 39, 21 June 1945

98 Box 39, 6 June 1945

99 Box 39, 20 May 1945

100 HC pp, 11 July 1945

Chapter VII Bart's Revenge

1 Interview, 23 July 1994

2 HC pp, 22 February 1946

3 HC pp, 15 March 1946

4 Roy Lewis, 'The *Daily Mirror*, Persuasion, Spring 1947

5 PB, 28 July 1945

6 *AYP*, 292

7 *WOTW*, 173

8 *WOTW*, 174

9 Box 38, *MS*, 4 August and 2 September 1944
10 3 August 1947
11 26 October 1946
12 *WOTW*, 177
13 *WOTW*, 178
14 *WOTW*, 189
15 *WOTW*, 180
16 HC memorandum on marriages to RDE
17 HC pp., marriage certificate 31 October 1945, both of 112D Cheyne Walk; marriage service 6 October 1945 in Serbian Orthodox Church.
18 *Pictorial*, 12 March 1939
19 Box 37, *MS*, 15 May 1940
20 Box 38, *MS*, 14 April 1943
21 *WMTN*, 29 January 1945
22 *WOTW*, 259
23 *AYP*, 99
24 *Daily Worker*, 30 April 1947
25 PB, 26 April 1948
26 *SP*, 171
27 *PB*, to AMK, 3 November 1946
28 *SP*, 170
29 PB, to AMK, n.d.
30 *SP*, 166
31 *SP*, 167
32 *SP*, 177
33 PB, 4 November 1947
34 *WOTW*, 195–6
35 *WOTW*, 198
36 PB, 12 February [1947]
37 *SP*, 162–3
38 Interview with Tom and Doris Langley
39 Frank Barton, *The Press of Africa: Persecution and Perseverance* (London, 1979), 33
40 PB, CHK to Colin King, 23 November 1949
41 *SP*, 123
42 *WOTW*, 174
43 *WOTW*, 183
44 *The Backbench Diaries of Richard Crossman* (ed. Janet Morgan), (London, 1981), 56
45 Box 39, 5 December 1949
46 HC pp, to Bill Soles, 14 December 1949
47 *AYP*, 100
48 *WOTW*, 184
49 Crossman, 56
50 HC pp, Mary Ellison, 8 December 1949
51 HC pp, 9 December 1949
52 Crossman, 96
53 HC pp, 11 December 1949
54 *WOTW*, 185
55 Interview, 20 August 1994
56 *WOTW*, 192
57 *AYP*, 105–6
58 Box 40, A. J. P. Taylor to CHK, 22 August 1960
59 *WOTW*, 187–8
60 *WOTW*, 188
61 *WOTW*, 186–7
62 *WOTW*, 187
63 *AYP*, 105
64 Crossman, 56
65 *AYP*, 102
66 Anthony Howard, *Crossman* (London, 1990), 129
67 *WOTW*, 192
68 *SP*, 149
69 Interview, 19 February 1996
70 PB, note by Dr I. Babatunde José
71 King, *Commonplace Book*, 25
72 *SP*, 150
73 Interview with Denis Forman, 27 January 1992
74 Box 40, back of photograph
75 *SP*, 141
76 PB, 11 November 1943
77 *SP*, 72
78 PB, Wednesday
79 Box 39, 7 October 1945
80 PB, to AMK, October 12 [1946]

81 PB, Nigel Falls, 'Living with Uncle Cecil', n.d.

82 PB, n.d., but during the war

83 PB, n.d.

84 HC pp, CHK to HC, 12 January 1944, though dated 1943

85 PB, CHK to AMK, 5 June 1945

86 PB, 29 December 1947

87 PB, 17 February 1947

88 Box 39, 28 November 1949

89 PB, Francis to CHK, 13 November 1946

90 Box 39, 4 November 1947

91 Box 39, quoted in CHK to Priscilla, 23 January 1951

92 PB, 28 July 1941

93 PB, Michaelmas term 1938

94 Box 39, n.d., but 1949

95 PB, 23 November 1949

96 PB, n.d., unsent

97 Francis to CHK, 2 May 1950

98 PB, Tuesday, circa August 1950

99 PB, Thursday, n.d.

100 PB, n.d., but circa 1949/50

101 WOTW, 390

102 Box 39, 4 November 1950

103 27 December 1950

104 Box 39, to Priscilla, 29 January 1951

105 PB, Nigel Falls

106 Edelman, The Mirror: a political history, 154

107 WOTW, 193

108 Crossman, 54–5

109 PABD!, 277

110 Francis Williams, The Right to Know (London, 1969), 141–2

111 Advertisers Weekly, 20 December 1951

112 22 December 1951

113 Box 39, paper unidentified, n.d.

114 PB, 23 December 1951

115 PABD!, 278

116 WOTW, 259

Chapter VIII The Eagle and the Lark

1 HC pp, to Max Aitken, 28 March 1952

2 HC pp, transcript of part of a letter from CHK to J. D. Patience, 27 March 1952

3 The Backbench Diaries of Richard Crossman (ed. Janet Morgan), (London, 1981) 110

4 Crossman, 110

5 Crossman, 96

6 Crossman, 110

7 WOTW, 199

8 Crossman, 153

9 HC pp. transcribed from a letter from CHK to J. D. Patience, 15 September 1951

10 WOTW, 199

11 HC pp, copy CHK to HC, 18 March 1953

12 WOTW, 203

13 SP, 174–5

14 SP, 182

15 WOTW, 198

16 WOTW, 198

17 WOTW, 201

18 SP, 180

19 WOTW, 201

20 SP, 180

21 SP, 179

22 WOTW, 201

23 WOTW, 202

24 WOTW, 203

25 Interview, 23 November 1996

26 HC pp, CHK to HC, 27 December 1952

27 HC pp, HC to CHK, 6 November 1952

28 HC pp, HC to CHK, 13 November 1952

29 HC pp, CHK to HC, 27 December 1952

30 HC pp, HC to CHK 29 December 1952

31 HC pp, HC to CHK, 21 January 1953

32 HC pp, HC to CHK, 29 December 1952

33 Quoted in Matthew Engels, *Tickle the Public* (London, 1996), 181

34 Engels, 181

35 Engels, 181

36 Keith Waterhouse, *Streets Ahead: Life After City Lights* (London, 1995), 66

37 Waterhouse, 66

38 Crossman, 508

39 Waterhouse, 64

40 Interview

41 *AYP*, 23

42 HC pp, CHK to HC, 18 March 1953

43 Waterhouse, 38

44 Mike Randall *The Funny Side of The Streets* (London, 1998), 55–6

45 Crossman, 142

46 Crossman, 149

47 HC pp, 13 August 1953

48 Crossman, 154

49 HC pp, CHK to HC, 13 August 1953

50 HC pp, 4 June 1952

51 Quoted in *PABD!*, 250–1

52 *PABD!*, 278

53 *PABD!*, 283

54 HC pp, CHK to HC, 18 March 1953

55 *PABD!*, 282–3

56 HC pp, 18 March 1953

57 *PABD!*, 285

58 Crossman, 261

59 *New Statesman*, 17 October 1953

60 *AYP*, 300–1

61 *AYP*, 303–4

62 *AYP*, 317

63 *AYP*, 31 and 317

64 *AYP*, 317

65 Crossman, 110

66 Interview

67 (London, 1996), 293

68 Interview, 16 November 1992

69 *WOTW*, 299

70 I am grateful to Bruce Arnold for this information

71 25 September 1955

72 Patrick Higgins, *Heterosexual Dictatorship: male homosexuality in postwar Britain*, 294–7

73 Darden Asbury Pyron, *Liberace: an American boy*, (Chicago, 2000), 225

74 Pyron, 227

75 *WOTW*, 237

76 *WOTW*, 236

77 Higgins, 282

78 Higgins, 283

79 Francis Williams, *The Right to Know*, 153

80 *AYP*, 54

81 *AYP*, 55

82 *AYP*, 142

83 Quoted in *AYP*, 148

84 *AYP*, 93

85 *AYP*, 92

86 Williams, 153

87 *AYP*, 342

88 *AYP*, 342

89 Box 36, WSC to CHK, 29 December 1952

90 HC pp, HC to WSC, 30 December 1952

91 Lord Moran, *Winston Churchill: The Struggle for Survival 1940–1965* (London, 1966), 17 August 1953

92 Moran, 26 January 1954

93 Crossman, 306

94 HC pp, HC to WSC, 22 July 1955

95 *SP*, 111

96 Donald Zec *Some Enchanted Egos* (London, 1966), 139–42

97 Crossman, 377

98 *WOTW*, 213

99 Crossman, 418

100 Crossman, 439

101 Box 40, CHK to Herbert Morrison, 15 December 1955

102 Box 40, Morrison to CHK, 29 December 1955

103 *SP*, 130

104 *SP*, 130

105 *WOTW*, 212–3

106 *WOTW*, 226–7

107 *AYP*, 111

108 HC pp, n.d.

109 HC pp, Donald Tyerman to HC, 26 September 1956

110 Box 40, CHK to Gaitskell, 6 November 1956

111 Box 40, Gaitskell to CHK, 9 November 1956

112 *WOTW*, 230

113 *AYP*, 157

114 *AYP*, 158

115 *SP*, 122

116 *WOTW*, 257–8

117 *AYP*, 169

Chapter IX His Uncle's Nephew

1 *AYP*, 173

2 *AYP*, 188–9

3 *SP*, 124

4 *Observer*, 28 February 1960

5 *AYP*, 192

6 Interview, 8 October 1968

7 Interview, 8 October 1968

8 *AYP*, 199–259 *passim*

9 29 January 1961

10 2 March 1961

11 *Queen*, 15 March 1961

12 8 March 1961

13 LK, CHK to LK, 19 October 1951

14 PB, Nigel Falls

15 Ruth Railton, *Daring to Excel* (London, 1992), 140

16 PB

17 Box 39, Enid Stokes to CHK, 17 December, n.y. but 1952

18 Interview

19 LK, n.d., but 1952

20 Box 40, CHK to Betty Pinney, 1954

21 Box 39, R. A. Skelton to CHK, 22 May 1953

22 Box 39, Enid Stokes to CHK, 17 December

23 Railton, 14

24 Railton, 138

25 Railton, 140

26 Railton, 189

27 Interview

28 Box 40, CHK to American Embassy, 20 May 1955

29 Box 40, 26 August 1955

30 Antonia White, *Diaries*, 301, 16 February 1956

31 Interview with Hugh Cudlipp

32 Interview with Hugh Cudlipp

33 LK, Enid Stokes to LK, February 1956

34 Box 40, R. A. Skelton to CHK, 15 February 1956

35 Box 40, CHK to R. A. Skelton, n.d.

36 Box 40, A. Humphrey Reeve

37 Dennis Barker, *Guardian*, 1 March 2001

38 Interview with Christabel Bielenberg, 26 September 1995

39 Nicholas Spice, *London Review of Books*, 6 January 1994

40 Interview

41 Interviews with Bruce Arnold and RDE

42 PB, n.d.

43 *Guardian*, 1 March 2001

44 PB, n.d., probably not sent

45 Box 40, Charles Neil to CHK, 10 April 1957

46 *Evening Standard*, 15 October 1962

47 PB, 24 October 1943

48 LK, H. C. H. Graves to MK, 11 February 1949

49 LK, Graves to CHK, 28 March 1949

50 Keith Waterhouse, *Streets Ahead*, 65

51 Dennis Hackett, 'In El Vino's Veritas', *Queen*, 16 January 1963

52 *UK Press Gazette*, 11 December 1967

53 LK, n.d., but 1953 or 1954

54 *Sunday Telegraph*, 'Peregrine Worsthorne's Week', date missing, but shortly after 31 October 1980

55 PB, George Lyttleton to MK, 24 October 1943

56 Box 42, MK to CHK, 4 May 1962

57 Interview, 13 March 1994

58 PB, MK to AMK, 15 February 1942?

59 Box 34, n.d., but 1928

Chapter X The Influence of Ruth

1 *The Economist*, 4 February 1961

2 *New Statesman*, 3 February 1961

3 'Journalist Tycoon', *Observer*, 18 June 1961

4 *WOTW*, 247–8

5 'Journalist Tycoon', *Observer*, 18 June 1961

6 Box 41, George Brown to CHK, 25 May 1961

7 Box 40, George Brown to CHK, 2 June 1960; CHK to George Brown, 13 June 1960

8 Box 41, CHK to George Brown, 6 June 1961

9 HC pp, *Inky Way Annual*, 1953

10 'The Journal of a Curious Citizen', *Truth*, 11 October 1953

11 Interview with Tony Delano

12 John Beavan in the *Independent*, 18 May 1998

13 Memo for RDE

14 Richard Crossman, *Diaries of a Cabinet Minister*, vol. 1, January 1958

15 Interview with Dr Edward McClellan

16 Beavan, *Independent*

17 HC pp, Jack Nener to HC, 21 March 1969

18 *WOTW*, 301

19 HC pp, memo to RDE

20 Jodi Cudlipp, 'Being at the ringside – and even in the ring', *British Journalism Review*, vol. 12, no. 2, 2001

21 Box 47, CHK to Arthur J. Ellison, 4 April 1967

22 *Without Fear or Favour*, 244

23 *WOTW*, 391

24 *WMTN*, 18 April 1942

25 Box 43, Sir George Joy to CHK and RK, 11 August 1962

26 Box 43, Celia Green to CHK, 11 April 1964

27 Box 43, 15 April 1964

28 Box 45, Celia Green to CHK, 11 February 1965 and CHK to Sir George Joy, 22 February 1965

29 Box 43, for instance John Beloff to CHK, 12 June 1964

30 Paul Johnson, 'Avoid small generals, but look out for tall blondes', *The Spectator*, 11 March 2000

31 Box 48, CHK to Sir George Joy, 5 July 1967

32 Box 48, R. G. Medhurst to CHK, 9 July 1967

33 21 February 1969

34 Interview, 27 February 1996

35 Interview, 19 February 1996

36 Interview, 26 February 1996

37 Interview, 20 August 1994

38 *New Statesman*, 28 October 1966

39 Box 47, 3 January 1966

40 *Sunday Times*, 16 February 1964

41 Box 42, speech on the sixtieth birthday of the *Daily Mirror*, 7 December 1963

42 *Stet*, July 1964

43 *WOTW*, 249

44 *Newsweek*, 30 September 1963

45 *Time & Tide*, 17–23 September 1964

46 Matthew Engels, *Tickle the Public*, 250

47 *Sunday Times*, 16 February 1964

48 Box 43, Sun Editorial Briefing Conference, 12 September 1964

49 Jean Rook, *The Cowardly Lioness* (London, 1989), 48–9

50 *France Observateur*, 24 September 1964

51 *World Press News*, 11 September 1964

52 Engels, 250

53 Box 40, Hugh Gaitskell to CHK, 7 October 1956

54 Box 43, CHK to Geoffrey Rippon, 4 December 1964

55 Crossman, 676, 14 March 1958

56 Crossman, 714, 8 October 1958

57 Crossman, 714–5, 17 October 1958

58 Crossman, 715, 17 October 1958

59 Crossman, 723, 27 November 1958

60 Crossman, 747–8, 14 May 1959

61 Crossman, 772, 27 August 1959

62 *WOTW*, 295

63 *Observer*, 1 November 1959

64 See *AYP* for a photograph

65 HC pp, 27 May 1960

66 Box 40, BBC press conference, 28 February 1958

67 Box 40, BBC press conference, 28 February 1961

68 Box 41, International Press Institute meeting at Chatham House, 25 January 1961

69 See, for instance, Peter Jenkins in the *Guardian*, 24 January 1966, on how under King's leadership the NPA 'for once faced up to blackmail'

70 *World Press News*, 24 May 1963

71 Box 42, no source given, 9 November 1963

72 Box 47, *Editor & Publisher*, 29 April 1967

73 Box 42, speech to African ministers, 24 July (1963?)

74 Box 43, CHK to Alfred Eggleston, 22 January 1964

75 Cf Frank Barton, *The Press of Africa: Persecution and Perseverance* (London, 1979)

76 HC pp, attached to a memorandum of 12 August 1965 to IPC directors and others

77 Box 42, CHK to Priscilla, 30 October 1963

78 Quoted in 'ON THE VERGE OF GREATNESS', *Sunday Mirror*, 24 November 1963

79 'ON THE VERGE OF GREATNESS', *Sunday Mirror*, 24 November 1963

80 *CKD*, 25 July 1965

81 *CKD*, 25 July 1965

82 W.F. Deedes, *Dear Bill: W. F. Deedes Reports* (London, 1997), 107

83 Crossman, 977, 15 February 1963

84 Alan Watkins, 'These unpredictable press barons still rule the jungle', *Independent on Sunday*, 20 August 2000

85 Speech to Liverpool Labour Party workers, 23 March 1963

86 HC pp., to Harold Wilson, 13 May 1968

87 Box 42, Harold Wilson to CHK, 4 October 1963

88 HC pp, HC to CHK, 18 February 1964

89 Box 43, 23 June 1964

90 HC pp., 27 July 1964

91 *WOTW*, 218

92 *Sun*, 17 September 1964

93 *Sun*, 23 September 1964

94 *Sun*, 30 September 1964

95 *Financial Times*, 16 October 1964

96 Pickering's note of a conversation with Wilson, 31 May 1969; Wilson had also told Crossman (II, 403, 30 June 1967) that this was the issue over which King fell out with him; Wilson confirmed the story in a letter to Cudlipp, 26 March 1976, though the details were slightly hazy; Cudlipp in *WOTW*, 345, says he saw a letter from King asking for the earldom.

97 PB, n.d., but probably early 1950s; written from Bird's Farm

98 Frank Waters, 1 January 1952, quoted in Stephen Koss, *The Rise and Fall of the Political Press in Britain*, II (London, 1984), 648

99 Interview

100 Box 44, diary page, 15 June 1964

101 Cudlipp, 'The Humble Seeker After Knowledge', in *Fleet Street* (London, 1964), 56

102 *WOTW*, 307

103 Antonia White, *Diaries 1958–1979* (London, 1992) 106

104 Box 41, Enid Stokes to CHK, 14 August 1961

105 PB, CHK to Priscilla, 9 November 1966

106 Box 46, transcript of an address given on 17 November 1966

107 White, 1 October 1966

108 Box 46, Cardinal Heenan to CHK, 22 November 1966

109 Box 43, CHK to Harold Wilson, 4 November 1964

110 Box 45, CHK to Harold Wilson, 27 November 1965

111 *Yorkshire Post*, 10 March 1965

112 Box 44, *Granada's Scene* at 6.30, 6 July 1965

113 *CKD*, 5 August 1965

114 *CKD*, 7 August 1965

115 Box 45, 28 July 1965

116 Minutes of Evidence, Q. 2298

117 Box 45, CHK to Jean Monnet, 26 February 1965

118 *CKD*, 15 November 1965

119 *CKD*, 32–3, 19 August 1965

120 Unilateral Declaration of Independence

121 *The Spectator*, 10 December 1965

122 *The Spectator*, 10 December 1965

123 Magnus Turnstile, 'King v. Wilson', *New Statesman*, 25 March 1966

124 20 March 1966

125 30 March 1966

126 *CKD*, 65

127 Box 47, Wednesday, n.d., but 13 April 1966

128 *CKD*, 15 April 1966

129 *CKD*, 19 April 1966

130 Interview for Granada, 10 October 1968

131 *The Times*, 1 July 1966

132 Box 47, CHK to George Brown, 17 June 1966

133 Box 47, 25 June 1966

134 *WOTW*, 293

135 *CKD*, 30 June 1966

136 *CKD*, 5 July 1966

137 *CKD*, 23 July 1966

138 Crossman, 115, 8 November 1966

139 *WOTW*, 294

140 *Birmingham Post*, 7 November 1966

141 *WOTW*, 296

142 *WOTW*, 296–8

143 *WOTW*, 298

144 *CKD*, 22 February 1967

145 Quoted in *CKD*, 5 May 1967

146 *CKD*, 18 September 1967

147 Quoted in *WOTW*, 300

148 *Observer*, 8 October 1967

149 *Morning Star*, 30 September 1967

150 *CKD*, 9 November 1967

151 *CKD*, 28 November 1967

152 *Observer*, 10 December 1967

153 *Financial Times*, 6 July 1965

154 Box 48, AGM of IPC, 12 July 1967

155 HC pp., Edward Pickering to HC, 1 December 1975

156 Interview with Ellis and Alma Birk, 26 February 1996

157 *WOTW*, 306

Chapter XI The Reluctant Assassin

1 Quoted in the *Guardian*, 31 May 1968

2 Interview for Granada

3 Interview with Ellis Birk

4 *WOTW*, 299

5 *WOTW*, 299

6 Roy Jenkins, *A Life at the Centre* (London, 1991), 253

7 Interview

8 *WOTW*, 302

9 *CKD*, 22 August 1967

10 *WOTW*, 323

11 *WOTW*, 304–5

12 *CKD*, 7 February 1968

13 Tony Benn, *Office Without Power, Diaries 1968–72* (London, 1988), 6 February 1968

14 *WOTW*, 310

15 *WOTW*, 311

16 Stephens put his recollections of this time with King on paper the following year: HC pp., Peter Stephens to HC, 4 July 1969; see also *WOTW*, 311–14

17 Stephens memo

18 *CKD*, 22 February 1968

19 WOTW, 316

20 *Guardian*, 23 February 1968

21 *CKD*, 24 February 1968

22 *The Spectator*, 23 February 1968

23 *WOTW*, 317

24 Stephens memo

25 *WOTW*, 318–22

26 From George Gale's review of *CKD*, quoted in *WOTW*, 321

27 HC pp, Edward Pickering to HC, 8 March 1976

28 *Observer*, 31 March 1968

29 *CKD*, 1 April 1968

30 *WOTW*, 322

31 *WOTW*, 322–3

32 *Punch*, 17 January 1968

33 HC pp, John Beavan to King and Cudlipp, 6 May 1968

34 HC pp, HC to CHK, n.d., but re. Sir Sigmund Warburg's letter of 1 March 1968

35 *WOTW*, 323

36 *WOTW*, 325

37 HC pp, HC to CHK, 29 April 1968

38 HC pp, HC to CHK, 30 April 1968

39 Philip Ziegler, *Mountbatten* (London, 1985), 659

40 *WOTW*, 326

41 Quoted in Hugh Cudlipp, 'The So-Called "Military Coup" of 1968', *Encounter*, September 1981; see also Louis Heren and Lord Zuckerman in *Encounter*, October 1981

42 Solly Zuckerman's diary entry, 15 July 1970, quoted in Ziegler, 660

43 Solly Zuckerman in the *Observer*, 2 September 1979

44 14 November 1975, quoted in Cudlipp's *Encounter* article

45 Ziegler, 660

46 Solly Zuckerman, 'A Reply', *Encounter*, October 1981

47 The early end to the meeting was confirmed by John Barrett, cf. Cudlipp's and Zuckerman's *Encounter* articles

48 Zuckerman in *Encounter*, October 1981

49 Cudlipp in *Encounter*, September 1981

50 Quoted in *Time*, 13 April 1981

51 *WOTW*, 330–1

52 23 August 1994 to the *Daily Telegraph*, whose obituary of John Beavan, Lord Ardwick, had suggested that he drafted 'Enough is Enough'

53 *WOTW*, 334

54 Box 49, transcript of the programme *Battle for the Boroughs*

55 HC pp, Ellis Birk to Frank Rogers, 15 May 1968

56 Jenkins, 254

57 *Daily Telegraph*, 14 May 1968

58 Richard Crossman, *Diaries of a Cabinet Minister*, III, 10 May 1968

59 *The Times*, 11 May 1968

60 *WOTW*, 341

61 HC pp, HC to CHK, 10 May 1968

62 *The Times*, 11 May 1968

63 *The Times*, 11 May 1968

64 *CKD*, 11 May 1968
65 Quoted in *East African Standard*, 16 March 1968
66 *Sunday Express*, 12 May 1968
67 Ben Pimlott, *Harold Wilson* (London, 1992), 507
68 Box 51, CHK to Desmond Donnelly, 'Strictly Private and Confidential', 14 May 1968
69 *Punch*, 22 May 1968
70 *Private Eye*, 24 May 1968
71 *New Statesman*, 24 May 1968
72 *Guardian*, 13 May 1968
73 Crossman, 13 May 1968
74 HC pp, Ellis Birk to Frank Rogers, 15 May 1968
75 HC pp, Ellis Birk to Frank Rogers, 15 May 1968
76 Ellis Birk to Frank Rogers, 15 May 1968
77 *WOTW*, 379
78 *WOTW*, 349
79 *WOTW*, 374
80 *WOTW*, 371–3
81 Interview with Jocelyn Stevens for Granada
82 Charles Wintour, *The Rise and Fall of Fleet Street* (London, 1989), 130
83 Printed in *WOTW*, 351
84 *WOTW*, 384
85 *WOTW*, 359
86 The interview, as reported in *WOTW*, was based on notes made shortly afterwards, now in HC pp.
87 Wintour, 131
88 *CKD*, 8 June 1968
89 *WOTW*, 355
90 'Dog Watches Dog', *UK Press Gazette*, 3 June 1968
91 *WOTW*, 357
92 *WOTW*, 358
93 *WOTW*, 359
94 Wintour, 132
95 Peter Paterson in the *Sunday Telegraph* said it was clear Cudlipp was confiding in Wilson at the Chancellor's party; the *Guardian*, 31 May 1968, was anxious to know when Wilson had heard of the plot
96 Michael Dove, *Sunday Express*, 2 June 1968
97 Laurence Marks, *Observer*, 2 June 1968
98 Stephen Aris, *Sunday Times*, 2 June 1968
99 *Sunday Telegraph*, 9 June 1968
100 'Dog Watches Dog', *UK Press Gazette*, 3 June 1968
101 *WOTW*, 378
102 HC pp, Peter Stephens, 4 July 1969, telling the story Ruth had told his wife

Chapter XII Lord Cudlipp and Mr King

1 *Observer*, 2 June 1968
2 Peter Wilsher, *Sunday Times*, 2 June 1968
3 *Sunday Express*, 2 June 1968
4 Hamlyn interview with Charles Wintour, quoted in Wintour
5 *CKD*, 2 July 1968
6 *WOTW*, 361
7 HC pp, n.d., but circa 20 July 1968
8 HC pp, 17 and 22 July 1968
9 *WOTW*, 362–8, gives a full account of the AGM
10 *Financial Times*, 24 July 1968
11 HC pp, *Proceedings at the Sixth Annual Meeting of the Members held at the Café Royal, Regent Street, London, W.I., on Tuesday, 23rd July, 1968, at 12 noon*
12 *CKD*, 8 June 1968
13 *CKD*, 18 June 1968
14 *CKD*, 25 July 1968
15 *The Spectator*, 26 July 1968
16 *Guardian*, 24 July 1968
17 *Investor's Chronicle*, 26 July 1968
18 *Daily Telegraph*, 23 July 1968

19 *Birmingham Post*, 24 July 1968

20 *CKD*, 31 December 1968

21 *Observer* magazine, 9 January 1977

22 Harold Wilson, *The Labour Government, 1964–1970* (London, 1971), 529

23 HC pp, Peter Stephens to HC, 4 July 1969

24 *CKD*, 24 April 1969

25 Talk delivered to the Society of Business Economists, 26 March 1971; published in *The Business Economist*, Summer 1971

26 HC pp, Peter Stephens to HC, 10 March 1972

27 *WOTW*, 395

28 HC pp, *JASMIN, Die Zeitschrift für das Leben zu zweit*, 21 December 1970

29 *CKD*, 11 December 1968 for their first meeting; and see *CKD*, 1970–4 *passim*

30 *CKD*, 11 March 1971

31 Ed Moloney and Andy Pollak, *Paisley* (Dublin, 1986), 322

32 Joe Cahill, quoted in Brendan Anderson, *Joe Cahill: a life in the IRA* (Belfast, 2002), 253

33 *CKD*, 23 December 1968

34 *CKD*, 12 February 1969

35 *CKD*, 20 June 1970

36 *CKD*, 21 June 1970

37 *CKD*, 22 January 1972

38 Anderson, 255

39 HC pp, Peter Stephens to HC, 10 March 1972

40 *CKD*, 15 August 1971

41 *CKD*, 4 February 1972

42 Cecil King, *On Ireland*, (London 1973) 40

43 *On Ireland*, 168

44 *CKD*, 2 June 1969

45 *Sunday Times*, 2 March 1969; *CKD*, 18 March 1969

46 HC pp, Max Aitken to CHK, February 1969

47 *WOTW*, 389

48 *The Economist*, 31 May 1969

49 Box 56, Needham to CHK, 13 June 1969

50 Christabel Bielenberg, *The Past is Myself*, (London, 1968)

51 *SP*, 90

52 Interview with Christabel Bielenberg

53 *The Economist*, 28 November 1970

54 *Observer*, 2 November 1970

55 *WOTW*, 392

56 *WOTW*, 392

57 *CKD*, 15 November 1972

58 *CKD*, 17 November 1972

59 *Punch*, 6–12 December 1972

60 *Sunday Times*, 19 October 1975

61 *CKD*, 16 October 1974

62 *Daily Telegraph*, 'The day Cecil King talked of treason', 21 April 1987

63 *CKD*, 7 November 1973

64 *The Economist*, 18 October 1975

65 *Observer*, 19 October 1975

66 *Independent*, 20 April 1987

67 PB, CHK to Priscilla, 16 December 1975

68 *WOTW*, 307

69 Interview

70 *WOTW*, 381

71 Interview

72 *New Statesman*, 15 November 1968

73 *WOTW*, 253

74 Terry Coleman, 28 August 1974, *Guardian*

75 *WOTW*, 252

76 *CKD*, 19 December 1968

77 Matthew Engels, *Tickle the Public*, 248

78 *Sunday Times*, 16 February 1964

79 John Pilger, *Heroes* (London 1986), 512–13

80 Engels, 253

81 HC pp, 12 October 1971

82 Interview

83 *The Economist*, 31 January 1970

84 Interview

85 *Sunday Times*, 26 January 1970

86 Bob Edwards, *Goodbye Fleet Street* (London, 1988) 208–9

87 *CKD*, 16 June 1970

88 Edwards, 206

89 Goodman in *British Journalism Review*, vol. 9, no. 3, 1998

90 HC pp, address at Sydney Jacobson's funeral, November 1988

91 *Guardian*, 18 May 1998

92 HC pp, HC to Don Ryder, 21 September 1972

93 HC pp, 2 October 1972

94 HC pp, Lee Howard to HC, 4 May 1971

95 Edwards, 210

96 HC pp, 'MANY CONGRATULATIONS ON YOUR WELL DESERVED HONOUR', 1 January 1973

97 Hansard, 17 March 1974

98 *Chichester Observer*, 2 March 1995

99 HC pp, innumerable memoranda to Robert Maxwell, 1984–6

100 *Daily Mail*, 5 December 1991

101 *Guardian*, 4 November 1976

102 *Observer*, 7 November 1976

103 *The Times*, 4 November 1974

104 HC pp, CHK to HC, 24 October 1971

105 HC pp, CHK to HC, 13 October 1976

106 PB, 13 November 1976

107 *SP*, 39

108 HC pp

109 HC pp, HC to CHK, 6 May 1980; CHK to HC, 15 May 1980

110 HC pp, CHK to HC, 31 March 1981

111 HC pp, HC to CHK, 3 April 1981

112 23 October 1981

113 Review of Piers Brendon, *The Life and Death of the Press Barons*, (London, 1982), in *Books & Bookmen*

114 Carey King

115 PB, CHK to Priscilla, 22 January 1978

116 LK, CHK to LK 27 September 1981

117 King, *Commonplace Book*, 14

118 RK, n.d.

119 To Lucinda King, n.d

120 HC pp, Stephens to HC, 2 May 1969

121 Interview for Granada

122 *Country Life*, 9 January 1975

123 PB, CHK to Priscilla, 2 June 1975

124 PB, CHK to Priscilla, 29 January 1976

125 *CKD*, 6 May 1970

126 *CKD*, 14 July 1971

127 *CKD*, 21 February 1979

128 LK, Colin to MK, 6 February 1972

129 PB, CHK to Priscilla, 21 September 1980

130 PB, RK to Priscilla, 16 August 1980

131 PB, CHK to Priscilla, 16 August 1980

132 PB, CHK to Priscilla, 21 September 1980

133 'Peregrine Worsthorne's Week', *Sunday Telegraph*, 31 October 1980

134 PB, CHK to Francis, 14 August 1980

135 PB, CHK to Francis, 22 April, probably 1981

136 PB, Francis to CHK, 26 March, probably 1981

137 PB, CHK to Francis, 15 December n.y.

138 PB, CHK to Priscilla, 13 November 1976

139 PB, CHK to Priscilla, 2 April, probably 1983

140 PB, RK to Priscilla, 16 August 1980

141 Interview

142 King, *Commonplace Book*, 44

143 PB, CHK to Francis 17 January 1984

144 PB, CHK to Priscilla, 24 July 1985

145 PB, CHK to Priscilla, 4 November 1986

146 HC pp, HC to Michael Boon, 26 November 1997

147 HC pp, 17 May 1998

Epilogue

1 PB, CHK to Priscilla, 23 August 1980
2 *Daily Times*, 20 April 1987
3 *London Daily News*, 28 April 1987
4 *Today*, 28 April 1987
5 Lynn Picknett, Clive Prince, Stephen Prior and Robert Brydon, *War of the Windsors: A Century of Unconstitutional Monarchy* (Edinburgh, 2002); to call this poorly researched would be a compliment
6 LK to RDE, mid-1990s

7 PB, CHK to Priscilla, 4 November 1985
8 RK to Lucinda King, Easter 1987
9 Nigel Falls to Priscilla, 10 December n.y.
10 Nicholas Spice, *London Review of Books*, 6 January 1994
11 RDE, CHK to Bruce Arnold, 10 October 1982
12 RDE, RK to Bruce Arnold, October 1982
13 *Guardian*, 1 March 2001

INDEX

Aboyne, Aberdeenshire 12, 51; *see also* Cushnie

Abrams, Mark 328

Acheson, Dean 399

Adamson, Joy: *Born Free* 310

Age (Melbourne) 226

Aldingbourne, Sussex 420

Alexander, A. V. 173

Altrincham, Lord *see* Grigg, John

Amalgamated Press, King buys 267, 268–70

American Society of Newspaper Editors 335

Amiel, Henri Frédéric: *Journal Intime* 107–8, 142–3, 344

Anderson, Lindsay 207

Andrews, Eamonn 426n

'Andy Capp' 265

Angell, Sir Norman 246

Anglo-Canadian Pulp & Paper Company 114, 276, 299

Answers 7, 54, 89

Ardwick, Baron *see* Beavan, John

Argus (Melbourne) 225, 226

Armstrong, Sir William 369

Arnold, Bruce 449

Ascroft, Eileen *see* Cudlipp, Eileen

Asquith, Herbert Henry: 2, 27, 28, 29–30, 201; letter quoted by King 69–70

Associated Newspapers 54, 63, 112

Association of Motion Picture Producers 208

Astor, John Jacob 54

Attlee, Clement 148, 154, 156, 191, 205, 262, 263, 351n, 406, 421

ATV 270n, 303, 321–2

Baistow, Tom 237n

Balcon, Sir Michael 207

Baldwin, Stanley 66, 71, 76, 112, 114, 128, 176, 376; and Edward VIII 109, 110, 111

Banda, Hastings 335

Bank of England: King's directorship of 344, 348, 361, 374–5, 376, 391

Barker, Dennis: obituary of Ruth King 293, 451

Barnes, Dr Ernest, Bishop of Birmingham 192

Barratt, John 370

Bartholomew, Harry Guy ('Bart') 72–4, 75, 100 and Nicholson 103–4; and Cudlipp 110, 112–13, 115, 116, 118, 132; and King 115, 121, 127, 144, 183, 185–7; meeting with Attlee 148, 154; bravery 162; becomes Chairman 183; resents King/Cudlipp relationship 194–5; takes revenge 198–201; buys Melbourne *Argus* 219, 225; enforced resignation 218–21, 222; portrayed in *Mirror* histories 241–2,

245, 324, 325, 380

Bather, A. G. 22, 33, 35, 36, 39

Beavan, John (*later* Baron Ardwick) 305, 314, 326, 338, 339, 346, 347, 363, 366, 411, 420n

Beaverbrook, William Maxwell Aitken, Baron: early career 201; editorial policies 201–3; assessment of Northcliffe 52–3; and politics 71, 165, 202, 203; and Cudlipp 172, 187, 203–4, 325n; personality assessed by Cudlip p 203; loathed by King 404 *and n*

Beeching, Lord 350, 351, 369

Beloff, John 318–19

Benn, Anthony Wedgwood 359–60, 374, 388, 444

Benney, Gerald: 448 *and n*

Berry, James *see* Kemsley, Lord

Berry, Michael 268, 299

Berry, Sir William *see* Camrose, Lord

Bevan, Aneurin 165, 203, 238, 263, 380

Beveridge, William Beveridge, Baron 246

Bevin, Ernest 150, 191

Beyfus, Sir Gilbert 251

BFI *see* British Film Institute

Bielenberg, Christabel 14–15, 137, 279, 288, 293–4, 405–6

Billings, Josh 263

Birk, Alma, Baroness 378, 380, 388

Birk, Ellis 274, 305; on travelling with King 276; dislike of Eileen Cudlipp 308; and King's behaviour and removal 321, 322, 353–4, 363, 374, 378, 381, 382, 383, 385, 388, 392, 393; and Cudlipp as chairman 356, 412, 424

Black, Sheila 424

Blackburn, Raymond 158n

Blackpool, Cudlipp in 94–9

Blunt, Dr, Bishop of Bradford 110, 192

Bolam, Silvester 204, 219, 231, 232, 233, 239, 240

Bonham-Carter, Lady Violet 406

Bosanquet, Reginald 388

Bower, Frank 237n

Brabourne, Lord 369–70

Bracken, Brendan 165, 173, 182

Braithwaite, Warwick 90–1, 131

Brando, Marlon 208

Brebner, J. H. 150

Brendon, Piers 428

British Film Institute (BFI): King as Chairman 206–8

Brown, George 249, 306, 328, 338, 347, 351, 352

Browne, Coral 100

Browne, Hon. John 61–2, 67

Brownlee, L. D. 72, 73, 74

Burgess, Guy 249

Burnet, Alastair 374

Burton, Christabel (*née* Harmsworth) 12, 39, 406; Rothermere to 109

Burton, Sir George xi, 293, 430*n*, 434 *and n*, 448

Burton, Sir Montague 79

Burton, Percy 12

Burton, Priscilla, Lady (*née* King, *then* Gore): xi; relationship with her father 134, 136, 174, 175, 212, 214, 276, 277, 300, 301, 343, 431, 434, 438, 439–40; and her grandmother 136; schooling 175, 194; at London University 212; 21st birthday 212; 213; at university in Montreal 217; first marriage 218; looks after Falls orphans 218; and Ruth King 284, 290, 292, 295, 301*n*, 344*n*; 307; 320*n*, 343; at IPC AGM 396*n*; second marriage 434; 439, 440;

Butler, R. A. 261

Butlin, Billy 273

Café Royal, London 237*n*, 329, 398, 419–20

Cahill, Joe 401–2, 403

Caird, Andrew 63

Callaghan, James 350, 351, 352, 356, 368 *and n*, 369, 376, 422

Campbell, Stuart ('Sam') 119, 152, 154, 163, 164, 186, 189

Campbell-Savours, Dale 444

Camrose, William Berry, Lord 54–5, 112, 268, 299

Capone, Al 308

Carreras, Jimmy 369

Cartwright, Gordon 397

Cassandra *see* Connor, William; Gale, George

Castle, Barbara 368

Cave, Paul 281

Chamberlain, Neville 125, 129, 144, 145, 146, 148, 198, 421; Rothermere to 77

Chancellor, Sir Christopher 271

Charles, Prince 257, 269

Cheyne Walk, London: No. 9 266–7; No. 109 209–10, 266, 276, 300

Chichester, Sussex 421

Chifley, Ben 196

Christiansen, Arthur 187, 198, 199, 303–4, 306

Churchill, Clementine 144

Churchill, Mary 144

Churchill, Randolph 246

Churchill, Winston: and Northcliffe 27; and Rothermere 31, 76–7; sympathetic to Edward VIII 109; relationship with *Mirror* 114, 127–8, 148, 154–60, 164–5; and King 144, 145, 146; *Pictorial* campaigns for 145–6; and Cudlipp 171, 172, 182, 425*n*; popularity in USA 184; written off by King 176–7 *and n*, 261; defeated in 1945 Election 188; and Beaverbrook 201; wins 1951 Election 205; libel action against *Mirror* 205, 222; 258–61

Citizen (Glasgow) 202

Clark, Lorna (*née* King) 435, 450–1

Clarke, Tom 29, 40

Clausewitz, Karl von 153

Clore, Charles 309

Cloud of Unknowing 44

Connor, William 101, 113, 181, 237*n*; as Cassandra 80, 111, 147, 154, 164, 165, 176, 182, 235, 406; and Liberace article and court case 250–1; knighted 346; death 364

Cooke, Betty *see* Pinney, Betty

Cooke, Canon G. A. 43, 44, 55–6, 61, 132–3, 134, 178

Cooke, Helen (Margaret King's mother) 47–8, 56, 57, 59, 61, 62, 67, 178

Cooke, Helen (Margaret King's sister) 47, 55, 142

Cooke, James 195, 196, 197, 199, 219, 247, 274, 392

Cooke, Mary 47, 61

Coope, John 183, 392

Cooper, Duff 130, 147

Counter-Inflation Publicity Unit 422

Cousins, Frank 317

Coward, Noel 105

Cowley, John 72, 74, 75, 108, 129; and King 66, 71, 148; and Cudlipp's feature pages 102, 104, 109, 119–20; death 183

Cripps, Isobel, Lady 318

Cripps, Sir Stafford 196, 404*n*

Crossman, Anne: on Cudlipp 234

Crossman, Richard: categorises Wykehamists 37; and Cudlipp 37, 198, 199, 204, 224–5, 226, 237–8, 239; column in *Pictorial* 204, 225; on King 219, 313, 332, 349; on Bartholomew's resignation 219–20; reviews Cudlipp's *Publish and Be Damned!* 245–6; and Cudlipp's 'Evil Men' series 247; on Churchill 260; and *Mirror*'s support for Labour 262, 263; and Eileen Cudlipp 307–8; 310; on Cudlipp's support for Labour 329–30; fired from *Pictorial* 332; critical of King's article on Wilson 376–7, 378, 380, 382–3

Croydon Times Group 221

Cudlipp, Bessie Amelia (Hugh's mother) 3–4, 82, 83, 84, 85

Cudlipp, Edith ('Bunny') (*née* Parnell) (Hugh's first wife) 89, 99, 100, 101, 131–2

Cudlipp, Eileen (Ascroft) (Hugh's second wife): 132; relationship with Cudlipp 132, 153, 193, 226, 238, 266, 267, 307, 308; works for Beaverbrook 202, 203, 204; 256; becomes Fleetway director 270, 304; varied opinions of 307–8; friendship with Jodi Hyland 309–10, 311, 312; death 311, 312

Cudlipp, Hugh (Hubert Kinsman) 1913–45: background and childhood 3–4, 81–2, 83–7; as reporter on *Penarth News* 87–90; and Bunny Parnell 88–9; changes name 90; on Cardiff *Evening Express* 90–2; on *Manchester Evening Chronicle* 92–100; engagement 99, 100, 101; joins *Sunday Chronicle* 100; joins *Mirror* 3, 80, 100–1, 102–3; as Features Editor 104–6, 108, 109; marries Bunny Parnell 131; and Bunny's death 132; and Eileen Ascroft 132; and Edward VIII 110–11; relationship with Cecil King 112; becomes Editor of *Pictorial* 115–16; transforms paper 117–25; writes as Charles Wilberforce 121–5; turns down Mackenzie's *Windsor Tapestry* 253–4; and Eden resignation scoop 125–7; visits Churchill 127; and outbreak of war 129; relationship with King strengthens 130–1; and Margot King 139; denounces Lloyd George 145; and Churchill's appointment as Prime Minister 146; Hulton's assessment of 146–7; enrages Churchill 147–8; hatred of Nazism 149; call-up postponed by King 149–50; joins up 150–1; army training

152–4, 167; engaged to Eileen 153; retains contact
with King 163, 164, 165, 167; edits *Sandhurst
Magazine* 168; joins *Santa Rosa* 168; launches *Ocean
News* 168–9; in Western Desert 170–1; letters
from King 170–1; produces *Union Jack* 171–2,
180–2; BBC broadcast praised by Beaverbrook
172; visits London 173; King wants him home
182–4, 186; marries Eileen Ascroft 193
1946–62: services competed for 187; returns to
Pictorial 187–8, 189; postwar successes 189, 191–3;
good working relationship with King 189–91,
194; 'spikes' King's Enugu riots cable 198; and
Bartholomew 196–7, 198–201; joins *Express* under
Beaverbrook 199, 200, 201, 202–4, 224; reinstated as *Pictorial* Editor 223, 224–5; Australian
visits 196–7, 225–9, 230; meets Packer 228–9,
and Sir Keith Murdoch 229; correspondence
and relationship with King (1952–3) 229–33, 236,
239; writes *Publish and Be Damned!* (1953) 66, 70,
239–46; enraged by Randolph Churchill 246–7;
and homosexuality 247–9, 251–3; and royalty
stories 253–8; and Churchill 258–61; collaboration with Sydney Jacobson 262–3; and Suez
crisis 264–5; inspiration for 'Andy Capp' 265; in
Russia (1958) 267; and takeover of
Amalgamated Press 268–9, 270; produces
Labour Party pamphlet 329; supports Labour in
1959 Election 328, 329–30; appointed Chairman
of Odhams 303–6; 'inexhaustible energies' 306–7;
relationship with Eileen 307; in love with Jodi
Hyland (*see* Cudlipp, Jodi) 308; moves into
Sonning house 312; publishes *At Your Peril* 265,
312; and Eileen's death 312
1963–98: marriage to Jodi 315–17; on King 321–2,
324, 337; and *Mirror's* 60th birthday 325; launches
Sun in place of *Herald* 326–8; becomes IPC
Deputy Chairman 355; supports Labour in
Election 328, 339; first visit to Africa (1965) 335;
and Wilson 338–9; and King's alarming behaviour 341–2, 354, 355–6, 357, 358, 361–3, 364–5,
366–7; tries to avert rift between King and
Wilson 348, 350, 372–3; and Mountbatten 'coup'
367–72, 427; and King's anti-Wilson articles 373,
374*n*, 376, 377; and King's removal 2, 381–9, 392–3;
as Chairman 390–2, 394, 411–12; and King's
AGM appearance 395, 396, 397, 398; speaks at
Foyle's Luncheon 404–5; sells *Sun* to Murdoch
413–15; resigns Chairmanship and returns to
editing 415–16; trip to Far East with Jodi and
Goodman 416, 417; fury at Murdoch 417–18;
retires (1973) 411, 418, 419–20; knighted and
ennobled 420; maiden speech in Lords 420; joins
Labour Party 421, and SDP 421*n*; lectures 420–1;
happy in retirement 421–2; accepts consultancy
from Maxwell 422–3; writes *Walking on the Water*
423–6; sends King *The Prerogative of the Harlot* and
keeps in touch 427–8; and author 439*n*, 449, 450;
last messages and death 441–2; obituary 312*n*;
rumours linking him with MI5 444–5
views on: Bartholomew 72, 73, 112, 113, 115–16, 195,
196; Beaverbrook 202, 203–4; Connor 101;
Cowley 72, 120; *Daily Mirror* 66, 135, 325–6; 'The
Green Light' 247, 253, 257; homosexuality 247,
249; King 1, 57–8, 66, 73–4, 106–7, 113, 135, 219,

266–7, 269, 283–4, 362–3; King and Margot 61*n*;
King and his mother 16–17; King's *Diaries*
407–8; King's life and his own 81, 82, 85, 87;
King's loathing of Beaverbrook 404*n*; Sir Keith
Murdoch 229; Nicholson 101–2, 103–4; politics
86, 93–4, 188, 192, 236, 328–33, 345; Rothermere
76; ; Wykehamists 37
Cudlipp, Jodi (*née* Hyland) (Hugh's third wife): xi;
background and early career 308; and Eileen
Cudlipp 270, 308; friendship with Eileen
309–10, 311; and Cudlipp 308, 309, 311; marriage
315–17; in China with Cudlipp 416, 417; and his
ennoblement 420*n*; and his retirement 420, 421,
422, 423; 441–2; on Cudlipp and King 358; on
Ruth King 320–1
Cudlipp, Percy (Hugh's brother): childhood 81, 82,
84; 'Cardiff's Boy Poet' 82–3; and Hugh 85; on
provincial newspapers 3, 5, 86, 87, 92; editor of
Evening Standard 80; advises Hugh to answer
Mirror advertisement 3, 80; as *Daily Herald* editor
147, 173, 305, 307; death 312
Cudlipp, Phyllis (Hugh's sister) *see* Stratton
Cudlipp, Reg (Hugh's brother) 5, 81, 82, 84, 86, 87,
90, 92, 93, 307, 421
Cudlipp, Willie (Hugh's father) 3, 81, 83, 84, 86
Culham Court, nr Henley-on-Thames 132–4, 143,
160–1, 175, 176, 178, 179, 208
Curzon, George Curzon, 1st Marquess 10
Curzon, Mary, Lady 10, 11
Cushnie, Aberdeenshire 69, 133, 134, 178, 275, 278, 292,
300, 301*n*

Daily Express 52, 112, 187, 199, 201, 202, 233, 246, 296,
297, 318, 390
Daily Gleaner (Jamaica) 79
Daily Graphic (Ghana) 206, 298
Daily Herald 147, 256, 305–6, 307, 326
Daily Mail: under Northcliffe 8–9, 26–7, 29; King
joins 40; taken over by Rothermere 54; King in
advertisement department 62–5; attacks Baldwin
71; supports Blackshirts 75; attitude to Germany
76, 77; contacts in high places 112; on King's
removal 392
Daily Mail Trust 72, 108
Daily Mirror: founded (1903) 26, 65; King joins 65;
political content under Rothermere 65–6, 75–6;
Rothermere sells shares in 71–2, 108; under
Triumvirate (Cowley, Roome, Lovell) 72; Bart's
contributions 72–3, 74 (*see* Bartholomew, Harry);
Cudlipp joins 100–1; and Edward VIII 109–12;
Churchill's relationship with *see under* Churchill,
Winston; banned from schools 175; wartime
reporting 144, 146, 163, 164–7; attacks Eton 179;
supports Labour in Election campaigns 188–9,
204–5; King elected Chairman 220, 221, 236; 50th
birthday celebrations 239; history (*Publish and Be
Damned!*) written by Cudlipp 239–46; loses
Liberace case 249–52; famous for 'Shock Issues'
252; royalty coverage 254–8; 'Spotlight' pamphlets 258; anti-Establishment crusade 261–2;
and Labour Party support 262–4, 328–31,
339–40; and Suez crisis 264–5; sponsors National
Youth Orchestra 280–1; Edelman's history 324–5,
380; famous attack on Khrushchev 332; and

union stoppages 333–4; and Macmillan 331, 339; and competition from *Sun* 412–14, 415 circulation (1914) 65, (1950) 204, (1953) 239, (1964) 325, (1968) 1, (171–3) 417–18; 'Andy Capp' 265; 'Jane' 180, 185, 332; *see also* Birk, Ellis; Bolam, Silvester; Connor, William; Cowley, John; Cudlipp, Hugh; Gale, George; Goodman, Geoffrey; Howard, Lee; Jennings, Richard; King, Cecil Harmsworth; Nener, Jack; Nicholson, Basil; Pickering, Sir Edward
Daily Mirror building, Holborn 1, 272–3
Daily Mirror (Sydney) 196
Daily News 29, 79
Daily Record 265, 373*n*
Daily Sketch 232, 246
Daily Telegraph 153, 247, 268, 375, 398, 444
Daily Telegraph (Sydney) 228
Daily Times (Nigeria) 197–8, 206, 444
Daily Worker 147, 156, 195
Dale, Derek 298
Darlow, Tom 100, 131, 132
Day, Robin 368*n*
Deedes, William 337
Delano, Tony 293, 313
De Mille, Cecil B. 208
Des Moines (USA), King in (1937) 114–15
Dickson, Ivey 288, 289, 290
Dinsdale, Dick 233–4
Donnelly, Desmond 379, 389
Douglas-Home, Sir Alec 336, 337, 339, 369, 421
Drawbell, James Wedgwood 100, 101, 107

East African Standard 390
Easter rebellion (Ireland, 1916) 27–8
Economist, The 255, 263, 265, 272, 303, 334, 374, 415
Edelman, Maurice: history of *Mirror* 324–5, 380
Eden, Anthony 121, 125–7, 145, 262, 264, 265, 421
Edward VIII: and Wallis Simpson 109–11, 202
Edwards, Bob 363*n*, 415, 416, 419–20, 423*n*, 441
Edwards, Ruth Dudley 439*n*, 441, 449–50
Eilbeck, James 230–1
Eisenhower, General Dwight D. 173
Elizabeth II: as Princess 192–3; Coronation 232, 239
Elizabeth, Queen (latterly the Queen Mother) 165–6, 193, 283
Elland, Percy 202
Ellerman, Sir John 392–3
Ellison, Mary 224
El Vino's (London) 113, 237 *and n*, 251, 296
Emerson, Ralph Waldo 447
Empire Paper Mills, Kent 65, 114
Encounter 427
Engel, Matthew 328, 413
Engels, Friedrich 94
Epstein, Jacob: 'Genesis' 96
Eton College 21 *and n*, 135, 176, 179, 213
Evening Express (Cardiff): Cudlipp at 90–2
Evening News 64
Evening Standard 3, 80, 120, 132, 202, 295, 380, 398

Faisal, King 399
Falcon, the (London pub) 237, 298
Falkender, Marcia 427
Falls, John 42

Falls, John (son) 42, 136, 137, 217
Falls, Nigel 217, 218, 274, 285, 290, 301, 448, 451
Falls, Patrick 217–18, 274, 285, 290, 291, 301, 451*n*
Falls, Sheila, *see* Spence
Falls, Sheila Geraldine (*née* King) (Cecil's sister) 9, 10, 13, 41–2
Faulkner, Brian 403
Financial Times 353, 390, 395, 398
Finnegan's, Barney (London pub) 237
Fisher, Dr Geoffrey, Archbishop of Canterbury 303, 367
Fleetway Publications 270, 271, 272, 303, 387
Fonteyn, Dame Margot 304
Foot, Hugh 197
Foot, Michael 203, 391
Forman, Denis 207, 208, 225, 276, 277, 285, 302
Foster, J. K. 87, 89–90
Foyle's Literary Luncheons 246, 404–5, 411
France Observateur 327
Frost Programme, The 365–6
Fuller, General 'Boney' 146, 152, 153, 172
Fyfe, Hamilton 65, 66

Gaitskell, Hugh 37, 263, 264–5, 305, 306, 328, 329, 337–8, 339
Gale, George 364, 366
Gandhi, Mahatma 196
Garro-Jones, G. M. 164
Gaulle, Charles de 345
General Elections: 1922 66; 1931 98; 1945 182, 188–9; 1950 204; 1951 205; 1959 328, 329–30, 331; 1964 339; 1966 346–7
General Strike (1926) 86
George V 58, 102
George VI 165–6, 193
Geraldine House, Fetter Lane 104, 161–2, 269
Glasgow Evening News 265
Glasgow Record 57–8
Goddard, Rayner, Lord Chief Justice 258
Goebbels, Joseph 125
Goering, Hermann 191
Gone With the Wind 207 *and n*
Goodman, Geoffrey 416–17, 422, 423*n*, 441
Goodman, Lord 423*n*
Gordon, John 204, 377, 394
Gore, St John 'Bobby' 217, 218, 295, 430
Gore, Priscilla *see* Burton, Priscilla, Lady
Gore, William 301, 435, 448
Gowon, General 399
Grade, Sir Lew 322, 323, 416, 417
Gray, Bernard 217*n*
Green, Celia 318
Greenhill, Sir Denis 409
Greenwell, George 162
Greenwood, Arthur 173
Greenwood, Walter 94
Grey, George 158*n*
Grigg, John 255
Grigg, P. J. 182
Grimaldi, G. H. 63
Guardian 222–3, 351, 361, 362, 363, 377, 378*n*, 389–90, 391, 394*n*, 397, 398, 444

Halifax, Lord 127

Hamlyn, Paul 383, 395 *and n*, 448, 449
Harding, Major-General 169–70
Hardy, Olif 20
Harmsworth, Alfred (Cecil's grandfather) 4, 6–7, 18
Harmsworth, Alfred (Cecil's cousin) 28
Harmsworth, Alfred Charles (Cecil's uncle) *see* Northcliffe, Viscount
Harmsworth, Cecil Harmsworth, Baron (Cecil's uncle and godfather) 5, 7, 9, 24, 27, 28, 30 *and n*, 31, 32, 35, 41, 78, 209, 341
Harmsworth, Desmond (Cecil's cousin) 57, 405
Harmsworth, Emily (*née* Maffett) (Cecil's aunt) 405
Harmsworth, Esmond (Cecil's cousin) *see* Rothermere, 2nd Viscount
Harmsworth, Geraldine Mary (*née* Maffett) (Cecil's grandmother) 4, 5–6, 9, 17, 28, 34, 39, 48–9, 67, 137
Harmsworth, Geoffrey (Cecil's cousin) 25
Harmsworth, Harold (Cecil's uncle) *see* Rothermere, Viscount
Harmsworth, Sir Hildebrand (Cecil's uncle) 7, 41
Harmsworth, Sir (Robert) Leicester (Cecil's uncle) 5, 7, 9, 14, 41, 67, 134, 209
Harmsworth, Ronald (Cecil's cousin) 57
Harmsworth, St John (Cecil's uncle) 18, 24, 39, 58; letter to Geraldine 56–7
Harmsworth, Vere (Cecil's cousin) 27, 29
Harmsworth, Vere Harold (Cecil's cousin) *see* Rothermere, 3rd Viscount
Harmsworth, Vyvyan (Cecil's cousin) 25, 31, 37
Hart, Basil Liddell 125, 152
Hartnell, Norman 256
Healey, Denis 351, 368 *and n*, 379
Healey, Edna 399
Heath, Edward: and King 328, 345–6, 347, 350, 361, 400, 402, 403; and Ruth King 402, 403, 426n, 448; told of Election date by King 407; and Cudlipp 420, 421
Heenan, Cardinal John 344
Higgins, Patrick: *Heterosexual Dictatorship...* 248, 252–3
Hitler, Adolf 76–7, 113–14, 124, 125, 144, 148–9, 177n
Hogg, Quintin 150
Hore-Belisha, Leslie 125, 130, 144, 152
Horsfall, Magdalene (*née* King) 4
Houghton, Douglas 356n
Howard, Lee 297–8, 414, 419
Hulton, Edward: assessment of Cudlipp 146–7
Hulton's 270
Hyland, Irene ('Fling') 308, 315, 421
Hyland, Jodi *see* Cudlipp, Jodi

Imperial Paper Mills 269
Imperial Tobacco 432
Ingram, Sarah (*née* King) 435
Innes, Ralph Hammond 181
International Publishing Company (IPC) 1, 318–19, 321, 326, 352–3, 355, 383, 394–8, 415, 424n
Investor's Chronicle 398
Irish Independent 28
Irish Republican Army (IRA) 401, 402–3, 404, 411, 429

Jack and Jill 268
Jacobson, Sydney: and Cudlipp 236, 237n, 262–3;

friendship with Gaitskell 264, and King 277; becomes Editor of *Sun* 326–7; and Labour Party support 329, 330; on Cudlipp and King 338; opposes 'Wilson Must Go' campaign 363; and Goodman 416; ennobled 420n; in Wilson's Counter-Inflation Publicity Unit 422
'Jane' (strip cartoon) 180, 185, 332
Jay, Douglas 351
Jeffreys, Pastor 85
Jenkins, Peter 351, 362
Jenkins, Roy 350, 356, 366, 368 *and n*, 369, 375–6, 377, 378 *and n*, 379, 389, 399n
Jennings, Richard ('W. M.') 113–14
Jinnah, Mohammed, President of Pakistan 196, 404
John Bull 100, 131, 132
Johnson, Paul 319, 324, 383, 424
Jones, David 308
Jordan, Philip 184
José, Babatunde 205–6, 443–4
Joy, Sir George 318, 319

Kaunda, Kenneth 335
Keegan, John 409, 444
Kelly-Iliffe 269
Kemsley, James Berry, Lord 97, 98, 99, 101, 230, 265, 266, 268, 271, 299
Kennedy, John F., US President 336
Khrushchev, Nikita 93, 267, 332
Kierkegaard, Sören 439
King, Alfred Curzon ('Bob') (Cecil's brother) 10, 11, 19, 32, 33–5
King, Carey (*née* Caroline Schofield) (Cecil's grand-daughter-in-law) 436–8, 440
King, Cecil Francis (Cecil's son) 134; and his father 133, 134, 139, 176–7, 183n, 214–15, 295, 298, 299–300, 301; on his mother 134, and grand-mother 136; at Winchester 135, 154, 211–12; joins up 212; and Oxford 214; works for Mirror group 222; and Ruth King 291–2; marriage 298; in Africa 298; children 300; at Fleetway Publications 298; and King's removal 387; moves into charity work 433; 433–4, 440
King, Cecil Harmsworth 1901–37: ancestry 4; birth 4, 5, 9–10; childhood 4, 10, 11–12, 13–14, 15–17, 18–20; at Surrey prep school 20–1; at Irish day school 21; interest in war 21, 27, 31; at Winchester 21, 22–3, 24–5, 31–3, 35–7, 59–60; and Easter rebellion (1916) 27–8; and brother's death 33–5; letters to mother 32–3, 35, 40, 41; lack of schoolfriends 36; at Oxford 35, 37–9, 40–1, 49; friendships 38, 41, 66–8, 69; helped by Northcliffe 39–40; and sister's death 42; engage-ment to Margaret 42–3, 44–5, 48–9; and Northcliffe's illness and death 49, 51, 52, 53, 54; in Scotland 55; gets news of Margaret from Needham 55–6, 57, 58–9; as a reporter 57–8; introduced to George V 58; develops psoriasis 58; and Margaret's family 60; wedding and hon-eymoon 61–2; joins *Daily Mail* 62–4; given direc-torship of Kent Paper Mills and holiday by Rothermere 65; early days with *Mirror* 65, 66, 70, 71, 72, 73–5; and Croydon newspapers 70; in Soviet Union 70–1; relationship with Bartholomew 73, 74, 75; and removal of

Brownlee 73–4; reputation grows 78, 79; in Africa 78–9; in New York 79; 101; relationship with Rothermere 108–9; appointed Director of *Sunday Pictorial* 108; relationship with Cudlipp 107, 112; and *Mirror*'s political coverage 108, 109, 114; in Canada and America 114–15, 128; makes Cudlipp Editor of *Pictorial* 115–16
1937–52: working relationship with Cudlipp 119–20, 121–2, 126–7; and propaganda 125; relationship with Churchill 127–8; fails to get war job 129–30; relationship with Cudlipp strengthens 130–1; moves to Culham Court 132–3, 143; relationship with his children 134–6, *see also* Burton, Lady, King, Cecil Francis, King, Colin *and* King, Michael; relationship with mother 137, 138; marital difficulties 132, 134, 138–41; begins war diary 144; and Churchill 144, 145–6; anti-Establishment 147–9; blocks Cudlipp's call-up 149–50; clashes with Churchill 154–60; in the Blitz 160–3; and Stuart Campbell 154,163, 164, 186; and *Mirror*'s wartime criticism of government 163–7; keeps in touch with Cudlipp 167, 170–1, 173; gives up Culham 178, 179; marital problems 179–80; and Cudlipp's return 182–3, 184, 187–8; in North and South America 184–6; thrilled by Election results 188–9; postwar relationship with Cudlipp 189–91, 194; sent to India 195–6, Australia 196, Africa 197–8, and Canada 196; Enugu riots cable 'spiked' by Cudlipp 198–9; and Cudlipp's sacking 199, 200–1; personality change in Africa 205–6; becomes Chairman of British Film Institute 206–8; and mother's death 208–9; and Margot 210, 213–14, 215–17; takes on the Falls orphans 217–18; displaces Bartholomew as Chairman 218–19, 220–3
1952–68: lures Cudlipp from Beaverbrook 223, 224; visits Australia 226–7; and Packer 228; correspondence and plans with Cudlipp (1952–3) 229–33, 236, 239; portrayed in Cudlipp's *Publish and Be Damned!* 241, 242–4, 245; contribution to *Mirror* 258; and expansion of *Mirror* group 265–6; transforms Amalgamated Press into Fleetway Publications 267, 268–70; takes over Odhams 271–2, 303, 304, 305; and *Daily Mirror* building 272–4; marital breakdown 274, 278–9; begins relationship with Ruth Railton 279 (*see* King, Ruth); asks Margot for divorce 282; passes running of *Daily Herald* to Cudlipp 305–6; and Jodi Hyland 309; and ATV music 321–3; and Edelman's history of *Mirror* 324–5; and launch of *Sun* 326, 327; dislike of Gaitskell 328; disparages Tory Cabinet 331; and the unions 333, 334; attacks Newspaper Publishers' Association and Press Council 333; and US press 334–5; and John F. Kennedy 336; and Douglas–Home 336–7; and *Mirror* coverage of Wilson 338–9, 344–5, 346–50, 352, 354; refuses life peerage 340–1; accepts directorships 344, 347–8, 351; relationship with Heath 345–6, 350, 402, 403; and IPC affairs 352–3; and his dismissal 353–4, 355–6; and Wilson 359–60, 364; sits for Sutherland 360; and Mountbatten 'coup' 367–72; and Wilson 372–80; 'Enough is Enough' article

373–5, 376, 380–1; final dismissal 1–2, 381–7; TV appearances 387–9; and press coverage 389–93
1968–87: activities post–dismissal 394–5; and Hamlyn and Ryder 395; IPC AGM 395–8; association with IPC 398–9; visits Mosley 399–400; likes Powell 400–1; interest in Northern Ireland and friendship with Paisley 401–2, 403–4; publication of *Strictly Personal* 404–6, 410, *With Malice Towards None* 406, *Without Fear or Favour* 407, and *Diaries* 407–10; moves to Dublin 410, 411; and Cudlipp's *Walking on the Water* 423–6; attitude to life in Dublin 428–9; and his family 430–1, 431, 434, 435–6; and deaths of Colin and Michael 432–3 *and n*; relationship with Laurence King 435–6, 437; 80th birthday speech 438–9; publishes *Commonplace Book* 439; changes will in Ruth's favour 445; death 440–1; funeral 441, 443–4; obituaries 444
views on: animals 135; Attlee 148, 406; Beaverbrook 404*n*; Churchill 261; Cudlipp as Chairman 415; *Daily Mirror* readers 413; father 14, 15, 18–19; friendships 38, 40, 69; homosexuality 194, 247, 248–9, 251–2; money 68, 133, 278, 300–2; mother 15, 16–17, 18–19, 24, 405; Northcliffe 39–40; Rothermere 76, 77; Stalin 236; Wilson 341
King, Colin Henry (Cecil's son) 134; and his father 133, 136, 279, 295, 299, 300, 431; at Eton 213; works in Quebec 276; and Ruth King 291; children 300; and Michael 432; death 431–2
King, Elinor Mary (Nora) (Cecil's sister) 9, 10, 13, 46; King to 78–9
King, Enid (Cecil's sister) *see* Stokes, Enid
King, Francis *see* King, Cecil Francis
King, Geraldine (*née* Harmsworth) (Cecil's mother): childhood 6, 18; love of father 6; marriage in India 7–8; character and personality 8, 18, 41; presented at court 9; birth of children in India 9, 10–11; and birth and naming of Cecil 9, 10; leaves India 11; in Ireland 14, 15–16; relationship with husband 15; as a parent 16–18; correspondence with Luke 21–2; and Luke's death 24, 43; correspondence with Cecil 27, 32–3, 35, 40, 41, 45; and John Falls 42, 136–7; approves of Cecil's fiancée 45–6; letters from Mrs Cooke 47–8; worried about finances 56; and her husband's death 67; gives Cecil money for Culham Court 132, 133; and her grandchildren 134, 136; despises *Mirror* and *Pictorial* 137; supportive of Margot 137–8; death 208; King's analysis of 208–9; obituary 7*n*
King, Geraldine (Cecil's granddaughter) 438*n*
King, Henry (Cecil's grandfather) 4
King, Henry (Harry) (Cecil's uncle) 4, 22
King, Hugo (Cecil's grandson) 217
King, Jenny (*née* Beckett) (Cecil's daughter–in–law) 298
King, Laurence (Cecil's grandson) 38, 258, 301, 435–6, 437, 438, 439, 440, 446, 448*n*
King, Libby (*née* Elizabeth Hobhouse, *then* Eden) (Cecil's daughter–in–law) 211, 274, 277, 291, 297, 300, 432–3
King, Lucas Henry ('Luke') (Cecil's brother) 9, 10, 13, 18, 19, 21–2, 23, 43

King, Sir Lucas White (Cecil's father) 4–5, 7–8, 10, 11, 12–13, 14–15, 38, 41, 46, 67

King, Margaret ('Margot') (née Cooke) (Cecil's first wife): character 47; meets and becomes engaged to Cecil King 42–3, 44–5; and her in-laws 45–7, 48–9; and Needham 55, 56, 57, 58–9; attachment to family annoys King 60; wedding and honeymoon 61–2;and early married life 60–1, 62, 65, 66; as parent 68, 134; in Africa (1935) 78, and America (1937) with King 114; at Culham 132–4, 178, 208; in Ireland with children 129, 179; relationship with her mother–in–law 137–8; and King and his infidelities 138–43; discourages King from becoming war correspondent 160; on Priscilla 175; dislikes King's newspapers 177–8; illness and exhaustion 178; spirituality 179, 343–4; relationship with King 179–80; takes on Falls orphans 217, 218; illness 209, 210, 278–9, 295; lives separate life from King 274; and King's request for divorce 282–3; and Ruth King 292, 321; agrees to divorce 295; recovery from depression 344, 430; death 434n

King, Michael Lucas (Cecil's son): birth 68; childhood 133, 134–5; at Eton 175, 176, 179; in Glasgow shipyard 179, 210; later career 210–11, 295–6, 297–8, 345, 353, 371n; and his father 133, 135, 175, 176, 295–8, 299, 300, 432–3; marries 211; children 217, 300; and Ruth King 291, 295, 301n, 430; death 432; obituaries 444

King, Priscilla, see Burton, Lady

King, Robin (Cecil's grandson) 435, 450–1

King, Roger (Cecil's grandson) 435, 446, 451n

King, Dame Ruth (née Railton) (Cecil's second wife): character 285–6, 437–8; musical ability 279–80, 288; founds and runs National Youth Orchestra 280–1, 288–90, 293–4; meets King 280; begins relationship 279, 281–2; and Margot 43; moves in with King 283, 284; and the Falls children 285, 287–8, 290–1; influence on King 19, 285, 293, 301, 302; and his children 291–2; continues musical career 292–3; marriage 295; psychic powers believed in by King 317–18, 319–21; disliked by his friends 321; King wants as musical director of ATV 321–3; encourages his megalomania 324, 341, 358, 365; increasing possessiveness 342; gives up musical directorship of NYO 342; becomes dame 344; approves of Heath 346; and King's dismissal 390, 393 and n, 394n; at IPC AGM 396; as mediator in Ireland 401–2, 403; relationship with Heath 402, 403, 426n; and mother–in–law 405; moves to Ireland with King 410 and n, 411, 428–30; denounces Cudlipp 426; hatred of Ireland 430, 437; gets rid of family correspondence 431n; 'cocoons' King from children and grandchildren 411, 434, 435–6, 437, 440, 446; and King's death 440–1, 443–4; disposes of his money 445–6; treatment of his family 446–8; traumatises Secker & Warburg 448–9, 449–50; death 450; will 450–1; obituary 293, 451

King, Sheila (Cecil's sister) see Falls, Sheila Geraldine

King, Sophie (née Eccleston) (Cecil's grandmother) 4, 19, 22

King, Sophie Geraldine ('Chirrie') (Cecil's sister) see Spencer, Sophie

King, Zena (née Woodward) (Cecil's granddaughter-in-law) 435

Kitchener, Horatio, Lord: Northcliffe's attack on 26–7, 165; death 28

Lamb, Larry 413

Lambert, Gavin 207, 208

Lancaster, Terry 441

Lanchester, Elsa 103

Langley, Doris 275, 276, 287–8, 290

Langley, Tom 275–6, 278, 287, 290

Laughton, Charles 103

Lawrence, Frederick Pethick 196

Lee, Jenny 380

Lehmann, Rosamond 134, 143

Leinster, torpedoing of 33, 34

Levin, Bernard 410

Liberace: wins lawsuit against Mirror 249–52

Lloyd George, David: becomes Minister of Munitions 27; discussions with Northcliffe 28, 29; pressurises him to go to USA 30; Cecil Harmsworth on his secretariat 31; elevates Harmsworth family 41; and Beaverbrook 201, 325n; Esmond Harmsworth his aide–de–camp 58; and Northcliffe 49–50, 52; and Cudlipp 93, 123, 145, 146, 425n

London Choir School 248

Louis, Joe 308

Lovell, Jimmy 72

Lysaght, Charles x

Lyttleton, George 176, 179, 296, 297

McAlpine, Sir Malcolm 147

McClellan, Edward 343

MacDonald, Ramsay 66

Mackendrick, Kerry 421

Mackendrick, Mercedes ('Merry') 421

Mackenzie, Compton: The Windsor Tapestry 253–4

Mackenzie, Kelvin 442

Maclean, Donald 249

Macleod, Iain 331

Macmillan, Harold 171, 331, 339, 350n 367, 423n

Manchester Evening News 298

Manchester Guardian 172, 298

Manningham–Buller, Sir Reginald 258

Mansergh, Margaret 405n

Margaret, Princess: and Peter Townsend 254–5

Marks, Derek 296

Marlowe, Thomas 63

Massey, Mr (Wesleyan parson) 83

Masterman, Sir John 38, 57

Mathias, Mr (schoolteacher) 87

Matthews, Amy 13, 14, 18

Maudling, Reginald 328, 346, 369

Maugham, William Somerset 105

Maxwell, Robert 413, 422–3

Mayhew, Christoper 407n

Melbourne Herald group 226, 227, 390

Miles, Tony 233

Millikin, C. Stephen 63

Milne, Ewart 44

Mirror see Daily Mirror

Moffat, Howard Unwin, Prime Minister of
    Rhodesia 79
Molloy, Mike 423n
Monckton, Sir Walter 130
Monnet, Jean 400
Montgomery, Field Marshal Bernard 172, 173
Moran, Lord 259
Morning Star 351–2
Morrison, Herbert 163–4, 165, 206–7, 263–4
Mortimer, Raymond 143
Mosley, Sir Oswald 75, 76, 78, 399–400
Mountbatten, Lord Louis 105, 203, 358–9, 367–72,
    425, 426 and n, 427, 444
Muggeridge, Malcolm 254, 255, 304, 396, 406
Mulally, Terence 360n
Murdoch, Sir Keith 226, 229
Murdoch, Rupert 229; Sun takeover 413–14, 415, 416,
    417–18
Murphy, William Martin 28
Mussolini, Benito 76, 77, 114

Nasser, Gamal, President of Egypt 264
National Coal Board 347–8, 350n, 351, 378, 381
National Exhibition of Children's Art 280
National Film Theatre 208
National Orchestra of Wales 90–1
National Parks Commission 347, 351
National Youth Orchestra 280–1, 283, 288–90, 342,
    344
Needham, Francis: friendship with King 38, 61,
    66–7, 69, 249; letters to King 49, 51, 52, 55, 57,
    58–9, 62, 63, 65, 69, 70, 300, 405
Nehru, Jawaharlal 196
Nener, Jack 230, 231, 233–4, 260, 314–15
New Statesman 72, 165, 222, 346, 380, 383, 412
New York Daily News 75, 101
New York Herald Tribune 259
New York Post 390
New York Times 124, 272
Newnes 270
News Chronicle group 184, 237n, 255, 265
News of the World 246, 247, 307, 413
Newsom, John 283
Newspaper Proprietors' Association/Newspaper
    Publishers' Association (NPA) 78, 148, 333 and n,
    334, 347
Newsweek 326
Nicholson, Basil D. 79, 80, 100–1, 102, 103–4, 342
Nkrumah, Kwame, President of Ghana 206
North, Rex 238
Northcliffe, Alfred Harmsworth, Viscount 1–2;
    childhood 6, 18; early career in journalism 7;
    and death of father 7; launches Daily Mail 8–9;
    adores mother 9, 17, 28; generous to brother-in-
    law 12; and Bartholomew 73; and nephews and
    nieces and their deaths 23, 25, 26, 29, 31, 34;
    achievements during World War I 25–7, 28,
    29–31, 165; and Irish question 28; becomes irra-
    tional about Germany 34, 37; and Lloyd George
    49–50, 52; on 'world whirl' 50–1; founds
    Newspaper Proprietors' Association 78; con-
    structs Geraldine House 104; illness and death
    51; funeral 51–2; assessments of 52–3; impor-
    tance to King 3, 5, 12, 13, 37, 39–40

Norton, Ezra 196, 225, 227–8, 229
Norton, John 227–8
Norton, Martin 277
NPA see Newspapers Proprietors' Association
Nyerere, Julius 335

Observer 269–70, 272, 304–5, 306, 331–2, 352, 364, 377
O'Connell, David (Daithí Ó Conaill) 402, 429, 443
Odhams 270–2, 303, 304, 305
Orléans, Charles d' 41, 68, 177

Packer, Sir Frank 228–9
Paisley, The Reverend Ian 401, 402–3, 404, 410, 411,
    429, 443, 448
Pantin, W. A. 38
Park Stile, Langley 68
Parnell, Edith ('Bunny') see Cudlipp, Edith
Parnell, Val 322–3
Parsons, Maurice 356
Patience, Jack 224
Paton, Harold 38, 52, 69, 249
Pavilion, Hampton Court 342, 410, 431
Penarth News, Cudlipp works for 87–90
People, 189, 254, 263 and n
Philip, Prince 192–3, 420
Phillips, S. J. (firm) 277
Pickering, Sir Edward: Editor of Express 297; joins
    Mirror 298, 321; on Michael King 297, 298; dis-
    likes Ruth King 321; on King's last years and
    removal from IPC 353, 354, 357, 363, 364, 376,
    381; and Mountbatten 367; succeeds Cudlipp
    394; on Cudlipp as Chairman 412, 415;
    announces Reed's control over IPC 415
Pictorial see Sunday Pictorial
Pilger, John 414
Pinney, Betty (née Cooke) 47, 68, 278–9
Pompidou, Georges 399
Powell, Dilys 208
Powell, Enoch 400–1
Poynters Hall, Totteridge 5, 12, 39
Press Council 333, 338
Preston, Peter 423–4
Printers' Pension Corporation 353
Private Eye, 315n, 379–80
Proops, Marjorie 256, 423n
Punch: on Northcliffe's world tour 50–1; Christmas
    poem on King 408

Queen 272, 274, 296, 303
Queen Charlotte's Ball 256
Queen Mary 104

Railton, Dame Ruth see King, Ruth
Read, Grantly Dick: How a Baby is Born 189
Reed (A. E.) Paper Group 1, 272, 353, 381, 384, 395,
    415, 423, 431
Reisz, Karel 207
Reith, John, Lord 130
Reuters 211, 271, 296
Reveille 221
Reynold's News 224
Rippon, Geoffrey 328
Robens, Alf, Lord 249, 328, 339, 350, 351, 352, 358,
    361, 362, 378, 402

Roberts, Frederick, Lord 22
Roebuck Hall, 13–14, 17
Rogers, Sir Frank: as Managing Director of IPC
321, 348, 397; on King in Africa 205; on Ruth
King's influence on King 321, 341; and King's
removal 2, 354, 359, 363, 374, 381, 382, 385–7; on
Cudlipp as Chairman 391n, 415
Rogers, Esma, Lady 383
Rommel, Field Marshal Erwin 169
Rook, Jean 327
Roome, Wally 72, 128
Roosevelt, Franklin D., US President 171
Rothermere, Esmond Harmsworth, 2nd Viscount
39, 58, 65, 77, 78, 112, 148, 187, 426–7
Rothermere, Harold Harmsworth, 1st Viscount:
joins Alfred on Answers 7; in World War I 2, 27;
and deaths of nephew and son 24, 31; elevated
to viscount 41; and Northcliffe's death 54–5;
generous to sister 68; political views 66, 71,
75–6; and Hitler 76–8; and Churchill 77; loses
interest in Mirror and Pictorial 71–2, 115, 120–1;
and King 5, 12, 61, 63, 65, 70, 108–9
Rothermere, Mary, Viscountess (née Share) 18
Rothermere, Vere Harmsworth, 3rd Viscount 426–7
Royal Commission on the Press 271, 334, 345
Royal Commission on Standards of Conduct in
Public Life 422
Royal Institution: King's lecture on ESP (1969) 320
Royal Southern Yacht Club, Chichester 421
Ryder, Don 2, 381, 384, 385–7, 395, 415–16

Sadleir, Michael 143
Sainsbury, Lord 350, 351
Saintsbury, Professor 170
Salford, Cudlipp in 93–4
Salisbury, 3rd Marquess 9
Sampson, Anthony 37
Sargent, Sir Malcolm 303–4
Savage Club, London 173
Scott, Thomas, Dean of Christ Church 23, 39
Secker & Warburg 448–50
Semphill, Cecilia 177
Shawcross, Lord 350
Shinwell, Emmanuel 406, 410
Simpson, Wallis: and Edward VIII 109–11, 202
Skelton, R. A. 279, 284–5
Smith, Ian 335, 346
Smith, Peter Dallas 333–4
Snoad, Harold 269
Soames, Christopher 258
Society for Psychical Research (SPR) 318
Southern Television 269
Spanish Civil War 114
Spectator, The 362, 398, 413
Spence, Sheila (née Falls) 217, 218, 274–5, 276, 285,
301; and Ruth King 287–8, 290, 291, 435, 451
Spencer, Sophie ('Chirrie') (née King) 10, 11, 208
Stalin, Joseph 236
Starkie, Enid 20, 41
Stephens, Peter 360, 361, 363, 400, 402, 403, 430
Stevens, Jocelyn 272, 274, 303, 304, 326, 355, 383
Stokes, Enid (née King): childhood in India 9, 10, 11;
holidays with grandmother 19; and Bob's death
34–5; and Cecil's engagement 46; letter to Cecil

(1942) 173–4; looks after Margot 213–14; loving
farewell to Cecil 343, death 342; misuse of
memoirs by King 405; memories of: Abercorn
Place 62, Cecil's childhood 16, 20, Cecil's mar-
ital problems 279, father 14, governess 13, grand-
mother 5–6, Harmsworth uncles 35, 39, mother
17, 18, Northcliffe 25, Roebuck Hall, near
Dublin 13–14, 19, Ruth King 284, 291, Sheila 19,
travelling with Cecil 276–7
Straits Times Annual 247
Stratton, Phyllis (née Cudlipp) 81, 421
Suez crisis 264–5
Sun 326–8, 339, 363, 373n, 412–13; taken over by
Murdoch 413–14, 415, 416, 417–18
Sun Pictorial (Melbourne) 226
Sunday Chronicle, Cudlipp at 100, 101
Sunday Companion 268
Sunday Dispatch 254, 255
Sunday Express 106, 202, 204, 222, 225, 377, 391
Sunday Mail 265
Sunday Mirror (formerly Sunday Pictorial, q.v.) 310–11, 345,
377, 419
Sunday Pictorial: founded 65; King becomes Advertise-
ment Director 70, and Director 108; circulation
dropping 115; Cudlipp becomes Editor 115–16;
transformed by Cudlipp 117–21; political coverage
121–4, 125–7, 128; Cudlipp on 'The New
Woman' 193; wartime reporting 144–8; campaigns for Churchill 145–6; as critic of privilege
147, 150; Churchill's complaints against 154–60;
popular with forces 163; risks suppression 163–4,
165, 166, 167; King becomes Editorial Director
183; Campbell resigns as Editor 186; success
under Cudlipp 187–8, 189–93; and Cudlipp's
dismissal 198–201; deteriorates under Philip Zec
201, 204; Crossman's column 204, 224–5; and
Cudlipp's return 224, 225, 237; King's plans and
appointments 230–1, 233; attack on Bevan 238–9;
campaign against homosexuality 247–9, 252–3;
royalty stories 253–5; banned in Ireland 275;
sponsors National Exhibition of Children's Art
280; renamed Sunday Mirror (q.v.) 310–11; circulation (1937) 115, (1946) 189, (1948) 195, (1949) 198
Sunday Telegraph 377, 392
Sunday Times 271, 325, 326, 334, 392, 415; serialisation
of King's Strictly Personal 404
Sutherland, Graham: King portrait 360, 411, 445, 450

Tavistock, Marquis of 256
Taylor, A. J. P. 202, 380; English History, 1914–1945
324–5
Teare, Dr Donald 312
television, commercial 266, 269, 270
Temperley, Joyce 142, 216
Thackeray, Sergeant 172
Thatcher, Margaret 429, 434
Thomas, Cecil 74, 75, 113, 144, 165, 201
Thompson, J. Walter 79, 101
Thomson, Roy, Lord 271–2, 305, 334
Thrower, J. Thurston 221
Tiarks, Henrietta 256
Time magazine 372
Times, The: under Northcliffe 25, 26; King's first
piece 40; sold to Astor 54; contacts in high

places 112; King quoted 344, 348, 371n; taken
over by Lord Thomson 334; on Wilson and
King 362 *and n*, 378n; on King's TV appearances
376; on King's removal 383, 392; on IPC AGM
398; King as consultant to 399n; Mayhew's letter
407n; Cudlipp's obituary 312n
Tolstoy, Leo 61
Townsend, Peter 154–5
Trades Union Congress (TUC) 305, 326
trades unions *see* unions
Trevor–Roper, Professor Hugh 38
Truth (Australian paper) 7n, 196, 225, 227
Turley (Irish chauffeur) 19, 275
Tussaud's, Louis (Blackpool) 96
Tyerman, Donald 264–5

UK Press Gazette 392
Union Jack 171–2, 180–2
unions, trades 303, 333–4, 413; *see also* Trades Union
Congress
United Empire Party 71

Valdar, Colin 231, 233, 245, 392
Valentine 268
Vansittart, Sir Robert 125
Vicky (cartoonist) 236, 237n
Victoria, Queen 9
Villon, François 141

'W. M.' *see* Jennings, Richard
Wah Kee 85
Walker, Patrick Gordon 356n
Wallace, Edgar 98
Walston, Harry 211
Warwick Castle 78
Waterhouse, Keith 233, 234–5, 255–6, 296, 423n, 441
Watkins, Alan 233, 235, 338, 346
Wavell, Archibald Wavell, 1st Earl 196
Week, The 156
Weinstock, Arnold 358
Wellington School 137
West, Nigel 371n
Western Mail 90
Weston, Garfield 158n
White, Antonia 133–4, 138, 139, 178, 282–3, 342–3,
344
White, Luke 4
Whiting, Audrey 233
Wickham, Kenneth 176
Wigg, Lord 380

'Wilberforce, Charles' *see* Cudlipp, Hugh
Williams, Reverend Austin 343
Williams, Francis 220–1, 252, 257, 305, 365–6, 379
Wilson, Harold: becomes leader of Labour Party
338; friendly relationship with King 338–9; offers
him life peerage 340; confers damehood on
Ruth King 344; appoints King to directorship
of Bank of England 344–5; Downing Street
parties 316; King's campaign against 2, 346–50,
352, 354, 359–60, 361, 368, 372–80; friendly
towards Cudlipp 382; and King's removal 388,
389, 390, 426n; on King 399; and colleagues' dis-
loyalty 407; recommends Cudlipp's ennoblement
420; requests setting up of Counter–Inflation
Publicity Unit 422
Wilson, Mary 383
Wilson, Peter 118–19, 181, 308
Wilson, Woodrow, US President 34, 49
Winchester School/Wykehamists 36–7, 38, 62, 120,
176, 211, 227, 228, 264; King at 21, 22–3, 24–5,
31–3, 35–7, 59–60
Winn, Godfrey 105, 106, 107, 108, 152–3
Winnie's (pub) 237, 296
Wintour, Charles 298
Wolfenden Report (1957) 249
Woman 271, 309
Woman's Illustrated 268, 270, 309
Woman's Journal 268
Woman's Mirror 304, 308, 309n, 310
Woman's Own 271, 309
Woman's Weekly 268, 271
Woodcock, Lucinda (*née* King) (Cecil's grandchild)
435, 446–7
World Press News 327
Worsthorne, Peregrine 297, 433
Wright, Peter 371n, 444
Wyatt, Woodrow 345

Yorkshire Post 255
Young, Hugo 408, 410

Zec, Donald 235, 261–2, 423n, 441
Zec, Philip: cartoons 164, 165, 188; appointed as
Cudlipp's successor 201, 224–5; and
Bartholomew's resignation 218, 219–20; and
Crossman 219–20, 224, 225, 238; introduces
King to Ruth Railton 280
Zinoviev letter 66
Zuckerman, Sir Solly 369, 370–1, 372